ORDER FORM

FILM DIRECTORS: A Complete Guide

STANDING ORDER _____Yes _____No

_____ copies @ $32.95 $ _____

Add $ 2.15 tax (CA only) $ _____

Shipping/ handling
add $3.50 per copy. $ _____

Canada/Mexico add
$4.50 per copy $ _____

All other countries add
$17.50 per copy airmail $ _____

TOTAL $ _____U.S.

MAKE CHECKS PAYABLE TO
LONE EAGLE PUBLISHING

PAYMENT IS BY: □ CHECK □ MONEY ORDER
□ VISA □ MASTERCARD

CARD NUMBER _____ / _____
EXPIRATION DATE

SIGNATURE _____
(EXACTLY AS IT APPEARS ON CARD)

Name _____
Firm _____
Address _____
City _____ State _____ Zip _____
Country _____

Please allow 4–6 weeks for delivery

ORDER FORM

FILM DIRECTORS: A Complete Guide

STANDING ORDER _____Yes _____No

_____ copies @ $32.95 $ _____

Add $ 2.15 tax (CA only) $ _____

Shipping/ handling
add $3.50 per copy. $ _____

Canada/Mexico add
$4.50 per copy $ _____

All other countries add
$17.50 per copy airmail $ _____

TOTAL $ _____U.S.

MAKE CHECKS PAYABLE TO
LONE EAGLE PUBLISHING

PAYMENT IS BY: □ CHECK □ MONEY ORDER
□ VISA □ MASTERCARD

CARD NUMBER _____ / _____
EXPIRATION DATE

SIGNATURE _____
(EXACTLY AS IT APPEARS ON CARD)

Name _____
Firm _____
Address _____
City _____ State _____ Zip _____
Country _____

Please allow 4–6 weeks for delivery

Did we forget you?
Does your listing need updating?

The 1985 edition of
FILM DIRECTORS A Complete Guide
is now in preparation.

**Fill out and mail this card
immediately and we'll send
you the form.**

Name _____
Address _____
City _____ State _____ Zip _____
Country _____

DON'T DELAY/MAIL TODAY!

Did we forget you?
Does your listing need updating?

The 1985 edition of
FILM DIRECTORS A Complete Guide
is now in preparation.

**Fill out and mail this card
immediately and we'll send
you the form.**

Name _____
Address _____
City _____ State _____ Zip _____
Country _____

DON'T DELAY/MAIL TODAY!

THE STUDIOS AT LAS COLINAS/
THE DALLAS COMMUNICATIONS COMPLEX

PREP IT

CAST IT

REHEARSE IT

LIGHT IT

SHOOT IT

WRAP IT

CUT IT

WE'VE GOT YOU COVERED ... FROM CONCEPT TO COMPLETION

The one-stop production facility in Texas

★ Three acoustically superior studios — 3000, 6000 & 15,000 square feet of production space

★ Competitively priced with no charge for overtime or power

★ Computerized lighting boards with memory control; hard and soft cycloramas

★ 24-hour security and easy access to full-service kitchen, construction area, star and cast dressing rooms, production offices, screening room and rehearsal hall

★ One of the largest film/video equipment suppliers in the world

★ Complete audio production facility for film & video and a modern video post house

★ Ancillary service companies for every production need

★ Leasing offices and service area available

★ Conveniently located just 10 minutes from Dallas/Fort Worth Airport and an abundance of 4-star hotels

The Studios at Las Colinas

Dallas Communications Complex
TEXAS

For studio information contact:
Harry B. Friedman II, President
Betty Buckley, Production Manager
One Dallas Communications Complex,
Irving, Texas 75039, 214/869-0700

For leasing information contact:
Bruce Fogerty, Vice President/Marketing
Two Dallas Communications Complex,
Irving, Texas 75039, 214/869-0700

FILM
DIRECTORS
A COMPLETE GUIDE

Compiled and Edited by Michael Singer

LONE EAGLE

Again, for JCB

Photographs of Martha Coolidge, Taylor Hackford, Lynne Littman and Ronald Neame by Toris Von Wolfe. Photograph of Ridley Scott by Steven Poster. Photograph of Paul Bartel courtesy of 20th Century Fox Studios. Black and white photos printed by Isgo Lepejian, Custom Black & White Photo Lab, Burbank, CA.

FILM DIRECTORS: A Complete Guide

LONE EAGLE PUBLISHING
9903 Santa Monica Blvd., Suite 204
Beverly Hills, CA 90212

Printed in the United States of America

Book designed by Liz Vietor

ISBN 0-943728-05-3
ISSN 0740-2872

NOTE: We have made every reasonable effort to ensure that the information contained herein is as accurate as possible. However, errors and omissions are sure to occur. We would appreciate your notifying us of any which you find.

*Lone Eagle Publishing is a division of Lone Eagle Productions, Inc.

TABLE OF CONTENTS

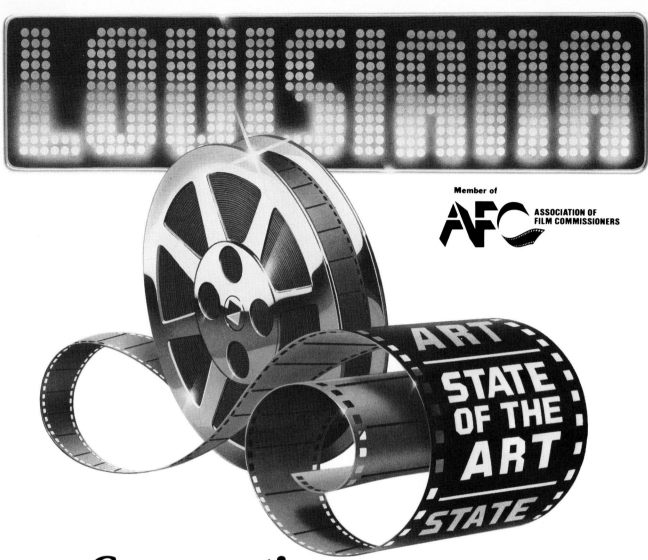

Cooperation, Locations, Contacts
and the
1984 World's Fair

STATE OF THE ART STATE

A
RIGHT-TO-WORK
STATE

Louisiana Film Commission

For information, call or write:
Barbara Coleman, *Director*
Louisiana Film Commission/Office of Commerce & Industry.
P.O. Box 44185. Dept. C2 Baton Rouge, LA 70804/(504) 342-5403

INTRODUCTION

This updated, revised and expanded second annual international edition of **FILM DIRECTORS: A Complete Guide** includes feature and telefeature credits for over 1200 filmmakers both domestic and foreign. As we said in the first edition the intention of this book is to provide an easy, practical and comprehensive reference to living film directors and their work.

Among our new features are:

- A new name. **DIRECTORS: A Complete Guide** said it all to those of us who work in the motion picture industry. *Directors* are, of course, *Film Directors*. But to the real world out there, the title was imprecise. So ... **FILM DIRECTORS: A Complete Guide** is the new name.

- FROM THE DIRECTOR'S CHAIR, a special section highlighting six prominent directors, interviewed by the editor especially for this book. FROM THE DIRECTOR'S CHAIR will become a permanent fixture of all future volumes, with new interviews each year.

- A cross-referenced index of over 12,000 film titles in alphabetical order followed by the names of their directors. This will help those who remember the title of a film, but not its director.

- Academy and Emmy Award nominees and winners among the directors listed in this book.

Some words of explanation about the listings:

DIRECTORS—The listings herein are selective by necessity, as the inclusion of every living person who ever made a full-length film would inflate the guide to encyclopaedic proportions. Selecting is not an easy task, and we're certainly open to suggestions. Although the listed directors are primarily active, also included are some retired greats, such as Frank Capra, Rouben Mamoulian and Henry Hathaway out of sheer respect for their places in film history. Foreign directors included are those whose films have had some distribution and recognition in the United States. We've also made an effort this year to include several independent filmmakers, as some of them will invariably become major directors in the not-too-distant future.

The reader should be reminded that because we list only full-length features and telefeatures, a director whose last credit in the book is ten years old could be one of the many who works constantly in episodic television.

Birthdates, birthplaces and contacts have been provided whenever possible, but it's well known that both birthdates and agents are subject to change without notice.

FILMS—One of the great frustrations of collecting data for this book is that certain films seem to materialize from movieland limbo. Just when a director's credits appear to be complete, some obscure title appears on T.V. at 2:15 A.M. on a Tuesday night and, *vòila,* we find out that it was directed by that same filmmaker in 1965, a Spanish-Bulgarian co-production! Needless to say, we've attempted to make these credits as complete as possible.

The criteria for listed films, in terms of running times, are explained in the **KEY TO ABBREVIATIONS.** Videotaped television dramas—many of which are now called "movies" by the networks—are not included. Although some truly impressive work has been done on video—particularly programs like Anthony Page's *THE MISSILES OF OCTOBER* and Edward Zwick's *SPECIAL BULLE-TIN*—we have to live up to our title.

TITLES—Films are often known by a multiplicity of titles in the course of international distribution. Since this is a U.S.-based book, American release titles are utilized, with alternate titles following in *italics*, e.g.

BUTCHER, BAKER, NIGHTMARE MAKER *NIGHT WARNING/MOMMA'S BOY* Royal American, 1981

In the case of films from England, Australia or other English-speaking foreign countries, a title in *italics* usually represents the original title in that country if different from its American release title, e.g.

THE ROAD WARRIOR *MAD MAX II* Warner Bros., 1982, Australian

For foreign films which were distributed in the United States, the American title is listed first, followed by the original foreign-language title, only if its meaning is substantially different from the English, e.g.

ALL SCREWED UP *TUTTO A POSTE E NIENTE IN ORDINE* New Line Cinema, 1974, Italian

Films that did not receive American distribution are generally listed under their original foreign-language titles (except, of course, those films which were actually released in the U.S. under those original titles), e.g.

LA BELLA DI ROMA Lux Film, 1955, Italian

or:

LA VIE CONTINUE Triumph/Columbia, 1982, French

DISTRIBUTORS AND PRODUCTION COMPANIES Original American distributors of feature films are listed, although movies often change their distributors through the course of time. For foreign films that received no U.S. distribution, the original distributors or production companies in their home countries are included whenever possible.

Telefeatures and television mini-series are identified with the names of their production companies rather than the networks on which they aired.

Production companies are also listed for features which have not yet found distributors.

YEAR OF RELEASE—This is often extremely hard to determine. Usually, a foreign film is released in the United States a year or two (sometimes more) after its initial appearance in its own country. Therefore, for the sake of accuracy, the *original* year of release is provided rather than the American release date. Nevertheless, there are often differences of opinion as to when certain films, domestic *and* foreign, were first exhibited. The dates herein may be at variance with other sources. Also, release dates for films not yet released are projections.

COUNTRY OF ORIGIN—These are the years of incredibly complex international co-production deals. How does one explain that a film made in England with an American director, French producer and international cast, but registered in Panama for tax purposes is, therefore, a Panamanian film? We have opted for realism based upon the nationalities of production personnel, and geographic locations of participating companies.

Once again, we would like to thank the staffs of the Academy of Motion Picture Arts & Sciences Margaret Herrick Library, and the UCLA Theatre Arts Library, for their fine and helpful service.

We've had a gratifying response to the first edition of **FILM DIRECTORS: A Complete Guide** from producers, students, actors, writers, technicians, publicists, financiers, theatre owners, exhibitors, buffs … *and* directors. Their suggestions and corrections have helped immensely. Once again we've included insert cards for that very purpose, and we urge readers to use them. With that kind of response, we cannot but improve year by year.

Michael Singer
Los Angeles
November 1983

FROM THE

DIRECTOR'S

CHAIR

TAYLOR HACKFORD

AN OFFICER AND A GENTLEMAN, one of 1982's most successful films, was only the second feature by a young director named Taylor Hackford. With a strong background in television journalism and documentaries—and an Oscar for a previous short film—Hackford brought excitement, sensuality and intense emotion to *AN OFFICER AND A GENTLEMAN*'s somewhat traditional story of life and love on a military base. Widely admired for its strong performances, the film brought an Academy Award to Louis Gossett, Jr. as Best Supporting Actor and a DGA nomination to the director himself.

AN OFFICER AND A GENTLEMAN also brought Taylor Hackford to a position of creative stability, allowing him to develop his own projects. The first of these, *AGAINST ALL ODDS*, is scheduled for release in 1984.

MICHAEL SINGER: You keep a pretty low profile in this day of celebrity directors. Is that intentional, or is publicity just not something you think much about?

TAYLOR HACKFORD: It's intentional. So far, I haven't had a need, and certainly don't have a desire, to do a lot of self-promotion. I've been lucky in that I've been able to make films—that's what I need to do. And because of *AN OFFICER AND A GENTLEMAN*, I've been able to start developing projects, which is important to me. I haven't had to go out and beat my chest and get articles written about me. I didn't hire a publicist, although I was approached by many, because I just didn't feel a need. Luckily, the DGA nominated me for their directors' award, which was an incredible honor for me. Everyone at the time said, "You've got to hire a publicist to go after the Academy so you can also get nominated for an Oscar." Frankly, it was probably more important to me to have been nominated by the DGA because they are my peers. Also, it's only my second film. I'm interested in building a body of work and not burning out on one or two films. If I find I can't get work, maybe then I'll have to go out and beat the bushes; but for the time being I'd rather keep a low profile.

You said that you "need" to make films. Of course, most filmmakers make movies because that's the only thing they want to do, but you had been in news and broadcast journalism. What turned you around? Had you always been interested in film, or was there a calling at some particular point?

Well, I think it has to do with evolution. I'd gone to college and ma-jored in International Relations—I've always been very political. I was in the Peace Corps . . . I thought I was going to be a lawyer . . . and the evolution in terms of changing that whole career outlook took a number of years. I started hanging out with some film students when I was a senior at USC, and got turned on to film and the power of the media. I loved feature films. For periods of my life I went to 15 films a week, which is a lot of film on a regular basis. But since my background was political and I was very knowledgeable about politics, I went into the only area that I was interested in, which was a combination. I started working at a public television station simultaneously doing investigative *and* political reporting. I also did rock and roll shows, because of my extensive background in music. It was kind of incongruous that the two things would fit together, but at KCET, where I worked, they were very understaffed and you had to do a lot of things. I've always been a real glutton for work. I love work, and given the opportunity, when some of the producers were doing one piece a week, I was doing five because I thought, "what an opportunity!" And it was, in fact, my film school. To me, I wasn't being exploited—I was exploiting an opportunity to go out and get a lot of experience, which I did. But you know, in the back of my mind always—although it was a bit of a dream at the time—was the thought that it would be wonderful to make dramatic films. A number of the long documentaries that I did were portrait documentaries that were actually composed. I mean, they were documentaries in the sense that they were based on real people, but I spent enough time with those people so that I

kind of composed them in a structural way. And those were much more dramatic than the normal kind of informational documentary. In those films, there was really something of substance, in getting someone who is a real person to let down his guard and reveal himself. It's immensely more difficult if you make it through and they do reveal themselves on camera. Much more difficult than working with actors, believe me, because normal barriers are very, very strong. An actor is trained to open up and let his insides come out. Real people don't want to do that. They have a barrier up and they want you to think of them as nice people. But "nice" people *can* be mean at times, or crazy, or depressed, and no one really wants to show that other side of themselves to the world in a film. If you're skilled enough to get them to do it, I think it's an immense accomplishment. I use that skill now when I work with actors. I consider myself a performance director. I work with actors, I want performances, I want to do story films that have real changes in character. you cannot, in films today—at least in films that I want to make—separate who the real person is from the actor. What I'm trying to do is reveal the actors in their roles, and that hearkens back to when I was making documentaries—trying to make those people I was dealing with reveal themselves. You've got to draw from your own experiences. And that's what I do.

After the documentaries, you left KCET and started making short films, didn't you?

I made one short film. You know, at a certain point working at a job . . . and I'm not making excuses, KCET was not a way station for me . . . I had a terrific time, able to do literally hundreds of mini-docs and news stories and rock and roll and jazz shows . . . but at a certain point . . . well, it was funny. We'd been doing an investigative show, a real good one, I think. We won a Peabody Award, I won a couple of Emmys, other producers on the show had won Emmys. It was a hard-hitting show. But, any time you go after people, you're going to get sued a lot. It puts a lot of pressure on a little television station. There was a policy change at the station where they leaned toward doing the kind of soft human interest features that commercial television was doing. And I said, jeez, what are we doing? We've got a good investigative unit, we're being recognized for what we're doing, why change? But it was clear that the pressure was just too much, and that they wanted to follow along the lines of commercial television. So I said the hell with it, and quit. I had to make a decision: either I was going to get a job working in news on commercial television as a network reporter, or I was going to take this dream of working in dramatic film and see if I could do it. You know, at a certain point you have to pretty well put up or shut up. I went out and starved for awhile, about 6 or 7 months, waiting for a dramatic film. I kept myself alive by doing the NASA coverage of the Jupiter shot. It was a bread and butter job, but it was fun. Finally, I got a job doing a short film for an organization that wanted to make sex education films for high schools. They wanted a documentary, but I convinced them that if I made it look like a documentary, only write it and cast it with actors, it would be more effective. They agreed, and I made a half-hour film called *TEENAGE FATHER*. It was made for classrooms, but it turned out really well. We showed it on television, in a movie house here, and it won an Academy Award for Best Dramatic Short. When people saw it, they said, well, this guy can probably work with actors, and that was my ticket. Then I was able to do *THE IDOLMAKER*.

Considering your background in music, was THE IDOLMAKER a project that you initiated or was it brought to you?

It was a project that was brought to me. Because of *TEENAGE FATHER* I got an agent . . . two agents really: Fred Specktor and Stephanie Brody of CAA, and they worked their asses off. They heard about *THE IDOLMAKER*—Gene Kirkwood and Howard Koch, Jr. had it at United Artists and were looking for a director. I met them, they saw my short film, liked it, heard about my background in music and hired me. They already had a screenplay, but not one the studio wanted to go ahead with. When I came in they wanted me to do a rewrite. I went through two drafts, the studio gave us a go, and we made the picture.

That was a fairly expensive looking movie, although I suspect it was very moderately budgeted.

It was between $4½ and $5 million. I think we got a lot of production value on the screen. Getting your first feature is a feat, and I felt incredibly lucky in that I knew the period very, very well. I taught the history of rock and roll at the Alternative College at USC. I have a real background in music and also, I'd done the concert films. It was a very nice opening film for me. At the same time I'm from California—I'm not Italian, nor am I from New York, and it was a film

based in that milieu. When you've done documentaries, you become very respectful of accuracy and reality. With films like *MEAN STREETS* around—and I mention that because I think it's a fabulous movie and one that really reflected that kind of New York milieu—you have a lot to live up to. So I went to New York and South Philadelphia, spent time in the Bronx, went to Brooklyn with Ray Sharkey, basically observing. Sometimes an outside point of view can really help. On the other hand, no one could have made *MEAN STREETS* the way Marty [Scorsese] did because he knew it so well. What I'm saying is that it was a terrific opportunity and I didn't take it likely.

My only quibble with THE IDOL-MAKER—and I'm sure you've heard this before—is that I wish the music had been more faithful to the actual sound of what was coming out of Philadelphia in the early 1960's.

You make the movie as best you can and try to put as much on the screen of what's inside you. Then you turn it out and hope for an audience.

I've got to take the heat on that one, because the music coming out of Philadelphia in the early 1960's to me, is one of the low points of rock and roll. I mean, Bobby Rydell was actually quite good, but this film was based in part on the careers of Frankie Avalon, Fabian and Bob Marcucci. And frankly, it would seem to me to be a one joke film if I'd put either the actual songs that Avalon and Fabian sang, or songs like it, into the film. You're right, there was a definite decision made not to go for total simplistic accuracy there, and we were trying to do something that would have some relevance today. Jeff Barry, who wrote the music, did a terrific job and of course, he did write some of the best songs ever in rock and roll after that period. We didn't use any synthesizers. We didn't use any kind of instrumentation that wasn't available then. Looking back on it, we suffered from doing a film that in essence, wasn't the Bob Marcucci story, or the Frankie Avalon and Fabian story. But it was close enough to it that it got tagged with that. Inevitably, people looked at it and said, well, this isn't exactly the Frankie Avalon and Fabian story. On the other hand, people who didn't like those guys put it down as a Frankie Avalon/Fabian story. We ended up falling between the cracks when in

fact, we were trying to make a film about a manager and his artists, which I think is a very interesting subject. From my point of view, as a first time director, it was a great experience.

When you were making AN OFFICER AND A GENTLEMAN, did you have any inkling of its eventual success as a monster hit?

Not at all. I don't think anybody who was working on the film did. Oftentimes studios will say, "Oh, this is a sure thing, this is going to be a monster." Unless they're doing *SUPERMAN*, or something like that, and even then it's never guaranteed, studios don't really know what's going to be a hit or not. I sincerely doubt whether Chartoff, Winkler and John Avildsen, when they were making *ROCKY* said, "This is going to be a hundred million dollar film." They might have believed in it—you have to believe in the film when you're going along. No one had any expectations for the *ROCKY*'s, the *OFFICER AND A GENTLEMAN*'s, even *STAR WARS* and certainly *E.T.*, which was turned down by other studios. You make the movie as best you can and try to put as much on the screen of what's inside of you. Then you turn it out there and hope for an audience. With *THE IDOLMAKER*, we never got that audience. The audiences that did see the film loved it, but we were never able to sell it enough to get them in the theatres despite the good word-of-mouth. With *AN OFFICER AND A GENTLEMAN*, Paramount was very smart. I have to give Don Simpson a lot of credit when he was head of production at Paramount. He liked the script—no one else at Paramount liked it, they didn't want to make it—but Don Simpson liked it, brought me in to direct the film and was a guiding force. He believed in it, but I don't think he thought it was going to be a big, successful movie. When it was finished, Frank Mancuso looked at it. He really had the sense that it could probably do big business. He designed a marketing campaign that I think was brilliant, and responsible for the business that it did. He's a very smart man, a very good marketer—the best. The film was good. I think it would have been successful. How successful I don't know—I think they did a lot to maximize its success.

And the word-of-mouth took care of the rest?

But *they* started the word-of-mouth! They screened the movie like crazy all over the country for everybody who would look, which was wise. You may be losing five bucks for one person, but if they go out and tell ten other people and five of them come, you made out pretty well. Mancuso understood that.

Was it an easy shoot for you?

No, it was hell. I loved it in the sense that we had a wonderful location and a good script to work with and a fabulous cast. But it was very difficult, very hard physically since we were in the Pacific Northwest on the Olympic Peninsula, where it rained all the time. There were immense personality conflicts on the film. The studio did not give us a great deal of support and wanted to fire me about six weeks into the film. The producer was not supportive at all, did everything he could to work against me on this. On every level, it was a hard film to do. But at the same time, there was a lot of vitality happening. And it worked. I must say, that to Richard [Gere] and Debra's [Winger] credit, when the studio wanted to fire me they said that they wouldn't work with another director. Paramount's a real tough outfit, but they're also a good studio—they know how to make movies. But in reality, I must tell you that at least in the making of the movie, it was not a particularly thrilling experience in the sense of having a lot of backup and support. On the other hand, I was able to make a movie I wanted. When it came to editing, Paramount did back me up. The movie that's up there is my film on every level, and I have no complaints there. Threats to the contrary, they did ultimately support me. At the same time, I gave them a good movie.

I know very little about *AGAINST ALL ODDS* except that it's supposedly based upon Jacques Tourneur's *OUT OF THE PAST*. When you went into production your film was also titled *OUT OF THE PAST*. Does the change in title signify a deliberate attempt to break away from the earlier version?

Yes. The idea of doing a remake is a tough one to begin with, but this is so different from the original. If a film has been done well, to do it again in the same period is a mistake. I felt the original film had wonderful characterizations—Robert Mitchum, Kirk Douglas and Jane Greer were great—but the story was convoluted and fell apart at the end. I updated it to the present. I took the core relationship from the original film— with a very strong man and a very dangerous woman—and plugged it into a brand new story. I wanted to do a film about power in Los Angeles. And I believe that somebody could go to these two movies on the same night and see two different films. For that reason, I didn't want it to be called *OUT OF THE PAST*. I didn't want people to come expecting to see the old movie redone. When the writer and I got finished, we looked at each other and said, "It's too bad we even called this a remake because it's so different." The bottom line is that those three characters are still there, and that was from the old film. Certain purist critics will say, "Oh God, the old films can never be improved upon," and we'll have to take the heat, something you don't have to do with an original screenplay. Hopefully, people will be open enough to see that there is some real value in this and difference from the original. It has some homage in it, but mostly it's taking the old film as a jumping-off point and really moving into new territory.

Are there any attempts to match or update the film noir style?

Not at all. I used Don Thorin again, my cinematographer on *AN OFFICER AND A GENTLEMAN*, but this has a very different look from *OFFICER*. It's a hard-edged, sharp style. It's tough to make a film in Los Angeles—I mean, so many films have been made here to begin with and television treats it every day. So to look at L.A. from a different perspective is hard. Finding locations which haven't been seen before is difficult. I think we've done it with this film. You really see the city from a unique point of view. A whole third of the film takes place in Mexico, in the Yucatan Peninsula. That should be very interesting because we started in Cozumel, on a little island called Isla Mujeres, and then we shot in two Mayan ruins which have never been filmed before. There's an immense amount of production value, and a sense of adventure from the audience's point of view. But there's no sentimentality in the L.A. footage, no mythologizing. I think too many people who have made films here come in and see this never-never land, and never really have a sense that this is as ruthless and vicious a place as any other city. I know that perspective, having been a reporter here looking at power and how it's manipulated. The movie business is a big part of this town but it's by no means the real power of this city. The people who wield that power are land rich and always have been. We deal with some of those people in the movie.

Was this an easier time for you than on *AN OFFICER AND A GENTLEMAN*?

Yeah . . . it wasn't an easy shoot . . . no film is an easy shoot. But I produced this movie, it was my project from the beginning. Columbia, who picked the film up, has been an incredibly good place to make a film, completely supportive all the way down the line. They believed in the movie and have allowed me to make the movie that was in my head. If it works, great. And if not, I have no excuses.

5

Photograph by Toris Von Wolfe

MARTHA COOLIDGE

One of 1983's nicest surprises was a funny, incisive and touching film called *VALLEY GIRL*, which won acclaim — and long-awaited recognition—for its director, Martha Coolidge.

Although *VALLEY GIRL* was her first widely distributed film, Coolidge's filmmaking background is prodigious. She won her first festival award in 1971, and no fewer than six of her films have been seen at multiple film festivals around the world. Her feature-length *NOT A PRETTY PICTURE*, a widely praised and very controversial film about rape, won the Blue Ribbon Award at the American Film Festival and the Gold Ducat Award at the Mannheim Film Festival. But financial and professional rewards have evaded her until the considerable critical and box-office success of *VALLEY GIRL*, which has now allowed her to complete an independent feature called *THE CITY GIRL*, and was no doubt responsible for her being chosen by Paramount Pictures to helm their *NATIONAL LAMPOON'S JOY OF SEX*.

MICHAEL SINGER: It seemed to me that you transcended the basic youth/sex genre with *VALLEY GIRL* and turned it into something different from what might originally have been intended.

MARTHA COOLIDGE: Well, it was [producers and co-writers] Andy Lane and Wayne Crawford's project and they always intended it to be a love story. They were a little worried that the girls wouldn't come off as real, and that's why they wanted me to direct it. I think that as a woman I was able to bring some reality to the girls, which is very important. I mean, I learned something from Roger Ebert and Gene Siskel on T.V., when they said that in all the other teenage comedy sex pictures the girls don't even have names! That is really shocking. Andy and Wayne were genuinely concerned about that . . . they wanted it to be better than it could have been. And I think the people who were genuinely surprised were the distributors. I don't think they expected a real movie.

How involved were you with the development of *VALLEY GIRL*?

Well, they did a rewrite with me and then added scenes. I wanted certain scenes in there, like Nicolas [Cage] and Deborah's [Foreman] breakup scene at the door. It wasn't in the script. I said, you can't have a love story where the couple breaks up without *showing* them breaking up. There was somewhat of a lack of focus, but they had written the

script quickly. So we worked on it together before we shot it.

A lot of people who knew of you before *VALLEY GIRL*— basically from *NOT A PRETTY PICTURE*, which is a very different kind of movie—were surprised to see your name connected with a title as commercial as *VALLEY GIRL*. Of course, it turned out better than expected. Are you surprised by what's been happening to you since it was released?

Oh no, I'm ready. I'm definitely ready. But on the other hand, it's always a surprise, I think, when things bring the unexpected. There are always surprises, and I'm not entirely used to it yet either. Somebody asks me how success feels, and I am shocked—is he talking to me? And then I thought, hell, I guess he's right. I'm working, which I'm glad to be doing, but I don't think it's been long enough for me to tell what it feels like. I'm ready, but when you're working on a movie and faced with a million problems, it doesn't make any difference whether you're successful or not. You're just working on a movie faced with a million problems.

Your newest film is *NATIONAL LAMPOON'S JOY OF SEX*...

You know I have another picture, don't you? It's called *THE CITY GIRL*.

That's something you've been working on for a long time, isn't it?

Two and a half years, but it's finished. It's very different from *VALLEY GIRL* and *JOY OF SEX*—a serious, dark picture about singles life in an urban city. It's about a young woman photographer who has modern romantic ideas—mostly sexual ideas—about men. And she has a boyfriend who is not like her fantasies. He's not cool, not hip and not beautiful in a way that she fantasizes. She's a photographer for kind of a hip publication not unlike *L.A. Weekly* combined with *Interview*—she does fashion and rock and roll and kind of new wave lifestyle pictures. She finally breaks up with her boyfriend and tries to go and live out her fantasies in the club life of Toronto. And nothing works out. It's very funny, but also a dark, multi-layered, very interesting movie. I really like it. It's totally independent, shot partly in L.A. and mostly in Toronto. Peter Bogdanovich bought it—he's the executive producer. It shut down in Canada, we ran out of money, the producers didn't know what to do. I tried to raise the money many times over until Peter saw it. He loved the picture, fully appreciated the kind of ordeal that I'd been through and bought it himself.

Your newest film, a comedy based on Alex Comfort's book, *The Joy of Sex*, has been through about a dozen producers.

And a lot of writers too.

Was the final script the product of a number of those writers?

Only one—Kathleen Rowell, who also wrote *THE OUTSIDERS*, so this is a real change of pace for her. Now *JOY OF SEX* is about two high school kids who decide that they want to have their first sexual experience. But since they're both very romantic, they want a *romantic* sexual experience. But they both keep getting sidetracked, and nothing works out. It's not a farce, but a very funny, naive and sweet picture.

With those two names—National Lampoon—in front of the title, one immediately wonders about excessive raunch.

No. The most intensive raunch is a scene where these guys are lighting their farts, but that's not in detail.

What the hell, if it was good enough for Bergman in *FANNY AND ALEXANDER* I guess it's good enough for *NATIONAL LAMPOON'S JOY OF SEX*. Did you have any trepidation when you were asked to direct the film?

7

Well, I was being offered a lot of youth comedies, and they were generally not good. I realized that I wanted to go ahead and work right away, for several reasons. One is that I spent so many years not working, and two, I needed to make some money too. So I figured okay, I'll do it . . . and I'm thrilled I'm doing comedy. I think comedy is extremely difficult to do. Kathleen is a very good friend of mine and we were going to develop something together. And it was one of my agents at William Morris who said that *JOY OF SEX* was coming up

---

Somebody asks me how success feels and I am shocked . . . is he talking to me?

---

and could be available, and that Kathleen wrote it. I mean, we were talking about doing something else, and she wasn't available to write it because she was working on *JOY OF SEX*! So it just seemed to make sense.

As a woman working on a big studio film, did you find yourself getting special treatment?

I don't think that people treated me any differently than any other picture I've done . . . people have generally respected me. Except they called me "Ma'am," which is strange. I think it stems from the old Hollywood tradition of calling the director "Sir."

Where are you from, and when did you start making movies?

I'm from New Haven, Connecticut, and I made my first film in my first year at college. And I really loved it. I had lots of friends, older than me by a year or two, who already were making films. I was directing theatre and acting, so I was already in the theatre world. I acted in a film that summer, then made four films in my sophomore year. Then in the third year I went into independent study, because they didn't really have a film department, and made a 16mm film as opposed to 8mm. Then I left school, went to New York, and worked in commercials and documentaries—mostly assistant editor, then editor, script girl . . . you know . . . everything. I also went to night school in film—NYU, the School of Visual Arts and Columbia Graduate School. At Columbia, in the spring of 1968, I was doing a 25-minute 16mm film with Michael Brandon about a guy who was drafted and was afraid to go to Vietnam. And then the whole school was shut down by the riots. I didn't get my

film finished that year, and ended up emigrating to Montreal to write and produce for television. I finally came back to NYU Graduate School in the master's program, and directed three or four films there, produced several and edited quite a few in 35mm. In my last year I produced my first film that got distribution, *PASSING QUIETLY THROUGH*, and directed my documentary *DAVID: OFF AND ON*. A teacher at NYU saw that film and hired me to direct an hour-long documentary about a free school in Long Island which became a special on PBS. I got very active in the New York film community and ended up getting a grant to make my next picture, which I called *OLD FASHIONED WOMAN*—it was a portrait of my grandmother and has been on PBS a lot. Then I got more grants and investors, and did *NOT A PRETTY PICTURE*. By then I was pretty well established in New York, I'd won a lot of prizes in the non-theatrical film world, lots of festivals, and started the Association of Independent Video and Film Makers with two other people. But I really, really wanted to make theatrical films . . . not to put down the films I made—I love them and I'd always like to be able to do it that way. But I wanted to work with actors. After *NOT A PRETTY PICTURE*, I decided to chuck it all and move to Los Angeles. Even though I was over-experienced in a way, I was an AFI intern with Robert Wise on *AUDREY ROSE*, which was a very interesting experience. I learned a lot. Finally, after going back and forth for a year, Francis Coppola and company come back from doing *APOCALYPSE NOW* in the Philippines and said they wanted to work with me. So I went into development on *PHOTOPLAY*, a rock and roll love story, which ended up being two and a half years of my life. After it got shelved, and several other development deals fell through, I got kind of disillusioned and moved back to Canada and immediately directed a mini-series for the CBC. Then I got *THE CITY GIRL*, which I told you about before. I've also written a screwball comedy with Colleen Camp called *TWELVE'S A CROWD*, which Peter Bogdanovich wants me to direct for his company.

You're one of the top women directors working in this town. How do you see yourself as far as that position is concerned?

I must say that I do very clearly see myself as a pioneer, as I do the other women directors. There is absolute truth to the fact that one woman's success is another woman's success. The guy who

hired me to do *VALLEY GIRL* went around and hired another woman director for his next picture. Also, I turned down a picture at a studio and they turned around and hired another woman who had never done a feature before.

Are you afraid that producers are going to typecast women directors?

I'm not afraid of it. They do that. I think it's good that I'm doing comedy, because comedy can break through some sexual lines. I really want people to see *THE CITY GIRL* because I think that will break through some other pre-conceived ideas. It's so much a woman's picture I can't even tell you. And it's not what anybody expects from a woman. It's absolutely a woman's picture — not soft, not light, not silly, not easy, not without violence and not without an edge. You know, a movie takes a lot out of you, and you can only make so many in your life. I want to do some comedies, and I want to do some serious pictures and I want to do some big pictures. I don't necessarily mean $40 million . . . when I say big, I mean big in scope. And I think you can say that I want to prove that I can do those things, that a woman can do things on that scale. I'd like to do science fiction, deal with special effects. I'm not a director because I want to do movies that stay in the Valley—I mean, when I approached the Valley, I approached it the way I would an historical subject. You have to get to know your material.

How have attitudes changed toward women directors?

In the past, a woman was not hired, in general, to do the kind of "B" pictures

---

When you're working on a movie faced with a million problems, it doesn't make any difference whether you're successful or not . . . you're just working on a movie faced with a million problems.

---

that young male directors were hired to do, and that generally had to do with the attitudes of the people financing those pictures. There are a couple of exceptions—Barbara Peeters and Stephanie Rothman. But in general, I found that in the past the attitude of the independent financiers was much worse than even the studios, who would at least talk to a woman director. They were open to political and societal pressure to take women seriously, whereas the cliched independent who chews on a cigar and worked his way up from nothing and thinks the woman should stay in the kitchen is not going to hire a woman—and he does what he wants with his money, you know? That's a very simplified explanation for why I think it's harder for women in the independents. Therefore, women directors in general have to make a leap that in many cases a male director doesn't, which is from educational films, documentaries, little things for television or children's films to—suddenly — features. The *VALLEY GIRL*'s are very hard to come by, almost unheard of for a woman. That's why I was so thrilled. I was being offered a commercial, independent, low-budget picture.

Do you think male directors are judged by different standards than women directors?

Yes. How many times has a woman done a picture that wasn't that good or wasn't a hit, and they said "Well, I'll never work with a woman again." Imagine if they said that about a man! "I'll never work with a *man* again"? Because he didn't have a hit? I really hope to God that if I ever make a really awful picture, they'll give me the space to do it in.

Do you think things have finally and truly changed?

They're changing. It's in the process and it's going to take a long time. I feel that it's a movement, and women changing their role in our society is simply an aspect of the social movement. But the point is, that women have seriously been changing their role in society for the last eighty years, and there is tremendous historical resistance to it, in women as well as men. There may be brilliant, talented women out there, but they are not as prepared by their background and their childhood and their histories to be leaders. Or something even more complicated than a leader, like a director—which is an in-between position—a person who is both under and over a lot of creative people. It's a very lonely, isolated position. But it *is* changing.

Photograph by Steven Poster

R I D L E Y   S C O T T

With just three films, British director Ridley Scott has established himself as one of filmdom's most original visual stylists. *THE DUELLISTS*, with its painterly evocations of a past world, led to the alternately beautiful and terrifying visions of the future in *ALIEN* and *BLADE RUNNER*. Along with Alan Parker, Adrian Lyne and his own brother Tony, Scott is a graduate of what has become film school for many English feature directors—television commercials. Working within the less constrictive boundaries of European advertising, these filmmakers developed a way of telling stories in striking, often concise images ... narrative through pictures rather than words.

Ridley Scott's latest project is a large scale fantasy film for Universal Pictures entitled *LEGEND*, many years in development.

MICHAEL SINGER: You've made three films, one set in the past, two in the future. You don't seem to be terribly interested in the here and now, rather creating alternate worlds for the audience. Is that accurate?
RIDLEY SCOTT: It's an accurate assessment almost coincidentally. I've got no intentions of locking myself into that pattern. I tend to be somebody who rather follows his nose along a route. I have had a route of being involved with science fiction movies, since *BLADE RUNNER* and *ALIEN* are science fiction or futuristic movies. It just fell that way. There was really no preconceived plan. I mean, I've got every intention, at some point in time when I've got this out of my system, of moving around to more contemporary material. But I think that nearly all the material I get locked into has a slightly exotic central core to it. And half the predicament is that the present day, the way I see it, isn't terribly interesting to me.

Your films have a very specific look to them, and it's as if you might have taken your visions somewhere else—on canvas, in sculpture or on a stage. Why film?

I've often asked that question myself because film, most of the time, is a lot of aggravation. If I were a writer I think I would probably stay with that, because writing in its physical form is the simplest art form. You have a pad, a piece of paper, a quiet room, and you can create your world. And it doesn't cost anybody anything, right? That's why I don't bother as a writer. I couldn't do it. I can write, but not to the degree that I can write screenplays. I started off as a painter. I did seven years of art school

and three and a half years as a painter. I found the painting process to be—at that particular time in my life—slightly directionless. I was standing there filling in a white canvas ... to what purpose? The occupation was too lonely. I think I needed people, to communicate with people and be happy about my own creativity. I can't stand my own company, and writing and painting are both lonely occupations, and static occupations. Obviously, the excitement of the obvious elements of cinema—the movement, the color, the sound—is much more exciting. Other than film, I think what I'd like to have done was to play in a band, because a musician to me is instant adrenalin and instant pleasure. Films take eighteen months to two years to turn around. The instant pleasure happens after that eighteen months and that's only if I feel I've got the film right which usually occurs sometime just at the end of the dubbing. The dub has just glued the film together and I think, "God, that's interesting," or, "Oh my God, it doesn't work." That's the biggest moment of pleasure. A musician gets his pleasure every night.

It's an interesting analogy. Musicians play together in bands, and filmmakers work in grand collaborative efforts. Your collaborations with designers and cinematographers have always been interesting.

Well, I don't ever try and pretend to be an expert in all fields. I know about quite a few which are involved in the film process—art direction, the way a film should look—and therefore I suppose I know a little bit about cinematography. I certainly know how it should look to me. But I prefer to collaborate, and therefore the whole thing becomes a much stronger

and richer process. And that's why, certainly in the last three films, including *LEGEND*, I've involved artists, illustrators or painters at a very early stage to illustrate the general feeling of the film. And these are usually very, very elaborate pieces of artwork. I'm very curious to actually go through that process as well as try something which is just about people in a contemporary environment. That would be a different kind of challenge.

When you were a boy, did you derive more inspiration from watching movies or reading books?

When I was a kid I was not the inveterate filmgoer, probably because of the part of the world I came from. Northern England isn't exactly big film buff territory, so I used to be a regular Saturday afternoon kid going in to see Hollywood movies and look at the great rolling credits at the beginning and end of the movie and wondering who did what. The thing I actually keyed into was the person called the art director. That was my first real long term connection with the idea that I might want to make films, because I think my strongest subject, early on, was painting.

I know that you had a project for a time called *KNIGHTS*. Were you ever influenced by the Matter of Britain—the Arthurian legends?

I don't know what makes any individual really tick, or what makes them gravitate towards one facet or the other, whether you are a contemporary person or have an affinity for the past. There is no specific answer to that question. I think as I began working seriously in advertising and commercials, I just found that I sort of gravitated towards period pieces, whether Victorian or earlier. I found that in England, the opportunity for me to explore all those kinds of periods was vast. Frequently I would change an idea or concept. I wanted to get into films, and the film that I found myself getting into was a Napoleonic period piece called *THE DUELLISTS*. I was shooting where Eleanor of Acquitaine used to live as part of her domain, and therefore I was actually walking through the forests and the fields everyday that were essentially Arthurian—where you mix fact with mythology. And I sort of keyed in on that. When I was doing *THE DUELLISTS*, I had the idea that I'd like to do something with knights, which nobody had actually done properly for many years. So we started planning something, and I went into a very highbrow version of that, which was

continued on page 19

Photograph by Toris Von Wolfe

LYNNE LITTMAN

Based upon audience reactions, *TESTAMENT* appears to be a film with the power to change people's minds—and the big surprise is that it was directed by first-time feature filmmaker—Lynne Littman.

A well-known director of documentaries including the Oscar winning *NUMBER OUR DAYS* — a compassionate look at the elderly Jews of Venice, California, Littman originally made *TESTAMENT* for the PBS American Playhouse series. But her extraordinary, intimate chronicle of nuclear war's effect on a middle-class American family, and the Northern California town in which they live, was picked up instead for major theatrical distribution by Paramount Pictures.

Littman, a multiple local Emmy Award winner for public affairs and news broadcast efforts, later served a term as an executive producer for network television movies before returning to her real passion—working behind the camera rather than a desk.

MICHAEL SINGER: Tell me something about the genesis of *TESTAMENT*.

LYNNE LITTMAN: *TESTAMENT* was a three-page story written by a woman named Carol Amen that I read one night in *Ms. Magazine*. The back of the magazine said that Ms. Amen lived in Sunnyvale, California. I called information there, got her phone number, and then proceeded to persuade her to sell me the rights to the story. Her story is deceptive—it's short but extremely complete. It truly was the basis for the film. We added the front part—the life of the family before the blast—but very much of that was indicated in the story itself. I was able to get funding from American Playhouse after six months of looking at other sources. We then hired John Sacret Young to write it. But I was certainly there . . . it was my baby from the beginning.

ced*TESTAMENT* is your first feature. Is it also the first time you worked with actors?

No, I did a half-hour dramatic short for the Children's Home Society which was completely scripted and acted. That was about two years ago.

How many other films have you made?

About forty documentaries, one of which, *NUMBER OUR DAYS*, won an Academy Award.

A couple of years ago, you veered off into television as a production executive. Why?

I made that career move because I'd just had a baby, and I knew that I wanted to stop making documentaries—at least for awhile. It seemed like a good opportunity to get a very well-paid education. And indeed, at some level, it was. I was executive producer of movies for television at ABC for about a year. But I'm just not an executive—unless it's connected to a project of my own. I'm fine as a producer of my own films, but I am not interested in power over other people. And that's what that job was about. It was less about getting films made than it was about power.

But don't you have power over many people as a director?

No. You are working *with* people. You don't have power *over* them. You're not deciding the fate of their lives. You're part of a team and you're the leader. That's not executive power, which is ridiculous. Good executives are probably as rare as good directors. Television especially—probably more than movies—is such a game, such a market-place, that it's not about making things, it's about selling things. My whole background is about making things, which is very different.

When did you start working in film?

I got into public television, because that was a place where women could work in 1964. I worked at *NET* in New

York on a series called *NET JOURNAL*, which was a public television version of the Edward R. Murrow show, that kind of investigative reporting. We did some wonderful full-length documentaries. I was a researcher and associate producer, and I fell in love with the process of making documentaries and with journalism. What I was struck by—and what continued in my life from then — was the way that people's lives changed because of your presence. That probably came to a kind of head when I worked with Barbara Myerhoff on *NUMBER OUR DAYS*, because we really changed those old people's lives. No, we didn't change their lives . . . their lives had been very full and rich without us. But we had a real effect on people's awareness of them, which was part of what Barbara's work as an anthropologist was about. What I finally found, when I worked on my last documentary—which was a film about mothers and daughters—was that I had gotten to the point where I was manipulating my subjects. And the minute that began to happen, I realized that I had better switch over. The minute you start telling your subjects what you want them to do, that you think you know better than they do what they should be saying—better write a script.

You mention changing people's lives. I think *TESTAMENT* is a movie that may change a lot of people's lives.

Well, it changed my life.

How?

My attitude towards the future is completely different. I've lost the sense of the future. In a very sneaky way, I think the threat of nuclear destruction has entered my consciousness, and I don't have a vision of the future. I am afraid that I have been . . . radiated in that sense.

You've lost the sense of the future . . . ?

Not as a professional. What I like about movies, the movies that I love, is that they've changed my view of life so that I come out of the theatre different from when I walked in. Not message films, but films that have some kind of insight about humanity, that make me think differently through the experiences of the characters. In a way, I think *NUMBER OUR DAYS* did that, and I think that *TESTAMENT* does it.

Did you feel that you were making a political film?

I felt I was making a film that I hoped would not end for people in the theatre. I hoped that the end of the film would be people sort of gushing out of the theatre and finishing the film themselves, saying, "We can't allow this to happen. This must not happen." That family in the film, flawed though it was, is pretty much a perfect family. They're certainly the updated version of the media ideal family. I think they're all complicated people, they're all smart. We were very careful not to make them clichés ... they're a lot like people I know. They function, they love each other, they have problems and they either will or will not survive as a family. It's very much about the problems and the issues that I face in my life now as a wife and mother. It's certainly not directly from my life, but it's not that far away either.

What were your ambitions for TESTAMENT when you first conceived of it?

It's like "The Little Engine That Could" ... we did not have goals for this film beyond American Playhouse, which I was absolutely thrilled about and would again be thrilled to make a film for. I mean, I would rather make an independent film that stands a chance of having my control and my vision intact. That seems to me a gift.

In the aftermath of TESTAMENT, more than likely than not you'll be deluged with scripts and offers from the studios. Are you afraid of that kind of success?

I'm not afraid of anything but not being good. I finish a project and my feeling is that I'll never have another idea and there'll never be another film — but I've had that through forty films.

Are you the kind of person who wonders when everybody's going to wake up and find out that you really don't have any talent after all?

Yes ... that this was a series of accidents. But the thing that I *know* I have is an enormous sense of perfection, and I'm also a workaholic ... so I have no question that things happen by chance ... they never, never, never do. I'm like a rabid dog when I get hold of a project that I want to do—I hook into it and don't let go until I get it done. Luckily, I surrounded myself with people who are just like me. Which means that you're never pulling anybody, you're just running like a pack of wild dogs, which is the most exhilarating, terrific feeling in the world. Especially when you're running

with a pack of *talented* wild dogs. There was a sense about this film, that it had to get made. We paid everybody minimum, but sent grips and gaffers copies of the script and enlisted them on the basis of their enthusiasm for the project. And they came ... people I'd never worked with before. The interesting thing is that I don't think very many people on the crew had ever worked for a woman before.

Were there any problems with the crew because of that?

I'm sure some had trepidation, but they kept it to themselves and were phenomenal. They were young and dedicated, and the process was a joy. The entire crew came to dailies almost every day. That's unheard of. That's how much they cared about what was getting on film.

What I like about movies— the movies that I love—is that they've changed my view of life so that I come out of the theatre different from when I walked in.

When did you know that the film was going beyond public television in terms of distribution? How did it come about?

The man who gave me the final third of the budget — I sold him all the distribution rights—had made an arrangement with American Playhouse that if he could make a theatrical distribution deal they would give him a certain period of time in which to first distribute the film theatrically before it went on American Playhouse. And indeed, he made his deal. I had nothing to do with it. This has been a dream come true, and continues to be. You see, I have never worked on anything that I wasn't in love with. I can't get my motors running unless I'm in love—I am either not professional enough or I'm lucky. Now, that means that the period in-between jobs is hell, because it's like I'm dead. Right now I feel like I'm running around trying to get pregnant. I'm trying to have an idea, another baby. Each one of these films feels like having a baby.

Are you interested in making films about women's issues?

My films will always be, hopefully, from my point of view. I am a woman. Therefore they will be. At this point in my life, my struggle is about men and women. I think as a woman I know a huge amount about women's issues and the reality of the way we're perceived in society, which has its own shocking education. But I'm also interested in men. So instead of films being male fantasies about women, there's a good chance they'll be female fantasies about men, or efforts at perceptions of reality.

Are you hoping that the White House asks for a print of TESTAMENT?

I think that the White House could see this film and absolutely view it as a justification for everything they're doing. See, the thing about this film is that it can justify everybody's feelings. People can come out saying "I must go build a bigger shelter," or they can say "I must arm against any possible nuclear attack." My hope is that they'll come out saying that we must prevent this from happening at any cost. But I certainly don't think it will change anybody's political persuasion.

But the film does come from a very definite point of view.

My background as a documentary filmmaker is the most important part of why I make films. It's about a certain sense of responsibility toward the material and toward the people who see them. I think movies are the most powerful medium. They certainly always were in my life. I think the images that you take away from movies, whether it's the way a man treats a woman or the way a woman treats a child or the way a boss treats an employee, are the images that we live with. And I think that I will always want to be responsible for the results. That doesn't mean to make myself self-important in terms of the power I have. But those images, and those huge screens of people doing things to each other, really impress people. And I want to be very sure that I'm proud of my own.

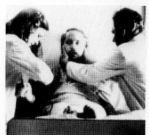

Photograph courtesy of 20th Century Fox

PAUL BARTEL

One of Hollywood's authentic mavericks, Paul Bartel has carved a niche in the hearts of audiences and critics alike with his unique blend of the macabre and the comic. His offbeat sensibilities have graced such films as *PRIVATE PARTS*, *DEATH RACE 2000* and the delightful *EATING RAOUL*. Starring with Mary Woronov as Paul and Mary Bland, America's original square, uptight and ultimately murderous couple, Bartel created a hilarious world of horrible gentility and misplaced priorities.

When not directing and acting in his own projects, Bartel can often be seen performing in several of his colleague's films, including *HOLLYWOOD BOULEVARD*, *PIRANHA*, *ROCK 'N' ROLL HIGH SCHOOL*, *GET CRAZY* and *HEART LIKE A WHEEL*.

MICHAEL SINGER: Let's talk about death.
PAUL BARTEL: Always a pleasure.

It seems to me that death is at the heart of most of your films. But it's treated in such a gleeful way that it takes the edge off. Are you particularly interested in death as a subject in film?

No, I don't think I am consciously interested in death. I *am* interested in comedy. And I think, probably, at the heart of a lot of comedy is fear of one kind or another. Surely fear of death is one of those main fears. Yes, in terms of *DEATH RACE 2000*, the whole idea of inflicting death more or less capriciously seemed to me a good basis for comedy. The premise of the movie was so grim that the only way I could deal with it was to exaggerate it outrageously, artificialize it and not take it seriously. That was also true of the premise of *PRIVATE PARTS*, much less so in *CANNONBALL*, where I really wasn't very interested in the premise of the movie at all. I'm interested in the horror genre, the suspense genre, and death is certainly an important aspect of those.

***EATING RAOUL* is a film that revels delightedly in a kind of hip bad taste.**

That comes from a blending of Dick's [Blackburn, Bartel's collaborator] and my sensibilities plus the sensibilities of the actors. The impetus for making *EATING RAOUL*, from my standpoint, was to do a film in which Mary Woronov and I could co-star. And because we aren't big names, we wanted to do something that would attract attention by its outrageousness and would entertain an audience on its own merits. I think that it catered to the aesthetics of the film, the desire to be outrageous and appeal to a young, hip audience. I would certainly be interested in making a more genteel comedy, but those are much harder to sell. Outrageousness is an exploitive quality in film.

Nevertheless, *EATING RAOUL* was in many ways a comedy of manners.

There's a synthesis of a genteel approach and raunchy and outrageous material, which was the basic production concept of the movie.

***EATING RAOUL* had one of the best senses of Los Angeles, from a comic point of view, that I've seen in a long while. Did you grow up here?**

No, I'm an East Coaster, from New Jersey. But I lived in New York for awhile and I think of myself as essentially a New Yorker with a New York sensibility.

But your approach to L.A. in *EATING RAOUL* is sort of a love/hate thing, a city both repugnant and vastly entertaining.

Well, I'm very fond of L.A. I do find plenty of food for satire here. But I'm not one of those New York L.A. haters. I really love it most of the time.

When did you know you were going to be a filmmaker?

I got interested in animation at a very early age. I used to go to the movies a lot and my favorite films were animated films. I loved Saturday cartoon matinees, the UPA films. When I came out to California for the first time, going to UCLA, I thought I wanted to be an animation director. But the bottom was falling out of the market for good, ambitious, sophisticated animation. And also, I became a little more interested in theatre and acting, as well as writing and live-action films. But animation was my first love and I still appreciate it.

Is it correct to assume that there's a certain influence of animated films on your live-action features?

It is certainly an element in the mix, specifically in *EATING RAOUL* and *DEATH RACE 2000*. Much less so in *CANNONBALL* and *PRIVATE PARTS*.

How did you get your first feature, *PRIVATE PARTS*, financed and made?

The administration at MGM at that time wanted to produce a series of very low-budget non-union pictures, and *PRIVATE PARTS* was one of them.

Were you pleased with the distribution? How much of the country saw *PRIVATE PARTS*?

Most of the major cities. But the title, which was chosen by the president, was a major miscalculation and the absence of any star names in it pretty much killed the film's chance for reaching a wide audience.

What was your original title?
BLOOD RELATIONS.

Was *DEATH RACE 2000* your concept or Roger Corman's?

Roger Corman's. When I came into it there was an unworkable script. We spent a year rewriting, abandoning and then putting it back into production again.

Can I assume that the original idea was not intended to be as funny as it turned out to be?

It was always intended to have a comic element. The first script was very bizarre and not particularly funny. Then Chuck Griffith brought a great deal of comedy into it, and my input was also basically comic. Roger was of two minds about it. He wanted it to be funny, but he didn't want it to be essentially a comedy and was trying to make a hard action film with comic overtones.

Did you have to fight for your vision?

Yes. I got in a certain number of things that I wanted. He ultimately had control of the editing, so he took out a lot of stuff that I would have liked to have had in. The finished film is very much a synthesis of his vision and mine. And people seem to enjoy the film, so I'm not unhappy with it.

It really has become one of the most popular cult films of the seventies. *MAD MAX* and *THE ROAD WARRIOR* would be unthinkable without it.

George Miller told me that *DEATH RACE 2000* was a big influence on *MAD MAX*. I like *MAD MAX*, but I think *THE ROAD WARRIOR* is the absolute apotheosis of that genre. I can't imagine any more perfect realization of that kind of movie. It's not my favorite kind of film, but *THE ROAD WARRIOR* is one of my favorite movies and George is high on my list of favorite directors.

You are often talked about in the same category as John Waters. You both celebrate bad taste and revel in a kind of junk nostalgia. Does that comparison bother you at all?

No, but I don't think it's particularly accurate. I met John recently and I think he's quite wonderful. In fact, we wrote a fairly large part for John in this new Paul and Mary Bland picture. He's very funny, and I think his movies are wonderfully funny and satirical, but I don't particularly identify. I see why people think that we are in some ways similar, but I think that my attitude toward the audience is different than his.

In what way?

I think he is more concerned with shocking and scandalizing than I am.

No, I don't think I'm consciously interested in death . . . I am interested in comedy. And I think, probably, at the heart of a lot of comedy is fear of one kind or another.

I went to see *EATING RAOUL* on opening night at a theatre in Westwood, and you were outside before the start of the film handing out promotional cookies which had a bite taken out of them. That seemed to be taking directorial involvement with a film's distribution several steps beyond what I've seen. Is working on the fringes of the industry something that you'd like to continue to do?

Well, I'd like to continue to be involved in the production of the kind of low-budget film which permits risk taking and innovation. I would also like to participate in some of the mainstream

productions with their economic benefits. My ideal would be to alternate between the two—do a low-budget, non-union picture independently and then work on a big-budget studio film.

Can you talk about your new project?

It's a light comedy about yellow journalism and political corruption in New York entitled *NOT FOR PUBLICATION*. It has none of the dark underpinnings of *EATING RAOUL*. It's a big change of pace. And indeed, the sequel to *EATING RAOUL*, which Dick is going to direct with me producing, is itself a much lighter film than *EATING RAOUL*. There's only one murder in it— and it's very early in the picture.

RIDLEY SCOTT *continued from page 11*

TRISTAN AND ISOLDE. We had it scripted, but I felt that at that particular time it was just too esoteric—I wouldn't dare go in and do something like that as a general audience movie. I was interested in Hollywood cinema. I was being totally blown away at that point by Francis Ford Coppola, George Lucas, Steven Spielberg, and I thought, what am I doing? Here I am planning a little, miniscule capsule. I like what *they* do. And now, five years later, I finally came up with a writer who had developed something. Immediate past attempts at what I'd call Arthurian material hadn't worked for me. I can elaborate on why I don't think they work, but I don't want to do that in case mine doesn't. But I think I've got it right. It's taken four or five years thinking, going from *TRISTAN AND ISOL-* *DE*, vaguely messing around with a project called *KNIGHTS*, which again, was too on the nose, too historical. I was trying to put more mystical magic into it rather than a strict historical piece about

> *I was totally blown away at that time by Francis Ford Coppola, George Lucas, Steven Spielberg and I thought, "What am I doing? . . . I like what **they** do."*

crusaders in North Africa. You can't do dialogue like, "My liege" and, "My lord" for a contemporary audience. And so what we've now come to is the story for

LEGEND. The final idea for *LEGEND*, in a funny kind of way, has taken twelve years. It's a compilation of various do's and don't's. It's a kind of combination of Cocteau's *BEAUTY AND THE BEAST* and Walt Disney . . .

That's quite a combination.
. . . meet *THE EXORCIST.*

RONALD NEAME

Director, producer, writer and cinematographer Ronald Neame—a self-described "jack of all trades"—has worked for, with and above some of the most distinguished names in movie history on both sides of the Atlantic. Previously allied with such luminaries as Noel Coward, David Lean, Anthony Havelock-Allen and Alec Guinness, Neame is himself a three time Academy Award nominee. Cineguild, the partnership formed in 1943 between Neame, Lean and Havelock-Allan, was responsible for such classics of the British screen as *BLITHE SPIRIT, BRIEF ENCOUNTER, GREAT EXPECTATIONS* and *OLIVER TWIST*. His creative association with Alec Guinness led to *THE HORSE'S MOUTH* and *TUNES OF GLORY*. Neame directed Judy Garland's last performance in *I COULD GO IN SINGING* and Maggie Smith's Oscar winning role in *THE PRIME OF MISS JEAN BRODIE*. Currently residing in Beverly Hills, Neame has organized a new production company with screenwriter Céline La Frenière.

MICHAEL SINGER: Considering your parentage, you really qualify as a child of the industry, can't you?

RONALD NEAME: I think so. My mother, Ivy Close, was an actress. And my father, Elwin Neame, became a director, cinematographer—everything. It's rather a romantic story in a way. My father was a very successful London photographer. He had a reputation for photographing all the beautiful girls. If a family had a lovely daughter they always sent her to my father to be photographed. And in 1910, the Daily Mirror—which is a London tabloid—decided to hold a world beauty competition, to find the "most beautiful girl in the world." They asked my father if he would photograph the twenty-five finalists in this competition. One of them was my mother. Of course, she won the competition, and my father married her. She was immediately offered a film contract, with Walter West Productions. So I was really, like Judy Garland—who was born in a trunk—born on a set practically.

When did you know for certain that like your parents, you were going to follow into films? Or had you ever considered doing anything else?

Well, when I was 12 years old, my father was killed in a motor accident. And since he was a one-man business—by that I mean everybody went to him to be photographed—when he was dead there was nothing. The money ran out because he didn't believe in insurance, so I had to go out to work. My uncle got me a job with the Anglo-Persian Oil Company. I became an office boy there at 14, but I didn't really enjoy it. And my mother, who was still acting a little bit, knew the studio manager at British International Pictures at Elstree Studios. So I left the Anglo-Persian Oil Company and went to work at Elstree Studios as a messenger boy. Now, you see, it's extraordinary how things change so much. Because my greatest ambition at that time was to be a very good assistant cameraman. That was my total ambition, really. And it always puzzles me when young men come in to see me about a job, and the first thing they say is, "Well, of course I'm going to direct." I would never have had the aspirations of ever becoming a chief cameraman, let alone a director. I mean, it just wouldn't enter my head. I got six pounds a week . . . oh, not to begin with—I started with two pounds-ten. When I became assistant cameraman, I worked for a man called Claude Friese-Greene. Now, we in England claim that William Friese-Greene invented the motion picture. Here, they claim Edison of course, and in France they claim Lumière. But I suspect they were all on to it, really, about the same time. But as far as we were concerned it was William, and I worked for his son. Claude drank very heavily. He would start drinking at about ten in the morning, and I had to take over doing quite a bit of lighting for the picture, and then he'd sort of pull himself together and take over again. But it was wonderful in a way for me, because I got the opportunity to learn all about lighting without any of the responsibilities. Then one day poor

Friese-Greene collapsed on the set and had to be taken to the hospital. The studio management—more out of meanness than anything else, since they didn't want to train another cameraman—asked if I thought I would be able to carry on. What I didn't know about lighting could fill volumes, but at that age—I was 21 at that time—I thought, well, I could do anything. And so I finished the picture, which was called *DRAKE OF ENGLAND*. Then I was offered a picture called *INVITATION TO THE WALTZ*. And from then on I became a cameraman, photographing quota quickies. You know about quota quickies? To protect the industry from American pictures, a certain percentage of screen time had to go to British films. The American companies were very clever. What they did was make their own British pictures. They were five thousand feet long and had to be made in a week. I worked for 20th Century-Fox. What happened was that 20th Century-Fox would engage a British producer and tell him, "We will give you six thousand pounds for a five thousand foot film." The producer would then make the film for five thousand pounds, which is a pound a foot, and he would then take the other thousand for himself as the producer. The movies were real stinkers, but they gave one tremendous training. Not only for people like myself, but performers like James Mason, Glynis Johns and Jessica Tandy as well. A lot of people who are now stars played in those quotas for nothing.

I suppose the pressures also forced a certain creativity to come up with something interesting and acceptable for so little time and money.

Well, it's extraordinary to see how proud we became of them, because it was not a question of "Have we made one of the best pictures?" Of course we hadn't. But our criteria was, "For one week's work, that was pretty bloody good." By law, the theatres only had to show them once a day. So they would put them on at the West End Theatre, or the Plaza, at 10:30 in the morning whilst the cleaners were cleaning the theatre, and then they wouldn't put it back on again. So nobody saw them.

People think of film being more business than art in this day and age, but with the quotas, it sounds like that's *only* what they were.

It was a pure ruse to get around the laws. Now, there were a few good British picture being made at the time. A producer named Gabriel Pascal was directing quotas, but he always went over budget, even on those. And it came to the point where he had wooed George Bernard Shaw—how I don't know—to give him all his properties for nothing. And when he was about to do *MAJOR BARBARA*, he had a terrible row with Freddie Young, who was the senior cameraman. I'd been doing second unit work in a steel factory in Newcastle with David Lean directing my unit. And David said, "You know, Ronnie, Freddie's leaving the picture. You ought to photograph it." Gabby told me to do some tests with Wendy Hiller, and I made her look so good that they gave me the picture.

Did you also shoot *PYGMALION*?

No, but I'm always being given credit for it. Harry Stradling photographed it.

I didn't know he was English.

He wasn't. He came over to England. At that time, all the big pictures in England, particularly those that had American financing, would only use American cameramen. We British cameramen, at that time, were considered to be just junior boys and not very good.

That's certainly changed over the years.

The war changed that, because all the American cameraman had to go back to American to do their thing and we young British characters got the opportunity. It was in the wartime that I became a top cameraman. Later, I trained people like Oswald Morris. See, Ozzie was my number boy when I was a focus puller. Then he was my focus puller when I was an operating cameraman. Then he was my operator when I was a lighting cameraman. And when I became a producer, I gave Ozzie his first lighting job.

In those years, all the top names in the British industry seemed to know each, work together, learn together and teach together. Does that explain the uniformly excellent work that began pouring out of England in the early 1940's, which continued until, say, the mid-1960's when things started to slide?

They started to go wrong before then, really. But we were a very small community, very small indeed. Most of us grew up together. And also, we had this wonderful character named Arthur Rank, who gave us complete and utter freedom. For example, I came to America for the first time in 1945. Arthur Rank sent me over to take a look at all the American stages and studios and to see what we needed in England to re-equip after the war, because we didn't even

have Mole Richardson lights. I got an arrogant notion in my head that I could make a picture that would please American audiences. So when I went back, I said to David Lean, who was then an editor, "How about you direct a picture and I'll produce it?" And he said, "That would be wonderful. What shall we make?" So together we found *GREAT EXPECTATIONS*. I went to Arthur Rank and said, "Arthur, David and I want to make *GREAT EXPECTATIONS*" and he said, "Okay, how much?" We said, "Three hundred and fifty thousand pounds," and he said, "Okay, go away and make it." And that was it. That applied to all those pictures—nobody saw any rushes or had anything to say. We had our freedom.

> *I went to Arthur Rank and said, "David [Lean] and I want to make GREAT EXPECTATIONS" and he said, "Okay, how much?" We said, "350,000 pounds," and he said, "Okay, go away and make it." And that was it. Nobody saw any rushes . . . we had our freedom.*

How closely did *OLIVER TWIST* follow the completion of *GREAT EXPECTATIONS*?

About a year.

Was the same creative unit used?

Yes and no. In the case of *GREAT EXPECTATIONS*, David and I did the screenplay ourselves. And indeed, we took screenplay credit, which I suppose was fair enough, but I still think it was Charles Dickens.

You tackled Dickens again in the musical *SCROOGE*.

Yes. Well, that was brought to me pretty well complete. I had just walked away from a picture with Darryl F. Zanuck, and was in the clear when Leslie Bricusse and Gordon Stulberg, who was then head of Cinema Center Films, asked me if I would do it. Then I got Albert Finney interested. It wasn't bad . . . I enjoyed it. I would have liked to have made another musical, but I never have since, although we nearly got *THE FANTASTICKS* off the ground last year. You know, it's difficult to get anything off the ground these days. The pictures that I like best, the pictures that I enjoyed the

most of my own work were *THE HORSE'S MOUTH* and *TUNES OF GLORY*. Now, they were made by sheer pieces of luck. There was a man in New York called Robert Dowling who was a multi-millionaire and whose corporation at that time owned the Empire State Building, the Carlyle Hotel and several other properties. He had been wooed by Alexander Korda to come into partnership. They financed a four picture deal with Alec Guinness, but in the middle of it Korda died. So there were two pictures left with Alec Guinness that Robert Dowling owned. Now, Dowling had gotten United Artists out of a big financial problem and had gone onto their Board of Directors. Guinness and I got together on *THE HORSE'S MOUTH* and went to Dowling with it. He pretty well insisted that United Artists finance it. Well, when we had a preview of *THE HORSE'S MOUTH* in New York, and it was a big success, Arthur Krim said to me "Ronnie, I don't know how you made *that* picture from *that* script." I said "Well I'll tell you, Arthur. *That* picture *was* that script. It's just that you didn't know how to read it." And I think that one of the sad things is that people don't know how to read scripts. A lot of lovely things get turned down because readers read them for the company, turned down and never seen by anyone else. It's only the most obvious scripts, it seems to me, that people understand. They understand car chases, explosions, buildings falling down, people being stabbed to death, people being screwed all over the place . . . but I don't think they can read anything that's subtle. They say to me, "Ronnie, why aren't you making films as good as those that you used to make?" I don't think that I've slipped. I think it's simply that I cannot get good material going.

Have you had some frustrating experiences over the past few years with properties that you've tried to activate?

Yes, indeed I have. I've got two now, both of which I think could make very nice small pictures. But it should be with an unknown cast—in the case of one it's two 17-year-old girls. You know, they'll say, "Get Brooke Shields and you can do it." It's a bit disheartening and of course, the thing is that fortunately—because of a bad picture of mine called *THE POSEIDON ADVENTURE*—I've made sufficient money that I don't have to worry about paying the rent. It tends to make you a little more choosy. I think, to hell with it, why should I make this? Sometimes you can be wrong. I didn't want to make *THE POSEIDON AD-*

VENTURE. I did my best to get out of that almost until the day we started shooting. And then when Gordon Stulberg phoned me in England six months later and said, "This film's going to make more money than all the rest of your films put together," I said, "You're out of your mind, Gordon."

When did you start making films in America?

The first film I made in America I only made half of. I was longing to come to Hollywood and make a picture, and I was offered a terrible thing called *THE SEVENTH SIN* that MGM was making

I have a feeling that you love actors, since your films have been filled with some great performances—I think of Guinness in *THE HORSE'S MOUTH,* John Mills and Guinness in *TUNES OF GLORY,* Maggie Smith in *THE PRIME OF MISS JEAN BRODIE* and Judy Garland in *I CAN GO ON SINGING.* That was her last film, wasn't it?

Yes. We had a great love-hate relationship. When she was fond of me, which was half the time, she used to call with Eleanor Parker. There was a big change of management going on at MGM, the whole place was in turmoil, and I found myself in the middle of it. I also found that my rushes were being seen before *I* saw them. I got into a terrible state and began to really lose control, and the fact that the material was so poor didn't help. After four or five weeks, I could see that the studio was unhappy, I was unhappy, everybody was unhappy. My agent at that time said, "Ronnie, you've taken enough of this. You should resign, pack up." Well, I knew that this was a kind of way of him saying, "Better leave, because if you don't they're going to ask you to." So I left the picture and Vincente Minnelli took it over. I thought that was the end of my career. I was absolutely convinced that that was it. And I remember going home that evening to the little house that I had rented on Miller Drive, very depressed. At about eight o'clock in the evening the telephone rang. I got on and the voice said, "Mr. Neame?" "Yes?," I said. He said, "My name is George Cukor. I'm phoning you because I imagine you must be feeling a bit low this evening." I said, "Well, to be honest with you, I'm devastated." He said, "Well, that's why I'm phoning. Don't worry about it. I was the director taken off of *GONE WITH THE WIND.* And it won't make any difference to your career." I thought, what a wonderful thing to do. I didn't know that man, yet he went to the

trouble to phone.
me "Pussycat." When she disliked me, which was half the time, she would say, "Get that goddamned British Henry Hathaway off the set!" You know about Henry Hathaway? He was the great bully at that time.

Of all the actors you've worked with, whom did you enjoy the most?

Well of course, enjoyment takes so many different forms, doesn't it? That's a difficult one to answer. I still think the greatest actor I've worked with is Alec Guinness. And I think I would have to say that I enjoyed working with Guinness more than anybody else. But for sheer fun and pleasure, I'd have to say Walter Matthau. He's such a funny man, never a dull moment when we're working together. He keeps the unit alive and full of fun when he's on the set. And I mean the right kind of fun. Who taught me the most? Guinness taught me a great deal about acting and actors. I was directing him in *THE PROMOTER,* which in English is called *THE CARD.* He got a bit difficult, a bit sulky over something and was being miserable. I asked him what was wrong. And he said, "Ronnie, would you like me to tell you something about actors that may help you as a director? Most so-called normal, ordinary human beings go through a period when they want to act. This period usually is between the ages of ten and fourteen. Little boys want to dress up as cowboys or Indians and go bang-bang-bang. Little girls borrow their mother's dresses, put on their mother's makeup and flounce around the place. At the age of about fourteen and fifteen they grow up through this adolescent period and they become scientists, clerks, doctors, dentists, cab drivers, bus drivers, anything you like. But the actor and actress, in that part of their mind that wants to act, remains terminally and forever fourteen. Therefore, even though I may be much better read than you, I may be more intellectual than you, I may be more intelligent than you . . . the part of me that wants to act is still fourteen. And I want to be treated like that. I want to be encouraged. I want to be told, 'Well done, Alec.' But occasionally, I also have to be spanked. I also have to be cut down to size. I also have to be put in my place and told to behave myself. And if you can treat actors like that, Ronnie, you won't go far wrong." And it's absolutely true. The trouble is, it's not always easy to treat a highly intelligent man like Guinness as a 14-year old! Now, Noel Coward taught me a great deal, and of course I loved working with him—he's godfather to my son Christopher, by the way.

Maggie Smith . . . I loved working with her because she's such a first-rate actress, but she can be a pain in the ass. I loved working with Judy Garland, but she could drive you around the bend too. Albert Finney is wonderful. I didn't get along very well with Gene Hackman. I don't think I was the right kind of director for him. He didn't quite understand my Britishness, I suppose. He said "I'm used to somebody shouting."

I guess he should have gotten Henry Hathaway.

Yes, I suppose so.

Your style of movie making can be described, if you'll permit me, as being old-fashioned in that one is rarely aware of overt technique. How would you characterize the difference between your style and that being used by most young filmmakers today?

I belong to a school that said, "There is no camera." In other words, what you're seeing is happening, but there is no camera. So we tried to cover up any camera movements. Although my camera tracks all the time, and it's never still, I would cover up all those movements, disguise them. Now, what's happened in the present generation is that instead of it being "There is no camera," it's become "I am a camera." I, me, am the camera. Modern filmmaking has a different kind of realism. It's got a documentary realism. It's got the realism of having grabbed the moment, instead of the realism of my generation, which was very much rehearsed.

It's interesting to me that although you know and recognize the more contemporary style of filmmaking, you make a conscious decision to do it your own way. That seems to indicate a kind of purity.

Well, I don't know. You see, Picasso—not that I would say any film director is like Picasso—came through the conventional, classical style of painting to what he finished up with. I would love to be able to change, but I've been so programmed that I can't.

TORIS VON WOLFE

FOTO-INTERNATIONALE
LOS ANGELES (213) 995-1876

DIRECTORS

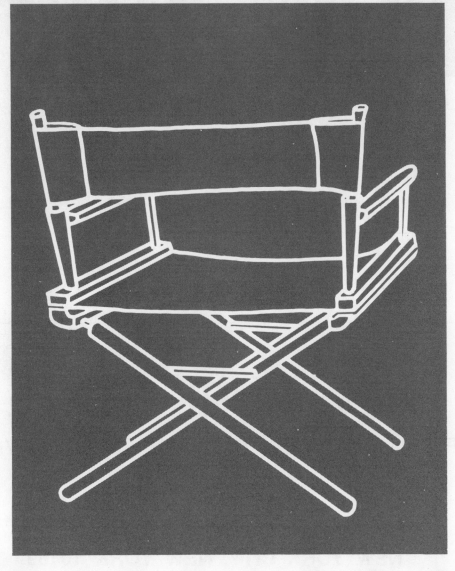

LISTINGS

NEW YORK

YOUR ONLY DIRECTION

NEW YORK STATE

OFFICE OF MOTION PICTURE AND TELEVISION
DEVELOPMENT

**230 PARK AVENUE
NEW YORK CITY, NEW YORK 10169
212-949-8514**

JAYNNE C. KEYES—DIRECTOR

PEPPER O'BRIEN   **TONY DIDIO**

BONNIE MCCRACKEN   **DONALD HILL**

KEY TO ABBREVIATIONS

(TF)   =   TELEFEATURE
Motion pictures made for television with an on-air running time of 1½ hours to 4½ hours on commercial television; or 1 hour to 4 hours on non-commercial television.

(CTF)   =   CABLE TELEFEATURE
Motion pictures made for cable television with an on-air running time of 1 hour to 4 hours.

(MS)   =   MINISERIES
Motion pictures made for television with an on-air running time of 4½ hours and more on commercial television; or 4 hours or more on non-commercial television.

(CMS)   =   CABLE MINISERIES
Motion pictures made for cable television with an on-air running time of 4 hours or more.

(FD)   =   FEATURE DOCUMENTARY
Documentary films made for theatrical distribution of feature length (1 or more hours).

(TD)   =   TELEVISION DOCUMENTARY
Documentary films made for television of feature length (1½ hours or more on commercial television, 1 hour or more on non-commercial television).

(CTD)   =   CABLE TELEVISION DOCUMENTARY
Documentary films made for cable television of feature length (1 or more hours).

(AF)   =   ANIMATED FEATURE

(ATF)   =   ANIMATED TELEFEATURE

KEY TO SYMBOLS

*   after a director's name denotes membership in the Directors Guild of America.

★   after a film title denotes a directorial Academy Award nomination.

★★   after a film title denotes directorial Academy Award win.

☆   after a film title denotes directorial Emmy Award nomination.

☆☆   after a film title denotes directorial Emmy Award win.

PAUL AARON *

Agent: Lee Muhl, ICM - Los Angeles, 213/550-4000
Attorney: William Kerstetter, Pollock, Bloom & Dekom, 9255 Sunset Blvd., Los
    Angeles, CA 90069, 213/278-8622

A DIFFERENT STORY   Avco Embassy, 1978
A FORCE OF ONE   American Cinema, 1979
THE MIRACLE WORKER (TF)   Katz-Gallin Productions/Half-Pint Productions,
    1979
THIN ICE (TF)   CBS Entertainment, 1981
MAID IN AMERICA (TF)   CBS Entertainment, 1982
DEADLY FORCE   Embassy, 1983
IMPLIED FORCE (TF)   The Jozak Company, 1983

GEORGE ABBOTT

b. June 25, 1887 - Forestville, New York
Business: 1270 Avenue of the Americas, New York, NY

WHY BRING THAT UP?   1929
HALF-WAY TO HEAVEN   1929
MANSLAUGHTER   1930
THE SEA GOD   1930
STOLEN HEAVEN   Paramount, 1931
SECRETS OF A SECRETARY   Paramount, 1931
MY SIN   1931
THE CHEAT   1931
TOO MANY GIRLS   RKO Radio, 1940
THE PAJAMA GAME   co-director with Stanley Donen, Warner Bros., 1957
DAMN YANKEES   co-director with Stanley Donen, Warner Bros., 1958

ROBERT J. ABEL *

b. March 10, 1937 - Cleveland, Ohio
Business: Robert Abel & Associates, 953 Highland Avenue, Hollywood, CA 90038,
    213/462-8100
Attorney: Sam Halpern, Bartman, Brown & Halpern, 1880 Century Park East - Suite
    1015, Los Angeles, CA 90067, 213/552-1093

ELVIS ON TOUR (FD)   co-director with Pierre Adidge, MGM, 1972
LET THE GOOD TIMES ROLL (FD)   co-director with Sidney Levin, Columbia,
    1973

JIM ABRAHAMS *

Business Manager: Abrahams Boy, Inc., 11777 San Vicente Blvd - Suite 600, Los
    Angeles, CA 90049, 213/820-1942

AIRPLANE!   co-director with David Zucker & Jerry Zucker, Paramount, 1980
TOP SECRET!   co-director with David Zucker & Jerry Zucker, Paramount, 1984

EDWARD ABROMS*

Messages: 805/495-0701
Agent: Skip Nicholson Agency - Sherman Oaks, 213/906-2700

THE IMPOSTER (TF)   Warner Bros. TV, 1975

AL ADAMSON

Business: Independent-International Pictures, 223 State Highway 18, East Brunswick,
   NJ, 201/249-8982

TWO TICKETS TO TERROR   Victor Adamson, 1964
GUN RIDERS   1969
BLOOD OF DRACULA'S CASTLE   Crown International, 1969
SATAN'S SADISTS   Independent-International, 1970
HELL'S BLOODY DEVILS   *THE FAKERS*   Independent-International, 1970
FIVE BLOODY GRAVES   Independent-International, 1971
HORROR OF THE BLOOD MONSTERS   Independent-International, 1971
THE FEMALE BUNCH   Dalia, 1971
LAST OF THE COMANCHEROS   Independent-International, 1971
BLOOD OF GHASTLY HORROR   Independent-International, 1972
THE BRAIN OF BLOOD   Hemisphere, 1972
DOOMSDAY VOYAGE   Futurama International, 1972
DRACULA VS. FRANKENSTEIN   Independent-International, 1973
THE DYNAMITE BROTHERS   Cinemation, 1974
GIRLS FOR RENT   Independent-International, 1974
THE NAUGHTY STEWARDESSES   Independent-International, 1975
STUD BROWN   Cinemation, 1975
BLAZING STEWARDESSES   Independent-International, 1975
JESSIE'S GIRLS   Manson International, 1976
BLACK HEAT   Independent-International, 1976
CINDERELLA 2000   Independent-International, 1977
BLACK SAMURAI   BLLJ International, 1977
SUNSET COVE   Cal-Am Artists, 1978
DEATH DIMENSION   Movietime, 1978
NURSE SHERRI   Independent-International, 1978
FREEZE BOMB   Movietime, 1980
CARNIVAL MAGIC   Krypton Corporation, 1982

PIERRE ADIDGE

JOE COCKER/MAD DOGS & ENGLISHMEN (FD)   MGM, 1971
ELVIS ON TOUR (FD)   co-director with Robert J. Abel, MGM, 1972

LOU ADLER*

Contact: Directors Guild of America - Los Angeles, 213/656-1220

UP IN SMOKE   Paramount, 1978
LADIES AND GENTLEMEN ... THE FABULOUS STAINS   Paramount, 1982

CHARLIE AHEARN

WILD STYLE   First Run Features, 1983

MOUSTAPHA AKKAD

b. Syria
Address: 2 Ennerdale Drive, London NW9 ODT, England, 01/205-3044

MOHAMMAD, MESSENGER OF GOD   *THE MESSAGE*   Tarik, 1977,
   Lebanese-British
LION OF THE DESERT   United Film Distribution, 1981, Libyan-British

ALAN ALDA *

b. January 28, 1936 - New York, New York
Agent: William Morris Agency - Beverly Hills, 213/274-7451

THE FOUR SEASONS   Universal, 1981

ADELL ALDRICH *

b. June 11, 1943 - Los Angeles, California
Business: The Aldrich Company, 606 N. Larchmont Blvd., Los Angeles, CA 90004,
    213/462-6511
Agent: Peter Giagni, APA - Los Angeles, 213/273-0744

DADDY, I DON'T LIKE IT LIKE THIS (TF)   CBS Entertainment, 1978
THE KID FROM LEFT FIELD (TF)   Gary Coleman Productions/Deena Silver-
    Kramer's Movie Company, 1979

ROBERT ALDRICH *

b. August 9, 1918 - Cranston, Rhode Island
Business: The Aldrich Company, 606 N. Larchmont Blvd., Los Angeles, CA 90004,
    213/462-6511
Agent: Stan Kamen, William Morris Agency - Beverly Hills, 213/274-7451

THE BIG LEAGUER   MGM, 1953
WORLD FOR RANSOM   Allied Artists, 1954
APACHE   United Artists, 1954
VERA CRUZ   United Artists, 1954
KISS ME DEADLY   United Artists, 1955
THE BIG KNIFE   United Artists, 1955
AUTUMN LEAVES   Columbia, 1956
ATTACK!   United Artists, 1956
TEN SECONDS TO HELL   United Artists, 1959, British
THE ANGRY HILLS   MGM, 1959, British
THE LAST SUNSET   Universal, 1961
WHAT EVER HAPPENED TO BABY JANE?   Warner Bros., 1962
SODOM AND GOMORRAH   20th Century-Fox, 1963, Italian-French-U.S.
4 FOR TEXAS   Warner Bros., 1963
HUSH ... HUSH, SWEET CHARLOTTE   Warner Bros., 1964
THE FLIGHT OF THE PHOENIX   20th Century-Fox, 1965
THE DIRTY DOZEN   MGM, 1967
THE LEGEND OF LYLAH CLARE   MGM, 1968
TOO LATE THE HERO   Cinerama Releasing Corporation, 1970
THE GRISSOM GANG   Cinerama Releasing Corporation, 1971
ULZANA'S RAID   Universal, 1972
EMPEROR OF THE NORTH EMPEROR OF THE NORTH POLE   20th
    Century-Fox, 1973
THE LONGEST YARD   Paramount, 1974
HUSTLE   Paramount, 1975
TWILIGHT'S LAST GLEAMING   Allied Artists, 1977, U.S.-West German
THE CHOIRBOYS   Universal, 1977
THE FRISCO KID   Warner Bros., 1979
... ALL THE MARBLES   MGM/United Artists, 1981

COREY ALLEN *

b. June 29, 1934 - Cleveland, Ohio
Agent: Contemporary-Korman Artists - Beverly Hills, 213/278-8250

PINOCCHIO   EUE, 1971
SEE THE MAN RUN (TF)   Universal TV, 1971
CRY RAPE! (TF)   Leonard Freeman Productions, 1973
YESTERDAY'S CHILD (TF)   co-director with Bob Rosenbaum, Paramount TV,
    1977
THUNDER AND LIGHTNING   20th Century-Fox, 1978
AVALANCHE   New World, 1979
STONE (TF)   Stephen J. Cannell Productions/Universal TV, 1979
THE MAN IN THE SANTA CLAUS SUIT (TF)   Dick Clark Productions, 1979
THE RETURN OF FRANK CANNON (TF)   QM Productions, 1980

IRWIN ALLEN *

b. June 12, 1916 - New York, New York
Agent: ICM - Los Angeles, 213/550-4000

THE SEA AROUND US (FD)   RKO Radio, 1951
THE ANIMAL WORLD (FD)   Warner Bros., 1956
THE STORY OF MANKIND   Warner Bros., 1957
THE LOST WORLD   20th Century-Fox, 1960
VOYAGE TO THE BOTTOM OF THE SEA   20th Century-Fox, 1961
FIVE WEEKS IN A BALLOON   20th Century-Fox, 1962
CITY BENEATH THE SEA (TF)   20th Century-Fox TV/Motion Pictures
    International, 1971
THE TOWERING INFERNO   action sequences only, 20th Century-Fox, 1974
THE SWARM   Warner Bros., 1978
BEYOND THE POSEIDON ADVENTURE   Warner Bros., 1979

WOODY ALLEN *

(Allen Stewart Konigsberg)

b. December 1, 1935 - Brooklyn, New York
Personal Manager: Jack Rollins/Charles Joffe, 130 West 57th Street, New York, NY,
    212/582-1940

WHAT'S UP, TIGER LILY?   American International, 1966
TAKE THE MONEY AND RUN   Cinerama Releasing Corporation, 1969
BANANAS   United Artists, 1971
EVERYTHING YOU ALWAYS WANTED TO KNOW ABOUT SEX* (*BUT
    WERE AFRAID TO ASK)   United Artists, 1972
SLEEPER   United Artists, 1973
LOVE AND DEATH   United Artists, 1975
ANNIE HALL ★★   United Artists, 1977
INTERIORS ★   United Artists, 1978
MANHATTAN   United Artists, 1979
STARDUST MEMORIES   United Artists, 1980
A MIDSUMMER NIGHT'S SEX COMEDY   Orion/Warner Bros., 1982
ZELIG   Orion/Warner Bros., 1983
BROADWAY DANNY ROSE   Orion, 1984
THE PURPLE ROSE OF CAIRO   Orion, 1984

PAUL ALMOND *

b. April 26, 1931 - Montreal, Quebec, Canada
Business: Quest Film Productions, Ltd., 1272 Redpath Drive, Montreal, Quebec H3G
    2K1, Canada, 514/849-7921

BACKFIRE   Anglo Amalgamated, 1962, British
THE DARK DID NOT CONQUER (TF)   CBC, 1963, Canadian
JOURNEY TO THE CENTRE (TF)   CBC, 1963, Canadian
ISABEL   Paramount, 1968, Canadian
ACT OF THE HEART   Universal, 1970, Canadian
JOURNEY   EPOH, 1972, Canadian
FINAL ASSIGNMENT   Almi Cinema 5, 1980, Canadian
UPS AND DOWNS   1983, Canadian

JOHN A. ALONZO *

b. 1934 - Dallas, Texas
Agent: Skip Nicholson Agency - Sherman Oaks, 213/906-2700

FM   Universal, 1978
CHAMPIONS ... A LOVE STORY (TF)   Warner Bros. TV, 1979
PORTRAIT OF A STRIPPER (TF)   Moonlight Productions/Filmways, 1979
BELLE STARR (TF)   Entheos Unlimited Productions/Hanna-Barbera Productions,
    1980
BLINDED BY THE LIGHT (TF)   Time-Life Films, 1980

EMMETT ALSTON

NEW YEAR'S EVIL   Cannon, 1981

ROBERT ALTMAN *

b. February 20, 1925 - Kansas City, Missouri
Business: Sandcastle 5 Productions, 128 Central Park South - Suite 4B, New York,
   NY 10019, 212/582-2970
Attorney: Eric Weissman, 9601 Wilshire Blvd., Los Angeles, CA, 213/858-7888
Business Manager: James W. Quinn, 11755 Addison Street, North Hollywood,
   CA 91607, 213/509-0259

THE DELINQUENTS   United Artists, 1957
THE JAMES DEAN STORY (FD)   co-director with George W. George, Warner
   Bros., 1957
NIGHTMARE IN CHICAGO (TF)   MCA-TV, 1964
COUNTDOWN   Warner Bros., 1968
THAT COLD DAY IN THE PARK   Commonwealth United, 1969, Canadian-U.S.
M*A*S*H ★   20th Century-Fox, 1970
BREWSTER McCLOUD   MGM, 1970
McCABE & MRS. MILLER   Warner Bros., 1971
IMAGES   Columbia, 1972, Irish
THE LONG GOODBYE   United Artists, 1973
THIEVES LIKE US   United Artists, 1974
CALIFORNIA SPLIT   Columbia, 1974
NASHVILLE ★   Paramount, 1976
BUFFALO BILL AND THE INDIANS or SITTING BULL'S
   HISTORYLESSON   United Artists, 1976
3 WOMEN   20th Century-Fox, 1977
A WEDDING   20th Century-Fox, 1978
A PERFECT COUPLE   20th Century-Fox, 1979
QUINTET   20th Century-Fox, 1979
HEALTH   20th Century-Fox, 1980
POPEYE   Paramount, 1980
COME BACK TO THE 5 & DIME JIMMY DEAN, JIMMY DEAN   Cinecom
   International, 1982
STREAMERS   United Artists Classics, 1983
THE UTTERLY MONSTROUS MIND-ROASTING SUMMER OF O.C. AND
   STIGGS   MGM/UA, 1984

JOE ALVES *

b. May 21, 1938 - San Leandro, California
Home: 4176 Rosario Road, Woodland Hills, CA 91364, 213/346-4624
Business: JAC of the Arts, Inc., 3000 Ocean Park Blvd. - Suite 1035, Santa Monica,
   CA 90405, 213/450-0437
Agent: Phil Gersh, The Gersh Agency - Beverly Hills, 213/274-6611

JAWS 3-D   Universal, 1983

ROD AMATEAU *

b. December 20, 1923 - New York, New York
Home: 133½ S. Linden Drive, Beverly Hills, CA 90212, 213/274-3865
Agent: Martin Baum, CAA - Los Angeles, 213/277-4545

THE BUSHWHACKERS   Realart, 1951
MONSOON   United Artists, 1952
PUSSYCAT, PUSSYCAT, I LOVE YOU   United Artists, 1970, British
THE STATUE   Cinerama Releasing Corporation, 1971, British
WHERE DOES IT HURT?   American Internationl, 1972, British
DRIVE IN   Columbia, 1976
THE SENIORS   Cinema Shares International, 1978
HITLER'S SON   1978, British
UNCOMMON VALOR (TF)   Brademan-Self Productions/Sunn Classic, 1983
HIGH SCHOOL U.S.A. (TF)   Hill-Mandelker Films, 1983

LINDSAY ANDERSON

b. April 17, 1923 - Bangalore, India
Address: 9 Stirling Mansions, Canfield Gardens, London W1, England

THIS SPORTING LIFE   Continental, 1962, British
IF ...   Paramount, 1969, British
O LUCKY MAN!   Warner Bros., 1973, British

continued

LINDSAY ANDERSON—continued
IN CELEBRATION   American Film Theatre, 1975, British-Canadian
BRITTANIA HOSPITAL   United Artists Classics, 1982, British

M I C H A E L   A N D E R S O N *

b. January 30, 1920 - London, England
Address: 1 Park Lane - Suite 609, 211 St. Patrick, Toronto, Canada, 416/977-8530
Agent: Chasin-Park-Citron - Los Angeles, 213/273-7190

PRIVATE ANGELO   co-director with Peter Ustinov, Associated British Picture
    Corporation, 1949, British
WATERFRONT WOMEN *WATERFRONT*   Rank, 1950, British
HELL IS SOLD OUT   Eros, 1951, British
NIGHT WAS OUR FRIEND   Monarch, 1951, British
WILL ANY GENTLEMAN?   Associated British Picture Corporation, 1953, British
THE HOUSE OF THE ARROW   Associated British Picture Corporation, 1953,
    British
THE DAM BUSTERS   Warner Bros., 1955, British
1984   Columbia, 1956, British
AROUND THE WORLD IN 80 DAYS ★   United Artists, 1956
BATTLE HELL *YANGTSE INCIDENT*   DCA, 1957, British
CHASE A CROOKED SHADOW   Warner Bros., 1958, British
SHAKE HANDS WITH THE DEVIL   United Artists, 1959, British
THE WRECK OF THE MARY DEARE   MGM, 1959
ALL THE FINE YOUNG CANNIBALS   MGM, 1960
THE NAKED EDGE   United Artists, 1961
FLIGHT FROM ASHIYA   United Artists, 1964
WILD AND WONDERFUL   Universal, 1964
OPERATION CROSSBOW   MGM, 1965, British-Italian
THE QUILLER MEMORANDUM   Paramount, 1966, British
THE SHOES OF THE FISHERMAN   MGM, 1968
POPE JOAN   Columbia, 1972, British
DOC SAVAGE, THE MAN OF BRONZE   Warner Bros., 1975
CONDUCT UNBECOMING   Allied Artists, 1975, British
LOGAN'S RUN   MGM/United Artists, 1975
ORCA   Paramount, 1976
DOMINIQUE   Sword and Sworcery Productions, 1979, British
THE MARTIAN CHRONICLES (TF)   Charles Fries Productions/Stonehenge
    Productions, 1980
MURDER BY PHONE   New World, 1983, Canadian

K E N   A N N A K I N *

b. August 10, 1914 - Beverley, England
Agent: The Cooper Agency - Los Angeles, 213/277-8422

HOLIDAY CAMP   Universal, 1947, British
MIRANDA   Eagle-Lion, 1948, British
BROKEN JOURNEY   Eagle-Lion, 1948, British
HERE COME THE HUGGETTS   General Film Distributors, 1948, British
QUARTET   co-director with Ralph Smart, Harold French & Arthur Crabtree,
    Eagle-Lion, 1948, British
VOTE FOR HUGGETT   General Film Distributors, 1949, British
THE HUGGETTS ABROAD   General Film Distributors, 1949, British
LANDFALL   Associated British Picture Corporation, 1949, British
TRIO   co-director with Harold French, Paramount, 1950, British
HOTEL SAHARA   United Artists, 1951, British
THE STORY OF ROBIN HOOD   co-director with Alex Bryce, RKO Radio,
    1952, U.S.-British
OUTPOST IN MALAYA *THE PLANTER'S WIFE*   United Artists, 1952,
    British
THE SWORD AND THE ROSE   RKO Radio, 1953, U.S.-British
DOUBLE CONFESSION   Stratford, 1953, British
YOU KNOW WHAT SAILORS ARE   United Artists, 1954, British
LAND OF FURY *THE SEEKERS*   Universal, 1955, British
LOSER TAKES ALL   British Lion, 1956, British
VALUE FOR MONEY   Rank, 1957, British
THREE MEN IN A BOAT   DCA, 1958, British
ACROSS THE BRIDGE   Rank, 1958, British
THIRD MAN ON THE MOUNTAIN   Buena Vista, 1959, U.S.-British
ELEPHANT GUN *NOR THE MOON BY NIGHT*   Lopert, 1959, British

continued

KEN ANNAKIN*—continued

SWISS FAMILY ROBINSON   Buena Vista, 1960
THE HELLIONS   Columbia, 1962, British
A COMING-OUT PARTY *VERY IMPORTANT PERSON*   Union, 1962, British
THE FAST LADY   Rank, 1962, British
CROOKS ANONYMOUS   Allied Artists, 1962, British
THE LONGEST DAY   co-director with Andrew Marton & Bernhard Wicki, 20th Century-Fox, 1962
THOSE MAGNIFICENT MEN IN THEIR FLYING MACHINES   20th Century-Fox, 1965, British
BATTLE OF THE BULGE   Warner Bros., 1965
UNDERWORLD INFORMERS *THE INFORMERS*   Continental, 1966, British
THE LONG DUEL   Paramount, 1967, British
THE BIGGEST BUNDLE OF THEM ALL   MGM, 1968, U.S.-Italian
THOSE DARING YOUNG MEN IN THEIR JAUNTY JALOPIES   Paramount, 1969, British-Italian-French
CALL OF THE WILD   Constantin, 1975, West German-Spanish
PAPER TIGER   Joseph E. Levine Presents, 1976, British
MURDER AT THE MARDI GRAS (TF)   The Jozak Company/Paramount TV, 1978
HAROLD ROBBINS' THE PIRATE (TF)   Howard W. Koch Productions/Warner Bros. TV, 1978
THE 5TH MUSKETEER   Columbia, 1979, Austrian
INSTITUTE FOR REVENGE (TF)   Gold-Driskill Productions/Columbia TV, 1979
CHEAPER TO KEEP HER   American Cinema, 1980
THE PIRATE MOVIE   20th Century-Fox, 1982, Australian

JEAN-JACQUES ANNAUD

b. October 1, 1943 - Jurisy, France
Agent: Jeff Berg, ICM - Los Angeles, 213/550-1440

BLACK AND WHITE IN COLOR *LA VICTOIRE EN CHANTANT*   Allied Artists, 1978, French-Ivory Coast-Swiss
COUP DE TETE *HOTHEAD*   Quartet, 1980, French
QUEST FOR FIRE   20th Century-Fox, 1982, Canadian-French

JOSEPH ANTHONY

b. May 24, 1912 - Milwaukee, Wisconsin

THE RAINMAKER   Paramount, 1956
THE MATCHMAKER   Paramount, 1958
CAREER   Paramount, 1959
ALL IN A NIGHT'S WORK   Paramount, 1961
CONQUERED CITY   American International, 1966, Italian
TOMORROW   Filmgroup, 1972

LOU ANTONIO*

b. January 23, 1934 - Oklahoma City, Oklahoma
Agent: CAA - Los Angeles, 213/277-4545

SOMEONE I TOUCHED (TF)   Charles Fries Productions, 1975
LANIGAN'S RABBI (TF)   Universal TV, 1976
THE GIRL IN THE EMPTY GRAVE (TF)   NBC-TV, 1977
SOMETHING FOR JOEY (TF)☆   MTM Productions, 1977
THE CRITICAL LIST (TF)   MTM Productions, 1978
A REAL AMERICAN HERO (TF)   Bing Crosby Productions, 1978
BREAKING UP IS HARD TO DO (TF)   Green-Epstein Productions/Columbia TV, 1979
SILENT VICTORY: THE KITTY O'NEILL STORY (TF)☆   Channing-Debin-Locke Company, 1979
THE CONTENDER (TF)   co-director with Harry Falk, Universal TV, 1980
WE'RE FIGHTING BACK (TF)   Highgate Pictures, 1981
THE STAR MAKER (TF)   Channing-Debin-Locke Company/Carson Productions, 1981
SOMETHING SO RIGHT (TF)   List-Estrin Productions/Tisch-Avnet Television, 1982

continued

LOU ANTONIO*—continued

BETWEEN FRIENDS (CTF)   HBO Premiere Films/Marian Rees Associates/Robert
Cooper Films III/List-Estrin Productions, 1983, U.S.-Canadian

MICHELANGELO ANTONIONI

b. September 29, 1912 - Ferrara, Italy
Contact: Ministry of Tourism & Education, Via Della Ferratella, No. 51, 00184
Rome, Italy, 06/7732

STORY OF A LOVE AFFAIR   New Yorker, 1950, Italian
I VINTI   Film Costellazione, 1953, Italian
LA SIGNORA SENZA CAMELIE   1953, Italian
LOVE IN THE CITY   co-director with Federico Fellini, Alberto Lattuada, Carlo
Lizzani, Francesco Maselli & Dino Risi, Italian Films Export, 1953, Italian
LE AMICHE   Trion Falcine/Titanus, 1955, Italian
IL GRIDO   Astor, 1957, Italian
L'AVVENTURA   Janus, 1961, Italian
LA NOTTE   Lopert, 1961, Italian-French
L'ECLISSE   Times, 1962, Italian-French
RED DESERT   Rizzoli, 1965, Italian-French
I TRE VOLTI   co-director, 1965, Italian
BLOW-UP ★   Premier, 1966, British-Italian
ZABRISKIE POINT   MGM, 1970
CHUNG KUO (FD)   1972, Italian
THE PASSENGER *PROFESSIONE: REPORTER*   MGM/United Artists, 1975,
Italian-French-Spanish-U.S.
THE MYSTERY OF OBERWALD   Sacis, 1981, Italian
IDENTIFICATION OF A WOMAN   Iter Film/Gaumont, 1982, Italian-French

MICHAEL APTED*

b. February 10, 1941 - Aylesbury, England
Agent: Michael Marcus, CAA - Los Angeles, 213/277-4545
Business Manager: Gary G. Cohen, 3520 Ocean Park Blvd. - Suite 100, Santa
Monica, CA, 213/452-0123

THE TRIPLE ECHO   Altura, 1973, British
STARDUST   Columbia, 1975, British
STRONGER THAN THE SUN (TF)   BBC, 1977, British
THE SQUEEZE   Warner Bros., 1977, British
AGATHA   Warner Bros., 1979, British
COAL MINER'S DAUGHTER   Universal, 1980
CONTINENTAL DIVIDE   Universal, 1981
P'TANG, YANG, KIPPERBANG   United Artists Classics, 1983, British
GORKY PARK   Orion, 1983

DARIO ARGENTO

b. 1943 - Italy
Contact: Ministry of Tourism & Education, Via Della Ferratella, No. 51, 00184
Rome, Italy, 06/7732

THE BIRD WITH THE CRYSTAL PLUMAGE   UMC, 1970, Italian-West
German
CAT O'NINE TAILS   National General, 1971, Italian-West German-French
FOUR FLIES ON GREY VELVET   Paramount, 1972, Italian-French
LE CINQUE GIORNATE   Seda Spettacoli, 1973, Italian
DEEP RED   Howard Mahler Films, 1976, Italian
SUSPIRIA   International Classics, 1977, Italian
INFERNO   20th Century-Fox, 1981, Italian
TENEBRAE   Titanus, 1982, Italian

ALAN ARKIN*

b. March 26, 1934 - New York, New York
Agent: Robinson, Luttrell & Associates - Beverly Hills, 213/275-6114
Business Manager: Saul B. Schneider - New York City, 212/489-0990

LITTLE MURDERS   20th Century-Fox, 1970
FIRE SALE   20th Century-Fox, 1977

ALLAN ARKUSH *

Home: 14134 Chandler Blvd., Van Nuys, CA 91401, 213/784-4830
Agent: Dennis Brody, William Morris Agency - Beverly Hills, 213/274-7451

HOLLYWOOD BOULEVARD   co-director with Joe Dante, New World, 1976
DEATHSPORT   co-director with Henry Suso, New World, 1978
ROCK 'N' ROLL HIGH SCHOOL   New World, 1979
HEARTBEEPS   Universal, 1981
GET CRAZY   Embassy, 1983

GEORGE ARMITAGE *

Agent: Mickey Freiberg, The Artists Agency - Los Angeles, 213/277-7779

PRIVATE DUTY NURSES   New World, 1972
HIT MAN   MGM, 1973
VIGILANTE FORCE   United Artists, 1976
HOT ROD (TF)   ABC Circle Films, 1979

GILLIAN ARMSTRONG

Address: c/o M&L Casting Consultants, 49 Darlinghurst Road, Kings Cross, NSW,
    2011, Australia, 02/358-3111

THE SINGER AND THE DANCER   Gillian Armstrong Productions, 1976,
    Australian
MY BRILLIANT CAREER   Analysis, 1980, Australian
STARSTRUCK   Cinecom International, 1982, Australian

GWEN ARNER *

Home: 223 33rd Street, Hermosa Beach, CA 90254, 213/376-3875
Agent: David, Hunter, Kimble, Parseghian & Rifkin - Los Angeles, 213/857-1234

MY CHAMPION   Shochiku, 1981, Japanese-U.S.
MOTHER'S DAY ON WALTON'S MOUNTAIN (TF)   Lorimar Productions/
    Amanda Productions, 1982

JACK ARNOLD *

b. October 14, 1916 - New Haven, Connecticut
Home: 4860 Nomad Drive, Woodland Hills, CA 91364
Agent: Abby Greshler, Diamond Artists Ltd. - Los Angeles, 213/278-8146

GIRLS IN THE NIGHT   Universal, 1953
IT CAME FROM OUTER SPACE   Universal, 1953
THE GLASS WEB   Universal, 1953
THE CREATURE FROM THE BLACK LAGOON   Universal, 1954
REVENGE OF THE CREATURE   Universal, 1955
THE MAN FROM BITTER RIDGE   Universal, 1955
TARANTULA   Universal, 1955
OUTSIDE THE LAW   Universal, 1956
RED SUNDOWN   Universal, 1956
THE INCREDIBLE SHRINKING MAN   Universal, 1957
THE TATTERED DRESS   Universal, 1957
MAN IN THE SHADOW   Universal, 1958
THE LADY TAKES A FLYER   Universal, 1958
THE SPACE CHILDREN   Paramount, 1958
MONSTER ON THE CAMPUS   Universal, 1958
THE MOUSE THAT ROARED   Columbia, 1959, British
NO NAME ON THE BULLET   Universal, 1959
BACHELOR IN PARADISE   MGM, 1961
THE LIVELY SET   Universal, 1964
A GLOBAL AFFAIR   MGM, 1964
HELLO DOWN THERE   Paramount, 1969
BLACK EYE   Warner Bros., 1974
THE GAMES GIRLS PLAY   General Films, 1975
BOSS NIGGER   Dimension, 1975
THE SWISS CONSPIRACY   SJ International, 1977
SEX AND THE MARRIED WOMAN (TF)   Universal TV, 1977

continued

JACK ARNOLD*—continued
MARILYN: THE UNTOLD STORY (TF)   co-director with John Flynn &
     Lawrence Schiller, Lawrence Schiller Productions, 1980

K A R E N   A R T H U R *

Agent: Peter Rawley, ICM - Los Angeles, 213/550-4165

LEGACY   Kino International, 1976
THE MAFU CAGE   Clouds Productions, 1979
CHARLESTON (TF)   Robert Stigwood Productions/RSO, Inc., 1979
RETURN TO EDEN (MS)   McElroy & McElroy/Hanna-Barbera Australia
     Productions, 1983, Australian

H A L   A S H B Y *

b. 1936 - Ogden, Utah
Contact: Directors Guild of America - Los Angeles, 213/656-1220

THE LANDLORD   United Artists, 1970
HAROLD AND MAUDE   Paramount, 1971
THE LAST DETAIL   Columbia, 1973
SHAMPOO   Columbia, 1975
BOUND FOR GLORY   United Artists, 1976
COMING HOME ★   United Artists, 1978
BEING THERE   United Artists, 1979
SECOND HAND HEARTS   Paramount, 1981
LOOKIN' TO GET OUT   Paramount, 1982
LET'S SPEND THE NIGHT TOGETHER (FD)   Embassy, 1983

W I L L I A M   A S H E R *

b. 1919
Agent: Fred Whitehead, ICM - Los Angeles, 213/550-4000

LEATHER GLOVES   co-director with Richard Quine, Columbia, 1948
THE SHADOW ON THE WINDOW   Columbia, 1956
THE 27TH DAY   Columbia, 1956
BEACH PARTY   American International, 1963
JOHNNY COOL   United Artists, 1963
MUSCLE BEACH PARTY   American International, 1963
BIKINI BEACH   American International, 1964
BEACH BLANKET BINGO   American International, 1965
HOW TO STUFF A WILD BIKINI   American International, 1965
FIREBALL 500   American International, 1966
BUTCHER, BAKER, NIGHTMARE MAKER *NIGHT WARNING/MOMMA'S
     BOY* Comworld, 1981

J O H N   A S T I N *

b. March 30, 1930 - Baltimore, Maryland
Home: P.O. Box 385, Beverly Hills, CA 90213
Agent: CAA - Los Angeles, 213/277-4545

OPERATION PETTICOAT (TF)   Universal TV, 1977
ROSSETTI AND RYAN: MEN WHO LOVE WOMEN (TF)   Universal TV,
     1977

R I C H A R D   A T T E N B O R O U G H *

b. August 29, 1923 - Cambridge, England
Business: Beaver Lodge, Richmond Green, Surrey, England, 01/940-7234
Agent: John Redway & Associates - London, 01/637-1612

OH! WHAT A LOVELY WAR   Paramount, 1969, British
YOUNG WINSTON   Columbia, 1972, British
A BRIDGE TOO FAR   United Artists, 1977, British
MAGIC   20th Century-Fox, 1978
GANDHI ★★   Columbia, 1982, British-Indian

R A Y   A U S T I N *

b. December 5, 1932 - London, England
Home: 8855 Hollywood Blvd., Los Angeles, CA 90068, 213/652-4400
Agent: Tom Chasin, Chasin-Park-Citron - Los Angeles, 213/273-7190
Business Manager: David G. Licht, 9171 Wilshire Blvd., Los Angeles, CA 90069,
    213/278-1920

IT'S THE ONLY WAY TO GO   Hallelujah, 1970, British
FUN AND GAMES   1971, British
VIRGIN WITCHES   Tigon, 1972, British
HOUSE OF THE LIVING DEAD   1973, British
TALES OF THE GOLD MONKEY (TF)   Universal TV/Belisarius Productions,
    1982
THE RETURN OF THE MAN FROM U.N.C.L.E. (TF)   Michael Sloan
    Productions/Viacom Productions, 1983
ROBIN HOOD (TF)   Charles Fries Productions/Bobka Productions, 1983

I G O R   A U Z I N S

Address: June Cann Management, 283 Alfred Street North, North Sydney, NSW,
    2060, Australia, 02/922-3066

ALL AT SEA (TF)   1977, Australian
HIGH ROLLING   Hexagon Productions, 1977, Australian
THE NIGHT NURSE   1978, Australian
WATER UNDER THE BRIDGE (MS)   Shotton Productions, 1980, Australian
TAURUS RISING (MS)   1982, Australian
WE OF THE NEVER NEVER   Triumph/Columbia, 1983, Australian

A R A M   A V A K I A N *

Agent: Fred Milstein, William Morris Agency - New York City, 212/586-5100

LAD: A DOG   co-director with Leslie H. Martinson, Warner Bros., 1961
END OF THE ROAD   Allied Artists, 1970
COPS AND ROBBERS   United Artists, 1973
11 HARROWHOUSE   20th Century-Fox, 1974, British

H O W A R D   (H I K M E T)   A V E D I S

Business: Hickmar Productions, The Burbank Studios, 4000 Warner Blvd., Burbank,
    CA 91522, 213/954-5104

THE STEPMOTHER   Crown International, 1973
THE TEACHER   Crown International, 1974
DR. MINX   Dimension, 1975
THE SPECIALIST   Crown International, 1975
SCORCHY   American International, 1976
TEXAS DETOUR   Cinema Shares International, 1978
THE FIFTH FLOOR   Film Ventures International, 1980
SEPARATE WAYS   Crown International, 1981
MORTUARY   Artists Releasing Corporation/Film Ventures International, 1983

H Y   A V E R B A C K *

b. 1925
Agent: CAA - Los Angeles, 213/277-4545

CHAMBER OF HORRORS   Warner Bros., 1966
WHERE WERE YOU WHEN THE LIGHTS WENT OUT?   MGM, 1968
I LOVE YOU, ALICE B. TOKLAS   Warner Bros., 1968
THE GREAT BANK ROBBERY   Warner Bros., 1969
SUPPOSE THEY GAVE A WAR AND NOBODY CAME?   Cinerama
    Releasing Corporation, 1970
RICHIE BROCKELMAN: MISSING 24 HOURS (TF)   Universal TV, 1976
THE LOVE BOAT II (TF)   Aaron Spelling Productions, 1977
MAGNIFICENT MAGNET OF SANTA MESA (TF)   Columbia TV, 1977
THE NEW MAVERICK (TF)   Cherokee Productions/Warner Bros. TV, 1978
A GUIDE FOR THE MARRIED WOMAN (TF)   20th Century-Fox TV, 1978
PEARL (TF)   Silliphant-Konigsberg Productions/Warner Bros. TV, 1978

continued

HY AVERBACK*—continued
THE NIGHT RIDER (TF)   Stephen J. Cannell Productions/Universal TV, 1979
SHE'S IN THE ARMY NOW (TF)   ABC Circle Films, 1981
THE GIRL, THE GOLD WATCH AND DYNAMITE (TF)   Fellows-Keegan
   Company/Paramount TV, 1981
WHERE THE BOYS ARE   Universal/AFD, 1984

JOHN G. AVILDSEN*

b. 1937 - Chicago, Illinois
Home: 45 East 89th Street - Suite 37A, New York, NY 10028, 212/534-5891
Agent: Marvin Moss Agency - Los Angeles, 213/274-8483

TURN ON TO LOVE   Haven International, 1969
GUESS WHAT WE LEARNED IN SCHOOL TODAY?   Cannon, 1970
JOE   Cannon, 1970
CRY UNCLE!   Cambist, 1971
OKAY BILL   Four Star Excelsior, 1971
THE STOOLIE   Jama, 1972
SAVE THE TIGER   Paramount, 1973
FORE PLAY   co-director with Bruce Malmuth & Robert McCarty, Cinema
   National, 1975
W.W. AND THE DIXIE DANCEKINGS   20th Century-Fox, 1975
ROCKY ★★   United Artists, 1976
SLOW DANCING IN THE BIG CITY   United Artists, 1978
THE FORMULA   MGM/United Artists, 1980
NEIGHBORS   Columbia, 1982
A NIGHT IN HEAVEN   20th Century-Fox, 1983
THE KARATE KID   Columbia, 1984

TOM AVILDSEN*

Home: 7501 Topeka Drive, Reseda, CA 91335
Agent: Marvin Moss Agency - Los Angeles, 213/274-8483

THINGS ARE TOUGH ALL OVER   Columbia, 1982

GEORGE AXELROD*

b. June 9, 1922 - New York, New York
Agent: Irving Paul Lazar - Beverly Hills, 213/275-6153

LORD LOVE A DUCK   United Artists, 1966
THE SECRET LIFE OF AN AMERICAN WIFE   20th Century-Fox, 1968

RANDALL BADAT*

Contact: Directors Guild of America - Los Angeles, 213/656-1220

SURF II   Arista, 1983

JOHN BADHAM *

b. 1939 - England
Agent: Adams, Ray & Rosenberg - Los Angeles, 213/278-3000

THE IMPATIENT HEART (TF)   Universal TV, 1971
ISN'T IT SHOCKING? (TF)   ABC Circle Films, 1973
THE LAW (TF)   Universal TV, 1974
THE GUN (TF)   Universal TV, 1974
REFLECTIONS OF MURDER (TF)   ABC Circle Films, 1974
THE GODCHILD (TF)   MGM TV, 1974
THE KEEGANS (TF)   Universal TV, 1976
THE BINGO LONG TRAVELING ALL STARS AND MOTOR
     KINGS   Universal, 1976
SATURDAY NIGHT FEVER   Paramount, 1977
DRACULA   Universal, 1979
WHOSE LIFE IS IT ANYWAY?   MGM/United Artists, 1981
BLUE THUNDER   Columbia, 1983
WARGAMES   MGM/UA, 1983

REZA BADIYI *

b. April 17, 1936 - Iran
Agent: Geoff Brandt, APA - Los Angeles, 213/273-0744

DEATH OF A STRANGER   Delta Commerz, 1972, West German-Israeli
THE EYES OF CHARLES SAND (TF)   Warner Bros. TV, 1972
TRADER HORN   MGM, 1973
THE BIG BLACK PILL (TF)   Filmways/NBC Entertainment, 1981
OF MICE AND MEN (TF)   Of Mice and Men Productions, 1981
WHITE WATER REBELS (TF)   CBS Entertainment, 1983
MURDER ONE, DANCER 0 (TF)   Mickey Productions, 1983
POLICEWOMAN CENTERFOLD (TF)   Moonlight Productions, 1983

MAX BAER, JR. *

b. December 4, 1937 - Oakland, California
Home: 213/989-5783
Business: Max Baer Productions, 10433 Wilshire Blvd., Los Angeles, CA 90024,
     213/470-2808

THE WILD McCULLOCHS   American International, 1975
ODE TO BILLY JOE   Warner Bros., 1976
HOMETOWN, U.S.A.   Film Ventures International, 1979

CHUCK BAIL *

Home: 1421 Morningside Drive, Burbank, CA 91506
Agent: Craig Rumar, F.A.M.E. - Los Angeles, 213/556-8071

BLACK SAMSON   Warner Bros., 1974
CLEOPATRA JONES AND THE CASINO OF GOLD   Warner Bros., 1975
GUMBALL RALLY   Warner Bros., 1976

GRAHAM BAKER

THE FINAL CONFLICT   20th Century-Fox, 1981
IMPULSE   20th Century-Fox, 1984

R O Y   W A R D   B A K E R

b. 1916 - London, England
Agent: Leading Artists, 60 St. James Street, London SW1, England

THE OCTOBER MAN   Eagle-Lion, 1947, British
THE WEAKER SEX   Eagle-Lion, 1948, British
PAPER ORCHID   1949, British
OPERATION DISASTER *MORNING DEPARTURE*   Universal, 1950, British
HIGHLY DANGEROUS   Lippert, 1951, British
I'LL NEVER FORGET YOU *THE HOUSE IN THE SQUARE*   20th Century-Fox, 1951, British
DON'T BOTHER TO KNOCK   20th Century-Fox, 1952
NIGHT WITHOUT SLEEP   20th Century-Fox, 1952
INFERNO   20th Century-Fox, 1953
PASSAGE HOME   1955, British
JACQUELINE   Rank, 1956, British
TIGER IN SMOKE   1956, British
THE ONE THAT GOT AWAY   Rank, 1958, British
A NIGHT TO REMEMBER   Rank, 1958, British
THE SINGER NOT THE SONG   Warner Bros., 1962, British
FLAME IN THE STREETS   Atlantic Pictures, 1962, British
THE VALIANT   co-director with Giorgio Capitani, United Artists, 1962, British-Italian
TWO LEFT FEET   1963, British
FIVE MILLION YEARS TO EARTH *QUARTERMASS AND THE PIT*   20th Century-Fox, 1968, British
THE ANNIVERSARY   20th Century-Fox, 1968, British
THE SPY KILLER (TF)   Halsan Productions, 1969
FOREIGN EXCHANGE (TF)   Halsan Productions, 1970
MOON ZERO TWO   Warner Bros., 1970, British
THE VAMPIRE LOVERS   American International, 1970, British
THE SCARS OF DRACULA   American Continental, 1971, British
DR. JEKYLL AND SISTER HYDE   American International, 1972, British
ASYLUM   Cinerama Releasing Corporation, 1972, British
THE VAULT OF HORROR   Cinerama Releasing Corporation, 1973, British
AND NOW THE SCREAMING STARTS   Cinerama Releasing Corporation, 1973, British
THE 7 BROTHERS MEET DRACULA *THE LEGEND OF THE SEVEN GOLDEN VAMPIRES*   Dynamite Entertainment, 1979, British
THE MONSTER CLUB   ITC, 1981, British
THE FLAME TREES OF THIKA (MS)   London Films Ltd./Consolidated Productions Ltd., 1982, British

R A L P H   B A K S H I *

b. 1939 - Brooklyn, New York
Business: Bakshi Productions, Inc., Paramount Studios, 5555 Melrose Avenue, Los Angeles, CA 90004, 213/468-5000

FRITZ THE CAT (AF)   American International, 1972
HEAVY TRAFFIC (AF)   American International, 1973
COONSKIN (AF)   Bryanston, 1974
WIZARDS (AF)   20th Century-Fox, 1977
THE LORD OF THE RINGS (AF)   United Artists, 1978
AMERICAN POP (AF)   Paramount, 1981
HEY GOOD LOOKIN' (AF)   Warner Bros., 1982
FIRE AND ICE (AF)   20th Century-Fox, 1983

F E R D I N A N D O   B A L D I

Contact: Ministry of Tourism & Education, Via Della Ferratella, No. 51, 00184 Rome, Italy, 06/7732

DAVID AND GOLIATH   co-director with Richard Pottier, Allied Artists, 1960, Italian
DUEL OF CHAMPIONS   co-director with Terence Young, Medallion, 1961, Italian-Spanish
BLINDMAN   20th Century-Fox, 1972, Italian
GET MEAN   Cee Note, 1976, Italian
NOVE OSPITI PER UN DELITTO   Overseas, 1976, Italian
THE SICILIAN CONNECTION   Joseph Green Pictures, 1977, Italian
L'INQUILINA DEL PIANO DI SOPRA   Fair Film, 1977, Italian

continued

FERDINANDO BALDI—continued

I PIRATI DELL'ISOLA VERDE   directed under pseudonym of Ted Kaplan, PBC,
1978, Italian-Spanish
LA SELVAGGIA (GEOMETRA PRINETTI SEL
VAGGIAMENTEOSVALDO)   Interfilm, 1978, Italian
LA RAGAZZA DEL VAGONE LETTO   1979, Italian
COMIN' AT YA   Filmways, 1981, U.S.-Spanish
TREASURE OF THE FOUR CROWNS   Cannon, 1983, U.S.-Spanish

PETER BALDWIN *

Agent: Frank Cooper, The Cooper Agency - Los Angeles, 213/277-8422

THE HARLEM GLOBETROTTERS ON GILLIGAN'S ISLAND (TF)   Sherwood
Schwartz Productions, 1981
THE BRADY GIRLS GET MARRIED (TF)   Sherwood Schwartz Productions,
1981

CARROLL BALLARD *

Contact: Directors Guild of America - Los Angeles, 213/656-1220

THE BLACK STALLION   United Artists, 1979
NEVER CRY WOLF   Buena Vista, 1983

ANNE BANCROFT *
(Anna Maria Louise Italiano)

b. September 17, 1931 - Bronx, New York
Business: Brooksfilms Limited, 20th Century-Fox, P.O. Box 900, Beverly Hills,
CA 90213, 213/203-1375

FATSO   20th Century-Fox, 1980

ALBERT BAND *
(Alfredo Antonini)

b. May 7, 1924 - Paris, France
Home: 8115 Amor Road, Los Angeles, CA 90046
Messages: 213/859-0034
Business: Empire International, 948 N. Fairfax Avenue, Los Angeles, CA 90046,
213/656-6610

THE YOUNG GUNS   Allied Artists, 1956
I BURY THE LIVING   United Artists, 1958
FACE OF FIRE   Allied Artists, 1959
THE AVENGER   Medallion, 1962, Italian-French
GRAND CANYON MASSACRE   1963, Italian
THE TRAMPLERS   Embassy, 1966, Italian
DRACULA'S DOG   Crown International, 1978
SHE CAME TO THE VALLEY   RGV Pictures, 1979

CHARLES BAND

Business: Empire International, 948 N. Fairfax Avenue, Los Angeles, CA 90046,
213/656-6610

THE ALCHEMIST   Ideal, 1980
PARASITE   Embassy, 1982
METALSTORM: THE DESTRUCTION OF JARED-SYN   Universal, 1983
RAGEWAR   Empire International, 1984

RICHARD L. BARE *

b. 1909 - Turlock, California
Home: 700 Harbor Island Drive, Newport Beach, CA 92660, 714/675-6269

SMART GIRLS DON'T TALK   Warner Bros., 1948
FLAXY MARTIN   Warner Bros., 1949
THE HOUSE ACROSS THE STREET   Warner Bros., 1949
THIS SIDE OF THE LAW   Warner Bros., 1950
RETURN OF THE FRONTIERSMAN   Warner Bros., 1950
PRISONERS OF THE CASBAH   Columbia, 1953
THE OUTLANDERS   Warner Bros., 1956
THE STORM RIDERS   Warner Bros., 1956
BORDER SHOWDOWN   Warner Bros., 1956
THE TRAVELLERS   Warner Bros., 1957
SHOOT-OUT AT MEDICINE BEND   Warner Bros., 1957
GIRL ON THE RUN   Warner Bros., 1958
THIS REBEL BREED   Warner Bros., 1960
WICKED, WICKED   MGM, 1973

BRUNO BARRETO

Contact: Conselho Nacional de Cinema, Rua Mayrink Veiga 28, Rio de Janeiro,
     Brazil, 2/233-8329

DONA FLOR AND HER TWO HUSBANDS   New Yorker, 1977, Brazilian
AMOR BANDIDO   Atlantic Releasing Corporation, 1982, Brazilian
GABRIELA   United Artists Classics, 1983, Brazilian-Italian

CHUCK BARRIS *

b. June 3 - Philadelphia, Pennsylvania
Home: 9100 Wilshire Blvd., Suite 411E, Beverly Hills, CA 90212, 213/278-9550

THE GONG SHOW MOVIE   Universal, 1980

ARTHUR BARRON

THE WRIGHT BROTHERS (TF)   PBS-TV, 1971
JEREMY   United Artists, 1973
BROTHERS   Warner Bros., 1977

PAUL BARTEL *

b. August 6, 1938 - Brooklyn, New York
Messages: 213/650-8878
Agent: Peter Rawley, ICM - Los Angeles, 213/550-4165

PRIVATE PARTS   MGM, 1972
DEATH RACE 2000   New World, 1975
CANNONBALL   New World, 1976
EATING RAOUL   20th Century-Fox International Classics, 1982
NOT FOR PUBLICATION   North Street Films, 1984

HALL BARTLETT *

b. November 27, 1922 - Kansas City, Missouri
Home: 861 Stone Canyon Road, Los Angeles, CA 90024, 213/476-3916
Business: Hall Bartlett Films, Inc., 9200 Sunset Blvd. - Suite 908, Los Angeles,
     CA 90069, 213/278-8883

UNCHAINED   Warner Bros., 1955
DRANGO   co-director with Jules Bricken, United Artists, 1957
ZERO HOUR   Paramount, 1957
ALL THE YOUNG MEN   Columbia, 1960
THE CARETAKERS   United Artists, 1963
CHANGES   Cinerama Releasing Corporation, 1969
THE WILD PACK *THE SANDPIT GENERALS*   American International, 1972
JONATHAN LIVINGSTON SEAGULL   Paramount, 1973
THE CHILDREN OF SANCHEZ   Lone Star, 1978, U.S.-Mexican

continued

HALL BARTLETT*—continued
LOVE IS FOREVER (TF)   Michael Landon-Hall Bartlett Films/NBC-TV/20th
Century-Fox TV, 1983

WILLIAM S. BARTMAN*

Home: 5517 Corteen Place, North Hollywood, CA 91607, 213/656-2541
Agent: Herb Tobias, Herb Tobias & Associates - Los Angeles, 213/277-6211

O'HARA'S WIFE   Davis-Panzer Productions, 1982

FRED BARZYK

Home: 12 Brook Street, Chelmsford, MA 01824, 617/256-4868
Business: Creative Television Associates, Inc., 1380 Soldiers Field Road, Brighton,
    MA 02135, 617/783-2103

BETWEEN TIME & TIMBUKTU (TF)   PBS, 1974
THE PHANTOM OF THE OPEN HEARTH (TF)   co-director with David R.
    Loxton, WNET-13 Television Laboratory/WGBH New Television Workshop,
    1976
CHARLIE SMITH AND THE FRITTER TREE (TF)   co-director with David R.
    Loxton, WNET-13 Television Laboratory/WGBH New Television Workshop,
    1978
THE LATHE OF HEAVEN (TF)   co-director with David R. Loxton, WNET-13
    Television Laboratory/Taurus Film, 1980

JULES BASS

Business: Rankin-Bass Productions, Inc., 1 East 53rd Street, New York, NY 10022,
    212/759-7721

MAD MONSTER PARTY (AF)   Embassy, 1967
THE WACKY WORLD OF MOTHER GOOSE (AF)   1968
THE HOBBIT (ATF)   co-director with Arthur Rankin, Jr., Rankin-Bass Productions,
    1977
RUDOLPH AND FROSTY (ATF)   co-director with Arthur Rankin Jr., Rankin-Bass
    Productions, 1979
THE RETURN OF THE KING (ATF)   co-director with Arthur Rankin, Jr., Rankin-
    Bass Productions, 1979
THE LAST UNICORN (AF)   co-director with Arthur Rankin, Jr., Jensen Farley
    Pictures, 1982
THE FLIGHT OF THE DRAGONS (ATF)   co-director with Arthur Rankin, Jr.,
    Rankin-Bass Productions, 1983
THE WIND IN THE WILLOWS (ATF)   co-director with Arthur Rankin, Jr.,
    Rankin-Bass Productions, 1983

SAUL BASS*

b. May 8, 1920 - New York, New York
Business: Saul Bass/Herb Yager & Associates, 7039 Sunset Blvd., Los Angeles,
    CA 90028, 213/466-9701

PHASE IV   Paramount, 1974

MICHAL BAT-ADAM

Contract: Israel Film Centre, Ministry of Industry & Trade, 30 Agron Street, P.O. Box
    299, Jerusalem 94190, Israel, 02/210433

EACH OTHER *MOMENTS*   Franklin Media, 1979, Israeli-French
THE THIN LINE   New Yorker, 1980, Israeli
YOUNG LOVE   GUY Film Productions Ltd., 1983, Israeli

ROBERT B. BEAN*

Business: 212/628-0500

MADE FOR EACH OTHER   20th Century-Fox, 1971

CHRIS BEARDE *

Address: 28106 Pacific Coast Highway, Malibu, CA   90265

HYSTERICAL   Embassy, 1982

WARREN BEATTY *

b. March 30, 1937 - Richmond, Virginia
Agent: William Morris Agency - Beverly Hills, 213/274-7451

HEAVEN CAN WAIT ★   co-director with Buck Henry, Paramount, 1978
REDS ★★   Paramount, 1981

GABRIELLE BEAUMONT *

Home: 3456 Alana Drive, Sherman Oaks, CA   91403, 213/906-0579
Agent: Joan Scott, Writers & Artists Agency - Los Angeles, 213/820-2240
Business: Individual Productions, Inc., 3701 Wilshire Blvd., Los Angeles, CA   90010,
   213/383-6996

THE GODSEND   Cannon, 1980, British
DEATH OF A CENTERFOLD: THE DOROTHY STRATTEN STORY
   (TF)   Wilc ox Productions/MGM TV, 1981
SECRETS OF A MOTHER AND DAUGHTER (TF)   The Shpetner Company,
   1983

HAROLD BECKER *

Agent: Adams, Ray & Rosenberg - Los Angeles, 213/278-3000

THE RAGMAN's DAUGHTER   Penelope Films, 1972, British
THE ONION FIELD   Avco Embassy, 1979
THE BLACK MARBLE   Avco Embassy, 1980
TAPS   20th Century-Fox, 1981
VISIONQUEST   Warner Bros., 1984

TERRY BEDFORD

Home: 9 Roderick Road, London NW3, England, 01/267-3220
Business Manager: Paul E. Esposito, Jennie & Co., 127 West 79th Street, New
   York, NY   10024, 212/595-5200

SLAYGROUND   Universal/AFD, 1983, British

JEAN-JACQUES BEINEIX

Contact: French Film Office, 745 Fifth Avenue, New York, NY   10151, 212/832-
   8860

DIVA   United Artists Classics, 1982, French
THE MOON IN THE GUTTER   Triumph/Columbia, 1983, French-Italian

EARL BELLAMY *

b. March 11, 1917 - Minneapolis, Minnesota
Agent: Herb Tobias & Associates - Los Angeles, 213/277-6211
Business Manager: Fred Barman, Los Angeles, 213/276-6666

SEMINOLE UPRISING   Columbia, 1955
BLACKJACK KETCHUM, DESPERADO   Columbia, 1956
TOUGHEST GUN IN TOMBSTONE   United Artists, 1958
STAGECOACH TO DANCERS' ROCK   Universal, 1962
FLUFFY   Universal, 1965
INCIDENT AT PHANTOM HILL   Universal, 1966
GUNPOINT   Universal, 1966
MUNSTER, GO HOME   Universal, 1966
THREE GUNS FOR TEXAS   co-director with David Lowell Rich & Paul Stanley,
   Universal, 1968
BACKTRACK   Universal, 1969

continued

EARL BELLAMY*—continued

THE PIGEON (TF)   Thomas-Spelling Productions, 1969
DESPERATE MISSION (TF)   20th Century-Fox TV, 1971
THE TRACKERS (TF)   Aaron Spelling Productions, 1971
SEVEN ALONE   Doty-Dayton, 1975
SIDECAR RACERS   Universal, 1975, Australian
PART 2 WALKING TALL   American International, 1975
AGAINST A CROOKED SKY   Doty-Dayton, 1975
FLOOD! (TF)   Irwin Allen Productions/20th Century-Fox TV, 1976
FIRE! (TF)   Irwin Allen Productions/20th Century-Fox TV, 1977
SIDEWINDER ONE   Avco Embassy, 1977
SPEEDTRAP   First Artists, 1978
DESPERATE WOMEN (TF)   Lorimar Productions, 1978
THE CASTAWAYS OF GILLIGAN'S ISLAND (TF)   Sherwood Schwartz
    Productions, 1979
VALENTINE MAGIC ON LOVE ISLAND (TF)   Dick Clark Productions/PKO/
    Osmond Television, 1980
MAGNUM THRUST   Shenandoah Films, 1981

MARCO BELLOCCHIO

b. 1939 - Piacenza, Italy
Contact: Ministry of Tourism & Education, Via Della Ferratella, No. 51, 00184
    Rome, Italy, 06/7732

FIST IN HIS POCKET   Peppercorn-Wormser, 1965, Italian
CHINA IS NEAR   Royal Films International, 1967, Italian
AMORE E RABBIA   co-director, 1969, Italian
NEL NOME DEL PADRE   1972, Italian
SBATTI IL MONSTRO IN PRIMA PAGINA   1972, Italian
FIT TO BE UNTIED   co-director, 1974, Italian
MATTA DA SLEGARE   11 Marzo Cinematografica, 1975, Italian
VICTORY MARCH   Summit Features, 1976, Italian-French
LES YEUX FERTILES   1977; French-Italian
IL GABBIANO (TF)   Indipendi Regionale, 1977, Italian
LA MACCHINA CINEMA   1978, Italian
LEAP INTO THE VOID   Summit Features, 1979, Italian
THE EYES, THE MOUTH   Triumph/Columbia, 1983, Italian-French
HENRY IV   Gaumont, 1983, Italian

JERRY BELSON*

Agent: William Morris Agency - Beverly Hills, 213/274-7451

JEKYLL AND HYDE ... TOGETHER AGAIN   Paramount, 1982

JACK BENDER*

Business Manager: Shagin & Hyman, 11777 San Vicente Blvd., Los Angeles,
    CA 90049, 213/820-7717

IN LOVE WITH AN OLDER WOMAN (TF)   Pound Ridge Productions/Charles
    Fries Productions, 1982
TWO KINDS OF LOVE (TF)   CBS, 1983

LASLO BENEDEK*

b. March 5, 1907 - Budapest, Hungary
Home: 70 Bank Street, New York, NY 10014

THE KISSING BANDIT   MGM, 1948
PORT OF NEW YORK   Eagle- Lion, 1949
DEATH OF A SALESMAN   Columbia, 1951
THE WILD ONE   Columbia, 1954
BENGAL BRIGADE   Columbia, 1954
KINDER, MUTTER UND EIN GENERAL   1955, West German
AFFAIR IN HAVANA   Allied Artists, 1957
MALAGA   Warner Bros., 1959, British
RECOURSE EN GRACE   1960, French
NAMU, THE KILLER WHALE   United Artists, 1966
DARING GAME   Paramount, 1968

continued

LASLO BENEDEK*—continued
THE NIGHT VISITOR   UMC, 1971
ASSAULT ON AGATHON   Nine Network, 1976

R I C H A R D   B E N E D I C T *

b. 1923
Home: 11730 Moorpark Street, Studio City, CA 91604
Messages: 213/769-9155
Agent: Craig Rumar, F.A.M.E. - Los Angeles, 213/556-8011

WINTER A GO-GO   Columbia, 1965
IMPASSE   United Artists, 1968

R I C H A R D   B E N J A M I N *

b. May 22, 1938 - New York, New York
Agent: Phil Gersh, The Gersh Agency - Beverly Hills, 213/274-6611

MY FAVORITE YEAR   MGM/UA, 1982
RACING WITH THE MOON   Paramount, 1984

R I C H A R D   B E N N E R *

Home: 228 West 4th Street, Apt. 4, New York, NY 10014, 212/620-5983
Agent: John Planco, William Morris Agency - New York City, 212/586-5100

OUTRAGEOUS!   Cinema 5, 1977, Canadian
HAPPY BIRTHDAY GEMINI   United Artists, 1980, U.S.-Canadian

R I C H A R D   C .   B E N N E T T *

Home: 17136 Index Street, Granada Hills, CA 91344, 213/363-3381
Agent: Ronald Lief, Contemporary-Korman Artists - Beverly Hills, 213/278-8250

HARPER VALLEY PTA   April Fools, 1978
THE ESCAPE OF A ONE-TON PET (TF)   Tomorrow Entertainment, 1978

R O B E R T   B E N T O N *

b. September 29, 1932 - Waxahachie, Texas
Agent: Sam Cohn, ICM - New York City, 212/556-6810

BAD COMPANY   Paramount, 1972
THE LATE SHOW   Warner Bros., 1976
KRAMER VS. KRAMER ★★   Columbia, 1979
STILL OF THE NIGHT   MGM/UA, 1982
THE TEXAS PROJECT   Tri-Star/Columbia, 1984

B R U C E   B E R E S F O R D

b. 1940 - Australia
Agent: William Morris Agency - Beverly Hills, 213/274-7451
Personal Manager: Cameron's Management, 120 Victoria Street, Kings Cross, NSW,
    2011, Australia, 02/358-6433

THE ADVENTURES OF BARRY McKENZIE   Columbia-Warners, 1973,
    Australian
BARRY McKENZIE HOLDS HIS OWN   EMI, 1974, Australian
SIDE BY SIDE   1976, Australian
DON'S PARTY   Satori, 1976, Australian
THE GETTING OF WISDOM   Atlantic Releasing Corporation, 1977, Australian
MONEY MOVERS   South Australian Film Corporation, 1979, Australian
BREAKER MORANT   New World/Quartet, 1980, Australian
THE CLUB   South Australian Film Corporation, 1981, Australian
PUBERTY BLUES   Universal Classics, 1981, Australian
TENDER MERCIES   Universal/AFD, 1983

ANDREW BERGMAN *

Home: 881 Seventh Avenue - Suite 834, New York, NY 10019, 212/582-9215
Agent: Lee Rosenberg, Adams, Ray & Rosenberg - Los Angeles, 213/278-3000

SO FINE Warner Bros., 1981

INGMAR BERGMAN

b. July 14, 1918 - Uppsala, Sweden
Contact: Swedish Film Institute, P.O. Box 27126, S-10252 Stockholm, Sweden, 08/
630510

CRISIS Svensk Filmindustri, 1945, Swedish
IT RAINS ON OUR LOVE Sveriges Folkbiografer, 1946, Swedish
THE LAND OF DESIRE Sveriges Folkbiografer, 1947, Swedish
NIGHT IS MY FUTURE Terrafilm, 1948, Swedish
PORT OF CALL Janus, 1948, Swedish
THE DEVIL'S WANTON Terrafilm, 1949, Swedish
THREE STRANGE LOVES *THIRST* Janus, 1949, Swedish
TO JOY Janus, 1950, Swedish
THIS CAN'T HAPPEN HERE Svensk Filmindustri, 1951, Swedish
ILLICIT INTERLUDE *SOMMARLEK* Janus, 1951, Swedish
SECRETS OF WOMEN Janus, 1952, Swedish
MONIKA Janus, 1953, Swedish
SAWDUST AND TINSEL *THE NAKED NIGHT* Janus, 1953, Swedish
A LESSON IN LOVE Janus, 1954, Swedish
DREAMS Janus, 1955, Swedish
SMILES OF A SUMMER NIGHT Janus, 1955, Swedish
THE SEVENTH SEAL Janus, 1957, Swedish
WILD STRAWBERRIES Janus, 1957, Swedish
SO CLOSE TO LIFE Janus, 1958, Swedish
THE MAGICIAN Janus, 1958, Swedish
THE VIRGIN SPRING Janus, 1960, Swedish
THE DEVIL'S EYE Janus, 1960, Swedish
THROUGH A GLASS DARKLY Janus, 1961, Swedish
WINTER LIGHT Janus, 1962, Swedish
THE SILENCE Janus, 1963, Swedish
ALL THESE WOMEN Janus, 1964, Swedish
PERSONA United Artists, 1966, Swedish
HOUR OF THE WOLF United Artists, 1968, Swedish
SHAME United Artists, 1968, Swedish
FARO DOCUMENT (TD) 1969, Swedish
THE RITUAL Janus, 1969, Swedish, originally made for television
THE PASSION OF ANNA United Artists, 1969, Swedish
THE TOUCH Cinerama Releasing Corporation, 1971, Swedish, originally made
for television
CRIES AND WHISPERS ★ New World, 1972, Swedish
SCENES FROM A MARRIAGE Cinema 5, 1973, Swedish, originally made for
television
THE MAGIC FLUTE Surrogate, 1975, Swedish, originally made for television
FACE TO FACE ★ Paramount, 1976, Swedish
THE SERPENT'S EGG Paramount, 1978, West German
AUTUMN SONATA New World, 1978, West German
FROM THE LIFE OF THE MARIONETTES Universal/AFD, 1980, West
German
FARO DOCUMENT 1979 (TD) Cinematograph, 1979, Swedish
FANNY AND ALEXANDER Embassy, 1983, Swedish-French-West German
AFTER THE REHEARSAL Triumph/Columbia, 1983, Swedish, originally made
for television

DAVID BERLATSKY *

Contact: Directors Guild of America - Los Angeles, 213/656-1220

THE FARMER Columbia, 1977

TED BERMAN

Business: Walt Disney Productions, 500 S. Buena Vista Street, Burbank, CA 91521, 213/845-3141

THE FOX AND THE HOUND (AF)   co-director with Art Stevens & Richard Rich, Buena Vista, 1981
THE BLACK CAULDRON (AF)   co-director with Art Stevens & Richard Rich, Buena Vista, 1985

ARMYAN BERNSTEIN *

Contact: Directors Guild of America - Los Angeles, 213/656-1220

WINDY CITY   Warner Bros., 1983

WALTER BERNSTEIN *

b. August 29, 1929 - Chicago, Illinois
Home: 320 Central Park West, New York, NY 10025, 212/724-1821
Agent: Sam Cohn, ICM - New York City, 212/556-6810

LITTLE MISS MARKER   Universal, 1980

CLAUDE BERRI
(Claude Langmann)

b. July 1, 1934 - Paris, France
Contact: French Film Office, 745 Fifth Avenue, New York, NY 10151, 212/832-8860

LE BAISERS   co-director, 1964, French
LE CHANCE ET L'AMOUR   co-director, 1964, French
THE TWO OF US *LE VIEL HOMME ET L'ENFANT*   Cinema 5, 1968, French
MARRY ME! MARRY ME! *MAZEL TOV OU LE MARIAGE*   Allied Artists, 1969, French
THE MAN WITH CONNECTIONS *LE PISTONNE*   Columbia, 1970, French
LE CINEMA DU PAPA   Columbia, 1971, French
LE SEX SHOP   Peppercorn-Wormser, 1973, French
MALE OF THE CENTURY   Joseph Green Pictures, 1975, French
THE FIRST TIME   EDP, 1976, French
ONE WILD MOMENT   Quartet/Films Incorporated, 1978, French
JE VOUS AIME   Renn Films/FR3/Cinevog, 1980, French
LA MAITRE D'ECOLE   AMLF, 1981, French
TCHAO PANTIN   AMLF, 1983, French

JOHN BERRY *

b. 1917 - New York, New York
Home: 299 West 12th Street, New York, NY 10014, 212/929-7134
Attorney: Ziffren, Brittenham, Gullen & Ingber - Los Angeles, 213/552-3388

MISS SUSIE SLAGLE'S   Paramount, 1945
FROM THIS DAY FORWARD   RKO Radio, 1946
CROSS MY HEART   Paramount, 1946
CASBAH   Universal, 1948
TENSION   MGM, 1949
HE RAN ALL THE WAY   United Artists, 1951
C'EST ARRIVE A PARIS   1952, French
CA VA BARDER   1954, French
JE SUIS UN SENTIMENTAL   1955, French
PANTALOONS *DON JUAN*   United Motion Picture Organizations, 1956, French-Spanish
OH, QUE MAMBO   1958, French
TAMANGO   Valiant, 1959, French
MAYA   MGM, 1966
A TOUT CASSER   1967, French
CLAUDINE   20th Century-Fox, 1974
THIEVES   Paramount, 1977
SPARROW   1978
THE BAD NEWS BEARS GO TO JAPAN   Paramount, 1978

continued

JOHN BERRY*—continued

ANGEL ON MY SHOULDER (TF)   Mace Neufeld Productions/Barney Rosenzweig Productions/Beowulf Productions, 1980
SISTER, SISTER (TF)   20th Century-Fox TV, 1982
HONEYBOY (TF)   Fan Fares Inc. Productions/Estrada Productions, 1982

B E R N A R D O   B E R T O L U C C I

b. March 16, 1940 - Parma, Italy
Contact: Ministry of Tourism & Education, Via Della Ferratella, No. 51, 00184 Rome, Italy, 06/7732

LA COMMARE SECCA   1962, Italian
BEFORE THE REVOLUTION   New Yorker, 1964, Italian
PARTNER   New Yorker, 1968, Italian
AMORE E RABBIA   co-director, 1969, Italian
THE SPIDER'S STRATAGEM   New Yorker, 1970, Italian
THE CONFORMIST   Paramount, 1971, Italian-French-West German
LAST TANGO IN PARIS ★   United Artists, 1973, Italian-French
1900   Paramount, 1977, Italian
LUNA   20th Century-Fox, 1979, Italian-U.S.
TRAGEDY OF A RIDICULOUS MAN   The Ladd Company/Warner Bros., 1982, Italian

J A M E S   B E S H E A R S

HOMEWORK   Jensen-Farley Pictures, 1982

E D W A R D   B I A N C H I *

Home: 36 Gramercy Park East, New York, NY 10003, 212/228-3668
Agent: Michael Black, ICM - Los Angeles, 213/550-4000

THE FAN   Paramount, 1981

T O N Y   B I L L *

b. August 23, 1940 - San Diego, California
Business: Tony Bill Productions, 73 Market Street, Venice, CA 90291, 213/396-5937
Agent: Robinson, Luttrell & Associates - Beverly Hills, 213/275-6114

MY BODYGUARD   20th Century-Fox, 1980
SIX WEEKS   Universal, 1982

B R U C E   B I L S O N *

b. May 19, 1928 - New York, New York
Agent: The Cooper Agency - Los Angeles, 213/277-8422

THE GIRL WHO CAME GIFT-WRAPPED (TF)   Spelling-Goldberg Productions, 1974
DEAD MAN ON THE RUN (TF)   Sweeney-Finnegan Productions, 1975
THE NEW DAUGHTERS OF JOSHUA CABE (TF)   Spelling-Goldberg Productions, 1976
BJ & THE BEAR (TF)   Universal TV, 1978
THE NORTH AVENUE IRREGULARS   Buena Vista, 1979
DALLAS COWBOYS CHEERLEADERS (TF)   Aubrey-Hammer Productions, 1979
PLEASURE COVE (TF)   Lou Shaw Productions/David Gerber Company/Columbia TV, 1979
THE GHOSTS OF BUXLEY HALL (TF)   Walt Disney Productions, 1980
CHATTANOOGA CHOO CHOO   Chattanooga Choo Choo Productions, 1984

KEVIN BILLINGTON

b. 1933 - England
Agent: A.D. Peters Ltd., 10 Buckingham Street, London WC2, England

INTERLUDE   Columbia, 1968, British
THE RISE AND RISE OF MICHAEL RIMMER   Warner Bros., 1970, British
THE LIGHT AT THE EDGE OF THE WORLD   National General, 1971, U.S.-
    Spanish
VOICES   Hemdale, 1973, British
AND NO ONE COULD SAVE HER (TF)   Associated London Films, 1973,
    British
ECHOES OF THE SIXTIES (TD)   ALA Productions, 1979
THE GOOD SOLDIER (TF)   Granada TV, 1983, British

JOHN BINDER *

Contact: Directors Guild of America - Los Angeles, 213/656-1220

UFORIA   Universal, 1983

MACK BING *

Agent: Eisenbach-Greene, Inc. - Los Angeles, 213/659-3420

ALL THE LOVING COUPLES   U-M, 1969
GABRIELLA   1974

PATRICIA BIRCH *

Agent: ICM - Los Angeles, 213/550-4000

GREASE 2   Paramount, 1982

BILL BIXBY *

b. January 22, 1934 - San Francisco, California
Personal Manager: Paul Brandon - Los Angeles, 213/273-6173

THE BARBARY COAST (TF)   Paramount TV, 1975
THREE ON A DATE (TF)   ABC Circle Films, 1978

NOEL BLACK *

b. 1937
Business: Highway Productions, 120 Greenfield Avenue, Los Angeles, CA 90049
Agent: Tom Chasin, Chasin-Park-Citron - Los Angeles, 213/273-7190

TRILOGY: THE AMERICAN BOY (TF)   ABC Stage 67, 1968
PRETTY POISON   20th Century-Fox, 1968
COVER ME BABE   20th Century-Fox, 1970
JENNIFER ON MY MIND   United Artists, 1971
MULLIGAN'S STEW (TF)   Paramount TV, 1977
MIRRORS   First American, 1978
A MAN, A WOMAN AND A BANK   Avco Embassy, 1979, Canadian
THE GOLDEN HONEYMOON (TF)   Learning in Focus, 1980
THE OTHER VICTIM (TF)   Shpetner Company, 1981
PRIME SUSPECT (TF)   Tisch-Avnet Television, 1982
THE ELECTRIC GRANDMOTHER (TF)   Highgate Pictures, 1982
HAPPY ENDINGS (TF)   Motown Productions, 1983
PRIVATE SCHOOL   Universal, 1983

MICHAEL BLAKEMORE

Contact: British Academy of Film & Television Arts, 195 Piccadilly, London W1,
    England, 01/734-0022

PRIVATES ON PARADE   Orion Classics, 1983, British

LES BLANK

b. November 27, 1935 - Tampa, Florida
Business: Flower Films, 10341 San Pablo Avenue, El Cerrito, CA 94530, 415/525-0942

CHULAS FRONTERAS (FD)   Brazos Films, 1976
ALWAYS FOR PLEASURE (FD)   Flower Films, 1978
BURDEN OF DREAMS (FD)   Flower Films, 1982

WILLIAM PETER BLATTY *

b. 1928 - New York, New York
Home: 23712 Malibu Colony, Malibu, CA 90265, 213/456-5081
Messages: 213/456-3317

THE NINTH CONFIGURATION   Warner Bros., 1979 - re-released under title
    TWINKLE, TWINKLE 'KILLER' KANE by United Film Distribution in 1980

JEFF BLECKNER *

Home: 4815 Dunman Avenue, Woodland Hills, CA 91364, 213/887-5938
Agent: Paul Heller, ICM - Los Angeles, 213/550-4311

RYAN'S FOUR (TF)   Fair Dinkum Inc./Groverton Productions/Paramount TV,
    1983
WHEN YOUR LOVER LEAVES (TF)   Major H Productions, 1983
CONCEALED ENEMIES (MS)   WGBH-Boston/Goldcrest Films & Television,
    1984

BERTRAND BLIER

b. March 14, 1939 - Paris, France
Contact: French Film Office, 745 Fifth Avenue, New York, NY 10151, 212/832-8860

HITLER CONNAIS PAS   1962, French
SI J'ETAIS UN ESPION   1967, French
GOING PLACES *LES VALSEUSES*   Cinema 5, 1974, French
FEMMES FATALES   New Line Cinema, 1977, French
GET OUT YOUR HANDKERCHIEFS   New Line Cinema, 1978, French
COLD CUTS   1979, French
BEAU PERE   New Line Cinema, 1981, French
LA FEMME DE MON POTE   AMLF, 1983, French

JEFFREY BLOOM

Agent: Adams, Ray & Rosenberg - Los Angeles, 213/278-3000

DOGPOUND SHUFFLE   Paramount, 1974, Canadian
THE STICK UP   Trident-Barber, 1978, British
BLOOD BEACH   Jerry Gross Organization, 1981
JEALOUSY (TF)   Charles Fries Productions/Alan Sacks Productions, 1983

GEORGE BLOOMFIELD *

b. Montreal, Quebec, Canada
Home: Admiral Road 50, Toronto, Ontario M5R215, Canada, 416/967-0826

JENNY   Cinerama Releasing Corporation, 1970
TO KILL A CLOWN   20th Century-Fox, 1972
CHILD UNDER A LEAF   Cinema National, 1975, Canadian
RIEL   CBC/Green River Productions, 1979, Canadian
NOTHING PERSONAL   American International, 1980 Canadian
DOUBLE NEGATIVE   Quadrant, 1981, Canadian

DON BLUTH

Business: Don Bluth Productions, 12229 Ventura Blvd., Studio City, CA 91604,
213/506-5440

THE SECRET OF NIMH (AF)   MGM/UA, 1982

BUDD BOETTICHER *
(Oscar Boetticher, Jr.)

b. July 29, 1916 - Chicago, Illinois
Contact: Directors Guild of America - Los Angeles, 213/656-1220

ONE MYSTERIOUS NIGHT   Columbia, 1944
THE MISSING JUROR   Columbia, 1944
A GUY, A GAL AND A PAL   Columbia, 1945
ESCAPE IN THE FOG   Columbia, 1945
YOUTH ON TRIAL   Columbia, 1945
THE FLEET THAT CAME TO STAY   Paramount, 1946
ASSIGNED TO DANGER   Eagle-Lion, 1948
BEHIND LOCKED DOORS   Eagle-Lion, 1948
THE WOLF HUNTERS   Monogram, 1949
BLACK MIDNIGHT   Monogram, 1949
KILLER SHARK   Monogram, 1950
THE BULLFIGHTER AND THE LADY   Republic, 1951
THE SWORD OF D'ARTAGNAN   Universal, 1951
THE CIMARRON KID   Universal, 1951
RED BALL EXPRESS   Universal, 1952
BRONCO BUSTER   Universal, 1952
HORIZONS WEST   Universal, 1952
CITY BENEATH THE SEA   Universal, 1953
SEMINOLE   Universal, 1953
THE MAN FROM THE ALAMO   Universal, 1953
EAST OF SUMATRA   Universal, 1953
WINGS OF THE HAWK   Universal, 1953
THE MAGNIFICENT MATADOR   20th Century-Fox, 1955
THE KILLER IS LOOSE   United Artists, 1956
SEVEN MEN FROM NOW   Warner Bros., 1956
THE TALL T   Columbia, 1957
DECISION AT SUNDOWN   Columbia, 1957
BUCHANAN RIDES ALONE   Columbia, 1958
RIDE LONESOME   Columbia, 1959
WESTBOUND   Warner Bros., 1959
COMANCHE STATION   Columbia, 1960
THE RISE AND FALL OF LEGS DIAMOND   Warner Bros., 1960
A TIME FOR DYING   Etoile, 1971
ARRUZA (FD)   Avco Embassy, 1972

PAUL BOGART *

b. November 21, 1919 - New York, New York
Business: Tiber Productions, Inc., 760 N. La Cienega Blvd., Los Angeles,
CA 90069, 213/652-0222
Agent: Irv Schechter Company - Beverly Hills, 213/278-8070

MARLOWE   MGM, 1969
HALLS OF ANGER   United Artists, 1970
SKIN GAME   Warner Bros., 1971
IN SEARCH OF AMERICA (TF)   Four Star Productions, 1971
CLASS OF '44   Warner Bros., 1973
CANCEL MY RESERVATION   Warner Bros., 1974
TELL ME WHERE IT HURTS (TF)   Tomorrow Entertainment, 1974
MR. RICCO   MGM, 1975
WINNER TAKE ALL (TF)   The Jozak Company, 1975
THE THREE SISTERS   NTA, 1977
OH, GOD! III   Warner Bros., 1984

PETER BOGDANOVICH

b. July 30, 1939 - Kingston, New York

TARGETS   Paramount, 1968
DIRECTED BY JOHN FORD (FD)   American Film Institute, 1971
THE LAST PICTURE SHOW ★   Columbia, 1971
WHAT'S UP, DOC?   Warner Bros., 1972
PAPER MOON   Paramount, 1973
DAISY MILLER   Paramount, 1974
AT LONG LAST LOVE   20th Century-Fox, 1975
NICKELODEON   Columbia, 1976
SAINT JACK   New World, 1979
THEY ALL LAUGHED   United Artists Classics, 1982

CLIFFORD BOLE *

Agent: Shapiro-Lichtman Agency - Los Angeles, 213/557-2244
Business Manager: Brad Marer & Associates - Los Angeles, 213/278-6690

T.J. HOOKER (TF)   Spelling-Goldberg Productions, 1982

ROBERT BOLT

b. August 15, 1924 - Sale, England
Contact: British Academy of Film & Television Arts, 195 Piccadilly, London W1,
    England, 01/734-0022

LADY CAROLINE LAMB   United Artists, 1973, British

SERGEI BONDARCHUK

b. September 25, 1920 - Belozersk, Ukraine, U.S.S.R.
Contact: State Committee of Cinematography of the U.S.S.R., Council of Ministers, 7
    Maly Gnesdnikovsky Pereulok, Moscow, U.S.S.R., 7 095/229-9912

FATE OF A MAN   Lopert, 1961, Soviet
WAR AND PEACE   Continental, 1968, Soviet
WATERLOO   Paramount, 1971, Italian-Soviet
THEY FOUGHT FOR THEIR MOTHERLAND   Mosfilm, 1974, Soviet
THE STEPPE   IFEX Film/Sovexport film, 1977, Soviet
RED BELLS: MEXICO IN FLAMES   Mosfilm/Conacite-2/RAI/Vides
    International/Cinefin, 1982, Soviet-Mexican-Italian
RED BELLS: I'VE SEEN THE BIRTH OF THE NEW WORLD   Mosfilm/
    Conacite-2/Vides International, 1983, Soviet-Mexican-Italian

PETER BONERZ *

Agent: CAA - Los Angeles, 213/277-4545

NOBODY'S PERFEKT   Columbia, 1981

JOHN BOORMAN *

b. January 18, 1933 - Shepperton, England
Business Manager: Edgar F. Gross, International Business Management - Los Angeles,
    213/277-4455

HAVING A WILD WEEKEND *CATCH US IF YOU CAN*   Warner Bros.,
    1965, British
POINT BLANK   MGM, 1967
HELL IN THE PACIFIC   Cinerama Releasing Corporation, 1968
LEO THE LAST   United Artists, 1970, British
DELIVERANCE ★   Warner Bros., 1972
ZARDOZ   20th Century-Fox, 1974, British
THE HERETIC: EXORCIST II   Warner Bros., 1977
EXCALIBUR   Orion/Warner Bros., 1981, British-Irish

PHILLIP BORSOS

Contact: Canadian Film & Television Association, 8 King Street, Toronto, Ontario M5C 1B5, Canada, 416/363-0296

THE GREY FOX   United Artists Classics, 1983, Canadian

JOHN BOULTING

b. November 21, 1913 - Bray, Buckinghamshire, England
Business: Charter Film Productions Ltd., 8A Glebe Place, London 5W351B, England, 01/352-6838

JOURNEY TOGETHER   RKO Radio, 1945, British
YOUNG SCARFACE *BRIGHTON ROCK*   Mayer-Kingsley, 1947, British
SEVEN DAYS TO NOON   Mayer-Kingsley, 1950, British
THE MAGIC BOX   Rank, 1952, British
CREST OF THE WAVE *SEAGULLS OVER SORRENTO*   co-director with
    Roy Boulting, MGM, 1954, British
PRIVATE'S PROGRESS   DCA, 1956, British
LUCKY JIM   Kingsley International, 1957, British
I'M ALL RIGHT, JACK   Columbia, 1960, British
THE RISK *SUSPECT*   co-director with Roy Boulting, Kingsley International,
    1961, British
HEAVEN'S ABOVE!   Janus, 1963, British
ROTTEN TO THE CORE   Cinema 5, 1965, British

ROY BOULTING *

b. November 21, 1913 - Bray, Buckinghamshire, England
Business: Charter Film Productions Ltd., 8A Glebe Place, London 5W351B, England, 01/352-6838
Agent: John Redway & Associates - London, 01/637-1612

TRUNK CRIME   Angelo, 1939, British
INQUEST   Grand National, 1939, British
PASTOR HALL   United Artists, 1940, British
THUNDER ROCK   English Films, 1942, British
DESERT VICTORY (FD)   Army Film Unit, 1943, British
TUNISIAN VICTORY (FD)   co-director with Frank Capra, Army Film Unit, 1943,
    British
BURMA VICTORY (FD)   Army Film Unit, 1945, British
THE OUTSIDER *THE GUINEA PIG*   Pathe, 1948, British
FAME IS THE SPUR   Two Cities, 1949, British
HIGH TREASON   Rank, 1951, British
SAILOR OF THE KING *SINGLE-HANDED*   20th Century-Fox, 1953, British
CREST OF THE WAVE *SEAGULLS OVER SORRENTO*   co-director with
    John Boulting, MGM, 1954
JOSEPHINE AND MEN   1955, British
RUN FOR THE SUN   United Artists, 1956, British
BROTHERS IN LAW   British Lion, 1957, British
HAPPY IS THE BRIDE   Kassler, 1959, British
MAN IN A COCKED HAT *CARLTON-BROWNE OF THE F.O.*   co-director
    with Jeffrey Dell, Show Corporation, 1960, British
A FRENCH MISTRESS   Films Around the World, 1960, British
THE RISK *SUSPECT*   co-director with John Boulting, Kingsley International,
    1961, British
THE FAMILY WAY   Warner Bros., 1967, British
TWISTED NERVE   National General, 1969, British
THERE'S A GIRL IN MY SOUP   Columbia, 1970, British
UNDERCOVERS HERO *SOFT BEDS AND HARD BATTLES*   United Artists,
    1975, British
THE LAST WORD   The Samuel Goldwyn Company, 1979

JENNY BOWEN

STREET MUSIC   Specialty, 1982

GEORGE BOWERS

THE HEARSE   Crown International, 1980
BODY AND SOUL   Cannon, 1982
MY TUTOR   Crown International, 1983

MARLON BRANDO*

b. April 3, 1924 - Omaha, Nebraska
Contact: Directors Guild of America - Los Angeles, 213/656-1220

ONE-EYED JACKS   Paramount, 1961

CHARLES BRAVERMAN*

Business: Braverman Productions, 4155 Witzel Drive, Sherman Oaks, CA 91423,
    213/783-8994

HIT AND RUN   Comworld, 1982

ROBERT BRESSON

b. September 25, 1907 - Bromont-Lamothe, France
Contact: French Film Office, 745 Fifth Avenue, New York, NY 10151, 212/832-
    8860

LES AFFAIRES PUBLIQUE   Arc Films, 1934, French
LES ANGES DU PECHE   Synops/Roland Tual, 1943, French
THE LADIES OF THE PARK   Brandon, 1945, French
DIARY OF A COUNTRY PRIEST   Brandon, 1950, French
A MAN ESCAPED   Continental, 1956, French
PICKPOCKET   New Yorker, 1959, French
THE TRIAL OF JOAN OF ARC   Pathe Contemporary, 1962, French
AU HASARD, BALTHAZAR   Cinema Ventures, 1966, French
MOUCHETTE   1967, French
UNE FEMME DOUCE   New Yorker, 1969, French
FOUR NIGHTS OF A DREAMER   New Yorker, 1972, French
LANCELOT OF THE LAKE   New Yorker, 1975, French-Italian
THE DEVIL, PROBABLY   1979, French
L'ARGENT   AMLF, 1983, French-Swiss

MARTIN BREST*

b. 1951 - New York, New York
Agent: The Ufland Agency - Beverly Hills, 213/273-9441

HOT TOMORROWS   American Film Institute, 1977
GOING IN STYLE   Warner Bros., 1979

MARSHALL BRICKMAN*

Business Manager: Bernstein & Freedman, 228 West 55th Street, New York,
    NY 10019

SIMON   Orion/Warner Bros., 1980
LOVESICK   The Ladd Company/Warner Bros., 1983

PAUL BRICKMAN*

Contact: Directors Guild of America - Los Angeles, 213/656-1220

RISKY BUSINESS   The Geffen Company/Warner Bros., 1983

ALAN BRIDGES

b. September 28, 1928 - Liverpool, England
Address: The Old Manor Farm, Church Street, Sunbury-on-Thames, Middlesex TW16
6RG, England, Tel.: Sunbury-on-Thames 80166
Agent: John Redway & Associates - London, 01/637-1612

ACT OF MURDER   Warner-Pathe/Anglo-Amalgamated, 1964, British
INVASION   Warner-Pathe/Anglo-Amalgamated, 1966, British
THE LIE   1970, British
THE HIRELING   Columbia, 1973, British
BRIEF ENCOUNTER (TF)   Carlo Ponti Productions/Cecil Clarke Productions,
1974, British
OUT OF SEASON   Athenaeum, 1975, British
AGE OF INNOCENCE   Rank, 1977, British-Canadian
LA PETITE FILLE EN VELOURS BLEU   1978, French
VERY LIKE A WHALE   Black Lion, 1981, British
THE RETURN OF THE SOLDIER   Golden Communications, 1982, British
PUDDN'HEAD WILSON (TF)   Gramwell Company, 1983, British
THE SHOOTING PARTY   Geoff Reeve Films & Television, 1984, British

BEAU BRIDGES *

(Lloyd Vernet Bridges III)

b. December 9, 1941 - Los Angeles, California
Agent: CAA - Los Angeles, 213/277-4545

THE KID FROM NOWHERE (TF)   Cates-Bridges Company, telefeature, 1982

JAMES BRIDGES *

b. February 3, 1936 - Paris, Arkansas
Agent: Steve Roth, CAA - Los Angeles, 213/277-4545
Business Manager: Ron Koblin - Beverly Hills, 213/854-4420

THE BABY MAKER   National General, 1970
THE PAPER CHASE   20th Century-Fox, 1973
9/30/55 *SEPTEMBER 30, 1955*   Universal, 1977
THE CHINA SYNDROME   Columbia, 1979
URBAN COWBOY   Paramount, 1980
MIKE'S MURDER   The Ladd Company/Warner Bros., 1984

BURT BRINCKERHOFF *

b. October 25, 1936
Agent: Fred Westheimer, William Morris Agency - Beverly Hills, 213/274-7451

TWO BROTHERS (TF)   KCET-TV, 1976
DOGS   R.C. Riddell, 1977
ACAPULCO GOLD   R.C. Riddell, 1978
THE CRACKER FACTORY (TF)   Roger Gimbel Productions/EMI TV, 1979
CAN YOU HEAR THE LAUGHTER? THE STORY OF FREDDIE PRINZE
(TF)   Roger Gimbel Productions/EMI TV, 1979
MOTHER AND DAUGHTER - THE LOVING WAR (TF)   Edgar J. Scherick
Associates, 1980
BRAVE NEW WORLD (TF)   Universal TV, 1980
THE DAY THE WOMEN GOT EVEN (TF)   Otto Salaman Productions/PKO,
1980
BORN TO BE SOLD (TF)   Ron Samuels Productions, 1981

REX BROMFIELD

Business: Bromfilms, Inc., 1237 Howe Street, Vancouver, British Columbia, Canada

LOVE AT FIRST SIGHT   Movietown, 1977, Canadian
TULIPS   co-director with Mark Warren & Al Waxman under the collective
pseudonym of Stan Ferris, Avco Embassy, 1981, Canadian
MELANIE   Jensen Farley Pictures, 1983, Canadian

PETER BROOK

b. March 21, 1925 - London, England
Address: c/o C.I.C.T., 9 Rue du Cirque, Paris 8, France

THE BEGGAR'S OPERA   Warner Bros., 1953, British
MODERATOR CANTABILE   Royal International, 1963, French-Italian
LORD OF THE FLIES   Continental, 1963, British
THE PERSECUTION AND ASSASSINATION OF JEAN-PAUL MARAT AS
    PERFORMED BY THE INMATES OF THE ASYLUM OF CHARENTON
    UNDER THE DIRECTION OF THE MARQUIS DE SADE *MARAT/
    SADE*   United Artists, 1967, British
TELL ME LIES   Continental, 1968, British
KING LEAR   Altura, 1971, British-Danish
MEETINGS WITH REMARKABLE MEN   Libra, 1979, British

ALBERT BROOKS *

b. July 22, 1947 - Los Angeles, California
Business Manager: Gelfand & Macnow - Los Angeles, 213/553-1707

REAL LIFE   Paramount, 1979
MODERN ROMANCE   Columbia, 1981

BOB BROOKS *

Home: 2 Stratford Studios, Stratford Road, London W8, England, 01/402-5561
Business: Bob Brooks Films Ltd. - London, 01/937-8597
Agent: Anthony Jones - London, 01/839-2556

TATTOO   20th Century-Fox, 1981

JAMES L. BROOKS *

b. May 9, 1940 - Brooklyn, New York
Business: Paramount Pictures, 5555 Melrose Avenue, Los Angeles, CA 90028,
    213/468-5899

TERMS OF ENDEARMENT   Paramount, 1983

JOSEPH BROOKS *

Business: Chancery Lane Films, Inc., 41-A East 74th Street, New York NY 10021,
    212/759-8720

YOU LIGHT UP MY LIFE   Columbia, 1977
IF EVER I SEE YOU AGAIN   Columbia, 1978
HEADIN' FOR BROADWAY   20th Century-Fox, 1980
INVITATION TO THE WEDDING   Chancery Lane Films, 1983, British

MEL BROOKS
(Melvin Kaminsky)

b. 1926 - New York, New York
Business: Brooksfilms Limited, 20th Century-Fox, P.O. Box 900, Beverly Hills,
    CA 90213, 213/203-1375

THE PRODUCERS   Avco Embassy, 1968
THE TWELVE CHAIRS   UMC, 1970
BLAZING SADDLES   Warner Bros., 1973
YOUNG FRANKENSTEIN   20th Century-Fox, 1974
SILENT MOVIE   20th Century-Fox, 1976
HIGH ANXIETY   20th Century-Fox, 1977
HISTORY OF THE WORLD, PART I   20th Century-Fox, 1981

RICHARD BROOKS *

b. May 18, 1912 - Philadelphia, Pennsylvania
Attorney: Gerald Lipsky - Beverly Hills, 213/878-4100

CRISIS   MGM, 1950
THE LIGHT TOUCH   MGM, 1951
DEADLINE - U.S.A.   MGM, 1952
BATTLE CIRCUS   MGM, 1953
TAKE THE HIGH GROUND   MGM, 1953
FLAME AND THE FLESH   MGM, 1954
THE LAST TIME I SAW PARIS   MGM, 1954
THE BLACKBOARD JUNGLE   MGM, 1955
THE LAST HUNT   MGM, 1956
THE CATERED AFFAIR   MGM, 1956
SOMETHING OF VALUE   MGM, 1957
CAT ON A HOT TIN ROOF ★   MGM, 1958
THE BROTHERS KARAMAZOV   MGM, 1958
ELMER GANTRY   United Artists, 1960
SWEET BIRD OF YOUTH   MGM, 1962
LORD JIM   Columbia, 1964
THE PROFESSIONALS ★   Columbia, 1966
IN COLD BLOOD ★   Columbia, 1967
THE HAPPY ENDING   United Artists, 1969
$ *DOLLARS*   Columbia, 1971
BITE THE BULLET   Columbia, 1975
LOOKING FOR MR. GOODBAR   Paramount, 1977
WRONG IS RIGHT   Columbia, 1982

BARRY BROWN *

Business: Brillig Productions, Inc., 300 Central Park West, New York, NY 10024,
    212/595-5454

THE WAY WE LIVE NOW   United Artists, 1970
CLOUD DANCER   Blossom, 1980

GEORG STANFORD BROWN *

b. June 24 - Havana, Cuba
Agent: ICM - Los Angeles, 213/550-4000

ROOTS: THE NEXT GENERATIONS (MS)   co-director with John Erman,
    Charles Dubin & Lloyd Richards, Wolper Productions, 1979
GRAMBLING'S WHITE TIGER (TF)   Jenner-Wallach Productions/Inter Planetary
    Productions, 1981

JIM BROWN

WASN'T THAT A TIME! (FD)   United Artists Classics, 1982

KIRK BROWNING *

b. May 28, 1921 - New York, New York
Home: 80 Central Park West, New York, NY 10023
Messages: 212/595-6474

BIG BLONDE (TF)   PBS-TV, 1980

FRANCO BRUSATI

Contact: Ministry of Tourism & Education, Via Della Ferratella, No. 51, 00184
    Rome, Italy, 06/7732

BREAD AND CHOCOLATE   World Northal, 1978, Italian
TO FORGET VENICE   Quartet, 1980, Italian-French
THE GOOD SOLDIER   Gaumont, 1982, Italian

LARRY BUCHANAN*

Home: 4159 Nogales Drive, Tarzana, CA 91356, 213/344-0976

FREE, WHITE AND 21   American International, 1963
UNDER AGE   Falcon International, 1964
A BULLET FOR PRETTY BOY   American International, 1970
GOODBYE, NORMA JEAN   Stirling Gold, 1976
HUGHES AND HARLOW: ANGELS IN HELL   Pro International, 1978
THE LOCH NESS HORROR   Omni-Leisure International, 1982

MARK BUNTZMAN

EXTERMINATOR 2   MGM/UA/Cannon, 1984

JUAN BUÑUEL

b. November 9, 1934 - Paris, France
Home: 6, Rue Leneveux, Paris 75014, France, Tel.: 540 53 94
Agent: Anne Alvarez Correa, 18, Rue Troyon, Paris 75017, France, Tel.: 755 80
    85

RENDEZVOUS WITH JOYOUS DEATH   United Artists, French
GIRL WITH RED BOOTS   French
LEONOR   Paramount, French

DEREK BURBIDGE

Contact: Directors Guild of Great Britain, 56 Whitfield Street, London WI, England,
    01/580-9592

URGH! A MUSIC WAR (FD)   Filmways, 1982
MEN WITHOUT WOMEN (FD)   1983

STUART BURGE

b. January 15, 1918 - Brentwood, England
Contact: Directors Guild of Great Britain, 56 Whitfield Street, London WI, England,
    01/580-9592

THERE WAS A CROOKED MAN   United Artists, 1962, British
UNCLE VANYA   Arthur Cantor, 1963, British
OTHELLO   Warner Bros., 1967, British
THE MIKADO   Warner Bros., 1967, British
JULIUS CAESAR   American International, 1971, British

MARTYN BURKE

Business: 113 N. San Vicente Blvd., Beverly Hills, CA 90211, 213/655-4115
Agent: ICM - New York City, 212/556-5600

THE CLOWN MURDERS   Canadian
POWER PLAY   Magnum International Pictures/Cowry Film Productions, 1978,
    Canadian-British
THE LAST CHASE   Crown International, 1981, Canadian

JAMES BURROWS*

b. December 30, 1940 - Los Angeles, California
Agent: Bob Broder, Broder-Kurland Agency - Los Angeles, 213/274-8921

MORE THAN FRIENDS (TF)   Reiner-Mishkin Productions/Columbia TV, 1978
PARTNERS   Paramount, 1982

WILLIAM J. BUSHNELL, JR.*

Business: Los Angeles Actors' Theatre, 1089 N. Oxford Avenue, Los Angeles,
CA 90029, 213/464-5603

PRISONERS   1973
THE FOUR DEUCES   Avco Embassy, 1974

ROBERT BUTLER*

b. November 17, 1927 - Los Angeles, California
Agent: Jim Wiatt, ICM - Los Angeles, 213/550-4273

THE COMPUTER WORE TENNIS SHOES   Buena Vista, 1970
THE BAREFOOT EXECUTIVE   Buena Vista, 1971
SCANDALOUS JOHN   Buena Vista, 1971
DEATH TAKES A HOLIDAY (TF)   Universal TV, 1971
NOW YOU SEE HIM, NOW YOU DON'T   Buena Vista, 1972
THE BLUE KNIGHT (TF)☆   Lorimar Productions, 1973
THE ULTIMATE THRILL   General Cinema, 1974
STRANGE NEW WORLD (TF)   Warner Brothers TV, 1975
DARK VICTORY (TF)   Universal TV, 1976
JAMES DEAN (TF)   The Jozak Company, 1976
MAYDAY AT 40,000 FEET (TF)   Andrew J. Fenady Associates/Warner
    Brothers TV, 1976
IN THE GLITTER PALACE (TF)   The Writer's Company/Columbia TV, 1977
HOT LEAD AND COLD FEET   Buena Vista, 1978
A QUESTION OF GUILT (TF)   Lorimar Productions, 1978
LACY AND THE MISSISSIPPI QUEEN (TF)   Lawrence Gordon Productions/
    Paramount TV, 1978
NIGHT OF THE JUGGLER   Columbia, 1980
UNDERGROUND ACES   Filmways, 1981
UP THE CREEK   Orion, 1984

JOHN BYRUM*

b. March 14, 1947 - Evanston, Illinois
Agent: CAA - Los Angeles, 213/277-4545
Business Manager: Bob Colbert, Guild Management - Los Angeles, 213/277-9711

INSERTS   United Artists, 1976, British
HEART BEAT   Orion/Warner Bros., 1980
THE RAZOR'S EDGE   Columbia, 1984

JAMES CAAN*

b. March 26, 1939 - Bronx, New York
Agent: CAA - Los Angeles, 213/277-4545
Business Manager: Licker & Pines, 9025 Wilshire Blvd., Beverly Hills, CA 90211,
    213/858-1276

HIDE IN PLAIN SIGHT   MGM/United Artists, 1980

MICHAEL CACOYANNIS

b. June 11, 1922 - Cyprus
Contact: Greek Film Centre, Panepistimiou Street, Athens 134, Greece, 1/363-4586

WINDFALL IN ATHENS   Audio Brandon, 1953, Greek
STELLA   Milas Films, 1955, Greek
THE FINAL LIE   Finos Films, 1958, Greek
OUR LAST SPRING   Cacoyannis, 1959, Greek
A GIRL IN BLACK   Kingsley International, 1959, Greek
THE WASTREL   Lux/Tiberia, 1960, Italian
ELECTRA   Lopert, 1962, Greek
ZORBA THE GREEK★   International Classics, 1964, Greek
THE DAY THE FISH CAME OUT   20th Century-Fox, 1967, British-Greek
THE TROJAN WOMEN   Cinerama Releasing Corporation, 1971, U.S.-Greek
THE STORY OF JACOB AND JOSEPH (TF)   Screen Gems/Columbia TV, 1974
ATTILA '74 (FD)   1975, Greek
IPHIGENIA   Cinema 5, 1977, Greek

MICHAEL CAFFEY *

Agent: Shapiro-Lichtman Agency - Los Angeles, 213/557-2244

SEVEN IN DARKNESS (TF)   Paramount TV, 1969
THE SILENT GUN (TF)   Paramount TV, 1969
THE DEVIL AND MISS SARAH (TF)   Universal TV, 1971
THE HANGED MAN (TF)   Fenady Associates/Bing Crosby Productions, 1974

CHRIS CAIN *

Business: 5901 Clover Heights, Malibu, CA 90265, 213/457-3261

BROTHER, MY SONG   Eagle International, 1976
GRAND JURY   CCF, 1976
THE BUZZARD   CCF, 1976
SIXTH AND MAIN   CCF, 1977
STONE BOY   20th Century-Fox International Classics, 1984

DOUGLAS CAMFIELD

b. London, England
Agent: London Management - London, 01/734-4192

IVANHOE (TF)   Norman Rosemont Productions/Columbia TV, 1982, U.S.-British

DONALD CAMMELL *

Agent: Steve Reuther, William Morris Agency - Beverly Hills, 213/274-7451

PERFORMANCE   co-director with Nicolas Roeg, Warner Bros., 1970, British
DEMON SEED   MGM/United Artists, 1977

JOE CAMP *

b. April 20, 1939 - St. Louis, Missouri
Business: Mulberry Square Productions, 10300 N. Central Expressway, Dallas, Texas 75231, 214/369-2430

BENJI   Mulberry Square, 1974
HAWMPS   Mulberry Square, 1976

FOR THE LOVE OF BENJI   Mulberry Square, 1978
THE DOUBLE McGUFFIN   Mulberry Square, 1979
OH HEAVENLY DOG   20th Century-Fox, 1980

continued

NORMAN CAMPBELL *

Home: 20 George Henry Blvd., Willowdale, Ontario M2J 1E2, Canada, 416/494-8576
Agent: Lee Gabler, ICM - Los Angeles, 213/550-4000

THE MAGIC SHOW   Producers Distributing Company, 1983, Canadian

MICHAEL CAMPUS *

Home: 2121 Kress Street, Los Angeles, CA 90046, 213/656-2648
Agent: Ron Mardigian, William Morris Agency - Beverly Hills, 213/274-7451
Business Manager: Licker & Pines, 9025 Wilshire Blvd., Beverly Hills, CA 90211,
    213/858-1276

Z.P.G.   Paramount, 1972
THE MACK   Cinerama Releasing Corporation, 1973
THE EDUCATION OF SONNY CARSON   Paramount, 1974
THE PASSOVER PLOT   Atlas, 1977, U.S.-Israeli

FRANK CAPRA *

b. May 18, 1897 - Palermo, Sicily
Home: P.O. Box 98, La Quinta, CA 92253

THE STRONG MAN   First National, 1926
LONG PANTS   First National, 1927
FOR THE LOVE OF MIKE   First National, 1927
THAT CERTAIN THING   Columbia, 1928
SO THIS IS LOVE   Columbia, 1928
THE MATINEE IDOL   Columbia, 1928
THE WAY OF THE STRONG   Columbia, 1928
SAY IT WITH SABLES   Columbia, 1928
SUBMARINE   Columbia, 1928
THE POWER OF THE PRESS   Columbia, 1928
THE YOUNGER GENERATION   Columbia, 1929
THE DONOVAN AFFAIR   Columbia, 1929
FLIGHT   Columbia, 1929
LADIES OF LEISURE   Columbia, 1930
RAIN OR SHINE   Columbia, 1930
DIRIGIBLE   Columbia, 1931
THE MIRACLE WOMAN   Columbia, 1931
PLATINUM BLONDE   Columbia, 1931
FORBIDDEN   Columbia, 1932
AMERICAN MADNESS   Columbia, 1932
THE BITTER TEA OF GENERAL YEN   Columbia, 1933
LADY FOR A DAY★   Columbia, 1933
IT HAPPENED ONE NIGHT★★   Columbia, 1934
BROADWAY BILL   Columbia, 1934
MR. DEEDS GOES TO TOWN★★   Columbia, 1936
LOST HORIZON   Columbia, 1937
YOU CAN'T TAKE IT WITH YOU★★   Columbia, 1938
MR. SMITH GOES TO WASHINGTON★   Columbia, 1939
MEET JOHN DOE   Warner Bros., 1941
PRELUDE TO WAR (FD)   U.S. Army, 1942
THE NAZIS STRIKE (FD)   co-director with Anatole Litvak, U.S. Army, 1942
DIVIDE AND CONQUER (FD)   co-director with Anatole Litvak, U.S. Army,
    1943
BATTLE OF BRITAIN (FD)   co-director, U.S. Army, 1943
BATTLE OF CHINA (FD)   co-director with Anatole Litvak, U.S. Army, 1943
THE NEGRO SOLDIER (FD)   U.S. Army, 1944
TUNISIAN VICTORY (FD)   co-director with Roy Boulting, Army Film Unit,
    1944, British
ARSENIC AND OLD LACE   Warner Bros., 1944
KNOW YOUR ENEMY: JAPAN (FD)   co-director with Joris Ivens, 1945
TWO DOWN AND ONE TO GO (FD)   1945
IT'S A WONDERFUL LIFE★   RKO Radio, 1946

continued

FRANK CAPRA*—continued

STATE OF THE UNION   MGM, 1948
RIDING HIGH   Paramount, 1950
HERE COMES THE GROOM   Paramount, 1951
A HOLE IN THE HEAD   United Artists, 1959
POCKETFUL OF MIRACLES   United Artists, 1961

JACK CARDIFF

b. September 18, 1914 - Yarmouth, England
Agent: Eric L'Epine Smith, 10 Wyndham Place, London WI, England, 01/724-0739

WEB OF EVIDENCE *BEYOND THIS PLACE*   Allied Artists, 1959, British
INTENT TO KILL   20th Century-Fox, 1959, British
HOLIDAY IN SPAIN   1960, British
SCENT OF MYSTERY   Todd, 1960, British
SONS AND LOVERS★   20th Century-Fox, 1960, British
MY GEISHA   Paramount, 1962
THE LION   20th Century-Fox, 1962, British
THE LONG SHIPS   Columbia, 1964, British-Yugoslavian
YOUNG CASSIDY   MGM, 1965, British
THE LIQUIDATOR   MGM, 1966, British
DARK OF THE SUN *THE MERCENARIES*   MGM, 1968, British
THE GIRL ON A MOTORCYCLE *NAKED UNDER LEATHER*   Claridge,
    1968, British-French
PENNY GOLD   Scotia-Barber, 1973, British
THE MUTATIONS   Columbia, 1974, British

JOHN ''BUD'' CARDOS*

Home: 19116 Enadia Way, Reseda, CA 91335, 213/343-4077
Agent: Craig Rumar, F.A.M.E. - Los Angeles, 213/556-8071

SOUL SOLDIER *THE RED, WHITE AND BLACK*   Fanfare, 1972
KINGDOM OF THE SPIDERS   Dimension, 1977
THE DARK   Film Ventures International, 1979
THE DAY TIME ENDED   Compass International, 1979
NIGHT SHADOWS   Artists Releasing Corporation/Film Ventures International,
    1984

GILLES CARLE

b. 1929 - Maniwaki, Quebec, Canada
Contact: Association des Realisateurs, 1406 Beaudry Street, Montreal, Quebec H2L
    4K4, Canada, 514/843-7770

LA VIE HEUREUSE DE LÉOPOLD Z   NFB, 1965, Canadian
PLACE A OLIVIER GUIMOND   Onyx Films, 1966, Canadian
PLACE AUX JEROLAS   Onyx Films, 1967, Canadian
LE VIOL D'UNE JEUNE FILLE DOUCE   Onyx-Fournier, 1968, Canadian
RED   Onyx Films/SMA, 1970, Canadian
LES MALES   Onyx Films/France Films, 1970, Canadian
LES CHEVALIERS   COFCI/ORTF, 1972, Canadian
LE VRAIE NATURE DE BERNADETTE   Les Productions Carle-Lamy, 1972,
    Canadian
LES CORPS CELESTES   Les Productions Carle-Lamy, 1973, Canadian
LA MORT D'UN BUCHERON   Les Productions Carle-Lamy, 1973, Canadian
LA TÊTE DE NORMANDE ST.   ONGE 1975, Canadian
THE ANGEL AND THE WOMAN   RSL Productions, 1977, Canadian
NORMANDE   Fred Baker Films, 1979, Canadian
FANTASTICA   Les Productions du Verseau/El Productions, 1980, Canadian
THE PLOUFFE FAMILY   ICC/Cine-London Productions, 1981, Canadian
THE GREAT CHESS MOVIE (FD)   co-director with Camille Coudari, 1982,
    Canadian
MARIA CHAPDELAINE   Astral Film Productions/Radio Canada/TFI, 1983,
    Canadian-French

LEWIS JOHN CARLINO*

b. January 1, 1932 - New York, New York
Agent: Michael Rosenfeld, CAA - Los Angeles, 213/277-4545

THE SAILOR WHO FELL FROM GRACE WITH THE SEA   Avco Embassy,
    1976, British
THE GREAT SANTINI *THE ACE*   Orion/Warner Bros., 1980
CLASS   Orion, 1983

JOHN CARPENTER*

b. January 16, 1948 - Carthage, New York
Home: P.O. Box 1334, North Hollywood, CA 91604
Agent: David Gersh, The Gersh Agency - Beverly Hills, 213/274-6611
Business Manager: Jim Jennings, Nanas, Stern, Biers & Company, 9454 Wilshire
    Blvd., Beverly Hills, CA 90212, 213/273-2501

DARK STAR   Jack H. Harris Enterprises, 1974
ASSAULT ON PRECINCT 13   Turtle Releasing Corporation, 1976
HALLOWEEN   Compass International, 1978
SOMEONE IS WATCHING ME (TF)   Warner Bros. TV, 1978
ELVIS (TF)   Dick Clark Productions, 1979
THE FOG   Avco Embassy, 1981
THE THING   Universal, 1982
JOHN CARPENTER'S CHRISTINE   Columbia, 1983

STEPHEN CARPENTER

PRANKS   co-director with Jeffrey Obrow, New Image, 1982
THE DORM THAT DRIPPED BLOOD   co-director with Jeffrey Obrow, Artists
    Releasing Corporation/Film Ventures International, 1983
THE POWER   co-director with Jeffrey Obrow, Artists Releasing Corporation/Film
    Ventures International, 1983

DAVID CARRADINE*

b. December 8, 1936 - Hollywood, California
Contact: Directors Guild of America - Los Angeles, 213/656-1220

YOU AND ME   Filmmakers International, 1975
AMERICANA   Crown International, 1983

MICHAEL CARRERAS

b. 1927 - London, England
Contact: British Academy of Film & Television Arts, 195 Piccadilly, London W1,
    England, 01/734-0022

THE STEEL BAYONET   United Artists, 1958, British
PASSPORT TO CHINA *VISA TO CANTON*   Columbia, 1961, British
THE SAVAGE GUNS   MGM, 1962, Spanish-U.S.
MANIAC   Columbia, 1963, British
WHAT A CRAZY WORLD   Warner-Pathe, 1963, British
THE CURSE OF THE MUMMY'S TOMB   Columbia, 1965, British
PREHISTORIC WOMEN *SLAVE GIRLS*   20th Century-Fox, 1967, British
THE LOST CONTINENT   20th Century-Fox, 1968, British
CALL HIM MR. SHATTER   Avco Embassy, 1975, British-Hong Kong

THOMAS CARTER*

Agent: ICM - Los Angeles, 213/550-4000

TRAUMA CENTER (TF)   Glen A. Larson Productions/Jeremac Productions/20th
    Century-Fox TV, 1983
AIR FORCE (TF)   Tisch-Avnet Productions, 1983

STEVE CARVER *

b. April 5, 1945 - Brooklyn, New York
Home: 1010 Pacific Avenue, Venice, CA   90291, 213/396-9905
Agent: Mike Greenfield, Charter Management - Los Angeles, 213/278-1690

THE ARENA   New World, 1974
BIG BAD MAMA   New World, 1974
CAPONE   20th Century-Fox, 1975
DRUM   United Artists, 1976
FAST CHARLIE ... THE MOONBEAM RIDER   Universal, 1979
STEEL   *LOOK DOWN AND DIE*   World Northal, 1980
AN EYE FOR AN EYE   Avco Embassy, 1981
LONE WOLF McQUADE   Orion, 1983

JOHN CASSAVETES *

b. December 9, 1929 - New York, New York
Agent: ICM - Los Angeles, 213/550-4000

SHADOWS   Lion International, 1961
TOO LATE BLUES   Paramount, 1962
A CHILD IS WAITING   United Artists, 1963
FACES   Continental, 1968
HUSBANDS   Columbia, 1970
MINNIE AND MOSKOWITZ   Universal, 1971
A WOMAN UNDER THE INFLUENCE★   Faces International, 1974
THE KILLING OF A CHINESE BOOKIE   Faces International, 1976
OPENING NIGHT   Faces International, 1979
GLORIA   Columbia, 1980
LOVE STREAMS   MGM/UA/Cannon, 1984

NICK CASTLE, JR. *

Home: 8458 Ridpath Drive, Los Angeles, CA   90046, 213/656-2470
Agent: Harry Ufland, The Harry J. Ufland Agency - Beverly Hills, 213/273-9441
Business Manager: Roy Skaff, Skaff & Kutcher, 17835 Ventura Blvd. - Suite 210,
     Encino, CA   91316, 213/344-4335

TAG   New World, 1982
THE LAST STARFIGHTER   Universal, 1983

GILBERT CATES *

b. June 6, 1934 - New York, New York
Business: Film/Jamel Productions, Inc., 195 S. Beverly Drive, Beverly Hills,
     CA   90212, 213/273-7773 or: 119 West 57th Street, New York,
     NY   10019, 212/765-1300
Agent: Fred Specktor, CAA - Los Angeles, 213/277-4545

RINGS AROUND THE WORLD (FD)   Columbia, 1967
I NEVER SANG FOR MY FATHER   Columbia, 1970
TO ALL MY FRIENDS ON SHORE (TF)   Jemmin & Jamel Productions, 1972
SUMMER WISHES, WINTER DREAMS   Columbia, 1973
THE AFFAIR (TF)   Spelling-Goldberg Productions, 1973
ONE SUMMER LOVE   *DRAGONFLY*   American International, 1976
JOHNNY, WE HARDLY KNEW YE (TF)   Talent Associates/Jamel Productions,
     1977
THE PROMISE   Universal, 1979
THE LAST MARRIED COUPLE IN AMERICA   Universal, 1980
OH, GOD! BOOK II   Warner Bros., 1980
COUNTRY GOLD (TF)   CBS Entertainment, 1982

JOSEPH CATES *

b. 1924
Business: Film/Jamel Productions, Inc., 195 S. Beverly Drive, Beverly Hills,
     CA 90212, 213/273-7773 or: 119 West 57th Street, New York, NY 10019,
     212/765-1300

GIRL OF THE NIGHT   Warner Bros., 1960
WHO KILLED TEDDY BEAR?   Magna, 1965
FAT SPY   Magna, 1966

LILIANA CAVANI

b. January 12, 1936 - Capri, Italy
Contact: Ministry of Tourism & Education, Via Della Ferratella, No. 51, 00184
     Rome, Italy, 06/7732

FRANCESCO D'ASSISI (TF)   1966, Italian
GALILEO   Fenice Cinematografica/Rizzoli Film/Kinozenter, 1968, Italian-Bulgarian
I CANNIBALI   1969, Italian
L'OSPITE   1971, Italian
THE NIGHT PORTER   Avco Embassy, 1974, Italian
MILAREPA   Lotar Film, 1974, Italian
OTRO IL BENE E IL MALE   Italnoleggio Cinematografico, 1978, Italian-French-
     West German
LA PELLE   Gaumont, 1981, Italian-French
BEYOND THE DOOR   Gaumont, 1982, Italian

JAMES CELLAN-JONES *

b. England
Home: 19 Cumberland Road, Kew, Surrey 13731, England, 01/940-8742
Agent: William Morris Agency - Beverly Hills, 213/274-7451

THE NELSON AFFAIR *A BEQUEST TO THE NATION*   Universal, 1973,
     British
CAESAR AND CLEOPATRA (TF)   NBC-TV, 1976, U.S.-British
THE DAY CHRIST DIED (TF)   Martin Manulis Productions/20th Century-Fox
     TV, 1980

CLAUDE CHABROL

b. June 24, 1930 - Paris, France
Contact: French Film Office, 745 Fifth Avenue, New York, NY 10151, 212/832-8860

LE BEAU SERGE   United Motion Picture Organization, 1958, French
THE COUSINS   Films Around the World, 1959, French
LEDA *WEB OF PASSION/A DOUBLE TOUR*   Times, 1959, French
LES BONNES FEMMES   Robert Hakim, 1960, French-Italian
LES GODELUREAUX   1961, French
SEVEN CAPITAL SINS   co-director with Jean-Luc Godard, Roger Vadim,
     Sylvaine Dhomme, Edouard Molinaro, Philippe De Broca, Jacques Demy, Marie-
     Jose Nat, Dominique Paturel, Jean-Marc Tennberg & Perrette Pradier, Embassy,
     1962, French-Italian
L'OEIL DU MALIN   1962, French-Italian
OPHELIA   New Line Cinema, 1962, French-Italian
LANDRU   Embassy, 1963, French-Italian
LES PLUS BELLES ESCROQUERIES DU MONDE   co-director, 1964, French-
     Italian-Japanese
LE TIGRE AIME LA CHAIR FRAICHE   1964, French-Italian
PARIS VU PAR ...   co-director, 1964, French
MARIE-CHANTAL CONTRE LE DOCTEUR KHA   1965, French-Italian-
     Moroccan
LE TIGRE SE PARFUME À LA DYNAMITE   1965, French-Spanish-Italian
LA LIGNE DE DEMARCATION   1966, French
THE CHAMPAGNE MURDERS *LE SCANDALE*   Universal, 1967, French
LA ROUTE DE CORINTHE   1967, French-Italian-West German
LES BICHES   VGC, 1968, French-Italian
LA FEMME INFIDELE   Allied Artists, 1968, French-Italian
THIS MAN MUST DIE   Allied Artists, 1969, French-Italian
LE BOUCHER   Cinerama Releasing Corporation, 1969, French-Italian
LA RUPTURE   New Line Cinema, 1970, French-Italian-Belgian

continued

CLAUDE CHABROL—continued

JUST BEFORE NIGHTFALL   Libra, 1971, French-Italian
TEN DAYS' WONDER   Levitt-Pickman, 1971, French
HIGH HEELS *DOCTEUR POPAUL*   1972, French-Italian
WEDDING IN BLOOD   New Line Cinema, 1973, French-Italian
DE GREY - LE BANC DE DESOLATION (TF)   1973, French
THE NADA GANG *NADA*   New Line Cinema, 1974, French-Italian
UNE PARTIE DE PLAISIR   Joseph Green Pictures, 1975, French
DIRTY HANDS *LES INNOCENTS AUX MAIN SALES*   New Line Cinema,
     1975, French-Italian-West German
LES MAGICIENS   1975, French
FOLIES BOURGEOISES   1976, French
ALICE OU LA DERNIERE FUGUE   Filmel-PHPG, 1977, French
LES LIENS DE SANG   Filmcorp, 1978, Canadian-French
VIOLETTE *VIOLETTE NOZIERE*   New Yorker, 1978, French
SPLINTERED   1980, French
LE CHEVAL D'ORGEUIL   Planfilm, 1980, French
LES FANTOMES DU CHAPELIER   Gaumont, 1982, French
THE BLOOD OF OTHERS (CMS)   HBO Premiere Films/ICC/Filmax Productions,
     1984, Canadian-French

D O N   C H A F F E Y *

b. August 5, 1917 - England
Home: 7020 La Presa Drive, Los Angeles, CA 90068, 213/851-0391
Agent: Ronald Lief, Contemporary-Korman Artists - Beverly Hills, 213/278-8250
Business Manager: Paul Gilbert, Oppenheim, Appel & Dixon - Los Angeles, 213/277-
     0400

THE MYSTERIOUS POACHER   General Film Distributors, 1950, British
THE CASE OF THE MISSING SCENE   General Film Distributors, 1951, British
SKID KIDS   Associated British Film Distributors/Children's Film Foundation,
     1953, British
TIME IS MY ENEMY   Independent Film Distributors, 1954, British
THE SECRET TENT   British Lion, 1956, British
THE GIRL IN THE PICTURE   Eros, 1957, British
THE FLESH IS WEAK   DCA, 1957, British
A QUESTION OF ADULTERY   Eros, 1958, British
THE MAN UPSTAIRS   Kingsley International, 1958, British
DANGER WITHIN   British Lion, 1959, British
DENTIST IN THE CHAIR   Ajay, 1960, British
LIES MY FATHER TOLD ME   Eire, 1960, British
NEARLY A NASTY ACCIDENT   Brittania, 1961, British
GREYFRIARS BOBBY   Buena Vista, 1961, U.S.-British
A MATTER OF WHO   Herts Lion, 1962, British
THE PRINCE AND THE PAUPER   Buena Vista, 1962, U.S.-British
THE WEBSTER BOY   RFI, 1963, British
THE HORSE WITHOUT A HEAD   Buena Vista, 1963, British
JASON AND THE ARGONAUTS   Columbia, 1963, British
THEY ALL DIED LAUGHING *A JOLLY BAD FELLOW*   Continental, 1963,
     British
THE THREE LIVES OF THOMASINA   Buena Vista, 1963, British-U.S.
THE CROOKED ROAD   7 Arts, 1965, British-Yugoslavian
ONE MILLION YEARS B.C.   20th Century-Fox, 1967, British
THE VIKING QUEEN   American International, 1967, British
A TWIST OF SAND   United Artists, 1968, British
CREATURES THE WORLD FORGOT   Columbia, 1971, British
CLINIC XCLUSIVE   Doverton, 1972, British
CHARLEY-ONE-EYE   Paramount, 1973, British
THE TERROR OF SHEBA *PERSECUTION*   Blueberry Hill, 1974, British
THE FOURTH WISH   South Australian Film Corporation, 1975, Australian
HARNESS FEVER   Walt Disney Productions, 1976, Australian
RIDE A WILD PONY *BORN TO RUN*   Buena Vista, 1976, U.S.-Australian
SURF   Trans-Atlantic Enterprises, 1977
PETE'S DRAGON   Buena Vista, 1977
THE MAGIC OF LASSIE   International Picture Show, 1978
THE GIFT OF LOVE (TF)   Osmond Productions, 1978
C.H.O.M.P.S.   American International, 1979
CASINO (TF)   Trellis Productions/Aaron Spelling Productions, 1980

EVERETT CHAMBERS *

b. August 19, 1926 - Montrose, California
Home: 182 East 95th Street, New York, N.Y. 10028, 212/534-1184
Business Manager: Arthur Gage, 1277 Sunset Plaza Drive, Los Angeles, CA 90069,
    213/652-4118

RUN ACROSS THE RIVER   Omat Corporation, 1959
THE LOLLIPOP COVER   Continental, 1964

MATTHEW CHAPMAN

b. September 2, 1950
Address: 38 Portland Road, London W11, England

HUSSY   Watchgrove Ltd., 1980, British
STRANGER'S KISS   Orion Classics, 1983

MICHAEL CHAPMAN *

Contact: Directors Guild of America - Los Angeles, 213/656-1220

ALL THE RIGHT MOVES   20th Century-Fox, 1983

MARVIN J. CHOMSKY *

b. May 23, 1929 - New York, New York
Agent: Len Hirshan, William Morris Agency - Beverly Hills, 213/274-7451
Business Manager: David B. Cohen, Plant, Cohen & Co., 9777 Wilshire Blvd.,
    Beverly Hills, CA 90212, 213/278-6171

ASSAULT ON THE WAYNE (TF)   Paramount TV, 1971
MONGO'S BACK IN TOWN (TF)   Bob Banner Associates, 1971
EVEL KNIEVEL   Fanfare, 1972
FIREBALL FORWARD (TF)   20th Century-Fox TV, 1972
FAMILY FLIGHT (TF)   Universal TV, 1972
FEMALE ARTILLERY (TF)   Universal TV, 1973
THE MAGICIAN (TF)   Paramount TV, 1973
MRS. SUNDANCE (TF)   20th Century-Fox TV, 1974
THE FBI STORY: THE FBI VERSUS ALVIN KARPIS, PUBLIC ENEMY
    NUMBER ONE (TF)   QM Productions/Warner Bros. TV, 1974
ATTACK ON TERROR: THE FBI VS. THE KLU KLUX KLAN (TF)   QM
    Productions, 1975
MACKINTOSH AND T.J.   Penland, 1975
LIVE A LITTLE, STEAL A LOT   MURPH THE SURF   American International,
    1975
KATE McSHANE (TF)   Paramount TV, 1975
BRINK'S: THE GREAT ROBBERY (TF)   QM Productions/Warner Bros. TV,
    1976
A MATTER OF WIFE ... AND DEATH (TF)   Columbia TV, 1976
LAW AND ORDER (TF)   Paramount TV, 1976
ROOTS (MS)☆   co-director with David Greene, John Erman & Gilbert Moses,
    Wolper Productions, 1977
LITTLE LADIES OF THE NIGHT (TF)   Spelling-Goldberg Productions, 1977
DANGER IN PARADISE (TF)   Filmways, 1977
HOLOCAUST (MS)☆☆   Titus Productions, 1978
GOOD LUCK, MISS WYCKOFF   Bel Air/Gradison, 1979
HOLLOW IMAGE (TF)   Titus Productions, 1979
DOCTOR FRANKEN (TF)   1980
ATTICA (TF)☆☆   ABC Circle Films, 1980
KING CRAB (TF)   Titus Productions, 1980
EVITA PERON (TF)   Hartwest Productions/Zephyr Productions, 1981
MY BODY, MY CHILD (TF)   Titus Productions, 1982
INSIDE THE THIRD REICH (TF)☆☆   ABC Circle Films, 1982
I WAS A MAIL ORDER BRIDE (TF)   Jaffe Productions/Tuxedo Limited
    Productions/MGM TV, 1982
TANK   Universal, 1984

THOMAS CHONG *

b. Edmonton, Canada
Business: C&C Brown Productions, Columbia Plaza, Burbank, CA 91505 213/954-3162

THE NEXT CHEECH & CHONG MOVIE   Universal, 1980
CHEECH & CHONG'S NICE DREAMS   Columbia, 1981
CHEECH & CHONG: STILL SMOKIN   Paramount, 1983
CHEECH & CHONG AS THE CORSICAN BROTHERS   Orion, 1984

ROGER CHRISTIAN

Contact: British Academy of Film & Television Arts, 195 Piccadilly, London W1,
    England, 01/734-0022

THE SENDER   Paramount, 1982, U.S.-British

BYRON CHUDNOW *

Home: 918 S. Westgate Avenue - Suite 4, Los Angeles, CA 90049, 213/820-1066

THE DOBERMAN GANG   Dimension, 1973
THE DARING DOBERMANS   Dimension, 1973
THE AMAZING DOBERMANS   Golden, 1976

MATT CIMBER
(Matteo Ottaviano)

SINGLE ROOM FURNISHED   Crown International, 1968
CALLIOPE   Moonstone, 1971
THE BLACK SIX   Cinemation, 1974
THE CANDY TANGERINE MAN   Moonstone, 1975
GEMINI AFFAIR   Moonstone, 1975
LADY COCOA   Dimension, 1975
THE WITCH WHO CAME FROM THE SEA   Moonstone, 1976
BUTTERFLY   Analysis, 1981
FAKE OUT   Analysis, 1983
A TIME TO DIE   Almi Films, 1983
HUNDRA   STAE/CMOD, 1983, Spanish
YELLOW HAIR AND THE PECOS KID   Cinestar/Continental Movie
    Productions, 1984, Spanish

MICHAEL CIMINO *

b. 1943
Agent: Stan Kamen, William Morris Agency - Beverly Hills, 213/274-7451
Attorney: Bruce Ramer - Los Angeles, 213/276-8087

THUNDERBOLT AND LIGHTFOOT   United Artists, 1974
THE DEER HUNTER★★   Universal, 1978
HEAVEN'S GATE   United Artists, 1980

RICHARD CIUPKA

Home: 71 Cornwall Street, Town of Mount Royal, Montreal, Quebec H3P 1M6,
    Canada, 514/738-9996

CURTAINS   directed under pseudonym of Jonathan Stryker, Jensen Farley
    Pictures, 1983, Canadian

BOB CLARK *

b. 1941 - New Orleans, Louisiana
Business: Brandywine Productions, 287A Park Avenue, Long Beach, CA 90803,
    213/438-6851
Business Manager: Harold Cohen - New York City, 212/550-0570

DEATHDREAM   1972, Canadian
CHILDREN SHOULDN'T PLAY WITH DEAD THINGS   Gemini Film, 1972,
    Canadian
DEATH OF NIGHT   Europix International, 1974, Canadian
BLACK CHRISTMAS *SILENT NIGHT, EVIL NIGHT/STRANGER IN THE
    HOUSE*   Warner Bros., 1975, Canadian
BREAKING POINT   20th Century-Fox, 1976, Canadian
MURDER BY DECREE   Avco Embassy, 1979, Canadian-British
TRIBUTE   20th Century-Fox, 1980, U.S.-Canadian
PORKY'S   20th Century-Fox, 1982, U.S.-Canadian
PORKY'S: THE NEXT DAY   20th Century-Fox, 1983, U.S.-Canadian
A CHRISTMAS STORY   MGM/UA, 1983, Canadian
RHINESTONE   20th Century-Fox, 1984

BRUCE CLARK

NAKED ANGELS   Favorite, 1969
THE SKI BUM   Avco Embassy, 1971
HAMMER   United Artists, 1972
GALAXY OF TERROR   New World, 1981

FRANK C. CLARK

BEYOND THE REEF   Universal, 1981

GREYDON CLARK

TOM   Four Star International, 1973
BLACK SHAMPOO   Dimension, 1976
THE BAD BUNCH   Dimension, 1976
SATAN'S CHEERLEADERS   World Amusement, 1977
HI-RIDERS   Dimension, 1978
ANGELS BRIGADE   Arista, 1980
WITHOUT WARNING   Filmways, 1980
THE RETURN   1981
JOYSTICKS   Jensen Farley Pictures, 1982
WACKO   Jensen Farley Pictures, 1983

JAMES B. CLARK *

Home: 10051-5 Valley Circle Blvd., Chatsworth, CA 91311, 213/998-0962

UNDER FIRE   20th Century-Fox, 1957
SIERRA BARON   20th Century-Fox, 1958
VILLA!   20th Century-Fox, 1958
THE SAD HORSE   20th Century-Fox, 1959
A DOG OF FLANDERS   20th Century-Fox, 1960
ONE FOOT IN HELL   20th Century-Fox, 1960
THE BIG SHOW   20th Century-Fox, 1961, U.S.-West German
MISTY   20th Century-Fox, 1961
FLIPPER   MGM, 1963
DRUMS OF AFRICA   MGM, 1963
ISLAND OF THE BLUE DOLPHINS   20th Century-Fox, 1964
AND NOW MIGUEL   Paramount, 1966
MY SIDE OF THE MOUNTAIN   Paramount, 1969
THE LITTLE ARK   National General, 1972

RON CLARK

Contact: Writers Guild of America, West - Los Angeles, 213/550-1000

THE FUNNY FARM   New World, 1983, Canadian

SHIRLEY CLARKE

b. 1925 - New York, New York
Business: UCLA Theatre Arts Department, 405 Hilgard Avenue, Los Angeles,
   CA 90024, 213/825-5761

DANCE IN THE SUN   1953
IN PARIS PARKS   1954
BULLFIGHT   1955
A MOMENT OF LOVE   1957
THE SKYSCRAPER   co-director with Willard Van Dyke, 1958
LOOPS   1958
BRIDGES-GO-ROUND   1959
A SCARY TIME   1960
THE CONNECTION   Films Around the World, 1962
THE COOL WORLD   Cinema 5, 1964
PORTRAIT OF JASON (FD)   Film-Makers, 1967

JAMES CLAVELL *

b. October 10, 1924 - Sydney, Australia
Agent: CAA - Los Angeles, 213/277-4545

FIVE GATES TO HELL   20th Century-Fox, 1959
WALK LIKE A DRAGON   Paramount, 1960
TO SIR, WITH LOVE   Columbia, 1967, British
THE SWEET AND THE BITTER   Monarch, 1968, British
WHERE'S JACK?   Paramount, 1969, British
THE LAST VALLEY   Cinerama Releasing Corporation, 1971, British

WILLIAM F. CLAXTON *

b. October 22, 1914 - California
Home: 1065 Napoli Drive, Pacific Palisades, CA 90272, 213/454-3246
Agent: Contemporary-Korman Artists - Beverly Hills, 213/278-8250

HALF PAST MIDNIGHT   20th Century-Fox, 1948
TUCSON   20th Century-Fox, 1949
ALL THAT I HAVE   Family Films, 1951
STAGECOACH TO FURY   20th Century-Fox, 1956
THE QUIET GUN   20th Century-Fox, 1957
YOUNG AND DANGEROUS   20th Century-Fox, 1957
ROCKABILLY BABY   20th Century-Fox, 1957
GOD IS MY PARTNER   20th Century-Fox, 1957
DESIRE IN THE DUST   20th Century-Fox, 1960
YOUNG JESSE JAMES   20th Century-Fox, 1960
LAW OF THE LAWLESS   Paramount, 1963
STAGE TO THUNDER ROCK   Paramount, 1964
NIGHT OF THE LEPUS   MGM, 1972

JACK CLAYTON *

b. 1921 - Brighton, England
Home: Heron's Flight, Highfield Park, Marlow, Buckinghamshire, England
Agent: Stan Kamen, William Morris Agency - Beverly Hills, 213/274-7451

ROOM AT THE TOP★   Continental, 1959, British
THE INNOCENTS   20th Century-Fox, 1962, British
THE PUMPKIN EATER   Royal International, 1964, British
OUR MOTHER'S HOUSE   MGM, 1967, British
THE GREAT GATSBY   Paramount, 1974
SOMETHING WICKED THIS WAY COMES   Buena Vista, 1983

TOM CLEGG

Contact: British Academy of Film & Television Arts, 195 Piccadilly, London W1,
   England, 01/734-0022

LOVE IS A SPLENDID ILLUSION   Schulman, 1970, British
SWEENEY 2   EMI, 1978, British
McVICAR   Crown International, 1981, British

continued

TOM CLEGG—continued
G'OLE! (FD)   Warner Bros., 1983, British

DICK CLEMENT *

b. September 5, 1937 - West Cliff-on-Sea, England
Home: 9700 Yoakum Drive, Beverly Hills, CA 90210, 213/276-4916
Business: Witzend Productions, 1600 N. Highland Avenue, Hollywood, CA 90028,
    213/462-6185

OTLEY   Columbia, 1969, British
A SEVERED HEAD   Columbia, 1971, British
CATCH ME A SPY   Rank, 1971, British
KEEP YOUR FINGERS CROSSED   1971, British
PORRIDGE   ITC, 1979, British
BULLSHOT!   HandMade Films, 1983, British

RENÉ CLEMENT

b. March 18, 1913 - Bordeaux, France
Contact: French Film Office, 745 Fifth Avenue, New York, NY 10151, 212/832-8860

LA BATAILLE DU RAIL   1946, French
LE PERE TRANQUILLE   1946, French
LES MAUDITS   1947, French
THE WALLS OF MALAPAGA   Films International of America, 1949, Italian-
    French
LE CHÂTEAU DE VERRE   1950, French-Italian
FORBIDDEN GAMES   Times, 1952, French
LOVERS, HAPPY LOVERS! *MONSIEUR RIPOIS/KNAVE OF*
    HEARTS   20th Century-Fox, 1954, French-British
GERVAISE   Continental, 1956, French
THIS ANGRY AGE   Columbia, 1958, Italian-French
PURPLE NOON   Times, 1960, French-Italian
QUELLE JOIE DE VIVRE   1961, French-Italian
THE DAY AND THE HOUR   MGM, 1962, French-Italian
JOY HOUSE *LES FELINS*   MGM, 1964, French
IS PARIS BURNING?   Paramount, 1966, French-U.S.
RIDER ON THE RAIN   Avco Embassy, 1970, French-Italian
THE DEADLY TRAP *LA MAISON SOUS LES ARBRES*   National General,
    1971, French-Italian
... AND HOPE TO DIE *LA COURSE DU LIEVRE A TRAVERS LES*
    CHAMPS   20th Century-Fox, 1972, French
LA BABY-SITTER   Titanus, 1975, Italian-French-Monocan

GRAEME CLIFFORD *

Agent: Geoffrey Sanford, Sanford-Beckett Agency - Los Angeles, 213/208-2100

FRANCES   Universal/AFD, 1982

PETER CLIFTON

Contact: British Academy of Film & Television Arts, 195 Piccadilly, London W1,
    England, 01/734-0022

POPCORN (FD)   Sherpix, 1969, U.S.-Australian
SUPERSTARS IN FILM CONCERT (FD)   National Cinema, 1971, British
THE SONG REMAINS THE SAME (FD)   co-director with Joe Massot, Warner
    Bros., 1976, British
THE LONDON ROCK & ROLL SHOW (FD)   1978, British
ROCK CITY *SOUND OF THE CITY: LONDON 1964-73 (FD)*   Columbia,
    1981, British

ROBERT CLOUSE*

Home: 454 Hotsprings Road, Santa Barbara, CA 93158, 805/969-4624
Agent: David Wardlow, ICM - Los Angeles, 213/550-4000

DARKER THAN AMBER   National General, 1970
DREAMS OF GLASS   Universal, 1970
ENTER THE DRAGON   Warner Bros., 1973, U.S.-Hong Kong
BLACK BELT JONES   Warner Bros., 1974
GOLDEN NEEDLES   American International, 1974
THE ULTIMATE WARRIOR   Warner Bros., 1976
THE AMSTERDAM KILL   Columbia, 1978, U.S.-Hong Kong
THE PACK   Warner Bros., 1978
GAME OF DEATH   Columbia, 1979, U.S.-Hong Kong
THE OMEGA CONNECTION (TF)   NBC-TV, 1979
THE KIDS WHO KNEW TOO MUCH (TF)   Walt Disney Productions, 1980
THE BIG BRAWL   Warner Bros., 1980
FORCE: FIVE   American Cinema, 1981
NIGHT EYES   Warner Bros., 1983, Canadian

LEWIS COATES

(Luigi Cozzi)

Contact: Ministry of Tourism & Education, Via Della Ferratella, No. 51, 00184
Rome, Italy, 06/7732

LA PORTIERA NUDA   CIA Cinematografica, 1975, Italian
L'ASSASSINO E COSTRETTO AD UCCIDERE ANCORA   Albione
Cinematografica/GIT International, 1976, Italian
DEDICATO A UNA STELLA   Euro, 1978, Italian
STARCRASH   New World, 1979, Italian
ALIEN CONTAMINATION   Cannon, 1980, Italian-West German
HERCULES   MGM/UA/Cannon, 1983, Italian
THE ADVENTURES OF HERCULES II   Cannon, 1983, Italian

PETER COE

b. April 18, 1929 - London, England
Contact: British Academy of Film & Television Arts, 195 Piccadilly, London W1,
England, 01/734-0022

LOCK UP YOUR DAUGHTERS   Columbia, 1969, British

ANNETTE COHEN

Home: 77 Roxborough Drive, Toronto, Ontario M4W 1X2, Canada, 416/364-4193
or 416/920-3745

LOVE   co-director with Nancy Dowd, Liv Ullmann & Mai Zetterling, Velvet Films,
1982, Canadian

HOWARD R. COHEN

SATURDAY THE 14TH   New World, 1981
SPACE RAIDERS   New World, 1983

LARRY COHEN*

b. July 15, 1945 - New York, New York
Home: 2111 Coldwater Canyon Blvd., Beverly Hills, CA 90210, 213/550-7942
Personal Manager: The Robert Littman Company - Los Angeles, 213/278-1572
Attorney: Skip Brittenham, Ziffren, Brittenham & Gullen, 2049 Central Park East, Los
Angeles, CA 90067, 213/552-3388

BONE   Jack H. Harris Enterprises, 1972
BLACK CAESAR   American International, 1973
HELL UP IN HARLEM   American International, 1973
IT'S ALIVE   Warner Bros., 1974
DEMON *GOD TOLD ME TO*   New World, 1977
IT LIVES AGAIN   Warner Bros., 1978

continued

LARRY COHEN*—continued
THE PRIVATE FILES OF J. EDGAR HOOVER   American International, 1978
FULL MOON HIGH   Filmways, 1981
Q   United Film Distribution, 1982
BLIND ALLEY   Hemdale, 1984

ROB COHEN*

b. April 12, 1949 - Cornwall-on-the-Hudson, New York
Home: 1383 Miller Place, Los Angeles, CA 90069, 213/654-6289
Messages: 213/954-6635
Business Manager: Lee Winkler, Global Business Management, 9000 Sunset Blvd. -
    Suite 1115, Los Angeles, CA 90069, 213/278-4141

A SMALL CIRCLE OF FRIENDS   United Artists, 1980
SCANDALOUS   Orion, 1984

HARLEY COKLISS

b. February 11, 1945 - San Diego, California
Address: 25 Milman Road, London NW6, England, 01/960-6769
Agent: Duncan Heath Associates - London, 01/937-9898

THAT SUMMER   Columbia, 1979, British
BATTLETRUCK   New World, 1982, U.S.-New Zealand

RICHARD A. COLLA*

b. April 18, 1918 - Milwaukee, Wisconsin
Agent: Fred Westheimer, William Morris Agency - Beverly Hills, 213/274-7451

THE WHOLE WORLD IS WATCHING (TF)   Universal TV, 1969
ZIGZAG   MGM, 1970
McCLOUD: WHO KILLED MISS U.S.A.? (TF)   Universal TV, 1970
THE OTHER MAN (TF)   Universal TV, 1970
SARGE: THE BADGE OR THE CROSS (TF)   Universal TV, 1971
THE PRIEST KILLER (TF)   Universal TV, 1971
FUZZ   United Artists, 1972
TENAFLY (TF)   Universal TV, 1973
THE QUESTOR TAPES (TF)   Universal TV, 1974
LIVE AGAIN, DIE AGAIN (TF)   Universal TV, 1974
THE TRIBE (TF)   Universal TV, 1974
THE UFO INCIDENT (TF)   Universal TV, 1975
OLLY OLLY OXEN FREE   Sanrio, 1978
BATTLESTAR GALACTICA   Universal, 1979
DON'T LOOK BACK (TF)   TBA Productions/Satie Productions/TRISEME, 1981

JAMES F. COLLIER*

Home: 11345 Brill Drive, Studio City, CA 91604, 213/986-1374

FOR PETE'S SAKE!   World Wide, 1966
HIS LAND   World Wide, 1967
TWO A PENNY   World Wide, 1970, British
CATCH A PEBBLE   World Wide, 1971, British
TIME TO RUN   World Wide, 1972
THE HIDING PLACE   World Wide, 1975
JONI   World Wide, 1980
THE PRODIGAL   World Wide, 1983

ROBERT COLLINS*

Agent: Bill Haber, CAA - Los Angeles, 213/277-4545

SERPICO: THE DEADLY GAME (TF)   Dino De Laurentiis Productions/
    Paramount TV, 1976
THE LIFE AND ASSASSINATION OF THE KINGFISH (TF)   Tomorrow
    Entertainment, 1977
WALK PROUD   Universal, 1979
GIDEON'S TRUMPET (TF)   Gideon Productions, 1980

continued

ROBERT COLLINS*—continued

SAVAGE HARVEST　　20th Century-Fox, 1981
OUR FAMILY BUSINESS (TF)　　Lorimar Productions, 1981
MONEY ON THE SIDE (TF)　　Green-Epstein Productions/Hal Landers
　　Productions/Columbia TV, 1982

LUIGI COMENCINI

Contact: Ministry of Tourism & Education, Via Della Ferratella, No. 51, 00184
　　Rome, Italy, 06/7732

PROIBITO RUBARE　　Lux Film, 1948, Italian
L'IMPERATORE DI CAPRI　　Lux Film, 1949, Italian
PERSIANE CHIUSE　　Rovere Film, 1951, Italian
HEIDI　　United Artists, 1952, Swiss
LA TRATTA DELLA BIANCHE　　Excelsa/Ponti/Dino De Laurentiis
　　Cinematografica, 1952, Italian
BREAD, LOVE AND DREAMS　　Italian Film Export, 1953, Italian
LA VALIGIA DEI SOGNI　　Mambretti, 1954, Italian
FRISKY *PANE, AMORE E GELOSIA*　　DCA, 1954, Italian
LA BELLA DI ROMA　　Lux Film, 1955, Italian
LA FINESTRA SUL LUNA PARK　　Noria Film, 1957, Italian
MARITI IN CITTA　　Oscar Film/Morino Film, 1957, Italian
MOGLI PERICOLOSE　　Morino/Tempo Film, 1958, Italian
UND DAS AM MONTAGMORGEN　　1959, West German
LA CORPRESE DELL'AMORE　　Morino/Tempo Film, 1959, Italian
EVERYBODY GO HOME!　　Royal Films International, 1960, Italian-French
A CAVALLO DELLA TIGRE　　Alfredo Bini, 1961, Italian
IL COMMISSARIO　　Dino De Laurentiis Cinematografica, 1962, Italian
BEBO'S GIRL　　Continental, 1963, Italian-French
TRE NOTTE D'AMORE　　co-director with Renato Costellani & Franco Rossi, Jolly
　　Film/Cormoran Film, 1964, Italian-French
LA MIA SIGNORINA　　co-director, Dino De Laurentiis Cinematografica, 1964,
　　Italian
BAMBOLE!　　co-director with Dino Risi, Franco Rossi & Mauro Bolognini, Royal
　　Films International, 1965, Italian
IL COMPAGNO DON CAMILLO　　Rizzoli Film/Francoriz/Omnia Film, 1965,
　　Italian-West German
LA BUGIARDA　　Ultra Film/Consortium Pathe/Tecisa, 1965, Italian-French-Spanish
INCOMPRESO　　1966, Italian
ITALIAN SECRET SERVICE　　1968, Italian
**INFANZIA, VOCAZIONE E PRIME ESPERIENZE DI GIACOMO CASANOVA -
　　VENEZIANO**　　1969, Italian
SENZA SAPERE NULLA DI LEI　　Rizzoli Film, 1969, Italian
LO SCOPONE SCIENTIFICO　　1972, Italian
DELITTO D'AMORE　　Documento Film, 1974, Italian
MIO DIO COME SONO CADUTA IN BASSO　　Dean Film, 1974, Italian
SUNDAY WOMAN　　20th Century-Fox, 1976, Italian-French
LA GODURIA　　co-director, 1976, Italian
BASTA CHE NON SI SAPPIA IN GIRO　　co-director with Nanni Loy & Luigi
　　Magni, Medusa, 1976, Italian
SIGNORE E SIGNORI BUONANOTTE　　co-director with Nanni Loy, Luigi
　　Magni, Mario Monicelli & Ettore Scola, Titanus, 1976, Italian
QUELLE STRANE OCCASIONI　　co-director, Cineriz, 1977, Italian
TILL MARRIAGE US DO PART　　Franklin Media, 1977, Italian
TRA MOGLIE E MARITO　　1977, Italian
IL GATTO　　United Artists, 1978, Italian
L'INGORGO　　Titanus, 1979, Italian-Spanish-West German
THEY ALL LOVED HIM　　Medusa, 1980, Italian
VOLTATI EUGENIO　　Gaumont, 1981, Italian-French
LOOKING FOR JESUS　　Intercontinental/Nouvelle Cinevog, 1982, Italian-French
CUORE (MS)　　RAI/Difilm/Antenne-2, 1984, Italian-French

RICHARD COMPTON*

Business Manager: Fred Altman - Beverly Hills, 213/278-4201

ANGELS DIE HARD　　New World, 1970
WELCOME HOME, SOLDIER BOYS　　20th Century-Fox, 1972
MACON COUNTY LINE　　American International, 1974
RETURN TO MACON COUNTY　　American International, 1975
MANIAC　　New World, 1977

continued

RICHARD COMPTON*—continued

DEADMAN'S CURVE (TF)   Roger Gimbel Productions/EMI TV, 1978
RAVAGES   Columbia, 1979
WILD TIMES (TF)   Metromedia Producers Corporation/Rattlesnake Productions,
    1980

KEVIN CONNOR*

b. July 14, 1940 - London, England
Business: Individual Productions, 870 N. Doheny Drive, Los Angeles, CA 90069,
    213/274-5121
Attorney: Burton Merrill Law Offices, 3701 Wilshire Blvd., Los Angeles, CA 90010,
    213/383-6996

FROM BEYOND THE GRAVE   Howard Mahler Films, 1975, British
THE LAND THAT TIME FORGOT   American International, 1975, British
AT THE EARTH'S CORE   American International, 1976, British
DIRTY KNIGHTS' WORK *A CHOICE OF WEAPONS*   Gamma III, 1976,
    British
THE PEOPLE THAT TIME FORGOT   American International, 1977, British
WARLORDS OF ATLANTIS   Columbia, 1978, British
ARABIAN ADVENTURE   AFD, 1979, British
MOTEL HELL   United Artists, 1980
GOLIATH AWAITS (TF)   Larry White Productions/Hugh Benson Productions/
    Columbia TV, 1981
THE HOUSE WHERE EVIL DWELLS   MGM/UA, 1982, U.S.-Japanese

WILLIAM CONRAD*

b. September 27, 1920 - Louisville, Kentucky
Agent: Rowland Perkins, CAA - Los Angeles, 213/277-4545

THE MAN FROM GALVESTON   Warner Bros., 1964
TWO ON A GUILLOTINE   Warner Bros., 1965
MY BLOOD RUNS COLD   Warner Bros., 1965
BRAINSTORM   Warner Bros., 1965
SIDE SHOW (TF)   Krofft Entertainment, 1981

JAMES L. CONWAY

b. October 27, 1950 - New York, New York
Agent: David, Hunter, Kimble, Parseghian & Rifkin - Los Angeles, 213/857-1234

IN SEARCH OF NOAH'S ARK   Sunn Classic, 1976
THE LINCOLN CONSPIRACY   Sunn Classic, 1977
THE INCREDIBLE ROCKY MOUNTAIN RACE (TF)   Sunn Classic Productions,
    1977
THE LAST OF THE MOHICANS (TF)   Sunn Classic Productions, 1977
BEYOND AND BACK   Sunn Classic, 1978
DONNER PASS: THE ROAD TO SURVIVAL (TF)   Sunn Classic Productions,
    1978
GREATEST HEROES OF THE BIBLE (MS)   Sunn Classic Productions, 1978
THE FALL OF THE HOUSE OF USHER   Sunn Classic, 1979
HANGAR 18   Sunn Classic, 1980
THE LEGEND OF SLEEPY HOLLOW (TF)   Sunn Classic, 1980
EARTHBOUND   Taft International, 1981
NASHVILLE GRAB (TF)   Taft International, 1981
THE BOOGENS   Jensen Farley Pictures, 1981
THE PRESIDENT MUST DIE   Jensen Farley Pictures, 1981

FIELDER COOK*

b. March 9, 1923 - Atlanta, Georgia
Home: 180 Central Park South, New York, NY 10019, 212/247-5100
Messages: 213/838-0500
Agent: Adams, Ray & Rosenberg - Los Angeles, 213/278-3000
Business Manager: Mortimer Leavy, Colton Weissberg, 505 Park Avenue, New York,
    NY 10022, 212/371-4350

PATTERNS   United Artists, 1956
HOME IS THE HERO   Showcorporation, 1961, Irish

continued

FIELDER COOK*—continued

A BIG HAND FOR THE LITTLE LADY   Warner Bros., 1966
HOW TO SAVE A MARRIAGE AND RUIN YOUR LIFE   Columbia, 1968
PRUDENCE AND THE PILL   20th Century-Fox, 1968, British
SAM HILL: WHO KILLED THE MYSTERIOUS MR. FOSTER?
    (TF)   Universal TV, 1971
GOODBYE, RAGGEDY ANN (TF)   Metromedia Producers Corporation, 1971
THE HOMECOMING (TF)☆   Lorimar Productions, 1971
THE HANDS OF CORMAC JOYCE (TF)   Crawford Productions/Foote, Cone &
    Belding, 1972
EAGLE IN A CAGE   National General, 1972, British-Yugoslavian
MIRACLE ON 34TH STREET (TF)   20th Century-Fox TV, 1973
FROM THE MIXED-UP FILES OF MRS. BASIL E. FRANKWEILER *THE*
    HIDEAWAYS   Cinema 5, 1973
THAT WAS THE WEST THAT WAS (TF)   Universal TV, 1974
MILES TO GO BEFORE I SLEEP (TF)   Tomorrow Entertainment, 1975
THE RIVALRY (TF)   NBC-TV, 1975
VALLEY FORGE (TF)   Clarion Productions/Columbia TV, 1975
BEAUTY AND THE BEAST (TF)   Palms Films Ltd., 1976, British
JUDGE HORTON AND THE SCOTTSBORO BOYS (TF)☆   Tomorrow
    Entertainment, 1976
A LOVE AFFAIR: THE ELEANOR AND LOU GEHRIG STORY (TF)   Charles
    Fries Productions/Stonehenge Productions, 1977
TOO FAR TO GO (TF)   Sea Cliff Productions, 1979
I KNOW WHY THE CAGED BIRD SINGS (TF)   Tomorrow Entertainment,
    1979
GAUGUIN THE SAVAGE (TF)   Nephi Productions, 1980
FAMILY REUNION (TF)   Creative Projects Inc./Columbia TV, 1981
WILL THERE REALLY BE A MORNING? (TF)   Jaffe-Blakely Films/Sama
    Productions/Orion TV, 1983
WHY ME? (TF)   Lorimar Productions, 1984

ALAN COOKE*

b. April 29, 1935 - London, England
Home: 2843 Nichols Canyon Road, Los Angeles, CA 90046, 213/851-7761
Agent: Martin Shapiro, Shapiro-Lichtman Agency - Los Angeles, 213/557-2244

FLAT TWO   Anglo-Amalgamated, 1962, British
THE MIND OF MR. SOAMES   Columbia, 1970, British
THE RIGHT PROSPECTUS (TF)   BBC-TV, 1972, British
BLODWEN HOME FROM RACHEL'S MARRIAGE (TF)   BBC-TV, 1976, British
THE HUNCHBACK OF NOTRE DAME (TF)   BBC-TV, 1978, British
RENOIR, MY FATHER (TF)   BBC-TV, 1979, British
COVER (MS)   ITC, 1980, British

MARTHA COOLIDGE*

b. August 17, 1946 - New Haven, Connecticut
Agent: William Morris Agency - Beverly Hills, 213/274-7451

NOT A PRETTY PICTURE   Films Incorporated, 1976
VALLEY GIRL   Atlantic Releasing Corporation, 1983
THE CITY GIRL   Moon Pictures, 1983
NATIONAL LAMPOON'S JOY OF SEX   Paramount, 1984

JACKIE COOPER*

b. September 15, 1921 - Los Angeles, California
Business: Jackie Enterprises, Inc., 9621 Royalton Drive, Beverly Hills, CA 90210
Agent: Bill Haber, CAA - Los Angeles, 213/277-4545

STAND UP AND BE COUNTED   Columbia, 1971
HAVING BABIES III (TF)   The Jozak Company/Paramount TV, 1978
PERFECT GENTLEMEN (TF)   Paramount TV, 1978
RAINBOW (TF)   Ten-Four Productions, 1978
SEX AND THE SINGLE PARENT (TF)   Time-Life Productions, 1979
MARATHON (TF)   Alan Landsburg Productions, 1980
WHITE MAMA (TF)   Tomorrow Entertainment, 1980
RODEO GIRL (TF)   Steckler Productions/Marble Arch Productions, 1980

continued

JACKIE COOPER*—continued

LEAVE 'EM LAUGHING (TF)   Julian Fowles Productions/Charles Fries
     Productions, 1981
ROSIE: THE ROSEMARY CLOONEY STORY (TF)   Charles Fries Productions/
     Alan Sacks Productions, 1982

H A L   C O O P E R *

Home: 2651 Hutton Drive, Beverly Hills, CA 90210, 213/271-8602
Agent: Major Talent Agency - Los Angeles, 213/820-5841

MILLION DOLLAR INFIELD (TF)   CBS Entertainment, 1982

S T U A R T   C O O P E R

b. 1942 - Hoboken, New Jersey
Agent: ICM, 22 Grafton Street, London, England

**LITTLE MALCOLM AND HIS STRUGGLE AGAINST THE
     EUNUCHS**   Multicetera Investments, 1974, British
OVERLORD   1975, British
THE DISAPPEARANCE   Levitt-Pickman, 1977, Canadian
A.D. - ANNO DOMINI (MS)   Procter & Gamble Productions/International Film
     Productions, 1984, U.S.-Italian

F R A N C I S   F O R D   C O P P O L A *

b. April 7, 1939 - Detroit, Michigan
Business: American Zoetrope, Sentinel Building, 916 Kearny Street, San Francisco,
     CA 94133, 415/789-7500

TONIGHT FOR SURE   Premier Pictures, 1961
DEMENTIA 13   American International, 1963
YOU'RE A BIG BOY NOW   7 Arts, 1966
FINIAN'S RAINBOW   Warner Bros., 1968
THE RAIN PEOPLE   Warner Bros., 1969
THE GODFATHER★   Paramount, 1972
THE CONVERSATION   Paramount, 1974
THE GODFATHER, PART II★★   Paramount, 1974
APOCALYPSE NOW★   United Artists, 1979
ONE FROM THE HEART   Columbia, 1982
THE OUTSIDERS   Warner Bros., 1983
RUMBLE FISH   Universal, 1983
THE COTTON CLUB   Orion, 1984

S E R G I O   C O R B U C C I

b. December 6, 1927 - Rome, Italy
Contact: Ministry of Tourism & Education, Via Della Ferratella, No. 51, 00184
     Rome, Italy, 06/7732

SALVATE MIA FIGLIA   Lauro; 1951; Italian
LA PECCATRICE DELL'ISOLA   Audax Film, 1953, Italian
TWO COLONELS   Comet, 1961, Italian
DUEL OF THE TITANS *ROMOLO E REMO*   Paramount, 1961, Italian
GOLIATH AND THE VAMPIRES *MACISTE CONTRO IL VAMPIRO*   co-
     director with Giacomo Gentilomo, American International, 1961, Italian
THE SLAVE *IL FIGLIO DI SPARTACUS*   MGM, 1962, Italian
IL PIU CORTO GIORNO   Titanus, 1963, Italian
MINNESOTA CLAY   Harlequin International, 1965, Italian-Spanish-French
DJANGO   BRC, 1966, Italian
NAVAJO JOE *UN DOLLARO A TESTA*   United Artists, 1966, Italian-Spanish
JOHNNY ORO   Sanson, 1966, Italian
THE HELLBENDERS   Embassy, 1966, Italian-Spanish
BERSAGLIO MOBILE   Rizzoli Film, 1967, Italian
IL GRANDE SILENZIO   Adelphia Cinematografica, 1967, Italian
THE MERCENARY   United Artists, 1969, Italian-Spanish
GLI SPECIALISTI   Adelphia Cinematografica, 1969, Italian
COMPAÑEROS *VAMOS A MATAR COMPAÑEROS*   Cinerama Releasing
     Corporation, 1971, Spanish-Italian
VIVA LA MUERTE ... TUA!   Tritone Filmind, 1971, Italian

continued

SERGIO CORBUCCI—continued

CHE C'ENTRIAMO NOI CON LA RIVOLUZIONE?   Fair Film, 1972, Italian
LA BANDA J & S - CRONACA CRIMINALE DEL FAR-WEST   1973, Italian
IL BESTIONE   C.C. Champion, Inc., 1974, Italian
BLUFF - STORIE DI TRUFFE E DI IMBRAGLIONE   Cineriz, 1975, Italian
UN GENIO, DUE COMPARI, UN POLLO   Titanus, 1975, Italian-French-West
    German
DE CHE SEGNO SEI?   PIC, 1976, Italian
IL SIGNOR ROBINSON - MONSTRUOSA STORIA D'AMORE E
    D'AVVENTURE   United Artists, 1976, Italian
TRE TIGRI CONTRA TRE TIGRI   Italian International Film, 1977, Italian
ECCO NOI PER ESEMPIO   CIDIF, 1977, Italian
LA MAZZETTA   United Artists, 1978, Italian
GIALLO NAPOLETANO   CIDIF, 1979, Italian
ATTI ATROCISSIMA DE AMORE E DI VENDETTA   1979, Italian
PARI E DISPARI   CIDIF, 1979, Italian
I DON'T UNDERSTAND YOU ANYMORE   Capital, 1980, Italian
I'M GETTING MYSELF A YACHT   Capital, 1981, Italian
A FRIEND IS A TREASURE   CEIAD, 1981, Italian
SUPER FUZZ   Avco Embassy, 1981, Italian
MY DARLING, MY DEAREST   PLM Film, 1982, Italian
THREE WISE KINGS   PLM Film, 1982, Italian
COUNT TACCHIA   DAC/Adige, 1982, Italian
SING SING   Columbia, 1983, Italian
LUI, LEI, MASCHIO E FEMMINA   Faso Film, 1984, Italian

N I C H O L A S   C O R E A *

b. April 7, 1943 - St. Louis, Missouri
Contact: Directors Guild of America - Los Angeles, 213/656-1220

THE ARCHER: FUGITIVE FROM THE EMPIRE (TF)   Mad-Dog Productions/
    Universal TV, 1981

R O G E R   C O R M A N

b. April 5, 1926 - Los Angeles, California
Business: New Horizons, 119 N. San Vicente Blvd., Beverly Hills, CA
    213/651-2374

FIVE GUNS WEST   American International, 1955
THE APACHE WOMAN   American International, 1955
THE DAY THE WORLD ENDED   American International, 1956
SWAMP WOMAN   Woolner Brothers, 1956
THE OKLAHOMA WOMAN   American International, 1956
THE GUNSLINGER   ARC, 1956
IT CONQUERED THE WORLD   American International, 1956
NOT OF THIS EARTH   Allied Artists, 1957
THE UNDEAD   American International, 1957
NAKED PARADISE   American International, 1957
ATTACK OF THE CRAB MONSTERS   Allied Artists, 1957
ROCK ALL NIGHT   American International, 1957
TEENAGE DOLL   Allied Artists, 1957
CARNIVAL ROCK   Howco, 1957
SORORITY GIRL   American International, 1957
THE VIKING WOMEN AND THE SEA SERPENT   American International,
    1957
WAR OF THE SATELLITES   Allied Artists, 1958
THE SHE GODS OF SHARK REEF   American International, 1958
MACHINE GUN KELLY   American International, 1958
TEENAGE CAVEMAN   American International, 1958
I, MOBSTER   20th Century-Fox, 1959
A BUCKET OF BLOOD   American International, 1959
THE WASP WOMAN   American International, 1959
SKI TROOP ATTACK   Filmgroup; 1960
THE HOUSE OF USHER   American International, 1960
THE LITTLE SHOP OF HORRORS   Filmgroup, 1960
THE LAST WOMAN ON EARTH   Filmgroup, 1960
CREATURE FROM THE HAUNTED SEA   Filmgroup, 1961
ATLAS   Filmgroup, 1961
THE PIT AND THE PENDULUM   American International, 1961
THE INTRUDER *I HATE YOUR GUTS*   Pathe American, 1962

continued

ROGER CORMAN—continued

THE PREMATURE BURIAL   American International, 1962
TALES OF TERROR   American International, 1962
TOWER OF LONDON   American International, 1962
THE RAVEN   American International, 1963
THE TERROR   American International, 1963
"X" - THE MAN WITH THE X-RAY EYES   American International, 1963
THE HAUNTED PALACE   American International, 1963
THE YOUNG RACERS   American International, 1963
THE SECRET INVASION   United Artists, 1964
THE MASQUE OF THE RED DEATH   American International, 1964, British-
     U.S.
THE TOMB OF LIGEIA   American International, 1965
THE WILD ANGELS   American International, 1966
THE ST. VALENTINE'S DAY MASSACRE   20th Century-Fox, 1967
THE TRIP   American International, 1967
TARGET: HARRY   directed under pseudonym of Harry Neill, ABC Pictures
     International, 1968
BLOODY MAMA   American International, 1970
GAS-S-S-SI . . .OR IT BECAME NECESSARY TO DESTROY THE WORLD
     IN ORDER TO SAVE IT!   American International, 1970
VON RICHTOFEN AND BROWN   United Artists, 1971

HUBERT CORNFIELD

b. February 9, 1929 - Istanbul, Turkey

SUDDEN DANGER   United Artists, 1955
LURE OF THE SWAMP   20th Century-Fox, 1957
PLUNDER ROAD   20th Century-Fox, 1957
THE THIRD VOICE   20th Century-Fox, 1959
ANGEL BABY   co-director with Paul Wendkos, Allied Artists, 1961
PRESSURE POINT   United Artists, 1962
THE NIGHT OF THE FOLLOWING DAY   Universal, 1969
LES GRAND MOYENS   1976, French

WILLIAM H. COSBY, JR.*

b. July 12, 1937 - Philadelphia, Pennsylvania
Agent: William Morris Agency - Beverly Hills, 213/274-7451

BILL COSBY, HIMSELF   20th Century-Fox International Classics, 1983

DON COSCARELLI*

b. February 17, 1954 - Tripoli, Libya
Business: Coscarelli-Pepperman Corporation, 15445 Ventura Blvd. - Suite 10,
     Sherman Oaks, CA 91413, 213/784-8822

JIM - THE WORLD'S GREATEST   Universal, 1976
KENNY AND COMPANY   20th Century-Fox, 1976
PHANTASM   Avco Embassy, 1979
THE BEASTMASTER   MGM/UA, 1982

GEORGE PAN COSMATOS*

Home: 2910 Seaview Road, Victoria, British Columbia V8N 1L1, Canada, 604/721-
     1675
Agent: Peter Meyer, William Morris Agency - Beverly Hills, 213/274-7451

MASSACRE IN ROME *RAPPRESAGLIA*   National General, 1973, Italian-
     French
THE CASSANDRA CROSSING   Avco Embassy, 1977, British-Italian-West
     German
RESTLESS   Joseph Brenner Associates, 1978
ESCAPE TO ATHENA   AFD, 1979, British
OF UNKNOWN ORIGIN   Warner Bros., 1983, Canadian

COSTA-GAVRAS
(See COSTA GAVRAS)

JACK COUFFER *

Agent: Ben Benjamin, ICM - Los Angeles, 213/550-4153

NIKKI, WILD DOG OF THE NORTH   Buena Vista, 1961, U.S.-Canadian
RING OF BRIGHT WATER   Cinerama Releasing Corporation, 1969, British
LIVING FREE   Columbia, 1972, British
THE DARWIN ADVENTURE   20th Century-Fox, 1972, British
THE LAST GIRAFFE (TF)   Westfall Productions, 1979

JEROME COURTLAND *

b. December 27, 1926 - Knoxville, Tennessee
Business: Walt Disney Productions, 500 S. Buena Vista Street, Burbank, CA 91521,
    213/845-3141

RUN, COUGAR, RUN   Buena Vista, 1972
DIAMONDS ON WHEELS   Buena Vista, 1972, U.S.-British
THE SKY TRAP (TF)   Walt Disney Productions, 1979

RAOUL COUTARD

b. September 16, 1924 - Paris, France
Contact: French Film Office, 745 Fifth Avenue, New York, NY 10151, 213/832-8860

HOA-BINH   Transvue, 1971, French
OPERATION LEOPARD   Bela Productions/FR3, 1980, French
S.A.S. MALKO "TERMINATE WITH EXTREME PREJUDICE"   UGC, 1983,
    French-West German

PAUL COX

Agent: Roberta Kent, S.T.E. Representation - Los Angeles, 213/550-3982
Agent: Cameron's Management, 120 Victoria Street, Kings Cross, NSW, 2011,
    Australia, 02/358-6433

LONELY HEARTS   The Samuel Goldwyn Company, 1982, Australian
MAN OF FLOWERS   Roadshow Distributors, 1983, Australian

WILLIAM CRAIN *

b. June 20, 1943
Business: P.O. Box 744, Beverly Hills, CA 90213
Agent: Chasin-Park-Citron - Los Angeles, 213/273-7190

BLACULA   American International, 1972
DR. BLACK, MR. HYDE   Dimension, 1976
THE WATTS MONSTER   Dimension, 1979
STANDING IN THE SHADOWS OF LOVE   Brandenberg-Crain Productions,
    1984

BARRY CRANE *

Business Manager: Brad Marer & Associates - Beverly Hills, 213/278-6690

THE HOUND OF THE BASKERVILLES (TF)   Universal TV, 1972

WES CRAVEN *

b. August 2, 1949 - Cleveland, Ohio
Business: Wesismore, Inc., 2309 Glynden Avenue, Venice, CA 90241, 213/397-
    4645
Agent: Marvin Moss Agency - Los Angeles, 213/274-8483

LAST HOUSE ON THE LEFT   Hallmark Releasing Corporation, 1973
THE HILLS HAVE EYES   Vanguard, 1977
STRANGER IN OUR HOUSE (TF)   Inter Planetary Pictures/Finnegan Associates,
    1978
DEADLY BLESSING   United Artists, 1981
SWAMP THING   Avco Embassy, 1982

RICHARD CRENNA *

b. November 30, 1926 - Los Angeles, California
Agent: CAA - Los Angeles, 213/277-4545

BETTER LATE THAN NEVER (TF)   Ten-Four Productions, 1979

CHARLES CRICHTON

b. August 6, 1910 - Wallasey, England
Contact: British Academy of Film & Television Arts, 195 Piccadilly, London W1,
    England, 01/734-0022

FOR THOSE IN PERIL   1944, British
PAINTED BOATS   1945, British
DEAD OF NIGHT   co-director with Alberto Cavalcanti, Basil Dearden & Robert
    Hamer, Universal, 1945, British
HUE AND CRY   Fine Arts, 1947, British
AGAINST THE WIND   Eagle Lion, 1948, British
ANOTHER SHORE   Rank, 1948, British
TRAIN OF EVENTS   co-director with Basil Dearden & Sidney Cole, Rank, 1949,
    British
DANCE HALL   Rank, 1950, British
THE LAVENDER HILL MOB   Universal, 1951, British
THE STRANGER IN BETWEEN *HUNTED*   Universal, 1952, British
THE TITFIELD THUNDERBOLT   Universal, 1953, British
THE LOVER LOTTERY   Continental, 1953, British
THE DIVIDED HEART   Republic, 1954, British
DECISION AGAINST TIME *THE MAN IN THE SKY*   MGM, 1956, British
LAW AND DISORDER   co-director with Henry Cornelius, Continental, 1958,
    British
FLOODS OF FEAR   Universal, 1958, British
THE BATTLE OF THE SEXES   Continental, 1959, British
THE BOY WHO STOLE A MILLION   Paramount, 1960, British
THE THIRD SECRET   20th Century-Fox, 1964, British
HE WHO RIDES A TIGER   Sigma III, 1966, British

MICHAEL CRICHTON *

b. October 23, 1942 - Chicago, Illinois
Agent: Michael Ovitz, CAA - Los Angeles, 213/277-4545

PURSUIT (TF)   ABC Circle Films, 1972
WESTWORLD   MGM, 1973
COMA   MGM/United Artists, 1978
THE GREAT TRAIN ROBBERY   United Artists, 1979, British
LOOKER   The Ladd Company/Warner Bros., 1981

DONALD CROMBIE

Business: Forest Home Films, 141 Penhurst Street, Willoughby, NSW, 2068,
    Australia, 02/411-4972

WHO KILLED JENNY LANGBY? (TF)   1974, Australian
DO I HAVE TO KILL MY CHILD? (TF)   1976, Australian
CADDIE   Atlantic Releasing Corporation, 1976, Australian
THE IRISHMAN   Forest Home Films, 1978, Australian

continued

DONALD CROMBIE—continued
CATHY'S CHILD   CB Productions, 1979, Australian
THE KILLING OF ANGEL STREET   Forest Home Films, 1981, Australian
KITTY AND THE BAGMAN   Quartet/Films Incorporated, 1982, Australian

DAVID CRONENBERG

Home: 184 Cottingham Street, Toronto, Ontario M4V 7C7, Canada, 416/961-3432

STEREO   Emergent Films, 1969, Canadian
CRIMES OF THE FUTURE   Emergent Films, 1970, Canadian
THEY CAME FROM WITHIN *SHIVERS*   Trans-America, 1976, Canadian
RABID   New World, 1977, Canadian
THE BROOD   New World, 1979, Canadian
FAST COMPANY   Topar, 1979, Canadian
SCANNERS   Avco Embassy, 1981, Canadian
VIDEODROME   Universal, 1983, Canadian
THE DEAD ZONE   Paramount, 1983, Canadian

ROBERT CULP *

b. August 16, 1930 - Berkeley, California
Home: 10880 Wilshire Blvd - Suite 2110, Los Angeles, CA 90024, 213/470-1315
Personal Manager: Hillard Elkins - Los Angeles, 213/858-6090

HICKEY AND BOGGS   United Artists, 1972

SEAN S. CUNNINGHAM *

b. December 31, 1941 - New York, New York
Home/Business: Sean S. Cunningham Films, Ltd., 155 Long Lots Road, Westport,
    CT 06880, 203/255-0666
Agent: Jeff Berg/Peter Rawley, ICM - Los Angeles, 213/550-4000

TOGETHER   Hallmark Releasing Corporation, 1971
THE CASE OF THE SMILING STIFFS   co-director with Brud Talbot, Seaberg,
    1974
SEX ON THE GROOVE TUBE   Newport, 1977
HERE COME THE TIGERS   American International, 1978
FRIDAY THE 13TH   Paramount, 1980
A STRANGER IS WATCHING   MGM/United Artists, 1982
SPRING BREAK   Columbia, 1983

DAN CURTIS *

b. August 12 - Bridgeport, Connecticut
Business: Dan Curtis Productions, 5555 Melrose Avenue, Hollywood, CA 90004,
    213/468-5000 ext. 5728
Business Manager: Michael Rutman, Breslauer, Jacobson & Rutman - Los Angeles,
    213/879-0167

HOUSE OF DARK SHADOWS   MGM, 1970
NIGHT OF DARK SHADOWS   MGM, 1971
THE NIGHT STRANGLER (TF)   ABC Circle Films, 1973
THE NORLISS TAPES (TF)   Metromedia Producers Corporation, 1973
SCREAM OF THE WOLF (TF)   Metromedia Producers Corporation, 1974
DRACULA (TF)   Universal TV/Dan Curtis Productions, 1974
MELVIN PURVIS: G-MAN (TF)   American International TV, 1974
THE GREAT ICE RIP-OFF (TF)   ABC Circle Films, 1974
TRILOGY OF TERROR (TF)   ABC Circle Films, 1975
THE KANSAS CITY MASSACRE (TF)   ABC Circle Films, 1975
BURNT OFFERINGS   United Artists, 1976
CURSE OF THE BLACK WIDOW (TF)   Dan Curtis Productions/ABC Circle
    Films, 1977
WHEN EVERY DAY WAS THE FOURTH OF JULY (TF)   Dan Curtis
    Productions, 1978
THE LAST RIDE OF THE DALTON GANG (TF)   NBC Productions/Dan Curtis
    Productions, 1979
MRS. R'S DAUGHTER (TF)   NBC Productions/Dan Curtis Productions, 1979
THE LONG DAYS OF SUMMER (TF)   Dan Curtis Productions, 1980
THE WINDS OF WAR (MS)☆   Paramount TV/Dan Curtis Productions, 1983

D

MORTON DA COSTA*
(Morton Tecosky)

b. March 7, 1914 - Philadelphia, Pennsylvania
Agent: Coleman-Rosenberg, 667 Madison Avenue, New York, NY, 212/838-0734

AUNTIE MAME   Warner Bros., 1958
THE MUSIC MAN   Warner Bros., 1962
ISLAND OF LOVE   Warner Bros., 1963

ROBERT DALVA*

b. April 14, 1942 - New York, New York
Home/Business: Dalva Films, 33 Walnut Avenue, Larkspur, CA 94939, 415/924-0164
Agent: Jim Berkus, 1900 Avenue of the Stars, Los Angeles, CA 90067, 213/277-9090

THE BLACK STALLION RETURNS   MGM/UA, 1983

DAMIANO DAMIANI

b. July 23, 1922 - Pasiano, Italy
Contact: Ministry of Tourism & Education, Via Della Ferratella, No. 51, 00184
    Rome, Italy, 06/7732

IL ROSSETTO   Europa Cinematografica/Explorer Film/EFPC, 1960, Italian-French
IL SICARIO   Europa Cinematografica/Galatea, 1961, Italian
ARTURO'S ISLAND   MGM, 1962, Italian
LA RIMPATRIATA   Galatea/22 Dicembre/Coronet, 1963, Italian-French
THE EMPTY CANVAS   Embassy, 1964, Italian
LA STREGA IN AMORE   Arco Film, 1966, Italian
MAFIA *IL GIORNO DELLA CIVETTA*   American International, 1968, Italian
A BULLET FOR THE GENERAL *QUIEN SABE?*   Avco Embassy, 1968,
    Italian-Spanish
UNA RAGAZZA PIUTTOSTO COMPLICATA   Produzioni Filmena/Fono Roma,
    1969, Italian
CONFESSIONS OF A POLICE CAPTAIN *CONFESSIONE DI UN
    COMMISSARIO*   1970, Italian
LA MOGLIE PIU BELLA   Explorer '58, 1970, Italian
L'ISTRUTTORIA E CHIUSA DIMENTICHI   Fair Film, 1971, Italian
IL SORRISO DEL GRANDE TENTATORE   Euro, 1972, Italian
GIROLIMONI - IL MOSTRO DI ROMA   Dino De Laurentiis Cinematografica,
    1972, Italian
THE DEVIL IS A WOMAN   20th Century-Fox, 1975, British-Italian
I AM AFRAID   Auro Cinematografica, 1977, Italian
GOODBYE AND AMEN   Cineriz, 1978, Italian-French
UN UOMO IN GINOCCHIO   Cineriz, 1979, Italian
TIME OF THE JACKALS   Capital, 1980, Italian
AMITYVILLE II: THE POSSESSION   Orion, 1982
LA PIOVRA   SACIS, 1983, Italian

MELVIN DAMSKI *

Home: 10533 Dunleer Drive, Los Angeles, CA 90064
Agent: David Gersh, The Gersh Agency - Beverly Hills, 213/274-6611

LONG JOURNEY BACK (TF)   Lorimar Productions, 1978
THE CHILD STEALER (TF)   The Production Company/Columbia TV, 1979
A PERFECT MATCH (TF)   Lorimar Productions, 1980
WORD OF HONOR (TF)   Georgia Bay Productions, 1981
AMERICAN DREAM (TF)   Mace Neufeld Productions/Viacom, 1981
FOR LADIES ONLY (TF)   The Catalina Production Group/Viacom, 1981
THE LEGEND OF WALKS FAR WOMAN (TF)   Roger Gimbel Productions/EMI
    TV/Raquel Welch Productions/Lee Levinson Productions, 1982
AN INVASION OF PRIVACY (TF)   Dick Berg-Stonehenge Productions/Embassy
    TV, 1983
YELLOWBEARD   Orion, 1983, British

MARC DANIELS *

Agent: Fred Westheimer, William Morris Agency - Beverly Hills, 213/274-7451

SQUEEZE A FLOWER   MGM-EMI, 1971, Australian
PLANET EARTH (TF)   Warner Bros. TV, 1974

HERBERT DANSKA *

Business: Emerald City Productions, Inc. - New York City, 212/666-4735

SWEET LOVE, BITTER *IT WON'T RUB OFF, BABY*   Peppercorn-Wormser,
    1967
RIGHT ON!   Leacock-Pennebaker, 1970

JOE DANTE *

Agent: David Gersh, The Gersh Agency - Beverly Hills, 213/274-6611

HOLLYWOOD BOULEVARD   co-director with Allan Arkush, New World, 1976
PIRANHA   New World, 1978
THE HOWLING   Avco Embassy, 1980
TWILIGHT ZONE - THE MOVIE   co-director with John Landis, Steven
    Spielberg & George Miller, Warner Bros., 1983
GREMLINS   Warner Bros., 1984

RAY DANTON *

b. September 19, 1931 - New York, New York
Business Manager: Joel Rosenbaum - Encino, 213/872-0231

THE DEATHMASTER   American International, 1972
CRYPT OF THE LIVING DEAD   Atlas, 1973
PSYCHIC KILLER   Avco Embassy, 1975

PHILIP D'ANTONI *

b. February 19, 1929 - New York, New York
Business: 8 East 63rd Street, New York, NY 10021, 212/688-4205

THE SEVEN UPS   20th Century-Fox, 1973

JOAN DARLING *
(Joan Kugell)

b. April 14, 1935 - Boston, Massachusetts
Agent: Ed Bondy, William Morris Agency - Beverly Hills, 213/274-7451

FIRST LOVE   Paramount, 1977
WILLA (TF)   co-director with Claudio Guzman, GJL Productions/Dove, Inc., 1979
THE CHECK IS IN THE MAIL   Robert Kaufman Productions, 1984

JULES DASSIN *

b. December 18, 1911 - Middleton, Connecticut
Home: 25 Anagnostopoulou Street, Athens, Greece, 3/629-751
Agent: Sue Mengers, ICM - Los Angeles, 213/550-4000

NAZI AGENT   MGM, 1942
THE AFFAIRS OF MARTHA   MGM, 1942
REUNION IN FRANCE   MGM, 1942
YOUNG IDEAS   MGM, 1943
THE CANTERVILLE GHOST   MGM, 1944
A LETTER FOR EVIE   MGM, 1945
TWO SMART PEOPLE   MGM, 1946
BRUTE FORCE   Warner Bros., 1947
THE NAKED CITY   Universal, 1948
THIEVES' HIGHWAY   RKO Radio, 1949
NIGHT AND THE CITY   20th Century-Fox, 1950, British
RIFIFI   Pathe, 1954, French
WHERE THE HOT WIND BLOWS *LA LOI*   MGM, 1960, French-Italian
NEVER ON SUNDAY★   Lopert, 1960, Greek
PHAEDRA   Lopert, 1962, Greek-U.S.-French
TOPKAPI   United Artists, 1964
10:30 P.M. SUMMER   Lopert, 1966, U.S.-Spanish
SURVIVAL '67   United, 1968, U.S.-Israeli
UP TIGHT   Paramount, 1968
PROMISE AT DAWN   Avco Embassy, 1970, French-U.S.
A DREAM OF PASSION   Avco Embassy, 1978, Greek-U.S.
CIRCLE OF TWO   World Northal, 1981, Canadian

HERSCHEL DAUGHERTY *

Home: 925 Santa Fe Drive, Encinitas, CA 92024
Messages: 914/753-6470

THE LIGHT IN THE FOREST   Buena Vista, 1958
THE RAIDERS   Universal, 1963
WINCHESTER '73 (TF)   Universal TV, 1967
THE VICTIM (TF)   Universal TV, 1972
SHE CRIED "MURDER" (TF)   Universal TV, 1973
TWICE IN A LIFETIME (TF)   Martin Rackin Productions, 1974

BOAZ DAVIDSON

Business: Cannon Group, 6464 Sunset Blvd., Los Angeles, CA 90038, 213/469-8124

AZIT THE PARATROOPER DOG   Liran Corporation, 1972, Israeli
CHARLIE AND A HALF   Filmonde, 1973, Israeli
LUPO GOES TO NEW YORK   Noah Films, 1977, Israeli
THE TZANANI FAMILY   Noah Films, 1978, Israeli
LEMON POPSICLE   Noah Films, 1981, Israeli
GOING STEADY (LEMON POPSICLE II)   Noah Films, 1981, Israeli
SEED OF INNOCENCE *TEEN MOTHERS*   Cannon, 1981
X-RAY   Cannon, 1981
HOT BUBBLEGUM (LEMON POPSICLE III)   Noah Films, 1981, Israeli
THE LAST AMERICAN VIRGIN   Cannon, 1982
PRIVATE POPSICLE (LEMON POPSICLE IV)   Noah Films, 1982, Israeli-West
   German

GORDON DAVIDSON *

b. May 7, 1933 - New York, New York
Business: 135 N. Grand Avenue, Los Angeles, CA 90012, 213/973-7388
Agent: William Morris Agency - Beverly Hills, 213/274-7451

THE TRIAL OF THE CATONSVILLE NINE   Cinema 5, 1972

MARTIN DAVIDSON *

b. November 7, 1939 - New York, New York
Agent: Jim Wiatt, ICM - Los Angeles, 213/550-4000

THE LORDS OF FLATBUSH   co-director with Stephen Verona, Columbia, 1974
ALMOST SUMMER   Universal, 1978
HERO AT LARGE   MGM/United Artists, 1980
EDDIE AND THE CRUISERS   Embassy, 1983

BARRY DAVIS

OPPENHEIMER (MS)   BBC-TV/WGBH-Boston, 1982, British-U.S.

DESMOND DAVIS

b. 1928 - London, England
Agent: John Redway & Associates - London, 01/637-1612

THE GIRL WITH GREEN EYES   United Artists, 1964, British
TIME LOST AND TIME REMEMBERED *I WAS HAPPY HERE*   Continental,
    1966, British
THE UNCLE   Lennart, 1966, British
SMASHING TIME   Paramount, 1967, British
A NICE GIRL LIKE ME   Avco Embassy, 1969, British
CLASH OF THE TITANS   MGM/United Artists, 1981, British
THE SIGN OF FOUR   Mapleton Films Ltd., 1983, British
THE COUNTRY GIRLS   London Films Ltd./Channel Four, 1983, British

OSSIE DAVIS

b. December 18, 1917 - Cogdell, Georgia
Agent: The Artists Agency - Los Angeles, 213/277-7779

COTTON COMES TO HARLEM   United Artists, 1970
BLACK GIRL   Cinerama Releasing Corporation, 1972
KONGI'S HARVEST   Tan Communications, 1973
GORDON'S WAR   20th Century-Fox, 1973
COUNTDOWN AT KUSINI   Columbia, 1976, U.S.-Nigerian

PETER DAVIS

Home: 325 Central Park West, New York, NY 10025

HEARTS AND MINDS (FD)   Warner Bros., 1975
MIDDLETOWN (TD)   PBS, 1982

ERNEST DAY

GREEN ICE   Universal/AFD, 1981, British
WALTZ ACROSS TEXAS   Atlantic Releasing Corporation, 1983

ROBERT DAY *

b. September 11, 1922 - Sheen, England
Agent: CAA - Los Angeles, 213/277-4545

THE GREEN MAN   DCA, 1957, British
STRANGERS' MEETING   Rank, 1957, British
THE HAUNTED STRANGLER *GRIP OF THE STRANGLER*   MGM, 1958,
    British
CORRIDORS OF BLOOD   MGM, 1958, British
FIRST MAN INTO SPACE   MGM, 1959, British
LIFE IN EMERGENCY WARD 10   Eros, 1959, British
BOBBIKINS   20th Century-Fox, 1960, British
TWO-WAY STRETCH   Showcorporation, 1960, British
TARZAN THE MAGNIFICENT   Paramount, 1960, British
CALL ME GENIUS *THE REBEL*   Continental, 1961, British
OPERATION SNATCH   Continental, 1962, British

continued

ROBERT DAY*—continued

TARZAN'S THREE CHALLENGES   MGM, 1963, British
SHE   MGM, 1965, British
TARZAN AND THE VALLEY OF GOLD   American International, 1966, U.S.-
    Swiss
TARZAN AND THE GREAT RIVER   Paramount, 1967
I THINK WE'RE BEING FOLLOWED   1967, British
THE HOUSE ON GREENAPPLE ROAD (TF)   QM Productions, 1970
RITUAL OF EVIL (TF)   Universal TV, 1970
BANYON (TF)   Warner Bros. TV, 1971
IN BROAD DAYLIGHT (TF)   Aaron Spelling Productions, 1971
MR. AND MRS. BO JO JONES (TF)   20th Century-Fox TV, 1971
THE RELUCTANT HEROES (TF)   Aaron Spelling Productions, 1971
THE GREAT AMERICAN BEAUTY CONTEST (TF)   ABC Circle Films, 1973
DEATH STALK (TF)   Wolper Productions, 1975
THE TRIAL OF CHAPLAIN JENSEN (TF)   20th Century-Fox TV, 1975
SWITCH (TF)   Universal TV, 1975
A HOME OF OUR OWN (TF)   QM Productions, 1975
TWIN DETECTIVES (TF)   Charles Fries Productions, 1976
KINGSTON: THE POWER PLAY (TF)   Universal TV, 1976
HAVING BABIES (TF)   The Jozak Company, 1976
BLACK MARKET BABY (TF)   Brut Productions, 1977
THE INITIATION OF SARAH (TF)   Charles Fries Productions, 1978
THE GRASS IS ALWAYS GREENER OVER THE SEPTIC TANK (TF)   Joe
    Hamilton Productions, 1978
MURDER BY NATURAL CAUSES (TF)   Richard Levinson-William Link
    Productions, 1979
WALKING THROUGH THE FIRE (TF)   Time-Life Films, 1979
THE MAN WITH BOGART'S FACE   SAM MARLOW, PRIVATE EYE   20th
    Century-Fox, 1980
PETER AND PAUL (TF)   Universal TV, 1981
SCRUPLES (TF)   Lou-Step Productions/Warner Brothers TV, 1981
MARIAN ROSE WHITE (TF)   Gerald Abrams Productions/Cypress Point
    Productions, 1982
RUNNING OUT (TF)   CBS Entertainment, 1983
YOUR PLACE OR MINE (TF)   Poolhouse Productions/Finnegan Associates,
    1983
CHINA ROSE (TF)   Robert Halmi Productions, 1983
COOK & PEARY: THE RACE TO THE POLE (TF)   Robert Halmi Productions,
    1983

LYMAN DAYTON

Business: Lyman Dayton Productions, 10850 Riverside Drive, North Hollywood,
    CA 91602, 213/980-7202

BAKER'S HAWK   Doty-Dayton, 1976
RIVALS   World Entertainment, 1979
THE STRANGER AT JEFFERSON HIGH (TF)   Lyman Dayton Productions,
    1981
THE AVENGING   Comworld, 1981

EMILE deANTONIO

b. 1920 - Scranton, Pennsylvania
Address: P.O. Box 1567, New York, NY 10017, 212/475-2630 or 212/674-5825

POINT OF ORDER (FD)   Point, 1963
RUSH TO JUDGMENT (FD)   Impact, 1967
AMERICA IS HARD TO SEE (FD)   1968
IN THE YEAR OF THE PIG (FD)   Pathe Contemporary, 1969
MILLHOUSE: A WHITE COMEDY   New Yorker, 1971
PAINTERS PAINTING (FD)   New Yorker, 1973
UNDERGROUND (FD)   co-director with Mary Lampson & Haskell Wexler, New
    Yorker, 1976
IN THE KING OF PRUSSIA   Turin Film Corporation, 1983

WILLIAM DEAR *

Home: 408/625-3696

TIMERIDER   Jensen Farley Pictures, 1983

JAMES DEARDEN

Contact: British Academy of Film & Television Arts, 195 Piccadilly, London W1,
England, 01/734-0022

THE COLD ROOM (CTF)   HBO Premiere Films/Cold Room Productions, 1983,
British

GIANFRANCO deBOSIO

Contact: Ministry of Tourism & Education, Via Della Ferratella, No. 51, 00184
Rome, Italy, 06/7732

LA BETIA   Titanus, 1972, Italian-Yugoslavian
MOSES THE LAWGIVER (MS)   ATV, Ltd./ITC/RAI, 1975, British-Italian
MOSES   Avco Embassy, 1976, British-Italian, feature film version of MOSES THE
LAWGIVER

PHILIPPE de BROCA

b. March 15, 1933 - Paris, France
Contact: French Film Office, 745 Fifth Avenue, New York, NY 10151, 212/832-
8860

LES JEUX DE L'AMOUR   1960, French
THE JOKER   Lopert, 1961, French
THE FIVE DAY LOVER   Kingsley International, 1961, French-Italian
SEVEN CAPITAL SINS   co-director with Jean-Luc Godard, Roger Vadim,
Sylvaine Dhomme, Edouard Molinaro, Claude Chabrol, Jacques Demy, Marie-
Jose Nat, Dominique Paturel, Jean-Marc Tennberg & Perrette Pradier, Embassy,
1962, French-Italian
CARTOUCHE   Embassy, 1962, French-Italian
LES VEINARDS   co-director, 1962, French
THAT MAN FROM RIO   Lopert, 1964, French-Italian
MALE COMPANION   International Classics, 1966, French-Italian
UP TO HIS EARS *LES TRIBULATIONS D'UN CHINOIS EN
CHINE*   Lopert, 1966, French-Italian
THE KING OF HEARTS   Lopert, 1967, French-Italian
THE OLDEST PROFESSION *LES PLUX VIEUX METIER DU MONDE*   co-
director with Franco Indovina, Mauro Bolognini, Michael Pfleghar, Claude
Autant-Lara & Jean-Luc Godard, Goldstone, 1968, French-Italian-West German
THE DEVIL BY THE TAIL   Lopert, 1969, French-Italian
GIVE HER THE MOON *LES CAPRICES DE MARIE*   United Artists, 1970,
French-Italian
TOUCH AND GO *LA ROUTE AU SOLEIL*   Libra, 1971, French
CHERE LOUISE   1972, French
LE MAGNIFIQUE   Cine III, 1974, French
INCORRIGIBLE   EDP, 1975, French
JULIE POT DE COLLE   1977, French
LE CAVALEUR   1978, French
DEAR DETECTIVE *DEAR INSPECTOR*   Cinema 5, 1978, French
PRACTICE MAKES PERFECT   Quartet/Films Incorporated, 1980, French
JUPITER'S THIGH   Quartet/Films Incorporated, 1981, French
PSY   Ariane Films/Antenne-2, 1981, French
L'AFRICAIN   Renn Productions, 1982, French
LOUISIANA (CMS)   HBO Premiere Films/ICC/Antenne-2/Gaumont/Filmax, 1983,
Canadian-French

F R A N K de F E L I T T A *

b. August 3, 1921 - New York, New York
Home: 3008 Paulcrest Drive, Los Angeles, CA 90046, 213/654-1310
Agent: Michael Marcus, CAA - Los Angeles, 213/277-4545

TRAPPED (TF)   Universal TV, 1973
THE TWO WORLDS OF JENNY LOGAN (TF)   Joe Wizan TV Productions/
     Charles Fries Productions, 1979
DARK NIGHT OF THE SCARECROW (TF)   Joe Wizan TV Productions, 1981

P H I L I P D e G U E R E *

Agent: Marvin Moss Agency - Los Angeles, 213/274-8483

DR. STRANGE (TF)   Universal TV, 1978

D O M D E L U I S E *

b. August 1, 1933 - Brooklyn, New York
Agent: CAA - Los Angeles, 213/277-4545

HOT STUFF   Columbia, 1979

J O N A T H A N D E M M E *

Agent: Arnold Stiefel, William Morris Agency - Beverly Hills, 213/274-7451
Business Manager: Lee Winkler, Global Business Management, 9000 Sunset Blvd. -
     Suite 1115, Los Angeles, CA 90069, 213/278-4141

CAGED HEAT   New World, 1974
CRAZY MAMA   New World, 1975
FIGHTING MAD   20th Century-Fox, 1976
CITIZENS BAND   *HANDLE WITH CARE*   Paramount, 1977
LAST EMBRACE   United Artists, 1979
MELVIN AND HOWARD   Universal, 1980
WHO AM I THIS TIME? (TF)   Rubicon Film Productions, 1982
SWING SHIFT   Warner Bros., 1984

P I E R R E D e M O R O

SAVANNAH SMILES   Embassy, 1983

J A C Q U E S D E M Y *

b. June 5, 1931 - Pont-Chateau, France
Home: 86 Rue Daguerre, Paris 75014, France, 322-32-36
Agent: The Lantz Office - Los Angeles, 213/858-1144

LOLA   Films Around the World, 1961, French
SEVEN CAPITAL SINS   co-director with Jean-Luc Godard, Roger Vadim,
     Sylvaine Dhomme, Edouard Molinaro, Philippe de Broca, Claude Chabrol, Marie-
     Jose Nat, Dominique Paturel, Jean-Marc Tennberg & Perrette Pradier, Embassy,
     1962, French-Italian
BAY OF THE ANGELS   Pathe Contemporary, 1964, French
THE UMBRELLAS OF CHERBOURG   Landau, 1964, French-West German
THE YOUNG GIRLS OF ROCHEFORT   Warner Bros., 1968, French
MODEL SHOP   Columbia, 1969
DONKEY SKIN   Janus, 1971, French
THE PIED PIPER   Paramount, 1972, British-West German
A SLIGHTLY PREGNANT MAN   SJ International, 1977, French
LADY OSCAR   Toho, 1978, Japanese-French
UN CHAMBRE EN VILLE   UGC, 1982, French

B R I A N   D E   P A L M A *

b. September 11, 1940 - Newark, New Jersey
Agent: ICM - Los Angeles, 213/550-4000
Business Manager: Richard Roemer, 605 Third Avenue, New York, NY 10158,
    212/972-1100

MURDER A LA MOD   Aries, 1968
GREETINGS   Sigma III, 1968
THE WEDDING PARTY   co-director with Wilford Leach & Cynthia Munroe,
    Powell Productions Plus/Ondine, 1969
DIONYSUS IN '69   co-director with Robert Fiore & Bruce Rubin, Sigma III,
    1970
HI, MOM!   Sigma III, 1970
GET TO KNOW YOUR RABBIT   Warner Bros., 1972
SISTERS   American International, 1973
PHANTOM OF THE PARADISE   20th Century-Fox, 1974
OBSESSION   Columbia, 1976
CARRIE   United Artists, 1976
THE FURY   20th Century-Fox, 1978
HOME MOVIES   United Artists Classics, 1980
DRESSED TO KILL   Filmways, 1980
BLOW OUT   Filmways, 1981
SCARFACE   Universal, 1983

J A C Q U E S   D E R A Y

(Jacques Deray Desrayaud)

b. February 19, 1929 - Lyons, France
Contact: French Film Office, 745 Fifth Avenue, New York, NY 10151, 212/832-8860

LE GIGOLO   1960, French
RIFIFI IN TOKYO   MGM, 1961, French-Italian
PAR UN BEAU MATIN D'ETE   1964, French
SYMPHONY FOR A MASSACRE   7 Arts, 1965, French-Italian
THAT MAN GEORGE! *L'HOMME DE MARRAKECH*   Allied Artists, 1966,
    French-Italian-Spanish
AVEC LA PEAU AUTRES   1967, French
THE SWIMMING POOL   Avco Embassy, 1970, French-Italian
BORSALINO   Paramount, 1970, French-Italian
DOUCEMENT LES BASSES   1971, French
THE OUTSIDE MAN   United Artists, 1973, French-U.S.
BORSALINO AND CO.   Medusa, 1974, French-Italian
FLIC STORY   Adel Productions/Lira Films/Mondial, 1975, French
LE GANG   1977, French
UN PAPILLON SUR L'EPAULE   Action Films, 1978, French
TROIS HOMMES A ABBATRE   Adel Production/Films A2, 1980, French
LE MARGINAL   Gaumont, 1983, French

J O H N   D E R E K *

(Derek Harris)

b. August 12, 1926 - Hollywood, California
Contact: Directors Guild of America - Los Angeles, 213/656-1220

ONCE BEFORE I DIE   7 Arts, 1967, U.S.-Filipino
A BOY ... A GIRL   Jack Hanson, 1968
CHILDISH THINGS   Filmworld, 1969
AND ONCE UPON A TIME *FANTASIES*   Joseph Brenner Associates, 1973
TARZAN, THE APE MAN   MGM/United Artists, 1981
BOLERO   MGM/UA/Cannon, 1983

C A L E B   D E S C H A N E L *

b. September 21, 1944 - Philadelphia, Pennsylvania
Contact: Directors Guild of America - Los Angeles, 213/656-1220

THE ESCAPE ARTIST   Orion/Warner Bros., 1982

TOM DeSIMONE

CHATTERBOX   American International, 1977
HELL NIGHT   Compass International, 1981
THE CONCRETE JUNGLE   Pentagon, 1982

ANDRE DE TOTH *
(Endre Toth)

b. 1910 - Mako, Hungary
Home: 3690 Barham Blvd., Los Angeles, CA 90068, 213/874-3548
Agent: Ronald Lief, Contemporary-Korman Artists - Beverly Hills, 213/278-8250

TOPRINI NASZ   1939, Hungarian
OT ORA 40 1939, **Hungarian**
KET LANY AZ UTCAN   1939, Hungarian
SEMMELWEIS   1939, Hungarian
HAT HET BOLDOGSAG   1939, Hungarian
PASSPORT TO SUEZ   Columbia, 1943
NONE SHALL ESCAPE   Columbia, 1944
DARK WATERS   United Artists, 1944
RAMROD   United Artists, 1947
THE OTHER LOVER   United Artists, 1947
PITFALL   United Artists, 1948
SLATTERY'S HURRICANE   20th Century-Fox, 1949
MAN IN THE SADDLE   Columbia, 1951
CARSON CITY   Warner Bros., 1952
SPRINGFIELD RIFLE   Warner Bros., 1952
LAST OF THE COMANCHES   Columbia, 1952
HOUSE OF WAX   Warner Bros., 1953
THE STRANGER WORE A GUN   Columbia, 1953
THUNDER OVER THE PLAINS   Warner Bros., 1953
RIDING SHOTGUN   Warner Bros., 1954
THE CITY IS DARK   Warner Bros., 1954
THE BOUNTY HUNTER   Warner Bros., 1954
TANGANYIKA   Universal, 1954
THE INDIAN FIGHTER   United Artists, 1955
MONKEY ON MY BACK   United Artists, 1957
HIDDEN FEAR   United Artists, 1957
THE TWO-HEADED SPY   Columbia, 1959
DAY OF THE OUTLAW   United Artists, 1959
MAN ON A STRING   Columbia, 1960
MORGAN THE PIRATE   MGM, 1960, British
THE MONGOLS   Colorama, 1961, Italian
GOLD FOR THE CAESARS   Colorama, 1962, Italian
PLAY DIRTY   United Artists, 1968, British

JOHN DEXTER

b. 1935 - England
Contact: British Academy of Film & Television Arts, 195 Piccadilly, London W1,
    England, 01/734-0022

THE VIRGIN SOLDIERS   Columbia, 1970, British
PIGEONS *THE SIDELONG GLANCES OF A PIGEON KICKER*   MGM,
    1970
I WANT WHAT I WANT   Cinerama Releasing Corporation, 1972, British

MAURY DEXTER *

b. 1927
Home: 1384 Camino Magenta, Thousand Oaks, CA 91360, 805/498-0540
Business Manager: Hank Tani - Thousand Oaks, 805/498-0540

THE HIGH POWERED RIFLE   20th Century-Fox, 1960
WALK TALL   20th Century-Fox, 1960
THE PURPLE HILLS   20th Century-Fox, 1961
WOMAN HUNT   20th Century-Fox, 1961
THE FIREBRAND   20th Century-Fox, 1962
AIR PATROL   20th Century-Fox, 1962
THE DAY MARS INVADED EARTH   20th Century-Fox, 1962

continued

MAURY DEXTER*—continued
HOUSE OF THE DAMNED   20th Century-Fox, 1962
HARBOR LIGHTS   20th Century-Fox, 1963
THE YOUNG SWINGERS   20th Century-Fox, 1963
POLICE NURSE   20th Century-Fox, 1963
YOUNG GUNS OF TEXAS   20th Century-Fox, 1963
SURF PARTY   20th Century-Fox, 1963
RAIDERS FROM BENEATH THE SEA   20th Century-Fox, 1964
WILD ON THE BEACH   20th Century-Fox, 1965
THE NAKED BRIGADE   Universal, 1965
MARYJANE   American International, 1968
THE MINI-SKIRT MOB   American International, 1968
BORN WILD   American International, 1968
HELL'S BELLES   American International, 1969

MICHAEL DINNER

Agent: Jack Rapke, CAA - Los Angeles, 213/277-4545

MISS LONELYHEARTS   H. Jay Holman Productions/American Film Institute, 1983

IVAN DIXON *

b. April 6, 1931 - New York, New York
Home: 3432 N. Marengo Avenue, Altadena, CA 91001, 213/681-1327

TROUBLE MAN   20th Century-Fox, 1972
THE SPOOK WHO SAT BY THE DOOR   United Artists, 1973
LOVE IS NOT ENOUGH (TF)   Universal TV, 1978

EDWARD DMYTRYK *

b. September 4, 1908 - Grand Forks, Canada
Agent: Kurt Frings - Beverly Hills, 213/274-8883

THE HAWK   Herman Wohl, 1935
TELEVISION SPY   Paramount, 1939
EMERGENCY SQUAD   Paramount, 1940
MYSTERY SEA RAIDERS   Paramount, 1940
GOLDEN GLOVES   Paramount, 1940
HER FIRST ROMANCE   Monogram, 1940
THE DEVIL COMMANDS   Columbia, 1941
UNDER AGE   Columbia, 1941
SWEETHEART OF THE CAMPUS   Columbia, 1941
THE BLONDE FROM SINGAPORE   Columbia, 1941
CONFESSIONS OF BOSTON BLACKIE   Columbia, 1941
SECRETS OF THE LONE WOLF   Columbia, 1941
COUNTER ESPIONAGE   Columbia, 1942
SEVEN MILES FROM ALCATRAZ   RKO Radio, 1942
THE FALCON STRIKES BACK   RKO Radio, 1943
HITLER'S CHILDREN   RKO Radio, 1943
CAPTIVE WILD WOMAN   Universal, 1943
BEHIND THE RISING SUN   RKO Radio, 1943
TENDER COMRADE   RKO Radio, 1943
MURDER MY SWEET   RKO Radio, 1945
BACK TO BATAAN   RKO Radio, 1945
TILL THE END OF TIME   RKO Radio, 1945
CROSSFIRE ★   RKO Radio, 1947
SO WELL REMEMBERED   RKO Radio, 1947
THE HIDDEN ROOM *OBSESSION*   British Lion, 1949, British
GIVE US THIS DAY *SALT TO THE DEVIL*   Eagle Lion, 1949, British
MUTINY   Universal, 1952
THE SNIPER   Columbia, 1952
EIGHT IRON MEN   Columbia, 1952
THE JUGGLER   Columbia, 1953
THE CAINE MUTINY   Columbia, 1954
BROKEN LANCE   20th Century-Fox, 1954
THE END OF THE AFFAIR   Columbia, 1954
SOLDIER OF FORTUNE   20th Century-Fox, 1955
THE LEFT HAND OF GOD   20th Century-Fox, 1955

continued

EDWARD DMYTRYK*—continued

THE MOUNTAIN   Paramount, 1956
RAINTREE COUNTY   MGM, 1957
THE YOUNG LIONS   20th Century-Fox, 1958
WARLOCK   20th Century-Fox, 1959
THE BLUE ANGEL   20th Century-Fox, 1959
WALK ON THE WILD SIDE   Columbia, 1962
THE RELUCTANT SAINT   Davis-Royal, 1962, Italian-U.S.
THE CARPETBAGGERS   Paramount, 1963
WHERE LOVE HAS GONE   Paramount, 1964
MIRAGE   Universal, 1965
ALVAREZ KELLY   Columbia, 1966
ANZIO   Columbia, 1968, Italian
SHALAKO!   Cinerama Releasing Corporation, 1968, British
BLUEBEARD   Cinerama Releasing Corporation, 1972, Italian-French-West German
THE HUMAN FACTOR   Bryanston, 1974, British-U.S.
HE IS MY BROTHER   Atlantic Releasing Corporation, 1976

R O G E R   D O N A L D S O N

Contact: New Zealand Film Commission, P.O. Box 11-546, Wellington, New Zealand,
    4/72-2360

SLEEPING DOGS   1977, New Zealand
SMASH PALACE   Atlantic Releasing Corporation, 1981, New Zealand
THE BOUNTY   Orion, 1984, British

S T A N L E Y   D O N E N *

b. April 13, 1924 - Columbia, South Carolina
Agent: Stan Kamen, William Morris Agency - Beverly Hills, 213/274/7451
Business Manager: Edward Traubner, Traubner & Flynn, 2049 Century Park East -
    Suite 2500, Los Angeles, CA 90067, 213/859-4221

ON THE TOWN   co-director with Gene Kelly, MGM, 1949
ROYAL WEDDING   MGM, 1951
SINGIN' IN THE RAIN   co-director with Gene Kelly, MGM, 1952
LOVE IS BETTER THAN NONE   MGM, 1952
FEARLESS FAGAN   MGM, 1952
GIVE A GIRL A BREAK   MGM, 1953
SEVEN BRIDES FOR SEVEN BROTHERS   MGM, 1954
DEEP IN MY HEART   MGM, 1954
IT'S ALWAYS FAIR WEATHER   co-director with Gene Kelly, MGM, 1955
FUNNY FACE   Paramount, 1957
THE PAJAMA GAME   co-director with George Abbott, Warner Bros., 1957
KISS THEM FOR ME   20th Century-Fox, 1957
INDISCREET   Warner Bros., 1958, British
DAMN YANKEES   co-director with George Abbott, Warner Bros., 1958
ONCE MORE, WITH FEELING   Columbia, 1960
SURPRISE PACKAGE   Columbia, 1960
THE GRASS IS GREENER   Universal, 1961
CHARADE   Universal, 1964
ARABESQUE   Universal, 1966, British-U.S.
TWO FOR THE ROAD   20th Century-Fox, 1967, British-U.S.
BEDAZZLED   20th Century-Fox, 1967, British
STAIRCASE   20th Century-Fox, 1969, British
THE LITTLE PRINCE   Paramount, 1974, British
LUCKY LADY   20th Century-Fox, 1975
MOVIE MOVIE   Warner Bros., 1978
SATURN 3   AFD, 1980
BLAME IT ON RIO   20th Century-Fox, 1983

W A L T E R   D O N I G E R *

b. July 1, 1917 - New York, New York
Home: 555 Huntley Drive, Los Angeles, CA 90048, 213/659-2787
Business: Bettina Productions Ltd. - Burbank, 213/954-2748
Agent: Adams, Ray & Rosenberg - Los Angeles, 213/278-3000

DUFFY OF SAN QUENTIN   Warner Bros., 1953
THE STEEL CAGE   United Artists, 1954

continued

WALTER DONIGER*—continued

THE STEEL JUNGLE   Warner Bros., 1955
UNWED MOTHER   Allied Artists, 1958
HOUSE OF WOMEN   Warner Bros., 1960
SAFE AT HOME!   Columbia, 1962
MAD BULL   co-director with Len Steckler, Steckler Productions/Filmways, 1977
KENTUCKY WOMAN (TF)   Walter Doniger Productions/20th Century-Fox TV, 1983

CLIVE DONNER*

b. January 21, 1926 - London, England
Agent: William Morris Agency - Beverly Hills, 213/274-7451

THE SECRET PLACE   Rank, 1957, British
HEART OF A CHILD   Rank, 1958, British
MARRIAGE OF CONVENIENCE   Allied Artists, 1961, British
THE SINISTER MAN   Allied Artists, 1961, British
SOME PEOPLE   American International, 1962, British
THE GUEST *THE CARETAKER*   Janus, 1963, British
NOTHING BUT THE BEST   Royal Films International, 1964, British
WHAT'S NEW PUSSYCAT?   United Artists, 1965, British
LUV   Columbia, 1967
HERE WE GO ROUND THE MULBERRY BUSH   Lopert, 1968, British
ALFRED THE GREAT   MGM, 1969, British
OLD DRACULA *VAMPIRA*   American International, 1975, British
SPECTRE (TF)   20th Century-Fox TV, 1977
THE THIEF OF BAGHDAD (TF)   Palm Films Ltd., 1979, British
THE NUDE BOMB   Universal, 1980
CHARLIE CHAN THE CURSE OF THE DRAGON QUEEN   American Cinema, 1980
OLIVER TWIST (TF)   Claridge Group Ltd./Grafton Films, 1982, British
THE SCARLET PIMPERNEL (TF)   London Films Ltd., 1982, British
ARTHUR THE KING (TF)   Martin Poll Productions/Comworld Productions/Jadran Film, 1983. U.S.-Yugoslavian
TO CATCH A KING (CTF)   HBO Premiere Films/Entertainment Partners/Gaylord Productions, 1984

RICHARD DONNER*

Business Manager: Gerald Breslauer, Breslauer, Jacobson & Rutman - Los Angeles, 213/879-0167

X-15   United Artists, 1961
SALT AND PEPPER   United Artists, 1968, British
LOLA *TWINKY*   American International, 1970, British-Italian
LUCAS TANNER (TF)   Universal TV, 1974
SENIOR YEAR (TF)   Universal TV, 1974
A SHADOW IN THE STREETS (TF)   Playboy Productions, 1975
SARAH T. - PORTRAIT OF A TEENAGE ALCOHOLIC (TF)   Universal TV, 1975
THE OMEN   20th Century-Fox, 1976
SUPERMAN   Warner Bros., 1978, U.S.-British
INSIDE MOVES   AFD, 1980
THE TOY   Columbia, 1982
LADYHAWKE   Warner Bros., 1984

JACK DONOHUE*

b. November 3, 1908 - New York, New York
Home: 13900 Panay Way, Suite R204, Marina Del Rey, CA 90291
Business Manager: Elliot Wax - Los Angeles, 213/273-8217

CLOSE-UP   Eagle Lion, 1948
THE YELLOW CAB MAN   MGM, 1950
WATCH THE BIRDIE   MGM, 1951
LUCKY ME   Warner Bros., 1954
BABES IN TOYLAND   Buena Vista, 1961
MARRIAGE ON THE ROCKS   Warner Bros., 1965
ASSAULT ON A QUEEN   Paramount, 1965

TOM DONOVAN *

Business: Director's Service, Inc., 650 Park Avenue, New York, NY 10021,
212/737-6910
Attorney: Thomas H. Ryan - New York City, 212/355-7003

THE LAST BRIDE OF SALEM (TF)   20th Century-Fox TV, 1974
TRISTAN AND ISOLT   Clar Productions, 1981, British

ROBERT DORNHELM

THE CHILDREN OF THEATRE STREET (FD)   Peppercorn-Wormser, 1977
SHE DANCES ALONE   Continental, 1982, U.S.-Austrian, British
DIGITAL DREAMS   Ripple Productions Ltd., 1983, British

GORDON DOUGLAS *

b. December 5, 1909 - New York, New York
Home: 6600 West 6th Street, Los Angeles, CA 90048
Business Manager: Robert Stilwell, Ryder, Stilwell, Inc., P.O. Box 92920, Los
Angeles, CA 90009, 213/937-5500

GENERAL SPANKY   co-director with Fred Newmayer, MGM, 1936
ZENOBIA   United Artists, 1939
SAPS AT SEA   United Artists, 1940
ROAD SHOW   co-director with Hal Roach & Hal Roach, Jr., United Artists,
1941
BROADWAY LIMITED   United Artists, 1941
NIAGARA FALLS   United Artists, 1941
THE DEVIL WITH HITLER   RKO Radio, 1942
THE GREAT GILDERSLEEVE   RKO Radio, 1942
GILDERSLEEVE'S BAD DAY   RKO Radio, 1943
GILDERSLEEVE ON BROADWAY   RKO Radio, 1943
GILDERSLEEVE'S GHOST   RKO Radio, 1944
A NIGHT OF ADVENTURE   RKO Radio, 1944
GIRL RUSH   RKO Radio, 1944
THE FALCON IN HOLLYWOOD   RKO Radio, 1944
ZOMBIES ON BROADWAY   RKO Radio, 1945
FIRST YANK INTO TOKYO   RKO Radio, 1945
DICK TRACY VS. CUEBALL   RKO Radio, 1946
SAN QUENTIN   RKO Radio, 1946
IF YOU KNEW SUSIE   RKO Radio, 1948
THE BLACK ARROW   Columbia, 1948
WALK A CROOKED MILE   Columbia, 1948
MR. SOFT TOUCH   co-director with Henry Levin, Columbia, 1949
THE DOOLINS OF OKLAHOMA   Columbia, 1949
THE NEVADAN   Columbia, 1950
FORTUNES OF CAPTAIN BLOOD   Columbia, 1950
ROGUES OF SHERWOOD FOREST   Columbia, 1950
KISS TOMORROW GOODBYE   United Artists, 1950
BETWEEN MIDNIGHT AND DAWN   Columbia, 1950
THE GREAT MISSOURI RAID   Paramount, 1951
ONLY THE VALIANT   Warner Bros., 1951
I WAS A COMMUNIST FOR THE FBI   Warner Bros., 1951
COME FILL THE CUP   Warner Bros., 1951
MARU MARU   Warner Bros., 1952
THE IRON MISTRESS   Warner Bros., 1952
SHE'S BACK ON BROADWAY   Warner Bros., 1953
THE CHARGE AT FEATHER CREEK   Warner Bros., 1953
SO THIS IS LOVE   Warner Bros., 1953
THEM   Warner Bros., 1954
YOUNG AT HEART   Warner Bros., 1954
THE McCONNELL STORY   Warner Bros., 1955
SINCERELY YOURS   Warner Bros., 1955
SANTIAGO   Warner Bros., 1956
THE BIG LAND   Warner Bros., 1957
BOMBERS B-52   Warner Bros., 1957
FORT DOBBS   Warner Bros., 1958
THE FIEND WHO WALKED THE WEST   20th Century-Fox, 1958
UP PERISCOPE   Warner Bros., 1959
YELLOWSTONE KELLY   Warner Bros., 1959
GOLD OF THE SEVEN SAINTS   Warner Bros., 1961

continued

GORDON DOUGLAS*—continued

THE SINS OF RACHEL CADE   Warner Bros., 1961
CLAUDELLE INGLISH   Warner Bros., 1961
FOLLOW THAT DREAM   United Artists, 1962
CALL ME BWANA   United Artists, 1963
ROBIN AND THE SEVEN HOODS   Warner Bros., 1964
RIO CONCHOS   20th Century-Fox, 1964
SYLVIA   Paramount, 1965
HARLOW   Paramount, 1965
STAGECOACH   20th Century-Fox, 1966
WAY ... WAY OUT!   20th Century-Fox, 1966
IN LIKE FLINT   20th Century-Fox, 1967
CHUKA   Paramount, 1967
TONY ROME   20th Century-Fox, 1967
THE DETECTIVE   20th Century-Fox, 1968
LADY IN CEMENT   20th Century-Fox, 1968
SKULLDUGGERY   Universal, 1970
BARQUERO   United Artists, 1970
THEY CALL ME MISTER TIBBS!   United Artists, 1970
SLAUGHTER'S BIG RIP-OFF   American International, 1973
NEVADA SMITH (TF)   Rackin-Hayes Productions/Paramount TV, 1975
VIVA KNIEVEL!   Warner Bros., 1978

KIRK DOUGLAS*

(Issur Danielovitch)

b. December 9, 1916 - Amsterdam, New York
Business: The Bryna Company, 141 El Camino Drive, Beverly Hills, CA 90212,
    213/274-5294

SCALAWAG   Paramount, 1973, U.S.-Italian
POSSE   Paramount, 1975

NANCY DOWD

b. Framingham, Massachusetts
Contact: Writers Guild of America, West - Los Angeles, 213/550-1000

LOVE   co-director with Annette Cohen, Liv Ullmann & Mai Zetterling, Velvet
    Films, 1982, Canadian

ROBERT DOWNEY

b. June, 1936
Business: 8497 Crescent Drive, Los Angeles, CA 90046
Attorney: Franklin, Wienrib, Rudell - New York City, 212/489-0680

BABO 73   1963
CHAFED ELBOWS   Grove Press, 1965
NO MORE EXCUSES   Rogosin, 1968
PUTNEY SWOPE   Cinema 5, 1969
POUND   United Artists, 1970
GREASER'S PALACE   Greaser's Palace, 1972
MAD MAGAZINE PRESENTS UP THE ACADEMY   Warner Brothers, 1980
MOONBEAM   Analysis, 1983

STAN DRAGOTI*

Business: EUE-Screen Gems, 3701 Oak Street, Burbank, CA 91505, 213/843-3221
Agent: CAA - Los Angeles, 213/277-4545

DIRTY LITTLE BILLY   Columbia, 1972
LOVE AT FIRST BITE   American International, 1979
MR. MOM   20th Century-Fox, 1983

ARTHUR DREIFUSS *

b. March 25, 1908 - Frankfurt am Main, Germany
Home: 3950 Los Feliz Blvd., Los Angeles, CA 90027, 213/652-5262
Agent: George Michaud, George Michaud Agency - Encino, 213/981-6680

DOUBLE DEAL   International Road Shows, 1939
MYSTERY IN SWING   International Road Shows, 1940
REG'LAR FELLERS   Producers Releasing Corporation, 1941
BABY FACE MORGAN   Producers Releasing Corporation, 1942
THE BOSS OF BIG TOWN   Producers Releasing Corporation, 1942
THE PAY-OFF   Producers Releasing Corporation, 1942
SARONG GIRL   Monogram, 1943
MELODY PARADE   Monogram, 1943
CAMPUS RHYTHM   Monogram, 1943
NEARLY EIGHTEEN   Monogram, 1943
THE SULTAN'S DAUGHTER   Monogram, 1944
EVER SINCE VENUS   Columbia, 1944
EDDIE WAS A LADY   Columbia, 1945
BOSTON BLACKIE BOOKED ON SUSPICION   Columbia, 1945
BOSTON BLACKIE'S RENDEZVOUS   Columbia, 1945
THE GAY SENORITA   Columbia, 1945
PRISON SHIP   Columbia, 1945
JUNIOR PROM   Monogram, 1946
FREDDIE STEPS OUT   Monogram, 1946
HIGH SCHOOL HERO   Monogram, 1946
VACATION DAYS   Monogram, 1947
BETTY CO-ED   Columbia, 1947
LITTLE MISS BROADWAY   Columbia, 1947
TWO BLONDES AND A REDHEAD   Columbia, 1947
SWEET GENEVIEVE   Columbia, 1947
GLAMOUR GIRL   Columbia, 1948
MARY LOU   Columbia, 1948
I SURRENDER DEAR   Columbia, 1948
AN OLD-FASHIONED GIRL   Eagle Lion, 1948
MANHATTAN ANGEL   Columbia, 1948
ALL AMERICAN PRO   Columbia, 1948
SHAMROCK HILL   Eagle Lion, 1949
THERE'S A GIRL IN MY HEART   Allied Artists, 1949
SECRET FILE   Triangle, 1955
ASSIGNMENT ABROAD   Triangle, 1956
LIFE BEGINS AT 17   Columbia, 1958
THE LAST BLITZKRIEG   Columbia, 1959
JUKE BOX RHYTHM   Columbia, 1959
THE QUARE FELLOW   Astor, 1962, Irish-British
RIOT ON SUNSET STRIP   American International, 1967
THE LOVE-INS   Columbia, 1967
FOR SINGLES ONLY   Columbia, 1968
A TIME TO SING   MGM, 1968
THE YOUNG RUNAWAYS   MGM, 1968

DAVID DRURY

Contact: British Academy of Film & Television Arts, 195 Piccadilly, London W1,
    England, 01/734-0022

FOREVER YOUNG   Enigma Productions, 1983, British

CHARLES S. DUBIN *

b. February 1, 1919 - New York, New York
Home: 651 Lorna Lane, Los Angeles, CA 90049
Agent: Bill Haber, CAA - Los Angeles, 213/277-4545

MISTER ROCK & ROLL   Paramount, 1957
TO DIE IN PARIS (TF)   co-director with Allen Reisner, Universal TV, 1968
MURDER ONCE REMOVED (TF)   Metromedia Productions, 1971
MURDOCK'S GANG (TF)   Don Fedderson Productions, 1973
MOVING VIOLATION   20th Century-Fox, 1976
THE DEADLY TRIANGLE (TF)   Columbia TV, 1977
TOPPER (TF)   Cosmo Productions/Robert A. Papazian Productions, 1979
ROOTS: THE NEXT GENERATIONS (MS)   co-director with John Erman, Lloyd
    Richards & Georg Stanford Brown, Wolper Productions, 1979

continued

CHARLES S. DUBIN*—continued

THE GATHERING, PART II (TF)   Hanna-Barbera Productions, 1979
THE MANIONS OF AMERICA (MS)   co-director with Joseph Sargent, Roger
    Gimbel Productions/EMI TV/Argonaut Films Ltd., 1981
MY PALIKARI (TF)   Center for TV in the Humanities, 1982

R O G E R   D U C H O W N Y *

Home: 5310 York Hill Drive, Hood River, Oregon 97031
Agent: CAA - Los Angeles, 213/277-4545

MURDER CAN HURT YOU! (TF)   Aaron Spelling Productions, 1970

P E T E R   J O H N   D U F F E L L

Agent: Merrily Kane Agency - Beverly Hills, 213/550-8874

PARTNERS IN CRIME   Allied Artists, 1961, British
THE HOUSE THAT DRIPPED BLOOD   Cinerama Releasing Corporation, 1971,
    British
ENGLAND MADE ME   Cine Globe, 1973, British
INSIDE OUT   Warner Bros., 1976, British
CAUGHT ON A TRAIN (TF)   BBC, 1980
EXPERIENCE PREFERRED, BUT NOT ESSENTIAL   The Samuel Goldwyn
    Company, 1983, British
THE FAR PAVILIONS (CMS)   Geoff Reeve & Associates/Goldcrest, 1984,
    British

M I C H A E L   D U G A N

MAUSOLEUM   MPM, 1983

J O H N   D U I G A N

Home Address: 57 Gipps Street, Balmain, NSW, 2041, Australia, 02/827-2756

THE FIRM MAN   John Duigan Productions, 1975, Australian
THE TRESPASSERS   Vega Film Productions, 1976, Australian
MOUTH TO MOUTH   1978, Australian
DIMBOOLA   Ko-An Productions, 1979, Australian
WINTER OF OUR DREAMS   Satori, 1981, Australian
FAR EAST   Filmco Australia, 1983, Australian
ONE NIGHT STAND   Astra Film Productions/Hoyts-Edgely, 1984, Australian

D A R Y L   D U K E *

b. Vancouver, Canada
Address: 4220 Evergreen Avenue, West Vancouver V7V 1H1, Canada,
    604/987-5029
Agent: Jack Gilardi, ICM - Los Angeles, 213/550-4000

THE SASKATCHEWAN (TF)   CBC, 1965, Canadian
THE PSYCHIATRIST: GOD BLESS THE CHILDREN (TF)   Universal TV,
    1970
PAYDAY   Cinerama Releasing Corporation, 1972
HAPPINESS IS A WARM CLUE (TF)   Universal TV, 1973
THE PRESIDENT'S PLANE IS MISSING (TF)   ABC Circle Films, 1973
I HEARD THE OWL CALL MY NAME (TF)   Tomorrow Entertainment, 1973
A CRY FOR HELP (TF)   Universal TV, 1975
THEY ONLY COME OUT AT NIGHT (TF)   MGM TV, 1975
GRIFFIN AND PHOENIX (TF)   ABC Circle Films, 1976
THE SILENT PARTNER   EMC Film/Aurora, 1979, Canadian
HARD FEELINGS   Astral Bellevue, 1981, Canadian
THE THORN BIRDS (MS)☆   David L. Wolper-Stan Margulies Productions/
    Edward Lewis Productions/Warner Brothers TV, 1983

R U D Y D U R A N D *

Business: Koala Productions, Ltd., 361 N. Canon Drive, Beverly Hills, CA 90212,
213/476-1649
Attorney: Greg Bautzer, Wyman, Rothman, Bautzer & Kuchel, 2049 Century Park
East, Los Angeles, CA 90067, 213/550-8000

TILT   Warner Bros., 1979

R O B E R T D U V A L L

b. January 5, 1931 - San Diego, California
Agent: Fred Specktor, CAA - Los Angeles, 213/277-4545
Personal Manager: 703/548-8100

WE'RE NOT THE JET SET (FD)   1975
ANGELO, MY LOVE   Cinecom International, 1983

B O B D Y L A N

(Robert Zimmerman)

b. May 24, 1941 - Duluth, Minnesota

RENALDO AND CLARA   Circuit, 1978

C H A R L E S E A S T M A N *

Messages: 213/376-0251
Agent: Michael Black/Jane Sindell, ICM - Los Angeles, 213/550-4000

THE ALL-AMERICAN BOY   Warner Bros., 1973

C L I N T E A S T W O O D *

b. May 31, 1930 - San Francisco, California
Business: Malpaso Productions, 1900 Avenue of the Stars - Suite 2270, Los
Angeles, CA 90067, 213/277-1900
Agent: Leonard Hirshan, William Morris Agency - Beverly Hills, 213/274-7451

PLAY MISTY FOR ME   Universal, 1971
HIGH PLAINS DRIFTER   Universal, 1972
BREEZY   Universal, 1973
THE EIGER SANCTION   Universal, 1974
THE OUTLAW JOSEY WALES   Warner Bros., 1976
THE GAUNTLET   Warner Bros., 1977
BRONCO BILLY   Warner Bros., 1980
FIREFOX   Warner Bros., 1982
HONKYTONK MAN   Warner Bros., 1982
SUDDEN IMPACT   Warner Bros., 1983

B L A K E   E D W A R D S *

b. July 26, 1922 - Tulsa, Oklahoma
Agent: Martin Baum, CAA - Los Angeles, 213/277-4545

BRING YOUR SMILE ALONG   Columbia, 1955
HE LAUGHED LAST   Columbia, 1956
MISTER CORY   MGM, 1957
THIS HAPPY FEELING   Universal, 1958
THE PERFECT FURLOUGH   Universal, 1959
OPERATION PETTICOAT   Universal, 1959
HIGH TIME   20th Century-Fox, 1960
BREAKFAST AT TIFFANY'S   Paramount, 1961
EXPERIMENT IN TERROR   Warner Bros., 1962
DAYS OF WINE AND ROSES   Warner Bros., 1962
THE PINK PANTHER   United Artists, 1964
A SHOT IN THE DARK   United Artists, 1964
THE GREAT RACE   Warner Bros., 1965
WHAT DID YOU DO IN THE WAR, DADDY?   United Artists, 1966
GUNN   Warner Bros., 1967
THE PARTY   United Artists, 1968
DARLING LILI   Paramount, 1970
WILD ROVERS   MGM, 1971
THE CAREY TREATMENT   MGM, 1972
THE TAMARIND SEED   Avco Embassy, 1974
RETURN OF THE PINK PANTHER   United Artists, 1975, British
THE PINK PANTHER STRIKES AGAIN   United Artists, 1976, British
REVENGE OF THE PINK PANTHER   United Artists, 1978, British
10   Orion/Warner Bros., 1979
S.O.B.   Paramount, 1981
VICTOR/VICTORIA   MGM/United Artists, 1982
TRAIL OF THE PINK PANTHER   MGM/UA, 1982
CURSE OF THE PINK PANTHER   MGM/UA, 1983
THE MAN WHO LOVED WOMEN   Columbia, 1983

V I N C E N T   E D W A R D S *

(Vincent Edward Zoimo)

b. July 9, 1928 - New York, New York
Agent: David Shapira & Associates - Sherman Oaks, 213/906-0322

MANEATER   Universal TV, 1973

J A N   E G L E S O N

BILLY IN THE LOWLANDS   Theatre Company of Boston, 1979
THE DARK END OF THE STREET   First Run Features, 1981
LITTLE SISTER (TF)   Shefida Productions, 1984

R O B E R T   E L F S T R O M

THE NASHVILLE SOUND (FD)   co-director with David Hoffman, 1970
JOHNNY CASH! THE MAN, HIS WORLD, HIS MUSIC (FD)   Continental,
     1970
PETE SEEGER ... A SONG AND A STONE (FD)   Theatre Exchange, 1972
THE GOSPEL ROAD   20th Century-Fox, 1973
MYSTERIES OF THE SEA (FD)   co-director with Al Giddings, Polygram
     Pictures/Ocean Films Ltd., 1980
MOSES PENDLETON PRESENTS MOSES PENDLETON (FD)   ABC Video
     Enterprises, 1982

LARRY ELIKANN *

b. July 4, 1923 - New York, New York
Business: The Larry Elikann Company, Inc., 100 S. Doheny Drive, Los Angeles,
   CA 90048, 213/271-4406
Agent: Bob Goodman, William Morris Agency - Beverly Hills, 213/274-7451

THE GREAT WALLENDAS (TF)   Daniel Wilson Productions, 1978
CHARLIE AND THE GREAT BALLOON CHASE (TF)   Daniel Wilson
   Productions, 1981

LANG ELLIOTT *

b. 1950 - Los Angeles, California
Home: 77 Chaumont Square, Atlanta, GA 30327, 404/352-0417
Business Manager: Myron Slobedien, Loeb & Loeb, 10100 Santa Monica Blvd. -
   Suite 2200, Los Angeles, CA 90067, 213/552-7765

THE PRIVATE EYES   New World, 1980

ROBERT ENDERS

Agent: Peter Crouch Associates, 59 Frith Street, London W1, England, 01/734-
   2167

STEVIE   First Artists, 1978, British

CY ENDFIELD

b. November, 1914 - South Africa
Contact: British Academy of Film & Television Arts, 195 Piccadilly, London W1,
   England, 01/734-0022

GENTLEMAN JOE PALOOKA   Monogram, 1946
STORK BITES MAN   United Artists, 1947, British
THE ARGYLE SECRETS   Film Classics, 1948, British
JOE PALOOKA IN THE BIG FIGHT   Monogram, 1949
THE UNDERWORLD STORY   United Artists, 1950
THE SOUND OF FURY   United Artists, 1950
TARZAN'S SAVAGE FURY   RKO Radio, 1952
COLONEL MARCH INVESTIGATES   Criterion, 1953, British
THE MASTER PLAN   directed under pseudonym of Hugh Raker, Astor, 1954,
   British
THE SECRET   Eros, 1955, British
CHILD IN THE HOUSE   Eros, 1956, British
HELL DRIVERS   Rank, 1957, British
SEA FURY   Lopert, 1958, British
JET STORM   United Producers Organization, 1959, British
MYSTERIOUS ISLAND   Columbia, 1961, British
HIDE AND SEEK   Universal, 1964, British
ZULU   Embassy, 1964, British
SANDS OF THE KALAHARI   Paramount, 1965, British
DE SADE   American International, 1969, U.S.-West German
UNIVERSAL SOLDIER   Hemdale, 1971, British

GEORGE ENGLUND *

b. June 22, 1926 - Washington, D.C.
Business: George Englund Productions, 4000 Warner Blvd., Burbank, CA 91522,
   213/954-3647
Business Manager: Dave Flynn, Traubner & Flynn, 2049 Century Park East - Suite
   2500, Los Angeles, CA 90067, 213/859-4221

THE UGLY AMERICAN   Universal, 1963
SIGNPOST TO MURDER   MGM, 1965
ZACHARIAH   Cinerama Releasing Corporation, 1970
SNOW JOB   Warner Bros., 1972
A CHRISTMAS TO REMEMBER (TF)   George Englund Productions, 1978
DIXIE: CHANGING HABITS (TF)   George Englund Productions, 1983

ROBERT ENRICO

b. April 13, 1931 - Lievin, France
Contact: French Film Office, 745 Fifth Avenue, New York, NY 10151, 212/832-
8860

AU COEUR DE LA VIE   1962, French
LA BELLE VIE   1963, French
THE WISE GUYS   Universal, 1965, French
THE LAST ADVENTURE *I TRE AVVENTURIERI*   Universal, 1969, Italian-
French
ZITA   Regional, 1968, French
HO!   1968, French
UN PEU ... BEAUCOUP ... PASSIONEMENT   1971, French
BOULEVARD DU RHUM   1972, French
LES CAIDS   1972, French
LE COMPAGNON INDESIRABLE   1973, French
LE SECRET   Cinema National, 1974, French
THE OLD GUN   Surrogate, 1976, French
COUP DE FOUDRE   1978, French
UN NEVEU SILENCIEUX   1978, French
IMPRINT OF GIANTS   Filmel/SNC/FR3, 1979, French
HEADS OR TAILS   Castle Hill, 1980, French
FOR THOSE I LOVED   20th Century-Fox, 1983, Canadian-French

JOHN ERMAN *

b. Chicago, Illinois
Agent: Bill Haber, CAA - Los Angeles, 213/277-4545
Business Manager: Plant & Cohen, 10900 Wilshire Blvd. - Suite 900, Los Angeles,
CA 90024, 213/824-2200

MAKING IT   20th Century-Fox, 1971
ACE ELI AND RODGER OF THE SKIES   directed under pseudonym of Bill
Sampson, 20th Century-Fox, 1973
LETTERS FROM THREE LOVERS (TF)   Spelling-Goldberg Productions, 1973
GREEN EYES (TF)   ABC, 1977
ROOTS (MS) ☆   co-director with David Greene, Marvin J. Chomsky & Gilbert
Moses, Wolper Productions, 1977
ALEXANDER: THE OTHER SIDE OF DAWN (TF)   Douglas Cramer
Productions, 1977
JUST ME & YOU (TF)   Roger Gimbel Productions/EMI, 1978
ROOTS: THE NEXT GENERATIONS (MS)   co-director with Charles S. Dubin,
Lloyd Richards & Georg Stanford Brown, Wolper Productions, 1979
MY OLD MAN (TF)   Zeitman-McNichol-Halmi Productions, 1979
MOVIOLA (MS) ☆   David L. Wolper-Stan Margulies Productions/Warner Bros.
TV, 1980
THE LETTER (TF)   Hajeno Productions/Warner Bros. TV, 1982
ELEANOR, FIRST LADY OF THE WORLD (TF)   Murbill Productions/Embassy
TV, 1982
ANOTHER WOMAN'S CHILD (TF)   CBS Entertainment, 1983
WHO WILL LOVE MY CHILDREN? (TF) ☆☆   ABC Circle Films, 1983
A STREETCAR NAMED DESIRE (TF)   Keith Barish Productions, 1983

RICHARD EYRE

Contact: Directors Guild of Great Britain, 56 Whitfield Street, London W1, England,
01/580-9592

THE PLOUGHMAN'S LUNCH   The Samuel Goldwyn Company, 1983, British
LOOSE CONNECTIONS   Umbrella Films/Virgin Films/NFFC, 1983, British

FERDINAND FAIRFAX

b. August 1, 1944 - London, England
Address: 62 Leathwaite Road, London SW11 6RS, England, 01/228-5339
Agent: Duncan Heath Associates - London, 01/937-9898

THE SPEED KING (TF)   BBC, British
WINSTON CHURCHILL - THE WILDERNESS YEARS (MS)   Southern
    Pictures Productions, 1983, British
NATE AND HAYES   Paramount, 1983, New Zealand

HARRY FALK *

Agent: William Morris Agency - Beverly Hills, 213/274-7451

THREE'S A CROWD (TF)   Screen Gems/Columbia TV, 1969
THE DEATH SQUAD (TF)   Spelling-Goldberg Productions, 1974
MEN OF THE DRAGON (TF)   Wolper Productions, 1974
THE ABDUCTION OF SAINT ANNE (TF)   QM Productions, 1975
MANDRAKE (TF)   Universal TV, 1979
CENTENNIAL (MS)   co-director with Bernard McEveety & Virgil Vogel, Universal
    TV, 1980
THE NIGHT THE CITY SCREAMED (TF)   David Gerber Company, 1980
THE CONTENDER (TF)   co-director with Lou Antonio, Universal TV, 1980
THE SOPHISTICATED GENTS (TF)   Daniel Wilson Productions, 1981
ADVICE TO THE LOVELORN (TF)   Universal TV, 1981
HEAR NO EVIL (TF)   Paul Pompian Productions/MGM TV, 1982
EMERALD POINT, N.A.S. (TF)   Richard and Esther Shapiro Productions/20th
    Century-Fox TV, 1983

JAMAA FANAKA

WELCOME HOME, BROTHER CHARLES   Crown International, 1975
EMMA MAE   Pro-International, 1977
PENITENTIARY   Jerry Gross Organization, 1980
PENITENTIARY II   MGM/UA, 1982

JAMES FARGO *

b. August 4, 1938 - Republic, Washington
Agent: Martin Shapiro, Shapiro-Lichtman Agency - Los Angeles, 213/557-2244
Business Manager: Howard Bernstein, Kaufman & Bernstein, 1900 Avenue of the
    Stars, Los Angeles, CA 90067, 213/277-1900

THE ENFORCER   Warner Bros., 1976
EVERY WHICH WAY BUT LOOSE   Warner Bros., 1978
CARAVANS   Universal, 1979, U.S.-Iranian
GAME FOR VULTURES   New Line Cinema, 1980, British
FORCED VENGEANCE   MGM/United Artists, 1982

FEDERICO FELLINI

b. January 20, 1920 - Rimini, Italy
Contact: Ministry of Tourism & Education, Via Della Ferratella, No. 51, 00184
    Rome, Italy, 06/7732

VARIETY LIGHTS   co-director with Alberto Lattuada, Pathe Contemporary,
    1950, Italian
THE WHITE SHEIK   Pathe Contemporary, 1952, Italian
I VITTELONI   API Productions, 1953, Italian
LOVE IN THE CITY   co-director with Michelangelo Antonioni, Alberto Lattuada,
    Carlo Lizzani, Francesco Maselli & Dino Risi, Italian Films Export, 1953, Italian
LA STRADA   Trans-Lux, 1954, Italian
IL BIDONE   Astor, 1955, Italian
NIGHTS OF CABIRIA   Lopert, 1957, Italian
LA DOLCE VITA ★   Astor, 1960, Italian
BOCCACCIO '70   co-director with Luchino Visconti & Vittorio De Sica,
    Embassy, 1962, Italian
8½ ★   Embassy, 1963, Italian
JULIET OF THE SPIRITS   Rizzoli, 1965, Italian-French-West German
SPIRITS OF THE DEAD *HISTOIRES EXTRAORDINAIRES*   co-director with
    Roger Vadim & Louis Malle, American International, 1969, French-Italian
FELLINI SATYRICON ★   United Artists, 1970, Italian-French
THE CLOWNS   Levitt-Pickman, 1971, Italian-French-West German, originally
    made for television
FELLINI'S ROMA   United Artists, 1972, Italian-French
AMARCORD ★   New World, 1974, Italian
CASANOVA *IL CASANOVA DI FEDERICO FELLINI*   Universal, 1977, Italian
ORCHESTRA REHEARSAL   New Yorker, 1979, Italian-West German, originally
    made for television
CITY OF WOMEN   New Yorker, 1981, Italian-French
AND THE SHIP SAILS ON   Triumph/Columbia, 1983, Italian-French

GEORG J. FENADY*

b. July 2, 1930 - Toledo, Ohio
Home: 602 N. Cherokee, Los Angeles, CA 90004, 213/466-5001
Business Manager: Mike Merrick - Los Angeles, 213/278-5354

ARNOLD   Cinerama Releasing Corporation, 1974
TERROR IN THE WAX MUSEUM   Cinerama Releasing Corporation, 1974
THE NIGHT THE BRIDGE FELL DOWN (TF)   Irwin Allen Productions/Warner
    Bros. TV, 1983
CAVE-IN! (TF)   Irwin Allen Productions/Warner Bros. TV, 1983

ABEL FERRARA

DRILLER KILLER   Rochelle Films, 1979
MS. 45   Rochelle Films, 1981
FEAR CITY   Bruce Cohn Curtis-Rebecca Productions, 1983

JOSE FERRER*
(Jose Vincente Ferrer de Otero y Cintron)

b. January 8, 1912 - Santurce, Puerto Rico
Business: 2 Penn Plaza - Suite 1825, New York, NY 10001, 212/947-9930

THE SHRIKE   Universal, 1955
THE COCKLESHELL HEROES   Columbia, 1956, British
THE GREAT MAN   Universal, 1956
I ACCUSE!   MGM, 1958
THE HIGH COST OF LOVING   MGM, 1958
RETURN TO PEYTON PLACE   20th Century-Fox, 1961
STATE FAIR   20th Century-Fox, 1962

MEL FERRER

b. August 25, 1917 - Elberon, New Jersey

THE GIRL OF THE LIMBERLOST   Columbia, 1945
VENDETTA   RKO Radio, 1950

continued

MEL FERRER—continued

THE SECRET FURY   RKO Radio, 1950
GREEN MANSIONS   MGM, 1959
CABRIOLA   Columbia, 1966, Spanish

MARCO FERRERI

b. May 11, 1928 - Milan, Italy
Contact: Ministry of Tourism & Education, Via Della Ferratella, No. 51, 00184
     Rome, Italy, 06/7732

EL PISITO   1958, Spanish
LOS CHICOS   1959, Spanish
EL COCHECITO   1960, Spanish
LE ITALIANE E L'AMORE   co-director with 11 others, Magic Film, 1961,
     Italian
THE CONJUGAL BED   *UNA STORIA MODERNA: L'APE
     REGINA*   Embassy, 1963, Italian-French
THE APE WOMAN   Embassy, 1964, Italian
CONTROSESSO   co-director with Franco Rossi, Jacques Romain, Gianni Puccini
     & Mino Guerrini, Adelphia Cinematografica/France Cinema Production, 1964,
     Italian-French
KISS THE OTHER SHEIK   *OGGI, DOMANI E DOPODEMANI*   co-director
     with Eduardo de Felippo & Luciano Salce, MGM, 1965, Italian-French
MARCIA NUNZIALE   Sancro Film/Transinter Film, 1966, Italian-French
L'HAREM   Sancro Film, 1967, Italian
THE MAN WITH THE BALLOONS   Sigma III, 1968, French-Italian
DILLINGER E MORTO   Pegaso Film, 1969, Italian
THE SEED OF MAN   SRL, 1970, Italian
L'UDIENZA   Vides, 1971, Italian
LIZA   Horizon, 1972, French-Italian
LA GRANDE BOUFFE   ABKCO, 1973, French-Italian
TOUCHEZ PAS LA FEMME BLANCHE   1974, French-Italian
THE LAST WOMAN   Columbia, 1976, Italian-French
BYE BYE MONKEY   Fida, 1978, Italian
CHIEDO ASILO   Gaumont, 1979, Italian-French-Tahitian
NO CHILD'S LAND   Sacis, 1980, Italian-French
TALES OF ORDINARY MADNESS   Fred Baker Films, 1983, Italian-French
THE STORY OF PIERA   UGC, 1983, Italian-French-West German
IL FUTURO E DONNA   Faso Film, 1984, Italian

KEN FINKLEMAN *

Contact: Directors Guild of America - Los Angeles, 213/656-1220

AIRPLANE II: THE SEQUEL   Paramount, 1983

ALBERT FINNEY

b. May 9, 1936 - Salford, England
Agent: ICM - Los Angeles, 213/550-4000

CHARLIE BUBBLES   Regional, 1968, British

SAM FIRSTENBERG

b. Israel

ONE MORE CHANCE   Cannon, 1981
REVENGE OF THE NINJA   MGM/UA/Cannon, 1983
NINJA III: THE DOMINATION   MGM/UA/Cannon, 1984

MAX FISCHER

Contact: Canadian Film & Television Association, 8 King Street, Toronto, Ontario
     M5C 1B5, Canada, 416/363-0296

THE LUCKY STAR   Pickman Films, 1981, Canadian
THE MAN IN 5A   Neighbour Film Inc., 1983, Canadian

BERND FISCHERAUER

Contact: German Film & TV Academy, Pommernallee 1, 1000 Berlin 19, West
   Germany, 030/303-6212

BLOOD AND HONOR: YOUTH UNDER HITLER (MS)   Daniel Wilson
   Productions/SWF Baden Baden/Taurus Film, 1982, U.S.-West German

DAVID FISHELSON

CITY NEWS   co-director with Zoe Zinman, Cinecom International, 1983

DAVID FISHER

LIAR'S MOON   Crown International, 1982

JACK FISK *

b. December 19, 1945 - Ipava, Illinois
Agent: Rick Nicita, CAA - Los Angeles, 213/277-4545

RAGGEDY MAN   Universal, 1981

RICHARD FLEISCHER *

b. December 8, 1916 - Brooklyn, New York
Agent: Phil Gersh, The Gersh Agency - Beverly Hills, 213/274-6611

CHILD OF DIVORCE   RKO Radio, 1946
BANJO   RKO Radio, 1947
DESIGN FOR DEATH   RKO Radio, 1948
SO THIS IS NEW YORK   United Artists, 1948
BODYGUARD   Columbia, 1948
MAKE MINE LAUGHS   RKO Radio, 1949
THE CLAY PIGEON   RKO Radio, 1949
FOLLOW ME QUIETLY   RKO Radio, 1949
TRAPPED   Eagle Lion, 1949
ARMORED CAR ROBBERY   RKO Radio, 1950
THE NARROW MARGIN   RKO Radio, 1952
THE HAPPY TIME   Columbia, 1952
ARENA   MGM, 1953
20,000 LEAGUES UNDER THE SEA   Buena Vista, 1954
VIOLENT SATURDAY   20th Century-Fox, 1955
THE GIRL IN THE RED VELVET SWING   20th Century-Fox, 1955
BANDIDO   United Artists, 1956
BETWEEN HEAVEN AND HELL   20th Century-Fox, 1956
THE VIKINGS   United Artists, 1958
THESE THOUSAND HILLS   20th Century-Fox, 1959
COMPULSION   20th Century-Fox, 1959
CRACK IN THE MIRROR   20th Century-Fox, 1960
THE BIG GAMBLE   20th Century-Fox, 1961
BARABBAS   Columbia, 1962, Italian
FANTASTIC VOYAGE   20th Century-Fox, 1966
DR. DOLITTLE   20th Century-Fox, 1967
THE BOSTON STRANGLER   20th Century-Fox, 1968
CHE!   20th Century-Fox, 1969
TORA! TORA! TORA!   co-director with Kinji Fukasaku, 20th Century-Fox,
   1970, U.S.-Japanese
10 RILLINGTON PLACE   Columbia, 1971, British
SEE NO EVIL   Columbia, 1971, British
THE LAST RUN   MGM, 1971
THE NEW CENTURIONS   Columbia, 1972
SOYLENT GREEN   MGM, 1972
THE DON IS DEAD   Universal, 1973
THE SPIKES GANG   United Artists, 1974
MR. MAJESTYK   United Artists, 1974
MANDINGO   Paramount, 1975
THE INCREDIBLE SARAH   Reader's Digest, 1976, British
CROSSED SWORDS *THE PRINCE AND THE PAUPER*   Warner Bros.,
   1978, British

continued

RICHARD FLEISCHER*—continued
ASHANTI   Columbia, 1970, Swiss-U.S.
THE JAZZ SINGER   AFD, 1980
TOUGH ENOUGH   20th Century-Fox, 1983
AMITYVILLE 3-D   Orion, 1983
CONAN, KING OF THIEVES   Universal, 1984

G O R D O N   F L E M Y N G

b. March 7, 1934 - Glasgow, Scotland
Address: 1 Albert Road, Wilmslow, Cheshire, England
Contact: Directors Guild of Great Britain, 56 Whitfield Street, London W1, England,
   01/580-9592

SOLD FOR SPARROW   Schoenfield, 1962, British
FIVE TO ONE   Allied Artists, 1963, British
JUST FOR FUN   Columbia, 1963
DR. WHO AND THE DALEKS   Continental, 1966, British
DALEKS - INVASION EARTH 2150 A.D.   Continental, 1966, British
THE SPLIT   MGM, 1968
GREAT CATHERINE   Warner Bros., 1968, British
THE LAST GRENADE   Cinerama Releasing Corporation, 1970, British
MIRAGE (TF)   Granada TV, 1978, British

T H E O D O R E   J .   F L I C K E R *

b. June 6, 1930 - Freehold, New Jersey
Business Manager: Freedman, Kinzelberg & Broder, 1801 Avenue of the Stars, Los
   Angeles, CA 90067, 213/277-0700

THE TROUBLEMAKER   Janus, 1964
THE PRESIDENT'S ANALYST   Paramount, 1967
UP IN THE CELLAR   American International, 1970
PLAYMATES (TF)   ABC Circle Films, 1972
GUESS WHO'S SLEEPING IN MY BED? (TF)   ABC Circle Films, 1973
JUST A LITTLE INCONVENIENCE (TF)   Universal TV, 1977
JACOB TWO-TWO MEETS THE HOODED FANG   Cinema Shares
   International, 1978, Canadian
LAST OF THE GOOD GUYS (TF)   Columbia TV, 1978
WHERE THE LADIES GO (TF)   Universal TV, 1980
SOGGY BOTTOM, U.S.A.   Cinemax Marketing & Distribution, 1981

J O H N   F L Y N N *

Home: 574 Latimer Road, Santa Monica, CA 90402, 213/454-6850
Agent: Jack Gilardi/Jeff Berg, ICM - Los Angeles, 213/550-4000
Business Manager: Paul Shaw, 2800 Olympic Blvd. - Suite 202, Santa Monica,
   CA 90404, 213/829-6805

THE SERGEANT   Warner Bros., 1968
THE JERUSALEM FILE   MGM, 1972, U.S.-Israeli
THE OUTFIT   MGM, 1974
ROLLING THUNDER   American International, 1978
DEFIANCE   American International, 1980
MARILYN: THE UNTOLD STORY (TF)   co-director with Jack Arnold &
   Lawrence Schiller, Lawrence Schiller Productions, 1980
TOUCHED   International Film Marketing, 1983

L A W R E N C E   D .   F O L D E S

b. November 4, 1959 - Los Angeles, California
Business: Star Cinema Production Group, Inc., 6253 Hollywood Blvd. - Suite 922,
   Los Angeles, CA 90028, 213/463-2000
Attorney: Ronald G. Gabler, 2029 Century Park East - Suite 1690, Los Angeles,
   CA 90067, 213/553-8848

MALIBU HIGH   Crown International, 1979
DON'T GO NEAR THE PARK   Cannon, 1981
THE GREAT SKYCOPTER RESCUE   Cannon, 1982
YOUNG WARRIORS   MGM/UA/Cannon, 1983

JAMES FOLEY

Contact: Writers Guild of America, West - Los Angeles, 213/550-1000

RECKLESS   MGM/UA, 1983

PETER FONDA*

b. February 23, 1939 - New York, New York
Agent: F.A.M.E. - Los Angeles, 213/656-7590
Business Manager: Nanas, Stern, Biers & Co. - Beverly Hills, 213/273-2501

THE HIRED HAND   Universal, 1971
IDAHO TRANSFER   Cinemation, 1975
WANDA NEVADA   United Artists, 1979

BRYAN FORBES*

b. July 22, 1926 - Stratford-Atte-Bow, England
Business: Pinewood Studios, Iver Heath, Bucks, England
Agent: William Morris Agency - Beverly Hills, 213/274-7451

WHISTLE DOWN THE WIND   Pathe-America, 1962, British
THE L-SHAPED ROOM   Columbia, 1963, British
SEANCE ON A WET AFTERNOON   Artixo, 1964, British
KING RAT   Columbia, 1965, British
THE WRONG BOX   Columbia, 1966, British
THE WHISPERERS   United Artists, 1967, British
DEADFALL   20th Century-Fox, 1968, British
THE MADWOMAN OF CHAILLOT   Warner Bros., 1969, British
LONG AGO TOMORROW *THE RAGING MOON*   Cinema 5, 1971, British
THE STEPFORD WIVES   Columbia, 1975
THE SLIPPER AND THE ROSE: THE STORY OF CINDERELLA   Universal,
    1976, British
INTERNATIONAL VELVET   MGM/United Artists, 1978, British
SUNDAY LOVERS   co-director with Edouard Molinaro, Dino Risi & Gene
    Wilder, MGM/United Artists, 1981, U.S.-British-Italian-French
CHANDLERTOWN *PHILIP MARLOWE - PRIVATE EYE (CMS)*   director
    with Peter Hunt, David Wickes & Sidney Hayers, HBO/David Wickes Television
    Ltd./London Weekend Television, 1983, British
BETTER LATE THAN NEVER   Warner Bros., 1983, British
THE NAKED FACE   MGM/UA/Cannon, 1984

CARL FOREMAN

b. July 23, 1914 - Chicago, Illinois
Contact: Writers Guild of America, West - Los Angeles, 213/550-1000

THE VICTORS   Columbia, 1963

MILOS FORMAN*

b. February 18, 1932 - Caslav, Czechoslovakia
Agent: Robert Lantz, The Lantz Office - New York City, 212/586-0200

COMPETITION   Brandon, 1963, Czech
BLACK PETER   Billings, 1964, Czech
LOVES OF A BLONDE   Prominent, 1966, Czech
THE FIREMAN'S BALL   Cinema 5, 1968, Czech
TAKING OFF   Universal, 1971
VISIONS OF EIGHT (FD)   co-director with Yuri Ozerov, Mai Zetterling, Arthur
    Penn, Michael Pfleghar, Kon Ichikawa, Claude Lelouch & John Schlesinger,
    Cinema 5, 1973
ONE FLEW OVER THE CUCKOO'S NEST★★   United Artists, 1976
HAIR   United Artists, 1979
RAGTIME   Paramount, 1981
AMADEUS   Orion, 1984

BILL FORSYTH *

b. Scotland
Contact: Directors Guild of America - Los Angeles, 213/656-1220

THAT SINKING FEELING   The Samuel Goldwyn Company, 1979, Scottish
GREGORY'S GIRL   The Samuel Goldwyn Company, 1982, Scottish
LOCAL HERO   Warner Bros., 1983, British

BOB FOSSE *

b. June 23, 1927 - Chicago, Illinois
Home: 58 West 58th Street, New York, NY 10019, 212/759-7323
Agent: ICM - New York City, 212/556-5600

SWEET CHARITY   Universal, 1969
CABARET★★   Allied Artists, 1972
LENNY★   United Artists, 1974
ALL THAT JAZZ★   20th Century-Fox, 1979
STAR 80   The Ladd Company/Warner Bros., 1983

ROBERT FOWLER *

Home: 3561 Canada Street, Los Angeles, CA 90065
Agent: Elliot Webb, ICM - Los Angeles, 213/550-4000

BELOW THE BELT   Atlantic Releasing Corporation, 1980

WILLIAM A. FRAKER *

b. 1923 - Los Angeles, California
Home: 2572 Outpost Drive, Hollywood, CA 90068

MONTE WALSH   National General, 1970
A REFLECTION OF FEAR   Columbia, 1973, British
THE LEGEND OF THE LONE RANGER   Universal/AFD, 1981

FREDDIE FRANCIS

b. 1917 - London, England
Address: 58 Wheatlands, Heston Village, Middlesex, England

TWO AND TWO MAKE SIX   Union, 1962, British
THE BRAIN *VENGEANCE*   Garrick, 1962, British-West German
PARANOIAC   Universal, 1964, British
NIGHTMARE   Universal, 1964, British
THE EVIL OF FRANKENSTEIN   Universal, 1964, British
TRAITOR'S GATE   Columbia, 1964, British-West German
DR. TERROR'S HOUSE OF HORRORS   Paramount, 1965, British
HYSTERIA   MGM, 1965, British
THE SKULL   Paramount, 1965, British
THE PSYCHOPATH   Paramount, 1966, British
THE DEADLY BEES   Paramount, 1967, British
THEY CAME FROM BEYOND SPACE   Embassy, 1967, British
TORTURE GARDEN   Columbia, 1968, British
DRACULA HAS RISEN FROM THE GRAVE   Warner Bros., 1969, British
MUMSY, NANNY, SONNY & GIRLY *GIRLY*   Cinerama Releasing
    Corporation, 1970, British
TROG   Warner Bros., 1970, British
THE HAPPENING OF THE VAMPIRE   1971, European
TALES FROM THE CRYPT   Cinerama Releasing Corporation, 1972, British
TALES THAT WITNESS MADNESS   Paramount, 1973, British
THE CREEPING FLESH   Columbia, 1973, British
SON OF DRACULA   Cinemation, 1974, British
CRAZE   Warner Bros., 1974, British
THE GHOUL   Rank, 1974, British
LEGEND OF THE WEREWOLF   Tyburn, 1975, British

KARL FRANCIS

Contact: Directors Guild of Great Britain, 56 Whitfield Street, London W1, England,
01/580-9592

THE MOUSE AND THE WOMAN   Facelift, 1981, British
GIRO CITY   Silvarealm/Rediffusion Films/Channel Four, 1982, British

MELVIN FRANK *

b. August 13, 1913 - Chicago, Illinois
Home: 9171 Wilshire Blvd. - Suite 530, Beverly Hills, CA 90212
Agent: William Morris Agency - Beverly Hills, 213/274-7451

THE REFORMER AND THE REDHEAD   co-director with Norman Panama,
MGM, 1950
CALLAWAY WENT THATAWAY   co-director with Norman Panama, MGM,
1951
STRICTLY DISHONORABLE   co-director with Norman Panama, MGM, 1951
ABOVE AND BEYOND   co-director with Norman Panama, MGM, 1952
KNOCK ON WOOD   co-director with Norman Panama, Paramount, 1954
THE COURT JESTER   co-director with Norman Panama, Paramount, 1956
THAT CERTAIN FEELING   co-director with Norman Panama, Paramount, 1956
THE JAYHAWKERS   Paramount, 1959
LI'L ABNER   Paramount, 1959
THE FACTS OF LIFE   United Artists, 1960
STRANGE BEDFELLOWS   Universal, 1965
BUONA SERA, MRS. CAMPBELL   United Artists, 1968
A TOUCH OF CLASS   Avco Embassy, 1973, British
THE PRISONER OF SECOND AVENUE   Warner Bros., 1975
THE DUCHESS AND THE DIRTWATER FOX   20th Century-Fox, 1976
LOST AND FOUND   Columbia, 1979

JOHN FRANKENHEIMER *

b. February 19, 1930 - Malba, New York
Business: John Frankenheimer Productions, 2800 Olympic Blvd., Santa Monica,
CA 90404, 213/829-0404
Agent: Jeff Berg, ICM - Los Angeles, 213/550-4205

THE YOUNG STRANGER   Universal, 1957
THE YOUNG SAVAGES   United Artists, 1961
ALL FALL DOWN   MGM, 1962
BIRDMAN OF ALCATRAZ   United Artists, 1962
THE MANCHURIAN CANDIDATE   United Artists, 1962
SEVEN DAYS IN MAY   Paramount, 1964
THE TRAIN   United Artists, 1965, U.S.-French-Italian
SECONDS   Paramount, 1966
GRAND PRIX   MGM, 1966
THE FIXER   MGM, 1968, British
THE EXTRAORDINARY SEAMAN   MGM, 1969
THE GYPSY MOTHS   MGM, 1969
I WALK THE LINE   Columbia, 1970
THE HORSEMEN   Columbia, 1971
THE ICEMAN COMETH   American Film Theatre, 1973
IMPOSSIBLE OBJECT   Valoria, 1973, French-Italian
99 AND 44/100% DEAD   20th Century-Fox, 1974
FRENCH CONNECTION II   20th Century-Fox, 1975
BLACK SUNDAY   Paramount, 1976
PROPHECY   Paramount, 1979
THE CHALLENGE   Embassy, 1982

RICHARD FRANKLIN *

b. July 15, 1948 - Melbourne, Australia
Contact: Directors Guild of America - Los Angeles, 213/656-1220

BELINDA   Aquarius, 1972, Australian
LOVELAND   Illustrated, 1973, Australian
THE TRUE STORY OF ESKIMO NELL *DICK DOWN UNDER*   Quest Films/
Filmways Australasian Distributors, 1975, Australian
FANTASM   Filmways Australasian, 1977, Australian

continued

RICHARD FRANKLIN*—continued

PATRICK   Cinema Shares International, 1979, Australian
ROAD GAMES   Avco Embassy, 1981, Australian
PSYCHO II   Universal, 1983
CLOAK AND DAGGER   Universal, 1984

JAMES FRAWLEY*

Business: Maya Films Ltd., 9220 Sunset Blvd., Los Angeles, CA 90069, 213/656-5075

THE CHRISTIAN LICORICE STORE   National General, 1971
KID BLUE   20th Century-Fox, 1973
DELANCEY STREET: THE CRISIS WITHIN (TF)   Paramount TV, 1975
THE BIG BUS   Paramount, 1976
THE MUPPET MOVIE   AFD, 1979, British
THE GREAT AMERICAN TRAFFIC JAM (TF)   Ten-Four Productions, 1980

HERB FREED

AWOL   BFB, 1972
HAUNTS   Intercontinental, 1977
BEYOND EVIL   IFI-Scope III, 1980
GRADUATION DAY   IFI-Scope III, 1981

JERROLD FREEDMAN*

Business: Chesapeake Films, Inc., 9220 Sunset Blvd. - Suite 206, Los Angeles, CA 90069, 213/275-3138

KANSAS CITY BOMBER   MGM, 1972
A COLD NIGHT'S DEATH (TF)   ABC Circle Films, 1973
BLOOD SPORT (TF)   Danny Thomas Productions, 1973
THE LAST ANGRY MAN (TF)   Screen Gems/Columbia TV, 1974
SOME KIND OF MIRACLE (TF)   Lorimar Productions, 1979
THIS MAN STANDS ALONE (TF)   Roger Gimbel Productions/EMI TV/Abby
   Mann Productions, 1979
THE STREETS OF L.A. (TF)   George Englund Productions, 1979
THE BOY WHO DRANK TOO MUCH (TF)   MTM Enterprises, 1980
BORDERLINE   AFD, 1980
THE VICTIMS (TF)   Hajeno Productions/Warner Bros. TV, 1982
LEGS (TF)   The Catalina Production Group/Radio City Music Hall Productions/
   Comworld Productions, 1983

ROBERT FREEDMAN*

Contact: Directors Guild of America - Los Angeles, 213/656-1220

GOIN' ALL THE WAY   Saturn International, 1982

RICK FRIEDBERG*

Agent: Jane Sindell, ICM - Los Angeles, 213/550-4000
Business Manager: M. Kenneth Suddleson, Loeb & Loeb, 10100 Santa Monica Blvd.,
   Los Angeles, CA 90067, 213/552-7781

PRAY TV *K-GOD*   Filmways, 1980
OFF THE WALL   Jensen Farley Pictures, 1983

DICK FRIEDENBERG

Agent: Writers & Artists Agency - Los Angeles, 213/820-2240

FRONTIER FREMONT   Sunn Classic, 1976
THE DEERSLAYER (TF)   Sunn Classic Productions, 1978
THE BERMUDA TRIANGLE   Sunn Classic, 1979

WILLIAM FRIEDKIN *

b. August 29, 1939 - Chicago, Illinois
Agent: Tony Fantozzi, William Morris Agency - Beverly Hills, 213/274-7451

GOOD TIMES   Columbia, 1967
THE BIRTHDAY PARTY   Continental, 1968, British
THE NIGHT THEY RAIDED MINSKY'S   United Artists, 1968
THE BOYS IN THE BAND   National General, 1970
THE FRENCH CONNECTION ★★   20th Century-Fox, 1971
THE EXORCIST ★   Warner Bros., 1973
SORCERER   Universal/Paramount, 1977
THE BRINK'S JOB   Universal, 1978
CRUISING   United Artists, 1980
DEAL OF THE CENTURY   Warner Bros., 1983

KIM HARLENE FRIEDMAN *

Business Manager: Marty Mickelson - Los Angeles, 213/858-1097

BEFORE AND AFTER (TF)   The Konigsberg Company, 1979

WILLIAM FRUET

Home: 51 Olive Street, Toronto, Ontario M6G 1T7, Canada, 416/535-3569

WEDDING IN WHITE   Avco Embassy, 1973, Canadian
THE HOUSE BY THE LAKE *DEATH WEEKEND*   American International,
    1977, Canadian
SEARCH AND DESTROY *STRIKING BACK*   Film Ventures International,
    1979
FUNERAL HOME *CRIES IN THE NIGHT*   MPM, 1981, Canadian
BAKER COUNTY USA *TRAPPED*   Jensen Farley Pictures, 1982
SPASMS   Producers Distribution Company, 1983, Canadian

ROBERT FUEST *

b. 1927 - London, England
Contact: Directors Guild of America - Los Angeles, 213/656-1220

JUST LIKE A WOMAN   Monarch, 1966, British
AND SOON THE DARKNESS   Levitt-Pickman, 1970, British
WUTHERING HEIGHTS   American International, 1971, British
THE ABOMINABLE DR. PHIBES   American International, 1971, British
DR. PHIBES RISES AGAIN   American International, 1972, British
THE LAST DAYS OF MAN ON EARTH *THE FINAL PROGRAMME*   New
    World, 1974, British
THE DEVIL'S RAIN   Bryanston, 1975, U.S.-Mexican
REVENGE OF THE STEPFORD WIVES (TF)   Edgar J. Scherick Productions,
    1980
APHRODITE   Prodis, 1983, French

SAMUEL FULLER *

b. August 12, 1911 - Worcester, Massachusetts
Agent: Chasin-Park-Citron - Los Angeles, 213/273-7190

I SHOT JESSE JAMES   Screen Guild, 1949
THE BARON OF ARIZONA   Lippert, 1950
THE STEEL HELMET   Lippert, 1951
FIXED BAYONETS!   20th Century-Fox, 1951
PARK ROW   United Artists, 1952
PICKUP ON SOUTH STREET   20th Century-Fox, 1953
HELL AND HIGH WATER   20th Century-Fox, 1954
HOUSE OF BAMBOO   20th Century-Fox, 1955
RUN OF THE ARROW   20th Century-Fox, 1957
FORTY GUNS   20th Century-Fox, 1957
CHINA GATE   20th Century-Fox, 1957
VERBOTEN!   Columbia, 1958
THE CRIMSON KIMONO   Columbia, 1959
UNDERWORLD U.S.A.   Columbia, 1961

continued

SAMUEL FULLER*—continued

MERRILL'S MARAUDERS   Warner Bros., 1962
SHOCK CORRIDOR   Allied Artists, 1963
THE NAKED KISS   Allied Artists, 1964
SHARK!   Heritage, 1970, U.S.-Mexican
DEAD PIGEON ON BEETHOVEN STREET   Emerson, 1972, West German
THE BIG RED ONE   United Artists, 1980
WHITE DOG   Paramount, 1982
THIEVES AFTER DARK   Parafrance, 1983, French

ALLEN FUNT*

b. 1914 - New York, New York
Contact: Directors Guild of America - New York City, 212/581-0370

WHAT DO YOU SAY TO A NAKED WOMAN?   United Artists, 1970
MONEY TALKS   United Artists, 1971

SIDNEY J. FURIE*

b. February 28, 1933 - Toronto, Canada
Business: Furie Productions, Inc., 9169 Sunset Blvd., Los Angeles, CA 90069
Agent: Paul Kohner, Inc. - Los Angeles, 213/550-1060

A DANGEROUS AGE   Ajay, 1959, Canadian
A COOL SOUND FROM HELL   1959, Canadian
DR. BLOOD'S COFFIN   United Artists, 1960, British
THE SNAKE WOMAN   United Artists, 1960, British
NIGHT OF PASSION   Astor, 1961, British
THREE ON A SPREE   United Artists, 1961, British
WONDERFUL TO BE YOUNG!   Paramount, 1961, British
THE BOYS   Gala, 1962, British
THE LEATHER BOYS   Allied Artists, 1964, British
SWINGERS' PARADISE   American International, 1964, British
THE IPCRESS FILE   Universal, 1965, British
THE APPALOOSA   Universal, 1966
THE NAKED RUNNER   Warner Bros., 1967, British
THE LAWYER   Paramount, 1970
LITTLE FAUSS AND BIG HALSY   Paramount, 1970
LADY SINGS THE BLUES   Paramount, 1972
HIT!   Paramount, 1973
SHEILA LEVINE IS DEAD AND LIVING IN NEW YORK   Paramount,/1975
GABLE AND LOMBARD   Universal, 1976
THE BOYS IN COMPANY C   Columbia, 1978
THE ENTITY   20th Century-Fox, 1983
PURPLE HEARTS ... A VIETNAM LOVE STORY   The Ladd Company/
     Warner Bros., 1984

ALAN GADNEY

b. January 1, 1941 - Dayton, Ohio
Business: Festival Films, P.O. Box 10180, Glendale, CA 91209, 213/222-8626

WEST TEXAS   American Media Productions/American Films Ltd., 1973
MOONCHILD   Filmmakers Ltd./American Films Ltd., 1974

GEORGE GAGE *

Business: George Gage Productions, 1303 N. Sierra Bonita Avenue, Los Angeles,
    CA 90046, 213/874-7400

SKATEBOARD   Universal, 1978
FEAR IN A HANDFUL OF DUST   Amitraj Productions, 1984

TIMOTHY GALFAS *

b. December 31, 1934 - Atlanta, Georgia
Home: 1366 San Ysidro Drive, Beverly Hills, CA 90210, 213/271-4915
Business Manager: Kaufman & Bernstein, 1900 Avenue of the Stars, Los Angeles,
    CA 90067, 213/277-1900

BOGARD   L-T Films, 1975
THE BLACK STREETFIGHTER   New Line Cinema, 1976
REVENGE FOR A RAPE (TF)   Albert S. Ruddy Productions, 1976
BLACK FIST   Worldwide, 1977
MANEATERS ARE LOOSE! (TF)   Mona Productions/Finnegan Associates, 1978
SUNNYSIDE   American International, 1979

HERB GARDNER

Contact: Writers Guild of America, East - New York City, 212/245-6180

THE GOODBYE PEOPLE   Embassy, 1983

JACK GARFEIN *

b. July 2, 1930 - Mukacevo, Czechoslovakia
Business: Actors & Directors Lab, 412 West 42nd Street, New York, NY 10036,
    212/695-5429

THE STRANGE ONE   END AS A MAN   Columbia, 1957
SOMETHING WILD   United Artists, 1961

PATRICK GARLAND

b. 1936 - London, England
Agent: Spokesmen, Ltd., 1 Craven Hill, London W2, England
Contact: Directors Guild of Great Britain, 56 Whitfield Street, London W1, England,
    01/580-9592

THE SNOW GOOSE (TF)   NBC, 1971
A DOLL'S HOUSE   Paramount, 1973, Canadian-U.S.

TONY GARNETT

Contact: British Academy of Film & Television Arts, 195 Piccadilly, London W1,
    England, 01/734-0022

PROSTITUTE   Mainline Pictures, 1981, British
HANDGUN   Warner Bros., 1983

LILA GARRETT *

b. New York, New York
Home: 1356 Laurel Way, Beverly Hills, CA 90212, 213/274-8041
Agent: Rowland Perkins, CAA - Los Angeles, 213/277-4545

TERRACES (TF)   Charles Fries Productions/Worldvision, 1977

COSTA GAVRAS *
(Konstantinos Gavras)

Home: 244 Rue St. Jacques, Paris 75005, France
Agent: Stan Kamen, William Morris Agency - Beverly Hills, 213/274-7451

THE SLEEPING CAR MURDERS   7 Arts, 1966, French
SHOCK TROOPS *UN HOMME DE TROP*   United Artists, 1968, French-
    Italian
Z ★   Cinema 5, 1969, French-Algerian
THE CONFESSION   Paramount, 1970, French
STATE OF SIEGE   Cinema 5, 1973, French
SPECIAL SECTION   Universal, 1975, French-Italian-West German
CLAIR DE FEMME   Atlantic Releasing Corporation, 1979, French
MISSING   Universal, 1982
HANNA K.   Universal Classics, 1983, French

THEODORE GERSHUNY

Contact: Writers Guild of America, East - New York City, 212/245-6180

LOVE, DEATH   1973
SILENT NIGHT, BLOODY NIGHT   Cannon, 1974
SUGAR COOKIES   Troma, 1977
DEATHOUSE   Cannon, 1981

NICHOLAS GESSNER

SOMEONE BEHIND THE DOOR   GSF, 1971, French
THE LITTLE GIRL WHO LIVES DOWN THE LANE   American International,
    1977, U.S.-Canadian-French
IT RAINED ALL NIGHT THE DAY I LEFT   Caneuram/Israfilm/COFCI, 1981,
    Canadian-Israeli-French

STEVEN GETHERS *

b. June 8, 1922
Agent: Adams, Ray & Rosenberg - Los Angeles, 213/278-3000

BILLY: PORTRAIT OF A STREET KID (TF)   Mark Carliner Productions, 1977
DAMIEN ... THE LEPER PRIEST (TF)   Tomorrow Entertainment, 1980
JACQUELINE BOUVIER KENNEDY (TF)   ABC Circle Films, 1981
CONFESSIONS OF A MARRIED MAN (TF)   Gloria Monty Productions/
    Comworld Productions, 1983

JOE GIANNONE

MADMAN   Jensen Farley Pictures, 1982

ALAN GIBSON

b. April 28, 1938 - Canada
Home: 55 Portland Road, London W11 4LR, England, 01/727-0354
Agent: Stone-Masser Talent Agents - Los Angeles, 213/275-9599

GOODBYE GEMINI   Cinerama Releasing Corporation, 1970, British
CRESCENDO   Warner Bros., 1972, British
DRACULA TODAY *DRACULA A.D. 1972*   Warner Bros., 1972, British
THE PLAYBOY OF THE WESTERN WORLD (TF)   BBC, 1975, British

continued

ALAN GIBSON—continued

COUNT DRACULA AND HIS VAMPIRE BRIDE *SATANIC RITES OF DRACULA*   Dynamite Entertainment, 1978, British
CHECKERED FLAG OR CRASH   Universal, 1978
A WOMAN CALLED GOLDA (TF)   Harve Bennett Productions/Paramount TV, 1982
WITNESS FOR THE PROSECUTION (TF)   Norman Rosemont Productions/ United Artists Productions, 1982, U.S.-British
HELEN AND TEACHER (TF)   20th Century-Fox TV/Castle Combe Productions, 1983, U.S.-British
MARTIN'S DAY   MGM/UA, 1984, Canadian

B R I A N   G I B S O N

Home: 65 Greenhill, Hampstead High Street, London NW3, England
Agent: A.D. Peters Ltd., 10 Buckingham Street, London WC2, England

BREAKING GLASS   Paramount, 1980, British

L E W I S   G I L B E R T *

b. March 6, 1920 - London, England
Address: 17 Sheldrake Place, Duchess of Bedford Walk, London W8, England
Attorney: Norman Tyre, Gang, Tyre & Brown - Los Angeles, 213/463-4863

THE LITTLE BALLERINA   General Film Distributors, 1947, British
ONCE A SINNER   Butcher, 1950, British
WALL OF DEATH *THERE IS ANOTHER SIDE*   Realart, 1951, British
THE SCARLET THREAD   Butcher, 1951, British
HUNDRED HOUR HUNT *EMERGENCY CALL*   Greshler, 1952, British
TIME GENTLEMEN PLEASE!   Eros, 1952, British
THE SLASHER *COSH BOY*   Lippert, 1953, British
JOHNNY ON THE RUN   co-director with Vernon Harris, Associated British Film Distributors/Children's Film Foundation, 1953, British
BREAK TO FREEDOM *ALBERT R.N.*   United Artists, 1953, British
THE GOOD DIE YOUNG   United Artists, 1954, British
THE SEA SHALL NOT HAVE THEM   United Artists, 1954, British
CAST A DARK SHADOW   DCA, 1955, British
REACH FOR THE SKY   Rank, 1956, British
PARADISE LAGOON *THE ADMIRABLE CRICHTON*   Columbia, 1957, British
CARVE HER NAME WITH PRIDE   Lopert, 1958, British
A CRY FROM THE STREETS   Tudor, 1959, British
FERRY TO HONG KONG   20th Century-Fox, 1959, British
SINK THE BISMARCK!   20th Century-Fox, 1960, British
SKYWATCH *LIGHT UP THE SKY*   Continental, 1960, British
LOSS OF INNOCENCE *THE GREENGAGE SUMMER*   Columbia, 1961, British
DAMN THE DEFIANT! *H.M.S. DEFIANT*   Columbia, 1962, British
THE SEVENTH DAWN   United Artists, 1964, U.S.-British
ALFIE   Paramount, 1966, British
YOU ONLY LIVE TWICE   United Artists, 1967, British
THE ADVENTURERS   Paramount, 1970
FRIENDS   Paramount, 1971, British-French
PAUL AND MICHELLE   Paramount, 1974, British-French
OPERATION DAYBREAK   Warner Bros., 1975, British
SEVEN NIGHTS IN JAPAN   EMI, 1976, British-French
THE SPY WHO LOVED ME   United Artists, 1977, British-U.S.
MOONRAKER   United Artists, 1979, British-French
EDUCATING RITA   Columbia, 1983, British

D A V I D   G I L E R *

Contact: Directors Guild of America - Los Angeles, 213/656-1220

THE BLACK BIRD   Columbia, 1975

STUART GILLARD

Agent: Century Artists - Beverly Hills, 213/273-4366

PARADISE   Avco Embassy, 1982, Canadian

TERRY GILLIAM

b. November 22, 1940 - Minneapolis, Minnesota
Address: 51 South Hill Park, London NW3, England

MONTY PYTHON AND THE HOLY GRAIL   co-director with Terry Jones,
    Cinema 5, 1974, British
JABBERWOCKY   Cinema 5, 1977, British
TIME BANDITS   Avco Embassy, 1981, British

FRANK D. GILROY *

b. October 13, 1925 - New York, New York
Agent: Ziegler, Diskant, Inc. - Los Angeles, 213/278-0700

DESPERATE CHARACTERS   ITC, 1971
JOHN O'HARA'S GIBBSVILLE (TF)   Columbia TV, 1975
THE TURNING POINT OF JIM MALLOY (TF)   David Gerber Company/
    Columbia TV, 1975
FROM NOON TILL THREE   United Artists, 1976
ONCE IN PARIS ...   Atlantic Releasing Corporation, 1978
REX STOUT'S NERO WOLFE (TF)   Emmett Lavery, Jr. Productions/Paramount
    TV, 1979

PETER GIMBEL *

b. February 14, 1928 - New York, New York
Business: Blue Gander, Inc., 10 East 63rd Street, New York, N.Y. 10021,
    212/753-9088
Agent: Robert Stein, Paul Kohner, Inc. - Los Angeles, 213/550-1060

BLUE WATER, WHITE DEATH (FD)   co-director with James Lipscomb,
    National General, 1971

MILTON MOSES GINSBERG

COMING APART   Kaleidoscope, 1969
THE WEREWOLF OF WASHINGTON   Diplomat, 1973

BOB GIRALDI *

Contact: Directors Guild of America - New York City, 212/581-0370

NATIONAL LAMPOON'S MOVIE MADNESS   co-director with Henry Jaglom,
    United Artists, 1982

BERNARD GIRARD *

b. 1930
Contact: Directors Guild of America - Los Angeles, 213/656-1220

THE GREEN-EYED BLONDE   Warner Bros., 1957
RIDE OUT FOR REVENGE   United Artists, 1958
AS YOUNG AS WE ARE   Paramount, 1958
THE PARTY CRASHERS   Paramount, 1958
A PUBLIC AFFAIR   Parade, 1962
DEAD HEAT ON A MERRY-GO-ROUND   Paramount, 1966
MAD ROOM   Columbia, 1969
HUNTERS ARE FOR KILLING (TF)   Cinema Center, 1970
THE HAPPINESS CAGE *THE MIND SNATCHERS*   Cinerama Releasing
    Corporation, 1972
GONE WITH THE WEST   International Cinefilm, 1975

DAVID GLADWELL

b. April 2, 1935 - Gloucester, England
Address: 8 Caldervale Road, London SW4, England
Contact: Directors Guild of Great Britain, 56 Whitfield Street, London W1, England,
    01/580-9592

REQUIEM FOR A VILLAGE   BFI Production Board, 1977, British
MEMOIRS OF A SURVIVOR   EMI, 1982, British

JOHN GLEN

b. May 15, 1932 - Sunbury on Thames, England
Address: 22 Wheelers Orchard, Chalfont Street, Peter, Buckinghamshire, England

FOR YOUR EYES ONLY   United Artists, 1981, British
OCTOPUSSY   MGM/UA, 1983, British

PETER GLENVILLE *

b. October 28, 1913 - London, England
Messages: 212/758-0800

THE PRISONER   Columbia, 1955, British
ME AND THE COLONEL   Columbia, 1958
SUMMER AND SMOKE   Paramount, 1961
TERM OF TRIAL   Warner Bros., 1963, British
BECKET ★   Paramount, 1964, British
HOTEL PARADISO   MGM, 1966, British
THE COMEDIANS   MGM, 1967, British

JIM GLICKENHAUS *

b. July 24, 1950 - New York, New York
Business: Glickenhaus Film, Inc., 1619 Broadway - Suite 303, New York,
    NY 10019, 212/265-1150
Agent: Sue Mengers, ICM - Los Angeles, 213/550-4264

THE ASTROLOGER   Interstar, 1979
THE EXTERMINATOR   Avco Embassy, 1980
THE SOLDIER   Embassy, 1982

JEAN-LUC GODARD

b. December 3, 1930 - Paris, France
Contact: French Film Office, 745 Fifth Avenue, New York, NY 10151, 212/832-
    8860

BREATHLESS *A BOUT DE SOUFFLE*   Films Around the World, 1960,
    French
A WOMAN IS A WOMAN   Pathe Contemporary, 1961, French
SEVEN CAPITAL SINS   co-director with Roger Vadim, Sylvaine Dhomme,
    Edouard Molinaro, Philippe De Broca, Claude Chabrol, Jacques Demy, Marie-
    Jose Nat, Dominique Paturel, Jean-Marc Tennberg & Perrette Pradier, Embassy,
    1962, French-Italian
MY LIFE TO LIVE   Pathe Contemporary, 1962, French
ROGOPAG   co-director, 1962, French
LE PETIT SOLDAT   West End, 1963, French
LES CARABINIERS   West End, 1963, French
CONTEMPT *LE MEPRIS*   Embassy, 1964, French-Italian
LES PLUS BELLES ESCROQUERIES DU MONDE   co-director, 1964, French-
    Italian-Japanese
BAND OF OUTSIDERS   Royal Films International, 1964, French
THE MARRIED WOMAN   Royal Films International, 1964, French
SIX IN PARIS   co-director, 1965, French
ALPHAVILLE   Pathe Contemporary, 1965, French
PIERROT LE FOU   Pathe Contemporary, 1965, French
MASCULINE FEMININE   Royal Films International, 1966, French-Swedish
MADE IN U.S.A.   Pathe Contemporary, 1966, French
TWO OR THREE THINGS I KNOW ABOUT HER   New Line Cinema, 1967,
    French

continued

JEAN-LUC GODARD—continued

THE OLDEST PROFESSION *LES PLUS VIEUX METIER DU MONDE*   co-director with Franco Indovina, Mauro Bolognini, Philippe de Broca, Michael Pfleghar, Claude Autant-Lara, Goldstone, 1967, Italian-French-West German
FAR FROM VIETNAM (FD)   co-director with Alain Resnais, William Klein, Agnes Varda, Joris Ivens & Claude Lelouch, New Yorker, 1967, French
LA CHINOISE   Leacock-Pennebaker, 1967, French
WEEKEND   Grove Press, 1968, French-Italian
UN FILM COMME LES AUTRES   1968, French
AMORE E RABBIA   co-director, 1969, Italian-French
LE GAI SAVOIR   EYR, 1969, French
ONE A.M.   Leacock-Pennebaker, 1969, French
COMMUNICATIONS   1969, French
SYMPATHY FOR THE DEVIL—1 + 1   New Line Cinema, 1969, British
BRITISH SOUNDS/SEE YOU AT MAO (TF)   co-director with Jean-Pierre Gorin, 1969, British
WIND FROM THE EAST   co-director with Jean-Pierre Gorin, New Line Cinema, 1969, French-Italian-West German
PRAVDA (FD)   co-director with Jean-Pierre Gorin, 1969, French-Czech
LOTTE IN ITALIA (FD)   co-director with Jean-Pierre Gorin, RAI, 1970, Italian
JUSQU'A LA VICTOIRE (FD)   co-director with Jean-Pierre Gorin, 1970, French
VLADIMIR ET ROSA   co-director with Jean-Pierre Gorin, 1971, French
TOUT VA BIEN   co-director with Jean-Pierre Gorin, New Yorker, 1972, French-Italian
LETTER TO JANE: INVESTIGATION OF A STILL   co-director with Jean-Pierre Gorin, New Yorker, 1972, French
MOI JE   1973, French
NUMERO DEUX   Zoetrope, 1975, French
LA COMMUNICATION (TF)   1976, French
COMMENT CA VA   1976, French
ICI ET AILLEURS   1977, French
EVERY MAN FOR HIMSELF *SAUVE QUI PEUT LA VIE*   New Yorker/Zoetrope, 1980, Swiss-French
PASSION   United Artists Classics, 1983, French-Swiss
PRENOM: CARMEN   Parafrance, 1983, French-Swiss

JIM GODDARD

Contact: Directors Guild of Great Britain, 56 Whitfield Street, London W1, England, 01/580-9592

A TALE OF TWO CITIES (TF)   Norman Rosemont Productions/Marble Arch Productions, 1980, U.S.-British
REILLY - ACE OF SPIES (TF)   co-director with Martin Campbell, Euston Films Ltd., 1983
KENNEDY (MS)   Central Independent Television Productions/Alan Landsburg Productions, 1983, British-U.S.

MENAHEM GOLAN

b. May 31, 1929 - Tiberias, Israel
Business: Cannon Group, 6464 Sunset Blvd. - Suite 1150, Hollywood, CA 90028, 213/469-8124

EL DORADO   1963, Israeli
TRUNK TO CAIRO   American International, 1967, Israeli-West German
THE GIRL FROM THE DEAD SEA   1967, Israeli
TEVYE AND HIS SEVEN DAUGHTERS   Noah Films, 1968, Israeli
FORTUNA   Trans-American, 1969, Israeli
WHAT'S GOOD FOR THE GOOSE   National Showmanship, 1969, British
MARGO   Cannon, 1970, Israeli
LUPO!   Cannon, 1970, Israeli
QUEEN OF THE ROAD   Noah Films, 1970, Israeli
KATZ AND KARASSO   Noah Films, 1971, Israeli
THE GREAT TELEPHONE ROBBERY   Noah Films, 1972, Israeli
ESCAPE TO THE SUN   Cinevision, 1972, Israeli-West German-French
KAZABLAN   MGM, 1973, Israeli
LEPKE   Warner Bros., 1975
DIAMONDS   Avco Embassy, 1975, U.S.-Israeli-Swiss
THE AMBASSADOR   Noah Films, 1976, Israeli
OPERATION THUNDERBOLT   Cinema Shares International, 1978, Israeli
THE URANIUM CONSPIRACY   Noah Films, 1978, Israeli-West German

continued

MENAHEM GOLAN—continued
THE MAGICIAN OF LUBLIN   Cannon, 1979, Israeli-West German-U.S.
THE APPLE   Cannon, 1980, U.S.-West German
ENTER THE NINJA   Cannon, 1981
OVER THE BROOKLYN BRIDGE   MGM/UA/Cannon, 1983

J A C K   G O L D

b. June 28, 1930 - London, England
Agent: ICM - Los Angeles, 213/550-4000

THE BOFORS GUN   Universal, 1968, British
THE RECKONING   Columbia, 1969, British
CATHOLICS (TF)   Sidney Glazier Productions, 1973, British
WHO?   Allied Artists, 1975, British-West German
MAN FRIDAY   Avco Embassy, 1975, British
ACES HIGH   Cinema Shares International, 1977, British
THE MEDUSA TOUCH   Warner Bros., 1978, British
THE SAILOR'S RETURN   Euston Films Ltd., 1978
THE NAKED CIVIL SERVANT (TF)   Thames TV, 1978, British
CHARLIE MUFFIN   Euston Films Ltd., 1980, British
LITTLE LORD FAUNTLEROY (TF)   Norman Rosemont Productions, 1980, U.S.-
     British
PRAYING MANTIS   Portman Productions/Channel Four, 1982, British
RED MONARCH   Enigma Films/Goldcrest Films & Television Ltd., 1983, British
GOOD AND BAD AT GAMES (TF)   Portman Quintet Productions, 1983,
     British

J A M E S   G O L D S T O N E *

b. June 8, 1931 - Los Angeles, California
Agent: John Gaines, APA - Los Angeles, 213/273-0744
Business Manager: Jess Morgan, Jess S. Morgan & Co., 6420 Wilshire Blvd., Los
     Angeles, CA 90048, 213/651-1601

SCALPLOCK (TF)   Columbia TV, 1966
CODE NAME: HERACLITUS (TF)   Universal TV, 1967
IRONSIDE (TF)   Universal TV, 1967
SHADOW OVER ELVERON (TF)   Universal TV, 1968
JIGSAW   Universal, 1968
A MAN CALLED GANNON   Universal, 1969
WINNING   Universal, 1969
A CLEAR AND PRESENT DANGER (TF) ☆   Universal TV, 1970
BROTHER JOHN   Columbia, 1971
RED SKY AT MORNING   Universal, 1971
CRY PANIC (TF)   Spelling-Goldberg Productions, 1974
DR. MAX (TF)   CBS, Inc., 1974
THINGS IN THEIR SEASON (TF)   Tomorrow Entertainment, 1974
JOURNEY FROM DARKNESS (TF)   Bob Banner Associates, 1975
ERIC (TF)   Lorimar Productions, 1975
SWASHBUCKLER   Universal, 1976
ROLLERCOASTER   Universal, 1977
STUDS LONIGAN (MS)   Lorimar Productions, 1979
WHEN TIME RAN OUT   Warner Bros., 1980
KENT STATE (TF) ☆☆   Inter Planetary Productions/Osmond Communications,
     1981
CHARLES & DIANA: A ROYAL LOVE STORY (TF)   St. Lorraine Productions,
     1982
CALAMITY JANE (TF)   CBS Entertainment, 1983
RITA HAYWORTH: THE LOVE GODDESS (TF)   The Susskind Co., 1983

B E R T   I .   G O R D O N *

b. September 24, 1922 - Kenosha, Wisconsin
Agent: The Gersh Agency - Beverly Hills, 213/274-6611

KING DINOSAUR   Lippert, 1955
BEGINNING OF THE END   Republic, 1957
CYCLOPS   American International, 1957
THE AMAZING COLOSSAL MAN   American International, 1957
ATTACK OF THE PUPPET PEOPLE   American International, 1958

continued

BERT I. GORDON*—continued

WAR OF THE COLASSAL BEAST   American International, 1958
THE SPIDER   American International, 1958
THE BOY AND THE PIRATES   United Artists, 1960
TORMENTED   Allied Artists, 1960
THE MAGIC SWORD   United Artists, 1962
VILLAGE OF THE GIANTS   Embassy, 1965
PICTURE MOMMY DEAD   Embassy, 1966
HOW TO SUCCEED WITH SEX   Medford, 1970
NECROMANCY   American International, 1972
THE MAD BOMBER   Cinemation, 1973
THE POLICE CONNECTION   DETECTIVE GERONIMO   1973
THE FOOD OF THE GODS   American International, 1976
EMPIRE OF THE ANTS   American International, 1977
THE COMING   1983

MICHAEL GORDON*

b. September 6, 1909 - Baltimore, Maryland
Home: 259 N. Layton Drive, Los Angeles, CA 90049, 213/476-2024
Business: UCLA Theatre Arts Department, 405 Hilgard Avenue, Los Angeles,
    CA 90024, 213/825-5761
Business Manager: Lynn Schweidel - Los Angeles, 213/651-2197

BOSTON BLACKIE GOES HOLLYWOOD   Columbia, 1942
UNDERGROUND AGENT   Columbia, 1942
ONE DANGEROUS NIGHT   Columbia, 1943
CRIME DOCTOR   Columbia, 1943
THE WEB   Universal, 1947
ANOTHER PART OF THE FOREST   Universal, 1948
AN ACT OF MURDER   Universal, 1948
THE LADY GAMBLES   Universal, 1949
WOMAN IN HIDING   Universal, 1950
CYRANO DE BERGERAC   United Artists, 1950
I CAN GET IT FOR YOUR WHOLESALE   20th Century-Fox, 1951
THE SECRET OF CONVICT LAKE   20th Century-Fox, 1951
WHEREVER SHE GOES   Mayer-Kingsley, 1953, Australian
PILLOW TALK   Universal, 1959
PORTRAIT IN BLACK   Universal, 1960
BOYS' NIGHT OUT   MGM, 1962
FOR LOVE OR MONEY   Universal, 1963
MOVE OVER, DARLING   20th Century-Fox, 1963
A VERY SPECIAL FAVOR   Universal, 1965
TEXAS ACROSS THE RIVER   Universal, 1966
THE IMPOSSIBLE YEARS   MGM, 1968
HOW DO I LOVE THEE?   Cinerama Releasing Corporation, 1970

BERRY GORDY*

Business: Motown Records Corporation, 6255 Sunset Blvd., Hollywood, CA 90028,
    213/468-3600

MAHOGANY   Paramount, 1975

CLAUDE GORETTA

b. June 23, 1929 - Geneva, Switzerland
Contact: Swiss Film Center, Muenstergasse 18, CH-8001 Zurich, Switzerland, 01/
    472-860

LE FOU   1970, Swiss
LE JOUR DES NOCES (TF)   1971, Swiss
L'INVITATION   Janus, 1973, Swiss
THE WONDERFUL CROOK   New Yorker, 1976, Swiss-French
THE LACEMAKER   New Yorker, 1977, Swiss-French
BONHEUR TOI-MEME   Phenix Films/FR3, 1980, French
THE GIRL FROM LORRAINE   LA PROVINCIALE   New Yorker, 1981, French
THE DEATH OF MARIO RICCI   New Line Showcase, 1983, Swiss-French

CARL GOTTLIEB *

b. March 18, 1938
Agent: Larry Grossman & Associates - Beverly Hills, 213/550-8127

CAVEMAN   United Artists, 1981

WILLIAM A. GRAHAM *

Home: 21510 Calle de Barco, Malibu, CA 90265
Agent: Fred Specktor, CAA - Los Angeles, 213/277-4545

THE DOOMSDAY FLIGHT (TF)   Universal TV, 1966
THE OUTSIDER (TF)   Universal TV, 1967
WATERHOLE #3   Paramount, 1967
CHANGE OF HABIT   Universal, 1968
THE LEGEND OF CUSTER (TF)   20th Century-Fox, 1968
SUBMARINE X-1   United Artists, 1969, British
TRIAL RUN (TF)   Universal TV, 1969
THEN CAME BRONSON (TF)   Universal TV, 1969
THE INTRUDERS (TF)   Universal TV, 1970
CONGRATULATIONS, IT'S A BOY! (TF)   Aaron Spelling Productions, 1971
THIEF (TF)   Metromedia Productions/Stonehenge Productions, 1971
MARRIAGE: YEAR ONE (TF)   Universal TV, 1971
JIGSAW (TF)   Universal TV, 1972
MAGIC CARPET (TF)   Universal TV, 1972
HONKY   Jack H. Harris Enterprises, 1972
COUNT YOUR BULLETS CRY FOR ME, BILLY   Brut Productions, 1972
BIRDS OF PREY (TF)   Tomorrow Entertainment, 1973
MR. INSIDE/MR. OUTSIDE (TF)   D'Antoni Productions, 1973
POLICE STORY (TF)   Screen Gems/Columbia TV, 1973
SHIRTS/SKINS (TF)   MGM TV, 1973
WHERE THE LILIES BLOOM   United Artists, 1974
TOGETHER BROTHERS   20th Century-Fox, 1974
GET CHRISTIE LOVE! (TF)   Wolper Productions, 1974
LARRY (TF)   Tomorrow Entertainment, 1974
TRAPPED BENEATH THE SEA (TF)   ABC Circle Films, 1974
BEYOND THE BERMUDA TRIANGLE (TF)   Playboy Productions, 1975
PERILOUS VOYAGE (TF)   Universal TV, 1976
SHARK KILL (TF)   D'Antoni-Weitz Productions, 1976
21 HOURS AT MUNICH (TF)   Filmways, 1976
PART 2 SOUNDER   Gamma III, 1976
MINSTREL MAN (TF)   Roger Gimbel Productions/EMI TV, 1977
THE AMAXING HOWARD HUGHES (TF)   Roger Gimbel Productions/EMI TV, 1977
CONTRACT ON CHERRY STREET (TF)   Columbia TV, 1977
CINDY (TF)   John Charles Walters Productions, 1978
ONE IN A MILLION: THE RON LeFLORE STORY (TF)   Roger Gimbel Productions/EMI TV, 1978
AND I ALONE SURVIVED (TF)   Jerry Leider-OJL Productions, 1978
TRANSPLANT (TF)   Time-Life Productions, 1979
ORPHAN TRAIN (TF)   Roger Gimbel Productions/EMI TV, 1979
GUYANA TRAGEDY: THE STORY OF JIM JONES (TF) ☆   The Konigsberg Company, 1980
RAGE (TF)   NBC, 1980
DEADLY ENCOUNTER (TF)   Rober Gimbel Productions/EMI TV, 1982
M.A.D.D.: MOTHERS AGAINST DRUNK DRIVERS (TF)   Universal TV, 1983
THE LAST NINJA (TF)   Paramount TV, 1983
HARRY TRACY   Quartet/Films Inc., 1983, Canadian
WOMEN OF SAN QUENTIN (TF)   David Gerber Company/MGM-UA TV, 1983

LEE GRANT *

(Lyova Rosenthal)

b. October 31, 1927 - New York, New York
Agent: Ed Bondy/Stan Kamen, William Morris Agency - Beverly Hills, 213/274-7451

TELL ME A RIDDLE   Filmways, 1980
THE WILLMAR 8 (FD)   California Newsreel, 1981
WHEN WOMEN KILL (CTD)   HBO/Joseph Feury Productions, 1983

ALEX GRASSHOFF*

b. December 10, 1930 - Boston, Massachusetts
Agent: Robinson-Weintraub & Associates - Los Angeles, 213/652-5802

YOUNG AMERICANS (FD)   Columbia, 1967
JOURNEY TO THE OUTER LIMITS (FD)   1974
THE LAST DINOSAUR (TF)   co-director with Tom Kotani, 1977, U.S.-Japanese
SMOKEY AND THE GOODTIME OUTLAWS   Howco International, 1978
J.D. & THE SALT FLAT KID   1978

WALTER GRAUMAN*

b. March 17, 1922 - Milwaukee, Wisconsin
Home: 244 Barlock Avenue, Los Angeles, CA 90049, 213/472-3160
Messages: 213/954-6535
Agent: Bob Broder, Broder-Kurland Agency - Los Angeles, 213/274-8291
Business Manager: Anita DeThomas, DeThomas & Associates, 1801 Avenue of the
    Stars - Suite 825, Los Angeles, CA 90067, 213/277-4866

THE DISEMBODIED   Allied Artists, 1957
LADY IN A CAGE   United Artists, 1964
633 SQUADRON   United Artists, 1964, British
A RAGE TO LIVE   United Artists, 1965
I DEAL IN DANGER   20th Century-Fox, 1966
DAUGHTER OF THE MIND (TF)   20th Century-Fox, 1969
THE LAST ESCAPE   United Artists, 1970
THE OLD MAN WHO CRIED WOLF (TF)   Aaron Spelling Productions, 1970
CROWHAVEN FARM (TF)   Aaron Spelling Productions, 1970
THE FORGOTTEN MAN (TF)   Walter Grauman Productions, 1971
PAPER MAN (TF)   20th Century-Fox TV, 1971
THEY CALL IT MURDER (TF)   20th Century-Fox TV, 1971
DEAD MEN TELL NO TALES (TF)   20th Century-Fox TV, 1971
THE STREETS OF SAN FRANCISCO (TF)   QM Productions, 1972
MANHUNTER (TF)   QM Productions, 1974
FORCE FIVE (TF)   Universal TV, 1975
MOST WANTED (TF)   QM Productions, 1976
ARE YOU IN THE HOUSE ALONE? (TF)   Charles Fries Productions, 1978
CRISIS IN MID-AIR (TF)   CBS Entertainment, 1979
THE GOLDEN GATE MURDERS (TF)   Universal TV, 1979
THE TOP OF THE HILL (TF)   Fellows-Keegan Company/Paramount TV, 1980
TO RACE THE WIND (TF)   Walter Grauman Productions, 1980
THE MEMORY OF EVA RYKER (TF)   Irwin Allen Productions, 1980
PLEASURE PALACE (TF)   Norman Rosemont Productions/Marble Arch
    Productions, 1980
JACQUELINE SUSANN'S VALLEY OF THE DOLLS 1981 (MS)   20th
    Century-Fox TV, 1981
BARE ESSENCE (MS)   Warner Bros. TV, 1982
ILLUSIONS (TF)   CBS Entertainment, 1983

MIKE GRAY*

Home: 1746 Deerhill, Topanga, CA 90290, 213/455-3233

WAVELENGTH   New World, 1983

GUY GREEN*

b. 1913 - Somerset, England
Agent: Phil Gersh, The Gersh Agency - Beverly Hills, 213/274-6611

RIVER BEAT   Lippert, 1954, British
POSTMARK FOR DANGER   *PORTRAIT OF ALISON*   RKO Radio, 1955,
    British
TEARS FOR SIMON   *LOST*   Republic, 1956, British
TRIPLE DECEPTION   *HOUSE OF SECRETS*   Rank, 1956, British
THE SNORKEL   Columbia, 1958, British
DESERT PATROL   *SEA OF SAND*   Universal, 1958, British
S.O.S. PACIFIC   Universal, 1960, British
THE ANGRY SILENCE   Valiant, 1960, British
THE MARK   Continental, 1961, British
LIGHT IN THE PIAZZA   MGM, 1962

continued

GUY GREEN*—continued

DIAMOND HEAD   Columbia, 1963
A PATCH OF BLUE   MGM, 1965
A MATTER OF INNOCENCE *PRETTY POLLY*   Universal, 1968, British
THE MAGUS   20th Century-Fox, 1968, British
A WALK IN THE SPRING RAIN   Columbia, 1970
LUTHER   American Film Theatre, 1974
JACQUELINE SUSANN'S ONCE IS NOT ENOUGH   Paramount, 1975
THE DEVIL'S ADVOCATE   Geria Films, 1978, West German
JENNIFER: A WOMAN'S STORY (TF)   Marble Arch Productions, 1979
THE INCREDIBLE JOURNEY OF DR. MEG LAUREL (TF)   Columbia TV, 1979
JIMMY B. & ANDRE (TF)   Georgia Bay Productions, 1980
INMATES: A LOVE STORY (TF)   Henerson-Hirsch Productions/Finnegan Associates, 1981
ISABEL'S CHOICE (TF)   Stuart Miller-Pantheon TV, 1981

WALON GREEN*

b. December 15, 1936 - Baltimore, Maryland
Contact: Directors Guild of America - Los Angeles, 213/656-1220

SPREE   co-director with Mitchell Leisen, United Producers, 1967
THE HELLSTROM CHRONICLE (FD)   Cinema 5, 1971
THE SECRET LIFE OF PLANTS (FD)   Paramount, 1978

PETER GREENAWAY

Contact: British Academy of Film & Television Arts, 195 Piccadilly, London W1, England, 01/734-0022

THE FALLS   British Film Institute, 1980, British
ACT OF GOD   British Film Institute, 1981, British
THE DRAUGHTMAN'S CONTRACT   United Artists Classics, 1983, British

DANFORD B. GREENE

THE SECRET DIARY OF SIGMUND FREUD   20th Century-Fox International Classics, 1984

DAVID GREENE*

b. February 22, 1921 - Manchester, England
Business: David Greene Productions, Inc., 106 S. Mansfield Avenue, Los Angeles, CA 90036, 213/939-4202
Agent: CAA - Los Angeles, 213/277-4545

THE SHUTTERED ROOM   Warner Bros., 1966, British
SEBASTIAN   Paramount, 1968, British
THE STRANGE AFFAIR   Paramount, 1968, British
I START COUNTING   United Artists, 1969, British
THE PEOPLE NEXT DOOR   Avco Embassy, 1970
MADAME SIN (TF)   ITC, 1971, British
GODSPELL   Columbia, 1973
THE COUNT OF MONTE CRISTO (TF)   Norman Rosemont Productions/ITC, 1975, U.S.-British
ELLERY QUEEN (TF)   Universal TV, 1975
RICH MAN, POOR MAN (MS)   co-director with Boris Sagal, Universal TV, 1976
ROOTS (MS) ☆☆   co-director with Marvin J. Chomsky, John Erman & Gilbert Moses, Wolper Productions, 1977
LUCAN (TF)   MGM TV, 1977
THE TRIAL OF LEE HARVEY OSWALD (TF)   Charles Fries Productions, 1977
GRAY LADY DOWN   Universal, 1978
FRIENDLY FIRE (TF) ☆☆   Marble Arch Productions, 1979
A VACATION IN HELL (TF)   David Greene Productions/Finnegan Associates, 1979
THE CHOICE (TF)   David Greene Productions/Finnegan Associates, 1981
HARD COUNTRY   Universal/AFD, 1981
WORLD WAR III (TF)   Finnegan Associates/David Greene Productions, 1982

continued

DAVID GREENE*—continued

REHEARSAL FOR MURDER (TF)   Levinson-Link Productions/Robert Papazian
Productions, 1982
TAKE YOUR BEST SHOT (TF)   Levinson-Link Productions/Robert Papazian
Productions, 1982
GHOST DANGING (TF)   Herbert Brodkin Productions/The Eugene O'Neill
Memorial Theatre Center/Titus Productions, 1983

B U D   G R E E N S P A N *

Business: Cappy Productions, 33 East 68th Street, New York, NY 10021, 212/
249-1800

WILMA (TF)   Cappy Productions, 1977

R O B E R T   G R E E N W A L D *

b. August 28, 1945 - New York, New York
Home: 53 27th Avenue, Venice, CA 90291, 213/392-5663
Messages: 213/552-9455
Business: Moonlight Productions, 100 Universal City Plaza, Universal City,
CA 91608, 213/508-4896
Agent: Gary Lucchesi, William Morris Agency - Beverly Hills, 213/274-7451

SHARON: PORTRAIT OF A MISTRESS (TF)   Moonlight Productions/
Paramount TV, 1977
KATIE: PORTRAIT OF A CENTERFOLD (TF)   Moonlight Productions/Warner
Bros. TV, 1978
FLATBED ANNIE & SWEETIE PIE: LADY TRUCKERS (TF)   Moonlight
Productions/Filmways, 1979
XANADU   Universal, 1980
FORTY DAYS FOR DANNY (TF)   Moonlight Productions/Filmways, 1982
IN THE CUSTODY OF STRANGERS (TF)   Moonlight Productions/Filmways,
1982

C H A R L E S   B .   G R I F F I T H

Agent: Jim Preminger Agency - Los Angeles, 213/475-9491

EAT MY DUST   New World, 1976
UP FROM THE DEPTHS   New World, 1979
DR. HECKLE AND MR. HYPE   Cannon, 1980
SMOKEY BITES THE DUST   New World, 1981

U L U   G R O S B A R D *

b. January 9, 1929 - Antwerp, Belgium
Home: 29 West 10th Street, New York, NY 10011
Agent: Sam Cohn, ICM - New York City, 212/556-5610

THE SUBJECT WAS ROSES   MGM, 1968
**WHO IS HARRY KELLERMAN AND WHY IS HE SAYING THOSE TERRIBLE
THINGS ABOUT ME?**   National General, 1971
STRAIGHT TIME   Warner Bros., 1978
TRUE CONFESSIONS   United Artists, 1981

R O B E R T   G U E N E T T E *

b. January 12, 1935 - Holyoke, Massachusetts
Business: 8489 West Third Street, Los Angeles, CA 90048 213/658-8450
Agent: The Sy Fischer Talent Co. - Los Angeles, 213/557-0388

THE TREE   Guenette, 1969
THE MYSTERIOUS MONSTERS   Sunn Classic, 1976
THE AMAZING WORLD OF PSYCHIC PHENOMENA   Sunn Classic, 1976
THE MAN WHO SAW TOMORROW   Warner Bros., 1981

JAMES WILLIAM GUERCIO*

Home: Caribou Ranch, Nederland, Colorado 80466, 303/258-3215
Agent: Jeff Berg, ICM - Los Angeles, 213/550-4205

ELECTRA GLIDE IN BLUE   United Artists, 1973

VAL GUEST

b. 1911 - London, England
Address: 11 Melina Place, London NW8, England, 01/286-5766

MISS LONDON LTD.   General Film Distributors, 1943, British
BEES IN PARADISE   General Film Distributors, 1944, British
GIVE US THE MOON   General Film Distributors, 1944, British
I'LL BE YOUR SWEETHEART   General Film Distributors, 1945, British
JUST WILLIAM'S LUCK   United Artists, 1947, British
WILLIAM COME TO TOWN   United Artists, 1948, British
MURDER AT THE WINDMILL   Grand National, 1949, British
MISS PILGRIM'S PROGRESS   Grand National, 1950, British
THE BODY SAID NO   Eros, 1950, British
MISTER DRAKE'S DUCK   United Artists, 1951, British
PENNY PRINCESS   Universal, 1952, British
LIFE WITH THE LYONS   Exclusive, 1954, British
THE RUNAWAY BUS   Eros, 1954, British
MEN OF SHERWOOD FOREST   Astor, 1954, British
DANCE LITTLE LADY   Renown, 1954, British
THEY CAN'T HANG ME   Independent Film Distributors, 1955, British
THE LYONS IN PARIS   Exclusive, 1955, British
BREAK IN THE CIRCLE   20th Century-Fox, 1955, British
THE CREEPING UNKNOWN *THE QUATERMASS EXPERIMENT*   United
    Artists, 1955, British
IT'S A WONDERFUL WORLD   Renown, 1956, British
THE WEAPON   Republic, 1956, British
CARRY ON ADMIRAL   Renown, 1957, British
ENEMY FROM SPACE *QUATERMASS II*   United Artists, 1957, British
THE ABOMINABLE SNOWMAN OF THE HIMALAYAS   20th Century-Fox,
    1957, British
THE CAMP ON BLOOD ISLAND   Columbia, 1958, British
UP THE CREEK   Dominant, 1958, British
FURTHER UP THE CREEK   Warner Bros., 1958, British
EXPRESSO BONGO   Continental, 1959, British
YESTERDAY'S ENEMY   Columbia, 1959
LIFE IS A CIRCUS   1960, British
HELL IS A CITY   Columbia, 1960, British
STOP ME BEFORE I KILL *THE FULL TREATMENT*   Columbia, 1961,
    British
THE DAY THE EARTH CAUGHT FIRE   Universal, 1962, British
JIGSAW   Beverly, 1962, British
80,000 SUSPECTS   Rank, 1963, British
CONTEST GIRL *THE BEAUTY JUNGLE*   Continental, 1964, British
WHERE THE SPIES ARE   MGM, 1965, British
CASINO ROYALE   co-director with Ken Hughes, John Huston, Joseph McGrath
    & Robert Parrish, Columbia, 1967, British
ASSIGNMENT K   Columbia, 1968, British
WHEN DINOSAURS RULED THE EARTH   Warner Bros., 1969, British
TOOMORROW   FRD, 1970, British
THE PERSUADERS   1971, British
AU PAIR GIRLS   Cannon, 1972, British
CONFESSIONS OF A WINDOW CLEANER   Columbia, 1974, British
KILLER FORCE   American International, 1975, British-Swiss
THE SHILLINGBURY BLOWERS *... AND THE BAND PLAYED ON*   Inner
    Circle, 1980, British
DANGEROUS DAVIES - THE LAST DETECTIVE   ITC/Inner Circle/
    Maidenhead Films, 1980, British
THE BOYS IN BLUE   MAM Ltd./Apollo Leisure Group, 1983, British

JOHN GUILLERMIN*

b. November 11, 1925 - London, England
Agent: ICM - Los Angeles, 213/550-4000

TORMENT   Adelphi, 1949, British
SMART ALEC   Grand National, 1951, British
TWO ON THE TILES   Grand National, 1951, British
FOUR DAYS   Grand National, 1951, British
BACHELOR IN PARIS *SONG OF PARIS*   Lippert, 1952, British
MISS ROBIN HOOD   Associated British Film Distributors, 1952, British
OPERATION DIPLOMAT   Butcher, 1953, British
ADVENTURE IN THE HOPFIELDS   British Lion/Children's Film Foundation,
    1954, British
THE CROWDED DAY   Adelphi, 1954, British
DUST AND GOLD   1955, British
THUNDERSTORM   Allied Artists, 1955, British
TOWN ON TRIAL   Columbia, 1957, British
THE WHOLE TRUTH   Columbia, 1958, British
I WAS MONTY'S DOUBLE   NTA Pictures, 1958, British
TARZAN'S GREATEST ADVENTURE   Paramount, 1959, British-U.S.
THE DAY THEY ROBBED THE BANK OF ENGLAND   MGM, 1960, British
NEVER LET GO   Rank, 1960, British
WALTZ OF THE TOREADORS   Continental, 1962, British
TARZAN GOES TO INDIA   MGM, 1962, British-U.S.-Swiss
GUNS AT BATASI   20th Century-Fox, 1964, British-U.S.
RAPTURE   International Classics, 1965, British-French
THE BLUE MAX   20th Century-Fox, 1966, British, U.S.
P.J.   Universal, 1968
HOUSE OF CARDS   Universal, 1969
THE BRIDGE AT REMAGEN   United Artists, 1969
EL CONDOR   National General, 1970
SKYJACKED   MGM, 1972
SHAFT IN AFRICA   MGM, 1973
THE TOWERING INFERNO   20th Century-Fox, 1974
KING KONG   Paramount, 1976
DEATH ON THE NILE   Paramount, 1978, British
MR. PATMAN   Film Consortium, 1980, Canadian

YILMAZ GUNEY

b. 1937 - Adana, Turkey
Contact: French Film Office, 745 Fifth Avenue, New York, NY 10151, 212/832-
    8860

MY NAME IS KERIM   Sahinler Film, 1967, Turkish
NURI THE FLEA   co-director with Serif Gedik, Guney Film, 1968, Turkish
BRIDE OF THE EARTH   Erman Film, 1968, Turkish
THE HUNGRY WOLVES   Iale Film, 1969, Turkish
AN UGLY MAN   Guney Film, 1969, Turkish
HOPE   Guney Film, 1970, Turkish
THE FUGITIVES   Alfan Film, 1971, Turkish
THE WRONGDOERS   Guney Film, 1971, Turkish
TOMORROW IS THE FINAL DAY   Irfan Film, 1971, Turkish
THE HOPELESS ONES   Akin Film, 1971, Turkish
PAIN   Azleyis Film, 1971, Turkish
ELEGY   Guney Film, 1971, Turkish
THE FATHER   Akun Film, 1971, Turkish
THE FRIEND   Guney Film, 1974, Turkish
ANXIETY   co-director with Serif Goren, Guney Film, 1974, Turkish
THE POOR ONES   co-director with Atif Yilmaz, Guney Film, 1975, Turkish
YOL   directed by Serif Goren, supervised by Yilmaz Guney, Triumph/Columbia,
    1982, Turkish-Swiss-West German
THE WALL   MK2/TF1, 1983, French

BILL GUNN

Contact: Writers Guild of America, East - New York City, 212/245-6180

STOP   Warner Bros., 1970
GANJA & HESS   Kelly-Jordan, 1973

ANDRE GUTTFREUND*

Contact: Directors Guild of America - Los Angeles, 212/656-1220

PARTNERS   Hurricane Gulch, 1981

CLAUDIO GUZMAN*

Home: 9785 Drake Lane, Beverly Hills, CA 90210, 213/278-8816

ANTONIO   Guzman Productions, 1973
LINDA LOVELACE FOR PRESIDENT   General Film, 1975
WILLA (TF)   co-director with Joan Darling, GJL Productions/Dove, Inc., 1979
THE HOSTAGE TOWER (TF)   Jerry Leider Productions, 1980
FOR LOVERS ONLY (TF)   Henerson-Hirsch Productions/Caesar's Palace
     Productions, 1982

TAYLOR HACKFORD*

Agent: Fred Specktor, CAA - Los Angeles, 213/277-4545
Attorney: Stuart Benjamin, Wyman, Rothman, Bautzer & Kuchel, 2049 Century Park
     East, Los Angeles, CA 90067, 213/556-8000

THE IDOLMAKER   United Artists, 1980
AN OFFICER AND A GENTLEMAN   Paramount, 1982
AGAINST ALL ODDS   Columbia, 1984

PIERS HAGGARD

b. 1939 - Scotland
Contact: Directors Guild of Great Britain, 56 Whitfield Street, London W1, England,
     01/580-9592

WEDDING NIGHT   American International, 1970, Irish
THE BLOOD ON SATAN'S CLAW *SATAN'S SKIN*   Cannon, 1971, British
THE QUATERMASS CONCLUSION   Euston Films Ltd., 1979, British
THE FIENDISH PLOT OF DR. FU MANCHU   Orion/Warner Bros., 1980,
     British
MRS. REINHARDT (TF)   BBC/WNET-13, 1981, British-U.S.
VENOM   Paramount, 1982, British

LARRY HAGMAN*

b. September 21, 1931 - Fort Worth, Texas
Business: MajLar Productions, Inc., 26 Malibu Colony, Malibu, CA 90265
Agent: Ed Bondy, William Morris Agency - Beverly Hills, 213/274-7451
Business Manager: Norman Marcus, Ernst & Whinney - Beverly Hills, 213/553-2800

BEWARE! THE BLOB *SON OF BLOB*   Jack H. Harris Enterprises, 1972

STUART HAGMANN*

b. September 2, 1942 - Sturgeon Bay, Wisconsin
Business: H.I.S.K. Productions, 10950 Ventura Blvd., Studio City, CA 91604, 213/
506-1700
Business Manager: Martin LeAnce - Beverly Hills, 213/275-0128

THE STRAWBERRY STATEMENT   MGM, 1970
BELIEVE IN ME   MGM, 1971
SHE LIVES (TF)   ABC Circle Films, 1973
TARANTULAS: THE DEADLY CARGO (TF)   Alan Landsburg Productions,
1977

RANDA HAINES*

Home: 2926½ Waverly Drive, Los Angeles, CA 90039, 213/662-7207
Agent: Bill Block, ICM - Los Angeles, 213/550-4000

THE JILTING OF GRANNY WEATHERALL (TF)   Learning in Focus, 1980
SOMETHING ABOUT AMELIA (TF)   Leonard Goldberg Productions, 1983

WILLIAM ''BILLY'' HALE*

Agent: William Morris Agency - Beverly Hills, 213/274-7451
Personal Manager: Martin Mickelson - Beverly Hills, 213/858-1097

HOW I SPENT MY SUMMER VACATION (TF)   Universal TV, 1967
GUNFIGHT IN ABILENE   Universal, 1967
JOURNEY TO SHILOH   Universal, 1968
NIGHTMARE (TF)   CBS, Inc., 1974
THE GREAT NIAGARA (TF)   Playboy Productions, 1974
CROSSFIRE (TF)   QM Productions, 1975
THE KILLER WHO WOULDN'T DIE (TF)   Paramount TV, 1976
STALK THE WILD CHILD (TF)   Charles Fries Productions, 1976
RED ALERT (TF)   The Jozak Company/Paramount TV, 1977
S.O.S. TITANIC (TF)   Roger Gimbel Productions/EMI TV/Argonaut Films Ltd.,
1979, U.S.-British
MURDER IN TEXAS (TF)   Dick Clark Productions/Billy Hale Films, 1981
ONE SHOE MAKES IT MURDER (TF)   The Fellows-Keegan Company/Lorimar
Productions, 1982
THE DEMON MURDER CASE (TF)   Dick Clark Productions/Len Steckler
Productions, 1983

JACK HALEY, JR.*

b. October 25, 1933 - Los Angeles, California
Business: 213/655-1106

NORWOOD   Paramount, 1970
THE LOVE MACHINE   Columbia, 1971
THAT'S ENTERTAINMENT! (FD)   MGM/United Artists, 1974
THAT'S ENTERTAINMENT, PART 2 (FD)   co-director with Gene Kelly, MGM/
United Artists, 1976
THAT'S DANCING! (FD)   MGM/UA, 1984

H.B. HALICKI

b. Dunkirk, New York
Business: H.B. Halicki Productions, P.O. Box 2123, Gardena, CA 90247, 213/327-
1744 or 213/770-1744

GONE IN 60 SECONDS   H.B. Halicki International, 1974
THE JUNKMAN   H.B. Halicki International, 1982
DEADLINE AUTO THEFT   H.B. Halicki International, 1983

ADRIAN HALL *

Home: 176 Pleasant Street, Providence, RI 02906, 401/421-4219
Personal Manager: Marion Simon, Trinity Square Repertory Company, Providence,
    RI 02903, 401/521-1100

THE HOUSE OF MIRTH (TF)   Cinelit Productions/WNET-13, 1981

PETER HALL

b. November 22, 1930 - Bury St. Edmunds, Suffolk, England
Address: The Wall House, Mongewall Park, Wallingford, Berkshire, England

WORK IS A FOUR LETTER WORD   Universal, 1968, British
A MIDSUMMER NIGHT'S DREAM   Eagle, 1968, British
PERFECT FRIDAY   Chevron, 1970, British
THE HOMECOMING   American Film Theatre, 1973, British
AKENFIELD (FD)   Angle Films, 1975, British

DANIEL HALLER *

b. 1926 - Los Angeles, California
Home: 5364 Jed Smith Road, Hidden Hills, CA 91302, 213/888-7936
Agent: Irv Schechter, Irv Schechter Company - Beverly Hills, 213/278-8070

DIE, MONSTER, DIE!   American International, 1965, U.S.-British
DEVIL'S ANGELS   American International, 1967
THE WILD RACERS   American International, 1968
PADDY   Allied Artists, 1970, Irish
PIECES OF DREAMS   United Artists, 1970
THE DUNWICH HORROR   American International, 1970
THE DESPERATE MILES (TF)   Universal TV, 1975
MY SWEET LADY (TF)   Universal TV, 1976
BLACK BEAUTY (MS)   Universal TV, 1978
LITTLE MO (TF)   Mark VII Ltd./Worldvision, 1978
BUCK ROGERS IN THE 25TH CENTURY   Universal, 1979
HIGH MIDNIGHT (TF)   The Mirisch Corporation/Universal TV, 1979
GEORGIA PEACHES (TF)   New World TV, 1980
FOLLOW THAT CAR   New World, 1981
MICKEY SPILLANE'S MARGIN FOR MURDER (TF)   Hammer Productions,
    1981
KNIGHT RIDER (TF)   Glen A. Larson Productions/Universal TV, 1982

DAVID HAMILTON

Contact: French Film Office, 745 Fifth Avenue, New York, NY 10151, 212/832-
    8860

BILITIS   Topar, 1976, French
TENDRE COUSINES   Crown International, 1980, French
LAURA   Les Films de L'Almacora, 1981, French
FIRST DESIRE   AMLF, 1983, French
UN ETE A SAINT TROPEZ (FD)   Fugio & Associates/JVC, 1983, French-
    Japanese

GUY HAMILTON *

b. September, 1922 - Paris, France
Agent: London Management - London, 01/493-1610

THE RINGER   British Lion, 1952, British
THE INTRUDER   Associated Artists, 1953, British
AN INSPECTOR CALLS   Associated Artists, 1954, British
THE COLDITZ STORY   Republic, 1955, British
CHARLEY MOON   British Lion, 1956, British
STOWAWAY GIRL   *MANUELA*   Paramount, 1957, British
THE DEVIL'S DISCIPLE   United Artists, 1959, British
A TOUCH OF LARCENY   Paramount, 1960, British
THE BEST OF ENEMIES   Columbia, 1962, Italian-British
MAN IN THE MIDDLE   20th Century-Fox, 1964, British-U.S.
GOLDFINGER   United Artists, 1964, British

continued

GUY HAMILTON*—continued
THE PARTY'S OVER   Allied Artists, 1966, British
FUNERAL IN BERLIN   Paramount, 1966, British
BATTLE OF BRITAIN   United Artists, 1969, British
DIAMONDS ARE FOREVER   United Artists, 1971, British
LIVE AND LET DIE   United Artists, 1973, British
THE MAN WITH THE GOLDEN GUN   United Artists, 1974, British
FORCE 10 FROM NAVARONE   American International, 1978
THE MIRROR CRACK'D   AFD, 1980, British
EVIL UNDER THE SUN   Universal/AFD, 1982, British

JOHN HANCOCK *

b. February 9, 1939 - Kansas City, Missouri
Home: 21531 Deerpath Lane, Malibu, CA 90265, 213/456-3627
Agent: David Wardlow, ICM - Los Angeles, 213/550-4000

LET'S SCARE JESSICA TO DEATH   Paramount, 1971
BANG THE DRUM SLOWLY   Paramount, 1973
BABY BLUE MARINE   Columbia, 1976
CALIFORNIA DREAMING   American International, 1979

CURTIS HANSON

Contact: Writers Guild of America, West - Los Angeles, 213/550-1000

THE AROUSERS   Asseyev-Hanson, 1976
THE LITTLE DRAGONS   Aurora, 1980
LOSIN' IT   Embassy, 1983, Canadian-U.S.

JOHN HANSON

NORTHERN LIGHTS   co-director with Rob Nilsson, Cine Manifest, 1979

JOSEPH C. HANWRIGHT *

Home: P.O. Box 2122, Ketchum, ID 83340, 208/726-3594

UNCLE JOE SHANNON   United Artists, 1979

JOSEPH HARDY *

b. March 8, 1929 - Carlsbad, New Mexico
Agent: Bill Haber, CAA - Los Angeles, 213/277-4545

GREAT EXPECTATIONS (TF)   Transcontinental Film Productions, 1974, British
A TREE GROWS IN BROOKLYN (TF)   20th Century-Fox TV, 1974
LAST HOURS BEFORE MORNING (TF)   Charles Fries Productions/MGM TV, 1975
THE SILENCE (TF)   Palomar Pictures International, 1975
JAMES AT 15 (TF)   20th Century-Fox TV, 1977
THE USERS (TF)   Aaron Spelling Productions, 1978
LOVE'S SAVAGE FURY (TF)   Aaron Spelling Productions, 1979
THE SEDUCTION OF MISS LEONA (TF)   Edgar J. Scherick Associates, 1980
DREAM HOUSE (TF)   Hill-Mandelker Films/Time-Life Productions, 1981
THE DAY THE BUBBLE BURST (TF)   Tamara Productions/20th Century-Fox TV/The Production Company, 1982
NOT IN FRONT OF THE CHILDREN (TF)   Tamtco Productions/The Edward S. Feldman Company, 1982
TWO MARRIAGES (TF)   Lorimar Productions/Raven's Claw Productions, 1983

ROBIN HARDY

Contact: British Academy of Film & Television Arts, 195 Piccadilly, London W1, England, 01/734-0022

THE WICKER MAN   Warner Bros., 1975, British

DEAN HARGROVE *

b. July 27, 1938 - Iola, Kansas
Agent: Major Talent Agency - Los Angeles, 213/820-5841

THE MANCHU EAGLE CAPER MYSTERY   United Artists, 1975
THE BIG RIP-OFF (TF)   Universal TV, 1975
THE RETURN OF THE WORLD'S GREATEST DETECTIVE (TF)   Universal
     TV, 1976
DEAR DETECTIVE (TF)   CBS, 1979

CURTIS HARRINGTON *

b. September 17, 1928 - Los Angeles, California
Contact: Directors Guild of America - Los Angeles, 213/656-1220

NIGHT TIDE   Universal, 1963
QUEEN OF BLOOD   American International, 1966
GAMES   Universal, 1967
HOW AWFUL ABOUT ALLAN (TF)   Aaron Spelling Productions, 1970
WHO SLEW AUNTIE ROO?   American International, 1971, British
WHAT'S THE MATTER WITH HELEN?   United Artists, 1971
THE CAT CREATURE (TF)   Screen Gems/Columbia TV, 1973
KILLER BEES (TF)   RSO Films, 1974
THE KILLING KIND   Media Trend, 1974
THE DEAD DON'T DIE (TF)   Douglas S. Cramer Productions, 1975
RUBY   Dimension, 1977
DEVIL DOG: THE HOUND OF HELL (TF)   Zeitman-Landers-Roberts
     Productions, 1978

DENNY HARRIS

Business: Denny Harris of California, Inc., 12166 W. Olympic Blvd., Los Angeles,
     CA 90064, 213/826-6265

SILENT SCREAM   American Cinema, 1980

HARRY HARRIS *

b. September 8, 1922 -Kansas City, Missouri
Agent: Ronald Lief, Contemporary-Korman Artists - Beverly Hills, 213/278-8250

THE RUNAWAYS (TF)   Lorimar Productions, 1975
THE SWISS FAMILY ROBINSON (TF)   Irwin Allen Productions/20th Century-
     Fox TV, 1975
RIVKIN: BOUNTY HUNTER (TF)   Chiarascurio Productions/Ten-Four
     Productions, 1981
A DAY FOR THANKS ON WALTON'S MOUNTAIN (TF)   Lorimar
     Productions/Amanda Productions, 1982

JAMES B. HARRIS *

b. August 3, 1928 - New York, New York
Business: James B. Harris Productions, 248½ Lasky Drive, Beverly Hills, CA 90212,
     213/273-4270

THE BEDFORD INCIDENT   Columbia, 1965
SOME CALL IT LOVING   Cine Globe, 1973
FAST-WALKING   Pickman Films, 1982

RICHARD HARRIS

b. October 1, 1932 - Limerick, Ireland
Agent: William Morris Agency - Beverly Hills, 213/274-7451

THE HERO *BLOOMFIELD*   Avco Embassy, 1972, Israeli-British

BRUCE HART *

b. January 15, 1938 - New York, New York
Home: 200 West 86th Street, New York, NY 10024, 212/724-1948
Agent: David Kennedy, ICM - New York City, 212/556-5761
Business Manager: Scott Shukat, The Shukat Co., Ltd., 340 West 55th Street, New
    York, NY 10019, 212/582-7614

SOONER OR LATER (TF)   Laughing Willow Company/NBC, 1979

HARVEY HART *

b. 1928 - Toronto, Canada
Home: 5 Sultan Street, Toronto, Ontario M5 I16, Canada, 416/960-2351
Agent: Bill Haber, CAA - Los Angeles, 213/277-4545
Business Manager: Marty Rosenthal, Kaufman & Bernstein, 1900 Avenue of the
    Stars - Suite 2270, Los Angeles, CA 90067, 213/277-1900

BUS RILEY'S BACK IN TOWN   Universal, 1965
DARK INTRUDER   Universal, 1965
SULLIVAN'S EMPIRE   co-director with Thomas Carr, Universal, 1967
THE SWEET RIDE   20th Century-Fox, 1968
THE YOUNG LAWYERS (TF)   Paramount TV, 1969
FORTUNE AND MEN'S EYES   MGM, 1971, Canadian
MAHONEY'S ESTATE (TF)   Topaz Productions, 1972, Canadian
THE PYX   Cinerama Releasing Corporation, 1973, Canadian
CAN ELLEN BE SAVED? (TF)   ABC Circle Films, 1974
MURDER OR MERCY (TF)   QM Productions, 1974
PANIC ON THE 5:22 (TF)   QM Productions, 1974
SHOOT   Avco Embassy, 1976, Canadian
STREET KILLING (TF)   ABC Circle Films, 1976
THE CITY (TF)   QM Productions, 1977
GOLDENROD (TF)   Talent Associates/Film Funding Ltd. of Canada, 1977, U.S.-
    Canadian
THE PRINCE OF CENTRAL PARK (TF)   Lorimar Productions, 1977
CAPTAINS COURAGEOUS (TF)   Norman Rosemont Productions, 1977
STANDING TALL (TF)   QM Productions, 1978
W.E.B. (TF)   NBC, 1978
LIKE NORMAL PEOPLE (TF)   Christiana Productions/20th Century-Fox TV,
    1979
THE ALIENS ARE COMING (TF)   Woodruff Productions/QM Productions,
    1980
JOHN STEINBECK'S EAST OF EDEN (MS)   Mace Neufeld Productions, 1981
THE HIGH COUNTRY   Crown International, 1981, Canadian
MASSARATI AND THE BRAIN (TF)   Aaron Spelling Productions, 1982
BORN BEAUTIFUL (TF)   Procter & Gamble Productions/Telecom Entertainment
    Inc., 1982
GETTING EVEN   New World, 1983, Canadian

ANTHONY HARVEY *

b. June 3, 1931 - London, England
Agent: Stan Kamen, William Morris Agency - Beverly Hills, 213/274-7451

DUTCHMAN   Continental, 1967, British
THE LION IN WINTER ★   Avco Embassy, 1968, British
THEY MIGHT BE GIANTS   Universal, 1971
THE GLASS MENAGERIE (TF)   Talent Associates, 1973
THE ABDICATION   Warner Bros., 1974, British
THE DISAPPEARANCE OF AIMEE (TF)   Tomorrow Entertainment, 1976
PLAYERS   Paramount, 1979
EAGLE'S WING   International Picture Show, 1980, British
RICHARD'S THINGS   New World, 1981, British
THE PATRICIA NEAL STORY (TF)   co-director with Anthony Page, Lawrence
    Schiller Productions, 1981
SVENGALI (TF)   Robert Halmi Productions, 1983
THE ULTIMATE SOLUTION OF GRACE QUIGLEY   MGM/UA/Cannon, 1984

HENRY HATHAWAY *

b. March 13, 1898 - Sacramento, California
Home Address: 888 Sarbonne Road, Los Angeles, CA 90077, 213/472-3684

HERITAGE OF THE DESERT   1932
WILD HORSE MESA   1932
UNDER THE TONTO RIM   1933
SUNSET PASS   1933
MAN OF THE FOREST   1933
TO THE LAST MAN   1933
THE THUNDERING HERD   1933
THE LAST ROUND-UP   1934
COME ON MARINES!   1934
THE WITCHING HOUR   Paramount, 1934
NOW AND FOREVER   Paramount, 1934
THE LIVES OF A BENGAL LANCER★   Paramount, 1935
PETER IBBETSON   Paramount, 1935
THE TRAIL OF THE LONESOME PINE   Paramount, 1936
GO WEST, YOUNG MAN   Paramount, 1936
SOULS AT SEA   Paramount, 1937
SPAWN OF THE NORTH   Paramount, 1938
THE REAL GLORY   United Artists, 1939
JOHNNY APOLLO   20th Century-Fox, 1940
BRIGHAM YOUNG, FRONTIERSMAN   20th Century-Fox, 1940
THE SHEPHERD OF THE HILLS   Paramount, 1941
SUNDOWN   United Artists, 1941
TEN GENTLEMEN FROM WEST POINT   20th Century-Fox, 1942
CHINA GIRL   20th Century-Fox, 1942
HOME IN INDIANA   20th Century-Fox, 1944
WING AND A PRAYER   20th Century-Fox, 1944
NOB HILL   20th Century-Fox, 1945
THE HOUSE ON 92ND STREET   20th Century-Fox, 1945
THE DARK CORNER   20th Century-Fox, 1946
13 RUE MADELEINE   20th Century-Fox, 1947
KISS OF DEATH   20th Century-Fox, 1947
CALL NORTHSIDE 777   20th Century-Fox, 1948
DOWN TO THE SEA IN SHIPS   20th Century-Fox, 1949
THE BLACK ROSE   20th Century-Fox, 1950, British-U.S.
YOU'RE IN THE NAVY NOW   20th Century-Fox, 1951
FOURTEEN HOURS   20th Century-Fox, 1951
RAWHIDE   20th Century-Fox, 1951
THE DESERT FOX   20th Century-Fox, 1951
DIPLOMATIC COURIER   20th Century-Fox, 1952
O. HENRY'S FULL HOUSE   co-director with Howard Hawks, Henry King, Henry
    Koster & Jean Negulesco, 20th Century-Fox, 1952
NIAGARA   20th Century-Fox, 1953
WHITE WITCH DOCTOR   20th Century-Fox, 1953
PRINCE VALIANT   20th Century-Fox, 1954
GARDEN OF EVIL   20th Century-Fox, 1954
THE RACERS   20th Century-Fox, 1955
THE BOTTOM OF THE BOTTLE   20th Century-Fox, 1956
23 PACES TO BAKER STREET   20th Century-Fox, 1956, British-U.S.
LEGEND OF THE LOST   United Artists, 1957
FROM HELL TO TEXAS   20th Century-Fox, 1958
WOMAN OBSESSED   20th Century-Fox, 1959
SEVEN THIEVES   20th Century-Fox, 1960
NORTH TO ALASKA   20th Century-Fox, 1960
HOW THE WEST WAS WON   co-director with John Ford & George Marshall,
    MGM, 1963
CIRCUS WORLD   Paramount, 1964
THE SONS OF KATIE ELDER   Paramount, 1965
NEVADA SMITH   Paramount, 1966
THE LAST SAFARI   Paramount, 1967, British
FIVE CARD STUD   Paramount, 1968
TRUE GRIT   Paramount, 1969
RAID ON ROMMEL   Universal, 1971
SHOOT-OUT   Universal, 1971
HANGUP *SUPER DUDE*   Universal, 1974

SIDNEY HAYERS *

b. Edinburgh, Scotland
Home: 10545 Wyton Drive, Los Angeles, CA 90024, 213/474-8984
Messages: 213/474-0945
Agent: Mark Lichtman, Shapiro-Lichtman Agency - Los Angeles, 213/557-2244
Business Manager: Susan Grode, 2049 Century Park East - Suite 1260, Los Angeles,
    CA 90067, 213/552-0592

VIOLENT MOMENT   Anglo-Amalgamated, 1959, British
THE WHITE TRAP   Anglo-Amalgamated, 1959, British
CIRCUS OF HORRORS   American International, 1960, British
THE MALPAS MYSTERY   Anglo-Amalgamated, 1960, British
ECHO OF BARBARA   Rank, 1961, British
BURN, WITCH, BURN *NIGHT OF THE EAGLE*   American International,
    1962, British
THIS IS MY STREET   Anglo-Amalgamated, 1963, British
THREE HATS FOR LISA   Anglo-Amalgamated, 1963, British
THE TRAP   Rank, 1966, British
FINDERS KEEPERS   United Artists, 1967, British
THE SOUTHERN STAR   Columbia, 1969, French-British
MISTER JERICO (TF)   ITC, 1970, British
IN THE DEVIL'S GARDEN *ASSAULT*   Hemisphere, 1971, British
THE FIRECHASERS   Rank, 1971, British
INN OF THE FRIGHTENED PEOPLE *TERROR FROM UNDER THE HOUSE/
REVENGE*   Hemisphere, 1973, British
DEADLY STRANGERS   Fox-Rank, 1974, British
DIAGNOSIS: MURDER   CIC, 1975, British
WHAT CHANGED CHARLEY FARTHING?   Stirling Gold, 1976, British
ONE WAY   Silhouette Film Productions, 1976
THE SEEKERS (TF)   Universal TV, 1978
THE LAST CONVERTIBLE (MS)   co-director with Jo Swerling, Jr. & Gus
    Trikonis, Roy Huggins Productions/Universal TV, 1979
CONDOMINIUM (TF)   Universal TV, 1980
CHANDLERTOWN *PHILIP MARLOWE - PRIVATE EYE (CMS)*   co-director
    with Bryan Forbes, Peter Hunt & David Wickes, HBO/David Wickes Television
    Ltd./London Weekend Television, 1983, British

JACK HAZAN

Contact: British Academy of Film & Television Arts, 195 Piccadilly, London W1,
    England, 01/734-0022

A BIGGER SPLASH   Lagoon Associates, 1975, British
RUDE BOY   co-director with David Mingay, Atlantic Releasing Corporation,
    1980, British

AMY HECKERLING *

Home: 1282 Devon Drive, Los Angeles, CA 90024, 213/271-9908
Agent: David Gersh, The Gersh Agency - Beverly Hills, 213/274-6611

FAST TIMES AT RIDGEMONT HIGH   Universal, 1982
JOHNNY DANGEROUSLY   20th Century-Fox, 1984

RICHARD T. HEFFRON *

Messages: 213/457-5323
Agent: Fred Specktor, CAA - Los Angeles, 213/277-4545

DO YOU TAKE THIS STRANGER? (TF)   Universal TV, 1971
FILLMORE (FD)   20th Century-Fox, 1972
TOMA (TF)   Universal TV, 1973
OUTRAGE! (TF)   ABC Circle Films, 1973
NEWMAN'S LAW   Universal, 1974
THE MORNING AFTER (TF)   Wolper Productions, 1974
THE ROCKFORD FILES (TF)   Universal TV, 1974
THE CALIFORNIA KID (TF)   Universal TV, 1974
LOCUSTS (TF)   Paramount TV, 1974
I WILL FIGHT NO MORE FOREVER (TF)   Wolper Productions, 1975
DEATH SCREAM (TF)   RSO Films, 1975
TRACKDOWN   United Artists, 1976

continued

RICHARD T. HEFFRON*—continued
FUTUREWORLD   American International, 1976
YOUNG JOE, THE FORGOTTEN KENNEDY (TF)   ABC Circle Films, 1977
OUTLAW BLUES   Warner Bros., 1977
SEE HOW SHE RUNS (TF)   CLN Productions, 1978
TRUE GRIT: A FURTHER ADVENTURE (TF)   Paramount TV, 1978
FOOLIN' AROUND   Columbia, 1978
A RUMOR OF WAR (TF)   Charles Fries Productions, 1980
A WHALE FOR THE KILLING (TF)   Play Productions/Beowulf Productions, 1981
I, THE JURY   20th Century-Fox, 1982
THE MYSTIC WARRIOR (MS)   David L. Wolper-Stan Margulies Productions/ Warner Bros. TV, 1983
A KILLER IN THE FAMILY (TF)   Stan Margulies Productions/Sunn Classic Pictures, 1983

JEROME HELLMAN*

b. September 4, 1928 - New York, New York
Business: Jerome Hellman Productions, 68 Malibu Colony Drive, Malibu, CA 90265, 213/456-3361

PROMISES IN THE DARK   Orion/Warner Bros., 1979

MONTE HELLMAN*

b. July 12, 1932 - New York, New York
Business: Monte Hellman Films, 265 N. Robertson Blvd., Beverly Hills, CA 90211, 213/278-2944
Agent: Mike Simpson, William Morris Agency - Beverly Hills, 213/274-7451

BEAST FROM HAUNTED CAVE   Allied Artists, 1959
BACK DOOR TO HELL   20th Century-Fox, 1964
FLIGHT TO FURY   1965
THE SHOOTING   American International, 1966
RIDE IN THE WHIRLWIND   American International, 1966
TWO-LANE BLACKTOP   Universal, 1971
COCKFIGHTER   *BORN TO KILL*   New World, 1974
CHINA 9 LIBERTY 37   Titanus, 1978, Italian

GUNNAR HELLSTROM*

Home: 10816-¾ Lindbrook Drive, Los Angeles, CA 90024, 213/474-6749
Business: Artistfilm, Toro, 14900 Nynashamn, Sweden, 0752-31135
Agent: F.A.M.E. - Los Angeles, 213/656-7590

THE NAME OF THE GAME IS KILL (TF)   Universal TV, 1968
MARK, I LOVE YOU (TF)   The Aubrey Company, 1980
RASKENSTAM   Sandrews, 1983, Swedish

DAVID HELPERN, JR.

I'M A STRANGER HERE MYSELF (FD)   October Films, 1974
HOLLYWOOD ON TRIAL (FD)   Lumiere, 1976
SOMETHING SHORT OF PARADISE   American International, 1979

DAVID HEMMINGS*

b. November 18, 1941 - Guildfold, England
Agent: Stone-Masser Talent Agents - Los Angeles, 213/275-9599

RUNNING SCARED   Paramount, 1972, British
THE 14   MGM-EMI, 1973, British
JUST A GIGOLO   United Artists Classics, 1978, West German
THE SURVIVOR   Hemdale, 1981, Australian
THE YOUND ADVENTURERS   *RACE TO THE YANKEE ZEPHYR*   Artists Releasing Corporation/Film Ventures International, 1983, New Zealand-British

FRANK HENENLOTTER

BASKET CASE   Analysis, 1982

BUCK HENRY *

b. 1930 - New York, New York
Agent: ICM - Los Angeles, 213/550-4000

HEAVEN CAN WAIT ★   co-director with Warren Beatty, Paramount, 1978
FIRST FAMILY   Warner Bros., 1980

JIM HENSON *

b. September 24, 1936 - Greenville, South Carolina
Business: 212/794-2400

THE GREAT MUPPET CAPER   Universal/AFD, 1981, British
THE DARK CRYSTAL   co-director with Frank Oz, Universal/AFD, 1982, British

MICHAEL HERZ

Business: Troma, Inc., 733 Ninth Avenue, New York, NY 10019, 212/757-4555

WAITRESS!   co-director with Samuel Weil, Troma, 1982
STUCK ON YOU!   co-director with Samuel Weil, Troma, 1983
THE FIRST TURN-ON!   co-director with Samuel Weil, Troma, 1983

JOHN HERZFELD *

Agent: Jack Rapke, CAA - Los Angeles, 213/277-4545

TWO OF A KIND   20th Century-Fox, 1983

WERNER HERZOG

b. 1942 - Sachrang, Germany
Contact: German Film & TV Academy, Pommernallee 1, 1000 Berlin 19, West
    Germany, 030/303-6212

DIE FLIEGENDEN ARZTE VON OSTAFRIKA   1968, West German
SIGNS OF LIFE   Werner Herzog Filmproduktion, 1968, West German
BEHINDERTE ZUNKUFT   1970, West German
EVEN DWARFS STARTED SMALL   New Line Cinema, 1971, West German
LAND OF SILENCE AND DARKNESS   New Yorker, 1972, West German
AGUIRRE, THE WRATH OF GOD   New Yorker, 1973, West German-Mexican-
    Peruvian
THE MYSTERY OF KASPAR HAUSER *EVERY MAN FOR HIMSELF AND
    GOD AGAINST ALL*   Cinema 5, 1974, West German
HEART OF GLASS   New Yorker, 1976, West German
STROSZEK   New Yorker, 1977, West German
FATA MORGANA   New Yorker, 1978, West German
WOYZECK   New Yorker, 1979, West German
NOSFERATU THE VAMPYRE   20th Century-Fox, 1979, West German-French-
    U.S.
GOD'S ANGRY MAN (TD)   1980, West German
FITZCARRALDO   New World, 1982, West German
WHERE THE GREEN ANTS DREAM   Orion Classics, 1984, West German-U.S.-
    Australian

GORDON HESSLER *

b. 1930 - Berlin, Germany
Home: 8910 Holly Place, Los Angeles, CA 90046, 213/654-9890
Agent: F.A.M.E. - Los Angeles, 213/656-7590

THE WOMAN WHO WOULDN'T DIE *CATACOMBS*   Warner Bros., 1965,
    British
THE OBLONG BOX   American International, 1969, British

continued

GORDON HESSLER*—continued
THE LAST SHOT YOU HEAR   20th Century-Fox, 1969, British
SCREAM AND SCREAM AGAIN   American International, 1970, British
CRY OF THE BANSHEE   American International, 1970, British
MURDERS IN THE RUE MORGUE   American International, 1971, British
EMBASSY   Hemdale, 1973, British
SCREAM, PRETTY PEGGY (TF)   Universal TV, 1973
SKYWAY TO DEATH (TF)   Universal TV, 1974
HITCHHIKE! (TF)   Universal TV, 1974
A CRY IN THE WILDERNESS (TF)   Universal TV, 1974
BETRAYAL (TF)   Metromedia Productions, 1974
THE GOLDEN VOYAGE OF SINBAD   Columbia, 1974, British
TRACCO DI VELENO IN UNA COPPA DI CHAMPAGNE   Arden, 1975,
    Italian
THE STRANGE POSSESSION OF MRS. OLIVER (TF)   The Shpetner
    Company, 1977
SECRETS OF THREE HUNGRY WIVES (TF)   Penthouse Productions, 1978
KISS MEETS THE PHANTOM OF THE PARK (TF)   Hanna-Barbera
    Productions/KISS Productions, 1978
BEGGERMAN, THIEF (TF)   Universal TV, 1980
THE SECRET WAR OF JACKIE'S GIRLS (TF)   Public Arts Productions/
    Penthouse Productions/Universal TV, 1980
ESCAPE FROM EL DIABLO   Cinema Presentations International, 1983, U.S.-
    Spanish-British

CHARLTON HESTON

b. October 4, 1923 - Evanston, Illinois
Agent: Chasin-Park-Citron - Los Angeles, 213/273-7190

ANTONY AND CLEOPATRA   Rank, 1973, British-Spanish-Swiss
MOTHER LODE   Agamemnon Films, 1982, Canadian

DOUGLAS HEYES *

Business Manager: Clarke Lilly Associates, 333 Apolena Avenue, Balboa Island,
    CA 92662, 714/833-3347

KITTEN WITH A WHIP   Universal, 1964
BEAU GESTE   Universal, 1966
THE LONELY PROFESSION (TF)   Universal TV, 1969
POWDERKEG (TF)   Filmways/Rodphi, 1969
DRIVE HARD, DRIVE FAST (TF)   Universal TV, 1973
CAPTAINS AND THE KINGS (MS)   co-director with Allen Reisner, Universal
    TV, 1976
ASPEN (MS)   Universal TV, 1977
THE FRENCH ATLANTIC AFFAIR (TF)   Aaron Spelling Productions/MGM TV,
    1979

DOUGLAS HICKOX *

Home: The White House, Ferry Lane, Wargrave, Berkshire, England, 073/522-2965
Agent: Shapiro-Lichtman Agency - Los Angeles, 213/557-2244

IT'S ALL OVER TOWN   British Lion, 1963, British
JUST FOR YOU   Columbia, 1963, British
ENTERTAINING MR. SLOANE   Continental, 1970, British
SITTING TARGET   MGM, 1972, British
THEATRE OF BLOOD   United Artists, 1973, British
BRANNIGAN   United Artists, 1975, British
SKY RIDERS   20th Century-Fox, 1976
ZULU DAWN   American Cinema, 1979, British
THE PHOENIX (TF)   Mark Carliner Productions, 1981
THE HOUND OF THE BASKERVILLES   Mapleton Films Ltd., 1983, British
THE MASTER OF BALLANTRAE (TF)   Larry White-Hugh Benson Productions/
    HTV/Columbia TV, 1984, U.S.-British

COLIN HIGGINS *

Agent: Steve Roth, CAA - Los Angeles, 213/277-4545

FOUL PLAY   Paramount, 1978
NINE TO FIVE   20th Century-Fox, 1980
THE BEST LITTLE WHOREHOUSE IN TEXAS   Universal, 1982

GEORGE ROY HILL *

b. December 20, 1922 - Minneapolis, Minnesota
Business: Pan Arts Productions, 4000 Warner Blvd., Burbank, CA 91522, 213/954-6000
Agent: William Morris Agency - Beverly Hills, 213/274-7451

PERIOD OF ADJUSTMENT   MGM, 1962
TOYS IN THE ATTIC   United Artists, 1963
THE WORLD OF HENRY ORIENT   United Artists, 1964
HAWAII   United Artists, 1966
THOROUGHLY MODERN MILLIE   Universal, 1967
BUTCH CASSIDY AND THE SUNDANCE KID ★   20th Century-Fox, 1969
SLAUGHTERHOUSE-FIVE   Universal, 1971
THE STING ★★   Universal, 1973
THE GREAT WALDO PEPPER   Universal, 1975
SLAP SHOT   Universal, 1977
A LITTLE ROMANCE   Orion/Warner Bros., 1979, U.S.-French
THE WORLD ACCORDING TO GARP   Warner Bros., 1982
THE LITTLE DRUMMER GIRL   Warner Bros., 1984

JACK HILL *

b. January 28, 1933 - Los Angeles, California
Home: 22014 De La Oja Street, Woodland Hills, CA 91364, 213/346-0110
Agent: Robinson-Weintraub & Associates - Los Angeles, 213/653-5802

BLOOD BATH   co-director with Stephanie Rothman, American International, 1966
PIT STOP   Distributors International, 1969
THE BIG DOLL HOUSE   New World, 1971
THE BIG BIRD CAGE   New World, 1972
COFFY   American International, 1973
FOXY BROWN   American International, 1974
THE SWINGING CHEERLEADERS   Centaur, 1974
SWITCHBLADE SISTERS   Centaur, 1975

JAMES HILL *

b. 1919 - England
Address: 1 Abdale Road, London W12, England, 01/743-7208
Agent: The Lantz Office - Los Angeles, 213/858-1144

THE STOLEN PLANS   Associated British Film Distributors/Children's Film Foundation, 1952, British
THE CLUE OF THE MISSING APE   Associated British Film Distributors/Children's Film Foundation, 1953, British
PERIL FOR THE GUY   British Lion/Children's Film, Foundation, 1956, British
MYSTERY IN THE MINE   Children's Film Foundation, 1959, British
THE KITCHEN   British Lion, 1961, British
THE DOCK BRIEF   MGM, 1962, British
LUNCH HOUR   Bryanston, 1962, British
SEASIDE SWINGERS *EVERY DAY'S A HOLIDAY*   Embassy, 1964, British
A STUDY IN TERROR   Columbia, 1966, British
BORN FREE   Columbia, 1966, British
THE CORRUPT ONES *THE PEKING MEDALLION*   Warner Bros., 1967, West German-French-Italian
CAPTAIN NEMO AND THE UNDERWATER CITY   MGM, 1970, British
AN ELEPHANT CALLED SLOWLY   American Continental, 1971, British
BLACK BEAUTY   Paramount, 1971, British-West German-Spanish
THE BELSTONE FOX *FREE SPIRIT*   Cine III, 1973, British
CHRISTIAN THE LION *THE LION AT WORLD'S END*   co-director with Bill Travers, Scotia American, 1974, British

continued

JAMES HILL*—continued

THE WILD AND THE FREE (TF)   BSR Productions/Marble Arch Productions,
1980
OWAIN GLYNDWR - PRINCE OF WALES (TF)   OPIX/S4C, 1983, British

WALTER HILL *

b. January 10, 1942 - Long Beach, California
Agent: Jeff Berg, ICM - Los Angeles, 213/550-4205

HARD TIMES   Columbia, 1975
THE DRIVER   20th Century-Fox, 1978
THE WARRIORS   Paramount, 1979
THE LONG RIDERS   United Artists, 1980
SOUTHERN COMFORT   20th Century-Fox, 1981
48 HRS.   Paramount, 1982
STREETS OF FIRE   Universal, 1984

ARTHUR HILLER *

b. November 22, 1923 - Edmonton, Canada
Agent: The Gersh Agency - Beverly Hills, 213/274-6611

THE CARELESS YEARS   United Artists, 1957
THE MIRACLE OF THE WHITE STALLIONS   Buena Vista, 1963
THE WHEELER DEALERS   MGM, 1963
THE AMERICANIZATION OF EMILY   MGM, 1964
PROMISE HER ANYTHING   Paramount, 1966
PENELOPE   MGM, 1966
TOBRUK   Universal, 1967
THE TIGER MAKES OUT   Columbia, 1967
POPI   United Artists, 1969
THE OUT-OF-TOWNERS   Paramount, 1970
LOVE STORY ★   Paramount, 1970
PLAZA SUITE   Paramount, 1971
THE HOSPITAL   United Artists, 1971
MAN OF LA MANCHA   United Artists, 1972, Italian-U.S.
THE CRAZY WORLD OF JULIUS VROODER   20th Century-Fox, 1974
THE MAN IN THE GLASS BOOTH   American Film Theatre, 1975
W.C. FIELDS AND ME   Universal, 1976
SILVER STREAK   20th Century-Fox, 1976
THE IN-LAWS   Columbia, 1979
NIGHTWING   Columbia, 1979
MAKING LOVE   20th Century-Fox, 1981
AUTHOR! AUTHOR!   20th Century-Fox, 1982
ROMANTIC COMEDY   MGM/UA, 1983
THE LONELY GUY   Universal, 1984

WILLIAM BYRON HILLMAN *

b. Chicago, Illinois
Home: P.O. Box 321, Tarzana, CA 91356, 213/705-3456
Agent: Scott Penney, Eisenbach, Greene, Inc. - Los Angeles, 213/659-3420

BETTA BETTA   Commonwealth United, 1971
THE TRAIL RIDE   Gulf States, 1973
THE PHOTOGRAPHER   Avco Embassy, 1974
THE MAN FROM CLOVER GROVE   American Cinema, 1977
THETUS   Rachel's Releasing Corporation, 1979
DOUBLE EXPOSURE   Crown International, 1982
CAMPUS CALL   New World, 1983

JACK B. HIVELY

THE ADVENTURES OF HUCKLEBERRY FINN (TF)   Sunn Classic Productions,
1981
CALIFORNIA GOLD RUSH (TF)   Sunn Classic Productions, 1981

MIKE HODGES *

Home: 25 Palace Court, London W2, England, 01/229-6135
Agent: Barry Krost, BKM Management, Inc. - Los Angeles, 213/550-7358

GET CARTER   MGM, 1971, British
PULP   United Artists, 1972, British
THE TERMINAL MAN   Warner Bros., 1974
FLASH GORDON   Universal, 1980, British
MISSING PIECES (TF)   Entheos Unlimited Productions/TTC, 1983

JACK HOFSISS *

b. September 28, 1950 - Brooklyn, New York
Contact: Directors Guild of America - New York City, 212/581-0370

I'M DANCING AS FAST AS I CAN   Paramount, 1982

ROD HOLCOMB *

Messages: 213/794-0700
Agent: Sylvia Gold/Elliot Webb, ICM - Los Angeles, 213/550-4000

CAPTAIN AMERICA (TF)   Universal TV, 1979
MIDNIGHT OFFERINGS (TF)   Stephen J. Cannell Productions, 1981
THE GREATEST AMERICAN HERO (TF)   Stephen J. Cannell Productions, 1981
THE QUEST (TF)   Stephen J. Cannell Productions, 1982
THE A TEAM (TF)   Stephen J. Cannell Productions, 1983
STITCHES   Marcucci-Kerr Productions, 1984

ALLAN HOLZMAN

FORBIDDEN WORLD   New World, 1982

ELLIOTT HONG

KILL THE GOLDEN GOOSE   Lone Star, 1979
THEY CALL ME BRUCE? *A FISTFUL OF CHOPSTICKS*   Artists Releasing Corporation/Film Ventures International, 1982

TOBE HOOPER *

Agent: John Gaines, APA - Los Angeles, 213/273-0744
Business Manager: Marvin Freedman, Freedman, Kinzelberg & Broder, 1801 Avenue of the Stars - Suite 911, Los Angeles, CA 90067, 213/277-0700

THE TEXAS CHAINSAW MASSACRE   Bryanston, 1974
EATEN ALIVE   Virgo International, 1977
SALEM'S LOT (TF)   Warner Bros. TV, 1979
THE FUNHOUSE   Universal, 1981
POLTERGEIST   MGM/UA, 1982

DENNIS HOPPER

b. May 17, 1936 - Dodge City, Kansas
Personal Manager: 213/656-7731

EASY RIDER   Columbia, 1969
THE LAST MOVIE   Universal, 1971
OUT OF THE BLUE   Discovery Films, 1982, Canadian

JERRY HOPPER *

b. July 29, 1907 - Guthrie, Oklahoma
Home: 815 Avenida Salvador, San Clemente, CA 92672

THE ATOMIC CITY   Paramount, 1952
HURRICANE SMITH   Paramount, 1952
PONY EXPRESS   Paramount, 1953
ALASKA SEAS   Paramount, 1954
SECRET OF THE INCAS   Paramount, 1954
NAKED ALIBI   Universal, 1954
SMOKE SIGNAL   Universal, 1955
THE PRIVATE WAR OF MAJOR BENSON   Universal, 1955
ONE DESIRE   Universal, 1955
THE SQUARE JUNGLE   Universal, 1956
NEVER SAY GOODBYE   Universal, 1956
TOY TIGER   Universal, 1956
THE MISSOURI TRAVELER   Buena Vista, 1958
BLUEPRINT FOR MURDER   Paramount, 1961
MADRON   Four Star-Excelsior, 1970, U.S.-Israeli

JOHN HOUGH *

b. November 21, 1941 - London, England
Business: Pinewood Studios, Iver Heath, Bucks, England, IVER 700, ext. 540
Agent: Joe Funicello, ICM - Los Angeles, 213/550-4000 or: John Redway &
     Associates - London, 01/637-1612

WOLFHEAD   1970, British
SUDDEN TERROR *EYEWITNESS*   National General, 1971, British
THE PRACTICE   1971, British
TWINS OF EVIL   Universal, 1972, British
TREASURE ISLAND   National General, 1972, British-French-West German-
     Spanish
THE LEGEND OF HELL HOUSE   20th Century-Fox, 1974, British
DIRTY MARY CRAZY LARRY   20th Century-Fox, 1974
ESCAPE TO WITCH MOUNTAIN   Buena Vista, 1975
RETURN FROM WITCH MOUNTAIN   Buena Vista, 1978
BRASS TARGET   MGM/United Artists, 1978
THE WATCHER IN THE WOODS   Buena Vista, 1980
THE INCUBUS   Artists Releasing Corporation/Film Ventures International, 1982,
     Canadian
TRIUMPHS OF A MAN CALLED HORSE   Jensen Farley Pictures, 1983, U.S.-
     Mexican

CY HOWARD *

b. September 27, 1915 - Milwaukee, Wisconsin
Home: 10230 Sunset Blvd., Los Angeles, CA 90024, 213/276-2615

LOVERS AND OTHER STRANGERS   Cinerama Releasing Corporation, 1970
EVERY LITTLE CROOK AND NANNY   MGM, 1972
IT COULDN'T HAPPEN TO A NICER GUY (TF)   The Jozak Company, 1974

RON HOWARD *

b. March 1, 1954 - Duncan, Oklahoma
Agent: TMI - Los Angeles, 213/273-4000

GRAND THEFT AUTO   New World, 1978
COTTON CANDY (TF)   Major H Productions, 1978
SKYWARD (TF)   Major H-Anson Productions, 1980
THROUGH THE MAGIC PYRAMID (TF)   Major H Productions, 1981
NIGHT SHIFT   The Ladd Company/Warner Bros., 1982
SPLASH   Buena Vista, 1984

KING HU

b. 1931 - Peking, China
Business: King Hu Film Productions, 10C Fa Po St., 2nd Floor, Yau Yat Cheun,
    Kowloon, Hong Kong, (3)81-8920, Cable: KINGSMOVIE

COME DRINK WITH ME   1966, Hong Kong
DRAGON GATE INN   1967, Hong Kong
A TOUCH OF ZEN   1968, Hong Kong
THE FATE OF LEE KHAN   1973, Hong Kong
THE VALIANT ONES   1974, Hong Kong
RAINING ON THE MOUNTAIN   1977, Hong Kong
LEGEND OF THE MOUNTAIN   1978, Hong Kong

TOM HUCKABEE

b. September 2, 1955 - Forth Worth, Texas
Business: Tiger Mountain Productions, Inc., 2136 N. Beachwood, Hollywood, CA,
    213/463-3831

TAKING TIGER MOUNTAIN   co-director with Kent Smith, Horizon, 1983

HUGH HUDSON

Address: Sussex House, 14 Upper Mall, London W6, England, 01/240-5684
Contact: Directors Guild of Great Britain, 56 Whitfield Street, London W1, England,
    01/580-9592

CHARIOTS OF FIRE ★   The Ladd Company/Warner Bros., 1981, British
GREYSTROKE: THE LEGEND OF TARZAN, LORD OF THE APES   Warner
    Bros., 1984, British

ROY HUGGINS*

b. July 18, 1914 - Litelle, Washington
Business: Public Arts, Inc., 1928 Mandeville Canyon, Los Angeles, CA 90049,
    213/476-7892

HANGMAN'S KNOT   Columbia, 1952
THE YOUNG COUNTRY (TF)   Universal TV, 1970

JOHN HUGHES

Contact: Writers Guild of America, West - Los Angeles, 213/550-1000

SIXTEEN CANDLES   Universal, 1984

KENNETH ''KEN'' HUGHES*

b. January 19, 1922 - Liverpool, England
Home: 950 N. Kings Road - Suite 364, Los Angeles, CA 90069, 213/654-2068
Agent: Eisenbach-Greene, Inc. - Los Angeles, 213/656-7126

WIDE BOY   Realart, 1952, British
HEAT WAVE *THE HOUSE ACROSS THE LAKE*   Lippert, 1954, British
BLACK 13   Archway, 1954, British
THE BRAIN MACHINE   RKO Radio, 1955, British
THE CASE OF THE RED MONKEY *LITTLE RED MONKEY*   Allied Artists,
    1955, British
THE DEADLIEST SIN *CONFESSION*   Allied Artists, 1955, British
THE ATOMIC MAN *TIMESLIP*   Allied Artists, 1955, British
JOE MACBETH   Columbia, 1956, British
WICKED AS THEY COME   Columbia, 1957, British
THE LONG HAUL   Columbia, 1957, British
JAZZ BOAT   Columbia, 1960, British
IN THE NICK   Columbia, 1960, British
THE TRIALS OF OSCAR WILDE   Kingsley International, 1960, British
PLAY IT COOLER   Columbia, 1961, British
THE SMALL WORLD OF SAMMY LEE   7 Arts, 1963, British
OF HUMAN BONDAGE   MGM, 1964, British
ARRIVEDERCI, BABY! *DROP DEAD, DARLING*   Paramount, 1966, British

continued

KENNETH "KEN" HUGHES*—continued
CASINO ROYALE   co-director with Val Guest, John Huston, Joseph McGrath &
    Robert Parrish, Columbia, 1967, British
CHITTY CHITTY BANG BANG   United Artists, 1968, British
CROMWELL   Columbia, 1970, British
THE INTERNECINE PROJECT   Allied Artists, 1974, British
ALFIE DARLING *OH! ALFIE*   1975, British
SEXTETTE   Crown International, 1978
NIGHT SCHOOL *TERROR EYES*   Paramount, 1981

T E R R Y   H U G H E S

Contact: Directors Guild of Great Britain, 56 Whitfield Street, London W1, England,
    01/580-9592

MONTY PYTHON LIVE AT THE HOLLYWOOD BOWL   Columbia, 1982,
    British
SUNSET LIMOUSINE (TF)   Witzend Productions/ITC, 1983

A N N   H U I

b. 1947 - Manchuria, China
Contact: Hong Kong International Film Festival, 5th Floor, High Block City Hall,
    Edinburgh Place, Hong Kong, (3)72-1193

THE SECRET   1979, Hong Kong
THE SPOOKY BUNCH   1980, Hong Kong
THE STORY OF WOO VIET   1981, Hong Kong
BOAT PEOPLE   Spectrafilm, 1983, Hong Kong

P E T E R   H U N T *

b. March 11, 1928 - London, England
Home: 2229 Roscomare Road, Los Angeles, CA 90077, 213/472-1911
Agent: Martin Shapiro, Shapiro-Lichtman Agency - Los Angeles, 213/557-2244

ON HER MAJESTY'S SECRET SERVICE   United Artists, 1969, British
GOLD   Allied Artists, 1974, British
SHOUT AT THE DEVIL   American International, 1976, British
GULLIVER'S TRAVELS   EMI, 1977, British-Belgian
THE BEASTS ARE ON THE STREETS (TF)   Hanna-Barbera Productions, 1978
DEATH HUNT   20th Century-Fox, 1981
CHANDLERTOWN *PHILIP MARLOWE - PRIVATE EYE (CMS)*   co-director
    with Bryan Forbes, Sidney Hayers & David Wickes, HBO/David Wickes
    Television Ltd./London Weekend Television, 1983, British
THE LAST DAYS OF POMPEII (MS)   David Gerber Company/Columbia TV,
    1984

P E T E R   H .   H U N T *

b. December 19, 1938 - Pasadena, California
Agent: Robert Lantz, The Lantz Office - New York City, 212/751-2107 or: Bill
    Haber, CAA - Los Angeles, 213/277-4545

1776   Columbia, 1972
FLYING HIGH (TF)   Mark Carliner Productions, 1978
BULLY   Maturo Image, 1978
WHEN SHE WAS BAD ... (TF)   Ladd Productions/Henry Jaffe Enterprises,
    1979
RENDEZVOUS HOTEL (TF)   Mark Carliner Productions, 1979
LIFE ON THE MISSISSIPPI (TF)   The Great Amwell Company/Nebraska ETV
    Network/WNET-13/Taurus Films, 1980
THE PRIVATE HISTORY OF A CAMPAIGN THAT FAILED (TF)   The Great
    Amwell Company/Nebraska ETV Network/WNET-13, 1981
THE MYSTERIOUS STRANGER (TF)   The Great Amwell Company/Nebraska
    ETV Network/WNET-13/MR Film/Taurus Films, 1982
SKEEZER (TF)   Margie-Lee Enterprises/The Blue Marble Company/Marble Arch
    Productions, 1982

TIM HUNTER *

Agent: Tina Nides, CAA - Los Angeles, 213/277-4545

TEX   Buena Vista, 1982

HARRY HURWITZ

Contact: Writers Guild of America, West - Los Angeles, 213/550-1000

THE PROJECTIONIST   Maron Films Limited, 1971
THE COMEBACK TRAIL   Dynamite Entertainment/Rearguard Productions, 1971
RICHARD   co-director with Lorees Yerby, Billings, 1972
CHAPLINESQUE, MY LIFE AND HARD TIMES   Xanadu, 1972
SAFARI 3000   United Artists, 1982

WARIS HUSSEIN *

b. 1938 - Lucknow, India
Agent: Elliot Webb, ICM - Los Angeles, 213/550-4000

THANK YOU ALL VERY MUCH *A TOUCH OF LOVE*   Columbia, 1969,
     British
QUACKSER FORTUNE HAS A COUSIN IN THE BRONX   UMC, 1970,
     British
MELODY *S.W.A.L.K.*   Levitt-Pickman, 1971, British
THE POSSESSION OF JOEL DELANEY   Paramount, 1972
HENRY VIII AND HIS SIX WIVES   Levitt-Pickman, 1973, British
DIVORCE HIS/DIVORCE HERS (TF)   World Film Services, 1973
AND BABY MAKES SIX (TF)   Alan Landsburg Productions, 1979
DEATH PENALTY (TF)   Brockway Productions/NBC Entertainment, 1980
THE HENDERSON MONSTER (TF)   Titus Productions, 1980
BABY COMES HOME (TF)   Alan Landsburg Productions, 1980
CALLIE & SON (TF)   Rosilyn Heller Productions/Hemdale Presentations/City
     Films/Motown Pictures Co., 1981
COMING OUT OF THE ICE (TF)   The Konigsberg Company, 1982
LITTLE GLORIA ... HAPPY AT LAST (TF)   Edgar J. Scherick Associates/
     Metromedia Producers Corporation, 1982, U.S.-Canadian-British
PRINCESS DAISY (MS)   NBC Productions, 1983
THE WINTER OF OUR DISCONTENT (TF)   Lorimar Productions, 1984

JIMMY HUSTON

Agent: Ben Conway & Associates - Los Angeles, 213/271-8133

DEATH RIVER   Omni, 1977
DARK SUNDAY   Intercontinental, 1978
BUCKSTONE COUNTY PRISON   Film Ventures International, 1978
SEABO   E.O. Corporation, 1978
FINAL EXAM   MPM, 1981
THE SLEUTH SLAYER   Private Eye Productions, 1984

JOHN HUSTON *

b. August 5, 1906 - Nevada, Montana
Agent: Paul Kohner, Inc. - Los Angeles, 213/550-1060
Business Manager: Jess S. Morgan & Company, 6420 Wilshire Blvd., Los Angeles,
     CA 90048, 213/651-1601

THE MALTESE FALCON   Warner Bros., 1941
IN THIS OUR LIFE   Warner Bros., 1942
ACROSS THE PACIFIC   Warner Bros., 1942
THE TREASURE OF THE SIERRA MADRE ★★   Warner Bros., 1948
KEY LARGO   Warner Bros., 1948
WE WERE STRANGERS   Columbia, 1949
THE ASPHALT JUNGLE ★   MGM, 1950
THE RED BADGE OF COURAGE   MGM, 1951
THE AFRICAN QUEEN ★   United Artists, 1952
MOULIN ROUGE ★   United Artists, 1952, British
BEAT THE DEVIL   United Artists, 1954, British
MOBY DICK   Warner Bros., 1956, British

continued

JOHN HUSTON*—continued

HEAVEN KNOWS, MR. ALLISON   20th Century-Fox, 1957
THE BARBARIAN AND THE GEISHA   20th Century-Fox, 1958
THE ROOTS OF HEAVEN   20th Century-Fox, 1958
THE UNFORGIVEN   United Artists, 1960
THE MISFITS   United Artists, 1961
FREUD   Universal, 1963
THE LIST OF ADRIAN MESSENGER   Universal, 1963
NIGHT OF THE IGUANA   MGM, 1964
THE BIBLE ... In the Beginning   20th Century-Fox, 1966, Italian
REFLECTIONS IN A GOLDEN EYE   Warner Bros., 1967
CASINO ROYALE   co-director with Val Guest, Ken Hughes, Joseph McGrath &
     Robert Parrish, Columbia, 1967, British
A WALK WITH LOVE AND DEATH   20th Century-Fox, 1969, British
SINFUL DAVEY   United Artists, 1969, British
THE KREMLIN LETTER   20th Century-Fox, 1970
FAT CITY   Columbia, 1972
THE LIFE AND TIMES OF JUDGE ROY BEAN   National General, 1973
THE MACKINTOSH MAN   Warner Bros., 1973, U.S.-British
THE MAN WHO WOULD BE KING   Allied Artists, 1975, British
WISE BLOOD   New Line Cinema, 1979
PHOBIA   Paramount, 1981, Canadian
VICTORY   Paramount, 1981
ANNIE   Columbia, 1982
UNDER THE VOLCANO   Universal Classics, 1984

B R I A N   G .   H U T T O N *

b. 1935 - New York, New York
Agent: Jack Gilardi, ICM - Los Angeles, 213/550-4135

WILD SEED   Universal, 1965
THE PAD (... AND HOW TO USE IT)   Universal, 1966
SOL MADRID   MGM, 1968
WHERE EAGLES DARE   MGM, 1969, British
KELLY'S HEROES   MGM, 1970, U.S.-Yugoslavian
X Y & ZEE ZEE & CO.   Columbia, 1972, British
NIGHT WATCH   Avco Embassy, 1973, British
THE FIRST DEADLY SIN   Filmways, 1980
HIGH ROAD TO CHINA   Warner Bros., 1983, U.S.-Yugoslavian

W I L L A R D   H U Y C K

Contact: Writers Guild of America, West - Los Angeles, 213/550-1000

MESSIAH OF EVIL   International Cinefilm, 1975
FRENCH POSTCARDS   Paramount, 1979
BEST DEFENSE   Paramount, 1984

P E T E R   H Y A M S *

b. July 26, 1943 - New York, New York
Agent: Leonard Hirshan, William Morris Agency - Beverly Hills, 213/274-7451

ROLLING MAN (TF)   ABC Circle Films, 1972
GOODNIGHT MY LOVE (TF)   ABC Circle Films, 1972
BUSTING   United Artists, 1974
OUR TIME   Warner Bros., 1974
PEEPER   20th Century-Fox, 1976
CAPRICORN ONE   20th Century-Fox, 1978
HANOVER STREET   Columbia, 1979
OUTLAND   The Ladd Company/Warner Bros., 1981
THE STAR CHAMBER   20th Century-Fox, 1983

I

KON ICHIKAWA

b. November 20, 1915 - Uji Yamda, Japan
Contact: Directors Guild of Japan, Tsukada Building, 8-33 Udagawa-cho, Shibuya-ku,
    Tokyo 150, Japan, 3/461-4411

A FLOWER BLOOMS   1948, Japanese
365 NIGHTS   1948, Japanese
DESIGN OF A HUMAN BEING   1949, Japanese
ENDLESS PASSION   1949, Japanese
SANSHIRO AT GINZA   1950, Japanese
THE HOT MARSHLAND   1950, Japanese
PURSUIT AT DAWN   1950, Japanese
NIGHTSHADE FLOWER   1951, Japanese
THE LOVER   1951, Japanese
THE MAN WITHOUT NATIONALITY   1951, Japanese
STOLEN LOVE   1951, Japanese
RIVER SOLO FLOWS   1951, Japanese
WEDDING MARCH   1951, Japanese
MR. LUCKY   1952, Japanese
THE YOUNG GENERATION   1952, Japanese
THE WOMAN WHO TOUCHED THE LEGS   1952, Japanese
THIS WAY - THAT WAY   1952, Japanese
MR. POO   1953, Japanese
THE BLUE REVOLUTION   1953, Japanese
THE YOUTH OF HEIJI SENIGATA   1953, Japanese
THE LOVERS   Toho, 1953, Japanese
ALL OF MYSELF   1954, Japanese
A BILLIONAIRE   1954, Japanese
TWELVE CHAPTERS ABOUT WOMEN   1954, Japanese
GHOST STORY OF YOUTH   1955, Japanese
THE HEART   1955, Japanese
THE BURMESE HARP   Brandon, 1956, Japanese
PUNISHMENT ROOM   1956, Japanese
BRIDGE OF JAPAN   1956, Japanese
THE CROWDED TRAIN   1957, Japanese
THE HOLE   1957, Japanese
THE MEN OF TOHOKU   1957, Japanese
ENJO   1958, Japanese
MONEY AND THREE BAD MEN   1958, Japanese
GOODBYE - GOOD DAY   1959, Japanese
ODD OBSESSION   Harrison Pictures, 1959, Japanese
FIRES ON THE PLAIN   1959, Japanese
POLICE AND SMALL GANGSTERS   1959, Japanese
A GINZA VETERAN   1960, Japanese
BONCHI   1960, Japanese
A WOMAN'S TESTAMENT   co-director, 1960, Japanese
HER BROTHER   1960, Japanese
TEN BLACK WOMEN   1961, Japanese
THE SIN   1962, Japanese
BEING TWO ISN'T EASY   1962, Japanese
AN ACTOR'S REVENGE   *THE REVENGE OF UKENO-JO*   1963, Japanese
ALONE ON THE PACIFIC   1963, Japanese
MONEY TAKLKS   1964, Japanese
TOKYO OLYMPIAD (FD)   American International, 1965, Japanese
THE TALE OF GENJI (MS)   1966, Japanese

continued

KON ICHIKAWA—continued

TOPO GIGIO E SEI LADRI   1967, Italian
TO LOVE AGAIN   1971, Japanese
MATATABI   1973, Japanese
VISIONS OF EIGHT (FD)   co-director with Yuri Ozerov, Mai Zetterling, Arthur Penn, Michael Pfleghar, Milos Forman, Claude Lelouch & John Schlesinger, Cinema 5, 1973
I AM A CAT   1975, Japanese
BETWEEN WIFE AND LADY   co-director with Shiro Toyoda, 1976, Japanese
THE INUGAMI FAMILY   1976, Japanese
THE DEVIL'S SONG OF BALL   1977, Japanese
QUEEN BEE   1978, Japanese
THE DEVIL'S ISLAND   1978, Japanese
THE PHOENIX   1979, Japanese
THE OLD CITY   Toho, 1980, Japanese
HINOTORI   Toho, 1980, Japanese
THE MAKIOKA SISTERS   Toho, 1983, Japanese
SASAMEYKI   1983, Japanese

E R I C   I D L E *

Contact: Directors Guild of America - Los Angeles, 213/656-1220

ALL YOU NEED IS CASH (TF)   co-director with Gary Weis, NBC, 1978, British

S H O H E I   I M A M U R A

b. 1926 - Tokyo, Japan
Contact: Directors Guild of Japan, Tsukada Building, 8-33 Udagawa-cho, Shibuya-ku, Tokyo 150, Japan, 3/461-4411

THE STOLEN DESIRE   1958, Japanese
LIGHTS OF NIGHT   1958, Japanese
THE ENDLESS DESIRE   1958, Japanese
MY SECOND BROTHER   1959, Japanese
PIGS AND BATTLESHIPS   1961, Japanese
THE INSECT WOMAN   1963, Japanese
INTENTIONS OF MURDER *UNHOLY DESIRE*   1964, Japanese
THE PORNOGRAPHER   1966, Japanese
A MAN VANISHES   1967, Japanese
THE PROFOUND DESIRE OF THE GODS   1968, Japanese
HISTORY OF POST-WAR JAPAN AS TOLD BY A BAR HOSTESS (FD)   1970, Japanese
KARAYUKI-SAN, THE MAKING OF A PROSTITUTE (FD)   1975, Japanese
VENGEANCE IS MINE   Shochiku, 1979, Japanese
EIJANAIKA   Shochiku, 1981, Japanese
THE BALLAD OF NARAYAMA   Toei, 1983, Japanese

J O H N   I R V I N *

Home: 6 Lower Common South, London SW15, England
Messages: 01/789-1514
Agent: William Morris Agency - Beverly Hills, 213/274-7451

TINKER, TAILOR, SOLDIER, SPY (TF)   BBC/Paramount TV, 1979, British
THE DOGS OF WAR   United Artists, 1981, U.S.-British
GHOST STORY   Universal, 1981
THE CHAMPIONS   Embassy, 1984, British

D A V I D   I R V I N G

GOOD-BYE, CRUEL WORLD   Sharp Features, 1982

RICHARD IRVING *

b. February 13, 1917 - New York, New York
Business: Hal Roach Studios, 1600 N. Fairfax Avenue, Los Angeles, CA 90046,
    213/850-0525
Business Manager: The Berke Management Co., 16255 Ventura Blvd., Encino,
    CA 91438, 213/990-2631

PRESCRIPTION: MURDER (TF)   Universal TV, 1968
ISTANBUL EXPRESS (TF)   Universal TV, 1968
BREAKOUT (TF)   Universal TV, 1970
RANSOM FOR A DEAD MAN (TF)   Universal TV, 1971
CUTTER (TF)   Universal TV, 1972
THE SIX-MILLION DOLLAR MAN (TF)   Universal TV, 1973
THE ART OF CRIME (TF)   Universal TV, 1975
EXO-MAN (TF)   Universal TV, 1977
SEVENTH AVENUE (MS)   co-director with Russ Mayberry, Universal TV, 1977

GERALD I. ISENBERG *

b. May 13, 1940 - Cambridge, Massachusetts
Home: 2208 Stradella Road, Los Angeles, CA 90077, 213/476-4146
Agent: Elliot Webb, ICM - Los Angeles, 213/550-4000

SEIZURE: THE STORY OF KATHY MORRIS (TF)   The Jozak Company, 1980

NEIL ISRAEL *

Contact: Directors Guild of America - Los Angeles, 213/656-1220

TUNNELVISION   co-director with Brad Swirnoff, World Wide, 1976
AMERICATHON   United Artists, 1979
BACHELOR PARTY   Bachelor Party Productions, 1984

JAMES IVORY *

b. June 7, 1928 - Berkeley, California
Home: 400 East 52nd Street, New York, NY 10022, 212/759-3694
Messages: 518/851-7808
Business: Merchant Ivory Productions, 250 West 57th Street - Suite 1913A, New
    York, NY 10019, 212/582-8049
Agent: Smith-Freedman & Associates - Los Angeles, 213/277-8464

THE HOUSEHOLDER   Royal Films International, 1963, Indian-U.S.
SHAKESPEARE WALLAH   Continental, 1966, Indian
THE GURU   20th Century-Fox, 1969, British-Indian
BOMBAY TALKIE   Dia Films, 1970, Indian
SAVAGES   Angelika, 1972
HELEN - QUEEN OF THE NAUTCH GIRLS (FD)   Merchant Ivory Productions,
    1973, Indian
MAHATMA AND THE MAD BOY   Merchant Ivory Productions, 1973, Indian
THE WILD PARTY   American International, 1975
AUTOBIOGRAPHY OF A PRINCESS (TF)   Merchant Ivory Productions, 1975
SWEET SOUNDS   Merchant Ivory Productions, 1976
ROSELAND   Cinema Shares International, 1977
THE 5:48 (TF)   PBS, 1979
HULLABALOO OVER GEORGIA & BONNIE'S PICTURES   Corinth, 1979
THE EUROPEANS   Levitt-Pickman, 1979, British
JANE AUSTEN IN MANHATTAN   Contemporary, 1980
QUARTET   New World, 1981, British-French
HEAT AND DUST   Universal Classics, 1983, British
THE BOSTONIANS   Merchant Ivory Productions, 1984

LEWIS JACKSON

Contact: Writers Guild of America, East - New York City, 212/245-6180

YOU BETTER WATCH OUT   Edward R. Pressman Productions, 1980

JOSEPH JACOBY

Agent: Shapiro-Lichtman Agency - Los Angeles, 213/557-2244

SHAME, SHAME, EVERBODY KNOWS HER NAME   JER, 1970
HURRY UP OR I'LL BE THIRTY   Avco Embassy, 1973
THE GREAT BANK HOAX   Warner Bros., 1978

JUST JAECKIN

b. 1940
Contact: French Film Office, 745 Fifth Avenue, New York, NY 10151, 212/832-8860

EMMANUELLE   Columbia, 1974, French
THE STORY OF O   Allied Artists, 1975, French
THE FRENCH WOMAN *MADAME CLAUDE*   Monarch 1979, French
THE LAST ROMANTIC LOVER   New Line Cinema, 1980, French
GIRLS   Caneuram Films, 1980, Canadian-French-Israeli
PRIVATE COLLECTIONS   co-director with Shuji Terayama & Walerian
    Borowczyk, Jeudi Films/Toei/French Movies, 1980, French-Japanese
LADY CHATTERLEY'S LOVER   Cannon, 1982, French-British
GWENDOLINE   Parafrance, 1983, French

STANLEY JAFFE *

Contact: Directors Guild of America - Los Angeles, 213/656-1220

WITHOUT A TRACE   20th Century-Fox, 1983

HENRY JAGLOM *

b. January 26, 1941 - London, England
Business: International Rainbow Pictures, 933 N. La Brea Avenue, Hollywood,
    CA 90038, 213/851-4811
Agent: Harry Ufland, The Ufland Agency - Beverly Hills, 213/273-9441

A SAFE PLACE   Columbia, 1971
TRACKS   Trio, 1977
SITTING DUCKS   Speciality Films, 1980
NATIONAL LAMPOON'S MOVIE MADNESS   co-director with Bob Giraldi,
    United Artists, 1981
CAN SHE BAKE A CHERRY PIE?   International Rainbow, 1983

JERRY JAMESON*

b. Hollywood, California
Agent: William Morris Agency - Beverly Hills, 213/274-7451

BRUTE CORPS   General Films, 1971
THE DIRT GANG   American International, 1972
THE BAT PEOPLE   American International, 1974
HEATWAVE! (TF)   Universal TV, 1974
THE ELEVATOR (TF)   Universal TV, 1974
HURRICANE (TF)   Metromedia Productions, 1974
TERROR ON THE 40TH FLOOR (TF)   Metromedia Productions, 1974
THE SECRET NIGHT CALLER (TF)   Charles Fries Productions/Penthouse
     Productions, 1975
THE DEADLY TOWER (TF)   MGM TV, 1975
THE LIVES OF JENNY DOLAN (TF)   Ross Hunter Productions/Paramount TV,
     1975
THE CALL OF THE WILD (TF)   Charles Fries Productions, 1976
THE INVASION OF JOHNSON COUNTY (TF)   Roy Huggins Productions/
     Universal TV, 1976
AIRPORT '77   Universal, 1977
SUPERDOME (TF)   ABC Circle Films, 1978
A FIRE IN THE SKY (TF)   Bill Driskill Productions, 1978
RAISE THE TITANIC   AFD, 1980, British-U.S.
HIGH NOON - PART II: THE RETURN OF WILL KANE (TF)   Charles Fries
     Productions, 1980
STAND BY YOUR MAN (TF)   Robert Papazian Productions/Peter Guber-Jon
     Peters Productions, 1981
KILLING AT HELL'S GATE (TF)   CBS Entertainment, 1981
HOTLINE (TF)   Wrather Entertainment International/Ron Samuels Productions,
     1982
STARFLIGHT: THE PLANE THAT COULDN'T LAND (TF)   Orgolini-Nelson
     Productions, 1983
COWBOY (TF)   Bercovici-St. Johns Productions/MGM TV, 1983
THIS GIRL FOR HIRE (TF)   Barney Rosenzweig Productions/Orion TV, 1983

MIKLOS JANCSO

b. September 27, 1921 - Vac, Hungary
Contact: Hungarofilm, 1054 Bathory utca lo., Budapest, Hungary, 36-1/31-7777

THE BELLS HAVE GONE TO ROME   Mafilm, 1958, Hungarian
THREE STARS   co-director, Mafilm, 1960, Hungarian
CANTATA   Studio Budapest, 1963, Hungarian
MY WAY HOME   Mafilm, 1964, Hungarian
THE ROUND-UP   Altura, 1965, Hungarian
THE RED AND THE WHITE   Brandon, 1967, Hungarian-Soviet
SILENCE AND CRY   Mafilm, 1967, Hungarian
THE CONFRONTATION   Mafilm, 1969, Hungarian
WINTER WIND *SIROKKO*   Marquise Film/Mafilm, 1969, French-Hungarian
LA PACIFISTA   Cinematografia Lombarda, 1970, Italian-French-West German
AGNUS DEI   Mafilm, 1971, Hungarian
LA TECNICA E IL RITO   RAI, 1971, Italian
RED PSALM   Mafilm, 1972, Hungarian
ROMA RIVUOLE CESARE   RAI, 1973, Italian
SZERELEM, ELEKTRA   Studio Hunnia, 1974, Hungarian
PRIVATE VICES - PUBLIC VIRTUE   1976, Italian-Yugoslavian
MASTERWORK   1977, Hungarian
HUNGARIAN RHAPSODY   Studio Dialog/Hungarofilm, 1978, Hungarian
ALLEGRO BARBARO   Mafilm, 1979, Hungarian
HEART OF A TYRANT   Sacis, 1981, Italian-Hungarian

DEREK JARMAN

Contact: British Academy of Film & Television Arts, 195 Piccadilly, London W1,
     England, 01/734-0022

SEBASTIANE   co-director with Paul Humfress, Discopat, 1977, British
JUBILEE   Libra, 1979, British
THE TEMPEST   World Northal, 1980, British
IN THE SHADOW OF THE SUN   ICA, 1981, British

CHARLES JARROTT *

b. June 6, 1927 - London, England
Agent: William Morris Agency - Beverly Hills, 213/274-7451
Business Manager: Jess S. Morgan & Company, 6420 Wilshire Blvd., Los Angeles,
    CA 90048, 213/651-1601

ANNE OF THE THOUSAND DAYS   Universal, 1969, British
MARY, QUEEN OF SCOTS   Universal, 1971, British
LOST HORIZON   Columbia, 1972
THE DOVE   Paramount, 1974
THE LITTLEST HORSE THIEVES *ESCAPE TO THE DARK*   Buena Vista,
    1977, U.S.-British
THE OTHER SIDE OF MIDNIGHT   20th Century-Fox, 1977
THE LAST FLIGHT OF NOAH'S ARK   Buena Vista, 1980
CONDORMAN   Buena Vista, 1981
THE AMATEUR   20th Century-Fox, 1981, Canadian

LIONEL JEFFRIES

b. 1926 - London, England
Agent: ICM - Los Angeles, 213/550-4000

THE RAILWAY CHILDREN   Universal, 1971, British
THE AMAZING MR. BLUNDEN   Goldstone, 1972, British
BAXTER!   National General, 1973, British
THE WATER BABIES   Pethurst International/Film Polski, 1978, British-Polish
WOMBLING FREE   Rank, 1979, British

NORMAN JEWISON *

b. July 21, 1926 - Toronto, Canada
Business: Knightsbridge Films, 18 Gloucester Street, Toronto, Ontario M4Y 1L5,
    Canada, 416/923-2787
Agent: William Morris Agency - Beverly Hills, 213/274-7451
Business Manager: Capell, Flekman, Coyne & Co. - Beverly Hills, 213/553-0310

40 POUNDS OF TROUBLE   Universal, 1962
THE THRILL OF IT ALL   Universal, 1963
SEND ME NO FLOWERS   Universal, 1964
THE ART OF LOVE   Universal, 1965
THE CINCINNATI KID   MGM, 1965
THE RUSSIANS ARE COMING THE RUSSIANS ARE COMING   United
    Artists, 1966
IN THE HEAT OF THE NIGHT ★   United Artists, 1967
THE THOMAS CROWN AFFAIR   United Artists, 1968
GAILY, GAILY   United Artists, 1969
FIDDLER ON THE ROOF ★   United Artists, 1971
JESUS CHRIST SUPERSTAR   Universal, 1973
ROLLERBALL   United Artists, 1975
F.I.S.T.   United Artists, 1978
... AND JUSTICE FOR ALL   Columbia, 1979
BEST FRIENDS   Warner Bros., 1982
A SOLDIER'S STORY   Columbia, 1984

ROBERT JIRAS

I AM THE CHEESE   Libra Cinema 5, 1983

ALEXANDRO JODOROWSKY

Contact: Direccion General de Radio, Television y Cinematografica de la Secretaria
    de Gobernacion, Atletas 2, Country Club, Mexico City 7DF, Mexico, 905/544-
    9580

FANDO AND LIS   Cannon, 1970, Mexican
EL TOPO   ABKCO, 1971, Mexican
THE HOLY MOUNTAIN   ABKCO, 1974, Mexican
TUSK   Yank Films-Films 21, 1980, French

ROLAND JOFFE

b. England
Agent: Merrily Kane Agency - Beverly Hills, 213/550-8874

THE SPONGERS (TF)   BBC, 1978, British
NO, MAMA, NO (TF)   BBC, 1979, British
UNITED KINGDOM (TF)   BBC, 1981, British
THE KILLING FIELDS   Warner Bros., 1984, British

ALAN JOHNSON

TO BE OR NOT TO BE   20th Century-Fox, 1983

JED JOHNSON

ANDY WARHOL'S BAD   New World, 1977

KENNETH JOHNSON *

b. October 26, 1942 - Pine Bluff, Arkansas
Attorney: Charles Silverberg, Silverberg, Rosen, Leon & Behr - Los Angeles, 213/
    277-4500

THE INCREDIBLE HULK (TF)   Universal TV, 1977
SENIOR TRIP (TF)   Kenneth Johnson Productions, 1981
V (TF)   Kenneth Johnson Productions/Warner Bros. TV, 1983

LAMONT JOHNSON *

b. 1920 - Stockton, California
Agent: John Gaines, APA - Los Angeles, 213/273-0744

THIN ICE   20th Century-Fox, 1961
A COVENANT WITH DEATH   Warner Bros., 1966
KONA COAST   Warner Bros., 1968
DEADLOCK (TF)   Universal TV, 1969
THE MACKENZIE BREAK   United Artists, 1970
MY SWEET CHARLIE (TF) ☆   Universal TV, 1970
A GUNFIGHT   Paramount, 1971
THE GROUNDSTAR CONSPIRACY   Universal, 1972, U.S.-Canadian
YOU'LL LIKE MY MOTHER   Universal, 1972
THAT CERTAIN SUMMER (TF) ☆   Universal TV, 1972
THE LAST AMERICAN HERO   20th Century-Fox, 1973
VISIT TO A CHIEF'S SON   United Artists, 1974
THE EXECUTION OF PRIVATE SLOVIK (TF) ☆   Universal TV, 1974
FEAR ON TRIAL (TF) ☆   Alan Landsburg Productions, 1975
LIPSTICK   Paramount, 1976
ONE ON ONE   Warner Bros., 1977
SOMEBODY KILLED HER HUSBAND   Columbia, 1978
PAUL'S CASE (TF)   Learning in Focus, 1979
OFF THE MINNESOTA STRIP (TF)   Cherokee Productions/Universal TV, 1980
CATTLE ANNIE AND LITTLE BRITCHES   Universal, 1981
CRISIS AT CENTRAL HIGH (TF)   Time-Life Productions, 1981
ESCAPE FROM IRAN: THE CANADIAN CAPER (TF)   Canamedia Productions,
    1981, Canadian
DANGEROUS COMPANY (TF)   The Dangerous Company/Finnegan Associates,
    1982
LIFE OF THE PARTY: THE STORY OF BEATRICE (TF)   Welch-Welch
    Productions/Columbia TV, 1982
SPACEHUNTER: ADVENTURES IN THE FORBIDDEN ZONE   Columbia,
    1983, Canadian-U.S.

AMY JONES

SLUMBER PARTY MASSACRE   Santa Fe, 1982
LOVE LETTERS   New World, 1983

DAVID JONES

b. February 19, 1934 - Poole, Dorset, England
Address: 26 Fitzjohns Avenue, London NW3, England

BETRAYAL   20th Century-Fox International Classics, 1983, British

EUGENE S. JONES *

Home: 461 Bellagio Terrace, Los Angeles, CA 90049, 213/476-6375
Attorney: Royal E. Blakeman, Pryor, Cashman, Sherman & Flynn, 415 Park Avenue,
    New York, NY 10022, 212/421-4100

A FACE OF WAR (FD)   Commonwealth, 1968
TWO MEN OF KARAMOJA *THE WILD AND THE BRAVE (FD)*   Tomorrow
    Entertainment, 1974
HIGH ICE (TF)   ESJ Productions, 1980

L.Q. JONES *

Business: 2144 N. Cahuenga Blvd., Hollywood, CA 90068, 213/463-4426
Agent: Mike Greenfield, Charter Management - Los Angeles, 213/278-1690

A BOY AND HIS DOG   Pacific Film Enterprises, 1975

TERRY JONES

b. 1942 - Colwyn Bay, Wales
Agent: Euroatlantic - London
Contact: Directors Guild of Great Britain, 56 Whitfield Street, London W1, England,
    01/580-9592

MONTY PYTHON AND THE HOLY GRAIL   co-director with Terry Gilliam,
    Cinema 5, 1974, British
MONTY PYTHON'S LIFE OF BRIAN   Orion/Warner Bros., 1979, British
MONTY PYTHON'S THE MEANING OF LIFE   Universal, 1983, British

GLENN JORDAN *

Business: Holiday Productions, 9401 Wilshire Blvd. - Suite 700, Beverly Hills,
    CA 90212, 213/278-7700
Agent: Bill Haber, CAA - Los Angeles, 213/277-4545

FRANKENSTEIN (TF)   Dan Curtis Productions, 1973
THE PICTURE OF DORIAN GRAY (TF)   Dan Curtis Productions, 1973
SHELL GAME (TF)   Thoroughbred Productions, 1975
ONE OF MY WIVES IS MISSING (TF)   Spelling-Goldberg Productions, 1975
DELTA COUNTY, U.S.A. (TF)   Leonard Goldberg Productions/Paramount TV,
    1977
SUNSHINE CHRISTMAS (TF)   Universal TV, 1977
IN THE MATTER OF KAREN ANN QUINLAN (TF)   Warren V. Bush
    Productions, 1977
THE DISPLACED PERSON (TF)   Learning in Focus, 1977
LES MISERABLES (TF) ☆   Norman Rosemont Productions/ITV Entertainment,
    1978
SON RISE: A MIRACLE OF LOVE (TF)   Rothman-Wohl Productions/Filmways,
    1979
THE FAMILY MAN (TF)   Time-Life Productions, 1979
THE WOMEN'S ROOM (TF)   Philip Mandelker Productions/Warner Bros. TV,
    1980
NEIL SIMON'S ONLY WHEN I LAUGH   Columbia, 1981
THE PRINCESS AND THE CABBIE (TF)   Freyda Rothstein Productions/Time-
    Life Productions, 1981
LOIS GIBBS AND THE LOVE CANAL (TF)   Moonlight Productions/Filmways,
    1982
THE BUDDY SYSTEM   20th Century-Fox, 1984
MASS APPEAL   Operation Cork Productions/Turman-Foster Company/Jalem
    Productions, 1984

NEIL JORDAN

Contact: Film Division - Department of Industry and Energy, Kildare Street, Dublin, Ireland, 1/78-9411

ANGEL   Triumph/Columbia, 1983, Irish

NATHAN JURAN*

b. September 1, 1907 - Austria
Home: 623 Via Horquilla, Palos Verdes Estates, CA 90274

THE BLACK CASTLE   Universal, 1952
GUNSMOKE   Universal, 1953
LAW AND ORDER   Universal, 1953
THE GOLDEN BLADE   Universal, 1953
TUMBLEWEED   Universal, 1953
HIGHWAY DRAGNET   Allied Artists, 1954
DRUMS ACROSS THE RIVER   Universal, 1954
THE CROOKED WEB   Columbia, 1955
THE DEADLY MANTIS   Universal, 1957
HELLCATS OF THE NAVY   Columbia, 1957
TWENTY MILLION MILES TO EARTH   Columbia, 1957
THE 7TH VOYAGE OF SINBAD   Columbia, 1958
GOOD DAY FOR A HANGING   Columbia, 1959
FLIGHT OF THE LOST BALLOON   Woolner Brothers, 1961
JACK THE GIANT KILLER   United Artists, 1962
SIEGE OF THE SAXONS   Columbia, 1963, British
FIRST MEN IN THE MOON   Columbia, 1964, British
EAST OF SUDAN   Columbia, 1964, British
LAND RAIDERS   Columbia, 1970
THE BOY WHO CRIED WEREWOLF   Universal, 1973

CLAUDE JUTRA

b. March 11, 1930 - Montreal, Quebec, Canada
Contact: Association Des Realisateurs, 1406 Beaudry Street, Montreal, Quebec H2L 4K4, Canada, 514/843-7770

LES MAINS NETTES   NFB, 1958, Canadian
LE NIGER - JEUNE REPUBLIQUE (FD)   NFB, 1961, Canadian
A TOUT PRENDE   Lopert, 1963, Canadian
COMMENT SAVOIR   NFB, 1966, Canadian
WOW!   NFB, 1969, Canadian
MON ONCLE ANTOINE   NFB/Gendon Films Ltd., 1970, Canadian
KAMOURASKA   New Line Cinema, 1974, Canadian
POUR LE MEILLEUR ET POUR LE PIRE   1975, Canadian
DREAMSPEAKER   1977, Canadian
SURFACING   Arista, 1981, Canadian
BY DESIGN   Atlantic Releasing Corporation, 1982, Canadian
BONHEUR D'OCCAFION   1983, Canadian
LE SILENCE, C'EST LE COMFORT   1984, Canadian

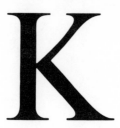

GEORGE KACZENDER

b. April 19, 1933 - Budapest, Hungary
Business: 2170 Century Park East - Suite 1608, Los Angeles, CA 90067, 213/
203-0710
Agent: Scott Penney, Eisenbach-Greene, Inc. - Los Angeles, 213/659-3420

DON'T LET THE ANGELS FALL   NFB, 1968, Canadian
THE GIRL IN BLUE *U-TURN*   Cinerama Releasing Corporation, 1974,
Canadian
IN PRAISE OF OLDER WOMEN   Avco Embassy, 1978, Canadian
AGENCY   Taft International, 1980, Canadian
YOUR TICKET IS NO LONGER VALID   RSL Productions/Ambassador, 1981,
Canadian
CHANEL SOLITAIRE   United Film Distribution, 1981, French-British

JEREMY PAUL KAGAN *

b. December 14, 1945 - Mt. Vernon, New York
Home: 2024 N. Curson Avenue, Los Angeles, CA 90046, 213/874-5175
Business: Our Own Company, c/o Pollock Bloom & Dekom, 9255 Sunset Blvd., Los
Angeles, CA 90069, 213/278-8622
Business Manager: The Brentwood Group, 11812 San Vicente Blvd. - Suite 200, Los
Angeles, CA 90049, 213/826-0909

UNWED FATHER (TF)   Wolper Productions, 1974
JUDGE DEE AND THE MONASTERY MURDERS (TF)   ABC Circle Films,
1974
KATHERINE (TF)   The Jozak Company, 1975
HEROES   Universal, 1977
SCOTT JOPLIN   Universal, 1977
THE BIG FIX   Universal, 1978
THE CHOSEN   20th Century-Fox International Classics, 1982
THE STING II   Universal, 1983

JEFF KANEW *

Business: Utopia Productions, 45 East 89th Street, New York, NY 10028, 212/
722-6968
Agent: Martin Bauer, William Morris Agency - New York City, 212/586-5100

BLACK RODEO (FD)   Cinerama Releasing Corporation, 1972
NATURAL ENEMIES   Cinema 5, 1979
EDDIE MACON'S RUN   Universal, 1983

MAREK KANIEVSKA

Contact: Directors Guild of Great Britain, 56 Whitfield Street, London W1, England,
01/580-9592

ANOTHER COUNTRY   Orion Classics, 1984, British

GARSON KANIN *

b. November 24, 1912 - Rochester, New York
Business: TFT Corporation, 200 West 57th Street - Suite 1203, New York,
    NY 10019
Agent: William Morris Agency - New York City, 212/586-5100

A MAN TO REMEMBER   RKO Radio, 1938
NEXT TIME I MARRY   RKO Radio, 1938
THE GREAT MAN VOTES   RKO Radio, 1939
BACHELOR MOTHER   RKO Radio, 1939
MY FAVORITE WIFE   RKO Radio, 1940
THEY KNEW WHAT THEY WANTED   Columbia, 1940
TOM, DICK AND HARRY   RKO Radio, 1941
THE TRUE GLORY   co-director with Carol Reed, Columbia, 1945
WHERE IT'S AT   United Artists, 1969
SOME KIND OF NUT   United Artists, 1969

HAL KANTER *

b. December 18, 1918 - Savannah, Georgia
Agent: Marvin Moss Agency - Los Angeles, 213/274-8483
Business Manager: James Harper, 13063 Ventura Blvd., Studio City, CA 91604

LOVING YOU   Paramount, 1957
I MARRIED A WOMAN   Universal, 1958
ONCE UPON A HORSE   Universal, 1958
FOR THE LOVE OF IT (TF)   Charles Fries Productions/Neila Productions, 1980

JONATHAN KAPLAN *

b. November 25, 1947 - Paris, France
Agent: William Morris Agency - Beverly Hills, 213/274-7451

THE STUDENT TEACHERS   New World, 1973
THE SLAMS   MGM, 1973
TRUCK TURNER   American International, 1974
NIGHT CALL NURSES   New World, 1974
WHITE LINE FEVER   Columbia, 1975
MR. BILLION   20th Century-Fox, 1976
OVER THE EDGE   Orion/Warner Bros., 1979
THE 11TH VICTIM (TF)   Marty Katz Productions/Paramount TV, 1979
THE HUSTLER OF MUSCLE BEACH (TF)   Furia-Oringer Productions, 1980
THE GENTLEMAN BANDIT (TF)   Highgate Pictures, 1981
HEART LIKE A WHEEL   20th Century-Fox, 1983
DEATH RIDE TO OSAKA (TF)   Hill-Mandelker Films, 1983

NELLY KAPLAN

b. 1936 - Buenos Aires, Argentina
Business: Cythere Films, 18 Rue Marbeuf, 75000 Paris, France, 1/562-7901
Attorney: Eric Weissman - Beverly Hills, 213/858-7888

GUSTAVE MOREAU (FD)   Cythere Films, 1961, French
ABEL GANCE HIER ET DEMAIN (FD)   Cythere Films, 1963, French
LE REGARD PICASSO (FD)   Cythere Films, 1966, French
A VERY CURIOUS GIRL *LE FIANCEE DU PIRATE*   Regional, 1970, French
PAPA LES PETITS BATEAUX   Cythere Films, 1971, French
NEA *NEA - A YOUNG EMMANUELLE*   Libra, 1976, French
CHARLES ET LUCIE   Nu-Image, 1980, French
ABEL GANCE ET SON NAPOLEON (FD)   Cythere Films, 1983, French

PHIL KARLSON *
(Philip Karlstein)

b. July 2, 1908 - Chicago, Illinois
Agent: The Gersh Agency - Beverly Hills, 213/274-6611

A WAVE, A WAC AND A MARINE   Monogram, 1944
THERE GOES KELLY   Monogram, 1945
G.I. HONEYMOON   Monogram, 1945

PHIL KARLSON*—continued

THE SHANGHAI COBRA   Monogram, 1945
DARK ALIBI   Monogram, 1946
LIVE WIRES   Monogram, 1946
THE MISSING LADY   Monogram, 1946
SWING PARADE OF 1946   Monogram, 1946
BEHIND THE MASK   Monogram, 1946
BOWERY BOMBSHELL   Monogram, 1946
WIFE WANTED   Monogram, 1946
BLACK GOLD   Allied Artists, 1947
KILROY WAS HERE   Monogram, 1947
LOUISIANA   Monogram, 1947
ADVENTURES IN SILVERADO   Columbia, 1948
ROCKY   Monogram, 1948
THUNDERHOOF   Columbia, 1948
THE LADIES OF THE CHORUS   Columbia, 1948
DOWN MEMORY LANE   Eagle Lion, 1949
THE BIG CAT   Eagle Lion, 1949
THE IROQUOIS TRAIL   United Artists, 1950
LORNA DOONE   Columbia, 1951
THE TEXAS RANGERS   Columbia, 1951
MASK OF THE AVENGER   Columbia, 1951
SCANDAL SHEET   Columbia, 1952
KANSAS CITY CONFIDENTIAL   United Artists, 1952
THE BRIGAND   Columbia, 1952
99 RIVER STREET   United Artists, 1953
THEY RODE WEST   Columbia, 1954
HELL'S ISLAND   Paramount, 1955
TIGHT SPOT   Columbia, 1955
FIVE AGAINST THE HOUSE   Columbia, 1955
THE PHENIX CITY STORY   Allied Artists, 1955
THE BROTHERS RICO   Columbia, 1957
GUNMAN'S WALK   Columbia, 1958
HELL TO ETERNITY   Allied Artists, 1960
KEY WITNESS   MGM, 1960
THE SECRET WAYS   Universal, 1961
THE YOUNG DOCTORS   United Artists, 1961
THE SCARFACE MOB   Desilu, 1962
KID GALAHAD   United Artists, 1962
RAMPAGE   Warner Bros., 1963
THE SILENCERS   Columbia, 1966
A TIME FOR KILLING   Columbia, 1967
THE WRECKING CREW   Columbia, 1968
HORNETS' NEST   United Artists, 1970
BEN   Cinerama Releasing Corporation, 1972
WALKING TALL   Cinerama Releasing Corporation, 1973
FRAMED   Paramount, 1974

ERIC KARSON*

Business: Karson-Higgins-Shaw Communications, Inc., 729 N. Seward Street, Hollywood, CA 90038, 213/461-3030

DIRT   co-director with Cal Naylor, American Cinema, 1979
THE OCTAGON   American Cinema, 1980

LAWRENCE KASDAN*

Attorney: Peter Benedek, Weissman, Wolff, Bergman, Coleman & Schulman - Beverly Hills, 213/858-7888

BODY HEAT   The Ladd Company/Warner Bros., 1981
THE BIG CHILL   Columbia, 1983

MILTON KATSELAS*

b. December 22, 1933 - Pittsburg, Pennsylvania
Agent: Tom Chasin, Chasin-Park-Citron - Los Angeles, 213/273-7190
Business Manager: Jerry Wolff, Lehmann-Wolff Accountancy Corporation - Los
    Angeles, 213/475-0595

BUTTERFLIES ARE FREE   Columbia, 1972
40 CARATS   Columbia, 1973
REPORT TO THE COMMISSIONER   United Artists, 1975
WHEN YOU COMIN' BACK, RED RYDER?   Columbia, 1979
STRANGERS: THE STORY OF A MOTHER AND A DAUGHTER
    (TF)   Chris-Rose Productions, 1979
THE RULES OF MARRIAGE (TF)   Entheos Unlimited Productions/Brownstone
Productions/20th Century-Fox TV, 1982

LEE H. KATZIN*

b. April 12, 1935 - Detroit, Michigan
Home: 13425 Java Drive, Beverly Hills, CA 90210, 213/278-7726
Agent: Ronald Lief, Contemporary-Korman Artists - Beverly Hills, 213/278-8250
Business Manager: Norman Greenbaum, Singer, Lewak, Greenbaum & Goldstein,
    10960 Wilshire Blvd. - Suite 826, Los Angeles, CA 90024, 213/477-3924

HONDO AND THE APACHES   MGM, 1967
HEAVEN WITH A GUN   MGM, 1969
WHAT EVER HAPPENED TO AUNT ALICE?   Cinerama Releasing Corporation,
    1969
THE PHYNX   Warner Bros., 1970
LE MANS   National General, 1970
ALONG CAME A SPIDER (TF)   20th Century-Fox TV, 1970
THE SALZBURG CONNECTION   20th Century-Fox, 1972
VISIONS ... (TF)   CBS, Inc., 1972
THE VOYAGE OF THE YES (TF)   Bing Crosby Productions, 1973
THE STRANGER (TF)   Bing Crosby Productions, 1973
ORDEAL (TF)   20th Century-Fox TV, 1973
SAVAGES (TF)   Spelling-Goldberg Productions, 1974
STRANGE HOMECOMING (TF)   Alpine Productions/Worldvision, 1974
THE LAST SURVIVORS (TF)   Bob Banner Associates, 1975
SKY HEI$T (TF)   Warner Bros. TV, 1975
QUEST (TF)   David Gerber Company/Columbia TV, 1976
THE MAN FROM ATLANTIS (TF)   Solow Production Company, 1977
RELENTLESS (TF)   CBS, Inc., 1977
THE BASTARD (TF)   Universal TV, 1978
ZUMA BEACH (TF)   Edgar J. Scherick Associates/Warner Bros. TV, 1978
TERROR OUT OF THE SKY (TF)   Alan Landsburg Productions, 1978
REVENGE OF THE SAVAGE BEES (TF)   1979
SAMURAI (TF)   Danny Thomas Productions/Universal TV, 1979
DEATH RAY 2000 (TF)   Woodruff Productions/QM Productions, 1981
THE NEIGHBORHOOD (TF)   David Gerber Company/Columbia TV, 1982

JONATHAN KAUFER

b. March 14, 1955 - Los Angeles, California

SOUP FOR ONE   Warner Bros., 1982

CHARLES KAUFMAN

Contact: Writers Guild of America, West - Los Angeles 213/550-1000

MOTHER'S DAY   United Film Distribution, 1980

PHILIP KAUFMAN*

b. October 23, 1936 - Chicago, Illinois
Contact: Directors Guild of America - Los Angeles, 213/656-1220

GOLDSTEIN   co-director with Benjamin Manaster, Altura, 1965
FEARLESS FRANK   American International, 1969
THE GREAT NORTHFIELD, MINNESOTA RAID   Universal, 1972

continued

PHILIP KAUFMAN*—continued
THE WHITE DAWN   Paramount, 1974
INVASION OF THE BODY SNATCHERS   United Artists, 1978
THE WANDERERS   Orion/Warner Bros., 1979
THE RIGHT STUFF   The Ladd Company/Warner Bros., 1983

R O B E R T   K A Y L O R *

Agent: Randy Herron, Herb Tobias & Associates - Los Angeles, 213/277-6211

DERBY (FD)   Cinerama Releasing Corporation, 1971
CARNY   United Artists, 1980

E L I A   K A Z A N *
(Elia Kazanjoglou)

b. September 7, 1909 - Constantinople, Turkey
Home: 22 West 68th Street, New York, NY   10023
Messages: 212/496-0422

A TREE GROWS IN BROOKLYN   20th Century-Fox, 1945
SEA OF GRASS   20th Century-Fox, 1947
BOOMERANG !   20th Century-Fox, 1947
GENTLEMAN'S AGREEMENT ★★   20th Century-Fox, 1947
PINKY   20th Century-Fox, 1949
PANIC IN THE STREETS   20th Century-Fox, 1950
A STREETCAR NAMED DESIRE ★   Warner Bros., 1951
VIVA ZAPATA !   20th Century-Fox, 1952
MAN ON A TIGHTROPE   20th Century-Fox, 1953
ON THE WATERFRONT ★★   Columbia, 1954
EAST OF EDEN ★   Warner Bros., 1955
BABY DOLL   Warner Bros., 1956
A FACE IN THE CROWD   Warner Bros., 1957
WILD RIVER   20th Century-Fox, 1960
SPLENDOR IN THE GRASS   Warner Bros., 1961
AMERICA AMERICA ★   Warner Bros., 1963
THE ARRANGEMENT   Warner Bros., 1969
THE VISITORS   United Artists, 1972
THE LAST TYCOON   Paramount, 1975

D O N   K E E S L A R

BOG   Marshall Films, 1978
THE CAPTURE OF GRIZZLY ADAMS (TF)   Sunn Classic Productions, 1982

A S A A D   K E L A D A *

Agent: Bob Broder, Broder-Kurland Agency - Los Angeles, 213/274-8921

THE FACTS OF LIFE GOES TO PARIS (TF)   Embassy TV, 1982

G E N E   K E L L Y *

b. August 23, 1912 - Pittsburgh, Pennsylvania
Contact: Directors Guild of America - Los Angeles, 213/656-1220

ON THE TOWN   co-director with Stanley Donen, MGM, 1949
SINGIN' IN THE RAIN   co-director with Stanley Donen, MGM, 1952
IT'S ALWAYS FAIR WEATHER   co-director with Stanley Donen, MGM, 1955
INVITATION TO THE DANCE   MGM, 1956
THE HAPPY ROAD   MGM, 1957
THE TUNNEL OF LOVE   MGM, 1958
GIGOT   20th Century-Fox, 1962
A GUIDE FOR THE MARRIED MAN   20th Century-Fox, 1967
HELLO, DOLLY !   20th Century-Fox, 1969
THE CHEYENNE SOCIAL CLUB   National General, 1970
THAT'S ENTERTAINMENT, PART 2   new sequences, MGM/United Artists, 1976

BURT KENNEDY*

b. September 3, 1922 - Muskegon, Michigan
Home: 13138 Magnolia Blvd., Sherman Oaks, CA 91403, 213/986-8759
Agent: David Shapira & Associates - Beverly Hills, 213/278-2742

THE CANADIANS   20th Century-Fox, 1961
MAIL ORDER BRIDE   MGM, 1963
THE ROUNDERS   MGM, 1965
THE MONEY TRAP   MGM, 1966
RETURN OF THE SEVEN   United Artists, 1966
WELCOME TO HARD TIMES   MGM, 1967
THE WAR WAGON   Universal, 1967
SUPPORT YOUR LOCAL SHERIFF   United Artists, 1969
YOUNG BILLY YOUNG   United Artists, 1969
THE GOOD GUYS AND THE BAD GUYS   Warner Bros., 1969
DIRTY DINGUS MAGEE   MGM, 1970
SUPPORT YOUR LOCAL GUNFIGHTER   United Artists, 1971
HANNIE CAULDER   Paramount, 1971, British
THE DESERTER   Paramount, 1971, Italian-Yugoslavian
THE TRAIN ROBBERS   Warner Bros., 1973
SHOOTOUT IN A ONE-DOG TOWN (TF)   Hanna-Barbera Productions, 1974
SIDEKICKS (TF)   Warner Bros. TV, 1974
ALL THE KIND STRANGERS (TF)   Cinemation TV, 1974
THE KILLER INSIDE ME   Warner Bros., 1976
HOW THE WEST WAS WON (MS)   co-director with Daniel Mann, MGM TV, 1977
THE RHINEMANN EXCHANGE (MS)   Universal TV, 1977
KATE BLISS & THE TICKER TAPE KID (TF)   Aaron Spelling Productions, 1978
THE WILD WILD WEST REVISITED (TF)   CBS Entertainment, 1979
THE CONCRETE COWBOYS (TF)   Frankel Films, 1979
MORE WILD WILD WEST   CBS Entertainment, 1980
THE HONOR GUARD *WOLF LAKE*   Wolf Lake Productions, 1981, Canadian

TOM KENNEDY

TIME WALKER   New World, 1983

IRVIN KERSHNER*

b. April 29, 1923 - Philadelphia, Pennsylvania
Home: P.O. Box 232, Route 7 North, Kent, CT 06757, 203/927-4483
Agent: Michael Marcus, CAA - Los Angeles, 213/277-4545
Business Manager: Charles Silverberg, Silverberg, Rosen, Leon & Behr, 2029 Century
     Park East - Suite 1900, Los Angeles, CA 90067, 213/277-4500

STAKEOUT ON DOPE STREET   Warner Bros., 1958
THE YOUNG CAPTIVES   Paramount, 1959
THE HOODLUM PRIEST   United Artists, 1961
A FACE IN THE RAIN   Embassy, 1963
THE LUCK OF GINGER COFFEY   Continental, 1964, Canadian
A FINE MADNESS   Warner Bros., 1966
THE FLIM-FLAM MAN   20th Century-Fox, 1967
LOVING   Columbia, 1970
UP THE SANDBOX   National General, 1972
S*P*Y*S   20th Century-Fox, 1974, British-U.S.
THE RETURN OF A MAN CALLED HORSE   United Artists, 1976
RAID ON ENTEBBE (TF) ☆   Edgar J. Scherick Associates/20th Century-Fox TV, 1977
EYES OF LAURA MARS   Columbia, 1978
THE EMPIRE STRIKES BACK   20th Century-Fox, 1980
NEVER SAY NEVER AGAIN   Warner Bros., 1983

BRUCE KESSLER*

b. March 23, 1936 - California
Home: 4444 Via Marina, Marina del Rey, CA 90291, 213/823-2394
Agent: The Cooper Agency - Los Angeles, 213/277-8422

ANGELS FROM HELL   American International, 1968
KILLERS THREE   American International, 1968

continued

BRUCE KESSLER—continued

THE GAY DECEIVERS   Fanfare, 1969
SIMON, KING OF WITCHES   Fanfare, 1971
MURDER IN PEYTON PLACE (TF)   20th Century-Fox TV, 1977
THE TWO-FIVE (TF)   Universal TV, 1978
DEATH MOON (TF)   Roger Gimbel Productions/EMI TV, 1978
CRUISE INTO TERROR (TF)   Aaron Spelling Productions, 1978

R O L A N D   K I B B E E *

b. February 15, 1914 - Monongahela, Pennsylvania
Agent: Major Talent Agency - Los Angeles, 213/820-5841

THE MIDNIGHT MAN   co-director with Burt Lancaster, Universal, 1974

M I C H A E L   K I D D *

b. August 12, 1919 - Brooklyn, New York
Agent: William Morris Agency - Beverly Hills, 213/274-7451

MERRY ANDREW   MGM, 1958

B R U C E   K I M M E L *

b. December 8, 1947 - Los Angeles, California
Home: 12230 Otsego Street, North Hollywood, CA 91607 213/760-3306
Business: Bruce Kimmel Productions, Inc., c/o Jorgenson & Co., 1801 Century Park
     East - Suite 1400, Los Angeles, CA 90067, 213/556-1730
Attorney: Rigrod & Surpin, 1880 Century Park East, Los Angeles, CA 90067, 213/
     552-1808

THE FIRST NUDIE MUSICAL   co-director with Mark Haggard, Paramount,
     1976
SPACESHIP *THE CREATURE WASN'T NICE*   Almi Cinema 5, 1982

A L L A N   K I N G

b. 1930 - Vancouver, Canada
Home: 397 Carlton Street, Toronto, Ontario M5A 2M3, Canada, 416/964-7284

PEMBERTON VALLEY (FD)   CBC, 1957, Canadian
A MATTER OF PRIDE (FD)   CBC, 1961, Canadian
COMING OF AGE IN IBIZA *RUNNING AWAY BACKWARDS (FD)*   CBC,
     1964, Canadian
WARRENDALE (FD)   Grove Press, 1968, Canadian
A MARRIED COUPLE (FD)   Aquarius, 1970, Canadian
COME ON CHILDREN (FD)   Allan King Associates, 1972, Canadian
WHO HAS SEEN THE WIND   Astral Bellevue, 1977, Canadian
ONE-NIGHT STAND   Janus, 1978, Canadian
SILENCE OF THE NORTH   Universal, 1981, Canadian

R I C H A R D   K I N O N *

Agent: Ellen Glick, ICM - Los Angeles, 213/550-4000

THE LOVE BOAT (TF)   co-director with Alan Myerson, Douglas S. Cramer
     Productions, 1976
THE NEW LOVE BOAT (TF)   Douglas S. Cramer Productions, 1977
ALOHA PARADISE (TF)   Aaron Spelling Productions, 1981

E P H R A I M   K I S H O N

Contact: Israel Film Centre, Ministry of Industry & Trade, 30 Agron Street, P.O. Box
     299, Jerusalem 94190, Israel, 02/210433

SALLAH   Palisades International, 1963, Israeli
THE BIG DIG   Canal, 1969, Israeli
THE POLICEMAN   Cinema 5, 1972, Israeli
FOX IN THE CHICKEN COOP   Hashu'alim Ltd., 1978, Israeli

ALF KJELLIN *

b. February 28, 1920 - Lund, Sweden
Home: 12630 Mulholland Drive, Beverly Hills, CA 90210, 213/273-6514
Agent: Neil Schanker, ICM - Los Angeles, 213/550-4000

GIRL IN THE RAIN   1955, Swedish
SEVENTEEN YEARS OLD   1957, Swedish
ENCOUNTERS AT DUSK   1957, Swedish
SWINGING AT THE CASTLE   1959, Swedish
ONLY A WAITER   1960, Swedish
PLEASURE GARDEN   1961, Swedish
SISKA   1962, Swedish
MIDAS RUN   Cinerama Releasing Corporation, 1969
THE McMASTERS   Chevron, 1970
THE DEADLY DREAM (TF)   Universal TV, 1971
THE GIRLS OF HUNTINGTON HOUSE (TF)   Lorimar Productions, 1973

ROBERT KLANE *

Contact: Directors Guild of America - Los Angeles, 213/656-1220

THANK GOD IT'S FRIDAY   Columbia, 1978

WILLIAM KLEIN

b. 1926 - New York, New York
Contact: French Film Office, 745 Fifth Avenue, New York, NY 10151, 212/832-
    8860

QUI ETES-VOUS POLLY MAGGOO?   1966, French
FAR FROM VIETNAM (FD)   co-director with Jean-Luc Godard, Joris Ivens, Alain
    Resnais & Agnes Varda, New Yorker, 1967, French
MISTER FREEDOM   1969, French
FLOAT LIKE A BUTTERFLY - STING LIKE A BEE (FD)   1969, French
FESTIVAL PANAFRICAIN (FD)   1969, French
ELDRIDGE CLEAVER (FD)   1970, French
LE COUPLE TEMOIN   1977, French

RANDAL KLEISER *

b. July 20, 1946
Business: Randal Kleiser Productions, 3855 Lankershim Blvd., North Hollywood,
    CA 91604, 213/760-6522
Personal Manager: Joel Dean, c/o Randal Kleiser Productions, 3855 Lankershim
    Blvd., North Hollywood, CA 91604, 213/760-6522

ALL TOGETHER NOW (TF)   RSO Films, 1975
DAWN: PORTRAIT OF A TEENAGE RUNAWAY (TF)   Douglas S. Cramer
    Productions, 1976
THE BOY IN THE PLASTIC BUBBLE (TF)   Spelling-Goldberg Productions,
    1976
THE GATHERING (TF) ☆   Hanna-Barbera Productions, 1977
GREASE   Paramount, 1978
THE BLUE LAGOON   Columbia, 1980
SUMMER LOVERS   Filmways, 1982
GRANDVIEW, U.S.A.   Warner Bros., 1984

MASAKI KOBAYASHI

b. February 14, 1916 - Hokkaido, Japan
Contact: Directors Guild of Japan, Tsukada Building, 8-33 Ugagawa-cho, Shibuya-ku,
    Tokyo 150, Japan, 3/461-4411

MY SON'S YOUTH   1952, Japanese
SINCERE HEART   1953, Japanese
ROOM WITH THICK WALLS   1953, Japanese
THREE LOVES   1954, Japanese
SOMEWHERE BENEATH THE WIDE SKY   1954, Japanese
BEAUTIFUL DAYS   1955, Japanese
THE FOUNTAINHEAD   1956, Japanese

continued

MASAKI KOBAYASHI—continued

I'LL BUY YOU   1956, Japanese
BLACK RIVER   1957, Japanese
THE HUMAN CONDITION, PART I (NO GREATER LOVE)   Shochiku, 1959, Japanese
THE HUMAN CONDITION, PART II (ROAD TO ETERNITY)   Shochiku, 1959, Japanese
THE HUMAN CONDITION, PART III (A SOLDIER'S PRAYER)   Shochiku, 1961, Japanese
THE INHERITANCE   Shochiku, 1962, Japanese
HARAKIRI SEPPUKU   Toho, 1962, Japanese
KWAIDAN   Continental, 1964, Japanese
REBELLION SAMURAI REBELLION   Toho, 1967, Japanese
HYMN TO A TIRED MAN   1968, Japanese
INN OF EVIL   1971, Japanese
FOSSILS   1975, Japanese
GLOWING AUTUMN   1979, Japanese
TOKYO SAIBAN (FD)   1983, Japanese

H O W A R D   W .   K O C H *

b. April 11, 1916 - New York, New York
Business: Paramount Pictures, 5555 Melrose Avenue, Hollywood, CA 90038, 213/468-5000

SHIELD FOR MURDER   co-director with Edmond O'Brien, United Artists, 1954
BIG HOUSE, U.S.A.   United Artists, 1955
UNTAMED YOUTH   Warner Bros., 1957
BOP GIRL   United Artists, 1957
JUNGLE HEAT   United Artists, 1957
THE GIRL IN BLACK STOCKINGS   United Artists, 1957
FORT BOWIE   United Artists, 1958
VIOLENT ROAD   Warner Bros., 1958
FRANKENSTEIN - 1970   Allied Artists, 1958
ANDY HARDY COMES HOME   MGM, 1958
THE LAST MILE   United Artists, 1959
BORN RECKLESS   Warner Bros., 1959
BADGE 373   Paramount, 1973

P A N C H O   K O H N E R

b. January 7, 1939 - Los Angeles, California
Contact: Writers Guild of America, West - Los Angeles, 213/550-1000

THE BRIDGE IN THE JUNGLE   United Artists, 1971, Mexican
MR. SYCAMORE   Film Ventures International, 1975

J A M E S   K O M A C K *

Agent: Larry Auerbach, William Morris Agency - Beverly Hills, 213/274-7451
Business Manager: Marvin "Dusty" Snyder, Oppenheim, Appel, Dixon & Co., 2029 Century Park East - Suite 1300, Los Angeles, CA 90067, 213/277-0400

HI-JINX   Hi-Jinx Productions, 1983

A N D R E I   K O N C H A L O V S K Y

b. August 20, 1937 - U.S.S.R.

A BOY AND A PIGEON   Mosfilm, 1960, Soviet
THE FIRST TEACHER   Mosfilm/Kirghizfilm, 1965, Soviet
ASYA'S HAPPINESS   Mosfilm, 1967, Soviet
A NEST OF GENTRY   Corinth, 1969, Soviet
UNCLE VANYA   Mosfilm, 1971, Soviet
A LOVER'S ROMANCE   Mosfilm, 1974, Soviet
SIBERIADE   IFEX Film, 1979, Soviet
MARIA'S LOVERS   MGM/UA/Cannon, 1984

B A R B A R A   K O P P L E *

Business: Cabin Creek Films, 58 East 11th Street, New York, NY 10003, 212/533-7157

HARLAN COUNTY, U.S.A. (FD)   Cabin Creek Films, 1976
KEEPING ON (TF)   Many Mansions Institute, 1983

J O H N   K O R T Y *

b. July 22, 1936 - Lafayette, Indiana
Business: Korty Films, Inc., 200 Miller Avenue, Mill Valley, CA 94941, 415/383-6900
Agent: William Morris Agency - Beverly Hills, 213/274-7451
Attorney: Peter Dekom, Pollock, Bloom & Dekom, 9255 Sunset Blvd., Los Angeles, CA 90064, 213/278-8622

CRAZY QUILT   Farallon, 1965
FUNNYMAN   New Yorker, 1967
RIVERRUN   Columbia, 1970
THE PEOPLE (TF)   Metromedia Productions/American Zoetrope, 1972
GO ASK ALICE (TF)   Metromedia Productions, 1973
CLASS OF '63 (TF)   Metromedia Productions/Stonehenge Productions, 1973
SILENCE   Cinema Financial of America, 1974
THE AUTOBIOGRAPHY OF MISS JANE PITTMAN (TF) ☆☆   Tomorrow Entertainment, 1974
ALEX & THE GYPSY   20th Century-Fox, 1976
FAREWELL TO MANZANAR (TF)   Korty Films/Universal TV, 1976
WHO ARE THE DE BOLTS? ... AND WHERE DID THEY GET 19 KIDS? (FD)   1977
THE MUSIC ROOM (TF)   Learning in Focus, 1977
FOREVER (TF)   Roger Gimbel Productions/EMI TV, 1978
OLIVER'S STORY   Paramount, 1979
A CHRISTMAS WITHOUT SNOW (TF)   Korty Films/The Konigsberg Company, 1980
TWICE UPON A TIME (AF)   co-director with Charles Swenson, The Ladd Company/Warner Bros., 1983
THE HAUNTING PASSION (TF)   BSR Productions/ITC, 1983

H E N R Y   K O S T E R *
(Hermann Kosterlitz)

b. May 1, 1905 - Berlin, Germany
Agent: Walter Kohner, Paul Kohner, Inc. - Los Angeles, 213/550-1060

DAS ABENTEUER DER THEA ROLAND   1932, German
DAS HASSLICHE MADCHEN   1933, German
PETER   1934, Austrian-Hungarian
KLEINE MUTTI   1934, Austrian-Hungarian
KATHARINA DIE LETZTE   1935, Austrian
DAS TAGEBUCH DER GELIEBTEN   1936, Austrian-Italian
THREE SMART GIRLS   Universal, 1936
100 MEN AND A GIRL   Universal, 1937
THE RAGE OF PARIS   Universal, 1938
THREE SMART GIRLS GROW UP   Universal, 1939
FIRST LOVE   Universal, 1939
SPRING PARADE   Universal, 1940
IT STARTED WITH EVE   Universal, 1941
BETWEEN US GIRLS   Universal, 1942
MUSIC FOR MILLIONS   MGM, 1944
TWO SISTERS FROM BOSTON   MGM, 1946
THE UNFINISHED DANCE   MGM, 1947
THE BISHOP'S WIFE★   RKO Radio, 1947
THE LUCK OF THE IRISH   20th Century-Fox, 1948
COME TO THE STABLE   20th Century-Fox, 1949
THE INSPECTOR GENERAL   Warner Bros., 1949
WABASH AVENUE   20th Century-Fox, 1950
MY BLUE HEAVEN   20th Century-Fox, 1950
HARVEY   Universal, 1950
NO HIGHWAY IN THE SKY *NO HIGHWAY*   20th Century-Fox, 1951
   British
MR. BELVEDERE RINGS THE BELL   20th Century-Fox, 1951
ELOPEMENT   20th Century-Fox, 1951

continued

HENRY KOSTER*—continued

O. HENRY'S FULL HOUSE   co-director with Henry Hathaway, Howard Hawks, Henry King & Jean Negulesco, 20th Century-Fox, 1952
STARS AND STRIPES FOREVER   20th Century-Fox, 1952
MY COUSIN RACHEL   20th Century-Fox, 1953
THE ROBE   20th Century-Fox, 1953
DESIREE   20th Century-Fox, 1954
A MAN CALLED PETER   20th Century-Fox, 1955
THE VIRGIN QUEEN   20th Century-Fox, 1955
GOOD MORNING, MISS DOVE   20th Century-Fox, 1955
D-DAY, THE SIXTH OF JUNE   20th Century-Fox, 1956
THE POWER AND THE PRIZE   MGM, 1956
MY MAN GODFREY   Universal, 1957
FRAULEIN   20th Century-Fox, 1958
THE NAKED MAJA   United Artists, 1959
THE STORY OF RUTH   20th Century-Fox, 1960
FLOWER DRUM SONG   Universal, 1961
MR. HOBBS TAKES A VACATION   20th Century-Fox, 1962
TAKE HER, SHE'S MINE   20th Century-Fox, 1963
DEAR BRIGITTE   20th Century-Fox, 1965
THE SINGING NUN   MGM, 1966

TOM KOTANI

THE LAST DINOSAUR (TF)   co-director with Alex Grasshoff, Rankin-Bass Productions, 1977, U.S.-Japanese
THE BERMUDA DEPTHS (TF)   Rankin-Bass Productions, 1978
THE IVORY APE (TF)   Rankin-Bass Productions, 1980, U.S.-Japanese
THE BUSHIDO BLADE   Aquarius, 1982, U.S.-Japanese

TED KOTCHEFF*

b. April 7, 1931 - Toronto, Canada
Agent: Jeff Berg, ICM - Los Angeles, 213/550-4000

TIARA TAHITI   Zenith International, 1962, British
LIFE AT THE TOP   Columbia, 1965, British
TWO GENTLEMENT SHARING   American International, 1969, British
OUTBACK *WAKE IN FRIGHT*   United Artists, 1971, Australian
BILLY TWO HATS   United Artists, 1972, British
THE APPRENTICESHIP OF DUDDY KRAVITZ   Paramount, 1974 Canadian
FUN WITH DICK & JANE   Columbia, 1977
WHO IS KILLING THE GREAT CHEFS OF EUROPE?   Warner Bros., 1978
NORTH DALLAS FORTY   Paramount, 1979
SPLIT IMAGE   Orion, 1982
FIRST BLOOD   Orion, 1982, Canadian
MISSING IN ACTION   Paramount, 1983

YAPHET KOTTO

b. November 15, 1937 - New York, New York

THE LIMIT *TIME LIMIT/SPEED LIMIT 65*   Cannon, 1972

BERNARD L. KOWALSKI*

b. August 2, 1929 - Brownsville, Texas
Home: 17524 Community Street, Northridge, CA 91324, 213/987-2433
Agent: Irv Schechter Company - Beverly Hills, 213/278-8070

HOT CAR GIRL   Allied Artists, 1958
NIGHT OF THE BLOOD BEAST   American International, 1958
THE GIANT LEECHES   American International, 1959
KRAKATOA, EAST OF JAVA   Cinerama Releasing Corporation, 1969
STILETTO   Avco Embassy, 1969
MACHO CALLAHAN   Avco Embassy, 1970
HUNTERS ARE FOR KILLING (TF)   1970
TERROR IN THE SKY (TF)   Paramount TV, 1971
BLACK NOON (TF)   Fenady Associates/Screen Gems, 1971
WOMEN IN CHAINS (TF)   Paramount TV, 1972

continued

BERNARD L. KOWALSKI*—continued

TWO FOR THE MONEY (TF)   Aaron Spelling Productions, 1972
THE WOMAN HUNTER (TF)   Bing Crosby Productions, 1972
SHE CRIED MURDER (TF)   1973
Sssssssss   Universal, 1973
IN TANDEM (TF)   D'Antoni Productions, 1974
FLIGHT TO HOLOCAUST (TF)   Aycee Productions/First Artists, 1977
THE NATIVITY (TF)   D'Angelo-Bullock-Allen Productions/20th Century-Fox TV, 1978
MARCIANO (TF)   ABC Circle Films, 1979
TURNOVER SMITH (TF)   Wellington Productions, 1980
NIGHTSIDE (TF)   Stephen J. Cannell Productions/Glen A. Larson Productions/ Universal TV, 1980

ROBERT KRAMER

Contact: French Film Office, 745 Fifth Avenue, New York, NY 10151, 212/832-8860

THE EDGE   Film-Makers, 1968
ICE   New Yorker, 1970
MILESTONES   co-director with John Douglas, Stone, 1975
BIRTH   1982, French
A TOUT ALLURE   INA, 1982, French

STANLEY KRAMER*

b. September 23, 1913 - New York, New York
Business: Stanley Kramer Productions, P.O. Box 158, Bellevue, Washington 90889, 206/454-1785
Personal Manager: Roy Kaufman, 1900 Avenue of the Stars, Los Angeles, CA 90067, 213/277-1900
Attorney: Gunther Schiff, 9665 Wilshire Blvd., Beverly Hills, CA 90212, 213/278-6500

NOT AS A STRANGER   United Artists, 1955
THE PRIDE AND THE PASSION   United Artists, 1957
THE DEFIANT ONES ★   United Artists, 1958
ON THE BEACH   United Artists, 1959
INHERIT THE WIND   United Artists, 1960
JUDGMENT AT NUREMBERG ★   United Artists, 1961
IT'S A MAD, MAD, MAD, MAD WORLD   United Artists, 1963
SHIP OF FOOLS   Columbia, 1965
GUESS WHO'S COMING TO DINNER ★   Columbia, 1969
THE SECRET OF SANTA VITTORIA   United Artists, 1969
R.P.M.*   Columbia, 1970
BLESS THE BEASTS & CHILDREN   Columbia, 1971
OKLAHOMA CRUDE   Columbia, 1973
THE DOMINO PRINCIPLE   Avco Embassy, 1977
THE RUNNER STUMBLES   20th Century-Fox, 1979

PAUL KRASNY*

b. August 8, 1935 - Cleveland, Ohio
Home: 3620 Goodland Drive, Studio City, CA 91604, 213/506-4200
Agent: Mark Lichtman, Shapiro-Lichtman Agency - Los Angeles, 213/557-2244

THE D.A.: CONSPIRACY TO KILL (TF)   Universal TV/Mark VII Ltd., 1971
THE ADVENTURES OF NICK CARTER (TF)   Universal TV, 1972
THE LETTERS (TF)   co-director with Gene Nelson, ABC Circle Films, 1973
CHRISTINA   International Amusements, 1974
BIG ROSE (TF)   20th Century-Fox TV, 1974
JOE PANTHER   Artists Creation & Associates, 1976
CENTENNIAL (MS)   co-director with Harry Falk, Bernard McEveety & Virgil Vogel, Universal TV, 1978
THE ISLANDER (TF)   Universal TV, 1978
WHEN HELL WAS IN SESSION (TF)   Aubrey-Hamner Productions, 1979
ALCATRAZ: THE WHOLE SHOCKING STORY (TF)   Pierre Cossette Productions, 1980
FUGITIVE FAMILY (TF)   Aubrey-Hamner Productions, 1980
TERROR AMONG US (TF)   David Gerber Company, 1981

continued

PAUL KRASNY*—continued

FLY AWAY HOME (TF)   An Lac Productions/Warner Bros. TV, 1981

J O H N   K R I S H

Contact: British Academy of Film & Television Arts, 195 Piccadilly, London W1,
England, 01/734-0022

THE SALVAGE GANG   Children's Film Foundation, 1958, British
THE WILD AFFAIR   Goldstone, 1963, British
THE UNEARTHLY STRANGER   American International, 1964, British
DECLINE AND FALL OF A BIRD WATCHER   20th Century-Fox, 1969, British
THE MAN WHO HAD POWER OVER WOMEN   Avco Embassy, 1971, British
JESUS   co-director with Peter Sykes, Warner Bros., 1979, British

W I L L I A M   K R O N I C K *

Home: 950 N. Kings Road, Los Angeles, CA 90069, 213/656-8150
Business: William Kronick Productions, 8489 W. Third Street, Los Angeles,
CA 90048, 213/651-2810

THE 500-POUND JERK (TF)   Wolper Productions, 1973
TO THE ENDS OF THE EARTH (FD)   Armand Hammer Productions, 1983

J E R E M Y   J O E   K R O N S B E R G *

Personal Manager: Leonard Grainger - Los Angeles, 213/858-1573
Attorney: Loeb & Loeb, 10100 Santa Monica Blvd., Los Angeles, CA 90067, 213/
552-7700

GOING APE!   Paramount, 1981

S T A N L E Y   K U B R I C K *

b. July 26, 1928 - Bronx, New York
Contact: Directors Guild of Great Britian, 56 Whitfield Street, London W1, England,
01/580-9592
Attorney: Louis C. Blau, Loeb & Loeb, 10100 Santa Monica Blvd., Los Angeles,
CA 90067, 213/552-7774

FEAR AND DESIRE   Joseph Burstyn, Inc., 1954
KILLER'S KISS   United Artists, 1955
THE KILLING   United Artists, 1956
PATHS OF GLORY   United Artists, 1957
SPARTACUS   Universal, 1960
LOLITA   MGM, 1962, British
**DR. STRANGELOVE OR: HOW I LEARNED TO STOP WORRYING AND
LOVE THE BOMB ★**   Columbia, 1964, British
2001: A SPACE ODYSSEY ★   MGM, 1968, British
A CLOCKWORK ORANGE ★   Warner Bros., 1971, British
BARRY LYNDON ★   Warner Bros., 1975, British
THE SHINING   Warner Bros., 1980, British

B U Z Z   K U L I K *

b. 1923 - New York, New York
Agent: Herb Tobias & Associates - Los Angeles 213/277-6211

THE EXPLOSIVE GENERATION   United Artists, 1961
THE YELLOW CANARY   20th Century-Fox, 1963
READY FOR THE PEOPLE   Warner Bros., 1964
WARNING SHOT   Paramount, 1968
SERGEANT RYKER   Universal, 1968
VILLA RIDES!   Paramount, 1968
RIOT   Paramount, 1969
VANISHED (TF)   Universal TV, 1971
OWEN MARSHALL, COUNSELOR AT LAW (TF)   Universal TV, 1971
BRIAN'S SONG (TF) ☆   Screen Gems/Columbia TV, 1971
TO FIND A MAN   Columbia, 1972
INCIDENT ON A DARK STREET (TF)   20th Century-Fox TV, 1973

continued

BUZZ KULIK*—continued

PIONEER WOMAN (TF)   Filmways, 1973
SHAMUS   Columbia, 1973
BAD RONALD (TF)   Lorimar Productions, 1974
REMEMBER WHEN (TF)   Danny Thomas Productions/The Raisin Company, 1974
CAGE WITHOUT A KEY (TF)   Columbia TV, 1975
MATT HELM (TF)   Columbia TV, 1975
BABE (TF) ☆   MGM TV, 1975
THE LINDBERGH KIDNAPPING CASE (TF)   Columbia TV, 1976
COREY: FOR THE PEOPLE (TF)   Columbia TV, 1977
KILL ME IF YOU CAN (TF)   Columbia TV, 1977
ZIEGFELD: THE MAN AND HIS WOMEN (TF)   Frankovich Productions/ Columbia TV, 1978
FROM HERE TO ETERNITY (MS)   Bennett-Katleman Productions/Columbia TV, 1979
THE HUNTER   Paramount, 1980
SIDNEY SHELDON'S RAGE OF ANGELS (TF)   Furia-Oringer Productions/NBC Productions, 1983
GEORGE WASHINGTON (MS)   David Gerber Company/MGM-UA TV, 1984

A K I R A   K U R O S A W A

b. March 23, 1910 - Tokyo, Japan
Contact: Directors Guild of Japan, Tsukada Building, 8-33 Udagawa-cho, Shibuya-ku, Tokyo 150, Japan, 3/461-4411

SANSHIRO SUGATA   Toho, 1943, Japanese
THE MOST BEAUTIFUL   Toho, 1944, Japanese
THOSE WHO TREAD ON THE TIGER'S TAIL   Toho, 1945, Japanese
SANSHIRO SUGATA - PART TWO   Toho, 1945, Japanese
NO REGRETS FOR OUR YOUTH   Toho, 1946, Japanese
THOSE WHO MAKE TOMORROW   Toho, 1946, Japanese
ONE WONDERFUL SUNDAY   Toho, 1947, Japanese
DRUNKEN ANGEL   Toho, 1948, Japanese
THE QUIET DUEL   Daiei, 1949, Japanese
STRAY DOG   Toho, 1949, Japanese
SCANDAL   Shochiku, 1959, Japanese
RASHOMON   RKO Radio, 1950, Japanese
THE IDIOT   Shochiku, 1951, Japanese
IKIRU   Brandon, 1952, Japanese
SEVEN SAMURAI   Landmark Releasing, 1954, Japanese
I LIVE IN FEAR   Brandon, 1955, Japanese
THE LOWER DEPTHS   Brandon, 1957, Japanese
THRONE OF BLOOD *THE CASTLE OF THE SPIDER'S WEB*   Brandon, 1957, Japanese
THE HIDDEN FORTRESS *THREE BAD MEN IN A HIDDEN FORTRESS*   Toho, 1958, Japanese
THE BAD SLEEP WELL   Toho, 1960, Japanese
YOJIMBO   Seneca International, 1961, Japanese
SANJURO   Toho, 1962, Japanese
HIGH AND LOW   Continental, 1963, Japanese
RED BEARD   Toho, 1965, Japanese
DODES'KA'DEN   Janus, 1970, Japanese
DERSU UZALA   New World, 1975, Soviet-Japanese
KAGEMUSHA: THE SHADOW WARRIOR   20th Century-Fox, 1980, Japanese

D I A N E   K U R Y S

Contact: French Film Office, 745 Fifth Avenue, New York, NY 10151, 212/832-8860

PEPPERMINT SODA   New Yorker, 1979, French
COCKTAIL MOLOTOV   Putnam Square, 1980, French
ENTRE NOUS *COUP DE FOUDRE*   United Artists Classics, 1983, French

MORT LACHMAN *

Business: Mort Lachman & Associates, 4115 "B" Warner Blvd., Burbank,
CA 91505, 213/769-6030
Agent: Bernie Weintraub, Robinson-Weintraub & Associates - Los Angeles, 213/653-5802

THE GIRL WHO COULDN'T LOSE (TF)☆☆   Filmways, 1975

HARVEY LAIDMAN *

Agent: Louis Bershad, Century Artists Ltd. - Beverly Hills, 213/273-4366
Business Manager: Marvin Freedman, Freedman, Kinzelberg & Broder, 1801 Avenue
of the Stars - Suite 911, Los Angeles, CA 90067, 213/277-0700

STEEL COWBOY (TF)   Roger Gimbel Productions/EMI TV, 1978

MARLENA LAIRD *

Home: 2729 Westshire Drive, Los Angeles, CA 90068, 213/465-6400
Agent: Irv Schechter Company - Beverly Hills, 213/278-8070

FRIENDSHIP, SECRETS AND LIES   co-director with Ann Zane Shanks,
Wittman-Riche Productions/Warner Bros. TV, 1979

FRANK LaLOGGIA

FEAR NO EVIL   Avco Embassy, 1981

MARY LAMPSON

UNDERGROUND (FD)   co-director with Emile de Antonio & Haskell Wexler,
New Yorker, 1976
UNTIL SHE TALKS (TF)   Alaska Street Productions, 1983

BURT LANCASTER *

b. November 2, 1913 - New York, New York
Agent: ICM - Los Angeles, 213/550-4000

THE MIDNIGHT MAN   co-director with Roland Kibbee, Universal, 1974

JOHN LANDIS *

Agent: Michael Marcus, CAA - Los Angeles, 213/277-4545

SCHLOCK   Jack H. Harris Enterprises, 1973
THE KENTUCKY FRIED MOVIE   United Film Distribution, 1977
NATIONAL LAMPOON'S ANIMAL HOUSE   Universal, 1978
THE BLUES BROTHERS   Universal, 1980

continued

JOHN LANDIS*—continued
AN AMERICAN WEREWOLF IN LONDON   Universal, 1981
TWILIGHT ZONE - THE MOVIE   co-director with Steven Spielberg, Joe Dante
     & George Miller, Warner Bros., 1983
TRADING PLACES   Paramount, 1983
COMING SOON (CTD)   Universal Pay TV, 1983

MICHAEL LANDON*

(Eugene Orowitz)

b. October 31, 1937 - Forest Hills, New York
Business Manager: Jay Eller, 1930 Century Park West - Suite 401, Los Angeles,
     CA 90067, 213/277-6408

IT'S GOOD TO BE ALIVE (TF)   Metromedia Productions, 1974
LITTLE HOUSE ON THE PRAIRIE (TF)   NBC Productions, 1974
THE LONELIEST RUNNER (TF)   NBC Productions, 1976
KILLING STONE (TF)   Universal TV, 1978
FATHER MURPHY (TF)   NBC Productions, 1981
SAM'S SON   Michael Landon Productions/Worldvision, 1984

ALAN LANDSBURG*

b. May 10, 1933 - New York, New York
Business: Alan Landsburg Productions, Inc., 1554 S. Sepulveda Blvd., Los Angeles,
     CA 90025, 213/473-9641

BLACK WATER GOLD (TF)   Metromedia Productions, 1970

RICHARD LANG*

Agent: Herb Tobias & Associates - Los Angeles, 213/277-6211

FANTASY ISLAND (TF)   Spelling-Goldberg Productions, 1977
THE HUNTED LADY (TF)   QM Productions, 1977
NOWHERE TO RUN (TF)   MTM Enterprises, 1978
NIGHT CRIES (TF)   Charles Fries Productions, 1978
DR. SCORPION (TF)   Universal TV, 1978
VEGA$ (TF)   Aaron Spelling Productions, 1978
THE WORD (MS)   Charles Fries Productions/Stonehenge Productions, 1978
THE MOUNTAIN MEN   Columbia, 1980
A CHANGE OF SEASONS   20th Century-Fox, 1980
MATT HOUSTON (TF)   Largo Productions/Aaron Spelling Productions, 1982
DON'T GO TO SLEEP (TF)   Aaron Spelling Productions, 1982
SHOOTING STARS (TF)   Aaron Spelling Productions, 1983

SIMON LANGTON

b. November 5, 1941 - Amersham, England
Agent: CAA - Los Angeles, 213/277-4545 or: Spokesmen, Ltd., 1 Craven Hill,
     London W2, England

SMILEY'S PEOPLE (MS)☆   BBC/Paramount TV, 1982, British
THE LOST HONOR OF KATHRYN BECK (TF)   Open Road Productions, 1983

STAN LATHAN*

Personal Manager: The Brillstein Company - Los Angeles, 213/275-6135

SAVE THE CHILDREN (FD)   Paramount, 1973
AMAZING GRACE   United Artists, 1974
THE SKY IS GRAY (TF)   Learning in Focus, 1980
DENMARK VESEY'S REBELLION (TF)   WPBT-Miami, 1982
GO TELL IT ON THE MOUNTAIN (TF)   Learning in Focus, 1984

ALBERTO LATTUADA

b. November 13, 1914 - Milan, Italy
Contact: Ministry of Tourism & Education, Via Della Ferratella, No. 51, 00184
    Rome, Italy, 06/7732

GIACOMO L'IDEALISTA   1942, Italian
LA FRECCIA NEL FIANCO   1943, Italian
LA NOSTRA GUERRA   1943, Italian
IL BANDITO   Lux Film, 1946, Italian
IL DELITTO DI GIOVANNI EPISCOPO   Lux Film, 1947, Italian
SENZA PIETA   Lux Film, 1948, Italian
LUCI DEL PO   1949, Italian
VARIETY LIGHTS   co-director with Federico Fellini, Pathe Contemporary, 1950,
    Italian
ANNA   Italian Films Export, 1951, Italian
IL CAPPOTTO   Faro Film, 1952, Italian
LA LUPA   Republic, 1953, Italian
LOVE IN THE CITY   co-director, Italian Films Export, 1953, Italian
LA SPIAGGIA   Titanus, 1954, Italian
SCUOLA ELEMENTARE   Titanus/Societe General de Cinematographie, 1954,
    Italian-French
GUENDALINA   Carlo Ponti/Les Films Marceau, 1957, Italian-French
TEMPEST   Paramount, 1958, Italian-French-Yugoslavian
I DOLCI INGANNI   Carlo Ponti/Titanus, 1960, Italian
LETTERA DI UNA NOVIZIA   Champion/Euro International, 1960, Italian
L'IMPREVISTO   Documento Film/Orsay Film, 1961, Italian-French
MAFIOSO   Zenith International, 1962, Italian
LA STEPPA   Zebra Film/Aera Film, 1962, Italian
LA MANDRAGOLA   Arco Film/Lux Compagnie Cinematographie, 1965, Italian-
    French
MATCHLESS   United Artists, 1966, Italian
DON GIOVANNI IN SICILIA   Adelphia, 1967, Italian
FRAULEIN DOKTOR   Paramount, 1969, Italian-Yugoslavian
L'AMICA   Fair Film, 1969, Italian
VENGA A PRENDERE IL CAFFE DA NOI   Mass Film, 1970, Italian
WHITE SISTER *BIANCO, ROSSO E . . .*   Columbia, 1971, Italian-French-
    Spanish
SONO STATO IO   Dear Film, 1973, Italian
LE FARO DA PADRE   Clesi Cinematografica, 1974, Italian
CUORE DI CANE   Italnoleggio, 1975, Italian
BRUCIATI DA COCENTE PASSIONE   Cineriz, 1976, Italian
OH, SERAFINA   Cineriz, 1976, Italian
COSI COME SEI   CEIAD, 1978, Italian-Spanish
THE CRICKET   PIC, 1979, Italian
THORN IN THE HEART   1981, Italian-French
CHRISTOPHER COLUMBUS (MS)   Rai/Clesi Cinematografica/Antenne-2/
    Bavaria/Lorimar Productions, 1984, Italian-West German-U.S.

FRANK LAUGHLIN*

Home: 213/476-7262
Business Manager: c/o Pal-Mel Productions, 9350 Wilshire Blvd. - Suite 400, Beverly
    Hills, CA 90212, 213/869-0497

THE TRIAL OF BILLY JACK   Taylor-Laughlin, 1974
THE MASTER GUNFIGHTER   Taylor-Laughlin, 1975

MICHAEL LAUGHLIN

STRANGE BEHAVIOR *DEAD KIDS*   World Northal, 1981, New Zealand-
    Australian
STRANGE INVADERS   Orion, 1983, Canadian

TOM LAUGHLIN*

b. 1938 - Minneapolis, Minnesota
Business: National Student Film Corporation, 4024 Radford Avenue, Studio City,
    CA 91604, 213/394-0286

THE PROPER TIME   Lopert, 1960
THE YOUNG SINNER   United Screen Arts, 1965

continued

TOM LAUGHLIN*—continued

BORN LOSERS   directed under pseudonym of T.C. Frank, American
     International, 1967
BILLY JACK   directed under pseudonym of T.C. Frank, Warner Bros., 1973
BILLY JACK GOES TO WASHINGTON   Taylor-Laughlin, 1978

A R N O L D   L A V E N *

b. February 23, 1922 - Chicago, Illinois
Home: 213/981-4551

WITHOUT WARNING   United Artists, 1952
VICE SQUAD   United Artists, 1953
DOWN THREE DARK STREETS   United Artists, 1954
THE RACK   MGM, 1956
THE MONSTER THAT CHALLENGED THE WORLD   United Artists, 1957
SLAUGHTER ON TENTH AVENUE   Universal, 1957
ANNA LUCASTA   United Artists, 1958
GERONIMO   United Artists, 1962
THE GLORY GUYS   United Artists, 1965
ROUGH NIGHT IN JERICHO   Universal, 1967
SAM WHISKEY   United Artists, 1969

J O E   L A Y T O N *

Personal Manager: Roy Gerber Associates, 9200 Sunset Blvd. - Suite 620, Los
     Angeles, CA 90069, 213/550-0100

RICHARD PRYOR LIVE ON THE SUNSET STRIP (FD)   Columbia, 1982

A S H L E Y   L A Z A R U S

Contact: British Academy of Film & Television Arts, 195 Piccadilly, London W1,
     England, 01/734-0022

FOREVER YOUNG, FOREVER FREE *E'LOLLIPOP*   Universal, 1976, British
GOLDEN RENDEZVOUS   Rank, 1977, British

W I L F O R D   L E A C H

THE WEDDING PARTY   co-director with Brian De Palma & Cynthia Munroe,
     Powell Productions Plus/Ondine, 1969
THE PIRATES OF PENZANCE   Universal, 1983

P H I L I P   L E A C O C K *

b. October 8, 1917 - London, England
Home: 914 Bienveneda Avenue, Pacific Palisades, CA 90272, 213/454-4188
Agent: Ronald Lief, Contemporary-Korman Artists - Beverly Hills, 213/278-8250

RIDERS OF THE NEW FOREST   Crown, 1946, British
THE BRAVE DON'T CRY   Mayer-Kingsley, 1952, British
ASSIGNMENT IN LONDON   Associated Artists, 1953, British
THE LITTLE KIDNAPPERS *THE KIDNAPPERS*   United Artists, 1954, British
ESCAPADE   DCA, 1955, British
THE SPANISH GARDENER   Rank, 1956, British
HIGH TIDE AT NOON   Rank, 1957, British
INNOCENT SINNERS   Rank, 1958, British
THE RABBIT TRAP   United Artists, 1959
LET NO MAN WRITE MY EPITAPH   Columbia, 1960
TAKE A GIANT STEP   United Artists, 1960
HAND IN HAND   Columbia, 1961, British
REACH FOR GLORY   Royal Films International, 1962, British
13 WEST STREET   Columbia, 1962
THE WAR LOVER   Columbia, 1962, British
TAMAHINE   MGM, 1964, British
ADAM'S WOMAN   Warner Bros., 1970, Australian
THE BIRDMEN (TF)   Universal TV, 1971
WHEN MICHAEL CALLS (TF)   Palomar International, 1972

continued

PHILIP LEACOCK*—continued

THE DAUGHTERS OF JOSHUA CABE (TF)   Spelling-Goldberg Productions, 1972
BAFFLED! (TF)   Arena Productions/ITC, 1973
THE GREAT MAN'S WHISKERS (TF)   Universal TV, 1973
DYING ROOM ONLY (TF)   Lorimar Productions, 1973
KEY WEST (TF)   Warner Bros. TV, 1973
KILLER ON BOARD (TF)   Lorimar Productions, 1977
WILD AND WOOLY (TF)   Aaron Spelling Productions, 1978
THE CURSE OF KING TUT'S TOMB (TF)   Stromberg-Kerby Productions/ Columbia TV/HTV West, 1980
ANGEL CITY (TF)   Factor-Newland Productions, 1980
THE TWO LIVES OF CAROL LETNER (TF)   Penthouse One Presentations, 1981
THE WILD WOMEN OF CHASTITY GULCH (TF)   Aaron Spelling Productions, 1982

P A U L   L E A F *

b. May 2, 1929 - New York, New York
Home: 924 23rd Street, Santa Monica, CA 90403, 213/829-2223
Agent: The Lantz Office - Los Angeles, 213/858-1144

TOP SECRET (TF)   Jemmin, Inc./Sheldon Leonard Productions, 1978
SERGEANT MATLOVICH VS. THE U.S. AIR FORCE (TF)   Tomorrow Entertainment, 1978

D A V I D   L E A N *

b. March 25, 1908 - Croydon, England
Contact: Directors Guild of Great Britain, 56 Whitfield Street, London W1, England, 01/580-9592

IN WHICH WE SERVE   co-director with Noel Coward, Universal, 1942, British
THIS HAPPY BREED   Universal, 1944, British
BLITHE SPIRIT   United Artists, 1945, British
BRIEF ENCOUNTER   Universal, 1946, British
GREAT EXPECTATIONS★   Universal, 1947, British
OLIVER TWIST   United Artists, 1948, British
ONE WOMAN'S STORY *THE PASSIONATE FRIENDS*   Universal, 1949, British
MADELEINE   Universal, 1950, British
BREAKING THE SOUND BARRIER *THE SOUND BARRIER*   United Artists, 1952, British
HOBSON'S CHOICE   United Artists, 1954, British
SUMMERTIME *SUMMER MADNESS★*   United Artists, 1955, British
THE BRIDGE ON THE RIVER KWAI★★   Columbia, 1957, British
LAWRENCE OF ARABIA★★   Columbia, 1962, British
DOCTOR ZHIVAGO★   MGM, 1965, British
RYAN'S DAUGHTER   MGM, 1970, British
A PASSAGE TO INDIA   Columbia, 1984, British

N O R M A N   L E A R *

b. July 27, 1922 - New Haven, Connecticut
Business: TAT Communications, 1901 Avenue of the Stars - Suite 1600, Los Angeles, CA 90067, 213/553-3600

COLD TURKEY   United Artists, 1971

J O A N N A   L E E *

Home: 135 S. Carmelina, Los Angeles, CA 90049, 213/270-3118
Agent: William Morris Agency - Beverly Hills, 213/274-7451
Business Manager: deThomas & Associates - Los Angeles, 213/277-4866

MIRROR, MIRROR (TF)   Christiana Productions, 1979
CHILDREN OF DIVORCE (TF)   Christiana Productions/Marble Arch Productions, 1980

ROBERT LEEDS *

Contact: Directors Guild of America - Los Angeles, 213/656-1220

RETURN OF THE BEVERLY HILLBILLIES (TF)   CBS, 1981

ERNEST LEHMAN *

b. 1920 - New York, New York
Business Manager: Henry J. Bamberger, 2049 Century Park East, Los Angeles,
  CA 90067, 213/553-0581

PORTNOY'S COMPLAINT   Warner Bros., 1972

DAVID LEIVICK

GOSPEL (FD)   co-director with Frederick Ritzenberg, 20th Century-Fox, 1983

CLAUDE LELOUCH

b. October 30, 1937 - Paris, France
Contact: French Film Office, 745 Fifth Avenue, New York, NY 10151, 212/832-
  8860

LE PROPRE DE L'HOMME   1960, French
L'AMOUR AVEC DES SI   1963, French
LA FEMME SPECTACLE   1964, French
TO BE A CROOK *UNE FILLE ET DES FUSILS*   Comet, 1965, French
LES GRAND MOMENTS   1965, French
A MAN AND A WOMAN ★   Allied Artists, 1966, French
LIVE FOR LIFE   United Artists, 1967, French
FAR FROM VIETNAM (FD)   co-director with Jean-Luc Godard, Joris Ivens,
  William Klein, Alain Resnais & Agnes Varda, New Yorker, 1967, French
GRENOBLE (FD)   co-director with Francois Reichenbach, United Producers of
  America, 1968, French
LIFE LOVE DEATH   Lopert, 1969, French
LOVE IS A FUNNY THING *UN HOMME QUI ME PLAIT*   United Artists,
  1970, French-Italian
THE CROOK   United Artists, 1971, French
SMIC, SMAC, SMOC   GSF, 1971, French
MONEY MONEY MONEY *L'AVENTURE C'EST L'AVENTURE*   GSF, 1972,
  French
HAPPY NEW YEAR *LA BONNE ANNEE*   Avco Embassy, 1973, French-
  Italian
VISIONS OF EIGHT (FD)   co-director with Yuri Ozerov, Mai Zetterling, Michael
  Pfleghar, Kon Ichikawa, Milos Forman & John Schlesinger, Cinema 5, 1973
AND NOW MY LOVE *TOUTE UNE VIE*   Avco Embassy, 1975, French-Italian
MARIAGE   1975, French
CAT AND MOUSE   Quartet, 1975, French
THE GOOD AND THE BAD   Paramount, 1976, French
SECOND CHANCE *SI C'ETAIT A REFAIRE*   United Artists Classics, 1976,
  French
ANOTHER MAN, ANOTHER CHANCE   United Artists, 1977, U.S.-French
ROBERT ET ROBERT   Quartet, 1978, French
A NOUS DEUX   1979, French-Canadian
BOLERO *LES UNS ET LES AUTRES*   Double 13, 1982, French
EDITH AND MARCEL   Miramax, 1983, French
VIVA LA VIE   UGC, 1984, French

JACK LEMMON *

b. February 8, 1925 - Boston, Massachusetts
Business: Jalem Productions, Inc., 141 El Camino - Suite 201, Beverly Hills,
  CA 90212, 213/278-7750
Agent: William Morris Agency - Beverly Hills, 213/274-7451
Business Manager: Marvin Freedman, Freedman, Kinzelberg & Broder, 1801 Avenue
  of the Stars - Suite 911, Los Angeles, CA 90067, 213/277-0700

KOTCH   Cinerama Releasing Corporation, 1971

M A L C O L M   L E O *

b. October 9, 1944 - New York, New York
Business: South Swell, Inc., 6536 Sunset Blvd., Los Angeles, CA 90028, 213/464-
    5193
Agent: Michael Poretzian, William Morris Agency - Beverly Hills, 213/274-7451

HEROES OF ROCK AND ROLL (TD)   co-director with Andrew Solt, ABC,
    1979
THIS IS ELVIS (FD)   co-director with Andrew Solt, Warner Bros., 1981
IT CAME FROM HOLLYWOOD (FD)   co-director with Andrew Solt, Paramount,
    1982

H E R B E R T   B .   L E O N A R D *

b. October 8, 1922
Home: 5300 Fulton Avenue, Van Nuys, CA 91401, 213/783-0457
Agent: ICM - Los Angeles, 213/550-4000

THE PERILS OF PAULINE   Universal, 1967
GOING HOME   MGM, 1971

J O H N   L E O N E *

Agent: William Morris Agency - Beverly Hills, 213/274-7451

THE GREAT SMOKEY ROADBLOCK *THE LAST OF THE*
    COWBOYS   Dimension, 1978

S E R G I O   L E O N E

b. 1921 - Rome, Italy
Contact: Ministry of Tourism & Education, Via Della Ferratella, No. 51, 00184
    Rome, Italy, 06/7732

THE COLOSSUS OF RHODES   MGM, 1960, Italian-French-Spanish
A FISTFUL OF DOLLARS   United Artists, 1967, Italian-Spanish-West German
FOR A FEW DOLLARS MORE   United Artists, 1967, Italian-Spanish-West
    German
THE GOOD, THE BAD AND THE UGLY   United Artists, 1968, Italian
ONCE UPON A TIME IN THE WEST   Paramount, 1969, Italian-U.S.
DUCK! YOU SUCKER *FISTFUL OF DYNAMITE*   United Artists, 1972,
    Italian-U.S.
ONCE UPON A TIME IN AMERICA   The Ladd Company/Warner Bros., 1984,
    U.S.-Italian-Canadian

M E R V Y N   L e R O Y *

b. October 15, 1900 - San Francisco, California
Business: Mervyn LeRoy Productions, c/o Finkel, Lewis & Joffe, 9200 Sunset Blvd. -
    Suite 1229, Los Angeles, CA 90069, 213/278-4441

NO PLACE TO GO   First National, 1927
FLYING ROMEOS   First National, 1928
HAROLD TEEN   First National, 1928
OH KAY!   First National, 1928
NAUGHTY BABY   First National, 1929
HOT STUFF   First National, 1929
BROADWAY BABIES   First National, 1929
LITTLE JOHNNY JONES   First National, 1929
PLAYING AROUND   First National, 1929
SHOWGIRL IN HOLLYWOOD   First National, 1930
NUMBERED MEN   First National, 1930
TOP SPEED   First National, 1930
LITTLE CAESAR   First National, 1931
GENTLEMAN'S FATE   First National, 1931
TOO YOUNG TO MARRY   First National, 1931
BROAD MINDED   First National, 1931
FIVE STAR FINAL   First National, 1931
LOCAL BOY MAKES GOOD   First National, 1931
TONIGHT OR NEVER   United Artists, 1931

continued

MERVYN LeROY*—continued

HIGH PRESSURE   Warner Bros., 1932
TWO SECONDS   First National, 1932
BIG CITY BLUES   Warner Bros., 1932
THREE ON A MATCH   First National, 1932
I AM A FUGITIVE FROM A CHAIN GANG   Warner Bros., 1932
HARD TO HANDLE   Warner Bros., 1933
ELMER THE GREAT   First National, 1933
GOLD DIGGERS OF 1933   Warner Bros., 1933
TUGBOAT ANNIE   MGM, 1933
THE WORLD CHANGES   First National, 1933
HI, NELLIE!   Warner Bros., 1934
HEAT LIGHTING   Warner Bros., 1934
HAPPINESS AHEAD   First National, 1934
SWEET ADELINE   Warner Bros., 1935
OIL FOR THE LAMPS OF CHINA   Warner Bros., 1935
PAGE MISS GLORY   Warner Bros., 1935
I FOUND STELLA PARISH   First National, 1935
ANTHONY ADVERSE   Warner Bros., 1936
THREE MEN ON A HORSE   First National, 1936
THE KING AND THE CHORUS GIRL   Warner Bros., 1937
THEY WON'T FORGET   Warner Bros., 1937
FOOLS FOR SCANDAL   Warner Bros., 1938
WATERLOO BRIDGE   MGM, 1940
ESCAPE   MGM, 1940
BLOSSOMS IN THE DUST   MGM, 1941
UNHOLY PARTNERS   MGM, 1941
JOHNNY EAGER   MGM, 1941
RANDOM HARVEST★   MGM, 1942
MADAME CURIE   MGM, 1943
THIRTY SECONDS OVER TOKYO   MGM, 1944
WITHOUT RESERVATIONS   RKO Radio, 1946
HOMECOMING   MGM, 1948
LITTLE WOMEN   MGM, 1949
ANY NUMBER CAN PLAY   MGM, 1949
EAST SIDE, WEST SIDE   MGM, 1950
QUO VADIS   MGM, 1951
LOVELY TO LOOK AT   MGM, 1952
MILLION DOLLAR MERMAID   MGM, 1952
LATIN LOVERS   MGM, 1953
ROSE MARIE   MGM, 1954
STRANGE LADY IN TOWN   Warner Bros., 1955
MISTER ROBERTS   co-director with John Ford, Warner Bros., 1955
THE BAD SEED   Warner Bros., 1956
TOWARD THE UNKNOWN   Warner Bros., 1956
NO TIME FOR SERGEANTS   Warner Bros., 1958
HOME BEFORE DARK   Warner Bros., 1958
THE FBI STORY   Warner Bros., 1959
WAKE ME WHEN IT'S OVER   20th Century-Fox, 1960
THE DEVIL AT 4 O'CLOCK   Columbia, 1961
A MAJORITY OF ONE   Warner Bros., 1962
GYPSY   Warner Bros., 1962
MARY, MARY   Warner Bros., 1963
MOMENT TO MOMENT   Universal, 1966

M A R K   L .   L E S T E R *

Business: 7932 Mulholland Drive, Los Angeles, CA 90046, 213/876-8783
Agent: Tom Chasin, Chasin-Park-Citron - Los Angeles, 213/273-7190

STEEL ARENA   L-T, 1973
TRUCK STOP WOMEN   L-T, 1974
THE WAY HE WAS   1975
BOBBI JO AND THE OUTLAW   American International, 1976
STUNTS   New Line Cinema, 1977
GOLD OF THE AMAZON WOMEN (TF)   Mi-Ka Productions, 1979
ROLLER BOOGIE   United Artists, 1979
CLASS OF 1984   United Film Distribution, 1982, Canadian
FIRESTARTER   Universal, 1984

R I C H A R D   L E S T E R *

b. January 19, 1932 - Philadelphia, Pennsylvania
Messages: 213/892-4477
Business: Twickenham Film Studios, St. Margarets, Middlesex, England
Agent: William Morris Agency - Beverly Hills, 213/274-7451

RING-A-DING RHYTHM *IT'S TRAD, DAD*   Columbia, 1962, British
THE MOUSE ON THE MOON   United Artists, 1963, British
A HARD DAY'S NIGHT   United Artists, 1964, British
THE KNACK ... AND HOW TO GET IT   Lopert, 1965, British
HELP!   United Artists, 1965, British
A FUNNY THING HAPPENED ON THE WAY TO THE FORUM   United
    Artists, 1966, British
TEENAGE REBELLION *MONDO TEENO*   co-director with Norman Herbert,
    Trans-American, 1967, British-U.S.
HOW I WON THE WAR   United Artists, 1967, British
PETULIA   Warner Bros., 1968, U.S.-British
THE BED SITTING ROOM   United Artists, 1969, British
THE THREE MUSKETEERS *THE QUEEN'S DIAMONDS*   20th Century-Fox,
    1974, British
JUGGERNAUT   United Artists, 1974, British
THE FOUR MUSKETEERS *MILADY'S REVENGE*   20th Century-Fox, 1975,
    British
ROYAL FLASH   20th Century-Fox, 1976, British
ROBIN AND MARIAN   Columbia, 1976, British
THE RITZ   Warner Bros., 1976
BUTCH AND SUNDANCE: THE EARLY DAYS   20th Century-Fox, 1979
CUBA   United Artists, 1979
SUPERMAN II   Warner Bros., 1981, U.S.-British
SUPPERMAN III   Warner Bros., 1983, U.S.-British
FINDERS KEEPERS   Warner Bros., 1984

W I L L I A M   A .   L E V E Y *

Agent: Peter Meyer, William Morris Agency - Beverly Hills, 213/274-7451

BLACKENSTEIN   LFG, 1973
SLUMBER PARTY '57   Cannon, 1977
THE HAPPY HOOKER GOES TO WASHINGTON   Cannon, 1977
SKATETOWN, U.S.A.   Columbia, 1979

A L A N   J .   L E V I *

Home: 13417 Inwood Drive, Sherman Oaks, CA 91423, 213/981-3417
Agent: William Morris Agency - Beverly Hills, 213/274-7451

GEMINI MAN (TF)   Universal TV, 1976
THE RETURN OF THE INCREDIBLE HULK (TF)   Universal TV, 1977
GO WEST, YOUNG GIRL (TF)   Bennett-Katleman Productions/Columbia TV,
    1978
THE IMMIGRANTS (TF)   Universal TV, 1978
THE LEGEND OF THE GOLDEN GUN (TF)   Bennett-Katleman Productions/
    Columbia TV, 1979
SCRUPLES (TF)   Lou-Step Productions/Warner Bros. TV, 1980
THE LAST SONG (TF)   Ron Samuels Productions/Motown Pictures, 1980

P E T E R   L E V I N *

Agent: Broder-Kurland Agency - Los Angeles, 213/274-8921
Business Manager: Alan Tivoli, Zeiderman, Oberman & Associates, 10313 N. Pico
    Blvd., Los Angeles, CA 90064, 213/551-1333

HEART IN HIDING (TF)   Filmways, 1973
PALMERSTOWN, U.S.A. (TF)   Haley-TAT Productions, 1980
THE COMEBACK KID (TF)   ABC Circle Films, 1980
RAPE AND MARRIAGE: THE RIDEOUT CASE (TF)   Stonehenge Productions/
    Blue Greene Productions/Lorimar Productions, 1980
THE MARVA COLLINS STORY (TF)   NRW Features, 1981
WASHINGTON MISTRESS (TF)   Lorimar Productions, 1982
THE ROYAL ROMANCE OF CHARLES AND DIANA (TF)   Chrysalis-Yellen
    Productions, 1982

SIDNEY LEVIN *

Agent: Smith-Gosnell Agency - Malibu, 213/456-6641

LET THE GOOD TIMES ROLL (FD)   co-director with Robert J. Abel, Columbia, 1973
THE GREAT BRAIN   Osmond Distribution Company, 1978

BARRY LEVINSON *

Contact: Directors Guild of America - Los Angeles, 213/656-1220

DINER   MGM/United Artists, 1982
THE NATURAL   Tri-Star/Columbia, 1984

GENE LEVITT *

b. May 28, 1920 - New York, New York
Agent: Adams, Ray & Rosenberg - Los Angeles, 213/278-3000
Business Manager: Henry J. Bamberger, 2049 Century Park East, Los Angeles, CA 90067, 213/553-0581

ANY SECOND NOW (TF)   Universal TV, 1969
RUN A CROOKED MILE (TF)   Universal TV, 1969
ALIAS SMITH AND JONES (TF)   Universal TV, 1971
COOL MILLION (TF)   Universal TV, 1972
THE PHANTOM OF HOLLYWOOD   MGM TV, 1974

EDMOND LEVY *

Home: 135 Central Park West, New York, NY 10023, 212/595-7666
Agent: Steve Weiss, William Morris Agency - Beverly Hills, 213/274-7451

MOM, THE WOLFMAN AND ME (TF)   Time-Life Productions, 1981

RALPH LEVY *

Agent: Irv Schechter Company - Beverly Hills, 213/278-8070

BEDTIME STORY   Universal, 1964
DO NOT DISTURB   20th Century-Fox, 1965

JERRY LEWIS *
(Joseph Levitch)

b. March 16, 1926 - Newark, New Jersey
Business: Jerry Lewis Films, Inc., 1888 Century Park East - Suite 830, Los Angeles, CA 90067, 213/552-2200
Agent: William Morris Agency - Beverly Hills, 213/274-7451

THE BELLBOY   Paramount, 1960
THE LADIES' MAN   Paramount, 1961
THE ERRAND BOY   Paramount, 1962
THE NUTTY PROFESSOR   Paramount, 1963
THE PATSY   Paramount, 1964
THE FAMILY JEWELS   Paramount, 1965
THREE ON A COUCH   Columbia, 1966
THE BIG MOUTH   Columbia, 1967
ONE MORE TIME   United Artists, 1970, British
WHICH WAY TO THE FRONT?   Warner Bros., 1970
HARDLY WORKING   20th Century-Fox, 1981
SMORGASBORD   Warner Bros., 1983

ROBERT M. LEWIS *

Agent: Allen Iezman, William Morris Agency - Beverly Hills, 213/274-7451
Business Manager: Frank Rohner - Los Angeles, 213/274-6182

THE ASTRONAUT (TF)   Universal TV, 1972
THE ALPHA CAPER (TF)   Universal TV, 1973

continued

ROBERT M. LEWIS*—continued

MONEY TO BURN (TF)   Universal TV, 1973
MESSAGE TO MY DAUGHTER (TF)   Metromedia Productions, 1973
PRAY FOR THE WILDCATS (TF)   ABC Circle Films, 1974
THE DAY THE EARTH MOVED (TF)   ABC Circle Films, 1975
THE INVISIBLE MAN (TF)   Universal TV, 1975
**GUILTY OR INNOCENT: THE SAM SHEPPARD MURDER CASE
   (TF)**   Universal TV, 1975
THE NIGHT THEY TOOK MISS BEAUTIFUL (TF)   Don Kirshner Productions,
   1977
RING OF PASSION (TF)   20th Century-Fox TV, 1980
S*H*E* (TF)   Martin Bregman Productions, 1980
IF THINGS WERE DIFFERENT (TF)   Bob Banner Associates, 1980
ESCAPE (TF)   Henry Jaffe Enterprises, 1980
A PRIVATE BATTLE (TF)   Procter & Gamble Productions/Robert Halmi
   Productions, 1980
FALLEN ANGEL (TF)   Green-Epstein Productions/Columbia TV, 1981
THE MIRACLE OF KATHY MILLER (TF)   Rothman-Wohl Productions/Universal
   TV, 1981
CHILD BRIDE OF SHORT CREEK (TF)   Lawrence Schiller-Paul Monash
   Productions, 1981
DESPERATE LIVES (TF)   Fellows-Keegan Company/Lorimar Productions, 1982
BETWEEN TWO BROTHERS (TF)   Turman-Foster Company/Finnegan
   Associates, 1982
COMPUTERCIDE (TF)   Anthony Wilson Productions, 1982
SUMMER GIRL (TF)   Bruce Lansbury Productions/Roberta Haynes Productions/
   Finnegan Associates, 1983
AGATHA CHRISTIE'S 'A CARIBBEAN MYSTERY' (TF)   Stan Margulies
   Productions/Warner Bros. TV, 1983
AGATHA CHRISTIE'S 'SPARKLING CYANIDE' (TF)   Stan Margulies
   Productions/Warner Bros. TV, 1983

JEFF LIEBERMAN *

Agent: Maron Rosenberg, The Lantz Office - Los Angeles, 213/858-1144

SQUIRM   American International, 1976
BLUE SUNSHINE   Cinema Shares International, 1979
JUST BEFORE DAWN   Picturmedia Limited, 1981

ROBERT LIEBERMAN *

Business: Harmony Pictures, 4242 Cahuenga Blvd., Los Angeles, CA 90068, 213/
   462-2121
Agent: Tom Chasin, Chasin-Park-Citron - Los Angeles, 213/273-7190

FIGHTING BACK (TF)   MTM Enterprises, 1980
WILL: G. GORDON LIDDY (TF)   A. Shane Company, 1982
TABLE FOR FIVE   Warner Bros., 1983

PETER LILIENTHAL

Contact: German Film & TV Academy, Pommernallee 1, 1000 Berlin 19, West
   Germany, 030/303-6212

DAVID   Kino International, 1979, West German
THE UPRISING   Kino International, 1981, El Salvador
DEAR MR. WONDERFUL   Joachim von Vietinghoff Produktion/Westdeutscher
   Rundfunk/Sender Freis Berlin, 1982, West German

MICHAEL LINDSAY-HOGG *

b. May 5, 1940 - New York, New York
Contact: Directors Guild of America - Los Angeles, 213/656-1220

LET IT BE (FD)   United Artists, 1970, British
NASTY HABITS   Brut Productions, 1977, British
BRIDESHEAD REVISITED (MS)☆   co-director with Charles Sturridge, Granada
   TV/WNET-13/NDR Hamburg, 1982, British-U.S.-West German
DOCTOR FISCHER OF GENEVA (TF)   Consolidated Productions/BBC, 1984,
   British

ART LINSON*

b. Chicago, Illinois
Contact: Directors Guild of America - Los Angeles, 213/656-1220

WHERE THE BUFFALO ROAM   Universal, 1980

AARON LIPSTADT

Business: California SHO Films, Ltd., 8961 Sunset Blvd., Los Angeles, CA 90069,
213/276-6668

ANDROID   California SHO Films, 1982

STEVEN LISBERGER*

b. April 1951 - Rye, New York
Home: 12345 Gorham Avenue, Los Angeles, CA 90049
Agent: Jeff Berg, ICM - Los Angeles, 213/550-4205

ANIMALYMPICS   Lisberger Studios, 1980 (AF)
TRON   Buena Vista, 1982

LYNNE LITTMAN*

Business: LDL Films, Inc., 8489 West Third Street, Los Angeles, CA 90048, 213/
658-5177
Agent: Fred Specktor, CAA - Los Angeles, 213/277-4545

TESTAMENT   Paramount, 1983

CARLO LIZZANI

b. April 3, 1917 - Rome, Italy
Contact: Ministry of Tourism & Education, Via Della Ferratella, No. 51, 00184
Rome, Italy, 06/7732

ACHTUNGI BANDITII   Cooperativa Spettori Produtti Cinematografici, 1951,
Italian
AI MARGINI DELLA METROPOLI   Elios Film, 1953, Italian
LOVE IN THE CITY   co-director, Italian Films Export, 1953
CRONACHE DI POVERI AMANTI   Cooperative Spettori Produtti
Cinematografici, 1954, Italian
LO SVITATO   Galatea/ENIC, 1956, Italian
BEHIND THE GREAT WALL *LA MURAGLIA CINESE (FD)*   Continental,
1958, Italian
ESTERINA   Italia Prod. Film, 1959, Italian
IL GOBBO   Dino De Laurentiis Cinematografica, 1960, Italian
IL CARABINIERE A CAVALLO   Maxima Film, 1961, Italian
IL PROCESSO DI VERONA   Duilio Cinematografica/Dino De Laurentiis
Cinematografica, 1963, Italian
LA VITA AGRA   Film Napoleon, 1964, Italian
AMORI PERICLOSI   co-director with Giulio Questi & Alfredo Giannetti, Zebra
Film/Fulco Film/Aera Film, 1964, Italian-French
LA CELESTINA P ... R ...   Aston Film, 1965, Italian
THE DIRTY GAME *GUERRE SECRETE*   co-director with Terence Young,
Christian-Jaque & Werner Klinger, American International, 1966, French-Italian-
West German
THRILLING   co-director with Ettore Scola & Gian Luigi Polidori, Dino De
Laurentiis Cinematografica, 1965, Italian
SVEGLIATI E UCCIDI   Sanson Film/Castoro Film, 1966, Italian
THE HILLS RUN RED *UN FIUME DI DOLLARI*   directed under pseudonym
of Lee W. Beaver, United Artists, 1966, Italian
REQUIESCANT   Castoro Film, 1967, Italian
THE VIOLENT FOUR *BANDITI A MILANO*   Paramount, 1968, Italian
L'AMANTE DI GRAMIGNA   Dino De Laurentiis Cinematografica, 1969, Italian
AMORE E RABBIA   co-director with Bernardo Bertolucci, Pier Paolo Pasolini,
Jean-Luc Godard & Marco Bellocchio, Castoro Film, 1969, Italian
BARBAGIA   Dino De Laurentiis Cinematografica, 1969, Italian
ROMA BENE   Castoro Film, 1971, Italian
TONINO NERA   Dino De Laurentiis Cinematografica, 1972, Italian

continued

CARLO LIZZANI—continued
CRAZY JOE   Columbia, 1974, Italian-U.S.
THE LAST FOUR DAYS *MUSSOLINI - ULTIMO ATTO*   Group 1, 1974, Italian
UOMINI MERCE   1976, Italian
SAN BABILA ORE 20: UN DELITTO INUTILE   Agora, 1976, Italian
KLEINHOFF HOTEL   Capitol, 1977, Italian
FONTAMARA   Sacis, 1980, Italian
CASA DEL TAPPETO GIALLO   Gaumont, 1983, Italian
ROME: THE IMAGE OF A CITY (FD)   Transworld Film, 1983, Italian
NUCLEO ZERO   Diamant Film/RAI, 1984, Italian

K E N N E T H   L O A C H

b. June 17, 1936 - Nuneaton, Warwickshire, England
Agent: Goodwin Associates, 19 London Street, London W2, England, 01/402-9137

POOR COW   National General, 1968, British
KES   United Artists, 1970, British
WEDNESDAY'S CHILD *Family Life*   Cinema 5, 1972, British
BLACK JACK   Boyd's Company, 1979, British
THE GAMEKEEPER   ATV, 1980, British
LOOKS AND SMILES   Black Lion Films/Kestrel Films/MK2, 1981, British-French

T O N Y   L O   B I A N C O *

b. New York, New York
Messages: 213/858-1144
Agent: Arnold Rifkin/Nicole David, David, Hunter, Kimble, Parseghian & Rifkin - Los Angeles, 213/857-1234

THE DOORMAN   Pinekona-Doorman Productions, 1983

J O S H U A   L O G A N

b. October 5, 1908 - Texarkana, Texas
Business: 435 East 52nd Street, New York, NY 10022, 212/PL. 2-1910

I MET MY LOVE AGAIN   co-director with Arthur Ripley, United Artists, 1938
PICNIC ★   Columbia, 1956
BUS STOP   20th Century-Fox, 1956
SAYONARA ★   Warner Bros., 1957
SOUTH PACIFIC   Magna, 1958
TALL STORY   Warner Bros., 1960
FANNY   Warner Bros., 1961
ENSIGN PULVER   Warner Bros., 1964
CAMELOT   Warner Bros., 1967
PAINT YOUR WAGON   Paramount, 1969

L O U I S   L O M B A R D O *

Home: 5455 Longridge Avenue, Van Nuys, CA 91401, 213/902-0422
Agent: Tony Ludwig, CAA - Los Angeles, 213/277-4545

RUSSIAN ROULETTE   Avco Embassy, 1975, U.S.-Canadian

U L L I   L O M M E L

b. West Germany
Business: New West Films, 1757 N. Curson Avenue, Hollywood, CA 90046, 213/876-1511
Publicity: Cassidy-Watson Associates, 1717 Vine Street, Hollywood, CA, 213/462-1739

TENDERNESS OF THE WOLVES   Monument, 1973, West German
BLANK GENERATION   International Harmony, 1979, West German
COCAINE COWBOYS   International Harmony, 1979, West German
THE BOOGEY MAN   Jerry Gross Organization, 1980
A TASTE OF SIN   Ambassador, 1983

continued

ULLI LOMMEL—continued
BRAINWAVES   MPM, 1983
THE DEVONSVILLE TERROR   MPM, 1983
STRANGERS IN PARADISE   New West, 1984

RICHARD LONCRAINE

b. October 20, 1946 - Cheltenham, England
Agent: Linda Seifert Associates, 8A Brunswick Gardens, London W8 4AJ, England,
    01/229-5163

FLAME   Goodtime Enterprises, 1975, British
THE HAUNTING OF JULIA *FULL CIRCLE*   Discovery Films, 1977, British-
    Canadian
BRIMSTONE AND TREACLE   United Artists Classics, 1982, British
THE MISSIONARY   Columbia, 1982, British

JERRY LONDON *

b. September 21, 1937 - Los Angeles, California Business: London Films, c/o
    Finnegan Associates, 4225 Coldwater Canyon Blvd., Studio City, CA 91604,
    213/985-0430
Agent: Bruce Vinokour, CAA - Los Angeles, 213/277-4545

KILLDOZER (TF)   Universal TV, 1974
McNAUGHTON'S DAUGHTER (TF)   Universal TV, 1976
COVER GIRLS (TF)   Columbia TV, 1977
ARTHUR HAILEY'S WHEELS (MS)   Universal TV, 1978
EVENING IN BYZANTIUM (TF)   Universal TV, 1978
WOMEN IN WHITE (MS)   NBC, 1979
SWAN SONG (TF)   Renee Valente Productions/Topanga Services Ltd./20th
    Century-Fox TV, 1980
SHOGUN (MS) ★   Paramount TV/NBC Entertainment, 1980, U.S.-Japanese
FATHER FIGURE (TF)   Finnegan Associates/Time-Life Productions, 1980
THE CHICAGO STORY (TF)   Eric Bercovici Productions/MGM TV, 1981
THE ORDEAL OF BILL CARNEY (TF)   Belle Company/Comworld Productions,
    1981
THE GIFT OF LIFE (TF)   CBS Entertainment, 1982
THE SCARLET AND THE BLACK (TF)   Bill McCutchen Productions/ITC/RAI,
    1983, U.S.-Italian
ARTHUR HAILEY'S HOTEL (TF)   Aaron Spelling Productions, 1983
CHIEFS (MS)   Highgate Pictures, 1984

JACK LORD *

(John Joseph Ryan)

b. December 30, 1928 - New York, New York
Home: 4999 Kahala Avenue, Honolulu, Hawaii 96816, 808/737-6060
Business: Lord & Lady Enterprises, Honolulu, Hawaii 96816, 808/735-5050
Business Manager: J. William Hayes, Executive Business Management, Inc., 132 S.
    Rodeo Drive, Beverly Hills, CA 90212, 213/858-2000

M STATION: HAWAII (TF)   Lord & Lady Enterprises, 1980

JOSEPH LOSEY *

b. January 14, 1909 - La Crosse, Wisconsin
Agent: Stan Kamen, William Morris Agency - Beverly Hills, 213/274-7451

THE BOY WITH GREEN HAIR   RKO Radio, 1948
THE LAWLESS   Paramount, 1950
M   Columbia, 1951
THE PROWLER   United Artists, 1951
THE BIG KNIGHT   United Artists, 1951
STRANGER ON THE PROWL   directed under pseudonym of Andrea Forzano,
    United Artists, 1952, U.S.-Italian
THE SLEEPING TIGER   directed under pseudonym of Victory Hanbury, Astor,
    1954, British
FINGER OF GUILT *THE INTIMATE STRANGER*   directed under pseudonym
    of Joseph Walton, RKO Radio, 1955, British

continued

JOSEPH LOSEY*—continued

TIME WITHOUT PITY   Astor, 1956, British
THE GYPSY AND THE GENTLEMAN   Rank, 1958, British
CHANCE MEETING *BLIND DATE*   Paramount, 1959, British
THE CONCRETE JUNGLE *THE CRIMINAL*   Fanfare, 1960, British
THESE ARE THE DAMNED *THE DAMNED*   Columbia, 1961, British
EVA   Times, 1962, French-Italian
THE SERVANT   Landau, 1964, British
KING AND COUNTRY   Allied Artists, 1965, British
MODESTY BLAISE   20th Century-Fox, 1966, British
ACCIDENT   Cinema 5, 1967, British
SECRET CEREMONY   Universal, 1968, British-U.S.
BOOM!   Universal, 1968, British-U.S.
FIGURES IN A LANDSCAPE   National General, 1971, British
THE GO-BETWEEN   Columbia, 1971, British
THE ASSASSINATION OF TROTSKY   Cinerama Releasing Corporation, 1972,
    French-Italian-British
A DOLL'S HOUSE   Tomorrow Entertainment, 1973, British-French
GALILEO   American Film Theatre, 1975, British-Canadian
THE ROMANTIC ENGLISHWOMAN   New World, 1975, British
MR. KLEIN   Quartet, 1977, French-Italian
LES ROUTES DU SUD   Parafrance, 1978, French
DON GIOVANNI   New Yorker, 1980, French
THE TROUT (LA TRUITE)   Triumph/Columbia, 1983, French

E M I L   L O T E A N U

b. November 6, 1936 - Bukovina, U.S.S.R.
Contact: State Committee of Cinematography of the U.S.S.R., Council of Ministers, 7
    Maly Gnesdikovsky Pereulok, Moscow, U.S.S.R., 7 095/229-9912

WAIT FOR US AT DAWN   Moldovafilm, 1963, Soviet
RED MEADOWS   Moldovafilm, 1966, Soviet
FRESCOS ON THE WHITE   Moldovafilm, 1968, Soviet
THIS INSTANT   Moldovafilm, 1969, Soviet
LAUTARY   Moldovafilm, 1972, Soviet
MY WHITE CITY   Moldovafilm, 1973, Soviet
INTO THE SUNSET   Mosfilm, 1976, Soviet
THE SHOOTING PARTY   Mosfilm, 1978, Soviet
PAVLOVA   Paramount, 1983, Soviet-U.S.

C H A R L I E   L O V E N T H A L

THE FIRST TIME   New Line Cinema, 1983

D I C K   L O W R Y *

Home: 704 N. Gardner Avenue - Suite 5, Los Angeles, CA 90046, 213/653-6115
Agent: Elliot Webb, ICM - Los Angeles, 213/550-4000

OHMS (TF)   Grant-Case-McGrath Enterprises, 1980
KENNY ROGERS AS THE GAMBLER (TF)   Kragen & Co., 1980
THE JAYNE MANSFIELD STORY (TF)   Alan Landsburg Productions, 1980
ANGEL DUSTED (TF)   NRW Features, 1981
COWARD OF THE COUNTY (TF)   Kraco Productions, 1981
A FEW DAYS IN WEASEL CREEK (TF)   Hummingbird Productions/Warner
    Bros., 1981
RASCALS AND ROBBERS: THE SECRET ADVENTURES OF TOM SAWYER
    AND HUCKELBERRY FINN (TF)   CBS Entertainment, 1982
MISSING CHILDREN: A MOTHER'S STORY (TF)   Kayden-Gleason
    Productions, 1982
LIVING PROOF: THE HANK WILLIAMS, JR. STORY (TF)   Procter &
    Gamble Productions/Telecom Entertainment/Melpomene Productions, 1983
SMOKEY AND THE BANDIT PART 3   Universal, 1983

D A V I D   R .   L O X T O N *

Home: 935 Park Avenue, New York, NY 10028, 212/249-0538
Business: Television Laboratory, WNET-13, 356 West 58th Street, New York,
    NY 10019, 212/560-3192

THE PHANTOM OF THE OPEN HEARTH (TF)   co-director with Fred Barzyk,
    WNET-13 Television Laboratory/WGBH New Television Workshop, 1976
CHARLIE SMITH AND THE FRITTER TREE (TF)   co-director with Fred Barzyk,
    WNET-13 Television Laboratory/WGBH New Television Workshop, 1978
THE LATHE OF HEAVEN (TF)   co-director with Fred Barzyk, WNET-13
    Television Laboratory/Taurus Film, 1980

N A N N I   L O Y

b. October 23, 1925 - Cagliari, Sardinia, Italy
Contact: Ministry of Tourism & Education, Via Della Ferratella, No. 51, 00184
    Rome, Italy, 06/7732

PAROLA DI LADRO   co-director with Gianni Puccini, Panal Film, 1957, Italian
IL MARITO   co-director with Gianni Puccini, Fortuna Film/Chamartin, 1957,
    Italian-Spanish
AUDACE COLPO DEI SOLITI IGNOTI   Titanus/Videss/SGC, 1959, Italian
UN GIORNO DA LEONI   Lux Film/Vides/Galatea, 1961, Italian
THE FOUR DAYS OF NAPLES   MGM, 1962, Italian
MADE IN ITALY   Royal Films International, 1965, Italian-French
IL PADRE DI FAMILIGLIA   Ultra/CFC/Marianne Productions, 1967, Italian-
    French
L'INFERNO DEL DESERTO   1969, Italian
ROSOLINO PATERNO SOLDATO   Dino De Laurentiis Cinematografica, 1970,
    Italian
WHY *DETENUTO IN ATTESTA DI GUIDIZIO*   Documento Film, 1971,
    Italian
LA GODURIA   1976, Italian
SIGNORE E SIGNORI BUONANOTTE   co-director with Luigi Comencini, Luigi
    Magni, Mario Monicelli & Ettore Scola, Titanus, 1976, Italian
IL CAFFE E UN PIACERE ... SE NON E BUONO CHE PLACERE
    E?   1978, Italian
INSIEME   1979, Italian
CAFE EXPRESS   Summit Features, 1980, Italian
TESTA OR CROCE   Filmauro, 1982, Italian
MI MANDA PICONE   Sacis, 1983, Italian

G E O R G E   L U C A S

b. January 14, 1944 - Modesto, California
Business: Lucasfilm Ltd., P.O. Box 668, San Anselmo, CA 94960

THX 1138   Warner Bros., 1971
AMERICAN GRAFFITI ★   Universal, 1973
STAR WARS ★   20th Century-Fox, 1977

S I D N E Y   L U M E T *

b. June 25, 1924 - Philadelphia, Pennsylvania
Agent: Sue Mengers, ICM - Los Angeles, 213/550-4264

TWELVE ANGRY MEN ★   United Artists, 1957
STAGE STRUCK   RKO Radio, 1958
THAT KIND OF WOMAN   Paramount, 1959
THE FUGITIVE KIND   United Artists, 1960
A VIEW FROM THE BRIDGE   Allied Artists, 1961, French-Italian
LONG DAY'S JOURNEY INTO NIGHT   Embassy, 1962
FAIL SAFE   Columbia, 1964
THE PAWNBROKER   Landau/Allied Artists, 1965
THE HILL   MGM, 1965, British
THE GROUP   United Artists, 1965
THE DEADLY AFFAIR   Columbia, 1967, British
BYE BYE BRAVERMAN   Warner Bros., 1968
THE SEA GULL   Warner Bros., 1968, British
THE APPOINTMENT   MGM, 1969
LAST OF THE MOBILE HOT-SHOTS   Warner Bros., 1970

continued

SIDNEY LUMET*—continued

KING: A FILMED RECORD ... MONTGOMERY TO MEMPHIS (FD)   co-
director with Joseph L. Mankiewicz, Maron Films Limited, 1970
THE ANDERSON TAPES   Columbia, 1971
CHILD'S PLAY   Paramount, 1972
THE OFFENSE   United Artists, 1973, British
SERPICO   Paramount, 1973
LOVIN' MOLLY   Columbia, 1974
MURDER ON THE ORIENT EXPRESS   Paramount, 1974, British
DOG DAY AFTERNOON ★   Warner Bros., 1975
NETWORK ★   MGM/United Artists, 1976
EQUUS   United Artists, 1977, British
THE WIZ   Universal, 1978
JUST TELL ME WHAT YOU WANT   Columbia, 1980
PRINCE OF THE CITY   Orion/Warner Bros., 1981
DEATHTRAP   Warner Bros., 1982
THE VERDICT ★   20th Century-Fox, 1982
DANIEL   Paramount, 1983

IDA LUPINO*

b. February 4, 1918 - London England
Business Manager: David Martin, 205 S. Beverly Drive - Suite 214, Beverly Hills,
CA 90212, 213/276-7071

OUTRAGE   RKO Radio, 1950
HARD, FAST AND BEAUTIFUL   RKO Radio, 1951
THE HITCH-HIKER   RKO Radio, 1953
THE BIGAMIST   Filmmakers, 1953
THE TROUBLE WITH ANGELS   Columbia, 1966

TONY LURASCHI

THE OUTSIDER   Paramount, 1980, U.S.-Irish

WILLIAM LUSTIG

MANIAC   Analysis, 1980
VIGILANTE   Artists Releasing Corporation/Film Ventures International, 1983

DAVID LYNCH*

Agent: CAA - Los Angeles, 213/277-4545

ERASERHEAD   Libra, 1978
THE ELEPHANT MAN ★   Paramount, 1980, British-U.S.
DUNE   Universal, 1984

PAUL LYNCH

b. November 6, 1946
Business: Questcam, Inc., 1460 Fourth Street, Santa Monica, CA 90401
Agent: David Gersh, The Gersh Agency - Beverly Hills, 213/274-6611
Attorney: Bruce Singman - Los Angeles, 213/276-2397

THE HARD PART BEGINS   Cinepix, 1974, Canadian
BLOOD AND GUTS   Ambassador, 1978, Canadian
PROM NIGHT   Avco Embassy, 1980, Canadian
HUMONGOUS   Avco Embassy, 1982, Canadian
CROSS-COUNTRY   New World, 1983, Canadian

ADRIAN LYNE*

Business Manager: Paul Esposito, Jennie & Co., 127 West 79th Street, New York,
NY 10024, 212/595-5200

FOXES   United Artists, 1980
FLASHDANCE   Paramount, 1983

M

ALEXANDER MACKENDRICK

b. 1912 - Boston, Massachusetts

TIGHT LITTLE ISLAND *WHISKEY GALORE!*   Rank, 1949, British
THE MAN IN THE WHITE SUIT   Rank, 1951, British
CRASH OF SILENCE *MANDY*   Universal, 1952, British
HIGH AND DRY *THE MAGGIE*   Universal, 1954, British
THE LADYKILLERS   Continental, 1956, British
SWEET SMELL OF SUCCESS   United Artists, 1957
A BOY TEN FEET TALL *SAMMY GOING SOUTH*   Paramount, 1963,
     British
A HIGH WIND IN JAMAICA   20th Century-Fox, 1965, British
DON'T MAKE WAVES   MGM, 1967

JOHN MACKENZIE

b. Scotland
Agent: Merrily Kane Agency - Beverly Hills, 213/550-8874

UNMAN, WITTERING & ZIGO   Paramount, 1971, British
ONE BRIEF SUMMER   Cinevision, 1972, British
MADE   International Co-productions, 1975, British
A SENSE OF FREEDOM (TF)   J. Isaacs Productions/STV, 1979, British
THE LONG GOOD FRIDAY   Embassy, 1982, British
BEYOND THE LIMIT   Paramount, 1983, British

DEZSO MAGYAR *

Agent: John Ptak/David Schiff, William Morris Agency - Beverly Hills, 213/859-4346

RAPPACINI'S DAUGHTER (TF)   Learning in Focus, 1980
SUMMER (TF)   Cinelit Productions/WNET-13, 1981
KING OF AMERICA (TF)   Center for Television in the Humanities, 1982

NORMAN MAILER

b. January 31, 1923 - Long Branch, New Jersey

WILD 90   Supreme Mix, 1968
BEYOND THE LAW   Grove Press, 1968
MAIDSTONE   Supreme Mix, 1971

DUSAN MAKAVEJEV

b. October 13, 1932 - Belgrade, Yugoslavia

MAN IS NOT A BIRD   Grove Press, 1965, Yugoslavian
LOVE AFFAIR; OR THE CASE OF THE MISSING SWITCHBOARD
     OPERATOR   Brandon, 1966, Yugoslavian
INNOCENCE UNPROTECTED   Grove Press, 1968, Yugoslavian
WR - MYSTERIES OF THE ORGANISM   Cinema 5, 1971, Yugoslavian
SWEET MOVIE   Biograph, 1975, French-Canadian-West German

continued

DUSAN MAKAVEJEV—continued
MONTENEGRO   Atlantic Releasing Corporation, 1981, Swedish

T E R R A N C E   M A L I C K *

b. October 30, 1944 - Illinois
Agent: Ziegler, Diskant, Inc. - Los Angeles, 213/278-0070

BADLANDS   Warner Bros., 1974
DAYS OF HEAVEN   Paramount, 1978

L O U I S   M A L L E *

b. October 30, 1932 - Thumeries, France
Business Manager: Gelfand, Rennert & Feldman, 489 Fifth Avenue, New York,
    NY 10017, 212/682-0234

FONTAINE DE VAUCLUSE   1953, French
STATION 307   1955, French
THE SILENT WORLD (FD)   co-director with Jacques-Yves Cousteau, Columbia,
    1956, French
FRANTIC *ASCENSEUR POUR L'ECHAFAUD*   Times, 1957, French
THE LOVERS   Zenith International, 1958, French
ZAZIE *ZAZIE DANS LE METRO*   Astor, 1960, French
A VERY PRIVATE AFFAIR   MGM, 1962, French-Italian
THE FIRE WITHIN   Governor, 1963, French
VIVA MARIAI   United Artists, 1965, French-Italian
THE THIEF OF PARIS *LE VOLEUR*   Lopert, 1967, French-Italian
SPIRITS OF THE DEAD *HISTOIRES EXTRAORDINAIRES*   co-director with
    Federico Fellini & Roger Vadim, American International, 1969, French-Italian
CALCUTTA (FD)   1969, French
PHANTOM INDIA (TD)   1969, French
MURMUR OF THE HEART *LE SOUFFLE AU COEUR*   Palomar, 1971,
    French
HUMAIN, TROP HUMAIN (FD)   New Yorker, 1972, French
LACOMBE LUCIEN   20th Century-Fox, 1974, French-Italian-West German
BLACK MOON   20th Century-Fox, 1975, French
PRETTY BABY   Paramount, 1978
ATLANTIC CITY ★   Paramount, 1981, Canadian-French
MY DINNER WITH ANDRE   New Yorker, 1981
CRACKERS   Universal, 1984

B R U C E   M A L M U T H *

b. February 4, 1934 - New York, New York
Business: Soularview Productions, Inc., 9981 Robbins Drive, Beverly Hills,
    CA 90212, 213/277-4555

FORE PLAY   co-director with John G. Avildsen & Robert McCarty, Cinema
    National, 1975
NIGHTHAWKS   Universal, 1981
THE MAN WHO WASN'T THERE   Paramount, 1983

R O U B E N   M A M O U L I A N *

b. October 8, 1898 - Tiflis, Georgia, Russia
Home: 1112 Schuyler Road, Beverly Hills, CA 90210

APPLAUSE   Paramount, 1929
CITY STREETS   Paramount, 1931
DR. JEKYLL AND MR. HYDE   Paramount, 1932
LOVE ME TONIGHT   Paramount, 1932
SONG OF SONGS   Paramount, 1933
QUEEN CHRISTINA   MGM, 1933
WE LIVE AGAIN   United Artists, 1934
BECKY SHARP   RKO Radio, 1935
THE GAY DESPERADO   United Artists, 1936
HIGH, WIDE, AND HANDSOME   Paramount, 1937
GOLDEN BOY   Columbia, 1939
THE MARK OF ZORRO   20th Century-Fox, 1940
BLOOD AND SAND   20th Century-Fox, 1941

continued

ROUBEN MAMOULIAN*—continued
RINGS ON HER FINGERS   20th Century-Fox, 1942
SUMMER HOLIDAY   MGM, 1948
SILK STOCKINGS   MGM, 1957

R O B E R T   M A N D E L *

Agent: CAA - Los Angeles, 213/277-4545

INDEPENDENCE DAY   Warner Bros., 1983
THE HAND ME DOWN KID (TF)   Highgate Pictures, 1983

J O S E P H   M A N D U K E *

Agent: Louis Bershad, Century Artists, Ltd. - Los Angeles, 213/273-4366

JUMP   Cannon, 1971
CORNBREAD, EARL AND ME   American International, 1975
KID VENGEANCE   Irwin Yablans, 1977, U.S.-Israeli
BEATLEMANIA   American Cinema, 1981

F R A N C I S   M A N K I E W I C Z

Contact: Association des Realisateurs, 1406 Beaudry Street, Montreal, Quebec H2L
     4K4, Canada, 514/843-7770

LE TEMPS D'UNE CHASSE   Cinepix, 1973, Canadian
LES BONS DEBARRAS—GOOD RIDDANCE   IFEX Film, 1981, Canadian
LES BEAUX SOUVENIRS   National Film Board of Canada, 1982, Canadian

J O S E P H   L .   M A N K I E W I C Z *

b. February 11, 1909 - Wilkes-Barre, Pennsylvania
Agent: Ben Benjamin (NY)/Luis Sanjurjo (LA), William Morris Agency, 212/556-5652
     or 213/550-4000
Business Manager: Arthur B. Greene, 666 Fifth Avenue, New York, NY 10103,
     212/246-1900

DRAGONWYCK   20th Century-Fox, 1946
SOMEWHERE IN THE NIGHT   20th Century-Fox, 1946
THE LATE GEORGE APLEY   20th Century-Fox, 1947
THE GHOST AND MRS. MUIR   20th Century-Fox, 1947
ESCAPE   20th Century-Fox, 1948
A LETTER TO THREE WIVES ★★   20th Century-Fox, 1949
HOUSE OF STRANGERS   20th Century-Fox, 1949
NO WAY OUT   20th Century-Fox, 1950
ALL ABOUT EVE ★★   20th Century-Fox, 1950
PEOPLE WILL TALK   20th Century-Fox, 1951
FIVE FINGERS ★   20th Century-Fox, 1952
JULIUS CAESAR   MGM, 1953
THE BAREFOOT CONTESSA   United Artists, 1954, U.S.-Italian
GUYS AND DOLLS   MGM, 1955
THE QUIET AMERICAN   United Artists, 1958
SUDDENLY LAST SUMMER   Columbia, 1960
CLEOPATRA   20th Century-Fox, 1963
THE HONEY POT   United Artists, 1967, British-U.S.-Italian
THERE WAS A CROOKED MAN   Warner Bros., 1970
KING: A FILMED RECORD ... MONTGOMERY TO MEMPHIS (FD)   co-
     director with Sidney Lumet, Maron Films Limited, 1970
SLEUTH ★   20th Century-Fox, 1972, British

T O M   M A N K I E W I C Z *

b. June 1, 1942 - Los Angeles, California
Contact: Directors Guild of America - Los Angeles, 213/656-1220

HART TO HART (TF)   Spelling-Goldberg Productions, 1979

ABBY MANN *
(Abraham Goodman)

b. 1927 - Philadelphia, Pennsylvania
Agent: Jerry Katzman, William Morris Agency - Beverly Hills, 213/274-7451

KING (MS) ☆   Abby Mann Productions/Filmways, 1978

DANIEL MANN *

b. August 8, 1912 - New York, New York
Agent: Grossman-Stalmaster Agency - Los Angeles, 213/657-3040
Business Manager: The Berke Management Co. - Encino, 213/990-2631

COME BACK, LITTLE SHEBA   Paramount, 1952
ABOUT MRS. LESLIE   Paramount, 1954
THE ROSE TATTOO   Paramount, 1955
I'LL CRY TOMORROW   MGM, 1955
TEAHOUSE OF THE AUGUST MOON   MGM, 1956
HOT SPELL   Paramount, 1958
THE LAST ANGRY MAN   Columbia, 1959
THE MOUNTAIN ROAD   Columbia, 1960
BUTTERFIELD 8   MGM, 1960
ADA   MGM, 1961
FIVE FINGER EXERCISE   Columbia, 1962
WHO'S GOT THE ACTION?   Paramount, 1962
WHO'S BEEN SLEEPING IN MY BED?   Paramount, 1963
JUDITH   Paramount, 1965, U.S.-British-Israeli
OUR MAN FLINT   20th Century-Fox, 1966
FOR LOVE OF IVY   Cinerama Releasing Corporation, 1968
A DREAM OF KINGS   National General, 1969
WILLARD   Cinerama Releasing Corporation, 1971
THE REVENGERS   National General, 1972, U.S.-Mexican
INTERVAL   Avco Embassy, 1973, U.S.-Mexican
MAURIE *BIG MO*   National General, 1973
LOST IN THE STARS   American Film Theatre, 1974
JOURNEY INTO FEAR   Stirling Gold, 1976, Canadian
HOW THE WEST WAS WON (MS)   co-director with Burt Kennedy, MGM TV, 1977
MATILDA   American International, 1978
PLAYING FOR TIME (TF)   Syzygy Productions, 1980
THE DAY THE LOVING STOPPED (TF)   Monash-Zeitman Productions, 1981

DELBERT MANN *

b. January 30, 1920 - Lawrence, Kansas
Agent: Leonard Hirshan, William Morris Agency - Beverly Hills, 213/274-7451

MARTY ★★   United Artists, 1965
THE BACHELOR PARTY   United Artists, 1957
DESIRE UNDER THE ELMS   Paramount, 1958
SEPARATE TABLES   United Artists, 1959
MIDDLE OF THE NIGHT   Columbia, 1959
THE DARK AT THE TOP OF THE STAIRS   Warner Bros., 1960
THE OUTSIDER   Universal, 1961
LOVER, COME BACK   Universal, 1962
THAT TOUCH OF MINK   Universal, 1962
A GATHERING OF EAGLES   Universal, 1963
DEAR HEART   Warner Bros., 1964
QUICK BEFORE IT MELTS   MGM, 1965
MISTER BUDDWING   MGM, 1966
FITZWILLY   United Artists, 1967
HEIDI (TF)   Omnibus Productions, 1968
THE PINK JUNGLE   Universal, 1968
DAVID COPPERFIELD (TF)   Omnibus Productions/Sagittarius Productions, 1970, British-U.S.
KIDNAPPED   American International, 1971, British
JANE EYRE (TF)   Omnibus Productions/Sagittarius Productions, 1971, British-U.S.
SHE WAITS (TF)   Metromedia Productions, 1972
NO PLACE TO RUN (TF)   ABC Circle Films, 1972
THE MAN WITHOUT A COUNTRY (TF)   Norman Rosemont Productions, 1973

continued

DELBERT MANN*—continued

A GIRL NAMED SOONER (TF)   Frederick Brogger Associates/20th Century-Fox
    TV, 1975
BIRCH INTERVAL   Gamma III, 1976
FRANCIS GARY POWERS: THE TRUE STORY OF THE U-2 SPY INCIDENT
    (TF)   Charles Fries Productions, 1976
TELL ME MY NAME (TF)   Talent Associates, 1977
BREAKING UP (TF) ☆   Time-Life Productions, 1978
LOVE'S DARK RIDE (TF)   Mark VII Ltd./Worldvision, 1978
HOME TO STAY (TF)   Time-Life Productions, 1978
THOU SHALT NOT COMMIT ADULTERY (TF)   Edgar J. Scherick Associates,
    1978
TORN BETWEEN TWO LOVERS (TF)   Alan Landsburg Productions, 1979
ALL QUIET ON THE WESTERN FRONT (TF)   Norman Rosemont Productions/
    Marble Arch Productions, 1979
TO FIND MY SON (TF)   Green-Epstein Productions/Columbia TV, 1980
NIGHT CROSSING   Buena Vista, 1982

MICHAEL MANN *

Agent: Jeff Berg, ICM - Los Angeles, 213/550-4000

THE JERICHO MILE (TF)   ABC Circle Films, 1979
THIEF   United Artists, 1981
THE KEEP   Paramount, 1983

TERRY MARCEL

b. 1942 - Oxford, England
Address: Gaston Bell Close, Richmond, Surrey, England
Contact: Directors Guild of Great Britain, 56 Whitfield Street, London W1, England,
    01/580-9592

THERE GOES THE BRIDGE   Vanguard, 1980, British
HAWK THE SLAYER   ITC, 1980, British
PRISONERS OF THE LOST UNIVERSE (CTF)   Marcel-Robertson Productions/
    Showtime, 1983, British

ALEX MARCH *

Contact: Directors Guild of America - Los Angeles, 213/656-1220

THE DANGEROUS DAYS OF KIOWA JONES (TF)   MGM TV, 1966
PAPER LION   United Artists, 1968
THE BIG BOUNCE   Warner Bros., 1969
FIREHOUSE (TF)   Metromedia Productions/Stonehenge Productions, 1972
MASTERMIND   Goldstone, 1977

STUART MARGOLIN *

b. January 31 - Davenport, Iowa
Home: P.O. Box 478, Ganges, British Columbia VOS 1EO, Canada, 604/537-2961
Agent: Lou Pitt, ICM - Los Angeles, 213/550-4000
Business Manager: Bash, Gesas & Co., 9401 Wilshire Blvd. - Suite 700, Beverly
    Hills, CA 90212, 213/278-7700

SUDDENLY, LOVE (TF)   Ross Hunter Productions, 1978
A SHINING SEASON (TF)   Green-Epstein Productions/T-M Productions/
    Columbia TV, 1979
BRET MAVERICK (TF)   Comanche Productions/Warner Bros. TV, 1981
THE LONG SUMMER OF GEORGE ADAMS (TF)   Warner Bros. TV, 1982
THE GLITTER DOME (TF)   HBO Premiere Films, 1984

PETER MARKLE

THE PERSONALS   New World, 1982
HOT DOG ... THE MOVIE   MGM/UA, 1984

ROBERT MARKOWITZ *

Business: Mustard Seed Pictures, 3037 Franklin Canyon Drive, Beverly Hills,
   CA 90210
Agent: Martin Caan, William Morris Agency - Beverly Hills, 213/859-4271

THE STORYTELLER (TF)   Universal TV, 1977
THE DEADLIEST SEASON (TF)   Titus Productions, 1977
VOICES   MGM/United Artists, 1979
THE WALL (TF)   Cinetex International/Time-Life Productions, 1982, U.S.-Polish
A LONG WAY HOME (TF)   Alan Landsburg Productions, 1981
PRAY TV (TF)   ABC Circle Films, 1982
PHANTOM OF THE OPERA (TF)   Robert Halmi Productions, 1983
MY MOTHER'S SECRET LIFE (TF)   ABC Circle Films, 1984

ARTHUR MARKS *

b. August 2, 1927 - Los Angeles, California
Business: Henry Plitt Productions, Inc., 1925 Century Park East, Los Angeles,
   CA 90067, 213/553-5307
Personal Business: Arm Service Company, Inc., Arthur Productions Inc., P.O. Box
   1305 Woodland Hills, CA 91365

CLASS OF '74   General Film Corporation, 1972
BONNIE'S KIDS   General Film Corporation, 1973
THE ROOM MATES   General Film Corporation, 1973
DETROIT 9000   General Film Corporation, 1973
A WOMAN FOR ALL MEN   General Film Corporation, 1975
BUCKTOWN   American International, 1975
FRIDAY FOSTER   American International, 1975
J.D.'S REVENGE   American International, 1976
THE MONKEY HUSTLE   American International, 1976

RICHARD MARQUAND

b. Wales
Agent: A.D. Peters Ltd., 10 Buckingham Street, London WC2, England

THE SEARCH FOR THE NILE (MS)   BBC/Time-Life Productions, 1972, British
THE LEGACY   Universal, 1979
BIRTH OF THE BEATLES (TF)   Dick Clark Productions, 1979, British-U.S.
EYE OF THE NEEDLE   United Artists, 1981, U.S.-British
RETURN OF THE JEDI   20th Century-Fox, 1983
UNTIL SEPTEMBER   MGM/UA, 1984

GARRY MARSHALL *

Agent: Joel Cohen - The Sy Fischer Company - Los Angeles, 213/557-0388
Business Manager: Alexander Grant & Co. - Beverly Hills, 213/658-5595

YOUNG DOCTORS IN LOVE   20th Century-Fox, 1982
SWEET GINGER BROWN   20th Century-Fox, 1984

CHARLES MARTIN *

b. 1916 - Newark, New Jersey
Home: 304 S. Elm Drive, Beverly Hills, CA 90212
Messages: 213/277-5843

NO LEAVE TO LOVE   MGM, 1946
MY DEAR SECRETARY   United Artists, 1948
DEATH OF A SCOUNDREL   RKO Radio, 1956
IF HE HOLLERS, LET HIM GO   Cinerama Releasing Corporation, 1968
HOW TO SEDUCE A WOMAN   Cenerama Releasing Corporation, 1974
ONE MAN JURY   Cal-Am Artists, 1978
DEAD ON ARRIVAL   Cinerama Shares International, 1979

L E S L I E   H .   M A R T I N S O N *

b. Boston, Massachusetts
Home: 2288 Coldwater Canyon Blvd., Beverly Hills, CA 90210, 213/271-4127
Agent: Shapiro-Litchman Agency - Los Angeles, 213/550-2244

THE ATOMIC KID   Republic, 1954
HOT ROD GIRL   American International, 1956
HOT ROD RUMBLE   Allied Artists, 1957
LAD: A DOG   co-director with Aram Avakian, Warner Bros, 1961
PT 109   Warner Bros., 1963
BLACK GOLD   Warner Bros., 1963
F.B.I. CODE 98   Warner Bros., 1964
FOR THOSE WHO THINK YOUNG   United Artists, 1964
BATMAN   20th Century-Fox, 1966
FATHOM   20th Century-Fox, 1967
THE CHALLENGERS (TF)   Universal TV, 1970
MRS. POLLIFAX - SPY   United Artists, 1971
HOW TO STEAL AN AIRPLANE (TF)   Universal TV, 1971
ESCAPE FROM ANGOLA   Doty-Dayton, 1976
CRUISE MISSILE   Eichberg Film/Cinelux-Romano Film/Mundial Film/Cine-Luce/
     Noble Productions/FPDC, 1978, West German-Spanish-U.S.-Iranian
RESCUE FROM GILLIGAN'S ISLAND (TF)   Sherwood Schwartz Productions,
     1978
THE KID WITH THE BROKEN HALO (TF)   Satellite Productions, 1982
THE KID WITH THE 200 I.Q. (TF)   Guillaume-Margo Productions/Zephyr
     Productions, 1983

A N D R E W   M A R T O N *

(Endre Marton)

b. January 26, 1904 - Budapest, Hungary
Home: 8856 Appian Way, Los Angeles, CA 90046, 213/654-1297
Agent: Paul Kohner, Inc. - Los Angeles, 213/271-5165

GYPSY COLT   MGM, 1954
PRISONER OF WAR   MGM, 1954
MEN OF THE FIGHTING LADY   MGM, 1954
GREEN FIRE   MGM, 1955
SEVEN WONDERS OF THE WORLD   co-director, Stanley Warner Cinema
     Corporation, 1956
UNDERWATER WARRIOR   MGM, 1958
THE LONGEST DAY   co-director with Ken Annakin & Bernhard Wicki, 20th
     Century-Fox, 1962
IT HAPPPENED IN ATHENS   20th Century-Fox, 1962
THE THIN RED LINE   Allied Artists, 1964
CRACK IN THE WORLD   Paramount, 1965, British
CLARENCE, THE CROSS-EYED LION   MGM, 1965
AROUND THE WORLD UNDER THE SEA   MGM, 1966
BIRDS DO IT   Columbia, 1966
AFRICA - TEXAS STYLE!   Paramount, 1967, British-U.S.

P A U L   M A S L A N S K Y *

b. November 23, 1933 - New York, New York
Business Manager: Leah Lynn Broidy - Los Angeles, 213/474-2795

SUGAR HILL   American International, 1974

Q U E N T I N   M A S T E R S *

b. July 12, 1946 - Australia
Agent: Cameron's Management, 120 Victoria Street, Potts Point, NSM, 2011,
     Australia, 02/358-6433

THUMB TRIPPING   Avco Embassy, 1973
THE STUD   Trans-American, 1978, British
THE PSI FACTOR   1981, British
A DANGEROUS SUMMER   Filmco Ltd., 1982, Australian
MIDNITE SPARES   Filmco Australia, 1983, Austrlian

NICO MASTORAKIS

THE NEXT ONE   Omega Productions, 1982, British-Greek
BLIND DATE   Omega Productions, 1983, British-Greek

ARMAND MASTROIANNI

HE KNOWS YOUR'RE ALONE   MGM/United Artists 1980
THE KILLING HOUR   Lansbury-Beruh Productions, 1983

VIVIAN MATALON*

Agent: Clifford Stevens, STE Representation Ltd. - New York City, 212/246-1030

PRIVATE CONTENTMENT (TF)   WNET-13/South Carolina Educational TV,
1982

WALTER MATTHAU
(Walter Matuschanskavasky)

b. October 1, 1920 - New York, New York
Agent: William Morris Agency - Beverly Hills, 213/274-7451

GANGSTER STORY   RCIP-States Rights, 1960

RONALD F. MAXWELL*

b. Tripoli, Libya
Agent: ICM - Los Angeles, 213/550-4000

VERNO: USO GIRL (TF) ☆   WNET-13, 1978
LITTLE DARLINGS   Paramount, 1980
THE NIGHT THE LIGHTS WENT OUT IN GEORGIA   Avco Embassy, 1981
KIDCO   20th Century-Fox, 1984

ELAINE MAY*
(Elaine Berlin)

b. April 21, 1932 - Philadelphia, Pennsylvania
Contact: Directors Guild of America - New York City, 212/581-0370

A NEW LEAF   Paramount, 1971
THE HEARTBREAK KID   20th Century-Fox, 1972
MIKEY AND NICKY   Paramount, 1977

RUSS MAYBERRY*

Agent: Sylvia Gold, ICM - Los Angeles, 213/550-4156

THE JESUS TRIP   EMCO, 1971
PROBE (TF)   Warner Bros. TV, 1972
A VERY MISSING PERSON (TF)   Universal TV, 1972
FER-DE-LANCE (TF)   Leslie Stevens Productions, 1974
SEVENTH AVENUE (MS)   co-director with Richard Irving, Universal TV, 1977
STONESTREET: WHO KILLED THE CENTERFOLD MODEL? (TF)   Universal
TV, 1977
THE 3,000 MILE CHASE (TF)   Universal TV, 1977
THE YOUNG RUNAWAYS (TF)   NBC, 1978
THE MILLION DOLLAR DIXIE DELIVERY (TF)   NBC, 1978
THE REBELS (MS)   Universal TV, 1979
UNIDENTITIED FLYING ODDBALL   Buena Vista, 1979
THE $5.20 AN HOUR DREAM (TF)   Thompson-Sagal Productions/Big Deal
Inc./Finnegan Associates, 1980
MARRIAGE IS ALIVE AND WELL (TF)   Lorimar Productions, 1980
REUNION (TF)   Barry Weitz Films, 1980
A MATTER OF LIFE AND DEATH (TF)   Big Deal Inc./Raven's Claw
Productions/Lorimar Productions, 1981
SIDNEY SHORR (TF)   Hajeno Productions/Warner Bros. TV, 1981

continued

RUSS MAYBERRY*—continued

THE FALL GUY (TF)   Glen A. Larson Productions/20th Century-Fox TV, 1981
SIDE BY SIDE: THE TRUE STORY OF THE OSMOND FAMILY
    (TF)   Osmond Productions/Comworld Productions, 1982
ROOSTER (TF)   Glen A. Larson Productions/Tugboat Productions/20th Century-
    Fox TV, 1982
MANIMAL (TF)   Glen A. Larson Productions/20th Century-Fox TV, 1983

T O N Y   M A Y L A M *

b. May 26, 1943 - London, England
Agent; APA - Los Angeles, 213/273-0744

WHITE ROCK (FD)   EMI, 1977, British
THE RIDDLE OF THE SANDS   Rank, 1979, British
THE BURNING   Orion, 1982
THE SINS OF DORIAN GRAY (TF)   Rankin-Bass Productions, 1983

A L B E R T   M A Y S L E S

b. November 26, 1926 - Brookline, Massachusetts

PSYCHIATRY IN RUSSIA (FD)   1955
YOUTH IN POLAND (FD)   co-director with David Maysles, 1962
SHOWMAN (FD)   co-director with David Maysles, 1962
WHAT'S HAPPENING: THE BEATLES IN THE USA (FD)   co-director with
    David Maysles, 1964
MEET MARLON BRANDO (FD)   co-director with David Maysles, 1965
WITH LOVE FROM TRUMAN (FD)   co-director with David Maysles, 1966
SALESMAN (FD)   co-director with David Maysles & Charlotte Zwerin, Maysles
    Film, 1969
GIMME SHELTER (FD)   co-director with David Maysles & Charlotte Zwerin,
    Cinema 5, 1971
CHRISTO'S VALLEY CURTAIN (FD)   co-director with David Maysles & Ellen
    Giffard, 1972
GREY GARDENS (FD)   co-director with David Maysles, Ellen Hovde & Muffie
    Meyer, 1975
RUNNING FENCE (FD)   co-director with David Maysles, 1977

D A V I D   M A Y S L E S

b. January 10, 1932 - Brookline, Massachusetts

YOUTH IN POLAND (FD)   co-director with Albert Maysles, 1957
SHOWMAN (FD)   co-director with Albert Maysles, 1962
WHAT'S HAPPENING: THE BEATLES IN THE USA (FD)   co-director with
    Albert Maysles, 1964
MEET MARLON BRANDO (FD)   co-director with Albert Maysles, 1965
WITH LOVE FROM TRUMAN (FD)   co-director with Albert Maysles, 1966
SALESMAN (FD)   co-director with Albert Maysles & Charlotte Zwerin, Maysles
    Film, 1969
GIMME SHELTER (FD)   co-director with Albert Maysles & Charlotte Zwerin,
    Cinema 5, 1971
CHRISTO'S VALLEY CURTAIN (FD)   co-director with Albert Maysles & Ellen
    Giffard, 1972
GREY GARDENS (FD)   co-director with Albert Maysles, & Ellen Hovde &
    Muffie Meyer, 1975
RUNNING FENCE (FD)   co-director with Albert Maysles, 1977

P A U L   M A Z U R S K Y *

b. April 25, 1930 - Brooklyn, New York
Agent: ICM - Los Angeles, 213/550-4000
Business Manager: B. Francis, 3283 Beverly Drive, Beverly Hills, CA.

BOB & CAROL & TED & ALICE   Columbia, 1969
ALEX IN WONDERLAND   MGM, 1970
BLUME IN LOVE   Warner Bros., 1973
HARRY AND TONTO   20th Century-Fox, 1974
NEXT STOP, GREENWICH VILLAGE   20th Century-Fox
AN UNMARRIED WOMAN   20th Century-Fox, 1978

continued

PAUL MAZURSKY*—continued

WILLIE AND PHIL   20th Century-Fox, 1980
TEMPEST   Columbia, 1982
MOSCOW ON THE HUDSON   Columbia, 1984

JIM McBRIDE*

Contact: Directors Guild of America - Los Angeles, 213/656-1220

DAVID HOLZMAN'S DIARY   Grove Press, 1967
MY GIRLFRIEND'S WEDDING   1968
GLEN AND RANDA   UMC, 1971
A HARD DAY FOR ARCHIE *HOT TIMES*   1973, re-released under title MY
   EROTIC FANTASIES in 1974 with additional footage by another director
BREATHLESS   Orion, 1983

ROBERT McCARTY

Home; 222 West 83rd Street, New York, NY 10024, 212/580-1034

I COULD NEVER HAVE SEX WITH A MAN WHO HAS SO LITTLE
   REGARD FOR MY HUSBAND   Cinema 5, 1973
FORE PLAY   co-director with John G. Avildsen & Bruce Malmuth, Cinema
   National, 1975

GEORGE McCOWAN*

Contact: Directors Guild of America - Los Angeles, 213/656-1220

THE MONK (TF)   Thomas-Spelling Productions, 1969
THE BALLAD OF AND CROCKER (TF)   Thomas-Spelling Productions, 1969
CARTER'S ARMY (TF)   Thomas-Spelling Productions, 1970
THE LOVE WAR (TF)   Thomas-Spelling Productions, 1970
THE OVER-THE-HILL GANG RIDES AGAIN (TF)   Thomas-Spelling Productions,
   1970
RUN, SIMON, RUN (TF)   Aaron Spelling Productions, 1970
LOVE, HATE, LOVE (TF)   Aaron Spelling Productions, 1971
CANNON (TF)   QM Productions, 1971
THE FACE OF FEAR (TF)   QM Productions, 1971
IF TOMORROW COMES (TF)   Aaron Spelling Productions, 1971
WELCOME HOME, JOHNNY BRISTOL (TF)   Cinema Center, 1972
THE MAGNIFICENT SEVEN RIDE!   United Artists, 1972
FROGS   American International, 1972
MURDER ON FLIGHT 502 (TF)   Spelling-Goldberg Productions, 1975
SHADOW OF THE HAWK   Columbia, 1976, Canadian
RETURN TO FANTASY ISLAND (TF)   Spelling-Goldberg Productions, 1978
THE RETURN OF THE MOD SQUAD (TF)   Thomas-Spelling Productions,
   1979
THE SHAPE OF THINGS TO COME   Film Ventures International, 1979,
   Canadian

DON McDOUGALL*

Home: 213/275-4578
Business Manager: R. Cohn - Los Angeles, 213/275-4577

ESCAPE TO MINDANAO (TF)   Universal TV, 1968
WILD WOMEN (TF)   Aaron Spelling Productions, 1970
THE AQUARIANS (TFO   Ivan Tors Productions, 1975
THE HEIST (TF)   Paramount TV, 1972
THE MARK OF ZORRO (TF)   20th Century-Fox TV, 1974
THE MISSING ARE DEADLY (TF)   Lawrence Gordon Productions, 1975

RODDY McDOWALL

b. September 17, 1928 - London, England
Agent: William Morris Agency - Beverly Hills, 213/274-7451

TAM LIN *THE DEVILS'S WIDOW*   American International, 1971

BERNARD McEVEETY *

Agent: Scott Penney, Eisenbach-Greene, Inc. - Los Angeles, 213/659-3420

RIDE BEYOND VENGEANCE   Columbia, 1966
A STEP OUT OF LINE (TF)   Cinema Center, 1971
THE BROTHERHOOD OF SATAN   Columbia, 1971
KILLER BY NIGHT (TF)   Cinema Center, 1972
NAPOLEON AND SAMANTHA   Buena Vista, 1972
ONE LITTLE INDIAN   Buena Vista, 1973
THE BEARS AND I   Buena Vista, 1974
THE MACAHANS (TF)   Albert S. Ruddy Productions/MGM TV, 1976
THE HOSTAGE HEART (TF)   Andrew J. Fenady Associates/MGM TV, 1977
DONOVAN'S KID (TF)   NBC, 1979
CENTENNIAL (MS)   co-director with Harry Falk, Paul Krasny & Virgil Vogel,
    Universal TV, 1979
ROUGHNECKS (TF)   Douglas Netter Productions/Metromedia Producers
    Corporations, 1980

VINCENT McEVEETY *

Home: 14561 Mulholland Drive, Los Angeles, CA 90077 213/783-4674

THIS SAVAGE LAND (TF)   1968
FIRECREEK   Warner Bros., 1968
CUTTER'S TRAIL (TF)   CBS Studio Center, 1970
THE MILLION DOLLAR DUCK   Buena Vista, 1971
THE BISCUIT EATER   Buena Vista, 1972
CHARLEY AND THE ANGEL   Buena Vista, 1972
WONDER WOMAN (TF)   Warner Bros. TV, 1974
SUPERDAD   Buena Vista, 1972
THE CASTAWAY COWBOY   Buena Vista, 1974
THE STRONGEST MAN IN THE WORLD   Buena Vista, 1975
THE LAST DAY (TF)   Paramount TV, 1975
THE TREASURE OF MATECUMBE   Buena Vista, 1976
GUS   Buena Vista, 1976
HERBIE GOES TO MONTE CARLO   Buena Vista, 1976
THE APPLE DUMPLING GANG RIDES AGAIN   Buena Vista, 1979
HERBIE GOES BANANAS   Buena Vista, 1980
AMY   Buena Vista, 1981
MCCLAIN'S LAW (TF)   Eric Bercovici Productions/Epipsychidion Inc., 1982

DARREN McGAVIN *

b. May 7, 1922 - Spokane, Washington
Home: 8643 Holloway Plaza, Los Angeles, CA 90069, 213/855-0271
Agent: Jack Gilardi, ICM - Los Angeles, 213/550-4000

HAPPY MOTHER'S DAY - LOVE, GEORGE   Cinema 5, 1973

PATRICK McGOOHAN *

b. May 19, 1928 - New York, New York
Contact: Directors Guild of America - Los Angeles, 213/656-1220

CATCH MY SOUL   Cinerama Releasing Corporation, 1974

JOSEPH McGRATH

Agent: ICM - London, 01/629-8080

CASINO ROYALE   co-director with Val Guest, Ken Hughes, John Huston &
    Robert Parrish, Columbia, 1967, British
30 IS A DANGEROUS AGE, CYNTHIA   Columbia 1968, British
THE BLISS OF MRS. BLOSSOM   Paramount, 1969, British
THE MAGIC CHRISTIAN   Commonwealth United, 1970, British
DIGBY, THE BIGGEST DOG IN THE WORLD   Cinerama Releasing
    Corporation, 1974, British
THE GREAT McGONAGALL   Scotia American, 1975, British
I'M NOT FEELING MYSELF TONIGHT   New Realm, 1976, British

JOSEPH McGRATH—continued

THE STRANGE CASE OF THE END OF CIVILISATION AS WE KNOW IT
(TF)   Shearwater Films/London Weekend TV, 1978, British
RISING DAMP   ITC 1980, British

THOMAS McGUANE *

Home: Hoffman Route, Livingston, Montana 59047
Agent: Jeff Berg, ICM - Los Angeles, 213/550-4000

92 IN THE SHADE   United Artists, 1975

ANDREW V. McLAGLEN *

b. July 28, 1920 - London, Englend
Agent; Ronald Lief, Contemporary-Korman Artists - Beverly Hills, 213/278-8250

GUN THE MAN DOWN   United Artists, 1956
MAN IN THE VAULT   Universal, 1956
THE ABDUCTORS   20th Century-Fox, 1957
FRECKLES   20th Century-Fox, 1960
THE LITTLE SHEPHERD OF KINGDOM COME   20th Century-Fox, 1961
McLINTOCKI   United Artists, 1963
SHENANDOAH   Universal, 1965
THE RARE BREED   Universal, 1966
MONKEYS, GO HOMEI   Buena Vista, 1967
THE WAY WEST   United Artists, 1967
THE BALLAD OF JOSIE   Universal, 1968
THE DEVIL'S BRIGADE   United Artists, 1968
BANDOLEROI   20th Century-Fox, 1968
HELLFIGHTERS   Universal, 1969
THE UNDEFEATED   20th Century-Fox, 1969
CHISUM   Warner Bros., 1970
ONE MORE TRAIN TO ROB   Universal, 1971
FOOLS' PARADE   Columbia, 1971
SOMETHING BIG   National General, 1971
CAHILL, U.S. MARSHAL   Warner Bros., 1973
MITCHELL   Allied Artists, 1975
THE LOG OF THE BLACK PEARL (TF)   Universal TV/Mark VII Ltd., 1975
STOWAWAY TO THE MOON (TF)   20th Century-Fox TV, 1975
BANJO HACKETT: ROAMIN' FREE (TF)   Bruce Lansbury Productions/Columbia
TV, 1976
THE LAST HARD MEN   20th Century-Fox, 1976
MURDER AT THE WORLD SERIES (TF)   ABC Circle Films, 1977
BREAKTHROUGH SERGEANT STEINER   Maverick Pictures International,
1978, West German
THE WILD GEESE   Allied Artists, 1979, British
ffolkes NORTH SEA HIJACK   Universal, 1980, British
THE SEA WOLVES   Paramount, 1981, British
THE SHADOW RIDERS (TF)   The Pegasus Group Ltd./Columbia TV, 1982
THE BLUE AND THE GRAY (MS)   Larry White-Lou Reda Productions/Columbia
TV, 1982
TRAVIS McGEE (TF)   Hajeno Productions/Warner Bros, TV, 1983
SAHARA   MGM/UA/Cannon, 1983

PETER MEDAK *

b. Budapest, Hungary
Home: 142 S. Bedford Drive, Beverly Hills, CA 90212
Agent: Jim Wiatt/Lou Pitt, ICM - Los Angeles, 213/550-4000
Business Manager: Fred Altman, Altman & Bemmel, 9229 Sunset Blvd., Los Angeles,
CA, 213/278-4201

NEGATIVES   Continental, 1968 British
A DAY IN THE DEATH OF JOE EGG   Columbia, 1972, British
THE RULING CLASS   Avco Embassy, 1972, British
THE THIRD GIRL FROM THE LEFT (TF)   Playboy Productions, 1973
GHOST IN THE NOONDAY SUN   Columbia, 1974, British
THE ODD JOB   Columbia, 1978, British
THE CHANGELING   AFD, 1980, Canadian
THE BABYSITTER (TF)   Moonlight Productions/Filmways, 1980

continued

PETER MEDAK*—continued

ZORRO, THE GAY BLADE   20th Century-Fox, 1981
MISTRESS OF PARADISE (TF)   Lorimar Productions, 1981
CRY FOR THE STRANGERS (TFO   David Gerber Company/MGM TV, 1982

DON MEDFORD*

Home: 1956 S. Bently Avenue, Los Angeles, CA 90025, 213/473-3439
Agent: Irv Schechter Company - Beverly Hills, 213/278-8070

TO TRAP A SPY   MGM, 1966
THE HUNTING PARTY   United Artists, 1970
INCIDENT IN SAN FRANSICSO (TF)   QM Productions, 1971
THE ORGANIZATION   United Artists, 1971
THE NOVEMBER PLAN   1976
THE CLONE MASTER (TF)   Mel Ferber Productions/Paramount TV, 1978
COACH OF THE YEAR (TF)   A. Shane Company, 1980
SIZZLE (TF)   Aaron Spelling Productions, 1981

BILL MELENDEZ

Business: Bill Melendez Productions, 439 N. Larchmont Blvd., Los Angeles,
    CA 90004, 213/463-4101

A BOY NAMED CHARLIE BROWN (AF)   National General, 1968
SNOOPY, COME HOME (AF)   National General, 1972
DICK DEADEYE, OR DUTY DONE (AF)   Intercontinental, 1976, British
RACE FOR YOUR LIFE, CHARLIE BROWN (AF)   Paramount, 1978
BON VOYAGE, CHARLIE BROWN (AND DON'T COME BACK!)
    (AF)   Paramount, 1980

GEORGE MENDELUK

Business: World Classic Pictures, 6263 Topia Drive, Malibu, CA 90265, 213/457-
    9911 or 213/457-5591

STONE COLD DEAD   Dimension, 1979, Canadian
THE KIDNAPPING OF THE PRESIDENT   Crown International, 1980, Canadian

KIETH MERRILL*

b. May 22, 1940 - Utah
Home: 11930 Rhus Ridge Road, Los Altos Hills, CA 94022, 415/941-8720

THE GREAT AMERICAN COWBOY (FD)   Sun Internnational, 1974
THREE WARRIORS   United Artists, 1978
TAKE DOWN   Buena Vista, 1979
WINDWALKER   Pacific International, 1980
MR. KRUEGER'S CHRISTMAS (TF)   Bonneville Productions, 1980
HARRY'S WAR   Taft International, 1981
THE CHEROKEE TRAIL (TF)   Walt Disney Productions, 1981

RADLEY METZGER

b. 1930

DARK ODYSSEY   co-director with William Kyriaskys, ERA, 1961
DICTIONARY OF SEX   1964
THE DIRTY GIRLS   1965
THE ALLEY CATS   1966
CARMEN, BABY   Audubon, 1967, U.S.-Yugoslavian-West German
THERESE AND IASBELLE   Audubon, 1968, West German-U.S.
CAMILLE 2000   Audubon, 1969, Italian
THE LICKERISH QUARTET   Audubon, 1970, U.S.-Italian-West German
LITTLE MOTHER   Audubon, 1972
SCORE   Audubon, 1973
NAKED CAME THE STRANGER   directed under pseudonym of Henry Paris,
    Catalyst, 1975
THE PRIVATE AFTERNOONS OF PAMELA MANN   directed under
    pseudonym of Henry Paris, Hudson Valley, 1975

continued

RADLEY METZGER—continued

ESOTIKA, EROTIKA, PSICOTIKA FAB   1975, Italian-Monocan
THE IMAGE   Audubon, 1976
THE OPENING OF MISTY BEETHOVEN   directed under pseudonym of Henry
     Paris, Catalyst, 1976
BARBARA BROADCAST   directed under pseudonym of Henry Paris, Crescent,
     1977
THE CAT AND THE CANARY   Quartet, 1978, British
THE TALE OF TIFFANY LUST   directed under pseudonym of Henry Paris,
     Entertainment Ventures, 1981

N I C H O L A S   M E Y E R *

b. New York, New York
Home: 2109 Stanley Hills Drive, Los Angeles, CA 90046

TIME AFTER TIME   Orion/Warner Bros., 1979
STAR TREK II: THE WRATH OF KHAN   Paramount, 1982
THE DAY AFTER (TF)   ABC Circle Films, 1983

R U S S   M E Y E R *

b. March 21, 1922 - Oakland, California
Business RM Films International Inc., P.O. Box 3748, Hollywood, CA 90028, 213/
     466-7791
Business Manager: Phillip Cooperman, Clokelman, Greenberg & Co., 7060 Hind
     Blvd., Los Angeles, CA 90028, 213/469-8241

THE IMMORAL MR. TEAS   Pedram, 1959
EVE AND THE HANDYMAN   Eve, 1961
EROTICA   Eve, 1961
THE IMMORAL WEST AND HOW IT WAS LOST   Eve, 1961
EUROPE IN THE RAW   Eve, 1963
HEAVENLY BODIES   Eve, 1963
KISS ME QUICK!   Eve, 1964
LORNA   Eve, 1965
ROPE OF FLESH   Eve, 1965
FANNY HILL: MEMOIRS OF A WOMAN OF PLEASURE   Pan World, 1965,
     U.S.-West German
MOTOR PSYCHO   Eve, 1965
FASTER PUSSYCAT, KILL! KILL!   Eve, 1965
MONDO TOPLESS   Eve, 1966
GOOD MORNING ... AND GOODBYE   Eve, 1967
COMMON LAW CABIN   Eve, 1967
FINDERS KEEPERS, LOVERS WEEPERS   Eve, 1968
RUSS MEYER'S VIXEN   Eve, 1968
CHERRY, HARRY AND RAQUEL   Eve, 1969
BEYOND THE VALLEY OF THE DOLLS   20th Century-Fox, 1970
THE SEVEN MINUTES   20th Century-Fox, 1971
SWEET SUZY! *BLACKSNAKE*   Signal 166, 1975
SUPERVIXENS   RM Films, 1975
RUSS MEYER'S UP!   RM Films, 1976
BENEATH THE VALLEY OF THE ULTRAVIXENS   RM Films, 1979
THE BREAST OF RUSS MEYER   RM Films, 1983

R I C H A R D   M I C H A E L S *

Agent: Adams, Ray & Rosenberg - Los Angeles, 213/278-3000
Business Manager: David G. Licht, 9171 Wilshire Blvd., Beverly Hills, CA 90210,
     213/278-1920

HOW COME NOBODY'S ON OUR SIDE?   American Films Ltd., 1975
DEATH IS NOT THE END   Libert Films International, 1976
ONCE AN EAGLE (MS)   co-director with E.W. Swackhammer, Universal TV,
     1976
CHARLIE COBB: NICE NIGHT FOR HANGING (TF)   Universal TV, 1977
HAVING BABIES II (TF)   The Jozak Company, 1977
THE REACH OF LOVE (TF)   1978
LEAVE YESTERDAY BEHIND (TF)   ABC Circle Films, 1978
MY HUSBAND IS MISSING (TF)   Bob Banner Associates, 1978
... AND YOUR NAME IS JONAH (TF)   Charles Fries Productions, 1979

continued

RICHARD MICHAELS*—continued
ONCE UPON A FAMILY (TF)   Universal TV, 1980
THE PLUTONIUM INCIDENT (TF)   Time-Life Productions, 1980
SCARED STRAIGHT! ANOTHER STORY (TF)   Golcen West TV, 1980
BERLIN TUNNEL 21 (TF)   Cypress Point Productions/Filmways, 1981
THE CHILDREN NOBODY WANTED (TF)   Blatt-Singer Productions, 1981
BLUE SKIES AGAIN   Warner Bros, 1983
ONE COOKS, THE OTHER DOESN'T (TF)   Kaleidoscope Films Ltd./Lorimar
Productions, 1983
SADAT (TF)   Blatt-Singer Productions/Columbia TV, 1983

G E O R G E   M I H A L K A

Home: 2030 Closse-Suite 4, Montreal, Quebec H3H 1Z9, Canada , 514/937-4740

MY BLODDY VALENTINE   Paramount, 1981, Canadian
PICK-UP SUMMER *PINBALL SUMMER*   Film Ventures International, 1821,
Canadian
SCANDALE   Vivafilm/Cine 360, 1982, Canadian

N I K I T A   M I K H A L K O V

b. U.S.S.R.
Contact: State Committee of Cinematography of the U.S.S.R., Council of Ministers, 7
Maly Gnesdiknovsky Pereulok, Moscow, U.S.S.R., 7 095/299-9912

AN UNFINISHED PIECE FOR PLAYER PIANO   Corinth, 1977, Soviet
A SLAVE OF LOVE   Cinema 5, 1978, Soviet
FIVE EVENINGS   IFEX Film, 1979, Soviet
OBLOMOV   IFEX Film, 1981, Soviet
FAMILY RELATIONS   Mosfilm, 1983, Soviet

C H R I S T O P H E R   M I L E S

b. April 19, 1939 - London, England
Home: 49 Berkeley Square, London N1, England, 01/491-2625
Contact: Directors Guild of Great Britain, 56 Whitfield Street, Londong W1, 01/580-
9592

UP JUMPED A SWAGMAN   Anglo-Amalgamated/Warner-Pathe, 1966, British
THE VIRGIN AND THE GYPSY   Chevron, 1970, British
TIME FOR LOVING   Hemdale, 1972, British
THE MAIDS   American Film Theatre, 1975, British-Canadian
THAT LUCKY TOUCH   Allied Artists, 1975, British
PRIEST OF LOVE   Filmways, 1981, British

J O H N   M I L I U S *

b. April 11, 1944 - St. Louis, Missouri
Agent: ICM - Los Angeles, 213/550-4000

DILLINGER   American International, 1973
THE WIND AND THE LION   MGM/United Artists, 1975
BIG WEDNESDAY   Warner Bros., 1978
CONAN THE BARBARIAN   Universal, 1982

G A V I N   M I L L A R

Contact: Directors Guild of Great Britain, 56 Whitfield Street, London W1, 01/580-
9592

SECRETS   The Samuel Goldwyn Company, 1983, British

STUART MILLAR *

b. 1929 - New York, New York
Home: 300 Central Park West - Suite 15G, New York, NY 10024, 212/873-5515

WHEN THE LEGENDS DIE   20th Century-Fox, 1972
ROOSTER COGBURN   Universal, 1975

DAVID MILLER *

b. November 28, 1909 - Paterson, New Jersey
Home: 1843 Thayer Avenue, Los Angeles, CA 90025, 213/474-8542
Agent: The Gersh Agency - Beverly Hills, 213/274-6611

BILLY THE KID   MGM, 1941
SUNDAY PUNCH   MGM, 1942
FLYING TIGERS   Republic, 1942
TOP O' THE MORNING   Paramount, 1948
LOVE HAPPY   United Artists, 1949
OUR VERY OWN   RKO Radio, 1950
SATURDAY'S HERO   Columbia, 1951
SUDDEN FEAR   RKO Radio, 1952
TWIST OF FATE *THE BEAUTIFUL STRANGER*   United Artists, 1954,
    British
DIANE   MGM, 1956
THE OPPOSITE SEX   MGM, 1956
THE STORY OF ESTHER COSTELLO   Columbia, 1957
HAPPY ANNIVERSARY   United Artists, 1959
MIDNIGHT LACE   Universal, 1961
BACK STREET   Universal, 1961
LONELY ARE THE BRAVE   Universal, 1962
CAPTAIN NEWMAN, M.D.   Universal, 1964
HAMMERHEAD   Columbia, 1968, British
HAIL, HERO!   National General, 1969
EXECUTIVE ACTION   National General, 1973
BITTERSWEET LOVE   Avco Embassy, 1976
LOVE FOR RENT (TF)   Warren V. Bush Productions, 1979
THE BEST PLACE TO BE (TF)   Ross Hunter Productions, 1979
GOLDIE AND THE BOXER (TF)   Orenthal Productions/Columbia TV, 1979
GOLDIE AND THE BOXER GO TO HOLLYWOOD (TF)   Orenthal
    Productions/Columbia TV, 1981

GEORGE MILLER

Business: Kennedy & Miller, Metro Theatre, 32 Orwell Street, Potts Point, NSW,
    2011, Australia, 02/357-2322

MAD MAX   American International, 1979, Australian
THE ROAD WARRIOR *MAD MAX II*   Warner Bros., 1982, Australian
TWILIGHT ZONE - THE MOVIE   co-director with John Landis, Steven
    Spielberg & Joe Dante, Warner Bros., 1983

GEORGE MILLER

Address: 3 Reed Street, Albert Park, Victoria, 3206, Australia, 03/690-5663

CASH AND COMPANY (MS)   1976, Australian
AGAINST THE WIND (MS)   co-director with Simon Wincer, 1978, Australian
THE LAST OUTLAW (MS)   1980, Australian
THE MAN FROM SNOWY RIVER   20th Century-Fox, 1982, Australian
ALL THE RIVERS RUN (CMS)   Crawford Productions/Nine Network/HBO,
    1983, Australian
THE AVIATOR   MGM/UA, 1984

JASON MILLER *

Contact: Directors Guild of America - Los Angeles, 213/656-1220

THAT CHAMPIONSHIP SEASON   Cannon, 1982

JONATHAN MILLER

Contact: British Academy of Film & Television Arts, 195 Piccadilly, London W1,
England, 01/734-0022

TAKE A GIRL LIKE YOU   Columbia, 1970, British

MICHAEL MILLER *

Agent: David Gersh, The Gersh Agency - Beverly Hills, 213/274-6611
Business Manager: Henry Levine, Henry Levine & Associates, 9100 Wilshire Blvd. -
Suite 517, Beverly Hills, CA 91210, 213/274-8691

STREET GIRLS   New World, 1975
JACKSON COUNTY JAIL   New World, 1976
OUTSIDE CHANCE (TF)   New World Productions/Miller-Begun Productions,
1978
SILENT RAGE   Columbia, 1982
NATIONAL LAMPOON'S CLASS REUNION   20th Century-Fox, 1983

ROBERT ELLIS MILLER *

b. July 18, 1932 - New York, New York
Agent: Paul Kohner, Inc. - Los Angeles, 213/550-1060
Business Manager: McGuire Management, 1901 Avenue of the Stars, Los Angeles,
CA 90067, 213/277-5902

ANY WEDNESDAY   Warner Bros., 1966
SWEET NOVEMBER   Warner Bros., 1967
THE HEART IS A LONELY HUNTER   Warner Bros., 1968
THE BUTTERCUP CHAIN   Warner Bros., 1970, British
BIG TRUCK AND POOR CLARE   Kastner-Ladd-Winkler/Pashanel-Topol-
Gottesman, 1972, U.S.-Israeli
THE GIRL FROM PETROVKA   Universal, 1974
JUST AN OLD SWEET SONG (TF)   MTM Enterprises, 1976
ISHI: THE LAST OF HIS TRIBE (TF)   Edward & Mildred Lewis Productions,
1978
THE BALTIMORE BULLET   Avco Embassy, 1980
MADAME X (TF)   Levenback-Riche Productions/Universal TV, 1981
REUBEN, REUBEN   Taft Entertainment, 1983

WALTER C. MILLER *

Home: 2401 Crest View Drive, Los Angeles, CA 90046, 213/656-2819

THE BORROWERS (TF)   Walt DeFaria Productions/20th Century-Fox TV, 1973
CAN I SAVE MY CHILDREN? (TF) ☆   Stanley L. Colbert Co-Production
Associates/20th Century-Fox TV, 1974

REGINALD MILLS

PETER RABBIT & TALES OF BEATRIX POTTER   MGM, 1971, British

STEVE MINER

b. June 18, 1951 - Chicago, Illinois
Business: Steven C. Miner Films Inc., 11372 Second Street - Suite 103, Santa
Monica, CA 90403, 213/393-0291
Agent: Mike Lynne, Blumenthal & Lynne, 488 Madison Avenue, New York,
NY 10022, 212/758-0190

FRIDAY THE 13TH PART 2   Paramount, 1981
FRIDAY THE 13TH PART 3   Paramount, 1982

DAVID MINGAY

Contact: British Academy of Film & Television Arts, 195 Piccadilly, London W1,
England, 01/734-0022

RUDE BOY   co-director with Jack Hazan, Atlantic Releasing Corporation, 1980,
British

VINCENTE MINNELLI*

b. February 28, 1910 - Chicago, Illinois
Home: 812 N. Crescent Drive, Beverly Hills, CA 90210, 213/276-8128
Agent: Paul Kohner, Inc. - Los Angeles, 213/550-1060
Business Manager: Nate Golden & Associates, 9601 Wilshire Blvd., Beverly Hills,
CA 90210, 213/278-1103

CABIN IN THE SKY   MGM, 1943
I DOOD IT   MGM, 1943
MEET ME IN ST. LOUIS   MGM, 1944
YOLANDA AND THE THIEF   MGM, 1945
THE CLOCK   MGM, 1945
ZIEGFELD FOLLIES   MGM, 1946
TILL THE CLOUDS ROLL BY   co-director with Richard Whorf, MGM, 1946
UNDERCURRENT   MGM, 1946
THE PIRATE   MGM, 1948
MADAME BOVARY   MGM, 1949
FATHER OF THE BRIDE   MGM, 1950
AN AMERICAN IN PARIS ★   MGM, 1951
FATHER'S LITTLE DIVIDEND   MGM, 1951
THE BAD AND THE BEAUTIFUL   MGM, 1952
THE STORY OF THREE LOVES   MGM, 1953
THE BAND WAGON   MGM, 1953
THE LONG, LONG TRAILER   MGM, 1954
BRIGADOON   MGM, 1954
THE COBWEB   MGM, 1955
KISMET   MGM, 1955
LUST FOR LIFE   MGM, 1956
TEA AND SYMPATHY   MGM, 1956
DESIGNING WOMAN   MGM, 1957
GIGI ★   MGM, 1958
THE RELUCTANT DEBUTANTE   MGM, 1958
SOME CAME RUNNING   MGM, 1959
HOME FROM THE HILL   MGM, 1960
BELLS ARE RINGING   MGM, 1960
THE FOUR HORSEMEN OF THE APOCALYPSE   MGM, 1962
TWO WEEKS IN ANOTHER TOWN   MGM, 1962
THE COURTSHIP OF EDDIE'S FATHER   MGM, 1963
GOODBYE, CHARLIE   20th Century-Fox, 1964
THE SANDPIPER   MGM, 1965
ON A CLEAR DAY YOU CAN SEE FOREVER   Paramount, 1970
A MATTER OF TIME   American International, 1976, U.S.-Italian

MOSHE MIZRAHI

Contact: French Film Office, 745 Fifth Avenue, New York NY 10151, 212/832-
8860

I LOVE YOU ROSA   Leisure Media, 1973, Israeli
THE HOUSE ON CHELOUCHE STREET   Productions Unlimited, 1974, Israeli
DAUGHTERSI DAUGHTERSI   Steinmann-Baxter, 1975, Israeli
RACHEL'S MAN   Allied Artists, 1976, Israeli
MADAME ROSA *LA VIE DEVANT SOI*   Atlantic Releasing Corporation,
1978, French
I SENT A LETTER TO MY LOVE   Atlantic Releasing Corporation, 1981,
French
LA VIE CONTINUE   Triumph/Columbia, 1982, French
YOUTH   1983, French
THE CHILDREN'S WAR   Stafford Productions, 1984

DAVID MOESSINGER *

Business: Universal Pictures, 100 Universal City Plaza, Universal City, CA 91608
Messages: 213/508-1112
Agent: Dan Richland, The Richland Agency - Los Angeles, 213/553-1257

MOBILE TWO (TF)   Universal TV/Mark VII Ltd., 1975

EDOUARD MOLINARO

b. May 13, 1928 Bordeaux, France
Contact: French Film Office, 745 Fifth Avenue, New York, NY 10151, 212/832-
    8860

BACK TO THE WALL   Ellis, 1958, French
DES FEMMES DISPARAISSENT   1959, French
UNE FILLE POUR L'ETE   1960, French
THE PASSION OF SLOW FIRE *LA MORT DE BELLE*   Trans-Lux, 1961,
    French
SEVEN CAPITAL SINS   co-director with Jean-Luc Godard, Roger Vadim,
    Sylvaine Dhomme, Philippe De Broca, Claude Chabrol, Jacques Demy, Marie-
    Jose Nat, Dominique Paturel, Jean-Marc Tennberg & Perrette Pradier, Embassy,
    1962, French-Italian
LES ENNEMIS   1962, French
ARSENE LUPIN CONTRE ARSENE LUPIN   1962, French
UNE RAVISSANTE IDIOTE   1964, French
MALE HUNT   Pathe Contemporary, 1965, French-Italian
QUAND PASSENT LES FAISANS   1965, French
TO COMMIT A MURDER *PEAU D'ESPION*   Cinerama Releasing Corporation,
    1967, French-Italian-West German
OSCAR   1968, French
HIBERNATUS   1969, French
MON ONCLE BENJAMIN   1969, French
LA LIBERTEEN CROUPE   1970, French
LES AVEUX LES PLUS DOUX   1971, French
LA MANDARINE   1972, French
A PAIN IN THE A–   Corwin-Mahler, 1973, French
LE GANG DES OTAGES   Gaumont, 1973, French
L'IRONIE DU SORT   1974, French
THE PINK TELEPHONE   SJ International, 1975, French
DRACULA PERE ET FILS   Gaumont, 1976, French
L'HOMME PRESSE   CIDIF, 1977, French
LA CAGE AUX FOLLES ★   United Artists, 1979, French-Italian
LA PITIE DANGEREUSE (TF)   Christine Gouze-Renal Progefi/Antenne-2, 1979,
    French
CAUSE TOUJOURS ... TU M'INTERESSE   Albina Productions, 1979, French
SUNDAY LOVERS   co-director with Bryan Forbes, Dino Risi & Gene Wilder,
    MGM/United Artists, 1981, U.S.-British-Italian-French
LA CAGE AUX FOLLES II   United Artists, 1981, French-Italian
FOR A MILLION BUCKS YOU'VE GOT NOTHING   UGC, 1982, French
I WON'T DANCE   MGM/UA, 1984

MARIO MONICELLI

b. May 15, 1915 - Rome, Italy
Contact: Ministry of Tourism & Education, Via Della Ferratella, No. 51, 00184
    Rome, Italy, 06/7732

AL DIAVOLO LA CELEBRITA   co-director with Steno, Produttori Associati,
    1949, Italian
TOTO CERCA CASA   co-director with Steno, ATA, 1949, Italian
VITA DA CANI   co-director with Steno, ATA, 1950, Italian
E ARRIVATO IL CAVALIERE   co-director with Steno, ATA/Excelsa Film, 1950,
    Italian
GUARDIE E LADRI   co-director with Steno, Carlo Ponti/Dino De Laurentiis
    Cinematografica/Golden Film, 1951, Italian
TOTO E I RE DI ROMA   co-director with Steno, Golden Film/Humanitas Film,
    1952, Italian
LE INFIDELI   co-director with Steno, Excelsa Film/Carlo Ponti/Dino De Laurentiis
    Cinematografica, 1953, Italian
PROIBITO   Documento Film/UGC/Cormoran Film, 1954, Italian
TOTO E CAROLINA   Rosa, 1955, Italian
UN EROE DEI NOSTRI TEMPI   Titanus/Vides, 1955, Italian

continued

MARIO MONICELLI—continued

DONATELLA   Sud Film, 1956, Italian
THE TAILOR'S MAID *PADRI E FIGLI*   Trans-Lux, 1957, Italian
IL MEDICO E LO STREGONE   Royal Film/Francinex, 1957, Italian-French
BIG DEAL ON MADONNA STREET *I SOLITI IGNOTTI*   United Motion
    Picture Organization, 1958, Italian
THE GREAT WAR   United Artists, 1959, Italian
THE PASSIONATE THIEF   Embassy, 1960, Italian
BOCCACCIO '70   co-director with Federico Fellini, Vittorio De Sica & Luchino
    Visconti, Embassy, 1962, Italian
THE ORGANIZER *I COMPAGNI*   Continental, 1963, Italian-French-Yugoslavian
HIGH INFIDELITY   co-director with Franco Rossi, Elio Petri & Luciano Salce,
    Magna, 1964, Italian-French
CASANOVA '70   Embassy, 1965, Italian-French
L'ARMATA BRANCALEONE   Fair Film, 1966, Italian
THE QUEENS *LE FATE*   co-director with Luciano Salce, Mauro Bolognini &
    Antonio Pietrangeli, Royal Films International, 1966, Italian-French
RAGAZZA CON LA PISTOLA   Documento Film, 1968, Italian
CAPRICCIO ALL'ITALIANA   co-director with Steno, Mauro Bolognini & Pier
    Paolo Pasolini, Dino De Laurentiis Cinematografica, 1968, Italian
TO'E MORTA LA NONNA   Vides, 1969, Italian
LE COPPIE   co-director with Alberto Sordi & Vittorio De Sica, Documento Film,
    1970, Italian
BRANCALEONE ALLE CROCIATE   Fair Film, 1970, Italian
LADY LIBERTY *MORTADELLA*   United Artists, 1971, Italian
VOGLIAMO I COLONNELLI   Dean Film, 1973, Italian
ROMANZO POPOLARE   Capitolina, 1975, Italian
MY FRIENDS   Allied Artists, 1975, Italian
CARO MICHELE   Cineriz, 1976, Italian
SIGNORE E SIGNORI BUONANOTTE   co-director with Luigi Comencini, Nanni
    Loy, Luigi Magni & Ettore Scola, Titanus, 1976, Italian
LA GODURIA   co-director, 1976, Italian
UN BORGHESE PICCOLO PICCOLI   Cineriz, 1977, Italian
VIVA ITALIAI *I NUOVI MOSTRI*   co-director with Dino Risi & Ettore Scola,
    Cinema 5, 1978, Italian
LOVERS AND LIARS *TRAVELS WITH ANITA*   Levitt-Pickman, 1979, Italian-
    French
HURRICANE ROSY   United Artists, 1979, Italian-French
THE MARQUIS OF GRILLO   Opera/RAI, 1981, Italian
AMICI MIEI II   Sacis, 1982, Italian
BERTOLDO BERTOLDINO E ... CACASENO   Gaumont, 1984, Italian

GIULIANO MONTALDO

Contact: Ministry of Tourism & Education, Via Della Ferratella, No. 51, 00184
    Rome, Italy, 06/7732

GRAND SLAM *AD OGNI COSTO*   Paramount, 1968, Italian-Spanish-West
    German
MACHINE GUN McCAIN *GLI INTOCCABILI*   Columbia, 1970, Italian
SACCO AND VANZETTI   UMC, 1971, Italian
L'AGNESE UN A MORIRE   Indipendenti Regionali, 1976, Italian
CLOSED CIRCUIT   Filmalpha/RAI, 1977, Italian
IL GIOCATTOLO   Titanus, 1979, Italian
MARCO POLO (MS)   RAI/Franco Cristaldi Productions/Vincenzo Labella
    Productions, 1982, Italian

RICHARD MOORE *

b. October 4, 1925 - Jacksonville, Illinois
Home: 213/459-4593

CIRCLE OF IRON   Avco Embassy, 1979

ROBERT MOORE *

b. August 17, 1927 - Detroit, Michigan
Agent: The Artists Agency - Los Angeles, 213/277-7779

THURSDAY'S GAME (TF)   ABC Circle Film, 1974
MURDER BY DEATH   Columbia, 1976

continued

ROBERT MOORE*—continued
THE CHEAP DETECTIVE   Columbia, 1978
CHAPTER TWO   Columbia, 1980

PHILIPPE MORA*

Agent: The Robert Littman Company - Beverly Hills, 213/278-1572

TROUBLE IN MOLOPOLIS   1972, British
SWASTIKA (FD)   Cinema 5, 1974, British
BROTHER, CAN YOU SPARE A DIME? (FD)   Dimension, 1975, Canadian
MAD DOG   *MAD DOG MORGAN*   Cinema Shares International, 1976,
    Australian
THE BEAST WITHIN   United Artists, 1982
THE RETURN OF CAPTAIN INVINCIBLE   *LEGEND IN LEOTARDS*   Jensen
    Farley Pictures, 1983, Australian
A BREED APART   Orion, 1983

RICK MORANIS

Address: 95 Forest Heights Blvd., Willowdale, Ontario, Canada, 416/968-2939

STRANGE BREW   co-director with Dave Thomas, MGM/UA, 1983, Canadian

JEANNE MOREAU

b. January 23, 1928 - Paris, France
Contact: French Film Office, 745 Fifth Avenue, New York, NY 10151, 212/832-
    8860

LUMIERE   New World, 1976, French
L'ADOLESCENTE   Landmark Releasing, 1979, French

DAVID BURTON MORRIS

PURPLE HAZE   Triumph/Columbia, 1983

HOWARD MORRIS*

b. September 4, 1919 - New York, New York
Agent: Tom Korman, Contemporary-Korman Artists - Beverly Hills, 213/278-8250

WHO'S MINDING THE MINT?   Columbia, 1967
WITH SIX YOU GET EGGROLL   National General, 1968
DON'D DRINK THE WATER   Avco Embassy, 1969
OHI BABY, BABY, BABY ... (TF)   Alan Landsburg Productions, 1974
GOIN' COCONUTS   Osmond Distribution, 1978

PAUL MORRISSEY

b. 1939 - New York, New York
Contact: Writers Guild of America, West - Los Angeles, 213/550-1000

FLESH   Warhol, 1968
TRASH   Warhol, 1970
ANDY WARHOL'S WOMEN   Warhol, 1971
HEAT   Warhol, 1972
L'AMOUR   co-director with Andy Warhol, Altura, 1973
ANDY WARHOL'S FRANKENSTEIN   *FLESH FOR
    FRANKENSTEIN*   Bryanston, 1974, Italian-French
ANDY WARHOL'S DRACULA   *BLOOD FOR DRACULA*   Bryanston, 1974,
    Italian-French
THE HOUND OF THE BASKERVILLES   Atlantic Releasing Corporation, 1979,
    British
MADAME WANG'S   1981
FORTY-DEUCE   Island Alive, 1983

GILBERT MOSES *

b. August 20, 1942 - Cleveland, Ohio
Agent: Shapiro-Lichtman Agency - Los Angeles, 213/557-2244

WILLIE DYNAMITE   Universal, 1974
ROOTS (MS) ☆   co-director with Marvin J. Chomsky, John Erman & David
  Greene, Wolper Productions, 1977
THE GREATEST THING THAT ALMOST HAPPENED (TF)   Charles Fries
  Productions, 1977
THE FISH THAT SAVED PITTSBURGH   United Artists, 1979

HARRY MOSES *

Business: CBS News, 524 West 57th Street, New York, NY 10019, 212/975-
  1885
Agent: Elliot Webb, ICM - Los Angeles, 213/550-4000
Business Manager: Richard Leibner, N.S. Bienstock - New York City, 212/765-3040

THORNWELL (TF)   MTM Enterprises, 1981

JOHN LLEWELLYN MOXEY *

b. 1920 - Burlingham, England
Personal Manager: Helen Kushnick, General Management Corporation - Beverly Hills,
  213/274-8805

HORROR HOTEL *CITY OF THE DEAD*   Trans-World, 1960, British
FOXHOLE IN CAIRO   Paramount, 1961, British
DEATH TRAP   Anglo-Amalgamated, 1962, British
THE 20,000 POUND KISS   Anglo-Amalgamated, 1963, British
RICOCHET   Warner-Pathe, 1963, British
DOWNFALL   Embassy, 1964, British
FACE OF A STRANGER   Warner-Pathe, 1964, British
STRANGLER'S WEB   Embassy, 1965, British
PSYCHO-CIRCUS *CIRCUS OF FEAR*   American International, 1967, British
THE TORMENTOR   ITC, 1967, British
SAN FRANCISCO INTERNATIONAL AIRPORT (TF)   Universal TV, 1970
THE HOUSE THAT WOULD NOT DIE (TF)   Aaron Spelling Productions,
  1970
ESCAPE (TF)   Paramount TV, 1971
THE LAST CHILD (TF)   Aaron Spelling Productions, 1971
A TASTE OF EVIL (TF)   Aaron Spelling Productions, 1971
THE DEATH OF ME YET! (TF)   Aaron Spelling Productions, 1971
THE NIGHT STALKER (TF)   ABC, Inc., 1972
HARDCASE (TF)   Hanna-Barbera Productions, 1972
THE BOUNTY MAN (TF)   ABC Circle Films, 1972
HOME FOR THE HOLIDAYS (TF)   ABC Circle Films, 1972
GENESIS II (TF)   Warner Bros. TV, 1973
THE STRANGE AND DEADLY OCCURENCE (TF)   Metromedia Productions,
  1974
WHERE HAVE ALL THE PEOPLE GONE? (TF)   Metromedia Productions,
  1974
FOSTER AND LAURIE (TF)   Charles Fries Productions, 1975
CHARLIE'S ANGELS (TF)   Spelling-Goldberg Productions, 1976
CONSPIRACY OF TERROR (TF)   Lorimar Productions, 1976
NIGHTMARE IN BADHAM COUNTY (TF)   ABC Circle Films, 1976
SMASH-UP ON INTERSTATE 5 (TF)   Filmways, 1976
PANIC IN ECHO PARK (TF)   Edgar J. Scherick Associates, 1977
INTIMATE STRANGERS (TF)   Charles Fries Productions, 1977
THE PRESIDENT'S MISTRESS (TF)   Stephen Friedman/King's Road
  Productions, 1978
THE COURAGE AND THE PASSION (TF)   David Gerber Company/Columbia
  TV, 1978
SANCTUARY OF FEAR (TF)   Marble Arch Productions, 1979
THE POWER WITHIN (TF)   Aaron Spelling Productions, 1979
THE SOLITARY MAN (TF)   Universal TV, 1979
EBONY, IVORY AND JADE (TF)   Frankel Films, 1979
THE CHILDREN OF AN LAC (TF)   Charles Fries Productions, 1980
THE MATING SEASON (TF)   Highgate Pictures, 1980
NO PLACE TO HIDE (TF)   Metromedia Producers Corporation, 1981
THE VIOLATION OF SARAH McDAVID (TF)   CBS Entertainment, 1981
KILLJOY (TF)   Lorimar Productions, 1981

continued

JOHN LLEWELLYN MOXEY*—continued

I, DESIRE (TF)   Green-Epstein Productions/Columbia TV, 1982
THE CRADLE WILL FALL (TF)   Cates Films Inc./Procter & Gamble
    Productions, 1983
THROUGH NAKED EYES (TF)   Charles Fries Productions, 1983

ALLAN MOYLE*

Home: 49 Park Avenue, New York, NY 10016, 212/685-0823
Messages: 212/279-9321
Agent: John Gaines, APA - Los Angeles, 213/273-0744

MONTREAL MAIN   co-director with Frank Vitale & Maxine McGillivray,
    President Films/Canadian Film Development Corporation, 1978, Canadian
THE RUBBER GUN   Schuman-Katzka, 1978, Canadian
TIMES SQUARE   AFD, 1980

RUSSELL MULCAHY

Contact: British Academy of Film & Television Arts, 195 Piccadilly, London W1,
    England, 01/734-0022

DEREK AND CLIVE GET THE HORN (FD)   Peter Cook Productions, 1981,
    British
RAZORBACK   Warner Bros., 1984, Australian

ROBERT MULLIGAN*

b. August 23, 1925 - Bronx, New York
Agent: Stan Kamen, William Morris Agency - Beverly Hills, 213/274-7451

FEAR STRIKES OUT   Paramount, 1957
THE RAT RACE   Paramount, 1960
THE GREAT IMPOSTER   Universal, 1961
COME SEPTEMBER   Universal, 1961
THE SPIRAL ROAD   Universal, 1962
TO KILL A MOCKINGBIRD ★   Universal, 1962
LOVE WITH THE PROPER STRANGER   Paramount, 1964
BABY, THE RAIN MUST FALL   Columbia, 1965
INSIDE DAISY CLOVER   Warner Bros., 1966
UP THE DOWN STAIRCASE   Warner Bros., 1967
THE STALKING MOON   National General, 1969
THE PURSUIT OF HAPPINESS   Columbia, 1971
SUMMER OF '42   Warner Bros., 1971
THE OTHER   20th Century-Fox, 1972
THE NICKEL RIDE   20th Century-Fox, 1975
BLOODBROTHERS   Warner Bros., 1979
SAME TIME, NEXT YEAR   Universal, 1979
KISS ME GOODBYE   20th Century-Fox, 1982

JIMMY T. MURAKAMI

Business: Murakami/Wolf/Swenson, Inc., 1463 Tamarind Avenue, Hollywood,
    CA 90028, 213/462-6473

BATTLE BEYOND THE STARS   New World, 1979

GEOFF MURPHY

Contact: New Zealand Film Commission, P.O. Box 11-546, Wellington, New Zealand,
    4/72-2360

WILDMAN   New Zealand
GOODBYE PORK PIE   The Samuel Goldwyn Company, 1981, New Zealand
UTU   Utu Productions/New Zealand Film Commission, 1983, New Zealand

DON MURRAY

b. July 29, 1929 - Hollywood, California
Agent: F.A.M.E. - Los Angeles, 213/656-7590

THE CROSS AND THE SWITCHBLADE   Dick Ross, 1970

FLOYD MUTRUX *

Contact: Directors Guild of America - Los Angeles, 213/656-1220

DUSTY AND SWEETS McGEE   Warner Bros., 1971
aloha, bobby and rose   Columbia, 1975
AMERICAN HOT WAX   Paramount, 1978
THE HOLLYWOOD KNIGHTS   Columbia, 1980

ALAN MYERSON *

Agent: David Gersh/Scott Harris, The Gersh Agency - Beverly Hills, 213/274-6611
Personal Manager: Shapiro-West - Beverly Hills, 213/278-8896

STEELYARD BLUES   Warner Bros., 1973
THE LOVE BOAT (TF)   co-director with Richard Kinon, Douglas S. Cramer
    Productions, 1976
PRIVATE LESSONS   Jensen Farley Pictures, 1981

ARTHUR H. NADEL *

Business: Filmation Studios, 18107 Sherman Way, Reseda, CA 91335, 213/345-
    7414
Attorney: Robert Kehr, Kehr, Siegel & Brifman - Los Angeles, 213/552-9681

CLAMBAKE   United Artists, 1967
UNDERGROUND   United Artists, 1970

IVAN NAGY *

b. January 23, 1938 - Budapest, Hungary
Business: American Skiagraph, Inc., 10128 Empyrean Way, Los Angeles,
    CA 90067, 213/552-4724
Agent: Jeff Cooper/Robby Wald, The Cooper Agency - Los Angeles, 213/277-8422

BAD CHARLESTON CHARLIE   International Cinema, 1973
MONEY, MARBLES AND CHALK   American International, 1973
FIVE MINUTES OF FREEDOM   Cannon, 1973
DEADLY HERO   Avco Embassy, 1976
MIND OVER MURDER (TF)   Paramount TV, 1979
ONCE UPON A SPY (TF)   David Gerber Company/Columbia TV, 1980
MIDNIGHT LACE (TF)   Four R Productions/Universal TV, 1981

continued

IVAN NAGY*—continued
A GUN IN THE HOUSE (TF)   Channing-Debin-Locke Company, 1981
JANE DOE (TF)   ITC, 1983

M I C H A E L   N A N K I N *

Home: 4333 Vantage Avenue, Studio City, CA 91604, 213/769-2863
Agent: Linne Radmin, The Associates - Los Angeles, 213/273-1133

MIDNIGHT MADNESS   co-director with David Wechter, Buena Vista, 1981

S I L V I O   N A R I Z Z A N O

b. February 8, 1928 - Montreal, Quebec, Canada
Home: 8400 De Longpre, Los Angeles, CA 90069, 213/654-9548
Agent: William Morris Agency - Beverly Hills, 213/274-7451

DIE! DIE! MY DARLING! *FANATIC*   Columbia, 1965, British
GEORGY GIRL   Columbia, 1967, British
BLUE   Paramount, 1968, British
LOOT   Cinevision, 1972, British
REDNECK   International Amusements, 1975, British-Italian
THE SKY IS FALLING   1976, Canadian
WHY SHOOT THE TEACHER   Quartet, 1977, Canadian
COME BACK, LITTLE SHEBA (TF)   Granada TV, 1977, British
THE CLASS OF MISS MacMICHAEL   Brut Productions, 1979, British
STAYING ON (TF)   Granada TV, 1980, British
CHOICES   1981, Canadian

G R E G O R Y   N A V A

EL NORTE   Cinecom International, 1983

C A L   N A Y L O R *

Home: 17606 Posetano Road, Pacific Palisades, CA 90272, 213/454-7229

DIRT   co-director with Eric Karson, American Cinema, 1979

R O N A L D   N E A M E *

b. April 23, 1911 - London, England
Home: 2317 Kimridge Road, Beverly Hills, CA 90210
Agent: John Gaines, APA - Los Angeles, 213/273-0744

TAKE MY LIFE   Eagle Lion, 1947, British
THE GOLDEN SALAMANDER   Eagle Lion, 1950, British
THE PROMOTER *THE CARD*   Universal, 1952, British
MAN WITH A MILLION *THE MILLION POUND NOTE*   United Artists, 1954, British
THE MAN WHO NEVER WAS   20th Century-Fox, 1956, British
THE SEVENTH SIN   MGM, 1957
WINDOM'S WAY   Rank, 1958, British
THE HORSE'S MOUTH   United Artists, 1959, British
TUNES OF GLORY   Lopert, 1960, British
ESCAPE FROM ZAHRAIN   Paramount, 1962
I COULD GO ON SINGING   United Artists, 1963, British
THE CHALK GARDEN   Universal, 1964, British
MISTER MOSES   United Artists, 1965, British
A MAN COULD GET KILLED   co-directed with Cliff Owen, Universal, 1966
GAMBIT   Universal, 1966
THE PRIME OF MISS JEAN BRODIE   20th Century-Fox, 1969, British
SCROOGE   National General, 1970, British
THE POSEIDON ADVENTURE   20th Century-Fox, 1972
THE ODESSA FILE   Columbia, 1974, British-West German
METEOR   American International, 1979
HOPSCOTCH   Avco Embassy, 1980
FIRST MONDAY IN OCTOBER   Paramount, 1981

H A L   N E E D H A M *

b. March 6, 1931 - Memphis, Tennessee
Business: 3518 Cahuenga Blvd. West, Hollywood, CA 90068, 213/876-8052
Agent: David Wardlow, Chasin-Park-Citron - Los Angeles, 213/273-7190

SMOKEY AND THE BANDIT   Universal, 1977
HOOPER   Warner Bros., 1978
THE VILLAIN   Columbia, 1979
DEATH CAR ON THE FREEWAY (TF)   Shpetner Productions, 1979
STUNTS UNLIMITED (TF)   Lawrence Gordon Productions/Paramount TV, 1980
SMOKEY AND THE BANDIT, PART II   Universal, 1980
THE CANNONBALL RUN   20th Century-Fox, 1981
MEGAFORCE   20th Century-Fox, 1982
STROKER ACE   Universal, 1983
CANNONBALL II   Warner Bros., 1984

J E A N   N E G U L E S C O *

b. February 26, 1900 - Craiova, Romania
Business Manager: Harold B. Weiser - Canoga Park, 213/998-2536

SINGAPORE WOMAN   Warner Bros., 1941
THE MASK OF DIMITRIOS   Warner Bros., 1944
THE CONSPIRATORS   Warner Bros., 1944
THREE STRANGERS   Warner Bros., 1946
NOBODY LIVES FOREVER   Warner Bros., 1946
HUMORESQUE   Warner Bros., 1947
DEEP VALLEY   Warner Bros., 1947
JOHNNY BELINDA ★   Warner Bros., 1948
ROAD HOUSE   20th Century-Fox, 1948
THE FORBIDDEN STREET *BRITANNIA MEWS*   20th Century-Fox, 1949
UNDER MY SKIN   20th Century-Fox, 1950
THREE CAME HOME   20th Century-Fox, 1950
THE MUDLARK   20th Century-Fox, 1950
TAKE CARE OF MY LITTLE GIRL   20th Century-Fox, 1951
PHONE CALL FROM A STRANGER   20th Century-Fox, 1952
LYDIA BAILEY   20th Century-Fox, 1952
LURE OF THE WILDERNESS   20th Century-Fox, 1952
O. HENRY'S FULL HOUSE   co-director with Howard Hawks, Henry King &
      Henry Koster, 20th Century-Fox, 1952
TITANIC   20th Century-Fox, 1953
HOW TO MARRY A MILLIONAIRE   20th Century-Fox, 1953
SCANDAL AT SCOURIE   MGM, 1953
THREE COINS IN THE FOUNTAIN   20th Century-Fox, 1954
A WOMAN'S WORLD   20th Century-Fox, 1954
DADDY LONG LEGS   20th Century-Fox, 1955
THE RAINS OF RANCHIPUR   20th Century-Fox, 1955
BOY ON A DOLPHIN   20th Century-Fox, 1957
THE GIFT OF LOVE   20th Century-Fox, 1958
A CERTAIN SMILE   20th Century-Fox, 1958
COUNT YOUR BLESSINGS   MGM, 1959
THE BEST OF EVERYTHING   20th Century-Fox, 1959
JESSICA   United Artists, 1962, U.S.-Italian-French
THE PLEASURE SEEKERS   20th Century-Fox, 1964
HELLO - GOODBYE   20th Century-Fox, 1970
THE INVINCIBLE SIX   Continental, 1970, U.S.-Iranian

D A V I D   N E L S O N *

b. October 24, 1936 - New York, New York
Business: Western International Media, 8732 Sunset Blvd., Los Angeles, CA 90038,
      213/659-5711

DEATH SCREAMS   ABA Productions, 1981
LAST PLANE OUT   New World, 1983

GARY NELSON *

Agent: CAA - Los Angeles, 213/277-4545

MOLLY AND LAWLESS JOHN   Producers Distribution Corporation, 1972
SANTEE   Crown International, 1973
THE GIRL ON THE LATE, LATE SHOW (TF)   Screen Gems/Columbia TV,
    1974
MEDICAL STORY (TF)   David Gerber Company/Columbia TV, 1975
PANACHE (TF)   Warner Bros. TV, 1976
WASHINGTON: BEHIND CLOSED DOORS (MS) ☆   Paramount TV, 1977
FREAKY FRIDAY   Buena Vista, 1977
TO KILL A COP (TF)   David Gerber Company/Columbia, TV, 1978
THE BLACK HOLE   Buena Vista, 1979
THE PRIDE OF JESSE HALLAM (TF)   The Konigsberg Company, 1981
SEVEN BRIDES FOR SEVEN BROTHERS (TF)   David Gerber Company/MGM-
    UA TV, 1982
JIMMY THE KID   New World, 1983
MURDER IN COWETA COUNTY (TF)   Telecom Entertainment/The
    International Picture Show Co., 1983
MICKEY SPILLANE'S 'MURDER ME, MURDER YOU' (TF)   Jay Bernstein
    Productions/Columbia TV, 1983
FOR LOVE AND HONOR (TF)   David Gerber Company/MGM-UA TV, 1983

GENE NELSON *

(Gene Berg)

b. March 24, 1920 - Seattle, Washington
Home: 3431 Vinton Avenue, Los Angeles, CA 90034, 213/837-0484
Agent: Contemporary-Korman Artists - Beverly Hills, 213/278-8250

HAND OF DEATH   20th Century-Fox, 1962
HOOTENANNY HOOT   MGM, 1962
KISSIN' COUSINS   MGM, 1964
YOUR CHEATIN' HEART   MGM, 1964
HARUM SCARUM   MGM, 1965
THE COOL ONES   Warner Bros., 1967
WAKE ME WHEN THE WAR IS OVER (TF)   Thomas-Spelling Productions,
    1969
THE LETTERS (TF)   co-director with Paul Krasny, ABC Circle Films, 1973

RALPH NELSON *

b. August 12, 1916 - New York, New York
Business: Rainbow Productions, 1514 Sinalda Drive, Montecito, CA 94022
Agent: Wilt Melnick, Chasin-Park-Citron - Los Angeles, 213/273-7190
Business Manager: Howard Bernstein, Kaufman & Bernstein, 1900 Avenue of the
    Stars, Los Angeles, CA 90067, 213/277-1900

REQUIEM FOR A HEAVYWEIGHT   Columbia, 1962
LILIES OF THE FIELD   United Artists, 1963
SOLDIER IN THE RAIN   Allied Artists, 1963
FATE IS THE HUNTER   20th Century-Fox, 1964
FATHER GOOSE   Universal, 1964
ONCE A THIEF   MGM, 1965
DUEL AT DIABLO   United Artists, 1966
COUNTERPOINT   Universal, 1968
CHARLY   Cinerama Releasing Corporation, 1968
... tick ... tick ... tick ...   MGM, 1970
SOLDIER BLUE   Avco Embassy, 1970
FLIGHT OF THE DOVES   Columbia, 1971, British
THE WRATH OF GOD   MGM, 1972
THE WILBY CONSPIRACY   United Artists, 1975, British
EMBRYO   Cine Artists, 1976
A HERO AIN'T NOTHIN' BUT A SANDWICH   New World, 1977
LADY OF THE HOUSE (TF)   co-director with Vincent Sherman, Metromedia
    Productions, 1978
BECAUSE HE'S MY FRIEND   1979
CHRISTMAS LILIES OF THE FIELD (TF)   Rainbow Productions/Osmond
    Productions, 1979
YOU CAN'T GO HOME AGAIN (TF)   CBS Entertainment, 1979

AVI NESHER

Contact: Israel Film Centre, Ministry of Tourism & Trade, 30 Agron Street, P.O. Box 299, Jerusalem 94190, Israel, 02/210433

THE TROUPE *HALAHAKA*   Eastways Productions, 1978, Israeli
DIZENGOFF 99   Shapira Films, 1979, Israeli
SHE   Continental Motion Pictures, 1983, Italian-U.S.

MIKE NEWELL

b. 1942
Address: 30 Cantelowes Road, London NW1, England, 01/485-1584
Agent: Duncan Heath Associates, 57 Redliffe Road, London SW10, England

THE MAN IN THE IRON MASK (TF)   Norman Rosemont Productions/ITC, 1977, U.S.-British
THE AWAKENING   Orion/Warner Bros., 1980
BLOOD FEUD (TF)   20th Century-Fox TV/Glickman-Selznick Productions, 1983
BAD BLOOD   Southern Pictures/New Zealand Film Commission, 1983, New Zealand

JOHN NEWLAND *

b. November 23, 1917 - Cincinnati, Ohio
Business: The Factor-Newland Production Corporation, 1438 Gower Street - Suite 250, Los Angeles, CA 90028, 213/467-1143
Agent: Herb Tobias & Associates - Los Angeles, 213/277-6211

THAT NIGHT   Universal, 1957
THE VIOLATORS   Universal, 1957
THE SPY WITH MY FACE   MGM, 1966
MY LOVER, MY SON   MGM, 1970, British
THE DEADLY HUNT (TF)   Four Star International, 1971
CRAWLSPACE (TF)   Titus Productions, 1972
DON'T BE AFRAID OF THE DARK (TF)   Lorimar Productions, 1972
WHO FEARS THE DEVIL *THE LEGEND OF HILLBILLY JOHN*   Jack H. Harris Enterprises, 1974
A SENSITIVE, PASSIONATE MAN (TF)   Factor-Newland Production Corporation, 1977
OVERBOARD (TF)   Factor-Newland Production Corporation, 1978
THE SUICIDE'S WIFE (TF)   Factor-Newland Production Corporation, 1979

ANTHONY NEWLEY

b. September 24, 1931 - London, England
Agent: ICM - Los Angeles, 213/550-4000

CAN HIERONYMOUS MERKIN EVER FORGET MERCY HUMPPE AND FIND TRUE HAPPINESS?   Regional, 1969, British
SUMMERTREE   Columbia, 1971

PAUL NEWMAN *

b. January 26, 1925 - Cleveland, Ohio
Business Manager: Traubner, Flynn, Philpott, Murphy & Kress, 2349 Century Park East - Suite 2500, Los Angeles, CA 90067, 213/277-3000

RACHEL, RACHEL   Warner Bros., 1968
SOMETIMES A GREAT NOTION *NEVER GIVE AN INCH*   Universal, 1971
THE EFFECT OF GAMMA RAYS ON MAN-IN-THE-MOON MARIGOLDS   20th Century-Fox, 1973
THE SHADOW BOX (TF)☆   The Shadow Box Film Company, 1980
HARRY AND SON   Orion, 1984

MIKE NICHOLS *
(Michael Igor Peschkowsky)

b. November 6, 1931 - Berlin, Germany
Agent: Sam Cohn, ICM - New York City, 212/556-6810
Attorney: Marvin B. Meyer, Rosenfeld, Meyer & Susman - Beverly Hills, 213/858-7700

WHO'S AFRAID OF VIRGINIA WOOLF? ★   Warner Bros., 1966
THE GRADUATE ★★   Avco Embassy, 1967
CATCH-22   Paramount, 1970
CARNAL KNOWLEDGE   Avco Embassy, 1971
THE DAY OF THE DOLPHIN   Avco Embassy, 1973
THE FORTUNE   Columbia, 1975
GILDA LIVE (FD)   Warner Bros., 1980
SILKWOOD   20th Century-Fox, 1983

ALLAN NICHOLLS

Contact: Writers Guild of America, West - Los Angeles, 213/550-1000

DEAD RINGER   Feature Films, 1982

JACK NICHOLSON *

b. April 22, 1937 - Neptune, New Jersey
Agent: Sandy Bresler, The Artists Agency - Los Angeles, 213/277-7779
Business Manager: Guild Management Corporation - Los Angeles, 213/277-9711

DRIVE, HE SAID   Columbia, 1971
GOIN' SOUTH   Paramount, 1979

PAUL NICOLAS
(Lutz Schaarwaechter)

BAD BLOOD JULIE DARLING   Twin Continental, 1982, Canadian-West German
CHAINED HEAT   Jensen Farley Pictures, 1983

GEORGE T. NIERENBERG

b. Roslyn Heights, New York

THE HOLLOW   1975
NO MAPS ON MY TAPS (FD)   1980
SAY AMEN, SOMEBODY (FD)   United Artists Classics, 1983

ROB NILSSON

NORTHERN LIGHTS   co-director with John Hanson, Cine Manifest, 1979
ON THE EDGE   Alliance Films, 1984

LEONARD NIMOY *

b. 1932 - Boston, Massachusetts
Agent: Merritt Blake, The Blake Agency - Beverly Hills, 213/278-6885

STAR TREK III: THE SEARCH FOR SPOCK   Paramount, 1984

B.W.L. NORTON *
(William Lloyd Norton)

b. August 13, 1943 - California
Agent: John Ptak, William Morris Agency - Beverly Hills, 213/274-7451

CISCO PIKE   Columbia, 1971
GARGOYLES (TF)   Tomorrow Entertainment, 1972
MORE AMERICAN GRAFFITI   Universal, 1979

NOEL NOSSECK *

Agent: David Gersh, The Gersh Agency - Beverly Hills, 213/274-6611

BEST FRIENDS   Crown International, 1973
LAS VEGAS LADY   Crown International, 1976
YOUNGBLOOD   American International, 1978
DREAMER   20th Century-Fox, 1979
KING OF THE MOUNTAIN   Universal, 1981
RETURN OF THE REBELS (TF)   Moonlight Productions/Filmways, 1981
THE FIRST TIME (TF)   Moonlight Productions, 1982
NIGHT PARTNERS (TF)   Moonlight Productions II, 1983

PHILLIP NOYCE

Agent: Cameron's Management, 120 Victoria Street, Kings Cross, NSW, 2011,
   Australia, 02/358-6433

BACKROADS   Cinema Ventures, 1978, Australian
NEWSFRONT   New Yorker, 1979, Australian
HEATWAVE   New Line Cinema, 1982, Australian

VICTOR NUÑEZ

GAL YOUNG UN   Nuñez Films, 1979
FLASH OF GREEN (TF)   Nuñez Films, 1984

TREVOR NUNN

b. January 14, 1940 - Ipswich, Suffolk, England
Contact: Directors Guild of Great Britain, 56 Whitfield Street, London W1, England,
   01/580-9592

HEDDA   Brut Productions, 1975, British

CHRISTIAN NYBY III *

b. June 1, 1941 - Glendale, California
Agent: Barry Perelman - Los Angeles, 213/275-6193

THE RANGERS (TF)   Universal TV/Mark VII Ltd., 1974
PINE CANYON IS BURNING (TF)   Universal TV, 1977

ARCH OBOLER

b. December 7, 1909 - Chicago, Illinois
Contact: Writers Guild of America, West - Los Angeles, 213/550-1000

BEWITCHED   MGM, 1945
STRANGE HOLIDAY   Producers Releasing Corporation. 1946

ARCH OBOLER continued

THE ARNELO AFFAIR   MGM, 1947
FIVE   Columbia, 1951
BWANA DEVIL   United Artists, 1952
THE TWONKY   United Artists, 1953
1 + 1: EXPLORING THE KINSEY REPORTS (FD)   1961, U.S.-Canadian
THE BUBBLE   Oboler Films, 1967
DOMO ARIGATO (FD)   Oboler Films, 1972

JEFFREY OBROW

PRANKS   co-director with Stephen Carpenter, New Image, 1982
THE DORM THAT DRIPPED BLOOD   co-director with Stephen Carpenter,
    New Image Releasing, 1983
THE POWER   co-director with Stephen Carpenter, Artists Releasing Corporation/
    Film Ventures International, 1984

JACK O'CONNELL

GREENWICH VILLAGE STORY   Lion International, 1963
REVOLUTION (FD)   Lopert, 1968
SWEDISH FLY GIRLS *CHRISTA*   American International, 1971, U.S.-Danish

JAMES O'CONNOLLY

Address: 61 Edith Grove, London SW10, England, 01/352-1242

THE HI-JACKERS   Butcher, 1964, British
SMOKESCREEN   Butcher, 1964, British
THE LITTLE ONES   Columbia, 1965, British
BERSERK!   Columbia, 1968, British
THE VALLEY OF GWANGI   Warner Bros., 1969, British
SOPHIE'S PLACE *CROOKS AND CORONETS*   Warner Bros., 1969, British
HORROR ON SNAPE ISLAND *BEYOND THE FOG*   Fanfare, 1972, British
MISTRESS PAMELA   Fanfare, 1974, British

MICHAEL O'DONOGHUE*

Agent: David Kennedy, ICM - New York City, 212/556-5600
Business Manager: Barry Secunda, Project X, 1619 Broadway - Suite 915, New
    York, NY 10019, 212/247-4790

MR. MIKE'S MONDO VIDEO   New Line Cinema, 1979

GERRY O'HARA

b. 1924 - Baston, Lincolnshire, England
Address: 8 Broomhouse Road, London SW6, England, 01/736-7869
Agent: CCA, 29 Dawes Road, London SW6, England, 01/381-3551

MODELS, INC. *THAT KIND OF GIRL*   Mutual, 1963, British
A GAME FOR THREE LOSERS   Embassy, 1963, British
THE PLEASURE GIRLS   Times, 1965, British
MAROC 7   Paramount, 1966, British
AMSTERDAM AFFAIR   Lippert, 1968, British
FIDELIA   1970, British
ALL THE RIGHT NOISES   20th Century-Fox, 1971, British
THE BRUTE   Rank, 1976, British
LEOPARD IN THE SNOW   New World, 1978, Canadian-British
THE BITCH   Brent Walker Productions, 1979, British
FANNY HILL   Playboy Enterprises, 1983, British

MICHAEL O'HERLIHY *

b. April 1, 1928 - Dublin, Ireland
Agent: Contemporary-Korman Artists - Beverly Hills, 213/278-8250

THE FIGHTING PRINCE OF DONEGAL   Buena Vista, 1966, British-U.S.
THE ONE AND ONLY GENUINE, ORIGINAL FAMILY BAND   Buena Vista, 1967
SMITH!   Buena Vista, 1969
DEADLY HARVEST (TF)   CBS, Inc., 1972
YOUNG PIONEERS (TF)   ABC Circle Films, 1976
KISS ME, KILL ME (TF)   Columbia TV, 1976
YOUNG PIONEERS' CHRISTMAS (TF)   ABC Circle Films, 1976
PETER LUNDY AND THE MEDICINE HAT STALLION (TF) Ed
    Friendly   Productions, 1977
BACKSTAIRS AT THE WHITE HOUSE (MS)   Ed Friendly Productions, 1979
THE FLAME IS LOVE (TF)   Ed Friendly Productions/Friendly-O'Herlihy Ltd., 1979
DALLAS COWBOYS CHEERLEADERS II (TF)   Aubrey-Hamner Productions, 1980
DETOUR TO TERROR (TF)   Orenthal Productions/Playboy Productions/Columbia TV, 1980
THE GREAT CASH GIVEAWAY GETAWAY (TF)   Penthouse Productions/Cine Guarantors, Inc., 1980
CRY OF THE INNOCENT (TF)   Tara Productions, 1980
DESPERATE VOYAGE (TF)   Barry Weitz Films/Joe Wizan TV Productions, 1980
A TIME FOR MIRACLES (TF)   ABC Circle Films, 1980
THE MILLION DOLLAR FACE (TF)   Nephi-Hamner Productions, 1981
I MARRIED WYATT EARP (TF)   Osmond TV Productions, 1983

TOM O'HORGAN *

Contact: Directors Guild of America - New York City, 212/581-0370

FUTZ   Commonwealth United, 1969
RHINOCEROS   American Film Theatre, 1974

JOEL OLIANSKY *

b. October 11, 1935 - New York, New York
Agent: Adams, Ray & Rosenberg - Los Angeles, 213/278-3000

THE COMPETITION   Columbia, 1980

LAURENCE OLIVIER

b. May 22, 1907 - Dorking, England
Address: 33/34 Chancery Lane, London WC2, England

HENRY V   Rank, 1945, British
HAMLET ★   Universal, 1946, British
RICHARD III   Lopert, 1956, British
THE PRINCE AND THE SHOWGIRL   Warner Bros., 1957, U.S.-British
THREE SISTERS   American Film Theatre, 1970, British

ERMANNO OLMI

b. July 24, 1931 - Bergamo, Italy
Contact: Ministry of Tourism & Education, Via Della Ferratella, No. 51, 00184 Rome, Italy, 06/7732

IL TEMPO SI E FERMATO   Sezione Cinema Edison Volta, 1959, Italian
THE SOUND OF TRUMPETS   Janus, 1961, Italian
THE FIANCES   Janus, 1963, Italian
AND THERE CAME A MAN   Brandon, 1965, Italian
UN CERTO GIORNO   Cinema Spa/Italnoleggio, 1968, Italian
I RECUPERANTI (TF)   RAI/Produzione Palumbo, 1969, Italian
DURANTE L'ESTATE (TF)   RAI, 1971, Italian
LA CIRCOSTANZA (TF)   RAI/Italnoleggio, 1974, Italian

continued

ERMANNO OLMI—continued

THE TREE OF WOODEN CLOGS   New Yorker, 1979, Italian, originally made
for television
KEEP WALKING   RAI/Gaumont, 1983, Italian-French
CAMMINACAMMINA   Grange Communications, 1983, Italian
MILANO '83 (FD)   1983, Italian·

R O N   O ' N E A L

b. September 1, 1937 - Utica, New York
Agent: 213/857-1234

SUPERFLY T.N.T.   Paramount, 1973

R O B E R T   V I N C E N T   O ' N E I L

Contact: Writers Guild of America, West - Los Angeles, 213/550-1000

ANGEL   New World, 1983

M A R C E L   O P H U L S

b. 1927 - Frankfurt, Germany
Contact: French Film Office, 745 Fifth Avenue, New York, NY 10151, 212/832-
8860

LOVE AT TWENTY   co-director with Francois Truffaut, Andrzej Wajda, Renzo
Rossellini & Shintaro Ishihara, Embassy, 1962, French-Italian-Japanese-Polish-
West German
BANANA PEEL   Pathe Contemporary, 1965, French-Italian
FEU A VOLONTE   1965, French-Italian
THE SORROW AND THE PITY (FD)   Cinema 5, 1972, French-Swiss-West
German
A SENSE OF LOSS (FD)   Cinema 5, 1972, U.S.-Swiss
THE MEMORY OF JUSTICE (FD)   Paramount, 1976, British-West German

N A G I S A   O S H I M A

b. March 31, 1932 - Kyoto, Japan
Contact: Directors Guild of Japan, Tsukada Building, 8-33 Udagawa-cho, Shibuya-ku,
Tokyo 150, Japan, 3/461-4411

A TOWN OF LOVE AND HOPE   Shochiku, 1959, Japanese
CRUEL STORY OF YOUTH   Shochiku, 1960, Japanese
THE SUN'S BURIAL   Shochiku, 1960, Japanese
NIGHT AND FOG IN JAPAN   Shochiku, 1960, Japanese
THE CATCH   Palace Productions/Taiho, 1961, Japanese
THE REVOLUTIONARY   Toei, 1962, Japanese
A SMALL CHILD'S FIRST ADVENTURE   Nissei Insurance Company, 1964,
Japanese
IT'S ME HERE, BELLETT   Society of Japanese Film Directors, 1964, Japanese
THE PLEASURES OF THE FLESH   Sozosha/Shochiku, 1965, Japanese
VIOLENCE AT NOON   Sozosha/Shochiku, 1966, Japanese
BAND OF NINJA   Sozosha/Art Theatre Guild, 1967, Japanese
A TREATISE IN JAPANESE BAWDY SONGS   Sozosha/Shochiku, 1967,
Japanese
JAPANESE SUMMER: DOUBLE SUICIDE   Sozosha/Shochiku, 1967, Japanese
DEATH BY HANGING   Grove Press, 1968, Japanese
THREE RESURRECTED DRUNKARDS   Sozosha/Shochiku, 1968, Japanese
DIARY OF A SHINJUKU BURGLAR   Grove Press, 1968, Japanese
BOY   Grove Press, 1969, Japanese
THE CEREMONY   New Yorker, 1974, Japanese
IN THE REALM OF THE SENSES   Surrogate Releasing, 1977, Japanese
EMPIRE OF PASSION *CORRIDA OF LOVE*   Barbary Coast, 1980, Japanese
MERRY CHRISTMAS, MR. LAWRENCE   Universal, 1983, British-Japanese

SAM O'STEEN *

b. November 6, 1923
Agent: The Ufland Agency - Beverly Hills, 213/273-9441
Business Manager: Robert Morgan, Tucker, Morgan & Martindale - Los Angeles,
213/274-0891

A BRAND NEW LIFE (TF)   Tomorrow Entertainment, 1973
I LOVE YOU, GOODBYE (TF)   Tomorrow Entertainment, 1974
QUEEN OF THE STARDUST BALLROOM (TF) ☆   Tomorrow Entertainment,
1975
HIGH RISK (TF)   Danny Thomas Productions/MGM TV, 1976
SPARKLE   Warner Bros., 1976
LOOK WHAT'S HAPPENED TO ROSEMARY'S BABY (TF)   Paramount TV,
1976
THE BEST LITTLE GIRL IN THE WORLD (TF)   Aaron Spelling Productions,
1981

GERD OSWALD *

b. June 9, 1916 - Berlin, Germany
Home: 237A Spalding Drive, Beverly Hills, CA 90212, 213/938-9436

A KISS BEFORE DYING   United Artists, 1956
THE BRASS LEGEND   United Artists, 1956
CRIME OF PASSION   United Artists, 1957
FURY AT SHOWDOWN   United Artists, 1957
VALERIE   United Artists, 1957
PARIS HOLIDAY   United Artists, 1958
SCREAMING MIMI   Columbia, 1958
AM TAG ALS DER REGEN KAM   1959, West German
BRAINWASHED   Allied Artists, 1960, West German
TEMPESTA SU CEYLON   co-director with Giovanni Roccardi, FICIT/Rapid Film,
1963, Italian-French
AGENT FOR H.A.R.M.   Universal, 1966
80 STEPS TO JONAH   Warner Bros., 1969
BUNNY O'HARE   American International, 1971
BIS ZUR BITTEREN NEIGE   1975, West German-Australian

GERARD OURY
(Max-Gerard Houry Tannenbaum)

b. April 29, 1919 - Paris, France
Contact: French Film Office, 745 Fifth Avenue, New York, NY 10151, 212/832-
8860

LA MAIN CHAUDE   Films de France, 1960, French
THE MENACE   Warner Bros., 1961, French
CRIME DOES NOT PAY   Embassy, 1962, French-Italian
THE SUCKER   Royal Films International, 1966, French-Italian
DON'T LOOK NOW ... WE'RE BEING SHOT AT *LA GRANDE
VADROVILLE*   Cinepix, 1966, French-British
THE BRAIN   Paramount, 1969, French-Italian
DELUSIONS OF GRANDEUR   Joseph Green Pictures, 1971, French
THE MAD ADVENTURES OF 'RABBI' JACOB   20th Century-Fox, 1974,
French-Italian
LA CARAPATE   Gaumont, 1978, French
LE COUP DU PARAPLUIE   Gaumont, 1980, French
L'AS DES AS   Gaumont/Cerito Rene Chateau, 1982, French-West German

CLIFF OWEN

b. April 22, 1919 - London, England
Address: 20 Marlborough Place, London NW8, England
Contact: Directors Guild of Great Britain, 56 Whitfield Street, London W1, 01/580-
9592

OFFBEAT   1961, British
A PRIZE OF ARMS   British Lion, 1961, British
THE WRONG ARM OF THE LAW   Continental, 1963, British
A MAN COULD GET KILLED   co-director with Ronald Neame, Universal, 1966
THAT RIVIERA TOUCH   Continental, 1966, British

continued

CLIFF OWEN—continued

WHAT HAPPENED AT CAMPO GRANDE? *THE MAGNIFICENT TWO*   Alan Enterprises, 1967, British
THE VENGEANCE OF SHE   20th Century-Fox, 1968, British
STEPTOE AND SON   MGM-EMI, 1972, British
OOH ... YOU ARE AWFUL   Lion International, 1973, British
NO SEX PLEASE - WE'RE BRITISH   Columbia-Warner, 1973, British
THE BAWDY ADVENTURES OF TOM JONES   Universal, 1975, British
GET CHARLIE TULLY   1976, British

F R A N K   O Z

Business: ATV Studios, Elstree, Hertfordshire, England

THE DARK CRYSTAL   co-director with Jim Henson, Universal/AFD, 1982, British
THE MUPPETS IN MANHATTAN   Tri-Star/Columbia, 1984

A N T H O N Y   P A G E *

b. September 21, 1935 - Bangalore, India
Agent: Adams, Ray & Rosenberg - Los Angeles, 213/278-3000
Business Manager: Richard M. Rosenthal - Los Angeles, 213/820-8585

INADMISSABLE EVIDENCE   Paramount, 1968, British
ALPHA BETA   Cine III, 1976, British
F. SCOTT FITZGERALD IN HOLLYWOOD (TF)   Titus Productions, 1976
I NEVER PROMISED YOU A ROSE GARDEN   New World, 1977
ABSOLUTION   Enterprise Pictures, 1979, British
THE LADY VANISHES   Rank, 1979, British
THE PATRICIA NEAL STORY (TF)   co-director with Anthony Harvey, Lawrence Schiller Productions, 1981
BILL (TF)   Alan Landsburg Productions, 1981
JOHNNY BELINDA (TF)   Dick Berg-Stonehenge Productions/Lorimar Productions, 1982
GRACE KELLY (TF)   The Kota Company/Embassy TV, 1983
BILL: ON HIS OWN (TF)   Alan Landsburg Productions, 1983

A L A N   J .   P A K U L A *

b. April 7, 1928 - New York, New York
Agent: Stan Kamen, William Morris Agency - Beverly Hills, 213/274-7451
Business Manager: The Pakula Company, 10889 Wilshire Blvd., Los Angeles, CA 90024, 213/208-3046

THE STERILE CUCKOO   Paramount, 1969
KLUTE   Warner Bros., 1971
LOVE AND PAIN and the whole damned thing   Columbia, 1973, British-U.S.

continued

ALAN J. PAKULA*—continued
THE PARALLAX VIEW   Paramount, 1974
ALL THE PRESIDENT'S MEN ★   Warner Bros., 1976
COMES A HORSEMAN   United Artists, 1978
STARTING OVER   Paramount, 1979
ROLLOVER   Orion/Warner Bros., 1981
SOPHIE'S CHOICE   Universal/AFD, 1982

T O N Y   P A L M E R

Address: 4 Kensington Park Gardens, London W11, England
Contact: Directors Guild of Great Britain, 56 Whitfield Street, London W1, England,
    01/580-9592

200 MOTELS   co-director with Frank Zappa, United Artists, 1971, British
BIRD ON A WIRE (FD)   EMI, 1974, British
THE SPACE MOVIE (FD)   International Harmony, 1980, British
WAGNER (MS)   London Trust Cultural Productions/RM Productions/Magyar TV,
    1983, British-Hungarian

B R U C E   P A L T R O W *

Business: MTM Enterprises, 4024 Radford Avenue, Studio City, CA   91604, 213/
    760-5000
Agent: Lee Gabler, ICM - Los Angeles, 213/550-4000
Attorney: Ken Meyer, Rosenfeld, Meyer & Susman - Beverly Hills, 213/858-7700

A LITTLE SEX   Universal, 1982

N O R M A N   P A N A M A *

b. April 21, 1914 - Chicago, Illinois
Agent: Mitchell Kaplan, Kaplan-Stahler Agency - Los Angeles, 213/653-4483

THE REFORMER AND THE REDHEAD   co-director with Melvin Frank, MGM,
    1950
STRICTLY DISHONORABLE   co-director with Melvin Frank, 1951
CALLAWAY WENT THATAWAY   co-director with Melvin Frank, MGM, 1951
ABOVE AND BEYOND   co-director with Melvin Frank, MGM, 1952
KNOCK ON WOOD   co-director with Melvin Frank, Paramount, 1954
THE COURT JESTER   co-director with Melvin Frank, Paramount, 1956
THAT CERTAIN FEELING   co-director with Melvin Frank, Paramount, 1956
THE TRAP   Paramount, 1959
THE ROAD TO HONG KONG   United States, 1962
NOT WITH MY WIFE, YOU DON'T!   Warner Bros., 1966
HOW TO COMMIT MARRIAGE   Cinerama Releasing Corporation, 1969
THE MALTESE BIPPY   MGM, 1969
COFFEE, TEA OR ME? (TF)   CBS, Inc., 1973
I WILL, I WILL ... FOR NOW   20th Century-Fox, 1976
BARNABY AND ME   Trans-Atlantic Enterprises, 1978

H E N R Y   P A R I S

(see RADLEY METZGER)

J E R R Y   P A R I S *

b. July 25, 1925 - San Francisco, California
Agent: CAA - Los Angeles, 213/277-4545

DON'T RAISE THE BRIDGE - LOWER THE RIVER   Columbia, 1968, British
NEVER A DULL MOMENT   Buena Vista, 1968
HOW SWEET IT IS!   National General, 1968
VIVA MAX!   Commonwealth United, 1969
THE GRASSHOPPER   National General, 1969
BUT I DON'T WANT TO GET MARRIED! (TF)   Aaron Spelling Productions,
    1970
THE FEMINIST AND THE FUZZ (TF)   Screen Gems/Columbia TV, 1970
TWO ON A BENCH (TF)   Universal TV, 1971
WHAT'S A NICE GIRL LIKE YOU ... ?   Universal TV, 1971

continued

JERRY PARIS*—continued

STAR SPANGLED GIRL   Paramount, 1971
CALL HER MOM (TF)   Screen Gems/Columbia TV, 1972
EVIL ROY SLADE (TF)   Universal TV, 1972
THE COUPLE TAKES A WIFE (TF)   Universal TV, 1972
EVERY MAN NEEDS ONE (TF)   ABC Circle Films, 1972
ONLY WITH MARRIED MEN (TF)   Spelling-Goldberg Productions, 1974
HOW TO BREAK UP A HAPPY DIVORCE (TF)   Charles Fries Productions,
     1976
MAKE ME AN OFFER (TF)   ABC Circle Films, 1980
LEO AND LOREE   United Artists, 1980

ALAN PARKER*

b. Feburary 14, 1944 - London, England
Business: The Alan Parker Film Company, Pinewood Studios, Iver Heath,
     Buckinghamshire, England
Agent: William Morris Agency - Beverly Hills, 213/274-7451

BUGSY MALONE   Paramount, 1976, British
MIDNIGHT EXPRESS ★   Columbia, 1978, British
FAME   MGM/United Artists, 1980
SHOOT THE MOON   MGM/United Artists, 1982
PINK FLOYD - THE WALL   MGM/UA, 1982, British

GORDON PARKS*

b. November 30, 1912 - Fort Scott, Kansas
Home: 860 U.N. Plaza, New York, NY 10017
Agent: ICM - Los Angeles, 213/550-4000

THE LEARNING TREE   Warner Bros., 1969
SHAFT   MGM, 1971
SHAFT'S BIG SCORE!   MGM, 1972
THE SUPER COPS   MGM, 1974
LEADBELLY   Paramount, 1976
SUPER COPS (TF)   MGM TV, 1976

EDWARD PARONE*

Agent: Alan Iezman, William Morris Agency - Beverly Hills, 213/274-7451

PROMISE HIM ANYTHING ... (TF)   ABC Circle Films, 1975
LETTERS FROM FRANK (TF)   The Jozak Company/Cypress Point Productions,
     1979

ROBERT PARRISH*

b. January 4, 1916 - Columbus, Georgia
Business Manager: Jess S. Morgan & Co., 6420 Wilshire Blvd., Los Angeles, CA
     90048, 213/651-1601

CRY DANGER   RKO Radio, 1951
THE MOB   Columbia, 1951
THE SAN FRANCISCO STORY   Warner Bros., 1952
ASSIGNMENT - PARIS   Columbia, 1952
MY PAL GUS   20th Century-Fox, 1952
SHOOT FIRST *ROUGH SHOOT*   United Artists, 1953, British
THE PURPLE PLAIN   United Artists, 1954, British
LUCY GALLANT   Paramount, 1955
FIRE DOWN BELOW   Columbia, 1957
SADDLE THE WIND   MGM, 1957
THE WONDERFUL COUNTRY   United Artists, 1959
IN THE FRENCH STYLE   Columbia, 1963, French-U.S.
UP FROM THE BEACH   20th Century-Fox, 1965
CASINO ROYALE   co-director with Val Guest, Ken Hughes, John Huston &
     Joseph McGrath, Columbia, 1967, Columbia
THE BOBO   Warner Bros., 1967, British
DUFFY   Columbia, 1968, British
JOURNEY TO THE FAR SIDE OF THE SUN *DOPPELGANGER*   Universal,
     1969, British

continued

ROBERT PARRISH*—continued

A TOWN CALLED BASTARD *A TOWN CALLED HELL* Scotia
International, 1971, British-Spanish
THE DESTRUCTORS *THE MARSEILLES CONTRACT* American
International, 1974, British-French

GORAN PASKALJEVIC

SPECIAL TREATMENT New Yorker, 1982, Yugoslavian
TWILIGHT TIME MGM/UA, 1983, U.S.-Yugoslavian

IVAN PASSER

b. Czechoslovakia
Attorney: Egon Dumler - New York City, 212/PL. 9-4580

INTIMATE LIGHTING Altura, 1969, Czech
BORN TO WIN United Artists, 1971
LAW AND DISORDER Columbia, 1974
CRIME AND PASSION American International, 1976
SILVER BEARS Columbia, 1978
CUTTER'S WAY *CUTTER AND BONE* United Artists Classics, 1981

MICHAEL PATE

b. 1920 - Sydney, Australia
Business: Pisces Productions, 21 Bundarra Road, Bellevue Hill, NSW, 2023, Australia,
02/30-4208

THE MANGO TREE Satori, 1977, Australian
TIM Satori, 1979, Australian

SHARAD PATEL

b. India
Agent: Soren Fischer Associates, 14 Glebe House, Fitzroy Mews, London W1P 5DP,
England, 01/437-6862

AMIN: THE RISE AND FALL *THE RISE AND FALL OF IDI AMIN* Twin
Continental, 1983, British-Kenyan

STEVEN PAUL

FALLING IN LOVE AGAIN International Picture Show Company, 1980
SLAPSTICK Entertainment Releasing Corporation/International Film Marketing,
1983

DAVID PAULSEN*

Telephone: 213/558-6064
Attorney: Mort Herbert, 6255 Sunset Blvd., Hollywood, CA 90028, 213/469-2994

SAVAGE WEEKEND *THE UPSTATE MURDERS* Cannon, 1976
SCHIZOID Cannon, 1980

RICHARD PEARCE*

Home: 767 Paseo Miramar, Pacific Palisades, CA 90271
Agent: Martin Bauer, William Morris Agency - Beverly Hills, 213/274-7451

THE GARDENER'S SON (TF) RIP/Filmhaus, 1977
SIEGE (TF) Titus Productions, 1978
NO OTHER LOVE (TF) Tisch-Avnet Productions, 1979
HEARTLAND Levitt-Pickman, 1979
THRESHOLD 20th Century-Fox International Classics, 1983, Canadian
SESSIONS (TF) Roger Gimbel Productions/EMI TV/Sarabande Productions,
1983

continued

RICHARD PEARCE*—continued
COUNTRY   Buena Vista, 1984

S A M   P E C K I N P A H *

b. February 21, 1925 - Fresno, California
Agent: Chasin-Park-Citron - Los Angeles, 213/273-7190
Business Manager: Kip Dellinger - Los Angeles, 213/273-1410

THE DEADLY COMPANIONS   Pathe-American, 1961
RIDE THE HIGH COUNTRY   MGM, 1962
MAJOR DUNDEE   Columbia, 1965
THE WILD BUNCH   Warner Bros., 1969
THE BALLAD OF CABLE HOGUE   Warner Bros., 1970
STRAW DOGS   Cinerama Releasing Corporation, 1972, British
THE GETAWAY   National General, 1972
JUNIOR BONNER   Cinerama Releasing Corporation, 1973
PAT GARRETT & BILLY THE KID   MGM, 1973
BRING ME THE HEAD OF ALFREDO GARCIA   United Artists, 1974
THE KILLER ELITE   United Artists, 1975
CROSS OF IRON   Avco Embassy, 1977, British-West German
CONVOY   United Artists, 1978
THE OSTERMAN WEEKEND   20th Century-Fox, 1983

L A R R Y   P E E R C E *

b. Bronx, New York
Agent: Fred Specktor, CAA - Los Angeles, 213/277-4545

ONE POTATO, TWO POTATO   Cinema 5, 1964
THE BIG T.N.T. SHOW (FD)   American International, 1966
THE INCIDENT   20th Century-Fox, 1967
GOODBYE, COLUMBUS   Paramount, 1969
THE SPORTING CLUB   Avco Embassy, 1971
A SEPARATE PEACE   Paramount, 1972
ASH WEDNESDAY   Paramount, 1973
THE STRANGER WHO LOOKS LIKE ME (TF)   Filmways, 1974
THE OTHER SIDE OF THE MOUNTAIN   Universal, 1975
TWO-MINUTE WARNING   Universal, 1976
THE OTHER SIDE OF THE MOUNTAIN - PART 2   Universal, 1978
THE BELL JAR   Avco Embassy, 1979
WHY WOULD I LIE?   MGM/United Artists, 1980
LOVE CHILD   The Ladd Company/Warner Bros., 1982
I TAKE THESE MEN (TF)   Lillian Gallo Productions/United Artists TV, 1983
HARD TO HOLD   Universal, 1983

B A R B A R A   P E E T E R S *

Business: The Big Movie Company, 4243 Bakeman Avenue, Studio City,
    CA 91602, 213/762-5883
Agent: Ronald Lief, Contemporary-Korman Artists, Beverly Hills, 213/278-8250

THE DARK SIDE OF TOMORROW   co-director with Jacque Beerson, Able,
    1970
BURY ME AN ANGEL   New World, 1972
SUMMER SCHOOL TEACHERS   New World, 1975
JUST THE TWO OF US   Boxoffice International, 1975
STARHOPS   First American, 1978
HUMANOIDS FROM THE DEEP   New World, 1980

A R T H U R   P E N N *

b. September 27, 1922 - Philadelphia, Pennsylvania
Agent: Sam Cohn, ICM - New York City, 212/556-5600

THE LEFT HANDED GUN   Warner Bros., 1958
THE MIRACLE WORKER ★   United Artists, 1962
MICKEY ONE   Columbia, 1965
THE CHASE   Columbia, 1966
BONNIE AND CLYDE ★   Warner Bros., 1967
ALICE'S RESTAURANT ★   United Artists, 1969

continued

ARTHUR PENN*—continued

LITTLE BIG MAN   National General, 1970
NIGHT MOVES   Warner Bros., 1975
THE MISSOURI BREAKS   United Artists, 1976
FOUR FRIENDS   Filmways, 1981

L E O   P E N N *

Agent: Herb Tobias & Associates - Los Angeles, 213/277-6211

QUARANTINED (TF)   Paramount TV, 1970
TESTIMONY OF TWO MEN (MS)   co-director with Larry Yust, Universal TV, 1977
THE DARK SECRET OF HARVEST HOME (TF)   Universal TV, 1978
MURDER IN MUSIC CITY (TF)   Frankel Films, 1979
HELLINGER'S LAW (TF)   Universal TV, 1981

D . A .   P E N N E B A K E R
(Don Alan Pennebaker)

b. 1930 - Evanston, Illinois
Business: Pennebaker Associates, 21 West 86th Street, New York, NY 10024, 212/496-9199

DON'T LOOK BACK (FD)   Leacock-Pennebaker, 1967
MONTEREY POP (FD)   Leacock-Pennebaker, 1967
COMPANY (FD)   Pennebaker Associates, 1970
SWEET TORONTO *KEEP ON ROCKIN' (FD)*   Pennebaker Associates, 1972
THE ENERGY WAR (TD)   Pennebaker Associates/Corporation for Public Broadcasting, 1979
ELLIOTT CARTER (FD)   Pennebaker Associates, 1980
DeLOREAN (TD)   Pennebaker Associates, 1981
ROCKABYE (TD)   Pennebaker Associates, 1983
ZIGGY STARDUST AND THE SPIDERS FROM MARS   20th Century-Fox International Classics/Miramax Films, 1983, filmed in 1973

G E O R G E   P E P P A R D *

b. October 1, 1928 - Detroit, Michigan
Business: Lime Tree Productions - Beverly Hills, 213/652-7011
Agent: David Shapira & Associates - Sherman Oaks, 213/906-0322

FIVE DAYS FROM HOME   Universal, 1977

E T I E N N E   P E R R I E R

Contact: French Film Office, 745 Fifth Avenue, New York, NY 10151, 212/832-8860

BOBOSSE   1959, Belgian
MEURTRE EN 45 TOURS   1960, Belgian
BRIDGE TO THE SUN   MGM, 1961, U.S.-French
SWORDSMAN OF SIENA   MGM, 1962, Italian-French
DIS-MOI QUI TUER   1965, Belgian
DES GARCONS ET DES FILLES   1968, French
RUBLO DE LOS CARAS   1969, Spanish
WHEN EIGHT BELLS TOLL   Cinerama Releasing Corporation, 1971, British
ZEPPELIN   Warner Bros., 1971, British
A MURDER IS A MURDER ... IS A MURDER   Levitt-Pickman, 1974, French
LA MAIN A COUPER   1974, French
LA CONFUSION DES SENTIMENTS (TF)   Christine Gouze-Renel Progefi/FR3, 1979, French

FRANK PERRY *

b. 1930 - New York, New York
Home: 655 Park Avenue, New York, NY 10021, 212/535-2910
Agent: Michael Black/Sam Cohn, ICM - Los Angeles/New York 213/550-4000 or
    212/556-5600

DAVID AND LISA ★   Continental, 1962
LADYBUG, LADYBUG   United Artists, 1963
THE SWIMMER   Columbia, 1968
LAST SUMMER   Allied Artists, 1969
TRILOGY   Allied Artists, 1969
DIARY OF A MAD HOUSEWIFE   Universal, 1970
DOC   United Artists, 1971
PLAY IT AS IT LAYS   Universal, 1972
MAN ON A SWING   Paramount, 1974
RANCHO DeLUXE   United Artists, 1975
DUMMY (TF)   The Konigsberg Company/Warner Bros. TV, 1979
SKAG (TF) ☆   NBC, 1980
MOMMIE DEAREST   Paramount, 1981
MONSIGNOR   20th Century-Fox, 1982

BILL PERSKY *

b. 1931 - New Haven, Connecticut
Agent: Ron Meyer, CAA - Los Angeles, 213/277-4545

ROLL, FREDDY, ROLLI (TF)   ABC Circle Films, 1974
HOW TO PICK UP GIRLSI (TF)   King-Hitzig Productions, 1978
SERIAL   Paramount, 1980
WAIT TILL YOUR MOTHER GETS HOME (TF)   Blue-Greene Productions/NBC
    Productions, 1983
TRACKDOWN: FINDING THE GOODBAR KILLER (TF)   Grosso-Jacobson
    Productions, 1983

WOLFGANG PETERSEN

Agent: Chasin-Park-Citron - Los Angeles, 213/273-7190

THE CONSEQUENCE   Libra, 1977, West German
BLACK AND WHITE LIKE DAY AND NIGHT   New Yorker, 1978, West
    German
DAS BOOT (THE BOAT) ★   Triumph/Columbia, 1981, West German
THE NEVER-ENDING STORY   Warner Bros., 1984, West German

CHRIS PETIT

Contact: British Academy of Film & Television Arts, 195 Piccadilly, London W1,
    England, 01/732-0022

RADIO ON   British Film Institute/Road Movies, 1979, British-West German
AN UNSUITABLE JOB FOR A WOMAN   Boyd's Co., 1982, British
FLIGHT TO BERLIN   Road Movies/British Film Institute/Channel Four, 1984,
    West German-British

DANIEL PETRIE *

b. November 26, 1920 - Glace Bay, Nova Scotia, Canada
Agent: Jack Gilardi, ICM - Los Angeles, 213/550-4000

THE BRAMBLE BUSH   Warner Bros., 1960
A RAISIN IN THE SUN   Columbia, 1961
THE MAIN ATTRACTION   MGM, 1962
STOLEN HOURS   United Artists, 1963
THE IDOL   Embassy, 1966, British
THE SPY WITH A COLD NOSE   Embassy, 1966, British
SILENT NIGHT, LONELY NIGHT (TF)   Universal TV, 1969
THE CITY (TF)   Universal TV, 1971
A HOWLING IN THE WOODS (TF)   Universal TV, 1971
MOON OF THE WOLF (TF)   Filmways, 1972
HEC RAMSEY (TF)   Universal TV/Mark VII Ltd., 1972

continued

DANIEL PETRIE*—continued

TROUBLE COMES TO TOWN (TF)   ABC Circle Films, 1973
THE NEPTUNE FACTOR   20th Century-Fox, 1973, Canadian
MOUSEY (TF)   Universal TV/Associated British Films, 1974, U.S.-British
THE GUN AND THE PULPIT (TF)   Danny Thomas Productions, 1974
BUSTER AND BILLIE   Columbia, 1974
RETURNING HOME (TF)   Lorimar Productions/Samuel Goldwyn Productions, 1975
ELEANOR AND FRANKLIN (TF) ☆☆   Talent Associates, 1976
SYBIL (TF)   Lorimar Productions, 1976
LIFEGUARD   Paramount, 1976
ELEANOR AND FRANKLIN: THE WHITE HOUSE YEARS (TF) ☆☆   Talent Associates, 1977
THE QUINNS (TF)   Daniel Wilson Productions, 1977
THE BETSY   Allied Artists, 1978
RESURRECTION   Universal, 1980
FORT APACHE, THE BRONX   20th Century-Fox, 1981
SIX PACK   20th Century-Fox, 1982
THE DOLLMAKER (TF)   Finnegan Associates/IPC Films, Inc., 1983

JOSEPH PEVNEY *

b. 1920 - New York, New York
Agent: Herb Tobias & Associates - Los Angeles, 213/277-6211
Business Manager: T.J. Smith - Granada Hills, 213/363-3341

SHAKEDOWN   Universal, 1950
UNDERCOVER GIRL   Universal, 1950
AIR CADET   Universal, 1951
IRON MAN   Universal, 1951
THE LADY FROM TEXAS   Universal, 1951
THE STRANGE DOOR   Universal, 1951
MEET DANNY WILSON   Universal, 1952
FLESH AND FURY   Universal, 1952
JUST ACROSS THE STREET   Universal, 1952
BECAUSE OF YOU   Universal, 1952
DESERT LEGION   Universal, 1953
IT HAPPENS EVERY THURSDAY   Universal, 1953
BACK TO GOD'S COUNTRY   Universal, 1953
YANKEE PASHA   Universal, 1954
PLAYGIRL   Universal, 1954
THREE RING CIRCUS   Paramount, 1954
SIX BRIDGES TO CROSS   Universal, 1955
FOXFIRE   Universal, 1955
FEMALE ON THE BEACH   Universal, 1955
AWAY ALL BOATS   Universal, 1956
CONGO CROSSING   Universal, 1956
ISTANBUL   Universal, 1956
TAMMY AND THE BACHELOR   Universal, 1957
THE MIDNIGHT STORY   Universal, 1957
MAN OF A THOUSAND FACES   Universal, 1957
TWILIGHT FOR THE GODS   Universal, 1958
TORPEDO RUN   MGM, 1958
CASH McCALL   Warner Bros., 1960
THE PLUNDERERS   Allied Artists, 1960
THE CROWDED SKY   Warner Bros., 1960
PORTRAIT OF A MOBSTER   Warner Bros., 1961
THE NIGHT OF THE GRIZZLY   Paramount, 1966
MY DARLING DAUGHTERS' ANNIVERSARY (TF)   Universal TV, 1973
WHO IS THE BLACK DAHLIA? (TF)   Douglas S. Cramer Productions, 1975
MYSTERIOUS ISLAND OF BEAUTIFUL WOMEN (TF)   Alan Landsburg Productions, 1977

JOHN PEYSER *

b. August 10, 1916 - New York, New York
Home: 19721 Redwing Street, Woodland Hills, CA 91364, 213/884-7730
Agent: Martin Shapiro, Shapiro-Lichtman Agency - Los Angeles, 213/557-2244

UNDERSEA GIRL   Allied Artists, 1958
THE MURDER MEN   MGM, 1964
THE YOUNG WARRIORS   Universal, 1967

continued

JOHN PEYSER*—continued

HONEYMOON WITH A STRANGER (TF)   20th Century-Fox TV, 1969
MASSACRE HARBOR   United Artists, 1970
CENTER FOLD GIRLS   Dimension, 1974
STUNT SEVEN (TF)   Martin Poll Productions, 1979

L E E   P H I L I P S *

Home: 11939 Gorham Avenue - Suite 104, Los Angeles, CA 90049, 213/820-
    7464
Agent: Martin Shapiro, Shapiro-Lichtman Agency - Los Angeles, 213/557-2244

GETTING AWAY FROM IT ALL (TF)   Palomar Pictures International, 1972
THE GIRL MOST LIKELY TO ... (TF)   ABC Circle Films, 1973
THE STRANGER WITHIN (TF)   Lorimar Productions, 1974
THE RED BADGE OF COURAGE (TF)   20th Century-Fox TV, 1974
SWEET HOSTAGE (TF)   Brut Productions, 1975
LOUIS ARMSTRONG - CHICAGO STYLE (TF)   Charles Fries Productions,
    1975
JAMES A. MICHENER'S DYNASTY (TF)   David Paradine TV, 1976
WANTED: THE SUNDANCE WOMAN (TF)   20th Century-Fox TV, 1976
THE SPELL (TF)   Charles Fries Productions, 1977
THE WAR BETWEEN THE TATES (TF)   Talent Associates, 1977
SPECIAL OLYMPICS (TF)   Roger Gimbel Productions/EMI TV, 1978
THE COMEDY COMPANY (TF)   Merrit Malloy-Jerry Adler Productions, 1978
SALVAGE (TF)   Bennett-Katleman Productions/Columbia TV, 1979
VALENTINE (TF)   Malloy-Philips Productions/Edward S. Feldman Company, 1979
HARDHAT AND LEGS (TF)   Syzygy Productions, 1980
CRAZY TIMES (TF)   Kayden-Gleason Productions/George Reeves Productions/
    Warner Bros. TV, 1981
ON THE RIGHT TRACK   20th Century-Fox, 1981
A WEDDING ON WALTON'S MOUNTAIN (TF)   Lorimar Productions/Amanda
    Productions, 1982
MAE WEST (TF) ☆   Hill-Mandelker Films, 1982
GAMES MOTHER NEVER TAUGHT YOU (TF)   CBS Entertainment, 1982
LOTTERY! (TF)   Rosner TV Productions/Orion TV, 1983
HAPPY (TF)   Bacchus Films Inc., 1983

C H A R L E S   B .   P I E R C E

THE LEGEND OF BOGGY CREEK   Howco International, 1973
BOOTLEGGERS   Howco International, 1974
WINTERHAWK   Howco International, 1975
THE WINDS OF AUTUMN   Howco International, 1976
THE TOWN THAT DREADED SUNDOWN   American International, 1977
GREYEAGLE   American International, 1977
THE NORSEMEN   American International, 1978
THE EVICTORS   American International, 1979
SACRED GROUND   Pacific International, 1983

F R A N K   P I E R S O N *

b. May 12, 1925 - New York, New York
Agent: Adams, Ray & Rosenberg - Los Angeles, 213/278-3000

THE LOOKING GLASS WAR   Columbia, 1970, British
THE NEON CEILING (TF)   Universal TV, 1971
A STAR IS BORN   Warner Bros., 1976
KING OF THE GYPSIES   Paramount, 1978

H A R O L D   P I N T E R

b. October 10, 1930 - London, England
Address: c/o ACTAC Ltd., 16 Cadogan Lane, London SW1, England

BUTLEY   American Film Theatre, 1974, British

ERNEST PINTOFF *

b. December 15, 1931 - Watertown, Connecticut
Agent: Ronald Lief, Contemporary-Korman Artists - Beverly Hills, 213/278-8250

HARVEY MIDDLEMAN, FIREMAN   Columbia, 1965
WHO KILLED MARY WHAT'S'ERNAME   Cannon, 1971
DYNAMITE CHICKEN   EYR, 1972
HUMAN FEELINGS (TF)   Crestview Productions/Worldvision, 1978
JAGUAR LIVES   American International, 1979
LUNCH WAGON *LUNCH WAGON GIRLS*   Seymour Borde Associates, 1981
ST. HELENS   Davis-Panzer Productions, 1981

S. LEE POGOSTIN

Agent: Paul Kohner, Inc. - Los Angeles, 213/550-1060

HARD CONTRACT   20th Century-Fox, 1969

SIDNEY POITIER *

b. February 20, 1924 - Miami, Florida
Business: Verdon-Cedric Productions, Ltd., 9350 Wilshire Blvd., Beverly Hills,
    CA 90212, 213/274-7253
Agent: Martin Baum, CAA - Los Angeles, 213/277-4545

BUCK AND THE PREACHER   Columbia, 1972
A WARM DECEMBER   National General, 1973
UPTOWN SATURDAY NIGHT   Warner Bros., 1974
LET'S DO IT AGAIN   Warner Bros., 1975
A PIECE OF THE ACTION   Warner Bros., 1977
STIR CRAZY   Columbia, 1980
HANKY PANKY   Columbia, 1982

ROMAN POLANSKI

b. August 18, 1933 - Paris, France
Contact: French Film Office, 745 Fifth Avenue, New York, NY 10151, 212/832-
    8860

KNIFE IN THE WATER   Kanawha, 1963, Polish
THE BEAUTIFUL SWINDLERS *LES PLUS BELLES ESCROQUERIES DU
    MONDE*   co-director with Ugo Grigoretti, Claude Chabrol & Hiromichi
    Horikawa, Jack Ellis Films, 1964, French-Italian-Japanese-Dutch
REPULSION   Royal Films International, 1965, British
CUL-DE-SAC   Sigma III, 1966, British
THE FEARLESS VAMPIRE KILLERS, OR PARDON ME BUT YOUR TEETH
    ARE IN MY NECK *DANCE OF THE VAMPIRES*   MGM, 1967, British
ROSEMARY'S BABY   Paramount, 1968
MACBETH   Columbia, 1971, British
WHAT?   Avco Embassy, 1973, Italian-French-West German
CHINATOWN ★   Paramount, 1974
THE TENANT   Paramount, 1976, French-U.S.
TESS ★   Columbia, 1980, French-British

BARRY POLLACK

COOL BREEZE   MGM, 1972
THIS IS A HIJACK   Fanfare, 1973

SYDNEY POLLACK *

b. July 1, 1934 - South Bend, Indiana
Agent: Michael Ovitz, CAA - Los Angeles, 213/277-4545
Attorney: Gary Hendler, Armstrong, Hendler & Hirsch - Los Angeles, 213/553-0305

THE SLENDER THREAD   Paramount, 1965
THIS PROPERTY IS CONDEMNED   Paramount, 1966
THE SCALPHUNTERS   United Artists, 1968
CASTLE KEEP   Columbia, 1969

continued

SYDNEY POLLACK*—continued
THEY SHOOT HORSES, DON'T THEY? ★   Cinerama Releasing Corporation,
   1969
JEREMIAH JOHNSON   Warner Bros., 1972
THE WAY WE WERE   Columbia, 1973
THE YAKUZA   Warner Bros., 1975
3 DAYS OF THE CONDOR   Paramount, 1975
BOBBY DEERFIELD   Columbia, 1977
THE ELECTRIC HORSEMAN   Columbia, 1979
ABSENCE OF MALICE   Columbia, 1981
TOOTSIE ★   Columbia, 1982

ABRAHAM POLONSKY*

b. December 5, 1910 - New York, New York
Agent: The Gersh Agency - Beverly Hills, 213/274-6611
Attorney: Shanks, Davis & Remer - New York City, 212/986-0440

FORCE OF EVIL   MGM, 1948
TELL THEM WILLIE BOY IS HERE   Universal, 1969
ROMANCE OF A HORSETHIEF   Allied Artists, 1971

GILLO PONTECORVO

b. November 19, 1919 - Pisa, Italy
Contact: Ministry of Tourism & Education, Via Della Ferratella, No. 51, 00184
   Rome, Italy, 06/7732

DIE WINDROSE   co-director, 1956, East German
LA GRANDE STRADA AZZURRA   Ge-Si Malenotti/Play Art/Eichberg/Triglav
   Film, 1957, Italian-Yugoslavian
KAPO   Vides/Zebra Film/Cineriz, 1960, Italian
BATTLE OF ALGIERS ★   Rizzoli, 1967, Italian-Algerian
BURNI *QUEIMADA!*   United Artists, 1970, Italian-French
OPERATION OGRO   CIDIF, 1979, Italian-Spanish-French

TED POST*

b. March 31, 1918 - Brooklyn, New York
Agent: ICM - Los Angeles, 213/550-4000
Business Manager: Norman Blumenthal, 3250 Ocean Park Blvd., Santa Monica,
   CA 90405

THE PEACEMAKER   United Artists, 1956
THE LEGEND OF TOM DOOLEY   Columbia, 1959
HANG 'EM HIGH   United Artists, 1968
BENEATH THE PLANET OF THE APES   20th Century-Fox, 1970
NIGHT SLAVES (TF)   Bing Crosby Productions, 1970
DR. COOK'S GARDEN (TF)   Paramount TV, 1970
YUMA (TF)   Aaron Spelling Productions, 1971
FIVE DESPERATE WOMEN (TF)   Aaron Spelling Productions, 1971
DO NOT FOLD, SPINDLE OR MUTILATE (TF)   Lee Rich Productions, 1971
THE BRAVOS (TF)   Universal TV, 1972
SANDCASTLES (TF)   Metromedia Productions, 1972
THE BABY   Scotia International, 1973, British
THE HARRAD EXPERIMENT   Cinerama Releasing Corporation, 1973
MAGNUM FORCE   Warner Bros., 1973
WHIFFS   20th Century-Fox, 1975
GOOD GUYS WEAR BLACK   American Cinema, 1978
GO TELL THE SPARTANS   Avco Embassy, 1978
DIARY OF A TEENAGE HITCHHIKER (TF)   The Shpetner Company, 1979
THE GIRLS IN THE OFFICE (TF)   ABC Circle Films, 1979
NIGHTKILL (TF)   Cine Artists, 1980
CAGNEY & LACEY (TF)   Mace Neufeld Productions/Filmways, 1981

GERALD   POTTERTON

Contact: Canadian Film & Television Association, 8 King Street, Toronto, Ontario
    M5C 1B5, Canada, 416/961-2288

THE RAINBOW BOYS   1975, Canadian
HEAVY METAL (AF)   Columbia, 1981, Canadian

MICHAEL   POWELL

b. September 30, 1905 - Canterbury, England

TWO CROWDED HOURS   Fox, 1931, British
MY FRIEND THE KING   Fox, 1931, British
RYNOX   Ideal, 1931, British
THE RASP   Fox, 1931, British
THE STAR REPORTER   Fox, 1931, British
HOTEL SPLENDIDE   Ideal, 1932, British
BORN LUCKY   MGM, 1932, British
C.O.D.   United Artists, 1932, British
HIS LORDSHIP   United Artists, 1932, British
THE FIRE RAISERS   Woolf & Freedman, 1933, British
THE NIGHT OF THE PARTY   Gaumont, 1934, British
RED ENSIGN   Gaumont, 1934, British
SOMETHING ALWAYS HAPPENS   Warner Bros., 1934, British
THE GIRL IN THE CROWD   First National, 1934, British
THE LOVE TEST   Fox British, 1935, British
LAZYBONES   Radio, 1935, British
SOME DAY   Warner Bros., 1935, British
HER LAST AFFAIRE   Producers Distributing Corporation, 1935, British
THE PRICE OF A SONG   Fox British, 1935, British
THE PHANTOM LIGHT   Gaumont, 1935, British
THE BROWN WALLET   First National, 1936, British
CROWN VS. STEVENS   Warner Bros., 1936, British
THE MAN BEHIND THE MASK   MGM, 1936, British
THE EDGE OF THE WORLD   British Independent Exhibitors' Distributors, 1937,
    British
U-BOAT 29 *THE SPY IN BLACK*   Columbia, 1939, British
THE LION HAS WINGS   co-director with Brian Desmond Hurst & Adrian
    Brunel, United Artists, 1939, British
THE THIEF OF BAGDAD   co-director with Ludwig Berger & Tim Whelan,
    United Artists, 1940, British
CONTRABAND *BLACKOUT*   Anglo-American, 1940, British
THE FORTY-NINTH PARALLEL *THE INVADERS*   Columbia, 1941, British
ONE OF OUR AIRCRAFT IS MISSING   co-director with Emeric Pressburger,
    United Artists, 1942, British
THE VOLUNTEER   co-director with Emeric Pressburger, Anglo, 1943, British
COLONEL BLIMP *THE LIFE AND DEATH OF COLONEL BLIMP*   co-
    director with Emeric Pressburger, GFO, 1943, British
A CANTERBURY TALE   co-director with Emeric Pressburger, Eagle-Lion, 1944,
    British
I KNOW WHERE I'M GOING   co-director with Emeric Pressburger, Universal,
    1945, British
STAIRWAY TO HEAVEN *A MATTER OF LIFE AND DEATH*   co-director
    with Emeric Pressburger, Universal, 1946, British
BLACK NARCISSUS   co-director with Emeric Pressburger, Universal, 1947,
    British
THE RED SHOES   co-director with Emeric Pressburger, Eagle-Lion, 1948, British
THE SMALL BACK ROOM *HOUR OF GLORY*   co-director with Emeric
    Pressburger, Snader Productions, 1948, British
THE WILD HEART *GONE TO EARTH*   co-director with Emeric Pressburger,
    RKO Radio, 1950, British
THE ELUSIVE PIMPERNEL   co-director with Emeric Pressburger, British Lion,
    1950, British
THE TALES OF HOFFMAN   co-director with Emeric Pressburger, Lopert, 1951,
    British
OH ROSALINDAI   co-director with Emeric Pressburger, Associated British Picture
    Corporation, 1955, British
PURSUIT OF THE GRAF SPEE *THE BATTLE OF THE RIVER PLATE*   co-
    director with Emeric Pressburger, Rank, 1956, British
NIGHT AMBUSH *ILL MET BY MOONLIGHT*   co-director with Emeric
    Pressburger, Rank, 1957, British
HONEYMOON *LUNA DE MIEL*   RKO Radio, 1958, Spanish
PEEPING TOM   Astor, 1960, British

continued

MICHAEL POWELL—continued

THE QUEEN'S GUARDS   20th Century-Fox, 1961, British
THEY'RE A WEIRD MOB   Williamson/Powell, 1966, Australian
AGE OF CONSENT   Columbia, 1970, Australian
THE TEMPEST   1974, Greek-British

MICHAEL PREECE *

Home: 12233 Everglade Street, Mar Vista, CA 90066, 213/390-6414
Business: Charbridge Productions, 1901 Avenue of the Stars -Suite 840, Los
    Angeles, CA 90067, 213/277-9511
Agent: Herb Tobias & Associates - Los Angeles, 213/277-6211

THE PRIZE FIGHTER   New World, 1979
PARADISE CONNECTION (TF)   Woodruff Productions/QM Productions, 1979

OTTO PREMINGER *

b. December 5, 1906 - Vienna, Austria
Business: Sigma Productions, Inc., 129 East 64th Street, New York, NY 10021,
    212/535-6001

DIE GROSSE LIEBE   1931, Austrian-German
UNDER YOUR SPELL   20th Century-Fox, 1936
DANGER - LOVE AT WORK   20th Century-Fox, 1937
MARGIN FOR ERROR   20th Century-Fox, 1943
IN THE MEANTIME, DARLING   20th Century-Fox, 1944
LAURA ★   20th Century-Fox, 1944
A ROYAL SCANDAL   20th Century-Fox, 1945
FALLEN ANGEL   20th Century-Fox, 1945
CENTENNIAL SUMMER   20th Century-Fox, 1946
FOREVER AMBER   20th Century-Fox, 1947
DAISY KENYON   20th Century-Fox, 1947
THE FAN   20th Century-Fox, 1949
WHIRLPOOL   20th Century-Fox, 1950
WHERE THE SIDEWALK ENDS   20th Century-Fox, 1950
THE 13TH LETTER   20th Century-Fox, 1951
ANGEL FACE   RKO Radio, 1953
THE MOON IS BLUE   United Artists, 1953
RIVER OF NO RETURN   20th Century-Fox, 1954
CARMEN JONES   20th Century-Fox, 1955
THE MAN WITH THE GOLDEN ARM   United Artists, 1955
THE COURT-MARTIAL OF BILLY MITCHELL   Warner Bros., 1955
SAINT JOAN   United Artists, 1957
BONJOUR TRISTESSE   Columbia, 1958
PORGY AND BESS   Columbia, 1959
ANATOMY OF A MURDER   Columbia, 1959
EXODUS   United Artists, 1960
ADVISE AND CONSENT   Columbia, 1962
THE CARDINAL ★   Columbia, 1963
IN HARM'S WAY   Paramount, 1964
BUNNY LAKE IS MISSING   Columbia, 1965, British
HURRY SUNDOWN   Paramount, 1967
SKIDOO   Paramount, 1968
TELL ME THAT YOU LOVE ME, JUNIE MOON   Paramount, 1970
SUCH GOOD FRIENDS   Paramount, 1971
ROSEBUD   United Artists, 1975
THE HUMAN FACTOR   United Artists, 1979, British

MICHAEL PRESSMAN *

b. July 1, 1950 - New York, New York
Agent: Rick Nicita, CAA - Los Angeles, 213/277-4545

THE GREAT TEXAS DYNAMITE CHASE   New World, 1976
THE BAD NEWS BEARS IN BREAKING TRAINING   Paramount, 1977
LIKE MOM, LIKE ME (TF)   CBS Entertainment, 1978
BOULEVARD NIGHTS   Warner Bros., 1979
THOSE LIPS, THOSE EYES   United Artists, 1980
SOME KIND OF HERO   Paramount, 1982
DOCTOR DETROIT   Universal, 1983

HAROLD PRINCE

b. July 30, 1928
Business: 1270 Avenue of the Americas, New York, NY, 212/399-0960

SOMETHING FOR EVERYONE   National General, 1970, British
A LITTLE NIGHT MUSIC   New World, 1978, Austrian-U.S.

ALBERT PYUN

THE SWORD AND THE SORCERER   Group 1, 1982
RADIOACTIVE DREAMS   Esparza Productions/ITM Productions, 1984

JOHN QUESTED

Business: Brent Walker Films, 9 Chesterfield Street, London WI, England

PHILADELPHIA, HERE I COME   Irish
HERE ARE LADIES   Arthur Cantor Films, 1971, Irish
LOOPHOLE   MGM/United Artists, 1981, British

RICHARD QUINE*

b. November 12, 1920 - Detroit, Michigan
Agent: Martin Baum, CAA - Los Angeles, 213/277-4545
Business Manager: Michael L. Laney, Laney, Weidenbaum & Ryder - Los Angeles,
    213/277-7611.

LEATHER GLOVES   co-director with William Asher, Columbia 1948
SUNNY SIDE OF THE STREET   Columbia, 1951
PURPLE HEART DIARY   Columbia, 1951
SOUND OFF   Columbia, 1952
RAINBOW 'ROUND MY SHOULDER   Columbia, 1952
ALL ASHORE   Columbia, 1953
SIREN OF BAGDAD   Columbia, 1953
CRUISIN' DOWN THE RIVER   Columbia, 1953
DRIVE A CROOKED ROAD   Columbia, 1954
PUSHOVER   Columbia, 1954
SO THIS IS PARIS   Universal, 1955
MY SISTER EILEEN   Universal, 1955
THE SOLID GOLD CADILLAC   Columbia, 1956
FULL OF LIFE   Columbia, 1957
OPERATION MAD BALL   Columbia, 1957
BELL, BOOK AND CANDLE   Columbia, 1958
IT HAPPENED TO JANE   Columbia, 1959
STRANGERS WHEN WE MEET   Columbia, 1960
THE WORLD OF SUZIE WONG   Paramount, 1960
THE NOTORIOUS LANDLADY   Columbia, 1962
PARIS WHEN IT SIZZLES   Paramount, 1964
SEX AND THE SINGLE GIRL   Warner Bros., 1965

continued

RICHARD QUINE*—continued
HOW TO MURDER YOUR WIFE   United Artists, 1965
SYNANON   Columbia, 1965
**OH DAD, POOR DAD, MOMMA'S HUNG YOU IN THE CLOSET AND I'M
      FEELING SO SAD**   Paramount, 1967
HOTEL   Warner Bros., 1967
A TALENT FOR LOVING   1969
THE MOONSHINE WAR   MGM, 1970
"W"   Cinerama Releasing Corporation, 1974, British
THE SPECIALISTS (TF)   Mark VII Ltd./Universal TV, 1975
THE PRISONER OF ZENDA   Universal, 1979

A N T H O N Y   Q U I N N

b. April 21, 1915 - Chihuahua, Mexico
Agent: William Morris Agency - Beverly Hills, 213/274-7451

THE BUCCANEER   Paramount, 1959

J O S E   Q U I N T E R O *

Agent: The Lantz Office - New York City, 212/586-0200

THE ROMAN SPRING OF MRS. STONE   Warner Bros., 1961

M I C H A E L   R A D F O R D

Contact: Directors Guild of Great Britain, 56 Whitfield Street, London WI, England,
      01/580-9592

VAN MORRISON IN IRELAND (FD)   Caledonia-Angle Films, 1981, British
ANOTHER TIME, ANOTHER PLACE   The Samuel Goldwyn Company, 1983,
      British

M I C H A E L   R A E

LASERBLAST   Irwin Yablans, 1978

B O B   R A F E L S O N *

b. 1934 - New York, New York
Business: 1400 N. Fuller Avenue, Hollywood, CA 90046
Agent: William Morris Agency - Beverly Hills, 213/274-7451

HEAD   Columbia, 1968
FIVE EASY PIECES   Columbia, 1970
THE KING OF MARVIN GARDENS   Columbia, 1972

continued

BOB RAFELSON*—continued
STAY HUNGRY   United Artists, 1976
THE POSTMAN ALWAYS RINGS TWICE   Paramount, 1981

S T E W A R T   R A F F I L L *

Contact: Directors Guild of America - Los Angeles, 213/656-1220

THE TENDER WARRIOR   Safari, 1971
THE ADVENTURES OF THE WILDERNESS FAMILY   Pacific International, 1975
ACROSS THE GREAT DIVIDE   Pacific International, 1976
THE SEA GYPSIES   Warner Bros., 1978
HIGH RISK   American Cinema, 1981
THE ICE PIRATES   MGM/UA, 1983

A L A N   R A F K I N *

Home: 1008 St. Bimini Circle, Palm Springs, CA, 619/323-4058
Personal Manager: The Brillstein Company - Los Angeles, 213/275-6135
Business Manager: Gelfand, Rennert & Feldman, 1880
Century Park East, Los Angeles, CA 90067, 213/553-1707

SKI PARTY   American International, 1965
THE GHOST AND MR. CHICKEN   Universal, 1966
THE RIDE TO HANGMAN'S TREE   Universal, 1967
NOBODY'S PERFECT   Universal, 1968
THE SHAKIEST GUN IN THE WEST   Universal, 1968
ANGEL IN MY POCKET   Universal, 1969
HOW TO FRAME A FIGG   Universal, 1971
LET'S SWITCH (TF)   Universal TV, 1975

S A M   R A I M I

THE EVIL DEAD   New Line Cinema, 1983

A L V I N   R A K O F F

b. Toronto, Canada
Business: Jara Productions Ltd., 1 The Orchard, Chiswick,
London W4 1JZ, England, 01/994-1269
Contact: Directors Guild of Great Britain, 56 Whitfield Street, London W1, England, 01/580-9592

PASSPORT TO SHAME   British Lion, 1959, British
ON FRIDAY AT ELEVEN   British Lion, 1961, West German-British
WORLD IN MY POCKET   MGM, 1962, West German-French-Italian
THE COMEDY MAN   Continental, 1964, British
CROSSPLOT   United Artists, 1969, British
HOFFMAN   Levitt-Pickman, 1971, British
SAY HELLO TO YESTERDAY   Cinerama Releasing Corporation, 1971, British
THE ADVENTURES OF DON QUIXOTE (TF)   Universal TV/BBC, 1973, U.S.-British
KING SOLOMON'S TREASURE   Filmco Limited, 1978, Canadian
CITY ON FIRE!   Avco Embassy, 1979, Canadian
DEATH SHIP   Avco Embassy, 1980, Canadian
DIRTY TRICKS   Avco Embassy, 1981, Canadian
A VOYAGE ROUND BY FATHER (TF)   Thames TV/D.L. Taffner Ltd., 1983, British
THE FIRST OLYMPICS—ATHENS 1896 (MS)   Larry White-Gary Allison Productions/Columbia TV, 1984

HAROLD RAMIS *

Agent: Jack Rapke, CAA - Los Angeles, 213/277-4545
Business Manager: David B. Kahn, 111 W. Washington Street, Chicago, ILL 60602, 312/346-4321

CADDYSHACK   Orion/Warner Bros., 1980
NATIONAL LAMPOON'S VACATION   Warner Bros., 1983

ARTHUR RANKIN, JR.

Business: Rankin-Bass Productions, Inc., 1 East 53rd Street, New York, NY 10022, 212/759-7721

WILLY McBEAN AND HIS MAGIC MACHINE (AF)   1967
THE HOBBIT (ATF)   co-director with Jules Bass, Rankin-Bass Productions, 1979
THE RETURN OF THE KING (ATF)   co-director with Jules Bass, Rankin-Bass Productions, 1979
THE LAST UNICORN (AF)   co-director with Jules Bass, Jensen Farley Pictures, 1982
THE FLIGHT OF THE DRAGONS (ATF)   co-director with Jules Bass, Rankin-Bass Productions, 1983
THE WIND IN THE WILLOWS (ATF)   co-director with Jules Bass, Rankin-Bass Productions, 1983

I.C. RAPOPORT *

Home: 559 Muskingum Avenue, Pacific Palisades, CA 90272, 213/454-3120
Agent: Elliot Webb, ICM - Los Angeles, 213/550-4301

THOU SHALT NOT KILL (TF)   Edgar J. Scherick Associates/Warner Bros. TV, 1982

IRVING RAPPER *

b. 1898 - London, England
Contact: Directors Guild of America - Los Angeles, 213/656-1220

SHINING VICTORY   Warner Bros., 1941
ONE FOOT IN HEAVEN   Warner Bros., 1941
THE GAY SISTERS   Warner Bros., 1942
NOW, VOYAGER   Warner Bros., 1942
THE ADVENTURES OF MARK TWAIN   Warner Bros., 1944
THE CORN IS GREEN   Warner Bros., 1945
RHAPSODY IN BLUE   Warner Bros., 1945
DECEPTION   Warner Bros., 1946
THE VOICE OF THE TURTLE   Warner Bros., 1947
ANNA LUCASTA   Columbia, 1949
THE GLASS MENAGERIE   Warner Bros., 1950
ANOTHER MAN'S POISON   United Artists, 1952, British
BAD FOR EACH OTHER   Columbia, 1954
FOREVER FEMALE   Paramount, 1954
STRANGE INTRUDER   Allied Artists, 1956
THE BRAVE ONE   Universal, 1956
MARJORIE MORNINGSTAR   Warner Bros., 1958
THE MIRACLE   Warner Bros., 1959
THE STORY OF JOSEPH AND HIS BRETHREN   Colorama, 1960, Italian
PONTIUS PILATE   US Films, 1962, Italian-French
THE CHRISTINE JORGENSEN STORY   United Artists, 1970
BORN AGAIN   Avco Embassy, 1978

STEVE RASH *

Business: Innovisions, Inc., 11751 Mississippi Avenue, Los Angeles, CA 90025, 213/478-3523

THE BUDDY HOLLY STORY   Columbia, 1978
UNDER THE RAINBOW   Orion/Warner Bros., 1981

S A T Y A J I T   R A Y

b. May 2, 1921 - Calcutta, India
Contact: Films Division, Ministry of Information & Broadcasting, 24 Dr G Beshmukh
    Marg, Bombay 40026, India, 36-1461

PATHER PANCHALI   Harrison, 1955, Indian
APARAJITO   Harrison, 1956, Indian
PARAS PATHAR   1957, Indian
THE MUSIC ROOM   Harrison, 1958, Indian
THE WORLD OF APU   Harrison, 1959, Indian
DEVI   Harrison, 1960, Indian
RABINDRANATH TAGORE   1961, Indian
TWO DAUGHTERS   Janus, 1961, Indian
KANCHENJUNGHA   Harrison, 1962, Indian
ABHIJAN   1962, Indian
MAHANAGAR   1963, Indian
CHARULATA *THE LONELY WIFE*   Trans-World, 1964, Indian
KAPURUSH-O-MAHAPURUSH   1966, Indian
NAYAK   1966, Indian
CHIDIAKHANA   1967, Indian
GOOPY GYNE BAGHA BYNE   Purnima Pictures, 1968, Indian
DAYS AND NIGHTS IN THE FOREST   Pathe Contemporary, 1970, Indian
THE ADVERSARY   Audio Brandon, 1971, Indian
SIMABADDHA   1972, Indian
DISTANT THUNDER   Cinema 5, 1973, Indian
THE MIDDLEMAN   Bauer International, 1976, Indian
THE CHESS PLAYERS   Creative, 1977, Indian
THE KINGDOM OF DIAMONDS   1980, Indian
SADGATI   1982, Indian

R O B E R T   R E D F O R D *

b. August 17, 1937 - Santa Monica, California
Business: Wildwood Enterprises, Inc., 4000 Warner Blvd., Burbank, CA 91522,
    213/954-3221
Agent: CAA - Los Angeles, 213/277-4545

ORDINARY PEOPLE ★★   Paramount, 1980

G E O F F R E Y   R E E V E

Contact: Directors Guild of Great Britain, 56 Whitfield Street, London WI, England,
    01/580-9592

PUPPET ON A CHAIN   co-director with Don Sharp, Cinerama Releasing
    Corporation, 1972, British
CARAVAN TO VACCARES   Bryanston, 1976, British-French

G O D F R E Y   R E G G I O

KOYAANISQATSI   Island Alive/New Cinema, 1983

M A R K   R E I C H E R T

UNION CITY   Kinesis, 1980

F R A N C O I S   R E I C H E N B A C H

b. July 3, 1922 - Paris, France
Contact: French Film Office, 745 Fifth Avenue, New York, NY 10151, 212/832-
    8860

L'AMERIQUE INSOLITE (FD)   1960, French
UN COEUR GROS COMME CA (FD)   1961, French
LES AMOUREAUX DU "FRANCE" (FD)   co-director with Pierre Grimblat,
    1963, French
GRENOBLE (FD)   co-director with Claude Lelouch, United Producers of America,
    1968, French
MEXICO MEXICO (FD)   1969, French

continued

FRANCOIS REICHENBACH—continued

ARTHUR RUBINSTEIN: LOVE OF LIFE (FD)   co-director with Gerard Patris,
New Yorker, 1970, French
L'INDISCRETE (FD)   1970, French
MEDICINE BALL CARAVAN (FD)   Warner Bros., 1971, French-U.S.
YEHUDI MENUHIN - ROAD OF LIGHT (FD)   co-director with Bernard Gavoty,
1971, French
LA RAISON DU PLUS FOU (FD)   co-director, 1973, French
DON'T YOU HEAR THE DOGS BARK? (FD)   1975, Mexican
SEX O'CLOCK USA (FD)   1976
ANOTHER WAY TO LOVE (FD)   1976
PELE (FD)   1977, French
HOUSTON, TEXAS (FD)   Camera One/TFI/Prisme Films, 1980, French
FRANCOIS REICHENBACH'S JAPAN (FD)   CIDIF, 1983, French

ALASTAIR REID

b. July 21, 1939 - Edinburgh, Scotland
Address: The Old Stores, Curload, Stoke, Taunton, Somerset, England
Agent: Douglas Rae Management - London, 01/836-3903

BABY LOVE   Avco Embassy, 1969, British
THE NIGHT DIGGER   MGM, 1971, British
SOMETHING TO HIDE   1971, British
THE FILE ON JILL HATCH (TF)   WNET-13/BBC, 1983, U.S.-British

CARL REINER *

b. March 20, 1922 - Bronx, New York
Home: 714 N. Rodeo Drive, Beverly Hills, CA
Business Manager: George Shapiro, 141 El Camino Drive, Beverly Hills, CA 90212,
213/278-8896

ENTER LAUGHING   Columbia, 1967
THE COMIC   Columbia, 1969
WHERE'S POPPA?   United Artists, 1970
THE ONE AND ONLY   Paramount, 1978
OH, GOD!   Warner Bros., 1978
THE JERK   Universal, 1979
DEAD MEN DON'T WEAR PLAID   Universal, 1979
THE MAN WITH TWO BRAINS   Warner Bros., 1983
ALL OF ME   Universal, 1984

ROB REINER *

b. 1947 - Beverly Hills, California
Agent: CAA - Los Angeles, 213/277-4545

SPINAL TAP   Embassy, 1984

ALLEN REISNER *

b. New York, New York
Home: 213/274-2844
Agent: George Chasin, Chasin-Park-Citron - Los Angeles, 213/273-7190
Business Manager: Neidorf & Perry - Los Angeles, 213/553-0171

ST. LOUIS BLUES   Paramount, 1958
ALL MINE TO GIVE *THE DAY THEY GAVE BABIES AWAY*   Universal,
1958
TO DIE IN PARIS (TF)   co-director with Charles Dubin, Universal TV, 1968
YOUR MONEY OR YOUR WIFE (TF)   Brentwood Productions, 1972
CAPTAINS AND THE KINGS (MS)   co-director with Douglas Heyes, Universal
TV, 1976
MARY JANE HARPER CRIED LAST NIGHT (TF)   Paramount TV, 1977
COPS AND ROBIN (TF)   Paramount TV, 1978
THE LOVE TAPES (TF)   Christiana Productions/MGM TV, 1980

KAREL REISZ *

b. July 21, 1926 - Ostrava, Czechoslovakia
Home: 11 Chalcot Gardens, Off-England's Lane, London NW3, England, 01/722-
     6848
Agent: Stan Kamen, William Morris Agency - Beverly Hills, 213/274-7451

WE ARE THE LAMBETH BOYS   Rank, 1958, British
SATURDAY NIGHT AND SUNDAY MORNING   Continental, 1961, British
NIGHT MUST FALL   Embassy, 1964, British
MORGAN! *MORGAN: A SUITABLE CASE FOR TREATMENT*   Cinema 5,
     1966, British
ISADORA *THE LOVES OF ISADORA*   Universal, 1969, British
THE GAMBLER   Paramount, 1974
WHO'LL STOP THE RAIN   United Artists, 1978
THE FRENCH LIEUTENANT'S WOMAN   United Artists, 1981, British

WOLFGANG REITHERMAN

Business: Walt Disney Productions, 500 S. Buena Vista Street, Burbank, CA 91521,
     213/845-3141

101 DALMATIONS (AF)   co-director with Hamilton S. Luke & Clyde Geronimi,
     Buena Vista, 1961
THE SWORD IN THE STONE (AF)   Buena Vista, 1963
THE JUNGLE BOOK (AF)   Buena Vista, 1967
THE ARISTOCATS (AF)   Buena Vista, 1970
ROBIN HOOD (AF)   Buena Vista, 1973
THE RESCUERS (AF)   Buena Vista, 1977

IVAN REITMAN *

b. October 26, 1946 - Czechoslovakia
Contact: Directors Guild of America - Los Angeles, 213/656-1220

FOXY LADY   Ivan Reitman Productions, 1971, Canadian
CANNIBAL GIRLS   American International, 1973, Canadian
MEATBALLS   Paramount, 1979, Canadian
STRIPES   Columbia, 1981

ALAIN RESNAIS

b. June 3, 1922 - Vannes, France
Contact: French Film Office, 745 Fifth Avenue, New York, NY 10151, 212/832-
     8860

HIROSHIMA, MON AMOUR   Zenith, 1959, French
LAST YEAR AT MARIENBAD   Astor, 1961, French-Italian
MURIEL   Lopert, 1963, French-Italian
LA GUERRE EST FINIE   Brandon, 1966, French-Swedish
FAR FROM VIETNAM   co-director with Jean-Luc Godard, William Klein, Claude
     Lelouch, Agnes Varda & Joris Ivens, New Yorker, 1967, French
JE T'AIME, JE T'AIME   New Yorker, 1968, French-Spanish
STAVISKY   Cinemation, 1974, French
PROVIDENCE   Cinema 5, 1977, French-Swiss
MON ONCLE D' AMERIQUE   New World, 1980, French
LIFE IS A BED OF ROSES *LA VIE EST UN ROMAN*   Spectrafilm, 1983,
     French

BURT REYNOLDS *

b. February 11, 1936 - Waycross, Georgia
Business: Burt Reynolds Productions, 8730 Sunset Blvd. - Suite 201, Los Angeles,
     CA 90069, 213/652-6005
Personal Manager: Clayton Enterprises, 8730 Sunset Blvd., Los Angeles, CA 90069,
     213/659-5186
Business Manager: Global Business Management - Beverly Hills, 213/278-4141

GATOR   United Artists, 1976
THE END   United Artists, 1978
SHARKY'S MACHINE   Orion/Warner Bros., 1982

continued

BURT REYNOLDS*—continued
STICK   Universal, 1984

GENE REYNOLDS*

Agent: Leonard Hanzer, Major Talent Agency - Los Angeles, 213/820-5841

IN DEFENSE OF KIDS (TF)   MTM Enterprises, 1983

KEVIN REYNOLDS*

b. January 17, 1952 - San Antonio, Texas
Business: Windmill Films, Inc., 5201 Lake Jackson, Waco, TX 76710, 213/506-
    1690
Agent: William Morris Agency - Beverly Hills, 213/274-7451

FANDANGO   Warner Bros., 1983

DAVID LOWELL RICH*

b. August 31, 1920 - New York, New York
Home: 465 Loring Avenue, Los Angeles, CA 90024, 213/279-1783
Agent: William Morris Agency - Beverly Hills, 213/274-7451
Business Manager: Wade Hansen, Boulder Brook, Inc., 3223 Laurel Canyon Blvd.,
    Studio City, CA 91604

NO TIME TO BE YOUNG   Columbia, 1957
SENIOR PROM   Columbia, 1958
HEY BOY! HEY GIRL!   Columbia, 1959
HAVE ROCKET, WILL TRAVEL   Columbia, 1959
SEE HOW THEY RUN (TF)   Universal TV, 1964
MADAME X   Universal, 1966
THE PLAINSMAN   Universal, 1966
ROSIE!   Universal, 1967
WINGS OF FIRE (TF)   Universal TV, 1967
THE BORGIA STICK (TF)   Universal TV, 1967
A LOVELY WAY TO DIE   Universal, 1968
THREE GUNS FOR TEXAS   co-director with Paul Stanley & Earl Bellamy,
    Universal, 1968
MARCUS WELBY, M.D. (TF)   Universal TV, 1969
EYE TO THE CAT   Universal, 1969
THE MASK OF SHEBA (TF)   MGM TV, 1970
BERLIN AFFAIR (TF)   Universal TV, 1970
THE SHERIFF (TF)   Screen Gems/Columbia TV, 1971
ASSIGNMENT: MUNICH (TF)   MGM TV, 1972
LIEUTENANT SCHUSTER'S WIFE (TF)   Universal TV, 1972
ALL MY DARLING DAUGHTERS (TF)   Universal TV, 1972
THAT MAN BOLT   co-director with Henry Levin, Universal, 1972
THE JUDGE AND JAKE WYLER (TF)   Universal TV, 1972
SET THIS TOWN ON FIRE (TF)   Universal TV, 1973
THE HORROR AT 37,000 FEET (TF)   CBS, Inc., 1973
BROCK'S LAST CASE (TF)   Talent Associates/Universal TV, 1973
CRIME CLUB (TF)   CBS, Inc., 1973
BEG, BORROW ... OR STEAL (TF)   Universal TV, 1973
SATAN'S SCHOOL FOR GIRLS (TF)   Spelling-Goldberg Productions, 1973
RUNAWAY! (TF)   Universal TV, 1973
DEATH RACE (TF)   Universal TV, 1973
THE CHADWICK FAMILY (TF)   Universal TV, 1974
THE SEX SYMBOL (TF)   Screen Gems/Columbia, 1974
ALOHA MEANS GOODBYE (TF)   Universal TV, 1974
THE DAUGHTERS OF JOSHUA CABE RETURN (TF)   Spelling-Goldberg
    Productions, 1975
ADVENTURES OF THE QUEEN (TF)   20th Century-Fox TV, 1975
YOU LIE SO DEEP, MY LOVE (TF)   Universal TV, 1975
BRIDGER (TF)   Universal TV, 1976
THE SECRET LIFE OF JOHN CHAPMAN (TF)   The Jozak Company, 1976
THE STORY OF DAVID (TF)   co-director with Alex Segal, Mildred Freed Alberg
    Productions/Columbia TV, 1976
SST - DEATH FLIGHT (TF)   ABC Circle Films, 1977
RANSOM FOR ALICE! (TF)   Universal TV, 1977
TELETHON (TF)   ABC Circle Films, 1977

continued

DAVID LOWELL RICH*—continued

THE DEFECTION OF SIMAS KUDIRKA (TF) ☆☆   The Jozak Company/
   Paramount TV, 1978
A FAMILY UPSIDE DOWN (TF)   Ross Hunter-Jacques Mapes Film/Paramount
   TV, 1978
LITTLE WOMEN (TF)   Universal TV, 1978
THE CONCORDE - AIRPORT '79 Universal, 1979
NURSE (TF)   Robert Halmi Productions, 1980
ENOLA GAY (TF)   The Production Company/Viacom, 1980
CHU CHU AND THE PHILLY FLASH   20th Century-Fox, 1981
THURSDAY'S CHILD (TF)   The Catalina Production Group/Viacom, 1983
THE FIGHTER (TF)   Martin Manulis Productions/The Catalina Production Group,
   1983
I WANT TO LIVE (TF)   United Artists Corporation, 1983

J O H N   R I C H *

b. July 6, 1925 - Rockaway Beach, New York
Agent: Leonard Hanzer, Major Talent Agency - Los Angeles, 213/820-5841
Business Manager: Marvin Freedman, Freedman, Kinzelberg & Broder, 1801 Avenue
   of the Stars - Suite 911, Los Angeles, CA 90067, 213/277-0700
Attorney: Arnold Burk, Gang, Tyre & Brown - Los Angeles, 213/557-7777

WIVES AND LOVERS   Paramount, 1963
THE NEW INTERNS   Columbia, 1964
ROUSTABOUT   Paramount, 1964
BOEING BOEING   Paramount, 1965
EASY COME, EASY GO   Paramount, 1967

R I C H A R D   R I C H

Business: Walt Disney Productions, 500 S. Buena Vista Street, Burbank, CA 91521,
   213/845-3141

THE FOX AND THE HOUND (AF)   co-director with Art Stevens & Ted
   Berman, Buena Vista, 1981
THE BLACK CAULDRON (AF)   co-director with Art Stevens & Ted Berman,
   Buena Vista, 1985

D I C K   R I C H A R D S *

b. 1936
Agent: Stan Kamen, William Morris Agency - Beverly Hills, 213/274-7451

THE CULPEPPER CATTLE CO.   20th Century-Fox, 1972
RAFFERTY AND THE GOLD DUST TWINS   Warner Bros., 1975
FAREWELL, MY LOVELY   Avco Embassy, 1975
MARCH OR DIE   Columbia, 1977, British
DEATH VALLEY   Universal, 1981
MAN, WOMEN AND CHILD   Paramount, 1983

L L O Y D   R I C H A R D S *

Home: 90 York Square, New Haven, CT 06511, 203/865-2933
Messages: 203/436-1586

ROOTS: THE NEXT GENERATIONS (MS)   co-director with John Erman,
   Charles S. Dubin & Georg Stanford Brown, Wolper Productions, 1979

T O N Y   R I C H A R D S O N *
(Cecil Antonio Richardson)

b. June 5, 1928 - Shipley, England
Business: 1478 N. Kings Road, Los Angeles, CA 90069

LOOK BACK IN ANGER   Warner Bros., 1958, British
THE ENTERTAINER   Continental, 1960, British
SANCTUARY   20th Century-Fox, 1961
A TASTE OF HONEY   Continental, 1962, British

continued

TONY RICHARDSON*—continued

THE LONELINESS OF THE LONG DISTANCE RUNNER   Continental, 1962,
British
TOM JONES ★★   Lopert, 1963, British
THE LOVED ONE   MGM, 1965
MADEMOISELLE   Lopert, 1966, French-British
THE SAILOR FROM GIBRALTER   Lopert, 1967, British
THE CHARGE OF THE LIGHT BRIGADE   United Artists, 1968, British
LAUGHTER IN THE DARK   Lopert, 1969, British-French
HAMLET   Columbia, 1969, British
NED KELLY   United Artists, 1970, British
A DELICATE BALANCE   American Film Theatre, 1973
DEAD CERT   United Artists, 1973, British
JOSEPH ANDREWS   Paramount, 1977, British
A DEATH IN CANAAN (TF)   Chris-Rose Productions/Warner Bros. TV, 1978
THE BORDER   Universal, 1982
THE HOTEL NEW HAMPSHIRE   Orion, 1984

WILLIAM RICHERT

Contact: Writers Guild of America, West - Los Angeles, 213/550-1000

FIRST POSITION (FD)   Roninfilm, 1973
WINTER KILLS   Avco Embassy, 1979
THE AMERICAN SUCCESS CO. *SUCCESS*   Columbia, 1979, West German-
U.S.

W.D. RICHTER

Contact: Writers Guild of America, West - Los Angeles, 213/550-1000

BUCKAROO BANZAI   20th Century-Fox, 1984

TOM RICKMAN

Contact: Writers Guild of America, West - Los Angeles, 213/550-1000

RIVER RATS   Deep River/Sundance Productions, 1984

DINO RISI

b. December 23, 1917 - Milan, Italy
Contact: Ministry of Tourism & Education, Via Della Ferratella, No. 51, 00184
Rome, Italy, 06/7732

VACANZE COL GANGSTER   Mambretti Film, 1952, Italian
VIALE DELLA SPERANZA   Mambretti Film/ENIC, 1953, Italian
LOVE IN THE CITY   co-director with Michelangelo Antonioni, Federico Fellini,
Alberto Lattuada, Carlo Lizzani & Francesco Maselli, Italian Films Export, 1953,
Italian
IL SEGNO DI VENERE   Titanus, 1955, Italian
SCANDAL IN SORRENTO *PANE, AMORE E ...*   DCA, 1955, Italian
POOR BUT BEAUTIFUL   Trans-Lux, 1956, Italian-French
LA NONNA SABELLA   Titanus/Franco-London Films, 1957, Italian-French
BELLE MA POVERE   Titanus, 1957, Italian
VENEZIA, LA LUNA E TU   Titanus/Societe Generale de Cinematographie,
1958, Italian-French
POVERI MILLIONARI   Titanus, 1958, Italian
IL VEDOVO   Paneuropa/Cino Del Duca, 1959, Italian
LOVE AND LARCENY *IL MATTATORE*   Major Film, 1960, Italian-French
UN AMORE A ROMA   CEI Incom/Fair Film/Laetitia Film/Les Films Cocinor/
Alpha Film, 1960, Italian-French-West German
A PORTE CHIUSE   Fair Film/Cinematografica Rire/Societe Generale de
Cinematographie/Ultra Film/Lyre Film/Roxy Film, 1960, Italian-French-West
German
UNA VITA DIFFICILE   Dino De Laurentiis Cinematografica, 1961, Italian
LA MARCIA SU ROMA   Fair Film/Orsay Films, 1962, Italian-French
THE EASY LIFE *IL SORPASSO*   Embassy, 1962, Italian
IL GIOVEDI   Dino De Laurentiis Cinematografica/Center Film, 1963, Italian
15 FROM ROME *I MOSTRI*   McAbee, 1963, Italian-French
IL GAUCHO   Fair Film/Clemente Lococo, 1964, Italian-Argentinian

continued

DINO RISI—continued

BAMBOLE!   co-director with Luigi Comencini, Franco Rossi & Mauro Bolognini, Royal Films International, 1965, Italian
I COMPLESSI   co-director with Franco Rossi & Luigi Filippo D'Amico, Documento Film/SPCE, 1965, Italian-French
WEEKEND, ITALIAN STYLE *L'OMBRELLONE*   Marvin Films, 1965, Italian-French-Spanish
I NOSTRI MARITI   co-director with Luigi Filippo D'Amico & Luigi Zampa, Documento Film, 1966, Italian
TREASURE OF SAN GENNARO *OPERAZIONE SAN GENNARO*   Paramount, 1966, Italian-French-West German
THE TIGER AND THE PUSSYCAT *IL TIGRE*   Embassy, 1967, Italian-U.S.
THE PROPHET   Joseph Green Pictures, 1967, Italian
STRAZIAMI DA MI BACI SAZIAMI   FIDA Cinematografica/Productions Jacques Roitfeld, 1968, Italian-French
VEDO NUDO   Dean Film/Jupiter Generale Cinematografica, 1969, Italian
IL GIOVANE NORMALE   Dean Film/Italnoleggio, 1969, Italian
THE PRIEST'S WIFE   Warner Bros., 1970, Italian-French
NOI DONNE SIAMO FATTE COSI   Apollo International Film, 1971, Italian
IN NOME DEL POPOLO ITALIANO   Apollo International Film, 1972, Italian
MORDI E FUGGI   C.C. Champion/Les Films Concordia, 1973, Italian-French
HOW FUNNY CAN SEX BE? *SESSOMATTO*   In-Frame, 1973, Italian
TELEFONI BIANCHI   Dean Film, 1975, Italian
SCENT OF A WOMAN   20th Century-Fox, 1976, Italian
ANIMA PERSA   Dean Film/Les Productions Fox Europe, 1977, Italian-French
LA STANZA DEL VESCOVO   Merope Film/Carlton Film Export/Societe Nouvelle Prodis, 1977, Italian-French
VIVA ITALIA! *I NUOVI MOSTRI*   co-director with Mario Monicelli & Ettore Scola, Cinema 6, 1978, Italian
PRIMO AMORE   Dean Film, 1978, Italian
CARO PAPA'   Dean Film/AMLF/Prospect Film, 1979, Italian-French-Canadian
SUNDAY LOVERS   co-director with Bryan Forbes, Edouard Molinaro & Gene Wilder, MGM/United Artists, 1980, U.S.-British-Italian-French
SONO FOTOGENICO   Dean Film/Marceau Cocinor, 1980, Italian-French
GHOST OF LOVE   Dean Film/AMLF/Roxy Film, 1981, Italian-French-West German
SESSO E VOLENTIERI   Dean Film, 1982, Italian
LA VITA CONTINUA (MS)   1983, Italian

MICHAEL RITCHIE*

b. 1938 - Waukesha, Wisconsin
Business Manager: Marvin Freedman, Freedman, Kinzelberg & Broder, 1801 Avenue of the Stars - Suite 911, Los Angeles, CA 90067, 213/277-0700

THE OUTSIDER (TF)   Universal TV, 1967
THE SOUND OF ANGER (TF)   Universal TV, 1968
DOWNHILL RACER   Paramount, 1969
PRIME CUT   National General, 1972
THE CANDIDATE   Warner Bros., 1972
SMILE   United Artists, 1975
THE BAD NEWS BEARS   Paramount, 1976
SEMI-TOUGH   United Artists, 1978
AN ALMOST PERFECT AFFAIR   Paramount, 1979
THE ISLAND   Universal, 1980
DIVINE MADNESS (TF)   The Ladd Company/Warner Bros., 1980
THE SURVIVORS   Columbia, 1983

MARTIN RITT*

b. March 2, 1920 - New York, New York
Agent: George Chasin, Chasin-Park-Citron - Los Angeles, 213/273-7190

EDGE OF THE CITY   MGM, 1957
NO DOWN PAYMENT   20th Century-Fox, 1957
THE LONG HOT SUMMER   MGM, 1958
THE BLACK ORCHID   Paramount, 1959
THE SOUND AND THE FURY   20th Century-Fox, 1959
FIVE BRANDED WOMEN   Paramount, 1960, Italian-Yugoslavian-U.S.
PARIS BLUES   United Artists, 1961
HEMINGWAY'S ADVENTURES OF A YOUNG MAN   20th Century-Fox, 1962

continued

MARTIN RITT*—continued

HUD ★   Paramount, 1963
THE OUTRAGE   MGM, 1964
THE SPY WHO CAME IN FROM THE COLD   Paramount, 1965, British
HOMBRE   20th Century-Fox, 1967
THE BROTHERHOOD   Paramount, 1968
THE MOLLY MAGUIRES   Paramount, 1970
THE GREAT WHITE HOPE   20th Century-Fox, 1970
SOUNDER   20th Century-Fox, 1972
PETE N' TILLIE   Universal, 1972
CONRACK   20th Century-Fox, 1974
THE FRONT   Columbia, 1976
CASEY'S SHADOW   Columbia, 1978
NORMA RAE   20th Century-Fox, 1979
BACK ROADS   Warner Bros., 1981
CROSS CREEK   Universal/AFD, 1983

FREDERICK RITZENBERG

GOSPEL (FD)   co-director with David Leivick, 20th Century-Fox, 1983

JOAN RIVERS*

b. 1937 - New York, New York
Personal Manager: Katz-Gallin-Morey Enterprises, 9255 Sunset Blvd. - Suite 1115,
    Los Angeles, CA 90069, 213/273-4210

RABBIT TEST   Avco Embassy, 1978

ALAIN ROBBE-GRILLET

b. August 18, 1922 - Brest, France
Home: 18 Boulevard Maillot, 92200 Neuilly, France, 1/722-3122

L'IMMORTELLE   Grove Press, 1963, French
TRANS-EUROP-EXPRESS   Trans-American, 1967, French
THE MAN WHO LIES   Grove Press, 1968, French-Czech
L'EDEN ET APRES   Como Films, 1971, French-Czech-Tunisian
GLISSMENTS PROGRESSIFS DU PLAISIR   SNETC, 1974, French
LE JEU AVEC LE FEU   Arcadie Productions, 1975, Italian-French
LA BELLE CAPTIVE   Argos Films, 1983, French

SEYMOUR ROBBIE*

Home: 9980 Liebe Drive, Beverly Hills, CA 90210, 213/274-6713
Agent: Sylvia Gold, ICM - Los Angeles, 213/550-4000

C.C. AND COMPANY   Avco Embassy, 1970
MARCO   Cinerama Releasing Corporation, 1974

JEROME ROBBINS*
(Jerome Rabinowitz)

b. October 11, 1918 - Weehawken, New Jersey
Business: New York City Ballet, 1 Lincoln Plaza, New York, NY, 212/870-5656

WEST SIDE STORY ★★   co-director with Robert Wise, United Artists, 1961

MATTHEW ROBBINS*

Contact: Directors Guild of America - Los Angeles, 213/656-1220

CORVETTE SUMMER   MGM/United Artists, 1978
DRAGONSLAYER   Paramount, 1981, U.S.-British

YVES ROBERT

b. June 19, 1920 - Saumur, France
Contact: French Film Office, 745 Fifth Avenue, New York, NY 10151, 212/832-8860

LES HOMMES NE PENSENT QU'A CA 1954, French
SIGNE ARSENE LUPIN   1959, French
LA FAMILLE FENOUILLARD   1961, French
LA GUERRE DES BOUTONS   LGE, 1962, French
BEBERT ET L'OMNIBUS   1963, French
LES COPAINS   1964, French
MONNAIRE DE SINGE   1965, French
VERY HAPPY ALEXANDER *ALEXANDER*   Cinema 5, 1968, French
CLERAMBARD   1969, French
THE TALL BLOND MAN WITH ONE BLACK SHOE   Cinema 5, 1972, French
SALUT L'ARTISTE   Exxel, 1973, French
RETURN OF THE TALL BLOND MAN WITH ONE BLACK SHOE   Lanir Releasing, 1974, French
PARDON MON AFFAIRE *AN ELEPHANT CA TROMPE ENORMEMENT*   First Artists, 1977, French
PARDON MON AFFAIRE, TOO! *NOUS IRONS TOUS AU PARADIS*   First Artists, 1978, French
COURAGE FUYONS   LGE, 1980, French

ALAN ROBERTS

Contact: Writers Guild of America, West - Los Angeles, 213/550-1000

THE ZODIAC COUPLES   co-director with Bob Stein, SAE, 1970
PANORAMA BLUE   Ellman Film Enterprises, 1974
YOUNG LADY CHATTERLEY   Intercontinental, 1977, British
THE HAPPY HOOKER GOES HOLLYWOOD   Cannon, 1980
FLASHDANCE FEVER   Shapiro Entertainment, 1983

CLIFF ROBERTSON *

b. September 9, 1925 - La Jolla, California
Agent: Michael Black, ICM - Los Angeles, 213/550-4000

J.W. COOP   Columbia, 1972
THE PILOT   Summit Features, 1981

HUGH A. ROBERTSON *

Home: 208A Terrace Vale Road, Good Wood Park, Trinidad, West Indies, 809/637-5994
Business: Sharc Productions, Ltd., 1 Valleton Avenue, Maraval, Trinidad, West Indies, 809/622-6580
Agent: Ron Mutchnick - Los Angeles, 213/659-3294

MELINDA   MGM, 1972
BIM   Sharc Productions, 1976, West Indian

FRANC RODDAM *

b. April 29 - Stockton, England
Agent: Spokesmen, Ltd., 1 Craven Hill, London W2, England
Contact: Directors Guild of America - Los Angeles, 213/656-1220

QUADROPHENIA   World Northal, 1979, British
THE LORDS OF DISCIPLINE   Paramount, 1983

NICOLAS ROEG *

b. December 15, 1928 - London, England
Home: 2 Oxford-Cambridge Mansions, Old Marylebone Road, London NW1, England,
   01/262-8612
Agent: Robert Littman Company - Beverly Hills, 213/278-1572

PERFORMANCE   co-director with Donald Cammell, Warner Bros., 1970, British
WALKABOUT   20th Century-Fox, 1971, British-Australian
DON'T LOOK NOW   Paramount, 1974, British-Italian
THE MAN WHO FELL TO EARTH   Cinema 5, 1976, British
BAD TIMING/A SENSUAL OBSESSION   World Northal, 1980, British
EUREKA   United Artists Classics, 1983, British

MICHAEL ROEMER

b. January 1, 1928 - Berlin, Germany

A TOUCH OF THE TIMES   1949
NOTHING BUT A MAN   co-director with Robert M. Young, Cinema 5, 1965
DYING (TD)   WGBH-Boston, 1976
PILGRIM, FAREWELL   Post Mills Productions, 1980

LIONEL ROGOSIN

b. 1924 - New York, New York

ON THE BOWERY (FD)   Film Representations, 1957
COME BACK, AFRICA (FD)   Rogosin, 1959
GOOD TIMES, WONDERFUL TIMES (FD)   Rogosin, 1966
BLACK ROOTS (FD)   Rogosin, 1970
BLACK FANTASY (FD)   Impact, 1972
WOODCUTTERS OF THE DEEP SOUTH (FD)   Rogosin, 1973

ERIC ROHMER
(Jean-Marie Maurice Scherer)

b. April 4, 1920 - Nancy, France
Contact: French Film Office, 745 Fifth Avenue, New York, NY 10151, 212/832-
   8860

LE SIGNE DU LION   1959, French
LA CARRIERE DE SUZANNE   Films du Losange, 1963, French
PARIS VU PAR ...   co-director, 1965, French
LA COLLECTIONNEUSE   Pathe Contemporary, 1967, French
MY NIGHT AT MAUD'S   Pathe Contemporary, 1970, French
CLAIRE'S KNEE   Columbia, 1971, French
CHLOE IN THE AFTERNOON   Columbia, 1972, French
THE MARQUISE OF O ...   New Line Cinema, 1976, French-West German
PERCEVAL   New Yorker, 1978, French
THE AVIATOR'S WIFE   New Yorker, 1980, French
LE BEAU MARIAGE   United Artists Classics, 1982, French
PAULINE AT THE BEACH   Orion Classics, 1983, French

SUTTON ROLEY *

Home: 777 Arden Road, Pasadena, CA 91106, 213/449-2491

SWEET, SWEET RACHEL (TF)   ABC, Inc., 1971
THE LONERS   Fanfare, 1972
SNATCHED (TF)   ABC Circle Films, 1973
SATAN'S TRIANGLE (TF)   Danny Thomas Productions, 1975
CHOSEN SURVIVORS   Columbia, 1974

EDDIE ROMERO

b. 1924 - Negros Oriental, Philippines
Contact: Philippine Motion Picture Producers Association, 514 Burke Building,
    Escolta Manila. Philippines, 2/48-7731

THE DAY OF THE TRUMPET   1957, U.S.-Filipino
THE RAIDERS OF LEYTE GULF   Hemisphere, 1963, Filipino-U.S.
MORE WITCH DOCTOR   20th Century-Fox, 1964, Filipino-U.S.
THE KIDNAPPERS *MAN ON THE RUN*   1964
THE WALLS OF HELL   co-director with Gerardo De Leon, Hemisphere, 1964,
    U.S.-Filipino
THE RAVAGERS   Hemisphere, 1965, U.S.-Filipino
BEAST OF BLOOD   Marvin Films, 1971, U.S.-Filipino
BLACK MAMA, WHITE MAMA   American International, 1973, U.S.-Filipino
BEYOND ATLANTIS   Dimension, 1973, U.S.-Filipino
SAVAGE SISTERS   American International, 1974, U.S.-Filipino
THE WOMAN HUNT   New World, 1975, U.S.-Filipino
SUDDEN DEATH   Topar, 1977, U.S.-Filipino
DESIRE   Hemisphere, 1983, Filipino
GANITO KAMI NOON, PAANO KAYO NGAYON?   1983, Filipino

GEORGE A. ROMERO

Business: Laurel Entertainment Inc., 928 Broadway, New York, NY 10010, 212/674-
    3800

NIGHT OF THE LIVING DEAD   Continental, 1968
THERE'S ALWAYS VANILLA   Cambist, 1972
THE CRAZIES *CODE NAME: TRIXIE*   Cambist, 1972
HUNGRY WIVES   Jack H. Harris Enterprises, 1973
MARTIN   Libra, 1978
DAWN OF THE DEAD   United Film Distribution, 1979
KNIGHTRIDERS   United Film Distribution, 1981
CREEPSHOW   Warner Bros., 1982

CONRAD ROOKS

CHAPPAQUA   Regional, 1968
SIDDHARTHA   Columbia, 1973

LES ROSE

Home: 17 Maple Avenue, Toronto, Ontario, Canada, 415/960-1829
Agent: Jeanine Edwards/Fifi Oscard - New York City, 212/764-1100

THREE CARD MONTE   Arista, 1977, Canadian
TITLE SHOT   Arista, 1979, Canadian
HOG WILD   Avco Embassy, 1980, Canadian
GAS   Paramount, 1981, Canadian
GORDON PINSENT AND THE LIFE AND TIMES OF EDWIN ALONZO
    BOYD (TF)   Poundmaker Productions, 1982, Canadian

MICKEY ROSE

Contact: Robinson-Weintraub Associates - Los Angeles, 213/653-5802

STUDENT BODIES   Paramount, 1981

MARTIN ROSEN

WATERSHIP DOWN (AF)   Avco Embassy, 1978, British
THE PLAGUE DOGS (AF)   Nepenthe Productions, 1982, British

ROBERT L. ROSEN

COURAGE   Sandy Howard/Adams Apple Productions, 1984

STUART ROSENBERG *

b. 1982 - New York, New York
Agent: William Morris Agency - Beverly Hills, 213/274-7451

MURDER, INC.   co-director with Burt Balaban, 20th Century-Fox, 1960
QUESTION 7   De Rochemont, 1961, U.S.-West German
FAME IS THE NAME OF THE GAME (TF)   Universal TV, 1966
ASYLUM FOR A SPY (TF)   Universal TV, 1967
COOL HAND LUKE   Warner Bros., 1967
THE APRIL FOOLS   National General, 1969
MOVE   20th Century-Fox, 1970
WUSA   Paramount, 1970
POCKET MONEY   National General, 1972
THE LAUGHING POLICEMAN   20th Century-Fox, 1973
THE DROWNING POOL   Warner Bros., 1975
VOYAGE OF THE DAMNED   Avco Embassy, 1977, British
LOVE AND BULLETS   AFD, 1979
THE AMITYVILLE HORROR   American International, 1979
BRUBAKER   20th Century-Fox, 1980
THE POPE OF GREENWICH VILLAGE   MGM/UA, 1984

RALPH ROSENBLUM *

Home: 344 West 84th Street, New York, NY 10024, 212/595-7975
Agent: The Gersh Agency - Beverly Hills, 213/274-6611

THE GREATEST MAN IN THE WORLD (TF)   Learning in Focus, 1979
ANY FRIEND OF NICHOLAS NICKLEBY IS A FRIEND OF MINE
    (TF)   Rubicon Productions, 1982

RICK ROSENTHAL *

Agent: The Gersh Agency - Beverly Hills, 213/274-6611

HALLOWEEN II   Universal, 1981
BAD BOYS   Universal/AFD, 1983
AMERICAN DREAMER   Warner Bros., 1984

ROBERT J. ROSENTHAL

Contact: Writers Guild of America, West - Los Angeles, 213/550-1000

MALIBU BEACH   Crown International, 1978
ZAPPED!   Embassy, 1982

FRANCESCO ROSI

b. November 15, 1922 - Naples, Italy
Contact: Ministry of Tourism & Education, Via Della Ferratella, No. 51, 00184
    Rome, Italy 06/7732

LA SFIDA   Lux/Vices/Suevia Film, 1958, Italian-Spanish
I MAGLIARI   Vides/Titanus, 1959, Italian
SALVATORE GIULIANO   CCM Films, 1962, Italian-French
LE MANI SULLA CITTA   Galatea Film, 1963, Italian
THE MOMENT OF TRUTH   Rizzoli, 1965, Italian-Spanish
MORE THAN A MIRACLE C'ERA UNA VOLTA   MGM, 1967, Italian-French
UOMINI CONTRO   Prima Cinematografica/Jadran Film, 1970, Italian-Yugoslavian
THE MATTEI AFFAIR   Paramount, 1973, Italian
LUCKY LUCIANO   Avco Embassy, 1974, Italian
IL CONTESTO   1975, Italian
ILLUSTRIOUS CORPSES   United Artists, 1976, Italian-French
EBOLI CHRIST STOPPED AT EBOLI   Franklin Media, 1980, Italian-French
THREE BROTHERS   New World, 1981, Italian
CARMEN   Gaumont, 1984, Italian-French

MARK ROSMAN

THE HOUSE ON SORORITY ROW   Artists Releasing Corporation/Film
Ventures International, 1983

HERBERT ROSS *

b. May 13, 1927 - New York, New York
Agent: William Morris Agency - Beverly Hills, 213/274-7451

GOODBYE, MR. CHIPS   MGM, 1969, British
THE OWL AND THE PUSSYCAT   Columbia, 1970
T.R. BASKIN   Paramount, 1971
PLAY IT AGAIN, SAM   Paramount, 1972
THE LAST OF SHEILA   Warner Bros., 1973
FUNNY LADY   Columbia, 1975
THE SUNSHINE BOYS   MGM/United Artists, 1975
THE SEVEN-PER-CENT SOLUTION   Universal, 1976, British
THE TURNING POINT ★   20th Century-Fox, 1977
THE GOODBYE GIRL   Warner Bros., 1977
CALIFORNIA SUITE   Columbia, 1978
NIJINSKY   Paramount, 1980
PENNIES FROM HEAVEN   MGM/United Artists, 1981
I OUGHT TO BE IN PICTURES   20th Century-Fox, 1982
MAX DUGAN RETURNS   20th Century-Fox, 1983
FOOTLOOSE   Paramount, 1984

BOBBY ROTH *

Home: 7957 Fareholm Drive, Los Angeles, CA 90068, 213/851-9702
Agent: John Burman, ICM - Los Angeles, 213/550-1000

INDEPENDENCE DAY   Unifilm, 1977
THE BOSS' SON   Circle Associates, 1980
CIRCLE OF POWER *MYSTIQUE/BRAINWASH/THE NAKED
    WEEKEND*   Televicine, 1983

STEPHANIE ROTHMAN

Contact: Writers Guild of America, West - Los Angeles, 213/550-1000

BLOOD BATH   co-director with Jack Hill, American International, 1966
IT'S A BIKINI WORLD   American International, 1967
THE STUDENT NURSES   New World, 1970
THE VELVET VAMPIRE   New World, 1971
GROUP MARRIAGE   Dimension, 1973
THE WORKING GIRLS   Dimension, 1974

RUSSELL ROUSE *

b. April 3, 1915 - New York, New York
Contact: Herman Rotsten, 620 N. Martel Avenue, Los Angeles, CA 90036, 213/
    655-0529
Attorney: Covey & Covey - Los Angeles, 213/272-0074

THE WELL   co-director with Leo Popkins, United Artists, 1951
THE THIEF   United Artists, 1952
WICKED WOMAN   United Artists, 1954
NEW YORK CONFIDENTIAL   Warner Bros., 1955
THE FASTEST GUN ALIVE   MGM, 1956
HOUSE OF NUMBERS   Columbia, 1957
THUNDER IN THE SUN   Paramount, 1959
A HOUSE IS NOT A HOME   Embassy, 1964
THE OSCAR   Embassy, 1966
THE CAPER OF THE GOLDEN BULLS   Embassy, 1967

JOSEPH RUBEN *

Home: 2680 Woodstock Road, Los Angeles, CA 90405, 213/392-9006
Agent: John Ptak, William Morris Agency - Beverly Hills, 213/274-7451

THE SISTER-IN-LAW   Crown International, 1975
THE POM-POM GIRLS   Crown International, 1976
JOYRIDE   American International, 1977
OUR WINNING SEASON   American International, 1978
GORP   American International, 1980
DREAMSCAPE   Bruce Cohn Curtis/Bella Productions, 1983

ALAN RUDOLPH *

Agent: Sue Mengers/Jim Wiatt, ICM - Los Angeles, 213/550-4000
Business Manager: William Goldstein - Los Angeles, 213/783-7671

WELCOME TO L.A.   United Artists/Lions Gate, 1977
REMEMBER MY NAME   Columbia/Lagoon Associates, 1979
ROADIE   United Artists, 1980
ENDANGERED SPECIES   MGM/UA, 1982
RETURN ENGAGEMENT (FD)   Island Alive, 1983
CHOOSE ME   Island Alive/New Image, 1984
SONGWRITER   Tri-Star/Columbia, 1984

RICHARD RUSH *

b. 1930
Agent: ICM - Los Angeles, 213/550-4000

TOO SOON TO LOVE   Universal, 1960
OF LOVE AND DESIRE   20th Century-Fox, 1963
FICKLE FINGER OF FATE   Pro International, 1967
THUNDER ALLEY   American International, 1967
HELL'S ANGELS ON WHEELS   American International, 1967
A MAN CALLED DAGGER   MGM, 1968
PSYCH-OUT   American International, 1968
THE SAVAGE SEVEN   American International, 1968
GETTING STRAIGHT   Columbia, 1970
FREEBIE AND THE BEAN   Warner Bros., 1974
THE STUNT MAN ★   20th Century-Fox, 1980

KEN RUSSELL *

b. July 3, 1927 - Southampton, England
Contact: Directors Guild of America - Los Angeles, 213/656-1220

FRENCH DRESSING   Warner-Pathe, 1963, British
BILLION DOLLAR BRAIN   United Artists, 1967, British
DANTE'S INFERNO (TF)   BBC, 1967, British
SONG OF SUMMER (TF)   BBC, 1968, British
THE DANCE OF THE SEVEN VEILS (TF)   BBC, 1970, British
WOMEN IN LOVE ★   United Artists, 1970, British
THE MUSIC LOVERS   United Artists, 1971, British
THE DEVILS   Warner Bros., 1971, British
THE BOY FRIEND   MGM, 1971, British
SAVAGE MESSIAH   MGM, 1972, British
MAHLER   Mayfair, 1974, British
TOMMY   Columbia, 1975, British
LISZTOMANIA   Warner Bros., 1975, British
VALENTINO   United Artists, 1977, British
ALTERED STATES   Warner Bros., 1980

MARK RYDELL *

b. March 23, 1934
Agent: William Morris Agency - Beverly Hills, 213/274-7451

THE FOX   Claridge, 1968
THE REIVERS   National General, 1969
THE COWBOYS   Warner Bros., 1972

continued

MARK RYDELL*—continued

CINDERELLA LIBERTY   20th Century-Fox, 1974
HARRY AND WALTER GO TO NEW YORK   Columbia, 1976
THE ROSE   20th Century-Fox, 1979
ON GOLDEN POND ★   Universal/AFD, 1981
THE RIVER   Universal, 1984

S

WILLIAM SACHS

Agent: Shapiro-Lichtman Agency - Los Angeles, 231/557-2244

SECRETS OF THE GODS   Film Ventures International, 1976
THERE IS NO THIRTEEN   Film Ventures International, 1977
THE INCREDIBLE MELTING MAN   American International, 1977
VAN NUYS BLVD.   Crown International, 1979
GALAXINA   Crown International, 1980

ALAN SACKS

Contact: Writers Guild of America, West - Los Angeles, 213/550-1000

DU BEAT-E-O   Sacks-Halpern Productions, 1984

HENRI SAFRAN

Contact: Mitch Consultancy, 98 Bay Road, Waverton, NSW, 2060, Australia, 02/
    922-6566

TROUBLE SHOOTER (MS)   1975, Australian
SOFTLY SOFTLY (MS)   1975, Australian
ELEPHANT BOY   1975, Australian
LOVE STORY (MS)   1976, Australian
STORM BOY   South Australian Film Corporation, 1976, Australian
NORMAN LOVES ROSE   Atlantic Releasing Corporation, 1981, Australian
THE WILD DUCK   Orion, 1983, Australian
BUSH CHRISTMAS   Quartet, 1983, Australian

GENE SAKS*

b. November 8, 1921 - New York, New York
Agent: John Planco, William Morris Agency - New York City, 212/586-5100
Business Manager: Wallin, Simon, Black & Co., 1350 Avenue of the Americas, New
    York, NY 10019

BAREFOOT IN THE PARK   Paramount, 1966
THE ODD COUPLE   Paramount, 1968
CACTUS FLOWER   Columbia, 1969
LAST OF THE RED HOT LOVERS   Paramount, 1972
MAME   Warner Bros., 1974

LUCIANO SALCE

b. September 22, 1922 - Italy
Contact: Ministry of Tourism & Education, Via Della Ferratella, No. 51, 00184
    Rome, Italy, 06/7732

LA PILLOLE DE ERCOLE   Maxima Film/Dino De Laurentiis Cinematografica,
    1960, Italian
IL FEDERALE   Dino De Laurentiis Cinematografica, 1961, Italian
CRAZY DESIRE *LA VOGLIA MATTA*   Embassy, 1962, Italian
LA CUCCAGNA   CIRAC/Agliani Cinematografica, 1962, Italian
THE HOURS OF LOVE   Cinema 5, 1963, Italian
THE LITTLE NUNS   Embassy, 1963, Italian
HIGH INFIDELITY   co-director with Mario Monicelli, Franco Rossi & Elio Petri,
    Magna, 1964, Italian-French
KISS THE OTHER SHEIK *OGGI, DOMANI E DOPODOMANI*   co-director
    with Marco Ferreri & Eduardo de Felippo, MGM, 1965, Italian-French
SLALOM   Fair Film/Cocinor/Copro Film, 1965, Italian-French-British
EL GRECO   20th Century-Fox, 1966, Italian-French
THE QUEENS *LE FATE*   co-director with Mario Monicelli, Mauro Bolognini, &
    Antonio Pietrangeli, Royal Films International, 1966, Italian-French
TI HO SPOSATO PER ALLEGRIA   Fair Film, 1967, Italian
LA PECORA NERA   Fair Film, 1969, Italian
COLPO DI STATO   Vides, 1969, Italian
**IL PROF. DR. GUIDO TERSILLI, PRIMARIO DELLA CLINICA VILLA
    CELESTE, CONVENSIONATA CON LE MUTUE**   San Marco, 1969,
    Italian
BASTA GUARDARLA   Fair Film, 1971, Italian
IL PROVINCIALE   Fair Film, 1971, Italian
IO E LUI   Dino De Laurentiis Cinematografica, 1973, Italian
TRAGICO FANTOZZI   Cineriz, 1975, Italian
IL SECONDO TRAGICO FANTOZZI   Cineriz, 1976, Italian
LA PRESIDENTESSA   Gold Film, 1976, Italian
L'ANATRA ALL'ARANCIA   Cineriz, 1976, Italian
ITALIANO COME ME   1977, Italian
IL ... BELPAESE   77 Cinematografica, 1977, Italian
DOVE VAI IN VACANZA?   co-director with Mauro Bolognini & Alberto Sordi,
    Cineriz, 1978, Italian
PROFESSOR KRANZ TEDESCO DI GERMANIA   Gold Film, 1979, Italian-
    Brazilian
RIAVANTI ... MARSCH!   PAC, 1980, Italian
RAG. ARTURO DE FANTI BANCARIO PRECARIO   PAC, 1980, Italian
THE INNOCENTS ABROAD (TF)   Nebraska ETV Network/The Great Amwell
    Company/WNET-13, 1983

JAMES SALTER

Agent: Ziegler, Diskant, Inc. - Los Angeles, 213/278-0700

THREE   United Artists, 1969, British

DENIS SANDERS *

b. January 21, 1929 - New York, New York
Home: 5033 Campanile Drive, San Diego, CA 92115, 619/583-8803 or 619/
    265-6575
Business: SRS Productions, 4224 Ellenita Avenue, Tarzana, CA 91356, 213/873-
    3171

CRIME AND PUNISHMENT, U.S.A.   Allied Artists, 1959
WAR HUNT   United Artists, 1961
ONE MAN'S WAY   United Artists, 1964
SHOCK TREATMENT   20th Century-Fox, 1964
ELVIS - THAT'S THE WAY IT IS (FD)   MGM, 1970
SOUL TO SOUL (FD)   Cinerama Releasing Corporation, 1971
INVASION OF THE BEE GIRLS   Centaur, 1973

JAY SANDRICH *

b. February 24, 1932 - Los Angeles, California
Home: 1 North Star - Suite 205, Marina del Rey, CA 90291, 213/392-7357
Agent: Michael Ovitz/Ron Meyer, CAA - Los Angeles, 213/277-4545
Business Manager: Bill Broder, Freedman, Kinzelberg & Broder, 1801 Avenue of the
    Stars - Suite 911, Los Angeles, CA 90067, 231/277-0700

THE CROOKED HEARTS (TF)   Lorimar Productions, 1972
WHAT ARE BEST FRIENDS FOR? (TF)   ABC Circle Films, 1973
NEIL SIMON'S SEEMS LIKE OLD TIMES   Columbia, 1980

JIMMY SANGSTER *

b. December 2, 1927 - England
Agent: Shapiro-Lichtman Agency - Los Angeles, 213/557-2244

THE HORROR OF FRANKENSTEIN   Levitt-Pickman, 1970, British
LUST FOR A VAMPIRE   American Continental, 1971, British
FEAR IN THE NIGHT   International Co-Productions, 1972, British

RICHARD C. SARAFIAN *

b. April 28, 1932 - New York, New York
Agent: Geoff Brandt, APA - Los Angeles, 213/273-0744
Business Manager: John Mitchell, Nanas, Stern & Biers, 9454 Wilshire Blvd., Los
    Angeles, CA 90048, 213/275-2701

TERROR AT BLACK FALLS   Beckman, 1962
ANDY   Universal, 1965
SHADOW ON THE LAND (TF)   Screen Gems/Columbia TV, 1968
RUN WILD, RUN FREE   Columbia, 1969, British
FRAGMENT OF FEAR   Columbia, 1971, British
MAN IN THE WILDERNESS   Warner Bros., 1971
VANISHING POINT   20th Century-Fox, 1971
LOLLY-MADONNA XXX   MGM, 1973
THE MAN WHO LOVED CAT DANCING   MGM, 1973
ONE OF OUR OWN (TF)   Universal TV, 1975
THE NEXT MAN   Allied Artists, 1976
A KILLING AFFAIR (TF)   Columbia TV, 1977
SUNBURN   Paramount, 1979, U.S.-British
DISASTER ON THE COASTLINER (TF)   Moonlight Productions/Filmways,
    1979
THE GOLDEN MOMENT: AN OLYMPIC LOVE STORY (TF)   Don Ohlmeyer
    Productions/Telepictures Corporation, 1980
THE GANGSTER CHRONICLES (TF)   Universal TV, 1981
SPLENDOR IN THE GRASS (TF)   Katz-Gallin Productions/Half-Pint Productions/
    Warner Bros. TV, 1981

JOSEPH SARGENT *
(Giuseppe Danielle Sorgente)

b. July 25, 1925 - Jersey City, New Jersey
Agent: Shapiro-Lichtman Agency - Los Angeles, 213/557-2244

ONE SPY TOO MANY   MGM, 1966
THE HELL WITH HEROES   Universal, 1968
THE SUNSHINE PATRIOT (TF)   Universal TV, 1968
THE IMMORTAL (TF)   Paramount TV, 1969
COLOSSUS: THE FORBIN PROJECT   Universal, 1970
TRIBES (TF) ☆   20th Century-Fox, 1970
MAYBE I'LL COME HOME IN THE SPRING (TF)   Metromedia Productions,
    1971
LONGSTREET (TF)   Paramount TV, 1971
MAN ON A STRING (TF)   Screen Gems/Columbia TV, 1972
THE MAN   Paramount, 1972
THE MARCUS-NELSON MURDERS (TF) ☆☆   Universal TV, 1973
THE MAN WHO DIED TWICE (TF)   Cinema Center, 1973
SUNSHINE (TF)   Universal TV, 1973
WHITE LIGHTNING   United Artists, 1973
THE TAKING OF PELHAM 1-2-3   United Artists, 1974
HUSTLING (TF)   Filmways, 1975

continued

JOSEPH SARGENT*—continued

FRIENDLY PERSUASION (TF)   International TV Productions/Allied Artists, 1975

THE NIGHT THAT PANICKED AMERICA (TF)   Paramount TV, 1975

MacARTHUR   Universal, 1977

GOLDENGIRL   Avco Embassy, 1979

AMBER WAVES (TF) ☆   Time-Life Productions, 1980

COAST TO COAST   Paramount, 1980

FREEDOM (TF)   Hill-Mandelker Films, 1981

THE MANIONS OF AMERICA (MS)   co-director with Charles S. Dubin, Roger Gimbel Productions/EMI TV/Argonaut Films Ltd., 1981

TOMORROW'S CHILD (TF)   20th Century-Fox TV, 1982

NIGHTMARES   Universal, 1983

CHOICES OF THE HEART (TF)   Katz-Gallin/Half-Pint Productions, 1983

MEMORIAL DAY (TF)   Charles Fries Productions, 1983

TERRIBLE JOE (TF)   Robert Halmi Productions, 1984

MICHAEL SARNE

b. August 6, 1939 - London, England
Address: 13 Airlie Gardens, London W8, England

LA ROUTE DE ST. TROPEZ   1966, French

JOANNA   20th Century-Fox, 1968, British

MYRA BRECKINRIDGE   20th Century-Fox, 1970

VERA VERAO   Relevo Productions, 1975, Brazilian

INTIMIDADE   Relevo Productions, 1976, Brazilian

THE PUNK   1978, British

PETER SASDY

b. Budapest, Hungary
Contact: Directors Guild of Breat Britian, 56 Whitfield Street, London W1, Endland, 01/580-9592

TASTE THE BLOOD OF DRACULA   Warner Bros., 1970, British

COUNTESS DRACULA   20th Century-Fox, 1972, British

HANDS OF THE RIPPER   Universal, 1972, British

DOOMWATCH   Avco Embassy, 1972, British

NOTHING BUT THE NIGHT   Cinema Systems, 1975, British

THE DEVIL WITHIN HER *I DON'T WANT TO BE BORN*   20th Century-Fox, 1976, British

WELCOME TO BLOOD CITY   EMI, 1977 British

THE LONELY LADY   Universal, 1983

RON SATLOF*

Agent: David Shapira & Associates - Beverly Hills, 213/278-2742

BENNY & BARNEY: LAS VEGAS UNDERCOVER (TF)   Universal TV, 1977

WAIKIKI (TF)   Aaron Spelling Productions, 1980

THE MURDER THAT WOULDN'T DIE (TF)   Universal TV, 1980

CARLOS SAURA

b. January 4, 1932 - Huesca, Spain
Contact: Direccion General del Libro y de la Cinematografia, Ministerio de Cultura, Paseo de la Castellana 109, Madrid 16, Spain, 1/455-5000

CUENCA   1959, Spanish

LOS GOLFOS   1962, Spanish

LLANTO POR UN BANDITO   1964, Spanish

THE HUNT   Trans-Lux, 1966, Spanish

PEPPERMINT FRAPPE   1967, Spanish

STRESS EN TRES TRES   1968, Spanish

HONEYCOMB *LA MADRIGUERA*   CineGlobe, 1969, Spanish

THE GARDEN OF DELIGHTS   Perry/Fleetwood, 1970, Spanish

ANA Y LOS LOBOS   1973, Spanish

COUSIN ANGELICA   New Yorker, 1974, Spanish

CRIA! *CRIA CUERVOS*   Jason Allen, 1976, Spanish

ELISA, VIDA MIA   Elias Querejeta Productions, 1977, Spanish

continued

CARLOS SAURA—continued
DEPRISA, DEPRISA   Films Moliere, 1981, Spanish-French
SWEET HOURS   New Yorker, 1982, Spanish
ANTONIETA   Gaumont/Conacine/Nuevo Cine, 1982, French-Mexican
CARMEN   Orion Classics, 1983, Spanish

CLAUDE SAUTET

b. February 23, 1924 - Montrouge, France
Contact: French Film Office, 745 Fifth Avenue, New York, NY 10151, 212/832-8860

BONJOUR SOURIRE   Vox, 1955, French
THE BIG RISK   United Artists, 1960, French-Italian
L'ARME A GAUCHE   1965, French
THE THINGS OF LIFE   Columbia, 1970, French
MAX ET LES FERRAILLEURS   1971, French
CESAR AND ROSALIE   Cinema 5, 1972, French-Italian-West German
VINCENT, FRANCOIS, PAUL AND THE OTHERS   Joseph Green Pictures, 1974, French-Italian
MADO   Joseph Green Pictures, 1976, French
A SIMPLE STORY   Quartet, 1979, French
A BAD SON   Sara Films/Antenne-2, 1980, French
GARCON   Sara Film/Renn Productions, 1983, French

TELLY SAVALAS*

b. 1926 - Garden City, New Jersey
Agent: Jack Gilardi, ICM - Los Angeles, 213/550-4000
Business Manager: Tucker, Morgan, Martindale, 9200 Sunset Blvd. - Suite 418, Los Angeles, CA 90069, 213/274-0981

BEYOND REASON   Goldfarb Distributors, 1982

JOHN SAYLES*

RETURN OF THE SECAUCUS SEVEN   Libra/Specialty Films, 1980
LIANNA   United Artists Classics, 1983
BABY IT'S YOU   Paramount, 1983

JOSEPH L. SCANLAN*

Home: 13900 Marquesa Way - Suite C-67, Marina del Rey, CA 90291, 213/306-3660
Agent: Scott Harris, The Gersh Agency - Beverly Hills, 231/274-6611

SPRING FEVER   Comworld, 1983, Canadian

GEORGE SCHAEFER*

b. December 16, 1920 - Wallingford, Connecticut
Home: 1040 Woodland Drive, Beverly Hills, CA 90210, 213/274-6017
Business: Schaefer-Karpf Productions, c/0 CAA, 1888 Century Park East, Los Angeles, CA 90067, 213/277-4545
Agent: CAA - Los Angeles, 213/277-4545

MACBETH   British Lion, 1961, British
PENDULUM   Columbia, 1969
GENERATION   Avco Embassy, 1969
DOCTOR'S WIVES   Columbia, 1971
A WAR OF CHILDREN (TF) ☆   Tomorrow Entertainment, 1972
F. SCOTT FITZGERALD AND "THE LAST OF THE BELLES" (TF)   Titus Productions, 1974
ONCE UPON A SCOUNDREL   Image International, 1974, U.S.-Mexican
IN THIS HOUSE OF BREDE (TF)   Tomorrow Entertainment, 1975
AMELIA EARHART (TF)   Universal TV, 1976
THE GIRL CALLED HATTER FOX (TF)   Roger Gimbel Productions/EMI TV, 1978
FIRST YOU CRY (TF)   MTM Enterprises, 1978

continued

GEORGE SCHAEFER*—continued

AN ENEMY OF THE PEOPLE   Warner Bros., 1978
WHO'LL SAVE OUR CHILDREN? (TF)   Time-Life Productions, 1978
BLIND AMBITION (TF)   Time-Life Productions, 1979
MAYFLOWER: THE PILGRIMS' ADVENTURE (TF)   Syzygy Productions, 1979
THE BUNKER (TF)   Time-Life Productions/SFP France/Antenne-2, 1981, U.S.-French
A PIANO FOR MRS. CIMINO (TF)   Roger Gimbel Productions/EMI TV, 1982
RIGHT OF WAY (CTF)   HBO Premiere Films, Schaefer-Karpf Productions/Post-Newsweek Video, 1983

FRANKLIN J. SCHAFFNER*

b. May 30, 1920 - Tokyo, Japan
Agent: CAA - Los Angeles, 213/277-4545

THE STRIPPER   20th Century-Fox, 1962
THE BEST MAN   Unitd Artists, 1964
THE WAR LORD   Universal, 1965
THE DOUBLE MAN   Warner Bros., 1968, British
PLANET OF THE APES   20th Century-Fox, 1968
PATTON ★★   20th Century-Fox, 1970
NICHOLAS AND ALEXANDRA   Columbia, 1971, British
PAPILLON   Allied Artists, 1973
ISLANDS IN THE STREAM   Paramount, 1977
THE BOYS FROM BRAZIL   20th Century-Fox, 1978
SPHINX   Orion/Warner Bros., 1981
YES, GIORGIO   MGM/UA, 1982

DON SCHAIN*

Home: 1817 N. Fuller Avenue, Los Angeles, CA 90046
Business: Derio Productions, Inc., 7942 Mulholland Drive, Los Angeles, CA 90046, 213/851-8140

GINGER   Joseph Brenner Associates, 1971
THE ADBUCTORS   Joseph Brenner Associates, 1972
A PLACE CALLED TODAY   Avco Embassy, 1972
GIRLS ARE FOR LOVING   Continental, 1973
TOO HOT TO HANDLE   Derio Productions, 1978

JERRY SCHATZBERG*

b. New York, New York
Agent: William Morris Agency - New York City, 212/586-5100
Business Manager: Herb Bard, Bard & Kass, 551 Fifth Avenue, New York, NY 10176, 212/599-2880

PUZZLE OF A DOWNFALL CHILD   Universal, 1970
PANIC IN NEEDLE PARK   20th Century-Fox, 1971
SCARECROW   Warner Bros., 1973
SWEET REVENGE *DANDY, THE ALL-AMERICAN GIRL*   MGM/United Artists, 1976
THE SEDUCTION OF JOE TYNAN   Universal, 1979
HONEYSUCKLE ROSE   Warner Bros., 1980
MISUNDERSTOOD   Accent/Keith Barish Productions, 1983

ROBERT SCHEERER*

b. Santa Barbara, California
Agent: The Cooper Agency - Los Angeles, 213/277-8422

HANS BRINKER (TF)   NBC, 1969
ADAM AT SIX A.M.   National General, 1970
THE WORLD'S GREATEST ATHLETE   Buena Vista, 1973
POOR DEVIL (TF)   Paramount TV, 1973
TARGET RISK (TF)   Universal TV, 1975
IT HAPPENED AT LAKEWOOD MANOR (TF)   Alan Landsburg Productions, 1977
HAPPILY EVER AFTER (TF)   Tri-Media II, Inc./Hamel-Somers Entertainment, 1978

continued

ROBERT SCHEERER*—continued
HOW TO BEAT THE HIGH COST OF LIVING   American International, 1980

MAXIMILIAN SCHELL

b. December 8, 1930 - Vienna, Austria
Agent: ICM - Los Angeles, 213/550-4000

FIRST LOVE   UMC, 1970, Swiss-West German
THE PEDESTRIAN   Cinerama Releasing Corporation, 1974, West German-Swiss-
    Israeli
END OF THE GAME   20th Century-Fox, 1976, West German-Italian
TALES FROM THE VIENNA WOODS   Cinema 5, 1979, Austrian-West
    German

HENNING SCHELLERUP

THE BLACK BUNCH   Entertainment Pyramid, 9173
SWEET JESUS, PREACHER MAN   MGM, 1973
THE BLACK ALLEYCATS   Entertainment Pyramid, 1974
THE TIME MACHINE (TF)   Sunn Classic Productions, 1978
IN SEARCH OF HISTORIC JESUS   Sunn Classic, 1979
BEYOND DEATH'S DOOR   Sunn Classic, 1979
THE LEGEND OF SLEEPY HOLLOW   Sunn Classic, 1979
THE ADVENTURES OF NELLIE BLY (TF)   Sunn Classic, 1981
CAMP-FIRE GIRLS   Rainbow Spectrum Film Co., 1984

FRED SCHEPISI *

b. December 26, 1939 - Melbourne, Australia
Contact: Directors Guild of America - Los Angeles, 213/656-1220

LIBIDO   co-director with John B. Murray, Tim Burstall & David Baker, Producers
    & Directors Guild of Australia, 1973, Australian
THE DEVIL'S PLAYGROUND   Entertainment Marketing, 1976, Australian
THE CHANT OF JIMMIE BLACKSMITH   New Yorker, 1978, Australian
BARBAROSA   Universal/AFD, 1982
ICEMAN   Universal, 1984

LAWRENCE J. SCHILLER *

b. December 28, 1936, New York, New York
Home: P.O. Box 5345, Beverly Hills, CA 90210, 213/906-0926
Agent: Jeff Berg, ICM - Los Angeles, 213/550-4000
Business Manager: Sloan & Kuppin - Los Angeles, 213/552-9192

THE LEXINGTON EXPERIENCE (FD)   Corda, 1971
THE AMERICAN DREAMER (FD)   co-director with L.M. Kit Carson, EYR, 1971
HEY, I'M ALIVE! (TF)   Charles Fries Productions/Worldvision, 1975
MARILYN: THE UNTOLD STORY (TF)   co-director with Jack Arnold & John
    Flynn, Lawrence Schiller Productions, 1980
THE EXECUTIONER'S SONG (TF)   Film Communications Inc., 1982

TOM SCHILLER *

Agent: Mike Hamilburg, Mitchell-Hamilburg Agency - Los Angeles, 213/657-1501

NOTHING LASTS FOREVER   MGM/UA, 1983

GEORGE SCHLATTER *

b. December 31, 1931
Business: Schlatter Productions, 8321 Beverly Blvd., Los Angeles, CA 90048, 213/
    655-1400
Agent: Tony Fantozzi, William Morris Agency - Beverly Hills, 213/274-7451

NORMAN ... IS THAT YOU?   MGM/United Artists, 1976

JOHN SCHLESINGER *

b. February 16, 1926 - London, England
Agent: Stan Kamen, William Morris Agency - Beverly Hills, 213/274-7451

A KIND OF LOVING   Continental, 1962 British
BILLY LIAR   Continental, 1963, British
DARLING ★   Embassy, 1965, British
FAR FROM THE MADDING CROWD   MGM, 1967, British
MIDNIGHT COWBOY ★★   United Artists, 1969
SUNDAY BLOODY SUNDAY ★   United Artists, 1970, British
VISIONS OF EIGHT (FD)   co-director with Yuri Ozerov, Mai Zetterling, Arthur
    Penn, Michael Pfleghar, Kon Ickikawa, Milos Forman & Claude Lelouch, Cinema
    5, 1973
THE DAY OF THE LOCUST   Paramount, 1975
MARATHON MAN   Paramount, 1976
YANKS   Universal, 1979, British
HONKY TONK FREEWAY   Universal/AFD, 1981

VOLKER SCHLONDORFF

b. 1939 - Wiesbaden, Germany
Contact: German Film & TV Academy, Pommernallee 1, 1000 Berlin 19, West
    Germany, 030/303-6212

YOUNG TORLESS   Kanawha, 1966, West German-French
A DEGREE OF MURDER   Universal, 1967, West German
MICHAEL KOHLHAAS   Columbia, 1969, West German
THE SUDDEN WEALTH OF THE POOR PEOPLE OF KOMBACH   New
    Yorker, 1970, West German
BAAL (TF)   Hessischer Rundfunk/Bayerischer Rundfunk/Hallelujah Film, 1970,
    West German
DIE MORAL DER RUTH HALBFASS   Hallelujah Film/Hessischer Rundfunk,
    1971, West German
A FREE WOMAN STROHFEUER   New Yorker, 1971, West German
UBERNACHTUNG IN TIROL (TF)   Hessischer Rundfunk, 1974, West German
GEORGINAS GRUNDE (TF)   West Deutscher Rundfunk/ORTF, 1975, West
    German-Austrian
THE LOST HONOR OF KATHARINA BLUM   co-director with Margaretha Von
    Trotta, New World, 1975, West German
COUP DE GRACE   Cinema 5, 1976, West German
NUR ZUM SPASS - NUR ZUM SPIEL (TD)   Kaleidoskop Valeska Gert/
    Bioskop Film, 1977
DEUTSCHLAND IM HERBST (FD)   co-director, Filmverlag der Autoren/
    Hallelujah Film/Kairos Film, 1978, West German
THE TIN DRUM   New World, 1980, West German
CIRCLE OF DECEIT DIE FALSCHUNG   United Artists Classics, 1982, West
    German-French
KRIEG UND FRIEDEN (FD)   co-director, Filmverlag der Autoren, 1983, West
    German
UN AMOUR DE SWANN   Gaumont, 1984, French-West German

DAVID SCHMOELLER

Agent: Shapiro-Lichtman Agency - Los Angeles, 213/557-2244

TOURIST TRAP   Compass International, 1979
THE SEDUCTION   Avco Embassy, 1981

ROBERT A. SCHNITZER

NO PLACE TO HIDE   American Films Ltd., 1975
THE PREMONITION   Avco Embassy, 1976

PAUL SCHRADER *

b. July 22, 1946 - Grand Rapids, Michigan
Agent: Jeff Berg, ICM - Los Angeles, 213/550-4000

BLUE COLLAR   Universal, 1978
HARDCORE   Columbia, 1979

continued

PAUL SCHRADER*—continued
AMERICAN GIGOLO   Paramount, 1980
CAT PEOPLE   Universal, 1982

B A R B E T   S C H R O E D E R

b. August 26, 1941 - Teheran, Iran
Business: Les Films du Losange, 26 Avenue Pierre de Serbie, Paris 75116, France,
    720-5412

MORE   Cinema 5, 1969, Luxembourg
THE VALLEY (OBSCURED BY CLOUDS)   Lagoon Associates, 1972, French
IDI AMIN DADA GENERAL IDI AMIN DADA (FD)   Tinc, 1974, French
MAITRESSE   Tinc, 1976, French
KOKO, A TALKING GORILLA (FD)   New Yorker, 1978, French
QUESTION DE CHANCE   Films du Galatee, 1983, French-West German

M I C H A E L   S C H U L T Z *

b. November 10, 1938 - Milwaukee, Wisconsin
Business: Crystalite Productions, Inc. P.O. Box 8659, San Marino, CA 91108, 213/
    282-4149

TOGETHER FOR DAYS   Olas, 1973
HONEYBABY, HONEYBABY   Kelly-Jordan, 1974
COOLEY HIGH   American International, 1975
CAR WASH   Universal, 1976
GREASED LIGHTNING   Warner Bros, 1977
WHICH WAY IS UP?   Universal, 1978
SGT. PEPPER'S LONELY HEARTS CLUB BAND   Universal, 1978
SCAVENGER HUNT   20th Century-Fox, 1979
CARBON COPY   Avco Embassy, 1981
BENNY'S PLACE (TF)   Titus Productions, 1982
FOR US, THE LIVING (TF)   Charles Fries Productions, 1983

J O E L   S C H U M A C H E R *

b. 1942 - New York, New York
Agent: ICM - Los Angeles, 213/550-4000

THE VIRGINIA HILL STORY (TF)   RSO Films, 1974
AMATEUR NIGHT AT THE DIXIE BAR & GRILL (TF)   Motown/Universal TV,
    1979
THE INCREDIBLE SHRINKING WOMAN   Universal, 1981
D.C. CAB   Universal, 1983

A R N O L D   S C H W A R T Z M A N

GENOCIDE (FD)   Simon Wiesenthal Center, 1982

E T T O R E   S C O L A

b. 1931 - Trevico, Italy
Contact: Ministry of Tourism & Education, Via Della Ferratella, No. 51, 00184
    Rome, Italy, 06/7732

LET'S TALK ABOUT WOMEN SE PERMETTE, PARLIAMO DI
    DONNE   Embassy, 1964, Italian-French
LA CONGIUNTURA   Fair Film/Les Films Concordia, 1965, Italian-French
THRILLING   co-director, 1966, Italian
THE DEVIL IN LOVE L'ARCIDIAVOLO   Warner Bros, 1966, Italian
RIUSCIRANNO I NOSTRI EROI A TROVARE L'AMICO MISTERIOSAMENTE
    SCOMPARSO IN AFRICA?   Documento Film, 1968, Italian
IL COMMISSARIO PEPE   Dean Film, 1969, Italian
THE PIZZA TRIANGLE DRAMMA DELLA GELOSIA - TUTTI I
    PARTICOLARI IN CRONICA   Warner Bros., 1970, Italian-Spanish
MY NAME IS ROCCO PAPALEO   Rumson, 1971, Italian
LA PIU BELLA SERATA DELLA MIA VITA   Dino De Laurentiis
    Cinematografica, 1972, Italian

continued

ETTORE SCOLA—continued

WE ALL LOVED EACH OTHER SO MUCH   Cinema 5, 1975, Italian
DOWN AND DIRTY *BRUTTI, SPORCHI E CATTIVI*   New Line Cinema,
   1976, Italian
SIGNORE E SIGNORI BUONANOTTE   co-director with Luigi Comencini, Nanni
   Loy, Luigi Magni & Mario Monicelli, Titanus, 1976, Italian
A SPECIAL DAY   Cinema 5, 1977, Italian
VIVA ITALIA! *I NUOVI MOSTRI*   co-director with Mario Monicelli & Dino
   Risi, Cinema 5, 1978, Italian
CHE SI DICE A ROMA   1979, Italian
LA TERRAZZA   United Artists, 1980, Italian-French
PASSIONE D'AMORE   Putnam Square, 1982, Italian-French
LA NUIT DE VARENNES   Triumph/Columbia, 1982, French-Italian
LE BAL   Titanus, 1983, Italian-French

M A R T I N   S C O R S E S E *

b. November 17, 1942 - Flushing, New York
Agent: The Ufland Agency - Beverly Hills, 213/273-9441

WHO'S THAT KNOCKING AT MY DOOR?   Joseph Brenner Associates, 1968
BOXCAR BERTHA   American International, 1972
MEAN STREETS   Warner Bros., 1973
ALICE DOESN'T LIVE HERE ANYMORE   Warner Bros., 1974
ITALIANAMERICAN (FD)   1974
TAXI DRIVER   Columbia, 1976
NEW YORK, NEW YORK   United Artists, 1977
AMERICAN BOY (FD)   1978
THE LAST WALTZ   United Artists, 1978
RAGING BULL ★   United Artists, 1978
THE KING OF COMEDY   20th Century-Fox, 1983

G E O R G E   C .   S C O T T *

b. October 18, 1927 - Wise, Virginia
Agent: Jane Deacy Agency - New York City, 212/752-4865
Business Manager: Becker & London - New York City, 212/541-7070

RAGE   Warner Bros., 1972
THE SAVAGE IS LOOSE   Campbell Devon, 1974

O Z   S C O T T *

Agent: Dennis Brady/Paul Yamamoto, William Morris Agency - Beverly Hills, 213/
   274-7451

BUSTIN' LOOSE   Universal, 1981
DREAMLAND   co-director with Nancy Baker & Joel Schulman, First Run
   Features, 1983

R I D L E Y   S C O T T *

b. England
Agent: CAA - Los Angeles, 213/277-4545

THE DUELLISTS   Paramount, 1978, British
ALIEN   20th Century-Fox, 1979, U.S.-British
BLADE RUNNER   The Ladd Company/Warner Bros., 1982

T O N Y   S C O T T

b. England
Contact: Directors Guild of America - Los Angeles, 213/656-1220

THE HUNGER   MGM/UA, 1983, British

ARTHUR ALLAN SEIDELMAN *

b. New York, New York
Agent: Joe Rosenberg, Writers & Artists Agency - Los Angeles, 213/820-2240
.Business: Entertainment Professionals, Inc. 1015 Gayley Avenue - Suite 1149, Los
    Angeles, CA 90024

CHILDREN OF RAGE   LSF, 1975, U.S.-Israeli
ECHOES   Entertainment Professionals, 1983

SUSAN SEIDELMAN

SMITHEREENS   New Line Cinema, 1982

ARNAUD SELIGNAC

DREAM ONE   Columbia, 1984, British-French

JACK M. SELL

b. September 15, 1954 - Albany, Georgia
Business: Sell Pictures, Inc. 9701 Wilshire Blvd., Beverly Hills, CA 90212, 213/
    659-2332
Attorney: Charles Biggam, 180 N. Ls Salle, Chicago, ILL 60601, 312/236-9119

THE PSYCHOTRONIC MAN   International Harmony, 1980
OUTTAKES   Sell Pictures, 1983

OUSMENE SEMBENE

BLACK GIRL   New Yorker, 1965, Senegalese
THE MONEY ORDER   1965, Senegalese
MANDABI   Grove Press, 1970, Senegalese
EMITAI   New Yorker, 1973, Senegalese
XALA   New Yorker, 1974, Senegalese
CEDDO   New Yorker, 1977, Senegalese

RALPH SENENSKY *

b. May 1, 1923 - Mason City, Iowa
Agent: The Gersh Agency - Beverly Hills, 213/274-6611

A DREAM FOR CHRISTMAS (TF)   Lorimar Productions, 1973
THE FAMILY KOVACK (TF)   Playboy Productions, 1974
DEATH CRUISE (TF)   Spelling-Goldberg Productions, 1974
THE FAMILY NOBODY WANTED (TF)   Universal TV, 1975
THE NEW ADVENTURES OF HEIDI (TF)   Pierre Cossette Enterprises, 1978
DYNASTY (TF)   Aaron Spelling Productions/Fox-Cat Productions, 1981

NICHOLAS SGARRO *

Agent: Louis Bershad, Century Artists Ltd. - Beverly Hills, 213/272-4366
Business Manager: Leslie Robbins, Geneva Management - Beverly Hills, 213/271-
    5295

THE HAPPY HOOKER   Cannon, 1975
THE MAN WITH THE POWER (TF)   Universal TV, 1977

KRISHNA SHAH *

b. May 10, 1938 - India
Home: P.O. Box 64515, Los Angeles, CA 90064

RIVALS   Avco Embassy, 1972
THE RIVER NIGER   Cine Artists, 1976
SHALIMAR   Judson Productions/Laxmi Productions, 1978, U.S.-Indian
CINEMA-CINEMA (FD)   Shahab Ahmed Productions, 1980, Indian

LINA SHANKLIN

SUMMERSPELL   Lina Shanklin Film, 1983

ANN ZANE SHANKS *

Home: 2237 N. New Hampshire, Los Angeles, CA 90027, 213/660-0121
Personal Manager: John Schulman, Weissman, Wolff, Bergman, Coleman, & Schulman
 - Beverly Hills, 213/858-7888
Business Manager: Al Rudick, Lazaron & Company - Beverly Hills, 213/273-8900

FRIENDSHIPS, SECRETS AND LIES (TF)   co-director with Marlena Laird,
 Wittman-Riche Productions/Warner Bros. TV. 1979

KEN SHAPIRO *

b. 1943 - New Jersey
Home: 2044 Stanley Hills Drive, Los Angeles, CA 90046 213/654-7471

THE GROOVE TUBE   Levitt-Pickman, 1974
MODERN PROBLEMS   20th Century-Fox, 1981

MELVIN SHAPIRO

SAMMY STOPS THE WORLD (FD)   Elkins, 1979

JIM SHARMAN

Contact: M&L Casting Consultants, 49 Darlinghurst Road, Kings Cross, NSW, 2100,
 Australia, 02/358-3111

SHIRLEY THOMPSON VERSUS THE ALIENS   Kolossal Piktures, 1972,
 Australian
SUMMER OF SECRETS   Greater Union Film Distribution, 1976, Australian
THE ROCKY HORROR PICTURE SHOW   20th Century-Fox, 1976, British
THE NIGHT THE PROWLER   International Harmony, 1978, Australian
SHOCK TREATMENT   20th Century-Fox, 1981, British

DON SHARP

b. April, 1922 - Hobart, Tasmania
Address: 80 Castelnau, Barnes, London SW13 9EX, England, 01/748-4333

THE GOLDEN AIRLINER   British Lion/Children's Film Foundation, 1955, British
THE ADVENTURES OF HAL 5   Children's Film Foundation, 1958, British
THE IN-BETWEEN AGE *THE GOLDEN DISC*   Allied Artists, 1958, British
THE PROFESSIONALS   American International, 1960, British
LINDA   British Lion, 1961, British
IT'S ALL HAPPENING *THE DREAM MAKER*   Universal, 1963, British
KISS OF THE VAMPIRE   Universal, 1963, British
THE DEVIL-SHIP PIRATES   Columbia, 1964, British
WITCHCRAFT   20th Century-Fox, 1964, British
THE FACE OF FU MANCHU   7 Arts, 1965, British
CURSE OF THE FLY   20th Century-Fox, 1965, British
RASPUTIN - THE MAD MONK *I KILLED RASPUTIN*   20th Century-Fox,
 1966, British-French-Italian
BANG, BANG, YOU'RE DEAD! *OUR MAN IN MARRAKESH*   American
 International, 1966, British
THE BRIDES OF FU MANCHU   7 Arts, 1966, British
THOSE FANTASTIC FLYING FOOLS *BLAST OFF/JULES VERNE'S ROCKET
 TO THE MOON*   American International, 1967, British
TASTE OF EXCITEMENT   Crispin, 1968, British
THE VIOLENT ENEMY   1969, British
PUPPET ON A CHAIN   co-director with Geoffrey Reeve, Cinerama Releasing
 Corporation, 1972, British
THE DEATH WHEELERS *PSYCHOMANIA*   Scotia International, 1973, British
DARK PLACES   Cinerama Releasing Corporation, 1974, British
HENNESSY   American International, 1975, British
CALLAN   Cinema National, 1975, British

continued

DON SHARP—continued

THE FOUR FEATHERS (TF)   Norman Rosemont Productions/Trident Films Ltd.,
   1978, U.S.-British
THE 39 STEPS   International Picture Show Company, 1978, British
BEAR ISLAND   Taft International, 1980, Canadian-British
SECRETS OF THE PHANTOM CAVERNS   Sandy Howard/Wishred Ltd., 1984

IAN SHARP

b. November 13, 1946 - Clitheroe, Lancashire, England
Address: 22 Westbere Road, London NW2, England
Agent: Duncan Heath Associates - London, 01/937-9898
Contact: Directors Guild of Great Britain, 56 Whitfield Street, London W1, England,
   01/580-9592

THE MUSIC MACHINE   Norfolk International Pictures/Target International
   Pictures, 1979, British
THE FINAL OPTION *WHO DARES WINS*   MGM/UA, 1983, British
ROBIN OF SHERWOOD (TF)   HTV/Goldcrest Films & Television, 1983, British

MELVILLE SHAVELSON *

b. April 1, 1917 - Brooklyn, New York
Business: Llenroc Productions, c/o Freedman, Kinzelberg & Broder, 1801 Avenue of
   the Stars - Suite 911, Los Angeles, CA 90067, 213/277-0700
Agent: Ron Mardigian, William Morris Agency - Beverly Hills, 213/274-7451

THE SEVEN LITTLE FOYS   Paramount, 1955
BEAU JAMES   Paramount, 1957
HOUSEBOAT   Paramount, 1958
THE FIVE PENNIES   Paramount, 1959
IT STARTED IN NAPLES   Paramount, 1960
ON THE DOUBLE   Paramount, 1961
THE PIDGEON THAT TOOK ROME   Paramount, 1962
A NEW KIND OF LOVE   Paramount, 1963
CAST A GIANT SHADOW   United Artists, 1966
YOUR, MINE AND OURS   United Artists, 1968
THE WAR BETWEEN MEN AND WOMEN   National General, 1972
MIXED COMPANY   United Artists, 1974
THE LEGEND OF VALENTINO (TF)   Spelling-Goldberg Productions 1975
THE GREAT HOUDINIS (TF)   ABC Circle Films, 1976
IKE (MS)   co-director with Boris Sagal, ABC Circle Films, 1979
THE OTHER WOMAN (TF)   CBS Entertainmant, 1983

JACK SHEA *

b. August 1, 1928 - New York, New York
Agent: Major Talent Agency - Los Angeles, 213/820-5841
Business Manager: Freedman, Kinzelberg & Broder, 1801 Avenue of the Stars - Suite
   911, Los Angeles, CA 90067, 213/277-0700

DAYTON'S DEVILS   Commonwealth United, 1968
THE MONITORS   Commonwealth United, 1969

DONALD SHEBIB

b. 1938 - Toronto, Canada
Address: 312 Wright Avenue, Toronto, Ontario M6R 1L9, Canada, 416/536-8969

GOIN' DOWN THE ROAD   Chevron, 1070, Canadian
RIP-OFF   Alliance, 1971, Canadian
BETWEEN FRIENDS   Eudon Productions, 1973, Canadian
SECOND WIND   Health and Entertainment Corporation of America, 1976,
   Canadian
THE FIGHTING MEN (TF)   CBC, 1977, Canadian
FISH HAWK   Avco Embassy, 1981, Canadian
HEARTACHES   MPM, 1982, Canadian
RUNNING BRAVE   directed under pseudonym of D.S. Everett, Buena Vista,
   1983, Canadian

RIKI SHELACH

Contact: Israel Film Centre, Ministry of Industry & Trade, 30 Agron Street, P.O. Box 299, Jerusalem 94190, Israel, 02/210433

THE LAST WINTER   Triumph/Columbia, 1983, Israeli

JAMES SHELDON *
(James Schleifer)

b. November 12 - New York, New York
Home: 9428 Lloydcrest Drive, Beverly Hills, CA 90210, 213/275-2210
Agent: Ronald Lief, Contemporary-Korman Artists - Beverly Hills, 213/278-8250

GIDGET GROWS UP (TF)   Screen Gems/Columbia TV, 1969
WITH THIS RING (TF)   The Jozak Company/Paramount TV, 1978
THE GOSSIP COLUMNIST (TF)   Universal TV, 1980

SIDNEY SHELDON *

b. February 11, 1917 - Chicago, Illinois
Agent: Mike Rosenfeld/Bill Haber/Rowland Perkins, CAA - Los Angeles, 213/277-4545
Business Manager: Gerald Breslauer, Breslauer, Jacobson & Rutman - Los Angeles, 213/879-0167

DREAM WIFE   MGM, 1953
THE BUSTER KEATON STORY   Paramount, 1957

JACK SHER *

b. March 16, 1913 - Minneapolis, Minnesota
Home: 9520 Dalegrove Drive, Beverly Hills, CA 90210, 213/273-2091
Agent: Michael Zimring, William Morris Agency - Beverly Hills, 213/274-7451

FOUR GIRLS IN TOWN   Universal, 1957
KATHY O'   Universal, 1958
THE WILD AND THE INNOCENT   Universal, 1959
THE THREE WORLDS OF GULLIVER   Columbia, 1960, British
LOVE IN A GOLDFISH BOWL   Paramount, 1961

EDWIN SHERIN *

b. January 15, 1930 - Danville, Pennsylvania
Home: Gordon Road, R.D. 2, Carmel, NY 10512, 914/225-4544
Agent: William Liff, William Morris Agency - New York City, 212/586-5100

VALDEZ IS COMING   United Artists, 1971
MY OLD MAN'S PLACE *GLORY BOY*   Cinerama Releasing Corporation, 1972

GARY A. SHERMAN *

Agent: Arnold Rifkin, David, Hunter, Kimble, Parseghian & Rifkin - Los Angeles, 213/857-1234
Business Manager: Jim Jorgensen & Company, 1801 Avenue of the Stars - Suite 235, Los Angeles, CA 90067, 213/556-1730

RAW MEAT *DEATH LINE*   American International, 1973
DEAD AND BURIED   Avco Embassy, 1981
VICE SQUAD   Avco Embassy, 1982
MYSTERIOUS TWO (TF)   Alan Landsburg Productions, 1982

G E O R G E   S H E R M A N *

b. July 14, 1908 - New York, New York
Personal Manager: Cleo Ranson, Ronsher Productions, 4314 Marina City Drive,
    Marina del Rey, CA 90291, 213/821-0693

WILD HORSE RODEO   Republic, 1938
THE PURPLE VIGILANTES   Republic, 1938
OUTLAWS OF SONORA   Republic, 1938
RIDERS OF THE BLACK HILLS   Republic, 1938
PALS OF THE SADDLE   Republic, 1938
OVERLAND STAGE RAIDERS   Republic, 1938
RHYTHM OF THE SADDLE   Republic, 1938
SANTA FE STAMPEDE   Republic, 1938
RED RIVER RANGE   Republic, 1938
MEXICALI ROSE   Republic, 1939
THE NIGHT RIDERS   Republic, 1939
THREE TEXAS STEERS   Republic, 1939
WYOMING OUTLAW   Republic, 1939
COLORADO SUNSET   Republic, 1939
NEW FRONTIER   Republic, 1939
COWBOYS FROM TEXAS   Republic, 1939
THE KANSAS TERRORS   Republic, 1939
ROVIN' TUMBLEWEEDS   Republic, 1939
SOUTH OF THE BORDER   Republic, 1939
GHOST VALLEY RAIDERS   Republic, 1940
ONE MAN'S LAW   Republic, 1940
THE TULSA KID   Republic, 1940
TEXAS TERRORS   Republic, 1940
COVERED WAGON DAYS   Republic, 1940
ROCKY MOUNTAIN RANGERS   Republic, 1940
UNDER TEXAS SKIES   Republic, 1940
THE TRAIL BLAZERS   Republic, 1940
LONE STAR RAIDERS   Republic, 1940
FRONTIER VENGEANCE   Republic, 1940
WYOMING WILDCAT   Republic, 1941
THE PHANTOM COWBOY   Republic, 1941
TWO GUN SHERIFF   Republic, 1941
DESERT BANDIT   Republic, 1941
KANSAS CYCLONE   Republic, 1941
DEATH VALLEY OUTLAWS   Republic, 1941
A MISSOURI OUTLAW   Republic, 1941
CITADEL OF CRIME   Republic, 1941
THE APACHE KID   Republic, 1941
ARIZONA TERRORS   Republic, 1942
STAGECOACH EXPRESS   Republic, 1942
JESSE JAMES JR.   Republic, 1942
THE CYCLONE KID   Republic, 1942
THE SOMBRERO KID   Republic, 1942
X MARKS THE SPOT   Republic, 1942
LONDON BLACKOUT MURDERS   Republic, 1942
THE PURPLE V   Republic, 1943
THE MANTRAP   Republic, 1943
THE WEST SIDE KID   Republic, 1943
MYSTERY BROADCAST   Republic, 1943
THE LADY AND THE MONSTER   Republic, 1944
STORM OVER LISBON   Republic, 1944
THE CRIME DOCTOR'S COURAGE   Columbia, 1945
THE GENTLEMAN MISBEHAVES   Columbia, 1946
RENEGADES   Columbia, 1946
TALK ABOUT A LADY   Columbia, 1946
THE BANDIT OF SHERWOOD FOREST   co-director with Henry Levin,
    Columbia, 1946
PERSONALITY KID   Columbia, 1947
SECRETS OF THE WHISTLER   Columbia, 1947
LAST OF THE REDMEN   Columbia, 1947
RELENTLESS   Columbia, 1948
BLACK BART   Universal, 1948
RIVER LADY   Universal, 1948
LARCENY   Universal, 1948
RED CANYON   Universal, 1949
CALAMITY JANE AND SAM BASS   Universal, 1949
YES SIR, THAT'S MY BABY   Universal, 1949
SWORD IN THE DESERT   Universal, 1949
SPY HUNT   Universal, 1950

continued

GEORGE SHERMAN*—continued

THE SLEEPING CITY   Universal, 1950
FEUDIN', FUSSIN' AND A-FIGHTIN'   Universal, 1950
COMANCHE TERRITORY   Universal, 1950
TOMAHAWK   Universal, 1951
TARGET UNKNOWN   Universal, 1951
THE RAGING TIDE   Universal, 1951
THE GOLDEN HORDE   Universal, 1951
STEEL TOWN   Universal, 1952
AGAINST ALL FLAGS   Universal, 1952
THE BATTLE AT APACHE PASS   Universal, 1952
BACK AT THE FRONT   Universal, 1952
THE LONE HAND   Universal, 1953
WAR ARROW   Universal, 1953
VEILS OF BAGDAD   Universal, 1953
BORDER RIVER   Universal, 1954
DAWN AT SOCORRO   Universal, 1954
CHIEF CRAZY HORSE   Universal, 1955
COUNT THREE AND PRAY   Universal, 1955
THE TREASURE OF PANCHO VILLA   Universal, 1955
COMANCHE   Universal, 1956
REPRISAL!   Columbia, 1956
THE HARD MAN   Columbia, 1957
THE LAST OF THE FAST GUNS   Universal, 1958
TEN DAYS TO TULARA   United Artists, 1958
THE SON OF ROBIN HOOD   20th Century-Fox, 1959
THE FLYING FONTAINES   Columbia, 1959
HELL BENT FOR LEATHER   Universal, 1960
FOR THE LOVE OF MIKE   20th Century-Fox, 1960
THE ENEMY GENERAL   Columbia, 1960
THE WIZARD OF BAGHDAD   20th Century-Fox, 1960
THE FIERCEST HEART   20th Century-Fox, 1961
PANIC BUTTON   Gorton, 1964
MURIETA   Warner Bros., 1965, Spanish
SMOKY   20th Century-Fox, 1966
BIG JAKE   National General, 1971

V I N C E N T   S H E R M A N *

b. July 16, 1906 - Vienna, Georgia
Home: 6355 Sycamore Meadows Drive, Malibu, CA 90265, 213/457-2229
Agent: Martin Baum, CAA - Los Angeles, 213/277-4545

THE RETURN OF DOCTOR X   Warner Bros., 1939
SATURDAY'S CHILDREN   Warner Bros., 1940
THE MAN WHO TALKED TOO MUCH   Warner Bros., 1940
FLIGHT FROM DESTINY   Warner Bros., 1941
UNDERGROUND   Warner Bros., 1941
ALL THROUGH THE NIGHT   Warner Bros., 1942
THE HARD WAY   Warner Bros., 1942
OLD ACQUAINTANCE   Warner Bros., 1943
IN OUR TIME   Warner Bros., 1944
MR. SKEFFINGTON   Warner Bros., 1945
PILLOW TO POST   Warner Bros., 1945
NORA PRENTISS   Warner Bros., 1947
THE UNFAITHFUL   Warner Bros., 1947
THE ADVENTURES OF DON JUAN   Warner Bros., 1949
THE HASTY HEART   Warner Bros., 1949
BACKFIRE   Warner Bros., 1950
THE DAMNED DON'T CRY   Warner Bros., 1950
HARRIET CRAIG   Columbia, 1950
GOODBYE, MY FANCY   Warner Bros., 1951
LONE STAR   MGM, 1952
AFFAIR IN TRINIDAD   Columbia, 1952
DIFENDO IL MIO AMORE   1956, Italian
THE GARMENT JUNGLE   Columbia, 1957
THE NAKED EARTH   20th Century-Fox, 1959
THE YOUNG PHILADELPHIANS   Warner Bros., 1959
ICE PALACE   Warner Bros., 1960
A FEVER IN THE BLOOD   Warner Bros., 1961
THE SECOND TIME AROUND   20th Century-Fox, 1961
THE YOUNG REBEL *CERVANTES*   American International, 1968, Italian-
   Spanish-French

VINCENT SHERMAN*—continued

THE LAST HURRAH (TF)   O'Connor-Becker Productions/Columbia TV, 1977
LADY OF THE HOUSE (TF)   co-director with Ralph Nelson, Metromedia
Productions, 1978
WOMEN AT WEST POINT (TF)   Green-Epstein Productions/Alan Sacks
Productions, 1979
BOGIE: THE LAST HERO (TF)   Charles Fries Productions, 1980
THE DREAM MERCHANTS (TF)   Columbia TV, 1980
TROUBLE IN HIGH TIMBER COUNTRY (TF)   Witt-Thomas Productions/
Warner Bros. TV, 1980

J A C K   S H O L D E R

ALONE IN THE DARK   New Line Cinema, 1982

S I G   S H O R E

Contact: Writers Guild of America, East - New York City, 212/245-6180

THAT'S THE WAY OF THE WORLD *SHINING STAR*   United Artists, 1975
THE ACT   Artists Releasing Corporation/Film Ventures International, 1983

C H A R L E S   S H Y E R *

Agent: ICM - Los Angeles, 213/550-4000

IRRECONCILABLE DIFFERENCES   Warner Bros., 1983

A N D Y   S I D A R I S *

b. February 20, 1932 - Chicago, Illinois
Home: 1891 Carla Ridge, Beverly Hills, CA 90210, 213/275-6282

THE RACING SCENE (FD)   Filmways, 1970
SEVEN   American International, 1979

G E O R G E   S I D N E Y *

b. October 4, 1916 - Long Island City, New York
Business: 9301 Wilshire Blvd., Beverly Hills, CA 90210, 213/550-7434

FREE AND EASY   MGM, 1941
PACIFIC RENDEZVOUS   MGM, 1942
PILOT NO. 5   MGM, 1943
THOUSANDS CHEER   MGM, 1943
BATHING BEAUTY   MGM, 1944
ANCHORS AWEIGH   MGM, 1945
THE HARVEY GIRLS   MGM, 1946
HOLIDAY IN MEXICO   MGM, 1946
CASS TIMBERLANE   MGM, 1947
THE THREE MUSKETEERS   MGM, 1948
THE RED DANUBE   MGM, 1949
KEY TO THE CITY   MGM, 1950
ANNIE GET YOUR GUN   MGM, 1950
SHOW BOAT   MGM, 1951
SCARAMOUCHE   MGM, 1952
YOUNG BESS   MGM, 1953
KISS ME KATE   MGM, 1953
JUPITER'S DARLING   MGM, 1955
THE EDDY DUCHIN STORY   Columbia, 1956
JEANNE EAGELS   Columbia, 1957
PAL JOEY   Columbia, 1957
WHO WAS THAT LADY?   Columbia, 1960
PEPE   Columbia, 1960
BYE BYE BIRDIE   Columbia, 1963
A TICKLISH AFFAIR   MGM, 1963
VIVA LAS VEGAS   MGM, 1964
THE SWINGER   Paramount, 1966
HALF A SIXPENCE   Paramount, 1968, British

D O N   S I E G E L *

b. October 26, 1912 - Chicago, Illinois
Agent: Len Hirshan - William Morris Agency - Beverly Hills, 213/274-7451
Business Manager: Manny Flekman, Flekman, Carlswell & Company, 9171 Wilshire
    Blvd. - Suite 530, Beverly Hills, CA 90210, 213/274-5847

THE VERDICT   Warner Bros., 1946
NIGHT UNTO NIGHT   Warner Bros., 1949
THE BIG STEAL   RKO Radio, 1949
DUEL AT SILVER CREEK   Universal, 1952
NO TIME FOR FLOWERS   RKO Radio, 1952
COUNT THE HOURS   RKO Radio, 1953
CHINA VENTURE   Columbia, 1953
RIOT IN CELL BLOCK 11   Allied Artists, 1954
PRIVATE HELL 36   Filmmakers, 1954
AN ANNAPOLIS STORY   Allied Artists, 1955
INVASION OF THE BODY SNATCHERS   Allied Artists, 1956
CRIME IN THE STREETS   Allied Artists, 1956
BABY FACE NELSON   Allied Artists, 1957
SPANISH AFFAIR   Paramount, 1958, Spanish
THE LINEUP   Columbia, 1958
THE GUN RUNNERS   United Artists, 1958
HOUND DOG MAN   20th Century-Fox, 1959
EDGE OF ETERNITY   Columbia, 1959
FLAMING STAR   20th Century-Fox, 1960
HELL IS FOR HEROES   Paramount, 1962
THE KILLERS   Universal, 1964
THE HANGED MAN (TF)   Universal TV, 1964
STRANGER ON THE RUN (TF)   Universal TV, 1967
MADIGAN   Universal, 1968
COOGAN'S BLUFF   Universal, 1968
DEATH OF A GUNFIGHTER   co-director with Robert Totten, both directed
    under pseudonym of Allen Smithee, Universal, 1969
TWO MULES FOR SISTER SARA   Universal, 1970, U.S.-Mexican
THE BEGUILED   Universal, 1971
DIRTY HARRY   Warner Bros., 1972
CHARLEY VARRICK   Universal, 1973
THE BLACK WINDMILL   Universal, 1974, British
THE SHOOTIST   Paramount, 1976
TELEFON   MGM/United Artists, 1977
ESCAPE FROM ALCATRAZ   Paramount, 1979
ROUGH CUT   Paramount, 1980
JINXED   MGM/UA, 1982

R O B E R T   J.   S I E G E L *

Contact: Directors Guild of America - New York City, 212/581-0370

PARADES   Cinerama Releasing Corporation, 1972

J A M E S   S I G N O R E L L I *

Contact: Directors Guild of America - New York City, 212/581-0370

EASY MONEY   Orion, 1983

J O A N   M I C K L I N   S I L V E R *

b. May 24, 1935 - Omaha, Nebraska
Business: Midwest Film Productions, 600 Madison Avenue, New York, NY 10022,
    212/355-0282
Agent: Arlene Donovan, ICM - New York City, 212/556-5600

HESTER STREET   Midwest Film Productions, 1975
BETWEEN THE LINES   Midwest Film Productions, 1977
HEAD OVER HEELS   United Artists, 1979, re-released in newly edited version
    by United Artists Classics in 1982 under title CHILLY SCENES OF WINTER
HOW TO BE A PERFECT PERSON (TF)   Highgate Pictures, 1984

R A P H A E L   D.   S I L V E R *

Business: Midwest Film Productions, 600 Madison Avenue, New York, NY 10022,
212/355-0282

ON THE YARD   Midwest Film Productions, 1979

E L L I O T   S I L V E R S T E I N *

b. 1927 - Boston, Massachusetts
Agent: Harold Cohn, Paul Kohner, Inc. - Los Angeles, 213/550-1060

BELLE SOMMARS   Columbia, 1962
CAT BALLOU   Columbia, 1965
THE HAPPENING   Columbia, 1967
A MAN CALLED HORSE   National General, 1970
DEADLY HONEYMOON *NIGHTMARE HONEYMOON*   MGM, 1974
THE CAR   Universal, 1977

F R A N C I S   S I M O N

THE CHICKEN CHRONICLES   Avco Embassy, 1977

A N T H O N Y   S I M M O N S

Business: West One Film Producers Ltd., 2 Lower James Street, London W1R 3PN,
England, 01/437-7015
Agent: ICM - London, 01/629-8080

YOUR MONEY OR YOUR WIFE   Rank, 1960, British
FOUR IN THE MORNING   West One, 1965, British
THE OPTIMISTS *THE OPTIMISTS OF NINE ELMS*   Paramount, 1973,
British
BLACK JOY   Hemdale, 1977, British

F R A N K   S I N A T R A *

b. December 12, 1915 - Hoboken, New Jersey
Contact: Directors Guild of America - Los Angeles, 213/656-1220

NONE BUT THE BRAVE   Warner Bros., 1964, U.S.-Japanese

A N D R E W   S I N C L A I R

Contact: British Academy of Film & Television Arts, 195 Piccadilly, London W1,
England, 01/732-0022

THE BREAKING OF BUMBO   Timon/ABPC, 1971, British
UNDER MILK WOOD   Altura, 1973, British
BLUE BLOOD   Mallard Productions, 1975, British

G E R A L D   S E T H   S I N D E L L

b. April 15, 1944 - Cleveland, Ohio
Home: 9566 Yoakum Drive, Beverly Hills, CA 90210, 213/275-3353
Attorney: Steve Burkow, Pollock, Bloom & Dekom, 9255 Sunset Blvd., Los Angeles,
CA 90069, 213/278-8622

DOUBLE-STOP   World Entertainment, 1967
HARPY (TF)   Cinema Center 100, 1970
TEENAGER   National Cinema, 1974
H.O.T.S.   Derio Productions, 1979

ALEXANDER SINGER *

b. 1932 - New York, New York
Agent: ICM - Los Angeles, 213/550-4000

A COLD WIND IN AUGUST   Lopert, 1961
PSYCHE 59   Royal Films International, 1964, British
LOVE HAS MANY FACES   Columbia, 1965
CAPTAIN APACHE   Scotia International, 1971, British
GLASS HOUSES   Columbia, 1972
THE FIRST 36 HOURS OF DR. DURANT (TF)   Columbia TV, 1975
TIME TRAVELERS (TF)   Irwin Allen Productions/20th Century-Fox TV, 1976
THE MILLION DOLLAR RIP-OFF (TF)   Charles Fries Productions, 1976
HUNTERS OF THE REEF (TF)   Writers Company Productions/Paramount TV,
    1978

HAL SITOWITZ *

Agent: Adams, Ray & Rosenberg - Los Angeles, 213/278-3000

A LAST CRY FOR HELP (TF)   Myrt-Hal Productions/Viacom, 1979

VILGOT SJOMAN

(David Harald Vilgot Sjoman)

b. December 2, 1924 - Stockholm, Sweden
Contact: Swedish Film Institute, P.O. Box 27126, 102 52 Stockholm, Sweden, 08/
    63-0510

THE SWEDISH MISTRESS   1962, Swedish
491   Peppercorn-Wormser, 1964, Swedish
THE DRESS   1964, Swedish
MY SISTER, MY LOVE *Syskonbadd 1782*   Sigma III, 1966, Swedish
STIMULANTIA   co-director, 1967, Swedish
I AM CURIOUS (YELLOW)   Grove Press, 1967, Swedish
I AM CURIOUS (BLUE)   Grove Press, 1968, Swedish
YOU'RE LYING   Grove Press, 1969, Swedish
BLUSHING CHARLIE   1970, Swedish
THE KARLSSON BROTHERS   1972, Swedish
TILL SEX DO US PART   Astro, 1973, Swedish
A HANDFUL OF LOVE   1974, Swedish
THE GARAGE   1975, Swedish
TABOO   1977, Swedish
LINUS AND THE MYSTERIOUS RED BRICK HOUSE   Svensk Filmindustri,
    1979, Swedish

JERZY SKOLIMOWSKI

b. May 5, 1938 - Warsaw, Poland
Contact: British Academy of Film & Television Arts, 195 Piccadilly, London W1,
    England, 01/732-0022

IDENTIFICATION MARKS: NONE   New Yorker, 1964, Polish
WALKOVER   New Yorker, 1965, Polish
BARRIER   Film Polski, 1966, Polish
LE DEPART   Pathe Contemporary, 1967, Belgian
HANDS UP!   1967, Polish
DIALOGUE   co-director, 1968, Czech
THE ADVENTURES OF GIRARD   United Artists, 1969, British-Swiss
DEEP END   Paramount, 1971, British-West German
KING, QUEEN, KNAVE   Avco Embassy, 1972, West German-British
THE SHOUT   Films Inc., 1979, British
MOONLIGHTING   Universal Classics, 1982, British

LANE SLATE *

Contact: Directors Guild of America - Los Angeles, 213/656-1220

CLAY PIGEON   co-director with Tom Stern, MGM, 1971
DEADLY GAME (TF)   MGM TV, 1977

JACK SMIGHT *

b. March 9, 1926 - Minneapolis, Minnesota
Agent: Kaplan-Stahler Agency - Los Angeles, 213/653-4483

I'D RATHER BE RICH   Universal, 1964
THE THIRD DAY   Warner Bros., 1965
HARPER   Warner Bros., 1966
KALEIDOSCOPE   Warner Bros., 1966, British
THE SECRET WAR OF HARRY FRIGG   Universal, 1968
NO WAY TO TREAT A LADY   Paramount, 1968
STRATEGY OF TERROR   Universal, 1969
THE ILLUSTRATED MAN   Warner Bros., 1969
RABBIT, RUN   Warner Bros., 1970
THE TRAVELING EXECUTIONER   MGM, 1970
THE SCREAMING WOMAN (TF)   Universal TV, 1972
BANACEK: DETOUR TO NOWHERE (TF)   Universal TV, 1972
THE LONGEST NIGHT (TF)   Universal TV, 1972
PARTNERS IN CRIME (TF)   Universal TV, 1973
DOUBLE INDEMNITY (TF)   Universal TV, 1973
LINDA (TF)   Universal TV, 1973
FRANKENSTEIN: THE TRUE STORY (TF)   Universal TV, 1973
AIRPORT 1975   Universal, 1974
MIDWAY   Universal, 1976
DAMNATION ALLEY   20th Century-Fox, 1977
ROLL OF THUNDER, HEAR MY CRY (TF)   Tomorrow Entertainment, 1978
FAST BREAK   Columbia, 1979
LOVING COUPLES   20th Century-Fox, 1980
REMEMBRANCE OF LOVE (TF)   Doris Quinlan Productions/Comworld
    Productions, 1982

CLIVE A. SMITH

Contact: Canadian Film & Television Association, 8 King Street, Toronto, Ontario
    M5C 1B5, Canada, 416/363-0296

ROCK & RULE (AF)   MGM/UA, 1983, Canadian

HOWARD SMITH

Business: The Village Voice, 842 Broadway, New York, NY 10003, 212/475-3300

MARJOE (FD)   co-director with Sarah Kernochan, Cinema 5, 1972
GIZMO! (FD)   New Line Cinema, 1977

ALFRED SOLE *

Home: 1641 N. Kings Road, Los Angeles, CA 90069, 213/656-9347
Personal Manager: Barry Krost, BKM Management - Los Angeles, 213/550-7358

ALICE, SWEET ALICE *COMMUNION/HOLY TERROR*   Allied Artists, 1977
TANYA'S ISLAND   IFEX Film/Fred Baker Films, 1981, Canadian
PANDEMONIUM   MGM/UA, 1982

ANDREW SOLT *

b. December 13, 1947 - London, England
Home: 1252 Shadybrook Drive, Beverly Hills, CA 90210

HEROES OF ROCK AND ROLL (TD)   co-director with Malcolm Leo, ABC,
    1979
THIS IS ELVIS (FD)   co-director with Malcolm Leo, Warner Bros., 1981
IT CAME FROM HOLLYWOOD (FD)   co-director with Malcolm Leo,
    Paramount, 1982

SUSAN SONTAG

DUET FOR CANNIBALS   Grove Press, 1969, Swedish
BROTHER CARL   New Yorker, 1972, Swedish
PROMISED LANDS (FD)   New Yorker, 1974, French

L A R R Y   G .   S P A N G L E R

THE SOUL OF NIGGER CHARLEY   Paramount, 1973
A KNIFE FOR THE LADIES   Bryanston, 1974
THE LIFE AND TIMES OF XAVIERA HOLLANDER   Mature, 1974
JOSHUA   Lone Star, 1976
SILENT SENTENCE   Intercontinental, 1983

P E N E L O P E   S P H E E R I S

THE DECLINE OF WESTERN CIVILIZATION (FD)   Spheeris Films Inc., 1981
THE WILD SIDE *SUBURBIA*   New World, 1983

S T E V E N   S P I E L B E R G *

b. December 18, 1947 - Cincinnati, Ohio
Agent: ICM - Los Angeles, 213/550-4000

NIGHT GALLERY (TF)   co-director with Boris Sagal & Barry Shear, Universal
    TV, 1969
DUEL (TF)   Universal TV, 1971
SOMETHING EVIL (TF)   Belford Productions/CBS International, 1972
SAVAGE (TF)   Universal TV, 1973
THE SUGARLAND EXPRESS   Universal, 1974
JAWS   Universal, 1975
CLOSE ENCOUNTERS OF THE THIRD KIND ★   Columbia, 1977
1941   Universal/Columbia, 1979
RAIDERS OF THE LOST ARK ★   Paramount, 1981
E.T. THE EXTRA-TERRESTRIAL ★   Universal, 1982
TWILIGHT ZONE - THE MOVIE   co-director with John Landis, Joe Dante &
    George Miller, Warner Bros., 1983
INDIANA JONES AND THE TEMPLE OF DOOM   Paramount, 1984

R O G E R   S P O T T I S W O O D E *

Home: 2451 Holly Drive, Los Angeles, CA 90068, 213/469-6679
Agent: Gary Lucchesi, William Morris Agency - Beverly Hills, 213/274-7451
Business Manager: Jay Trulman, Jay Trulman Accountancy Corporation, 1930
    Century Park West - Suite 3000, Los Angeles, CA 90067, 213/553-7300

TERROR TRAIN   20th Century-Fox, 1980, Canadian
THE PURSUIT OF D.B. COOPER   Universal, 1982
THE RENEGADES (TF)   Lawrence Gordon Productions/Paramount TV, 1982
UNDER FIRE   Orion, 1983

G . D .   S P R A D L I N

Agent: The Mishkin Agency - Los Angeles, 213/274-5261

THE ONLY WAY HOME   Regional, 1972

R O B I N   S P R Y

b. 1939 - Toronto, Canada
Home: 5330 Durocher, Montreal, Quebec H2V 3Y1, Canada, 514/277-1503

PROLOGUE   Vaudeo, 1969, Canadian
ACTION: THE OCTOBER CRISIS (FD)   1974, Canadian
DRYING UP THE STREETS   CBC, 1978, Canadian
HIT AND RUN   Agora Productions, 1981, Canadian
SUZANNE   20th Century-Fox, 1982, Canadian

RAYMOND ST. JACQUES
(James Arthur Johnson)

b. 1930 - Hartford, Connecticut
Agent: Contemporary-Korman Artists - Beverly Hills, 213/278-8250

BOOK OF NUMBERS   Avco Embassy, 1973

CHRISTOPHER ST. JOHN

TOP OF THE HEAP   Fanfare, 1972

SYLVESTER STALLONE*

b. July 6, 1946 - New York, New York
Agent: Ron Meyer, CAA - Los Angeles, 213/277-4545

PARADISE ALLEY   Universal, 1978
ROCKY II   United Artists, 1979
ROCKY III   MGM/UA, 1982
STAYING ALIVE   Paramount, 1983

PAUL STANLEY*

Agent: David Shapira & Associates - Beverly Hills, 213/278-2742

CRY TOUGH   United Artists, 1959
THREE GUNS FOR TEXAS   co-director with David Lowell Rich & Earl Bellamy,
     Universal, 1968
SOLE SURVIVOR (TF)   Cinema Center, 1969
RIVER OF MYSTERY (TF)   Universal TV, 1971
NICKY'S WORLD (TF)   Tomorrow Entertainment, 1974
CRISIS IN SUN VALLEY (TF)   Columbia TV, 1978
THE ULTIMATE IMPOSTER (TF)   Universal TV, 1979

RINGO STARR
(Richard Starkey)

b. July 7, 1940 - Liverpool, England
Business: Wobble Music Ltd., 17 Berkeley Street, London W1, England

BORN TO BOOGIE (FD)   MGM-EMI, 1972, British

JACK STARRETT

b. November 2, 1936 - Refugio, Texas

RUN, ANGEL, RUN!   Fanfare, 1969
THE LOSERS   Fanfare, 1970
CRY BLOOD, APACHE   Golden Eagle International, 1970
NIGHT CHASE (TF)   Cinema Center, 1970
THE STRANGE VENGEANCE OF ROSALIE   20th Century-Fox, 1972
SLAUGHTER   American International, 1972
CLEOPATRA JONES   Warner Bros., 1973
GRAVY TRAIN *THE DION BROTHERS*   Columbia, 1974
RACE WITH THE DEVIL   20th Century-Fox, 1975
A SMALL TOWN IN TEXAS   American International, 1976
FINAL CHAPTER - WALKING TALL   American International, 1977
ROGER & HARRY: THE MITERA TARGET (TF)   Bruce Lansbury Productions/
     Columbia TV, 1977
NOWHERE TO HIDE (TF)   Mark Carliner Productions/Viacom, 1977
THADDEUS ROSE AND EDDIE (TF)   CBS, Inc., 1978
BIG BOB JOHNSON AND HIS FANTASTIC SPEED CIRCUS (TF)   Playboy
     Productions/Paramount TV, 1978
MR. HORN (TF)   Lorimar Productions, 1979
SURVIVAL OF DANA (TF)   EMI TV, 1979
KISS MY GRITS *A TEXAS LEGEND/SUMMER HEAT*   Ambassador, 1982

JEFF STEIN

THE KIDS ARE ALRIGHT (FD)   New World, 1979, British

DAVID STEINBERG *

Agent: Stan Kamen, William Morris Agency - Beverly Hills, 213/274-7451
Business Manager: Neal Levin, Neal Levin Company - Beverly Hills, 213/858-8300

PATERNITY   Paramount, 1981
GOING BERSERK   Universal, 1983, Canadian

DANIEL STEINMANN

SAVAGE STREETS   MPM, 1984

LEONARD B. STERN *

b. December 23, 1923 - New York, New York
Agent: William Morris Agency - Beverly Hills, 213/274-7451
Business Manager: Gerwin, Jamner & Pariser - Los Angeles, 213/652-0222

ONCE UPON A DEAD MAN (TF)   Universal TV, 1971
THE SNOOP SISTERS (TF)   Universal TV, 1972
JUST YOU AND ME, KID   Columbia, 1979

SANDOR STERN *

b. July 13, 1936 - Timmins, Ontario, Canada
Home: 9116½ Pico Blvd., Los Angeles, CA 90035, 213/275-0180
Agent: Elliot Webb, ICM - Los Angeles, 213/550-4000

THE SEEDING OF SARAH BURNS (TF)   Michael Klein Productions, 1979
MUGGABLE MARY: STREET COP (TF)   CBS Entertainment, 1982
MEMORIES NEVER DIE (TF)   Groverton Productions/Scholastic Productions/
    Universal TV, 1982

STEVEN H. STERN *

b. November 1, 1937 - Ontario, Canada
Home: 4321 Clear Valley Drive, Encino, CA 91436, 213/788-3607
Agent: John Gaines, APA - Los Angeles, 213/273-0744

B.S. I LOVE YOU   20th Century-Fox, 1971
NEITHER BY DAY NOR BY NIGHT   Motion Pictures International, 1972, U.S.-
    Israeli
THE HARRAD SUMMER   Cinerama Releasing Corporation, 1974
ESCAPE FROM BOGEN COUNTY (TF)   Paramount TV, 1977
THE GHOST OF FLIGHT 401 (TF)   Paramount TV, 1978
DOCTORS' PRIVATE LIVES (TF)   David Gerber Company/Columbia TV, 1978
GETTING MARRIED (TF)   Paramount TV, 1978
FAST FRIENDS (TF)   Columbia TV, 1979
ANATOMY OF A SEDUCTION (TF)   Moonlight Productions/Filmways, 1979
YOUNG LOVE, FIRST LOVE (TF)   Lorimar Productions, 1979
RUNNING   Columbia, 1979, Canadian-U.S.
PORTRAIT OF AN ESCORT (TF)   Moonlight Productions/Filmways, 1980
THE DEVIL AND MAX DEVLIN   Buena Vista, 1981
MIRACLE ON ICE (TF)   Moonlight Productions/Filmways, 1981
A SMALL KILLING (TF)   Orgolini-Nelson Productions/Motown Productions,
    1982
THE AMBUSH MURDERS (TF)   David Goldsmith Productions/Charles Fries
    Productions, 1982
PORTRAIT OF A SHOWGIRL (TF)   Hamner Productions, 1982
NOT JUST ANOTHER AFFAIR (TF)   Ten-Four Productions, 1982
FORBIDDEN LOVE (TF)   Gross-Weston Productions, 1982
RONA JAFFE'S MAZES AND MONSTERS (TF)   McDermott Productions/
    Procter & Gamble Productions, 1982
BABY SISTER (TF)   Moonlight Productions II, 1983
STILL THE BEAVER (TF)   Bud Austin Productions/Universal TV, 1983

continued

STEVEN H. STERN*—continued

AN UNCOMMON LOVE (TF)   Beechwood Productions/Lorimar Productions, 1983

ART STEVENS

Business: Walt Disney Productions, 500 S. Buena Vista Street, Burbank, CA 91521, 213/845-3141

THE FOX AND THE HOUND (AF)   co-director with Ted Berman & Richard Rich, Buena Vista, 1981
THE BLACK CAULDRON (AF)   co-director with Ted Berman & Richard Rich, Buena Vista, 1985

DAVID STEVENS

Contact: Australian Film Commission, 9229 Sunset Blvd., Los Angeles, CA 90069, 213/275-7074

THE JOHN SULLIVAN STORY (TF)   1980, Australian
NUMBER 96 (MS)   1974, Australian
THE SULLIVANS (MS)   co-director with Simon Wincer, 1980, Australian
A TOWN LIKE ALICE (MS)   Seven Network/Victorian Film Corporation, 1981, Australian
THE CLINIC   Film House/Generation Films, 1982, Australian
UNDERCOVER   Filmco, 1983, Australian

LESLIE STEVENS*

b. February 3, 1924 - Washington, D.C.
Business: Leslie Stevens Productions, 1107 Glendon Avenue, Los Angeles, CA 90024, 213/479-2770

PRIVATE PROPERTY   Citation, 1960
INCUBUS   1961
HERO'S ISLAND   United Artists, 1962
DELLA   Four Star, 1964
FANFARE FOR A DEATH SCENE   Four Star, 1967
I LOVE A MYSTERY (TF)   Universal TV, 1973

ROBERT STEVENSON*

b. 1905 - London, England
Business: Walt Disney Productions, 500 S. Buena Vista Street, Burbank, CA 91521, 213/845-3141

HAPPILY EVER AFTER   Gaumont, 1932, British
FALLING FOR YOU   Woolf & Freedman, 1933, British
JACK OF ALL TRADES   Gaumont, 1936, British
NINE DAYS A QUEEN *TUDOR ROSE*   Gaumont, 1936, British
THE MAN WHO LIVED AGAIN *THE MAN WHO CHANGED HIS MIND*   Gaumont, 1936, British
KING SOLOMON'S MINES   Gaumont, 1937, British
NON-STOP NEW YORK   General Film Distributors, 1937, British
TO THE VICTOR *OWD BOB*   Gaumont, 1938, British
THE WARE CASE   Associated British Film Distributors, 1939, British
A YOUNG MAN'S FANCY   Associated British Film Distributors, 1939, British
RETURN TO YESTERDAY   Associated British Film Distributors, 1939, British
TOM BROWN'S SCHOOLDAYS   RKO Radio, 1940
BACK STREET   Universal, 1941
JOAN OF PARIS   RKO Radio, 1942
FOREVER AND A DAY   co-director with Rene Clair, Edmund Goulding, Cedric Hardwicke, Frank Lloyd, Victor Saville & Herbert Wilcox, RKO Radio, 1943
JANE EYRE   RKO Radio, 1944
DISHONORED LADY   United Artists, 1947
TO THE ENDS OF THE EARTH   RKO Radio, 1948
THE WOMAN ON PIER 13 *I MARRIED A COMMUNIST*   RKO Radio, 1949
WALK SOFTLY, STRANGER   RKO Radio, 1950
MY FORBIDDEN PAST   RKO Radio, 1951
THE LAS VEGAS STORY   RKO Radio, 1952

continued

ROBERT STEVENSON*—continued

JOHNNY TREMAIN   Buena Vista, 1957
OLD YELLER   Buena Vista, 1957
DARBY O'GILL AND THE LITTLE PEOPLE   Buena Vista, 1959
KIDNAPPED   Buena Vista, 1960, British-U.S.
THE ABSENT-MINDED PROFESSOR   Buena Vista, 1960
IN SEARCH OF THE CASTAWAYS   Buena Vista, 1962, British-U.S.
SON OF FLUBBER   Buena Vista, 1963
THE MISADVENTURES OF MERLIN JONES   Buena Vista, 1964
MARY POPPINS ★   Buena Vista, 1964
THE MONKEY'S UNCLE   Buena Vista, 1965
THAT DARN CAT   Buena Vista, 1965
THE GNOME-MOBILE   Buena Vista, 1967
BLACKBEARD'S GHOST   Buena Vista, 1968
THE LOVE BUG   Buena Vista, 1969
BEDKNOBS AND BROOMSTICKS   Buena Vista, 1971
HERBIE RIDES AGAIN   Buena Vista, 1974
THE ISLAND AT THE TOP OF THE WORLD   Buena Vista, 1974
ONE OF OUR DINOSAURS IS MISSING   Buena Vista, 1975, U.S.-British
THE SHAGGY D.A.   Buena Vista, 1976

JOHN STIX

FAMILY BUSINESS (TF)   Screenscope Inc./South Carolina Educational TV
    Network, 1983

ANDREW L. STONE*

b. July 16, 1902 - Oakland, California
Home: 10478 Wyton Drive, Los Angeles, CA 90024, 213/279-2497
Agent: Calder Agency - Los Angeles, 213/845-7434

SOMBRAS DE GLORIA   Sono Arts, 1930
HELL'S HEADQUARTERS   Capitol, 1932
THE GIRL SAID NO   Grand National, 1937
STOLEN HEAVEN   Paramount, 1938
SAY IT IN FRENCH   Paramount, 1938
THE GREAT VICTOR HERBERT   Paramount, 1939
THERE'S MAGIC IN MUSIC   Paramount, 1941
STORMY WEATHER   20th Century-Fox, 1943
HI DIDDLE DIDDLE   RKO Radio, 1943
SENSATIONS OF 1945   United Artists, 1944
BEDSIDE MANNER   United Artists, 1945
THE BACHELOR'S DAUGHTER   United Artists, 1946
FUN ON A WEEKEND   United Artists, 1947
HIGHWAY 301   Warner Bros., 1950
CONFIDENCE GIRL   United Artists, 1951
THE STEEL TRAP   20th Century-Fox, 1952
A BLUEPRINT FOR MURDER   20th Century-Fox, 1953
THE NIGHT HOLDS TERROR   Columbia, 1955
JULIE   MGM, 1956
CRY TERROR!   MGM, 1958
THE DECKS RAN RED   MGM, 1958
THE LAST VOYAGE   MGM, 1960
RING OF FIRE   MGM, 1961
THE PASSWORD IS COURAGE   MGM, 1963, British
NEVER PUT IT IN WRITING   Allied Artists, 1964, British
THE SECRET OF MY SUCCESS   MGM, 1965, British
SONG OF NORWAY   Cinerama Releasing Corporation, 1970
THE GREAT WALTZ   MGM, 1972

OLIVER STONE*

b. November 15, 1946 - New York, New York
Agent: Jeff Berg, ICM - Los Angeles, 213/550-4000
Business Manager: Licker & Pines, 9025 Wilshire Blvd., Beverly Hills, CA 90211,
    213/858-1276

SEIZURE   Cinerama Releasing Corporation, 1974, Canadian
THE HAND   Orion/Warner Bros., 1981

B A R B R A   S T R E I S A N D *

b. 1942 - New York, New York
Agent: William Morris Agency - Beverly Hills, 213/274-7451

YENTL   MGM/UA, 1983

J O S E P H   S T R I C K *

b. July 6, 1923 - Braddock, Pennsylvania
Home: 266 River Road, Grandview, NY 10960, 914/359-9527
Business: Trans-Lux Corporation, 625 Madison Avenue, New York, NY 10022,
    212/751-3110

THE BIG BREAK   1953
THE SAVAGE EYE   co-director with Ben Maddow & Sidney Meyers, Trans-Lux,
    1959
THE BALCONY   Continental, 1963
ULYSSES   Continental, 1967
TROPIC OF CANCER   Paramount, 1970
ROAD MOVIE   Grove Press, 1974
A PORTRAIT OF THE ARTIST AS A YOUNG MAN   Howard Mahler Films,
    1979

B R I A N   S T U A R T

SORCERESS   New World, 1982

M E L   S T U A R T *

b. September 2, 1928
Home: 11508 Thurston Circle, Los Angeles, CA 90049, 213/476-2634

IF IT'S TUESDAY, THIS MUST BE BELGIUM   United Artists, 1969
I LOVE MY WIFE   Universal, 1970
WILLY WONKA AND THE CHOCOLATE FACTORY   Paramount, 1971,
    British
ONE IS A LONELY NUMBER   MGM, 1972
WATTSTAX (FD)   Columbia, 1973
BRENDA STARR (TF)   Wolper Productions, 1976
MEAN DOG BLUES   American International, 1978
RUBY AND OSWALD (TF)   Alan Landsburg Productions, 1978
THE TRIANGLE FACTORY FIRE SCANDAL (TF)   Alan Landsburg
    Productions/Don Kirshner Productions, 1979
THE CHISHOLMS (MS)   Alan Landsburg Productions, 1979
THE WHITE LIONS   Alan Landsburg Productions, 1979
SOPHIA LOREN: HER OWN STORY (TF)   Roger Gimbel Productions/EMI TV,
    1980

J O H N   S T U R G E S *

b. January 3, 1911 - Oak Park, Illinois
Agent: William Morris Agency - Beverly Hills, 213/274-7451

THUNDERBOLT   co-director with William Wyler, Monogram, 1945
THE MAN WHO DARED   Columbia, 1946
SHADOWED   Columbia, 1946
ALIAS MR. TWILIGHT   Columbia, 1946
FOR THE LOVE OF RUSTY   Columbia, 1947
KEEPER OF THE BEES   Columbia, 1947
BEST MAN WINS   Columbia, 1948
THE SIGN OF THE RAM   Columbia, 1948
THE WALKING HILLS   Columbia, 1949
THE CAPTURE   RKO Radio, 1950
MYSTERY STREET   MGM, 1950
RIGHT CROSS   MGM, 1950
THE MAGNIFICENT YANKEE   MGM, 1950
KIND LADY   MGM, 1951
THE PEOPLE AGAINST O'HARA   MGM, 1951
IT'S A BIG COUNTRY   co-director with Charles Vidor, Richard Thorpe, Don
    Hartman, Don Weis, Clarence Brown & William Wellman, MGM, 1952

continued

JOHN STURGES*—continued
THE GIRL IN WHITE   MGM, 1952
JEOPARDY   MGM, 1953
FAST COMPANY   MGM, 1953
ESCAPE FROM FORT BRAVO   MGM, 1953
BAD DAY AT BLACK ROCK ★   MGM, 1955
UNDERWATER!   RKO Radio, 1955
THE SCARLET COAT   MGM, 1955
BACKLASH   MGM, 1956
GUNFIGHT AT THE O.K. CORRAL   Paramount, 1957
THE LAW AND JAKE WADE   MGM, 1958
THE OLD MAN AND THE SEA   Warner Bros., 1958
LAST TRAIN FROM GUN HILL   Paramount, 1959
NEVER SO FEW   MGM, 1959
THE MAGNIFICENT SEVEN   United Artists, 1960
BY LOVE POSSESSED   United Artists, 1961
SERGEANTS 3   United Artists, 1962
A GIRL NAMED TAMIKO   Paramount, 1963
THE GREAT ESCAPE   United Artists, 1963
THE SATAN BUG   United Artists, 1965
THE HALLELUJAH TRAIL   United Artists, 1965
HOUR OF THE GUN   United Artists, 1967
ICE STATION ZEBRA   MGM, 1968
MAROONED   Columbia, 1969
JOE KIDD   Universal, 1972
CHINO *THE VALDEZ HORSES*   Intercontinental, 1973, Italian-Spanish-French
McQ   Warner Bros., 1974
THE EAGLE HAS LANDED   Columbia, 1977, British

CHARLES STURRIDGE

Contact: British Academy of Film & Television Arts, 195 Piccadilly, London W1, England, 01/732-0022

BRIDESHEAD REVISITED (MS) ☆   co-director with Michael Lindsay-Hogg, Granada TV/WNET-13/NDR Hamburg, 1982, British-U.S.-West German
RUNNERS   The Samuel Goldwyn Company, 1983, British

JEREMY SUMMERS

Agent: Eric L'Epine Smith - London, 01/724-0759

DEPTH CHARGE   British Lion, 1960, British
CROOKS IN CLOISTERS   Warner-Pathe, 1964, British
FERRY CROSS THE MERSEY   United Artists, 1965, British
SAN FERRY ANN   British Lion, 1966, British
DATELINE DIAMONDS   Rank, 1966, British
HOUSE OF 1,000 DOLLS   American International, 1967, British
FIVE GOLDEN DRAGONS   Warner-Pathe, 1968, British
THE VENGEANCE OF FU MANCHU   Warner Bros., 1968, British
FALLEN HERO (TF)   Granada TV, 1979, British
TOURIST (TF)   Castle Combe Productions/Paramount TV, 1980
A KIND OF LOVING (TF)   Granada TV, 1981, British

E.W. SWACKHAMER*

Agent: Shapiro-Lichtman Agency - Los Angeles, 213/557-2244

IN NAME ONLY (TF)   Screen Gems/Columbia TV, 1969
MAN AND BOY   Levitt-Pickman, 1972
GIDGET GETS MARRIED (TF)   Screen Gems/Columbia TV, 1972
DEATH SENTENCE (TF)   Spelling-Goldberg Productions, 1974
DEATH AT LOVE HOUSE (TF)   Spelling-Goldberg Productions, 1976
ONCE AN EAGLE (MS)   co-director with Richard Michaels, Universal TV, 1976
NIGHT TERROR (TF)   Charles Fries Productions, 1977
SPIDER-MAN (TF)   Charles Fries Productions, 1977
THE DAIN CURSE (MS) ☆   Martin Poll Productions, 1978
THE WINDS OF KITTY HAWK (TF)   Charles Fries Productions, 1978
VAMPIRE (TF)   MTM Enterprises, 1979
THE DEATH OF OCEAN VIEW PARK (TF)   Furia-Oringer Productions/Playboy Productions, 1979

continued

E.W. SWACKHAMER*—continued

REWARD (TF)   Jerry Adler Productions/Espirit Enterprises/Lorimar Productions, 1980
TENSPEED AND BROWNSHOE (TF)   Stephen J. Cannell Productions, 1980
THE OKLAHOMA CITY DOLLS (TF)   IKE Productions/Columbia TV, 1981
LONGSHOT   GG Productions, 1981
COCAINE AND BLUE EYES (TF)   Orenthal Productions/Columbia TV, 1983
MALIBU (TF)   Hamner Productions/Columbia TV, 1983
CARPOOL (TF)   Charles Fries Productions/Cherryhill Productions, 1983
THE ROUSTERS (TF)   Stephen J. Cannell Productions, 1983

CHARLES   SWENSON

Business: Murakami/Wolf/Swenson, Inc., 1463, Tamarind Avenue, Hollywood,
     CA   90028, 213/462-6473

THE MOUSE AND HIS CHILD (AF)   co-director with Fred Wolf, Sanrio, 1977
TWICE UPON A TIME (AF)   co-director with John Korty, The Ladd Company/
     Warner Bros., 1983

JO   SWERLING,   JR.*

b. June 18, 1931 - Los Angeles, California
Home: 5400 Jed Smith Road, Hidden Hills, CA   91302, 213/888-7231
Messages: 213/465-5800
Business: Stephen J. Cannell Prods., 5555 Melrose Avenue, Los Angeles,
     CA   90028 213/468-5000
Agent: Sam Adams, Adams, Ray & Rosenberg - Los Angeles, 213/278-3000

THE LAST CONVERTIBLE (MS)   co-director with Sidney Hayers & Gus
     Trikonis, Roy Huggins Productions/Universal TV, 1979

DAVID   SWIFT*

b. 1919 - Minneapolis, Minnesota
Business Manager: Peter Dekom, Pollock, Bloom & Dekom, 9255 Sunset Blvd., Los
     Angeles, CA   90069, 213/278-8622

POLYANNA   Buena Vista, 1960
THE PARENT TRAP   Buena Vista, 1961
THE INTERNS   Columbia, 1962
LOVE IS A BALL   United Artists, 1962
UNDER THE YUM YUM TREE   Columbia, 1963
GOOD NEIGHBOR SAM   Columbia, 1964
HOW TO SUCCEED IN BUSINESS WITHOUT REALLY TRYING   United
     Artists, 1967

SAUL   SWIMMER

FORCE OF IMPULSE   Sutton, 1961
MRS. BROWN, YOU'VE GOT A LOVELY DAUGHTER   MGM, 1968, British
COMETOGETHER   Allied Artists, 1971, U.S.-Italian
THE CONCERT FOR BANGLADESH (FD)   20th Century-Fox, 1972
THE BLACK PEARL   Diamond, 1977
WE WILL ROCK YOU (FD)   Mobilevision/Yellowbill, 1983, Canadian

BRAD   SWIRNOFF

Contact: Writers Guild of America, West - Los Angeles, 213/550-1000

TUNNELVISION   co-director with Neil Israel, World Wide, 1976
AMERICAN RASPBERRY   Cannon, 1980

HANS-JURGEN SYBERBERG

b. December 8, 1935 - Germany
Contact: German Film & TV Academy, Pommernallee 1, 1000 Berlin 19, West
    Germany, 030/303-6212

LUDWIG: REQUIEM FOR A VIRGIN KING   Zoetrope, 1973, West German
KARL MAY   7MS Film Gesellschaft, 1976, West German
WINIFRED WAGNER (FD)   Bauer International, 1978, West German
HITLER: A FILM FROM GERMANY   Zoetrope, 1980, West German
PARSIFAL   Triumph/Columbia, 1983, French-West German

PETER SYKES

b. June 17, 1939 - Melbourne, Australia
Address: 66 Highgate Hill - No. 6, London NW19, England, 01/272-1664

THE COMMITTEE   Planet, 1968, British
DEMONS OF THE MIND   MGM-EMI, 1972, British
THE HOUSE IN NIGHTMARE PARK   MGM-EMI, 1973, British
STEPTOE AND SON RIDE AGAIN   MGM-EMI, 1973, British
LEGEND OF SPIDER FOREST *VENOM*   New Line Cinema, 1974, British
TO THE DEVIL A DAUGHTER   EMI, 1976, British
CRAZY HOUSE   Constellation, 1977, British
JESUS   co-director with John Krish, Warner Bros., 1979, British
THE SEARCH FOR ALEXANDER THE GREAT (MS)   Time-Life Productions/
    Video Arts TV Productions, 1981, U.S.-British

PAUL SYLBERT *

Home: 52 East 64th Street - Suite 3, New York, NY   10021
Messages: 212/308-9078

THE STEAGLE   Avco Embassy, 1971

ISTVAN SZABO

b. 1938 - Budapest, Hungary
Agent: Carole Dowling, William Morris Agency - New York City, 212/903-1182

AGE OF ILLUSIONS   Brandon, 1964, Hungarian
FATHER   Continental, 1966, Hungarian
LOVE FILM   Mafilm, 1970, Hungarian
25, FIREMAN'S STREET   Budapest Studio, 1970, Hungarian
PREMIERE (TF)   Hungarian TV, 1974, Hungarian
BUDAPEST TALES   Mafilm, 1976, Hungarian
CONFIDENCE   Mafilm, 1979, Hungarian
THE GREEN BIRD   Manfred Durniok Film, 1979, West German
MEPHISTO   Analysis, 1980, Hungarian-West German

JEANNOT SZWARC *

b. November 21, 1939 - Paris, France
Business: Terpsichore Productions, 10100 Santa Monica Blvd., Los Angeles,
    CA 90067, 213/553-8200
Agent: Shapiro-Lichtman Agency - Los Angeles, 213/557-2244

NIGHT OF TERROR (TF)   Paramount TV, 1972
THE WEEKEND SUN (TF)   Paramount TV, 1972
THE DEVIL'S DAUGHTER (TF)   Paramount TV, 1973
YOU'LL NEVER SEE ME AGAIN (TF)   Universal TV, 1973
LISA, BRIGHT AND DARK (TF)   Bob Banner Associates, 1973
A SUMMER WITHOUT BOYS (TF)   Playboy Productions, 1973
THE SMALL MIRACLE (TF)   FCB Productions/Alan Landsburg Productions,
    1973
EXTREME CLOSE-UP   National General, 1973
CRIME CLUB (TF)   Universal TV, 1975
BUG   Paramount, 1975
CODE NAME: DIAMOND HEAD (TF)   QM Productions, 1977
JAWS 2   Universal, 1978
SOMEWHERE IN TIME   Universal, 1980

continued

JEANNOT SZWARC*—continued
ENIGMA   Embassy, 1982, British-French
SUPERGIRL   Warner Bros., 1984, British

T

JEAN-CHARLES TACCHELLA

b. September 23, 1925 - Cherbourg, France
Home: 8 bis Boulevard de Lesseps, Versailles 78000, France, 3/950-4764
Agent: Jean-Paul Faure, Agence IPF, 2 Rue Jules Chaplain, Paris, France, 325-5163

VOYAGE TO GRAND TARTARIE   New Line Cinema, 1973, French
COUSIN COUSINE   Libra, 1975, French
THE BLUE COUNTRY   Quartet, 1977, French
IT'S A LONG TIME THAT I'VE LOVED YOU *SOUPCON*   Durham/Pike,
    1979, French
CROQUE LA VIE   UPCT, 1981, French

ALAIN TANNER

b. 1929 - Geneva, Switzerland
Contact: Swiss Film Center, Muenstergasse 18, CH-8001 Zurich, Switzerland, 01/
    472-860

CHARLES, DEAD OR ALIVE   New Yorker, 1969, Swiss-French
LA SALAMANDRE   New Yorker, 1971, Swiss
LA RETOUR D'AFRIQUE   1972, Swiss
THE MIDDLE OF THE WORLD   New Yorker, 1974, Swiss
JONAH WHO WILL BE 25 IN THE YEAR 2000   New Yorker, 1976, Swiss
MESSIDOR   New Yorker, 1979, Swiss-French
LIGHT YEARS AWAY   New Yorker, 1981, Swiss-French
IN THE WHITE CITY   Gray City, 1983, Swiss

DANIEL TARADASH*

b. January 29, 1913 - Louisville, Kentucky
Agent: Ben Benjamin, ICM - Los Angeles, 213/550-4000

STORM CENTER   Columbia, 1956

ANDREI TARKOVSKY

b. April 4, 1932 - Moscow, U.S.S.R.
Contact: State Committee of Cinematography of the USSR, Council of Ministers, 7
    Maly Gnesdnikovsky Pereulok, Moscow, USSR, 7 095/229-9912

THE ROLLER AND THE VIOLIN   Mosfilm, 1960, Soviet
MY NAME IS IVAN   Shore International, 1962, Soviet
ANDREI RUBLEV   Columbia, 1968, Soviet
SOLARIS   Mosfilm, 1972, Soviet

continued

ANDREI TARKOVSKY—continued

THE MIRROR   Mosfilm, 1974, Soviet
STALKER   New Yorker/Media Transactions Corporation, 1979, Soviet
NOSTALGHIA   Grange Communications, 1983, Italian-Soviet

BERTRAND TAVERNIER

b. April 25, 1941 - Lyons, France
Contact: French Film Office, 745 Fifth Avenue, New York, NY 10151, 212/832-8860

THE CLOCKMAKER OF ST. PAUL   Joseph Green Pictures, 1974, French
LET JOY REIGN SUPREME *QUE LA FETE COMMENCE ...*   SJ International, 1975, French
THE JUDGE AND THE ASSASSIN   Libra, 1976, French
SPOILED CHILDREN   Corinth, 1977, French
FEMMES FATALES   1979, French
DEATH WATCH   Quartet, 1980, French-West German
A WEEK'S VACATION *UNE SEMAINE DE VACANCES*   Biograph, 1982, French
COUP DE TORCHON (CLEAN SLATE)   Biograph/Quartet/Films Inc./The Frank Moreno Company, 1982, French
MISSISSIPPI '82   Little Bear Productions/Odessa Films, 1983, French
MONSIEUR L'ADMIRAL VA BIENTOT MOURIR   Sara Films/Films Ad, 1984, French

PAOLO TAVIANI

b. 1931 - San Miniato, Italy
Contact: Ministry of Culture & Education, Via Della Ferratella, No. 51, 00184 Rome, Italy, 06/7732

UN UOMO DA BRUCIARE   co-director with Vittorio Taviani & Valentino Orsini, Moira Film/Ager Film/Sancro Film, 1963, Italian
I FUORILEGGE DEL METRAIMONIO   co-director with Vittorio Taviani & Valentino Orsini, Ager Film/Filmcoop/D'errico Film, 1963, Italian
SOVVERSIVI   co-director with Vittorio Taviani, Ager Film, 1967, Italian
SOTTO IL SEGNO DELLO SCORPIONE   co-director with Vittorio Taviani, Ager Film, 1969, Italian
SAN MICHELE AVEVA UN GALLO (TF)   co-director with Vittorio Taviani, Igor Film/RAI, 1971, Italian
ALLONSANFAN   co-director with Vittorio Taviani, Una Cooperativa Cinematografica, 1974, Italian
PADRE PADRONE   co-director with Vittorio Taviani, New Yorker, 1977, Italian, originally made for television
THE MEADOW   co-director with Vittorio Taviani, New Yorker, 1979, Italian-French
THE NIGHT OF THE SHOOTING STARS *LA NOTTE DI SAN LORENZO*   co-director with Vittorio Taviani, United Artists Classics, 1981, Italian
XAOS   co-director with Vittorio Taviani, Sacis, 1984, Italian

VITTORIO TAVIANI

b. 1929 - San Miniato, Italy
Contact: Ministry of Culture & Education, Via Della Ferratella, No. 51, 00184 Rome, Italy, 06/7732

UN UOMO DA BRUCIARE   co-director with Paolo Taviani & Valentino Orsini, Moira Film/Ager Film/Sancro Film, 1963, Italian
I FUORILEGGE DEL METRAIMONIO   co-director with Paolo Taviani & Valentino Orsini, Ager Film/Filmcoop/D'errico Film, 1963, Italian
SOVVERSIVI   co-director with Paolo Taviani, Ager Film, 1967, Italian
SOTTO IL SEGNO DELLO SCORPIONE   co-director with Paolo Taviani, Ager Film, 1969, Italian
SAN MICHELE AVEVA UN GALLO (TF)   co-director with Paolo Taviani, Igor Film/RAI, 1971, Italian
ALLONSANFAN   co-director with Paolo Taviani, Una Cooperativa Cinematografica, 1974, Italian
PADRE PADRONE   co-director with Paolo Taviani, New Yorker, 1977, Italian, originally made for television

continued

VITTORIO TAVIANI—continued
THE MEADOW   co-director with Paolo Taviani, New Yorker, 1979, Italian-French
THE NIGHT OF THE SHOOTING STARS *LA NOTTE DI SAN*
    LORENZO   co-director with Paolo Taviani, United Artists Classics, 1981,
    Italian
XAOS   co-director with Paolo Taviani, Sacis, 1984, Italian

DON TAYLOR *

b. December 13, 1920 - Freeport, Pennsylvania
Agent: The Gersh Agency - Beverly Hills, 213/274-6611

EVERTHING'S DUCKY   Columbia, 1961
RIDE THE WILD SURF   Columbia, 1964
JACK OF DIAMONDS   MGM, 1967, U.S.-West German
SOMETHING FOR A LONELY MAN (TF)   Universal TV, 1968
THE FIVE MAN ARMY   MGM, 1970, Italian
WILD WOMEN (TF)   Aaron Spelling Productions, 1970
ESCAPE FROM THE PLANET OF THE APES   20th Century-Fox, 1971
HEAT OF ANGER (TF)   Metromedia Productions, 1972
TOM SAWYER   United Artists, 1973
NIGHT GAMES (TF)   Paramount TV, 1974
HONKY TONK (TF)   MGM TV, 1974
ECHOES OF A SUMMER   Cine Artists, 1976, U.S.-Canadian
THE MAN-HUNTER (TF)   Universal TV, 1976
THE GREAT SCOUT AND CATHOUSE THURSDAY   American International,
    1976
A CIRCLE OF CHILDREN (TF)   Edgar J. Scherick Associates/20th Century-Fox
    TV, 1977
THE ISLAND OF DR. MOREAU   American International, 1977
DAMIEN - OMEN II   20th Century-Fox, 1978
THE GIFT (TF)   The Jozak Company/Cypress Point Productions/Paramount TV,
    1979
THE FINAL COUNTDOWN   United Artists, 1980
THE PROMISE OF LOVE (TF)   Pierre Cossette Productions, 1980
BROKEN PROMISE (TF)   1981
RED FLAG: THE ULTIMATE GAME (TF)   Marble Arch Productions, 1981
DROP-OUT FATHER (TF)   CBS Entertainment, 1982
LISTEN TO YOUR HEART (TF)   CBS Entertainment, 1983
SEPTEMBER GUN (TF)   QM Productions/Taft Entertainment/Brademan-Self
    Productions, 1983

JUD TAYLOR *

b. February 25, 1940
Agent: CAA - Los Angeles, 213/277-4545

FADE-IN   Paramount, 1968
WEEKEND OF TERROR (TF)   Paramount TV, 1970
SUDDENLY SINGLE (TF)   Chris-Rose Productions, 1971
REVENGE (TF)   Mark Carliner Productions, 1971
THE ROOKIES (TF)   Aaron Spelling Productions, 1972
SAY GOODBYE, MAGGIE COLE (TF)   Spelling-Goldberg Productions, 1972
HAWKINS ON MURDER   Arena-Leda Productions/MGM TV, 1973
WINTER KILL (TF)   Andy Griffith Enterprises/MGM TV, 1974
THE DISAPPEARANCE OF FLIGHT 412 (TF)   Cinemobile Productions, 1975
SEARCH FOR THE GODS (TF)   Warner Bros. TV, 1975
FUTURE COP (TF)   Paramount TV, 1976
RETURN TO EARTH (TF)   King-Hitzig Productions, 1976
WOMAN OF THE YEAR (TF)   MGM TV, 1976
TAIL GUNNER JOE (TF) ☆   Universal TV, 1977
MARY WHITE (TF)   Radnitz/Mattel Productions, 1977
CHRISTMAS MIRACLE IN CAUFIELD, U.S.A. (TF)   20th Century-Fox TV,
    1977
THE LAST TENANT (TF)   Titus Productions, 1978
LOVEY: A CIRCLE OF CHILDREN, PART II (TF)   Time-Life Productions, 1978
FLESH AND BLOOD (TF)   The Jozak Company/Cypress Point Productions/
    Paramount TV, 1979
CITY IN FEAR (TF)   directed under pseudonym of Allen Smithee, Trans World
    International, 1980
ACT OF LOVE (TF)   Cypress Point Productions/Paramount TV, 1980
MURDER AT CRESTRIDGE (TF)   Jaffe-Taylor Productions, 1981

continued

JUD TAYLOR*—continued

A QUESTION OF HONOR (TF)   Roger Gimbel Productions/EMI TV/Sonny
Grosso Productions, 1982
PACKIN' IT IN (TF)   Roger Gimbel Productions/Thorn EMI TV/Jones-Reiker Ink
Corporation, 1983

ROBERT TAYLOR

THE NINE LIVES OF FRITZ THE CAT (AF)   American International, 1974
HEIDI'S SONG (AF)   Paramount, 1982

LEWIS TEAGUE*

Agent: The Gersh Agency - Beverly Hills, 213/274-6611

DIRTY O'NEIL   co-director with Howard Freen, American International, 1974
THE LADY IN RED   New World, 1979
ALLIGATOR   Group 1, 1980
FIGHTING BACK   Paramount, 1982
CUJO   Warner Bros., 1983

JULIEN TEMPLE

Contact: Directors Guild of Great Britian, 56 Whitfield Street, London W1, England,
01/580-9592

THE GREAT ROCK 'N' ROLL SWINDLE   Kendon Films/Matrix Best/Virgin
Records, 1980, British
THE SECRET POLICEMAN'S OTHER BALL (FD)   Miramax, 1981, British
IT'S ALL TRUE (TF)   Island Pictures/BBC, 1983, British

JOAN TEWKESBURY*

b. 1937 - Redlands, California
Agent: Jeff Berg/Jane Sindell, ICM - Los Angeles, 213/550-4000

OLD BOYFRIENDS   Avco Embassy, 1979
THE TENTH MONTH (TF)   Joe Hamilton Productions, 1979
THE ACORN PEOPLE (TF)   Rollins-Joffe-Morra-Brezner Productions, 1980

PETER TEWKSBURY

b. 1924

SUNDAY IN NEW YORK   MGM, 1964
EMIL AND THE DETECTIVES   Buena Vista, 1964
DOCTOR, YOU'VE GOT TO BE KIDDING   MGM, 1967
STAY AWAY, JOE   MGM, 1968
THE TROUBLE WITH GIRLS   MGM, 1969
SECOND CHANCE (TF)   Metromedia Productions, 1972

DAVE THOMAS

Address: 18 Saintfield, Don Mills, Ontario M3C 2M5, 416/487-8296

STRANGE BREW   co-director with Rick Moranis, MGM/UA, 1983, Canadian

GERALD THOMAS

b. December 10, 1920 - Hull, England
Business: Pinewood Studios, Iver Heath, Buckinghamshire, England, IVER 651700
Contact: Directors Guild of Great Britain, 56 Whitfield Street, London W1, England,
01/580-9592

CIRCUS FRIENDS   British Lion/Children's Film Foundation, 1956, British
TIMELOCK   DCA, 1957, British
THE CIRCLE THE VICIOUS CIRCLE   Kassler, 1957, British
THE DUKE WORE JEANS   Anglo-Amalgamated, 1958, British

continued

GERALD THOMAS—continued

CHAIN OF EVENTS   British Lion, 1958, British
CARRY ON SERGEANT   Governor, 1958, British
CARRY ON NURSE   Governor, 1959, British
PLEASE TURN OVER   Columbia, 1959, British
WATCH YOUR STERN   Magna, 1960, British
BEWARE OF CHILDREN *NO KIDDING*   American International, 1960, British
CARRY ON CONSTABLE   Governor, 1960, British
ROOMMATES *RAISING THE WIND*   Herts-Lion International, 1961, British
CARRY ON REGARDLESS   Anglo-Amalgamated, 1961, British
A SOLITARY CHILD   British Lion, 1961, British
TWICE ROUND THE DAFFODILS   Anglo-Amalgamated, 1962, British
CARRY ON CRUISING   Governor, 1962, British
THE SWINGIN' MAIDEN *THE IRON MAIDEN*   Columbia, 1962, British
NURSE ON WHEELS   Janus, 1963, British
CARRY ON CABBY   Anglo-Amalgamated/Warner-Pathe, 1963, British
CARRY ON JACK   Anglo-Amalgamated/Warner-Pathe, 1964, British
CARRY ON SPYING   Governor, 1964, British
CARRY ON CLEO   Governor, 1964, British
THE BIG JOB   Anglo-Amalgamated/Warner-Pathe, 1966, British
CARRY ON COWBOY   Anglo-Amalgamated/Warner-Pathe, 1966, British
CARRY ON SCREAMING   Anglo-Amalgamated/Warner-Pathe, 1966, British
FOLLOW THAT CAMEL   Schoenfeld Film Distributing, 1967, British
CARRY ON DOCTOR   Rank, 1968, British
CARRY ON ... UP THE KHYBER   Rank, 1969, British
CARRY ON CAMPING   Rank, 1969, British
CARRY ON UP THE JUNGLE   Rank, 1970, British
CARRY ON AGAIN, DOCTOR   Rank, 1970, British
CARRY ON AT YOUR CONVENIENCE   Rank, 1971, British
CARRY ON HENRY   Rank, 1971, British
CARRY ON LOVING   Rank, 1971, British
CARRY ON ABROAD   Rank, 1972, British
CARRY ON MATRON   Rank, 1972, British
BLESS THIS HOUSE   Rank, 1973, British
CARRY ON BEHIND   Rank, 1976, British
CARRY ON ENGLAND   Rank, 1976, British
CARRY ON EMMANUELLE   Rank, 1978, British
THAT'S CARRY ON   Rank, 1978, British

RALPH THOMAS

b. August 10, 1915 - Hull, England
Contact: Directors Guild of Great Britain, 56 Whitfield Street, London W1, England,
    01/580-9592

HELTER SKELTER   General Film Distributors, 1949, British
ONCE UPON A DREAM   General Film Distributors, 1949, British
TRAVELLER'S JOY   General Film Distributors, 1949, British
THE CLOUDED YELLOW   General Film Distributors, 1950, British
ISLAND RESCUE *APPOINTMENT WITH VENUS*   Universal, 1951, British
THE ASSASSIN *THE VENETIAN BIRD*   United Artists, 1952, British
THE DOG AND THE DIAMONDS   Associated British Film Distributors/
    Children's Film Foundation, 1953, British
A DAY TO REMEMBER   Republic, 1953, British
DOCTOR IN THE HOUSE   Republic, 1954, British
MAD ABOUT MEN   General Film Distributors, 1954, British
DOCTOR AT SEA   Republic, 1955, British
ABOVE US THE WAVES   Republic, 1955, British
THE IRON PETTICOAT   MGM, 1956, British
CHECKPOINT   Rank, 1956, British
DOCTOR AT LARGE   Universal, 1957, British
CAMPBELL'S KINGDOM   Rank, 1957, British
A TALE OF TWO CITIES   Rank, 1958, British
THE WIND CANNOT READ   20th Century-Fox, 1958, British
THE 39 STEPS   20th Century-Fox, 1959, British
UPSTAIRS AND DOWNSTAIRS   20th Century-Fox, 1959, British
COMSPIRACY OF HEARTS   Paramount, 1960, British
DOCTOR IN LOVE   Governor, 1960, British
NO LOVE FOR JOHNNIE   Embassy, 1961, British
NO, MY DARLING DAUGHTER   Zenith, 1961, British
A PAIR OF BRIEFS   Rank, 1962, British
YOUNG AND WILLING *THE WILD AND THE WILLING*   Universal, 1962,
    British

continued

RALPH THOMAS—continued
DOCTOR IN DISTRESS   Governor, 1963, British
AGENT 8 3/4 *HOT ENOUGH FOR JUNE*   Continental, 1963, British
McGUIRE, GO HOME! *THE HIGH BRIGHT SUN*   Continental, 1964, British
CARNABY, M.D. *DOCTOR IN CLOVER*   Continental, 1965, British
DEADLIER THAN THE MALE   Universal, 1966, British
SOME GIRLS DO   United Artists, 1968, British
THE HIGH COMMISSIONER *NOBODY RUNS FOREVER*   Cinerama
   Releasing Corporation, 1968, British
DOCTOR IN TROUBLE   Rank, 1970, British
PERCY   MGM, 1971, British
QUEST FOR LOVE   Rank, 1971, British
IT'S A 2'6" ABOVE THE GROUND WORLD   British Lion, 1972, British
THE LOVE BAN   1973, British
IT'S NOT THE SIZE THAT COUNTS *PERCY'S PROGRESS*   Joseph
   Brenner Associates, 1974, British
A NIGHTINGALE SANG IN BERKELEY SQUARE   S. Benjamin Fisz
   Productions/Nightingale Productions, 1980, British

R A L P H   L .   T H O M A S

Address: 365 Markham Street, Toronto, Ontario M6G 2K8, England, 416/922-8700

TYLER (TF)   CBC, 1977, Canadian
CEMENTHEAD (TF)   CBC, 1978, Canadian
A PAID VACATION (TF)   CBC, 1979, Canadian
TICKET TO HEAVEN   United Artists Classics, 1981, Canadian
THE TERRY FOX STORY (CTF)   HBO Premiere Films/Robert Cooper Films II,
   1983, Canadian

J .   L E E   T H O M P S O N *

b. 1914 - Bristol, England
Home: 21932 W. Pacific Coast Highway, Malibu, CA 90265
Agent: Chasin-Park-Citron - Los Angeles, 213/273-7190

MURDER WITHOUT CRIME   Associated British Picture Corporation, 1950,
   British
THE YELLOW BALLOON   Allied Artists, 1952, British
THE WEAK AND THE WICKED   Allied Artists, 1954, British
COCKTAILS IN THE KITCHEN *FOR BETTER OR WORSE*   Associated
   British Picture Corporation, 1954, British
AS LONG AS THEY'RE HAPPY   Rank, 1955, British
AN ALLIGATOR NAMED DAISY   Rank, 1955, British
BLONDE SINNER *YIELD TO THE NIGHT*   Allied Artists, 1956, British
THE GOOD COMPANIONS   Rank, 1957, British
WOMAN IN A DRESSING GOWN   Warner Bros., 1957, British
DESERT ATTACK *ICE COLD IN ALEX*   20th Century-Fox, 1958 British
NO TREES IN THE STREET   Associated British Picture Corporation, 1959,
   British
TIGER BAY   Continental, 1959, British
FLAME OVER INDIA *NORTH WEST FRONTIER*   20th Century-Fox, 1959,
   British
I AIM AT THE STARS   Columbia, 1960, U.S.-West German
THE GUNS OF NAVARONE ★   Columbia, 1961, U.S.-British
CAPE FEAR   Universal, 1962
TARAS BULBA   United Artists, 1962
KINGS OF THE SUN   United Artists, 1963
WHAT A WAY TO GO!   20th Century-Fox, 1964
JOHN GOLDFARB, PLEASE COME HOME   20th Century-Fox, 1965
RETURN FROM THE ASHES   United Artists, 1965, British-U.S.
EYE OF THE DEVIL   MGM, 1967, British
BEFORE WINTER COMES   Columbia, 1969, British
THE CHAIRMAN   20th Century-Fox, 1969, British
MACKENNA'S GOLD   Columbia, 1969
BROTHERLY LOVE *COUNTRY DANCE*   MGM, 1970, British
CONQUEST OF THE PLANET OF THE APES   20th Century-Fox, 1972
A GREAT AMERICAN TRAGEDY (TF)   Metromedia Productions, 1972
BATTLE FOR THE PLANET OF THE APES   20th Century-Fox, 1973
HUCKLEBERRY FINN   United Artists, 1974
THE BLUE KNIGHT (TF)   Lorimar Productions, 1975
THE REINCARNATION OF PETER PROUD   American International, 1975

continued

J. LEE THOMPSON*—continued
ST. IVES   Warner Bros., 1976
WIDOW (TF)   Lorimar Productions, 1976
THE WHITE BUFFALO   United Artists, 1977
THE GREEK TYCOON   Universal, 1978
THE PASSAGE   United Artists, 1979, British
CABOBLANCO   Avco Embassy, 1981
HAPPY BIRTHDAY TO ME   Columbia, 1981, Canadian
CODE RED (TF)   Irwin Allen Productions/Columbia TV, 1981
10 TO MIDNIGHT   Cannon, 1983
THE EVIL THAT MEN DO   Tri-Star/Columbia, 1984
THE AMBASSADOR   MGM/UA/Cannon, 1984

R O B E R T   C.   T H O M P S O N *

b. May 31, 1937 - Palmyra, New York
Home: 4536 Mary Ellen Avenue, Sherman Oaks, CA 91423, 213/995-0273
Messages: 213/501-3714
Agent: Debee Klein, Irv Schechter Company - Beverly Hills, 213/278-8070
Business Manager: Platt, Blue & Lucove, 23047 Ventura Blvd., Woodland Hills, CA,
   213/883-7296

BUD AND LOU (TF)   Bob Banner Associates, 1978

J E R R Y   T H O R P E *

b. 1930
Home: 865 S. Bundy Drive, Los Angeles, CA 90049
Business: Blinn-Thorpe Productions, 4024 Radford Avenue, Studio City, CA 91604,
   213/760-5201
Agent: Leonard Hanzer, Major Talent Agency - Los Angeles, 213/820-5841

THE VENETIAN AFFAIR   MGM, 1968
DAY OF THE EVIL GUN   MGM, 1968
DIAL HOT LINE (TF)   Universal TV, 1970
LOCK, STOCK AND BARREL (TF)   Universal TV, 1971
THE CABLE CAR MURDER (TF)   Warner Bros. TV, 1971
KUNG FU (TF)   Warner Bros. TV, 1972
COMPANY OF KILLERS *THE PROTECTORS*   Universal, 1972
SMILE JENNY, YOU'RE DEAD (TF)   Warner Bros. TV, 1974
THE DARK SIDE OF INNOCENCE (TF)   Warner Bros. TV, 1976
I WANT TO KEEP MY BABY (TF)   CBS, Inc., 1976
THE POSSESSED (TF)   Warner Bros. TV, 1977
STICKIN' TOGETHER (TF)   Blinn-Thorpe Productions/Viacom, 1978
A QUESTION OF LOVE (TF)   Viacom, 1978
THE LAZARUS SYNDROME (TF)   Blinn-Thorpe Productions/Viacom, 1979
ALL GOD'S CHILDREN (TF)   Blinn-Thorpe Productions/Viacom, 1980

E R I C   T I L L *

Home: 62 Chaplin Crescent, Toronto, Ontario M5P 1A3, Canada, 416/488-4068
Agent: Charles Hunt, Oscard Associates - New York City, 212/764-1100

A GREAT BIG THING   Argofilms, 1967, British
HOT MILLIONS   MGM, 1968, British
THE WALKING STICK   MGM, 1970, British
A FAN'S NOTES   Warner Bros., 1972, Canadian
ALL THINGS BRIGHT AND BEAUTIFUL *IT SHOULDN'T HAPPEN TO A
   VET*   World Northal, 1978, British
WILD HORSE HANK   1979, Canadian
AN AMERICAN CHRISTMAS CAROL (TF)   ABC, 1979
MARY AND JOSEPH: A STORY OF FAITH (TF)   Lorimar Productions/CIP-
   Europaische Treuhand AG, 1979, U.S.-West German
IMPROPER CHANNELS   Crown International, 1981, Canadian
IF YOU COULD SEE WHAT I HEAR   Jensen Farley Pictures, 1982, Canadian

JAMES TOBACK *

Home: 11 East 87th Street, New York, NY 10028, 212/427-5606
Agent: Jeff Berg, ICM - Los Angeles, 213/550-4000
Business Manager: David Kaufman, Kaufman & Nachbar, 100 Merrick Road, Rockville
   Centre, NY, 516/536-5760

FINGERS   Brut Productions, 1978
LOVE AND MONEY   Paramount, 1982
EXPOSED   MGM/UA, 1983

BURT TOPPER *

b. July 31, 1928 - New York, New York
Business: 213/651-1320
Agent: Ben Conway & Associates - Los Angeles, 213/271-8133

HELL SQUAD   American International, 1958
TANK COMMANDOS   American International, 1959
THE DIARY OF A HIGH SCHOOL BRIDE   American International, 1959
WAR IS HELL   Allied Artists, 1964
THE STRANGLER   Allied Artists, 1964
THE DEVIL'S 8   American International, 1968
THE HARD RIDE   American International, 1971
THE DAY THE LORD GOT BUSTED   American, 1976

ROBERT TOTTEN *

b. February 5, 1937 - Los Angeles, California
Home: 13819 Riverside Drive, Sherman Oaks, CA 91403, 213/788-4242
Agent: Herb Tobias & Associates - Los Angeles, 213/277-6211

THE QUICK AND THE DEAD   Beckman, 1963
DEATH OF A GUNFIGHTER   co-director with Don Siegel, both directed under
   pseudonym of Allen Smithee, Universal, 1967
THE WILD COUNTRY   Buena Vista, 1971
THE RED PONY (TF)   Universal TV/Omnibus Productions, 1973
HUCKLEBERRY FINN (TF)   ABC Circle Films, 1975
PONY EXPRESS RIDER   Doty-Dayton, 1976
THE SACKETTS (TF)   Douglas Netter Enterprises/M.B. Scott Productions/
   Shalako Enterprises, 1979

ROBERT TOWNE *

Contact: Directors Guild of America - Los Angeles, 213/656-1220

PERSONAL BEST   The Geffen Company/Warner Bros., 1982

BUD TOWNSEND *

Home: 5917 Blairstone Drive, Culver City, CA 90230, 213/870-1559
Agent: The Gersh Agency - Beverly Hills, 213/274-6611

NIGHTMARE IN WAX   Crown International, 1969
THE FOLKS AT RED WOLF INN   *TERROR HOUSE*   Scope III, 1972
ALICE IN WONDERLAND   General National Enterprises, 1976
COACH   Crown International, 1978
LOVESCENE   Playboy Enterprises, 1983

PAT TOWNSEND

Business: Crown International Pictures, 292 S. La Cienega Blvd., Beverly Hills,
   CA 90211, 213/657-6700

THE BEACH GIRLS   Crown International, 1982

JEAN-CLAUDE TRAMONT *

Agent: Michael Black, ICM - Los Angeles, 213/550-4000

FOCAL POINT   Warner Bros./Columbia, 1977, French
ALL NIGHT LONG   Universal, 1981

JOHN TRENT *

Home: 50 Dale Avenue, Toronto, Ontario M4W 1K8, Canada, 416/924-8863
Agent: The Gersh Agency - Beverly Hills, 213/274-6611

THE BUSHBABY   MGM, 1970, British
HOMER   National General, 1970, Canadian
THE MAN WHO WANTED TO LIVE FOREVER (TF)   Palomar Pictures
     International, 1970
JALNA (TF)   CBC/Thames TV, 1972, Canadian-British
SUNDAY IN THE COUNTRY   American International, 1973, British
IT SEEMED LIKE A GOOD IDEA AT THE TIME   Selective Cinema, 1974,
     Canadian
FIND THE LADY   Danton, 1975, Canadian
RIEL (TF)   CBC, 1977, Canadian
CROSSBAR (TF)   CBC, 1978, Canadian
MIDDLE AGE CRAZY   20th Century-Fox, 1980, Canadian-U.S.
BEST REVENGE   Lorimar Distribution International, 1983, Canadian

JESUS SALVADOR TREVINO

Home: 2358 Yorkshire Drive, Los Angeles, CA 90065
Messages: 213/256-8408

SEGUIN (TF)   KCET, 1982

GUS TRIKONIS *

b. New York, New York
Agent: Herb Tobias & Associates - Los Angeles, 213/277-6211

FIVE THE HARD WAY   Fantascope, 1969
THE SWINGING BARMAIDS   Premiere, 1975
SUPERCOCK   Hagen-Wayne, 1975
NASHVILLE GIRL   New World, 1976
MOONSHINE COUNTY EXPRESS   New World, 1977
NEW GIRL IN TOWN   New World, 1977
THE EVIL   New World, 1978
THE DARKER SIDE OF TERROR (TF)   Shaner-Ramrus Productions/Bob Banner
     Associates, 1979
SHE'S DRESSED TO KILL (TF)   Grant-Case-McGrath Enterprises/Barry Weitz
     Films, 1979
THE LAST CONVERTIBLE (MS)   co-director with Sidney Hayers & Jo
     Swerling, Jr., Roy Huggins Productions/Universal TV, 1979
FLAMINGO ROAD (TF)   MF Productions/Lorimar Productions, 1980
TOUCHED BY LOVE   Columbia, 1980
ELVIS AND THE BEAUTY QUEEN (TF)   David Gerber Company/Columbia TV,
     1981
TAKE THIS JOB AND SHOVE IT   Avco Embassy, 1981
TWIRL (TF)   Charles Fries Productions, 1981
MISS ALL-AMERICAN BEAUTY (TF)   Marian Rees Associates, 1982
DEMPSEY (TF)   Charles Fries Productions, 1983
DANCE OF THE DWARFS   Dove, Inc., 1983
FIRST AFFAIR (TF)   CBS Entertainment, 1983

JAN TROELL

b. July 23, 1931 - Limhamn, Skane, Sweden
Contact: Swedish Film Institute, P.O. Box 27126, 102 52 Stockholm, Sweden, 08/
     63-0510

4 X 4   co-director, 1965, Swedish-Finnish-Norwegian-Danish
HERE'S YOUR LIFE   Brandon, 1966, Swedish

continued

JAN TROELL—continued

EENY, MEENY, MINY, MO *WHO SAW HIM DIE?*   Svensk Filmindustri,
   1968, Swedish
THE EMIGRANTS *UTVANDRARNA* ★   Warner Bros., 1972, Swedish
THE NEW LAND *NYBYGGARNA*   Warner Bros., 1973, Swedish
ZANDY'S BRIDE   Warner Bros., 1974
BANG!   1977, Swedish
HURRICANE   Paramount, 1979
THE FLIGHT OF THE EAGLE   Summit Features, 1982, Swedish-West German-
   Norwegian

FRANCOIS TRUFFAUT

b. February 6, 1932 - Paris, France
Contact: French Film Office, 745 Fifth Avenue, New York, NY   10151, 212/832-
   8860

THE 400 BLOWS   Zenith, 1959, French
SHOOT THE PIANO PLAYER   Astor, 1960, French
JULES AND JIM   Janus, 1961, French
LOVE AT TWENTY   co-director with Renzo Rossellini, Shintaro Ishihara, Marcel
   Ophuls & Andrzej Wajda, Embassy, 1962, French-Italian-Japanese-Polish-West
   German
THE SOFT SKIN   Cinema 5, 1964, French
FAHRENHEIT 451   Universal, 1967, British
THE BRIDE WORE BLACK   Lopert, 1968, French-Italian
STOLEN KISSES   Lopert, 1969, French
MISSISSIPPI MERMAID   United Artists, 1970, French-Italian
THE WILD CHILD   United Artists, 1970, French
BED AND BOARD *DOMICILE CONJUGAL*   Columbia, 1971, French
TWO ENGLISH GIRLS *LES DEUX ANGLAISES ET LE
   CONTINENT*   Janus, 1972, French
SUCH A GORGEOUS KID LIKE ME   Columbia, 1973, French
DAY FOR NIGHT *LA NUIT AMERICAINE* ★   Warner Bros., 1973, French-
   Italian
THE STORY OF ADELE H.   New World, 1975, French
SMALL CHANGE *L'ARGENT DE POCHE*   New World, 1976, French
THE MAN WHO LOVED WOMEN   Cinema 5, 1977, French
THE GREEN ROOM   New World, 1978, French
LOVE ON THE RUN   New World, 1979, French
THE LAST METRO   United Artists Classics, 1980, French
THE WOMAN NEXT DOOR   United Artists Classics, 1981, French
VIVEMENT DIMANCHE   Spectrafilm, 1983, French

DOUGLAS TRUMBULL*

Business: Brock/Trumbull, 1335 Maxella Avenue, Venice, CA   90291, 213/823-
   0433

SILENT RUNNING   Universal, 1972
BRAINSTORM   MGM/UA, 1983

SLAVA TSUKERMAN

b. Moscow, U.S.S.R.

LIQUID SKY   Cinevista, 1983

MICHAEL TUCHNER*

b. June 24, 1934 - Berlin, Germany
Agent: Mike Marcus, CAA - Los Angeles, 213/277-4545 or Douglas Rae
   Management - London, 01/836-3903

VILLAIN   MGM, 1971, British
FEAR IS THE KEY   Paramount, 1973, British
MR. QUILP   Avco Embassy, 1975, British
THE LIKELY LADS   EMI, 1976, British
SUMMER OF MY GERMAN SOLDIER (TF)   Highgate Productions, 1978
HAYWIRE (TF)   Pando Productions/Warner Bros. TV, 1980

continued

MICHAEL TUCHNER*—continued
THE HUNCHBACK OF NOTRE DAME (TF)   Norman Rosemont Productions/
    Columbia TV, 1982, U.S.-British
PAROLE (TF)   RSO Films, 1982
TRENCHCOAT   Buena Vista, 1983
ADAM (TF)   Alan Landsburg Productions, 1983

S A N D Y   T U N G

A MARRIAGE   Cinecom International, 1983

L A W R E N C E   T U R M A N *

b. 1926 - Los Angeles, California
Business: Universal Studios, 100 Universal City Plaza, Universal City, CA 91608,
    213/508-3182

MARRIAGE OF A YOUNG STOCKBROKER   20th Century-Fox, 1971
SECOND THOUGHTS   Universal, 1983

U

L I V   U L L M A N N

b. December 16, 1939 - Tokyo, Japan
Agent: Paul Kohner, Inc. - Los Angeles, 213/550-1060

LOVE   co-director with Annette Cohen, Nancy Dowd & Mai Zetterling, Velvet
    Films, 1982, Canadian

P E T E R   U S T I N O V *

b. April 16, 1921 - London, England
Agent: William Morris Agency - Beverly Hills, 213/274-7451

SCHOOL FOR SECRETS   General Film Distributors, 1946, British
VICE VERSA   General Film Distributors, 1948, British
PRIVATE ANGELO   co-director with Michael Anderson, Associated British
    Picture Corporation, 1949, British
ROMANOFF AND JULIET   Universal, 1961
BILLY BUDD   Allied Artists, 1962, British
LADY L   MGM, 1966, U.S.-Italian-French
HAMMERSMITH IS OUT   Cinerama Releasing Corporation, 1972
MEMED   Peter Ustinov Productions Ltd./Jadran Films, 1983, British-Yugoslavian

JAMIE UYS

Contact: Department of Interior, Civitas Building, Struben Street, Pretoria 0002, South Africa, 12/48-2551

DINGAKA   Embassy, 1965, South African
AFTER YOU, COMRADE   Continental, 1967, South African
LOST IN THE DESERT   Columbia-Warner, 1971, South African
BEAUTIFUL PEOPLE *ANIMALS ARE BEAUTIFUL PEOPLE (FD)*   Warner Bros., 1974, South African
THE GODS MUST BE CRAZY   Jensen Farley Pictures, 1982, South African
BEAUTIFUL PEOPLE II (FD)   1983, South African

ROGER VADIM
(Roger Vadim Plemiannikov)

b. January 26, 1928 - Paris, France
Contact: French Film Office, 745 Fifth Avenue, New York, NY 10151, 212/832-8860

AND GOD CREATED WOMAN   Kingsley International, 1956, French
NO SUN IN VENICE *SAIT-ON JAMAIS?*   Kingsley International, 1957, French-Italian
THE NIGHT HEAVEN FELL *LES BIJOUTIERS DU CLAIR DE LUNES*   Kingsley International, 1957, French-Italian
LES LIAISONS DANGEREUSES   Astor, 1959, French-Italian
BLOOD AND ROSES *ET MOURIR DE PLAISIR*   Paramount, 1960, Italian
PLEASE, NOT NOW! *LA BRIDE SUR LE COU*   20th Century-Fox, 1961, French
SEVEN CAPITAL SINS   co-director with Jean-Luc Godard, Sylvaine Dhomme, Edouard Molinaro, Philippe De Broca, Claude Chabrol, Jacques Demy, Marie-Jose Nat, Dominique Paturel, Jean-Marc Tennberg & Perrette Pradier, Embassy, 1962, French-Italian
LOVE ON A PILLOW *LE REPOS DU GUERRIER*   Royal Films International, 1962, French-Italian
OF FLESH AND BLOOD *LES GRANDS CHEMINS*   Times, 1963, French-Italian
VICE AND VIRTUE   MGM, 1963, French
NUTTY, NAUGHTY CHATEAU *CHATEAU EN SUEDE*   Lopert, 1963 French-Italian
CIRCLE OF LOVE *LA RONDE*   Continental, 1964, French
THE GAME IS OVER *LA CUREE*   Royal Films International, 1966, French-Italian
SPIRITS OF THE DEAD *HISTOIRES EXTRAORDINAIRES*   co-director with Federico Fellini & Louis Malle, American International, 1968, Italian-French
BARBARELLA   Paramount, 1968, Italian-French
PRETTY MAIDS ALL IN A ROW   MGM, 1971
HELLE   1972, French
MS. DON JUAN *DON JUAN ETAIT UNE FEMME*   Scotia American, 1973, French
CHARLOTTE *LA JEUNE FILLE ASSASSINEE*   Gamma III, 1974, French

continued

ROGER VADIM—continued
UNE FEMME FIDELE   1976, French
NIGHT GAMES   Avco Embassy, 1980, French
THE HOT TOUCH   Astral Bellevue, 1981, Canadian
SURPRISE PARTY   Uranium Films, 1982, French
COME BACK   Comeci, 1983, French

LUIS VALDEZ *

Contact: Directors Guild of America - Los Angeles, 213/656-1220

ZOOT SUIT   Universal, 1981

BRUCE VAN DUSEN

COLD FEET   Cinecom International, 1983

BUDDY VAN HORN *

Home: 4409 Ponca Avenue, Toluca Lake, CA 91602
Messages: 213/462-2301

ANY WHICH WAY YOU CAN   Warner Bros., 1980

MELVIN VAN PEEBLES *

b. 1932 - Chicago, Illinois
Business: Yeah, Inc., 850 Seventh Avenue, New York, NY 10019, 212/489-6570

THE STORY OF A THREE-DAY PASS   Sigma III, 1968, French
WATERMELON MAN   Columbia, 1970
SWEET SWEETBACK'S BAADASSSSSS SONG   Cinemation, 1971

AGNES VARDA

b. May 30, 1928 - Brussels, Belgium
Home: 354 Indiana Avenue, Venice, CA, 213/392-7700

LA POINTE COURTE   1954, French
CLEO FROM 5 TO 7   Zenith, 1962, French
LE BONHEUR   Clover, 1965, French
LES CREATURES   New Yorker, 1966, French-Swedish
FAR FROM VIETNAM (FD)   co-director with Jean-Luc Godard, Claude Lelouch,
    Alain Resnais, William Klein & Joris Ivens, New Yorker, 1967, French
LIONS LOVE   Raab, 1969
NAUSICAA (TF)   1970, French
DAGUERREOTYPES (FD)   1975, French
ONE SINGS, THE OTHER DOESN'T   Cinema 5, 1977, French
MUR MURS (FD)   Cine-Tamaris, 1981
DOCUMENTEUR: AN EMOTION PICTURE   Cine-Tamaris, 1981

PAUL VERHOEVEN

Business: Riverside Pictures B.V., Koningslaan 17, 1075 AA Amsterdam, Netherlands,
    20/640-401
Agent: Marion Rosenberg, The Lantz Office - Los Angeles, 213/858-1144

WAT ZIEN IK   Rob Houwer Film, 1972, Dutch
TURKISH DELIGHT   Cinemation, 1974, Dutch
KEETJE TIPPEL   Cinema National, 1976, Dutch
SOLDIER OF ORANGE   The Samuel Goldwyn Company, 1979, Dutch
SPETTERS   The Samuel Goldwyn Company, 1981, Dutch
THE FOURTH MAN   Spectrafilm, 1983, Dutch

HENRI VERNEUIL
(Achod Malakian)

b. October 15, 1920 - Rodosto, Turkey
Business: V. Films, 12 Bis Rue Keppler, 75016 Paris, France, 723-5068

LA TABLE AUX CREVES   1951, French
BRELAN D'AS   1952, French
FORBIDDEN FRUIT   Films Around the World, 1952, French
LE BOULANGER DE VALORGUE   1953, French
CARNAVAL   1953, French
THE MOST WANTED MAN IN THE WORLD *ENNEMI PUBLIC NO. 1*   Astor, 1953, French-Italian
THE SHEEP HAS FIVE LEGS   United Motion Picture Organization, 1954, French
LES AMANTS DU TAGE   1955, French
DES GENS SANS IMPORTANCE   1955, French
PARIS-PALACE-HOTEL   1956, French
WHAT PRICE MURDER *UNE MANCHE ET LA BELLE*   United Motion Picture Organization, 1957, French
MAXIME   Interworld, 1958, French
THE BIG CHIEF   Continental, 1959, French-Italian
THE COW AND I *LA VACHE ET LE PRISONNIER*   Zenith, 1959, French-West German
L'AFFAIRE D'UNE NUIT   1960, French
LA FRANCAISE ET L'AMOUR   co-director, 1960, French
LE PRESIDENT   1961, French-Italian
THE LIONS ARE LOOSE   Franco-London, 1961, French-Italian
A MONKEY IN WINTER   MGM, 1962, French
ANY NUMBER CAN WIN *MELODIE EN SOUS-SOL*   MGM, 1963, French
GREED IN THE SUN   MGM, 1964, French
WEEKEND AT DUNKIRK *WEEKEND A ZUYDCOOTE*   20th Century-Fox, 1965, French-Italian
THE 25TH HOUR   MGM, 1967, French-Italian-Yugoslavian
GUNS FOR SAN SEBASTIAN *LA BATAILLE DE SAN SEBASTIAN*   MGM, 1968, French-Italian-Mexican
THE SICILIAN CLAN   20th Century-Fox, 1970, French
THE BURGLARS   Columbia, 1972, French-Italian
THE SERPENT *NIGHT FLIGHT TO MOSCOW*   Avco Embassy, 1973, French-Italian-West German
THE NIGHT CALLER *PEUR SUR LA VILLE*   Columbia, 1975, French
LE CORPS DE MON ENNEMI   1976, French
I AS IN ICARUS   V Films/SFP/Antenne-2, 1979, French
MILLE MILLIARDS DE DOLLARS   V Films/Films A2, 1982, French
LES MORFALOUS   AAA, 1984, French

STEPHEN F. VERONA *

b. September 11, 1940 - Illinois
Home: 1251 Stone Canyon Road, Los Angeles, CA 90024
Messages: 213/476-7387

THE LORDS OF FLATBUSH   co-director with Martin Davidson, Columbia, 1974
PIPE DREAMS   Avco Embassy, 1976
BOARDWALK   Atlantic Releasing Corporation, 1979
TALKING WALLS   Drummond Productions, 1983

DANIEL VIGNE

Contact: French Film Office, 745 Fifth Avenue, New York, NY 10151, 212/832-8860

THE RETURN OF MARTIN GUERRE   European International, 1983, French

VIRGIL W. VOGEL *

b. Peoria, Illinois
Agent: David Shapira & Associates - Beverly Hills, 213/278-2742

THE MOLE PEOPLE   Universal, 1956
THE KETTLES ON OLD McDONALD'S FARM   Universal, 1957

continued

VIRGIL W. VOGEL*—continued
THE LAND UNKNOWN   Universal, 1957
THE SWORD OF ALI BABA   Universal, 1965
THE RETURN OF JOE FORRESTER (TF)   Columbia TV, 1975
THE DEPUTIES (TF)   1976
LAW OF THE LAND (TF)   QM Productions, 1976
CENTENNIAL (MS)   co-director with Paul Krasny, Harry Falk & Bernard
    McEveety, Universal TV, 1978
POWER (TF)   co-director with Barry Shear, David Gerber Company/Columbia TV,
    1980
PORTRAIT OF A REBEL: MARGARET SANGER (TF)   Marvin Minoff
    Productions/David Paradine TV, 1980
BEULAH LAND (MS)   co-director with Harry Falk, David Gerber Company/
    Columbia TV, 1980
TODAY'S FBI (TF)   David Gerber Company, 1981

D A N I E L   W A C H S M A N N

Contact: Israel Film Centre, Ministry of Industry & Trade, 30 Agron Street, P.O. Box
    299, Jerusalem 94190, Israel, 02/210433

TRANSIT   Jacob Goldwasser Productions, 1979, Israeli
HOT WIND *HAMSIN*   Hemdale, 1982, Israeli

M I C H A E L   W A D L E I G H *

Contact: Directors Guild of America - Los Angeles, 213/656-1220

WOODSTOCK (FD)   Warner Bros., 1970
WOLFEN   Orion/Warner Bros., 1981

J A N E   W A G N E R *

b. February 2, 1935 - Morristown, Tennessee
Home: 213/275-5161
Agent: Ron Mardigian/Stan Kamen, William Morris Agency - Beverly Hills, 213/274-
    7451

MOMENT BY MOMENT   Universal, 1978

R A L P H   W A I T E *

b. June 22, 1928 - White Plains, New York
Agent: Ron Meyer, CAA - Los Angeles, 213/277-4545
Business Manager: Global Business Management, 9000 Sunset Blvd. - Suite 1115,
    Los Angeles, CA 90069, 213/278-4141

ON THE NICKEL   Rose's Park, 1980

A N D R Z E J   W A J D A

b. March 6, 1926 - Suwalki, Poland
Contact: French Film Office, 745 Fifth Avenue, New York, NY 10151, 212/832-8860

A GENERATION   WFF Wroclaw, 1954, Polish
JE VAIS VERS LE SOLEIL   WFD Warsaw, 1955, French-Polish
KANAL   Frankel, 1957, Polish
ASHES AND DIAMONDS   Janus, 1958, Polish
LOTNA   KADR Unit, 1959, Polish
INNOCENT SORCERERS   KADR Unit, 1960, Polish
SAMSON   Droga-KADR Unit, 1961, Polish
SIBERIAN LADY MACBETH   Avala Film, 1961, Polish
LOVE AT TWENTY   co-director with Francois Truffaut, Renzo Rossellini, Shintaro Ishihara & Marcel Ophuls, Embassy, 1962, French-Italian-Japanese-Polish-West German
ASHES   1965, Polish
GATES TO PARADISE   1967, British
EVERYTHING FOR SALE   New Yorker, 1968, Polish
HUNTING FLIES   1969, Polish
LANDSCAPE AFTER BATTLE   New Yorker, 1970, Polish
THE BIRCH-WOOD   1971, Polish
PILATUS UND ANDERE (TF)   1972, West German
THE WEDDING   Film Polski, 1972, Polish
THE PROMISED LAND   Film Polski, 1974, Polish
SHADOW LINE   1976, Polish
MAN OF MARBLE   New Yorker, 1977, Polish
WITHOUT ANESTHETIC   New Yorker, 1979, Polish
THE GIRLS FROM WILKO   1979, Polish-French
THE CONDUCTOR   Film Polski, 1980, Polish
ROUGH TREATMENT   Film Polski, 1980, Polish
MAN OF IRON   United Artists Classics, 1981, Polish
DANTON   Triumph/Columbia, 1983, French
EINE LIEBE IN DEUTSCHLAND   Gaumont, 1983, West German-French

N A N C Y   W A L K E R *

b. May 10, 1922 - Philadelphia, Pennsylvania
Agent: Tom Korman, Contemporary-Korman Artists - Beverly Hills, 213/278-8250

CAN'T STOP THE MUSIC   AFD, 1980

P E T E R   W A L K E R

Address: 23 Down Street - Flat 4, Mayfair, London W1, England, 01/493-7440
Contact: Directors Guild of Great Britain, 56 Whitfield Street, London W1, England, 01/580-9592

STRIP POKER   Miracle, 1969, British
COOL IT CAROLI   Miracle, 1970, British
MAN OF VIOLENCE   Miracle, 1971, British
THE FLESH AND BLOOD SHOW   Tigon, 1972, British
THE FOUR DIMENSIONS OF GRETA   Hemdale, 1972, British
TIFFANY JONES   Hemdale, 1973, British
HOUSE OF WHIPCORD   Miracle, 1974, British
FRIGHTMARE   Miracle, 1975, British
HOUSE OF MORTAL SIN   Miracle, 1976, British
THE COMEBACK   Enterprise, 1978, British
HOME BEFORE MIDNIGHT   Heritage/EMI, 1979, British
HOUSE OF THE LONG SHADOWS   MGM/UA/Cannon, 1983, British

T O M M Y   L E E   W A L L A C E *

Agent: David Gersh, The Gersh Agency - Beverly Hills, 213/274-6611

HALLOWEEN III: SEASON OF THE WITCH   Universal, 1982

HERB WALLERSTEIN *

Business: 20th Century-Fox Film Corporation, Box 900, Beverly Hills, CA 90213,
213/277-2211
Agent: Lew Sherrell Agency - Los Angeles, 213/461-9955

SNOWBEAST (TF)   Douglas Cramer Productions, 1977

FRED WALTON *

Contact: Directors Guild of America - Los Angeles, 213/656-1220

WHEN A STRANGER CALLS   Columbia, 1979
HADLEY'S REBELLION   ADI Marketing, 1983

SAM WANAMAKER *

b. June 14, 1919 - Chicago, Illinois
Home: The Surrey Dispensary, 42 Trinity Street, London SE1 4J6, England, 01/407-
3712
Agent: Ed Limato, William Morris Agency - Beverly Hills, 213/274-7451

THE FILE ON THE GOLDEN GOOSE   United Artists, 1969, British
THE EXECUTIONER   Columbia, 1970, British
CATLOW   MGM, 1971, U.S.-Spanish
SINBAD AND THE EYE OF THE TIGER   Columbia, 1977, British
MY KIDNAPPER, MY LOVE (TF)   Roger Gimbel Productions/EMI TV, 1980
THE KILLING OF RANDY WEBSTER (TF)   Roger Gimbel Productions/EMI TV,
1981

WAYNE WANG

A MAN, A WOMAN, AND A KILLER   co-director with Rick Schmidt, 1975
CHAN IS MISSING   New Yorker, 1982
DIM SUM   CIM Productions, 1983

DAVID S. WARD *

b. October 25, 1945
Home: 246 21st Street, Santa Monica, CA 90402
Agent: Jeff Berg, ICM - Los Angeles, 213/550-4000

CANNERY ROW   MGM/United Artists, 1981

CLYDE WARE *

b. December 22, 1934 - West Virginia
Home: 1252 N. Laurel Avenue, Los Angeles, CA 90046, 213/650-8205
Agent: CAA - Los Angeles, 213/277-4545
Business Manager: Jerry Sutter - Beverly Hills, 213/272-4243

NO DRUMS, NO BUGLES   Cinerama Releasing Corporation, 1971
THE STORY OF PRETTY BOY FLOYD (TF)   Universal TV, 1974
THE HATFIELDS AND THE McCOYS (TF)   Charles Fries Productions, 1975
THREE HUNDRED MILES FOR STEPHANIE (TF)   Edward S. Feldman
Company/Yellow Ribbon Productions/PKO, 1981

ANDY WARHOL
(Andrew Warhola)

b. August 8, 1927 - Cleveland, Ohio

KISS   Film-Makers, 1963
EAT   Film-Makers, 1963
SLEEP   Film-Makers, 1963
HAIRCUT   Film-Makers, 1963
TARZAN AND JANE REGAINED ... SORT OF   co-director, Film-Makers,
1964
DANCE MOVIE   Film-Makers, 1964

continued

ANDY WARHOL—continued

BLOW JOB   Film-Makers, 1964
BATMAN DRACULA   Film-Makers, 1964
SALOME AND DELILAH   Film-Makers, 1964
SOAP OPERA   co-director, Film-Makers, 1964
COUCH   Film-Makers, 1964
13 MOST BEAUTIFUL WOMEN   Film-Makers, 1964
HARLOT   Film-Makers, 1964
THE LIFE OF JUANITA CASTRO   Film-Makers, 1965
EMPIRE   Film-Makers, 1965
POOR LITTLE RICH GIRL   Film-Makers, 1965
SCREEN TEST   Film-Makers, 1965
VINYL   Film-Makers, 1965
BEAUTY #2   Film-Makers, 1965
BITCH   Film-Makers, 1965
PRISON   Film-Makers, 1965
SPACE   Film-Makers, 1965
THE CLOSET   Film-Makers, 1965
HENRY GELDZAHLER   Film-Makers, 1965
TAYLOR MEAD'S ASS   Film-Makers, 1965
FACE   Film-Makers, 1965
MY HUSTLER   Film-Makers, 1965
CAMP   Film-Makers, 1965
SUICIDE   Film-Makers, 1965
DRUNK   Film-Makers, 1965
OUTER AND INNER SPACE   Film-Makers, 1966
HEDY *HEDY THE SHOPLIFTER*   Film-Makers, 1966
PAUL SWAN   Film-Makers, 1966
MORE MILK, EVETTE *LANA TURNER*   Film-Makers, 1965
THE VELVET UNDERGROUND AND NICO   Film-Makers, 1966
KITCHEN   Film-Makers, 1966
LUPE   Film-Makers, 1966
EATING TOO FAST   Film-Makers, 1966
THE CHELSEA GIRLS   Film-Makers, 1966
I, A MAN   Film-Makers, 1967
BIKE BOY   Film-Makers, 1967
NUDE RESTAURANT   Film-Makers, 1967
FOUR STARS *24-HOUR MOVIE*   Film-Makers, 1967
IMITATION OF CHRIST   Film-Makers, 1967
THE LOVES OF ONDINE   Warhol, 1968
LONESOME COWBOYS   Sherpix, 1968
BLUE MOVIE *FUCK*   Factory, 1969
WOMEN IN REVOLT   Warhol, 1972
L'AMOUR   co-director with Paul Morrissey, Altura, 1973

C H A R L E S   M A R Q U I S   W A R R E N *

b. December 16, 1917 - Baltimore, Maryland
Home: 1130 Tower Road, Beverly Hills, CA 90210
Agent: Evarts Ziegler, Ziegler, Diskant, Inc. - Los Angeles, 213/278-0070

LITTLE BIG HORN   Lippert, 1951
HELLGATE   Lippert, 1952
ARROWHEAD   Paramount, 1953
FLIGHT TO TANGIER   Paramount, 1953
SEVEN ANGRY MEN   Allied Artists, 1955
TENSION AT TABLE ROCK   Universal, 1956
THE BLACK WHIP   20th Century-Fox, 1956
TROOPER HOOK   United Artists, 1957
BACK FROM THE DEAD   20th Century-Fox, 1957
THE UNKNOWN TERROR   20th Century-Fox, 1957
COPPER SKY   20th Century-Fox, 1957
RIDE A VIOLENT MILE   20th Century-Fox, 1957
DESERT HELL   20th Century-Fox, 1958
CATTLE EMPIRE   20th Century-Fox, 1958
BLOOD ARROW   20th Century-Fox, 1958
CHARRO!   National General, 1969

MARK WARREN *

Business Manager: Sheila Lane Reed, 211 S. Beverly Drive, Beverly Hills,
      CA 90212, 213/273-3442

COME BACK CHARLESTON BLUE   Warner Bros., 1972
TULIPS   co-director with Rex Bromfield & Al Waxman, all directed under
      pseudonym of Stan Ferris, Avco Embassy, 1981, Canadian
THE KINKY COACHES AND THE POM-POM
      PUSSYCATS *CRUNCH*   Summa Vista, 1981, Canadian

JOHN WATERS

b. Baltimore, Maryland

MONDO TRASHO   Film-Makers, 1970
PINK FLAMINGOS   Saliva Films, 1974
FEMALE TROUBLE   New Line Cinema, 1975
DESPERATE LIVING   New Line Cinema, 1977
POLYESTER   New Line Cinema, 1981

PETER WATKINS

b. October 29, 1935 - Norbiton, England
Contact: British Academy of Film & Television Arts, 195 Piccadilly, London W1,
      England, 01/732-0022

CULLODEN (TF)   BBC, 1964, British
THE WAR GAME   Pathe Contemporary, 1966, British
PRIVILEGE   Universal, 1967, British
GLADIATORS   1969, Swedish
PUNISHMENT PARK   Sherpix, 1971, British
EDVARD MUNCH   New Yorker, 1976, Swedish-Norwegian
EVENING LAND   Panorama-ASA, 1977, Danish

PAUL WATSON

Contact: British Academy of Film & Television Arts, 195 Piccadilly, London W1,
      England, 01/732-0022

THE ROTHKO CONSPIRACY (TF)   BBC/Lionheart TV, 1983, British

ROY WATTS

HAMBONE AND HILLIE   Sandy Howard/Adams Apple Productions, 1984

PETER WEBB

Contact: Directors Guild of Great Britain, 56 Whitfield Street, London W1, England,
      01/580-9592

BUTCH MINDS THE BABY   Park Village Productions, 1980, British
GIVE MY REGARDS TO BROAD STREET   20th Century-Fox, 1984, British

NICHOLAS WEBSTER *

b. July 24 - Spokane, Washington
Home: 4135 Fulton Avenue, Sherman Oaks, CA 91403, 213/784-5690

GONE ARE THE DAYS! *PURLIE VICTORIOUS*   Trans-Lux, 1963
SANTA CLAUS CONQUERS THE MARTIANS   Embassy, 1964
MISSION MARS   Allied Artists, 1968
NO LONGER ALONE   World Wide, 1978, British

DAVID WECHTER *

b. June 27, 1956 - Los Angeles, California
Home: 4508 Farmdale Avenue, North Hollywood, CA 91602, 213/762-6585
Agent: Doug Draizin, APA - Los Angeles, 213/273-0744

MIDNIGHT MADNESS   co-director with Michael Nankin, Buena Vista, 1980

STEPHEN WEEKS

b. 1948
Address: Penhow Castle, Nr. Newport, Gwent., Penhow 400800, England

GAWAIN AND THE GREEN KNIGHT   United Artists, 1972, British
I, MONSTER   Cannon, 1974, British
SWORD OF THE VALIANT   MGM/UA/Cannon, 1983, British

SAMUEL WEIL

Business: Troma, Inc., 733 Ninth Avenue, New York, NY 10019, 212/757-4555

SQUEEZE PLAY!   Troma, 1980
WAITRESS!   co-director with Michael Herz, Troma, 1982
STUCK ON YOU!   co-director with Michael Herz, Troma, 1983
THE FIRST TURN-ON!   co-director with Michael Herz, Troma, 1983

CLAUDIA WEILL *

b. 1947 - New York, New York
Business: Cyclops Films, Inc., 1697 Broadway, New York, NY 10019, 212/265-1375

THE OTHER HALF OF THE SKY: A CHINA MEMOIR (FD)   co-director with
    Shirley MacLaine, 1975
GIRLFRIENDS   Warner Bros., 1978
IT'S MY TURN   Columbia, 1980

PETER WEIR

b. August 8, 1944 - Sydney, Australia
Business: McElroy & McElroy, 1-3 Atchison Street, St. Leonards, NSW, 2065,
    Australia, 02/438-4555
Agent: William Morris Agency - Beverly Hills, 213/274-7451

THREE TO GO   co-director with Brian Hannant & Oliver Howes, Commonwealth
    Film Unit Production, 1971, Australian
THE CARS THAT EAT PEOPLE *THE CARS THAT ATE PARIS*   New Line
    Cinema, 1974, Australian
PICNIC AT HANGING ROCK   Atlantic Releasing Corporation, 1975, Australian
THE PLUMBER   Barbary Coast, 1978, Australian, originally made for television
THE LAST WAVE   World Northal, 1978, Australian
GALLIPOLI   Paramount, 1981, Australian
THE YEAR OF LIVING DANGEROUSLY   MGM/UA, 1983, Australian

DON WEIS *

b. May 13, 1922 - Milwaukee, Wisconsin
Agent: Irving Salkow Agency - Beverly Hills, 213/276-3141

BANNERLINE   MGM, 1951
IT'S A BIG COUNTRY   co-director with Charles Vidor, Richard Thorpe, John
    Sturges, Don Hartman, Clarence Brown & William Wellman, MGM, 1951
JUST THIS ONCE   MGM, 1952
YOU FOR ME   MGM, 1952
I LOVE MELVIN   MGM, 1953
REMAINS TO BE SEEN   MGM, 1953
A SLIGHT CASE OF LARCENY   MGM, 1953
THE AFFAIRS OF DOBIE GILLIS   MGM, 1953
HALF A HERO   MGM, 1953
THE ADVENTURES OF HAJJI BABA   20th Century-Fox, 1954
RIDE THE HIGH IRON   Columbia, 1957

continued

DON WEIS*—continued

MR. PHARAOH AND HIS CLEOPATRA   1959
THE GENE KRUPA STORY   Columbia, 1960
CRITIC'S CHOICE   Warner Bros., 1963
LOOKING FOR LOVE   MGM, 1964
PAJAMA PARTY   American International, 1964
BILLIE   United Artists, 1965
THE GHOST IN THE INVISIBLE BIKINI   American International, 1966
THE KING'S PIRATE   Universal, 1967
THE LONGEST 100 MILES (TF)   Universal TV, 1967
NOW YOU SEE IT, NOW YOU DON'T (TF)   Universal TV, 1968
**DID YOU HEAR THE ONE ABOUT THE TRAVELING
    SALESLADY?**   Universal, 1968
DEADLOCK (TF)   Universal TV, 1969
THE MILLIONAIRE (TF)   Don Fedderson Productions, 1978
ZERO TO SIXTY   First Artists, 1978
THE MUNSTERS' REVENGE (TF)   Universal TV, 1981

GARY WEIS*

Contact: Directors Guild of America - Los Angeles, 213/656-1220

ALL YOU NEED IS CASH (TF)   co-director with Eric Idle, Rutles Corps
    Productions, 1978, British
WHOLLY MOSES   Columbia, 1980
YOUNG LUST   RSO Films, 1982
MARLEY (FD)   Island Alive, 1984

ORSON WELLES

b. May 6, 1916 - Kenosha, Wisconsin

CITIZEN KANE   RKO Radio, 1941
THE MAGNIFICENT AMBERSONS   RKO Radio, 1942
THE STRANGER   RKO Radio, 1946
THE LADY FROM SHANGHAI   Columbia, 1948
MACBETH   Republic, 1948
OTHELLO   United Artists, 1952, U.S.-Italian
MR. ARKADIN   Warner Bros., 1955, Spanish-Swiss
TOUCH OF EVIL   Universal, 1958
THE TRIAL   Astor, 1963, French-Italian-West German
CHIMES AT MIDNIGHT *FALSTAFF*   Peppercorn-Wormser, 1967, Spanish-
    Swiss
THE IMMORTAL STORY   Altura, 1969, French, originally made for television
F FOR FAKE   Specialty, 1977, French-Iranian-West German
THE OTHER SIDE OF THE WIND   1983

WIM WENDERS*

b. 1945 - Dusseldorf, West Germany
Agent: Paul Kohner, Inc. - Los Angeles, 213/550-1060
Business Manager: Jess S. Morgan & Company, 6420 Wilshire Blvd., Los Angeles,
    CA 90048, 213/651-1601

SUMMER IN THE CITY *DEDICATED TO THE KINKS*   1970, West German
THE GOALIE'S ANXIETY AT THE PENALTY KICK   Bauer International,
    1972, West German
THE SCARLET LETTER   Bauer International, 1973, West German-Spanish
ALICE IN THE CITIES   New Yorker, 1974, West German
THE WRONG MOVE   New Yorker, 1975, West German
KINGS OF THE ROAD   Bauer International, 1976, West German
THE AMERICAN FRIEND   New Yorker, 1977, West German-French
LIGHTNING OVER WATER (NICK'S MOVIE)   co-director with Nicholas Ray,
    Pari Films, 1980, West German-Swiss-U.S.
THE STATE OF THINGS   Gray City, 1982, U.S.-West German-Portuguese
HAMMETT   Orion/Warner Bros., 1982
PARIS, TEXAS   Road Movies/Argos Film, 1984, West German-U.S.

P A U L   W E N D K O S *

b. September 20, 1922 - Philadelphia, Pennsylvania
Home: 19706 Pacific Coast Highway, Malibu, CA 90265
Agent: Fred Specktor, CAA - Los Angeles, 213/277-4545

THE BURGLAR   Columbia, 1957
THE CASE AGAINST BROOKLYN   Columbia, 1958
TARAWA BEACHHEAD   Columbia, 1958
GIDGET   Columbia, 1959
FACE OF A FUGITIVE   Columbia, 1959
BATTLE OF THE CORAL SEA   Columbia, 1959
BECAUSE THEY'RE YOUNG   Columbia, 1960
GIDGET GOES HAWAIIAN   Columbia, 1961
ANGEL BABY   Allied Artists, 1961
TEMPLE OF THE SWINGING DOLL   20th Century-Fox, 1961
GIDGET GOES TO ROME   Columbia, 1963
RECOIL   Lion, 1963
JOHNNY TIGER   Universal, 1966
ATTACK ON THE IRON COAST   United Artists, 1968, U.S.-British
HAWAII FIVE-O (TF)   Leonard Freeman Productions, 1968
GUNS OF THE MAGNIFICENT SEVEN   United Artists, 1969
FEAR NO EVIL (TF)   Universal TV, 1969
CANNON FOR CORDOBA   United Artists, 1970
THE BROTHERHOOD OF THE BELL (TF)   Cinema Center, 1970
THE MEPHISTO WALTZ   20th Century-Fox, 1971
TRAVIS LOGAN, D.A. (TF)   QM Productions, 1971
A TATTERED WEB (TF)   Metromedia Productions, 1971
A LITTLE GAME (TF)   Universal TV, 1971
A DEATH OF INNOCENCE (TF)   Mark Carliner Productions, 1971
THE DELPHI BUREAU (TF)   Warner Bros. TV, 1972
THE FAMILY RICO (TF)   CBS, Inc., 1972
HAUNTS OF THE VERY RICH (TF)   ABC Circle Films, 1972
FOOTSTEPS (TF)   Metromedia Productions, 1972
THE STRANGERS IN 7A (TF)   Palomar Pictures International, 1972
HONOR THY FATHER (TF)   Metromedia Productions, 1973
TERROR ON THE BEACH (TF)   20th Century-Fox TV, 1973
THE UNDERGROUND MAN (TF)   Paramount TV, 1974
THE LEGEND OF LIZZIE BORDEN (TF)   Paramount TV, 1975
DEATH AMONG FRIENDS (TF)   Douglas S. Cramer Productions/Warner Bros.
     TV, 1975
SPECIAL DELIVERY   American International, 1976
THE DEATH OF RICHIE (TF)   Henry Jaffe Enterprises, 1977
SECRETS (TF)   The Jozak Company, 1977
GOOD AGAINST EVIL (TF)   Frankel-Bolen Productions/20th Century-Fox TV,
     1977
HAROLD ROBBINS' 79 PARK AVENUE (MS)   Universal TV, 1978
BETRAYAL (TF)   Roger Gimbel Productions/EMI TV, 1978
A WOMAN CALLED MOSES (TF)   Henry Jaffe Enterprises, 1978
THE ORDEAL OF PATTY HEARST (TF)   Finnegan Associates/David Paradine
     TV, 1979
ACT OF VIOLENCE (TF)   Emmett G. Lavery, Jr. Productions/Paramount TV,
     1979
THE ORDEAL OF DR. MUDD (TF)   BSR Productions/Marble Arch Productions,
     1980
A CRY FOR LOVE (TF)   Charles Fries Productions/Alan Sacks Productions,
     1980
THE FIVE OF ME (TF)   Jack Farren Productions/Factor-Newland Production
     Corporation, 1981
GOLDEN GATE (TF)   Lin Bolen Productions/Warner Bros. TV, 1981
FARRELL FOR THE PEOPLE (TF)   InterMedia Entertainment/TAL Productions/
     MGM-UA TV, 1982
COCAINE: ONE MAN'S SEDUCTION (TF)   Charles Fries Productions/David
     Goldsmith Productions, 1983
INTIMATE AGONY (TF)   Henerson-Hirsch Productions/Robert Papazian
     Productions, 1983
BOONE (TF)   Lorimar Productions, 1983
CELEBRITY (MS)   NBC Productions, 1984

J E F F   W E R N E R *

Home: 4212 Teesdale Avenue, Studio City, CA 91604, 213/769-8651
Messages: 213/464-3511
Agent: Melinda Jason, The Artists Agency - Los Angeles, 213/277-7779

CHEERLEADERS' WILD WEEKEND   Dimension, 1979
DIE LAUGHING   Orion/Warner Bros., 1980

P E T E R   W E R N E R *

b. January 17, 1947 - New York, New York
Business: A Joyful Noise Unlimited, 359 20th Street, Santa Monica, CA 90402,
    213/395-4383
Agent: Robert Stein, Berkus, Cosay, Handley & Stein - Los Angeles, 213/277-9090

FINDHORD (FD)   Moving Pictures, 1976
BATTERED (TF)   Henry Jaffe Enterprises, 1978
AUNT MARY (TF)   Henry Jaffe Enterprises, 1979
DON'T CRY, IT'S ONLY THUNDER   Sanrio, 1981, U.S.-Japanese
PRISONERS   20th Century-Fox, 1983, New Zealand

L I N A   W E R T M U L L E R
(Arcangela Felice Assunta Wertmuller von Elgg)

b. August 14, 1928 - Rome, Italy
Contact: Ministry of Tourism & Education, Via Della Ferratella, No. 51, 00184
    Rome, Italy, 06/7732

I BALISCHI   22 Dicembre/Galatea, 1963, Italian
LET'S TALK ABOUT MEN QUESTA VOLTA PARLIAMO DI
    UOMINI   Allied Artists, 1965, Italian
RITA LA ZANZARA   Mondial, 1966, Italian
NON STUZZICATE LA ZANZARA   Mondial, 1967, Italian
THE SEDUCTION OF MIMI MIMI METALLURGICO FERITO
    NELL'ONORE   New Line Cinema, 1972, Italian
LOVE AND ANARCHY FILM D'AMORE E D'ANARCHIA   Peppercorn-
    Wormser, 1973, Italian
ALL SCREWED UP TUTTO A POSTE E NIENTE IN ORDINE   New Line
    Cinema, 1974, Italian
SWEPT AWAY BY AN UNUSUAL DESTINY IN THE BLUE SEA OF
    AUGUST   Cinema 5, 1974, Italian
SEVEN BEAUTIES PASQUALINO SETTEBELLEZZE ★   Cinema 5, 1976,
    Italian
THE END OF THE WORLD IN OUR USUAL BED IN A NIGHT FULL OF
    RAIN   Warner Bros., 1978, Italian-U.S.
BLOOD FEUD FATTO DI SANGUE FRA DUE UOMINI PER CAUSA DI
    UNA VEDOVA (SI SOSPETTANO MOVENTI POLITICI)   AFD, 1980,
    Italian
SCHERZO DEL DESTINO IN AGGUATO DIETRO L'ANGOLO COME UN
    BRIGANTE DI STRADA   Gaumont, 1983, Italian

E R I C   W E S T O N *

Messages: 213/650-5965

EVILSPEAK   The Frank Moreno Company, 1982
MARVIN AND TIGE   20th Century-Fox International Classics, 1983

H A S K E L L   W E X L E R *

b. 1926 - Chicago, Illinois
Business: 716 N. Alfred Street, Los Angeles, CA 90069, 213/655-6800

MEDIUM COOL   Paramount, 1969
BRAZIL: A REPORT ON TORTURE (FD)   co-director with Saul Landau, 1971
INTRODUCTION TO THE ENEMY (FD)   co-director, 1974
UNDERGROUND (FD)   co-director with Emile De Antonio & Mary Lampson,
    New Yorker, 1976
BUS II (FD)   co-director with Bonnie Bass Parker & Tom Tyson, 1983

CLAUDE WHATHAM

Address: Camp House, Camp, Miserden, Stroud, Gloucestershire, England

THAT'LL BE THE DAY   EMI, 1974, British
ALL CREATURES GREAT AND SMALL (TF)   Talent Associates/EMI TV,
   1975, British
SWALLOWS AND AMAZONS   LDS, 1977, British
SWEET WILLIAM   Kendon Films, 1980, British
HOODWINK   CB Films, 1981, Australian
MURDER IS EASY (TF)   David L. Wolper-Stan Margulies Productions/Warner
   Bros. TV, 1982

JIM WHEAT

Business: New Empire Films, 650 N. Bronson - Suite 144, Los Angeles, CA 90004,
   213/461-8535

LIES   co-director with Ken Wheat, New Empire, 1983

KEN WHEAT

Business: New Empire Films, 650 N. Bronson - Suite 144, Los Angeles, CA 90004,
   213/461-8535

LIES   co-director with Jim Wheat, New Empire, 1983

WILLIAM WIARD*

Agent: Adams, Ray & Rosenberg - Los Angeles, 213/278-3000

SCOTT FREE (TF)   Cherokee Productions/Universal TV, 1976
SKI LIFT TO DEATH (TF)   The Jozak Company/Paramount TV, 1982
THE GIRL, THE GOLD WATCH AND EVERYTHING (TF)   Fellows-Keegan
   Company/Paramount TV, 1980
TOM HORN   Warner Bros., 1980
THIS HOUSE POSSESSED (TF)   Mandy Productions, 1981
HELP WANTED: MALE (TF)   QM Productions/Brademan-Self Productions, 1982
FANTASIES (TF)   Mandy Productions, 1982
DEADLY LESSONS (TF)   Leonard Goldberg Productions, 1983

DAVID WICKES

Business: David Wickes Television Ltd., Twickenham Film Studios, St. Margaret's,
   Twickenham, Middlesex TW1 2AW, England, 01/892-4477

SWEENEY   EMI, 1977, British
SILVER DREAM RACER   Almi Cinema 5, 1980, British
CHANDLERTOWN *PHILIP MARLOWE - PRIVATE EYE*   co-director with
   Sidney Hayers, Bryan Forbes & Peter Hunt, HBO/David Wickes Television Ltd./
   London Weekend Television, 1983, British

BERNHARD WICKI*

b. October 28, 1919 - St. Polten, Austria
Home: Weissgerberstrasse 2, Munich 23, West Germany, 49/348-998
Business: Munich - 49/263-745

WARUM SIND SIE GEGEN UNS?   1958, West German
THE BRIDGE   Allied Artists, 1959, West German
DAS WUNDER DES MALACHIAS   1961, West German
THE LONGEST DAY   co-director with Ken Annakin & Andrew Marton, 20th
   Century-Fox, 1962
THE VISIT   20th Century-Fox, 1964, West German-Italian-French-U.S.
MORITURI *THE SABOTEUR, CODE NAME "MORITURI"*   20th Century-
   Fox, 1965
DAS FALSCHE GEWICHT   1971, West German
DIE EROBERUNG DER ZITADELLE   1977, West German

BO WIDERBERG

b. June 8, 1930 - Malmo, Sweden
Contact: Swedish Film Institute, P.O. Box 27126, 102 52 Stockholm, Sweden, 08/
   63-0510

THE BABY CARRIAGE   Europa Film, 1962, Swedish
RAVEN'S END   New Yorker, 1963, Swedish
LOVE 65   Europa Film, 1965, Swedish
THIRTY TIMES YOUR MONEY   Europa Film, 1965, Swedish
ELVIRA MADIGAN   Cinema 5, 1967, Swedish
THE WHITE GAME   co-director, 1968, Swedish
ADALEN '31   Paramount, 1971, Swedish-U.S.
JOE HILL   Paramount, 1971, Swedish-U.S.
STUBBY   1974, Swedish
MAN ON THE ROOF   Cinema 5, 1977, Swedish
VICTORIA   1979, Swedish-West German

KEN WIEDERHORN

SHOCK WAVES   Joseph Brenner Associates, 1977
KING FRAT   Mad Makers, 1979
EYES OF A STRANGER   Warner Bros., 1981
SUMMERTIME   Penny Lane Productions, 1983

CORNEL WILDE *

b. October 13, 1915 - New York, New York
Home: 10433 Wilshire Blvd., Los Angeles, CA 90024, 213/474-3589
Messages: 213/466-3428
Business Manager: Jess S. Morgan & Company, 6420 Wilshire Blvd., Los Angeles,
   CA 90048, 213/651-1601

STORM FEAR   United Artists, 1956
THE DEVIL'S HAIRPIN   Paramount, 1957
MARACAIBO   Paramount, 1958
THE SWORD OF LANCELOT *LANCELOT AND GUINEVERE*   Universal,
   1963, British
THE NAKED PREY   Paramount, 1966, U.S.-South African
BEACH RED   United Artists, 1967
NO BLADE OF GRASS   MGM, 1970, British
SHARK'S TREASURE   United Artists, 1975

BILLY WILDER *
(Samuel Wilder)

b. June 22, 1906 - Vienna, Austria
Agent: Paul Kohner, Inc. - Los Angeles, 213/550-1060
Business Manager: Equitable Investment Corporation - Los Angeles, 213/469-2975

MAUVAISE GRAINE   co-director with Alexander Esway, 1933, German
THE MAJOR AND THE MINOR   Paramount, 1942
FIVE GRAVES TO CAIRO   Paramount, 1943
DOUBLE INDEMNITY ★   Paramount, 1944
THE LOST WEEKEND ★★   Paramount, 1945
THE EMPEROR WALTZ   Paramount, 1948
A FOREIGN AFFAIR   Paramount, 1948
SUNSET BOULEVARD ★★   Paramount, 1950
THE BIG CARNIVAL *ACE IN THE HOLE*   Paramount, 1951
STALAG 17 ★   Paramount, 1953
SABRINA ★   Paramount, 1954
THE SEVEN YEAR ITCH   20th Century-Fox, 1955
THE SPIRIT OF ST. LOUIS   Warner Bros., 1957
LOVE IN THE AFTERNOON   Allied Artists, 1957
WITNESS FOR THE PROSECUTION ★   United Artists, 1958
SOME LIKE IT HOT ★   United Artists, 1959
THE APARTMENT ★★   United Artists, 1960
ONE, TWO, THREE   United Artists, 1961
IRMA LA DOUCE   United Artists, 1963
KISS ME, STUPID   Lopert, 1964
THE FORTUNE COOKIE   United Artists, 1966

continued

BILLY WILDER*—continued
THE PRIVATE LIFE OF SHERLOCK HOLMES   United Artists, 1970, U.S.-British
AVANTI I   United Artists, 1972, U.S.-Italian
THE FRONT PAGE   Universal, 1974
FEDORA   United Artists, 1979, West German-French
BUDDY BUDDY   MGM/United Artists, 1981

G E N E   W I L D E R *
(Jerry Silberman)

b. June 11, 1935 - Milwaukee, Wisconsin
Business: 9350 Wilshire Blvd. - Suite 400, Beverly Hills, CA 90212, 213/277-2211

THE ADVENTURE OF SHERLOCK HOLMES' SMARTER BROTHER   20th Century-Fox, 1975
THE WORLD'S GREATEST LOVER   20th Century-Fox, 1977
SUNDAY LOVERS   co-director with Bryan Forbes, Edouard Molinaro & Dino Risi, MGM/United Artists, 1981, U.S.-British-French-Italian
WOMAN IN RED   Orion, 1984

G O R D O N   W I L E S *

Home: 17123 Adlon Road, Encino, CA 91436, 213/788-2536

GINGER IN THE MORNING   National Film, 1974

O S C A R   W I L L I A M S *

Home: 856 S. St. Andrews Place, Los Angeles, CA 90005, 213/387-6487

THE FINAL COMEDOWN   New World, 1972
FIVE ON THE BLACK HAND SIDE   United Artists, 1973
HOT POTATO   Warner Bros., 1976

P A U L   W I L L I A M S *

b. 1944 - New York, New York
Messages: 213/451-5485
Business Manager: Henry Holmes, 1901 Avenue of the Stars, Los Angeles, CA 90067, 213/203-0900

OUT OF IT   United Artists, 1969
THE REVOLUTIONARY   United Artists, 1970
DEALING: OR THE BERKELEY-TO-BOSTON FORTY-BRICK LOST-BAG BLUES   Warner Bros., 1972
NUNZIO   Universal, 1978
MISS RIGHT   NIR, 1981, Italian

R I C H A R D   W I L L I A M S *

b. March 19, 1933 - Toronto, Canada
Messages: 213/851-8060
Business: Richard Williams Animation, 13 Soho Square, London W1V 5FB, England, 01/437-4455
Richard Williams Animation, 3193 Cahuenga Blvd. West, Hollywood, CA 90068, 213/851-8060

RAGGEDY ANN AND ANDY (AF)   20th Century-Fox, 1977

F R E D   W I L L I A M S O N

b. March 5, 1938 - Gary, Indiana
Business: Po' Boy Productions, 5907 W. Pico Blvd., West Los Angeles, CA 90035, 213/855-1285

ADIOS AMIGO   Atlas, 1976
MEAN JOHNNY BARROWS   Atlas, 1976

continued

FRED WILLIAMSON—continued

DEATH JOURNEY   Atlas, 1976
NO WAY BACK   Atlas, 1976
MR. MEAN   Lone Star/Po' Boy, 1977, Italian-U.S.
ONE DOWN TWO TO GO   Almi Films, 1982
THE LAST FIGHT   Marvin Films, 1983
THE BIG SCORE   Almi Distribution, 1983

G O R D O N   W I L L I S *

Business Manager: Ron Taft - New York City, 212/586-8844

WINDOWS   United Artists, 1979

H U G H   W I L S O N

Personal Manager: The Brillstein Company - Los Angeles, 213/275-6135
Business Manager: John Mucci & Associates - Los Angeles, 213/273-1301

POLICE ACADEMY   The Ladd Company/Warner Bros., 1984

R I C H A R D   W I L S O N *

b. December 25, 1915 - McKeesport, Pennsylvania
Home: 501 Ocean Front, Santa Monica, CA 90402, 213/395-0012
Agent: Arnold Greene, Eisenbach, Greene, Inc. - Los Angeles, 213/659-3420

MAN WITH THE GUN   United Artists, 1955
THE BIG BOODLE   United Artists, 1957
RAW WIND IN EDEN   Universal, 1958
AL CAPONE   Allied Artists, 1959
PAY OR DIE   Allied Artists, 1960
WALL OF NOISE   Warner Bros., 1963
INVITATION TO A GUNFIGHTER   United Artists, 1964
THREE IN THE ATTIC   American International, 1968

S I M O N   W I N C E R

Business: Michael Edgley International, 190 Exhibition Street, Melbourne, Victoria
    3000, Australia, 03/63-5108

TANDARRA (MS)   1976, Australian
THE SULLIVANS (MS)   co-director with David Stevens, 1976, Australian
AGAINST THE WIND (MS)   co-director with George Miller, 1978, Australian
THE DAY AFTER HALLOWEEN *SNAPSHOT*   Group 1, 1979, Australian
HARLEQUIN   New Image, 1980, Australian
PHAR LAP   20th Century-Fox, 1983, Australian

M I C H A E L   W I N N E R *

b. 1935 - London, England
Business: 6-8 Sackville Street, London W1X 1DD, England
Contact: Directors Guild of Great Britain, 56 Whitfield Street, London W1, England,
    01/580-9592

CLIMB UP THE WALL   New Realm, 1960, British
SHOOT TO KILL   New Realm, 1960, British
OLD MAC   Carlyle, 1961, British
SOME LIKE IT COOL   Carlyle, 1961, British
OUT OF THE SHADOW   New Realm, 1961, British
PLAY IT COOL   Allied Artists, 1962, British
THE COOL MIKADO   United Artists, 1962, British
WEST 11   Warner-Pathe, 1963, British
THE GIRL GETTERS *THE SYSTEM*   American International, 1964, British
YOU MUST BE JOKING!   Columbia, 1965, British
THE JOKERS   Universal, 1967, British
I'LL NEVER FORGET WHAT'S 'IS NAME   Regional, 1968, British
HANNIBAL BROOKS   United Artists, 1969, British
THE GAMES   20th Century-Fox, 1970, British
LAWMAN   United Artists, 1971

continued

MICHAEL WINNER*—continued

CHATO'S LAND   United Artists, 1972
THE NIGHTCOMERS   Avco Embassy, 1972, British
THE MECHANIC   United Artists, 1972
SCORPIO   United Artists, 1973
THE STONE KILLER   Columbia, 1973
DEATH WISH   Paramount, 1974
WON TON TON, THE DOG WHO SAVED HOLLYWOOD   Paramount, 1976
THE SENTINEL   Universal, 1977
THE BIG SLEEP   United Artists, 1978, British
FIREPOWER   AFD, 1979, British
DEATH WISH II   Filmways, 1982
THE WICKED LADY   MGM/UA/Cannon, 1983, British
SCREAM FOR HELP   Lorimar Distribution International, 1984

D A V I D   W I N T E R S *

Business: Harlequin Productions, 6525 Sunset Blvd., Hollywood, CA 90028, 213/
    464-0461

RACQUET   Cal-Am Artists, 1979
JAYNE MANSFIELD - AN AMERICAN TRAGEDY   1981
FANATIC   Twin Continental, 1983

H E R B E R T   W I S E *

Home: 13 Despard Road, London N19 5NP, England, 01/272-5047
Agent: Tim Corrie, Fraser & Dunlop Ltd., 91 Regent Street, London W1, England,
    01/734-7311

TO HAVE AND TO HOLD   Warner-Pathe, 1963, British
THE LOVERS!   British Lion, 1973, British
THE GATHERING STORM (TF)   BBC/Clarion Productions/Levien Productions,
    1974, British
SKOKIE (TF) ☆   Titus Productions, 1981

R O B E R T   W I S E *

b. September 10, 1914 - Winchester, Indiana
Business: Robert Wise Productions, Sunset Gower Studios, 1438 N. Gower Street,
    Hollywood, CA 90028, 213/461-3864
Agent: The Gersh Agency - Beverly Hills, 213/274-7451

THE CURSE OF THE CAT PEOPLE   co-director with Gunther von Fritsch, RKO
    Radio, 1944
MADEMOISELLE FIFI   RKO Radio, 1944
THE BODY SNATCHER   RKO Radio, 1945
A GAME OF DEATH   RKO Radio, 1945
CRIMINAL COURT   RKO Radio, 1946
BORN TO KILL   RKO Radio, 1947
MYSTERY IN MEXICO   RKO Radio, 1948
BLOOD ON THE MOON   RKO Radio, 1948
THE SET-UP   RKO Radio, 1949
TWO FLAGS WEST   20th Century-Fox, 1950
THREE SECRETS   Warner Bros., 1950
THE HOUSE ON TELEGRAPH HILL   20th Century-Fox, 1951
THE DAY THE EARTH STOOD STILL   20th Century-Fox, 1951
THE CAPTIVE CITY   United Artists, 1952
SOMETHING FOR THE BIRDS   MGM, 1952
THE DESERT RATS   20th Century-Fox, 1953
DESTINATION GOBI   20th Century-Fox, 1953
SO BIG   Warner Bros., 1953
EXECUTIVE SUITE   MGM, 1954
HELEN OF TROY   Warner Bros., 1955, Italian-French
TRIBUTE TO A BAD MAN   MGM, 1956
SOMEBODY UP THERE LIKES ME   MGM, 1957
THIS COULD BE THE NIGHT   MGM, 1957
UNTIL THEY SAIL   MGM, 1957
RUN SILENT, RUN DEEP   United Artists, 1958
I WANT TO LIVE! ★   United Artists, 1958
ODDS AGAINST TOMORROW   United Artists, 1959

continued

ROBERT WISE*—continued

WEST SIDE STORY ★★   co-director with Jerome Robbins, United Artists, 1961
TWO FOR THE SEESAW   United Artists, 1962
THE HAUNTING   MGM, 1963, British-U.S.
THE SOUND OF MUSIC ★★   20th Century-Fox, 1965
THE SAND PEBBLES   20th Century-Fox, 1966
STAR! *THOSE WERE THE HAPPY TIMES*   20th Century-Fox, 1968
THE ANDROMEDA STRAIN   Universal, 1971
TWO PEOPLE   Universal, 1973
THE HINDENBURG   Universal, 1975
AUDREY ROSE   United Artists, 1977
STAR TREK - THE MOTION PICTURE   Paramount, 1979

F R E D E R I C K   W I S E M A N

b. January 1, 1930
Home/Business: Zipporah Films, Inc., 1 Richdale Avenue - Suite 4, Cambridge,
     MASS 02140, 617/576-3603

TITICUT FOLLIES (FD)   Zipporah Films, 1967
HIGH SCHOOL (FD)   Zipporah Films, 1968
LAW AND ORDER (FD)   Zipporah Films, 1969
HOSPITAL (FD)   Zipporah Films, 1970
BASIC TRAINING (FD)   Zipporah Films, 1971
ESSENE (FD)   Zipporah Films, 1972
JUVENILE COURT (FD)   Zipporah Films, 1973
PRIMATE (FD)   Zipporah Films, 1974
WELFARE (FD)   Zipporah Films, 1975
MEAT (FD)   Zipporah Films, 1976
CANAL ZONE (FD)   Zipporah Films, 1977
SINAI FIELD MISSION (FD)   Zipporah Films, 1978
MANOEUVRE (FD)   Zipporah Films, 1979
MODEL (FD)   Zipporah Films, 1980
SERAPHITA'S DIARY   Zipporah Films, 1982
THE STORE (FD)   Zipporah Films, 1983

W I L L I A M   W I T N E Y *

b. May 15, 1910 - Lawton, Okalhoma
Agent: Lew Deuser, Armstrong-Deuser Agency - Beverly Hills, 213/553-8611

THE TRIGGER TRIO   Republic, 1937
HI-YO SILVER   co-director with John English, Republic, 1940
HEROES OF THE SADDLE   Republic, 1940
OUTLAWS OF PINE RIDGE   Republic, 1942
THE YUKON PATROL   co-director with John English, Republic, 1942
HELLDORADO   Republic, 1946
APACHE ROSE   Republic, 1947
BELLS OF SAN ANGELO   Republic, 1947
SPRINGTIME IN THE SIERRAS   Republic, 1947
ON THE SPANISH TRAIL   Republic, 1947
THE GAY RANCHERO   Republic, 1948
UNDER CALIFORNIA SKIES   Republic, 1948
EYES OF TEXAS   Republic, 1948
THE FAR FRONTIER   Republic, 1949
THE LAST MUSKETEER   Republic, 1952
THE OUTCAST   Republic, 1954
HEADLINE HUNTERS   Republic, 1955
CITY OF SHADOWS   Republic, 1955
A STRANGE ADVENTURE   Republic, 1956
PANAMA SAL   Republic, 1957
YOUNG AND WILD   Republic, 1958
JUVENILE JUNGLE   Republic, 1958
THE COOL AND THE CRAZY   American International, 1958
THE BONNIE PARKER STORY   American International, 1958
PARATROOP COMMAND   American International, 1959
SECRET OF THE PURPLE REEF   20th Century-Fox, 1960
MASTER OF THE WORLD   American International, 1961
THE LONG ROPE   20th Century-Fox, 1961
APACHE RIFLES   20th Century-Fox, 1964
THE GIRLS ON THE BEACH   Paramount, 1965
ARIZONA RAIDERS   Columbia, 1965

continued

WILLIAM WITNEY*—continued
FORTY GUNS TO APACHE PASS   Columbia, 1967
I ESCAPED FROM DEVIL'S ISLAND   United Artists, 1973
DARKTOWN STRUTTERS *GET DOWN AND BOOGIE*   New World, 1975

PETER WITTMAN

ELLIE   Rudine-Wittman Films, 1984

IRA WOHL

BEST BOY (FD)   IFEX Film, 1980

DAN WOLMAN

b. October 28, 1941 - Jerusalem, Israel
Contact: Israel Film Centre, Ministry of Industry & Trade, 30 Agron Street, P.O. Box
    299, Jerusalem 94190, Israel, 02/210433

THE MORNING BEFORE SLEEP   Toda Films, 1969, Israeli
THE DREAMER   Cannon, 1970, Israeli
FLOCH   Aldan Films/Floch Ltd., 1972, Israeli
MY MICHAEL   Alfred Plaine, 1976, Israeli
HIDE AND SEEK   1980, Israeli
NANA   MGM/UA/Cannon, 1983, Italian-U.S.
BABY LOVE (LEMON POPSICLE V)   Noah Films, 1983, Israeli
SOLDIER OF THE NIGHT   Cannon, 1983, Israeli

JOANNE WOODWARD*

b. 1930 - Thomasville, Georgia
Agent: CAA - Los Angeles, 213/277-4545

COME ALONG WITH ME (TF)   Rubicon Productions, 1982

CASPER WREDE

Contact: British Academy of Film & Television Arts, 195 Piccadilly, London W1,
    England, 01/734-0022

PRIVATE POTTER   MGM, 1964, British
ONE DAY IN THE LIFE OF IVAN DENISOVICH   Cinerama Releasing
    Corporation, 1971, British-Norwegian
THE TERRORISTS *RANSOM*   20th Century-Fox, 1975, British

TOM WRIGHT*

Agent: Tony Ludwig, CAA - Los Angeles, 213/277-4545

TORCH SONG   UCO Productions/Torch Productions, 1984, U.S.-Mexican

DONALD WRYE*

Agent: John Ptak, William Morris Agency - Beverly Hills, 213/274-7451

THE MAN WHO COULD TALK TO KIDS (TF)   Tomorrow Entertainment,
    1973
BORN INNOCENT (TF)   Tomorrow Entertainment, 1974
DEATH BE NOT PROUD (TF)   Good Housekeeping Productions/Westfall
    Productions, 1975
THE ENTERTAINER (TF)   RSO Films, 1976
IT HAPPENED ONE CHRISTMAS (TF)   Universal TV, 1977
ICE CASTLES   Columbia, 1979
HOUSE OF GOD *H.O.G.*   United Artists, 1981
FIRE ON THE MOUNTAIN (TF)   Bonnard Productions, 1982
DIVORCE WARS: A LOVE STORY (TF)   Wrye-Konigsberg Films/Warner Bros.
    TV, 1982

continued

DONALD WRYE*—continued
THE FACE OF RAGE (TF)   Hal Sitowitz Productions/Viacom, 1983

JIM WYNORSKI

b. August 14, 1950 - Long Island, New York
Business: Henry Plitt Productions, 1925 Century Park East - Suite 300, Los Angeles,
  CA 90067, 213/553-5307

THE LOST EMPIRE   Harwood Productions, 1983

TRACY KEENAN WYNN*

b. February 28, 1945 - Los Angeles, California
Agent: ICM - Los Angeles, 213/550-4000

HIT LADY (TF)   Spelling-Goldberg Productions, 1974

PETER YATES*

b. July 24, 1929 - Aldershot, England
Business: Tempest Productions, 1775 Broadway - Suite 621, New York,
  NY 10019, 212/974-1158
Agent: Tom Chasin, Chasin-Park-Citron - Los Angeles, 213/273-7190

SUMMER HOLIDAY   American International, 1963, British
ONE WAY PENDULUM   Lopert, 1964, British
ROBBERY   Avco Embassy, 1967, British
BULLITT   Warner Bros., 1968
JOHN AND MARY   20th Century-Fox, 1969
MURPHY'S WAR   Paramount, 1971, British
THE HOT ROCK   20th Century-Fox, 1972
THE FRIENDS OF EDDIE COYLE   Paramount, 1973
FOR PETE'S SAKE   Columbia, 1974
MOTHER, JUGS AND SPEED   20th Century-Fox, 1976
THE DEEP   Columbia, 1977
BREAKING AWAY ★   20th Century-Fox, 1979
EYEWITNESS   20th Century-Fox, 1981
KRULL   Columbia, 1983, U.S.-British
THE DRESSER   Columbia, 1983, British

LINDA YELLEN*

Business: Chrysalis-Yellen Productions - New York City, 212/675-5566
Agent: Sy Fischer Company - Los Angeles, 213/557-0388

COME OUT, COME OUT!   1969
LOOKING UP   Levitt-Pickman, 1977

continued

LINDA YELLEN*—continued

JACOBO TIMERMAN: PRISONER WITHOUT A NAME, CELL WITHOUT A NUMBER (TF)   Chrysalis-Yellen Productions, 1983

B U D   Y O R K I N *
(Alan David Yorkin)

b. February 22, 1926 - Washington, Pennsylvania
Contact: Directors Guild of America - Los Angeles, 213/656-1220

COME BLOW YOUR HORN   Paramount, 1963
NEVER TOO LATE   Warner Bros., 1965
DIVORCE AMERICAN STYLE   Columbia, 1967
INSPECTOR CLOUSEAU   United Artists, 1968, British
START THE REVOLUTION WITHOUT ME   Warner Bros., 1970, British
THE THIEF WHO CAME TO DINNER   Warner Bros., 1972

Y A K Y   Y O S H A

Business: Yaky Yosha Ltd., 29 Lilienblum Street, Tel Aviv 65133, Israel, 03/659108

SHALOM   Yaky Yosha Ltd., 1973, Israeli
ROCKINGHORSE   Sus-Etz, 1978, Israeli
THE VULTURE   New Yorker, 1981, Israeli
DEAD END STREET   Lelo Motza Ltd., 1982, Israeli
SUNSTROKE   Shapira Films, 1984, Israeli

F R E D D I E   Y O U N G

b. 1902 - England
Contact: British Academy of Film & Television Arts, 195 Piccadilly, London W1, England, 01/734-0022

ARTHUR'S HALLOWED GROUND   Enigma Productions/Goldcrest Films & Television, 1983, British

J E F F R E Y   Y O U N G *

Contact: Directors Guild of America - New York City, 212/581-0370

BEEN DOWN SO LONG IT LOOKS LIKE UP TO ME   Paramount, 1971

R O B E R T   M .   Y O U N G *

b. November 22, 1924 - New York, New York
Home: 125 West 76th Street, New York, NY 10023, 212/757-4580
Business: Bobwin Associates, Inc., 245 West 55th Street, New York, NY 10019, 212/757-4580
Agent: ICM - New York City, 212/556-6810

NOTHING BUT A MAN   co-director with Michael Roemer, Cinema 5, 1965
ALAMBRISTA I   Bobwin/Films Haus, 1977
SHORT EYES   The Film League, 1978
RICH KIDS   United Artists, 1979
ONE-TRICK PONY   Warner Bros., 1980
THE BALLAD OF GREGORIO CORTEZ   Embassy, 1983

R O G E R   Y O U N G *

Home: 213/506-6687
Agent: Broder-Kurland Agency - Los Angeles, 213/274-8921

BITTER HARVEST (TF) ☆   Charles Fries Productions, 1981
AN INNOCENT LOVE (TF)   Steve Binder Productions, 1982
DREAMS DON'T DIE (TF)   Hill-Mandelker Films, 1982
TWO OF A KIND (TF)   Lorimar Productions, 1982
HARDCASTLE AND McCORMICK (TF)   Stephen J. Cannell Productions, 1983
LASSITER   Warner Bros., 1984

TERENCE YOUNG *

b. June 20, 1915 - Shanghai, China
Agent: Kurt Frings - Beverly Hills, 213/274-8881

MEN OF ARNHEM (FD)   co-director with Brian Desmond Hurst, Army Film Unit,
  1944, British
CORRIDOR OF MIRRORS   Universal, 1948, British
ONE NIGHT WITH YOU   Universal, 1948, British
WOMAN HATER   Universal, 1948, British
THEY WERE NOT DIVIDED   General Film Distributors, 1950, British
VALLEY OF THE EAGLES   Lippert, 1951, British
THE FRIGHTENED BRIDE THE TALL HEADLINES   Beverly, 1952, British
PARATROOPER THE RED BERET   Columbia, 1953, British
THAT LADY   20th Century-Fox, 1954, British
STORM OVER THE NILE   co-director with Zoltan Korda, Columbia, 1955,
  British
SAFARI   Columbia, 1956, British
ZARAK   Columbia, 1956, British
ACTION OF THE TIGER   MGM, 1957, British
TANK FORCE NO TIME TO DIE   Columbia, 1958, British
SERIOUS CHARGE   Eros, 1959, British
BLACK TIGHTS   Magna, 1960, French
PLAYGIRL AFTER DARK TOO HOT TO HANDLE   Topaz, 1960, British
DUEL OF CHAMPIONS   co-director with Ferdinando Baldi, Medallion, 1961,
  Italian-Spanish
DR. NO   United Artists, 1962, British
FROM RUSSIA WITH LOVE   United Artists, 1963, British
THE AMOROUS ADVENTURES OF MOLL FLANDERS   Paramount, 1965,
  British
THUNDERBALL   United Artists, 1965, British
THE DIRTY GAME GUERRE SECRETE   co-director with Christian-Jaque,
  Carlo Lizzani & Werner Klinger, American International, 1966, French-Italian-
  West German
TRIPLE CROSS   Warner Bros., 1966, British-French
THE POPPY IS ALSO A FLOWER   Comet, 1966, European
WAIT UNTIL DARK   Warner Bros., 1967
L'AVVENTURIERO   Arco Film, 1967, Italian
MAYERLING   MGM, 1969, British-French
THE CHRISTMAS TREE   Continental, 1969, French-Italian
COLD SWEAT DE LA PART DES COPAINS   Emerson, 1970, French
RED SUN   National General, 1972, French-Italian-Spanish
THE VALACHI PAPERS JOE VALACHI: I SEGRETI DI COSA
  NOSTRA   Columbia, 1972, Italian-French
WAR GODDESS LE GUERRIERE DEL SNO NUDA   American International,
  1973, Italian
THE KLANSMAN   Paramount, 1974
SIDNEY SHELDON'S BLOODLINE   Paramount, 1979
INCHON I   MGM/UA, 1982, South Korean
THE JIGSAW MAN   MGM/UA, 1983, British

LARRY YUST *

Agent: Ben Benjamin, ICM - Los Angeles, 213/550-4000

TRICK BABY   Universal, 1973
HOMEBODIES   Avco Embassy, 1974
TESTIMONY OF TWO MEN (TF)   co-director with Leo Penn, Universal TV,
  1977

Z

K R Z Y S Z T O F   Z A N U S S I

b. July 17, 1939 - Warsaw, Poland
Contact: Ministry of Culture and Fine Arts (Central Board of Cinematography), 21/23
Krakowskie Przedmiescie, 00-0071 Warsaw, Poland, 26-7489

THE STRUCTURE OF CRYSTALS   1969, Polish
FAMILY LIFE   1971, Polish
BEHIND THE WALL   1971, Polish
ILLUMINATION   1973, Polish
THE CATAMOUNT KILLING   1974
A WOMAN'S DECISION   Tinc, 1975, Polish
CAMOUFLAGE   Libra, 1977, Polish
THE SPIRAL   1978, Polish
WAYS IN THE NIGHT   TeleCulture, 1980, West German
THE CONSTANT FACTOR   New Yorker, 1980, Polish
CONTRACT   New Yorker, 1981, Polish
FROM A FAR COUNTRY (POPE JOHN PAUL II) (TF)   Trans World Film/
ITC/RAI/Film Polski, 1981, British-Italian-Polish
IMPERATIV (TF)   Telefilm Saar, 1982, West German

F R A N K   Z A P P A

b. December 21, 1940 - Baltimore, Maryland

200 MOTELS   co-director with Tony Palmer, United Artists, 1971, British
BABY SNAKES   Intercontinental Absurdities, 1979

F R A N C O   Z E F F I R E L L I *

b. February 12, 1923 - Florence, Italy
Agent: William Morris Agency - Beverly Hills, 213/274-7451

LA BOHEME   Warner Bros., 1965, Swiss
FLORENCE - DAYS OF DESTRUCTION (FD)   1966, Italian
THE TAMING OF THE SHREW   Columbia, 1967, Italian-British
ROMEO AND JULIET ★   Paramount, 1968, Italian-British
BROTHER SUN SISTER MOON   Paramount, 1973, Italian-British
JESUS OF NAZARETH (MS)   Sir Lew Grade Productions/ITC, 1978, British-
Italian
THE CHAMP   MGM/United Artists, 1979
ENDLESS LOVE   Universal, 1981
LA TRAVIATA   Universal Classics, 1982, Italian

R O B E R T   Z E M E C K I S *

b. 1952 - Chicago, Illinois
Agent: CAA - Los Angeles, 213/277-4545

I WANNA HOLD YOUR HAND   Universal, 1977
USED CARS   Columbia, 1980
ROMANCING THE STONE   20th Century-Fox, 1984

MAI ZETTERLING

b. May 24, 1925 - Vasteras, Sweden
Agent: Douglas Rae Management - London, 01/836-3903

LOVING COUPLES   Prominent, 1964, Swedish
NIGHT GAMES   Mondial, 1966, Swedish
DOCTOR GLAS   20th Century-Fox, 1968, Danish
THE GIRLS   New Line Cinema, 1969, Swedish
VINCENT THE DUTCHMAN   1972, Swedish
VISIONS OF EIGHT (FD)   co-director with Yuri Ozerov, Arthur Penn, Michael
     Pfleghar, Kon Ichikawa, Milos Forman, Claude Lelouch & John Schlesinger,
     Cinema 5, 1973
LOVE   co-director with Annette Cohen, Nancy Dowd & Liv Ullmann, Velvet Films,
     1982, Canadian
SCRUBBERS   Orion Classics, 1983, British

HOWARD ZIEFF *

b. 1943 - Los Angeles, California
Agent: Steven Roth, CAA - Los Angeles, 213/277-4545

SLITHER   MGM, 1973
HEARTS OF THE WEST   MGM/United Artists, 1975
HOUSE CALLS   Universal, 1978
THE MAIN EVENT   Warner Bros., 1979
PRIVATE BENJAMIN   Warner Bros., 1980
UNFAITHFULLY YOURS   20th Century-Fox, 1983

RAFAL ZIELINSKI

Contact: Canadian Film & Television Association, 8 King Street, Toronto, Ontario
     M5C 1B5, Canada, 416/363-0296

BABE   Rafal Productions, 1980, Canadian
SCREWBALLS   New World, 1983, Canadian

VERNON ZIMMERMAN *

Business Manager: Eric Weissman - Beverly Hills, 213/274-8011

DEADHEAD MILES   Paramount, 1971
UNHOLY ROLLERS   American International, 1972
FADE TO BLACK   American Cinema, 1980

ZOE ZINMAN

CITY NEWS   co-director with David Fishelson, Cinecom International, 1983

FRED ZINNEMANN *

b. April 29, 1907 - Vienna, Austria
Address: 128 Mount Street, London W1, England
Agent: Stan Kamen, William Morris Agency - Beverly Hills, 213/274-7451

THE WAVE (FD)   co-director with Emilio Gomez Muriel, Strand, 1935, Mexican
KID GLOVE KILLER   MGM, 1942
EYES IN THE NIGHT   MGM, 1942
THE SEVENTH CROSS   MGM, 1944
LITTLE MR. JIM   MGM, 1946
MY BROTHER TALKS TO HORSES   MGM, 1947
THE SEARCH ★   MGM, 1948, U.S.-Swiss
ACT OF VIOLENCE   MGM, 1949
THE MEN   Columbia, 1950
TERESA   MGM, 1951
HIGH NOON ★   United Artists, 1952
THE MEMBER OF THE WEDDING   Columbia, 1953
FROM HERE TO ETERNITY ★★   Columbia, 1953
OKLAHOMA!   Magna, 1955
A HATFUL OF RAIN   20th Century-Fox, 1957

continued

FRED ZINNEMANN*—continued

THE NUN'S STORY ★   Warner Bros., 1959
THE SUNDOWNERS ★   Warner Bros., 1960
BEHOLD A PALE HORSE   Columbia, 1964
A MAN FOR ALL SEASONS ★★   Columbia, 1966, British
THE DAY OF THE JACKAL   Universal, 1973, British-French
JULIA ★   20th Century-Fox, 1977
FIVE DAYS ONE SUMMER   The Ladd Company/Warner Bros., 1982, British

P E T E R   Z I N N E R

b. July 24, 1919 - Vienna, Austria

THE SALAMANDER   ITC, 1981, British-Italian-U.S.

D A V I D   Z U C K E R *

Business Manager: Shagin & Hyman, 11777 San Vicente Blvd., Los Angeles,
    CA 90049, 213/820-7717

AIRPLANE!   co-director with Jim Abrahams & Jerry Zucker, Paramount, 1980
TOP SECRET!   co-director with Jim Abrahams & Jerry Zucker, Paramount, 1984

J E R R Y   Z U C K E R *

Business Manager: Shagin & Hyman, 11777 San Vicente Blvd., Los Angeles,
    CA 90049, 213/820-7717

AIRPLANE!   co-director with Jim Abrahams & David Zucker, Paramount, 1980
TOP SECRET!   co-director with Jim Abrahams & David Zucker, Paramount,
    1984

A L B E R T   Z U G S M I T H *

b. April 24, 1910 - Atlantic City, New Jersey
Home: 1210 N. Wetherly Drive, Los Angeles, CA 90069, 213/275-8221
Messages: 213/276-6627
Agent: Peter Miller - Peter Miller Agency - New York City, 212/221-8329

COLLEGE CONFIDENTIAL   Universal, 1960
SEX KITTENS GO TO COLLEGE   Allied Artists, 1960
THE PRIVATE LIVES OF ADAM AND EVE   Universal, 1960
DONDI   Allied Artists, 1961
CONFESSIONS OF AN OPIUM EATER *EVILS OF CHINATOWN*   Allied
    Artists, 1962
THE INCREDIBLE SEX REVOLUTION   1965
MOVIE STAR AMERICAN STYLE OR LSD - I HATE YOU   1966
ON HER BED OF ROSES   1966
THE VERY FRIENDLY NEIGHBORS   1969
TWO ROSES AND A GOLDEN ROD   1969

F R A N K   Z U N I G A *

Business: Pisces Productions, Inc. - North Hollywood, 213/766-2517

THE WILDERNESS FAMILY PART II   Pacific International, 1978
HEARTBREAKER   Monarex/Emerson Film Enterprises, 1983
THE GOLDEN SEAL   The Samuel Goldwyn Company, 1983
WHAT COLOR IS THE WIND   Pisces Productions, 1984

E D W A R D   Z W I C K *

Home: 309 Sumac Lane, Santa Monica, CA 90402, 213/459-5116
Agent: Norman Kurland, Broder-Kurland Agency - Los Angeles, 213/274-8921
Business Manager: Arnold Bernstein, Bernstein/Fox Accountancy, 1900 Avenue of
    the Stars - Suite 1650, Los Angeles, CA 90067, 213/277-3373

PAPER DOLLS (TF)   Leonard Goldberg Productions, 1982
HAVING IT ALL (TF)   Hill-Mandelker Films, 1982

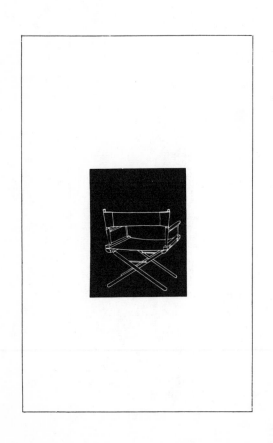
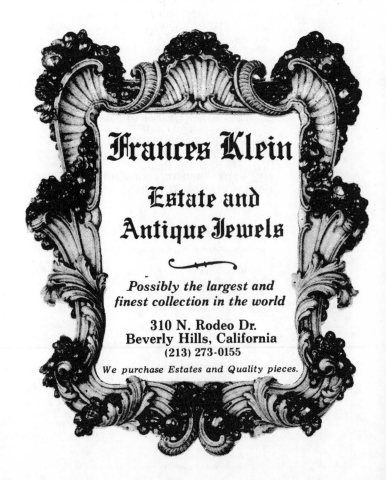
320

I N D E X

DIRECTORS • FILM TITLES • AGENTS • ADVERTISERS

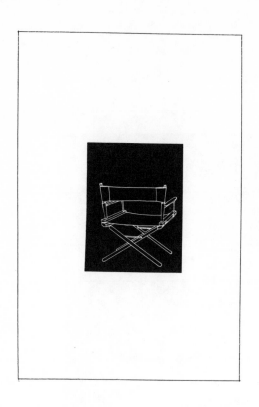

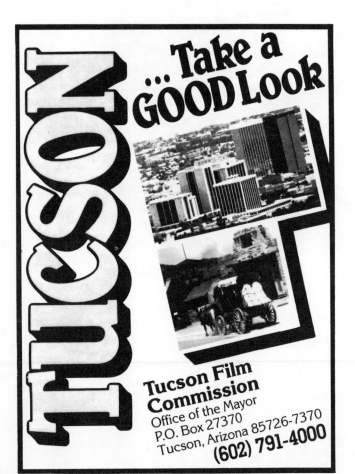

322

Index of Directors

IN MEMORIAM

LUIS BUÑUEL

GEORGE CUKOR

LAWRENCE DOHENY

MARTY FELDMAN

STEVE GORDON

BOB KELLJAN

VIC MORROW

ELIO PETRI

JACQUES TATI

IVAN TORS

KING VIDOR

JACK WEBB

324

Index of film titles

NOTE: This is *not* a title index to every film ever made, just to the films listed in this book.

ATOMIC KID, THE .... Leslie H. Martinson
ATOMIC MAN, THE ...... Kenneth "Ken" Hughes
ATTACK! .... Robert Aldrich
ATTACK OF THE CRAB MONSTERS .... Roger Corman
ATTACK OF THE PUPPET PEOPLE .... Bert I. Gordon
ATTACK ON TERROR: THE FBI VS. THE KLU KLUX KLAN (TF) .... Marvin J. Chomsky
ATTACK ON THE IRON COAST .. Paul Wendkos
ATTI ATROCISSIMA DE AMORE E DI VENDETTA .... Sergio Corbucci
ATTICA (TF)☆☆ .... Marvin J. Chomsky
ATTILA '74 (FD) .... Michael Cacoyannis
AU COEUR DE LA VIE .... Robert Enrico
AU HASARD, BALTHAZAR .... Robert Bresson
AU PAIR GIRLS .... Val Guest
AUDACE COLPO DEI SOLITI IGNOTI .... Nanni Loy
AUDREY ROSE .... Robert Wise
AUNT MARY (TF) .... Peter Werner
AUNTIE MAME .... Morton Da costa
AUTHOR! AUTHOR! .... Arthur Hiller
AUTOBIOGRAPHY OF A PRINCESS (TF) .... James Ivory
AUTOBIOGRAPHY OF MISS JANE PITTMAN (TF) ☆☆, THE .... John Korty
AUTUMN LEAVES .... Robert Aldrich
AUTUMN SONATA .... Ingmar Bergman
AVALANCHE .... Corey Allen
AVANTI! .... Billy Wilder
AVEC LA PEAU AUTRES .... Jacques Deray
AVENGER, THE .... Albert Band
AVENGING, THE .... Lyman Dayton
AVIATOR'S WIFE, THE .... Eric Rohmer
AVIATOR, THE .... George Miller
AWAKENING, THE .... Mike Newell
AWAY ALL BOATS .... Joseph Pevney
AWOL .... Herb Freed
AZIT THE PARATROOPER DOG ... Boaz Davidson

B

B.S. I LOVE YOU .... Steven H. Stern
BAAL (TF) .... Volker Schlondorff
BABE .... Rafal Zielinski
BABE (TF) ☆ .... Buzz Kulik
BABES IN TOYLAND .... Jack Donohue
BABO 73 .... Robert Downey
BABY BLUE MARINE .... John Hancock
BABY CARRIAGE, THE .... Bo Widerberg
BABY COMES HOME (TF) .... Waris Hussein
BABY DOLL .... Elia Kazan
BABY FACE MORGAN .... Arthur Dreifuss
BABY FACE NELSON .... Don Siegel
BABY IT'S YOU .... John Sayles
BABY LOVE .... Alastair Reid
BABY LOVE (LEMON POPSICLE V) .... Dan Wolman
BABY MAKER, THE .... James Bridges
BABY SISTER (TF) .... Steven H. Stern
BABY SNAKES .... Frank Zappa
BABY, THE .... Ted Post
BABY, THE RAIN MUST FALL .. Robert Mulligan
BABYSITTER (TF), THE .... Peter Medak
BACHELOR IN PARADISE .... Jack Arnold
BACHELOR IN PARIS .... John Guillermin
BACHELOR MOTHER .... Garson Kanin
BACHELOR PARTY .... Neil Israel
BACHELOR PARTY, THE .... Delbert Mann
BACHELOR'S DAUGHTER, THE .... Andrew L. Stone
BACK AT THE FRONT .... George Sherman
BACK DOOR TO HELL .... Monte Hellman
BACK FROM THE DEAD .... Charles Marquis Warren
BACK ROADS .... Martin Ritt
BACK STREET .... David Miller
BACK TO BATAAN .... Edward Dmytryk
BACK TO GOD'S COUNTRY ...... Joseph Pevney
BACK TO THE WALL .... Edouard Molinaro
BACKFIRE .... Paul Almond
BACKLASH .... John Sturges
BACKROADS .... Phillip Noyce
BACKSTAIRS AT THE WHITE HOUSE (MS) .... Michael O'herlihy
BACKTRACK .... Earl Bellamy
BAD AND THE BEAUTIFUL, THE .... Vincente Minnelli
BAD BLOOD .... Mike Newell
BAD BOYS .... Rick Rosenthal
BAD BUNCH, THE .... Greydon Clark
BAD CHARLESTON CHARLIE .... Ivan Nagy
BAD COMPANY .... Robert Benton
BAD DAY AT BLACK ROCK ★ ...... John Sturges
BAD FOR EACH OTHER .... Irving Rapper
BAD NEWS BEARS GO TO JAPAN, THE .... John Berry
BAD NEWS BEARS IN BREAKING TRAINING, THE .... Michael Pressman
BAD NEWS BEARS, THE .... Michael Ritchie
BAD RONALD (TF) .... Buzz Kulik
BAD SEED, THE .... Mervyn Leroy
BAD SLEEP WELL, THE .... Akira Kurosawa
BAD SON, A .... Claude Sautet
BAD TIMING/A SENSUAL OBSESSION .... Nicolas Roeg
BADGE 373 .... Howard W. Koch
BADLANDS .... Terrance Malick
BAFFLED! (TF) .... Philip Leacock
BAKER COUNTY USA .... William Fruet
BAKER'S HAWK .... Lyman Dayton
BALCONY, THE .... Joseph Strick
BALLAD OF AND CROCKER (TF), THE .... George Mccowan
BALLAD OF CABLE HOGUE, THE .... Sam Peckinpah
BALLAD OF GREGORIO CORTEZ, THE .... Robert M. Young
BALLAD OF JOSIE, THE ..... Andrew V. Mclaglen
BALLAD OF NARAYAMA, THE .... Shohei Imamura
BALTIMORE BULLET, THE ..... Robert Ellis Miller
BAMBOLE! .... Dino Risi
BANACEK: DETOUR TO NOWHERE (TF) .... Jack Smight
BANANA PEEL .... Marcel Ophuls
BANANAS .... Woody Allen
BAND OF NINJA .... Nagisa Oshima
BAND OF OUTSIDERS .... Jean-Luc Godard
BAND WAGON, THE .... Vincente Minnelli
BANDIDO .... Richard Fleischer
BANDIT OF SHERWOOD FOREST, THE .... George Sherman
BANDITI A MILANO .... Carlo Lizzani
BANDOLERO! .... Andrew V. Mclaglen
BANG! .... Jan Troell
BANG, BANG, YOU'RE DEAD! .... Don Sharp
BANG THE DRUM SLOWLY .... John Hancock
BANJO .... Richard Fleischer
BANJO HACKETT: ROAMIN' FREE (TF) .... Andrew V. Mclaglen
BANNERLINE .... Don Weis
BANYON (TF) .... Robert Day
BARABBAS .... Richard Fleischer
BARBAGIA .... Carlo Lizzani
BARBARA BROADCAST .... Radley Metzger
BARBARELLA .... Roger Vadim
BARBARIAN AND THE GEISHA, THE .... John Huston
BARBAROSA .... Fred Schepisi
BARBARY COAST (TF), THE .... Bill Bixby
BARE ESSENCE (MS) .... Walter Grauman
BAREFOOT CONTESSA, THE .... Joseph L. Mankiewicz
BAREFOOT EXECUTIVE, THE .... Robert Butler
BAREFOOT IN THE PARK .... Gene Saks
BARNABY AND ME .... Norman Panama
BARON OF ARIZONA, THE .... Samuel Fuller
BARQUERO .... Gordon Douglas
BARRIER .... Jerzy Skolimowski
BARRY LYNDON ★ .... Stanley Kubrick
BARRY MCKENZIE HOLDS HIS OWN .... Bruce Beresford
BASIC TRAINING (FD) .... Frederick Wiseman
BASKET CASE .... Frank Henenlotter
BASTA CHE NON SI SAPPIA IN GIRO .... Luigi Comencini
BASTA GUARDARLA .... Luciano Salce
BASTARD (TF), THE .... Lee H. Katzin
BAT PEOPLE, THE .... Jerry Jameson
BATHING BEAUTY .... George Sidney
BATMAN .... Leslie H. Martinson
BATMAN DRACULA .... Andy Warhol
BATTERED (TF) .... Peter Werner
BATTLE AT APACHE PASS, THE .... George Sherman
BATTLE BEYOND THE STARS .... Jimmy T. Murakami
BATTLE CIRCUS .... Richard Brooks
BATTLE FOR THE PLANET OF THE APES .... J. Lee Thompson
BATTLE HELL .... Michael Anderson
BATTLE OF ALGIERS ★ .... Gillo Pontecorvo
BATTLE OF BRITAIN .... Guy Hamilton
BATTLE OF BRITAIN (FD) .... Frank Capra
BATTLE OF CHINA (FD) .... Frank Capra
BATTLE OF THE BULGE .... Ken Annakin
BATTLE OF THE CORAL SEA ..... Paul Wendkos
BATTLE OF THE RIVER PLATE, THE .... Michael Powell
BATTLE OF THE SEXES, THE .. Charles Crichton
BATTLESTAR GALACTICA .... Richard A. Colla
BATTLETRUCK .... Harley Cokliss
BAWDY ADVENTURES OF TOM JONES, THE .... Cliff Owen
BAXTER! .... Lionel Jeffries
BAY OF THE ANGELS .... Jacques Demy
BEACH BLANKET BINGO .... William Asher
BEACH GIRLS, THE .... Pat Townsend
BEACH PARTY .... William Asher
BEACH RED .... Cornel Wilde
BEAR ISLAND .... Don Sharp
BEARS AND I, THE .... Bernard Mceveety
BEAST FROM HAUNTED CAVE .... Monte Hellman
BEAST OF BLOOD .... Eddie Romero
BEAST WITHIN, THE .... Philippe Mora
BEASTMASTER, THE .... Don Coscarelli
BEASTS ARE ON THE STREETS (TF), THE .... Peter Hunt
BEAT THE DEVIL .... John Huston
BEATLEMANIA .... Joseph Manduke
BEAU GESTE .... Douglas Heyes
BEAU JAMES .... Melville Shavelson
BEAU PERE .... Bertrand Blier
BEAUTIFUL DAYS .... Masaki Kobayashi
BEAUTIFUL PEOPLE .... Jamie Uys
BEAUTIFUL PEOPLE II (FD) .... Jamie Uys
BEAUTIFUL STRANGER, THE .... David Miller
BEAUTIFUL SWINDLERS, THE .. Roman Polanski
BEAUTY #2 .... Andy Warhol
BEAUTY AND THE BEAST (TF) ...... Fielder Cook
BEAUTY JUNGLE, THE .... Val Guest
BEBERT ET L'OMNIBUS .... Yves Robert
BEBO'S GIRL .... Luigi Comencini
BECAUSE HE'S MY FRIEND .... Ralph Nelson
BECAUSE OF YOU .... Joseph Pevney
BECAUSE THEY'RE YOUNG .... Paul Wendkos
BECKET ★ .... Peter Glenville
BECKY SHARP .... Rouben Mamoulian
BED AND BOARD .... Francois Truffaut
BED SITTING ROOM, THE .... Richard Lester
BEDAZZLED .... Stanley Donen
BEDFORD INCIDENT, THE .... James B. Harris
BEDKNOBS AND BROOMSTICKS .... Robert Stevenson
BEDSIDE MANNER .... Andrew L. Stone
BEDTIME STORY .... Ralph Levy
BEEN DOWN SO LONG IT LOOKS LIKE UP TO ME .... Jeffrey Young
BEES IN PARADISE .... Val Guest
BEFORE AND AFTER (TF) .... Kim Harlene Friedman
BEFORE THE REVOLUTION .... Bernardo Bertolucci
BEFORE WINTER COMES .... J. Lee Thompson
BEG, BORROW ... OR STEAL (TF) .... David Lowell Rich
BEGGAR'S OPERA, THE .... Peter Brook
BEGGERMAN, THIEF (TF) .... Gordon Hessler
BEGINNING OF THE END .... Bert I. Gordon
BEGUILED, THE .... Don Siegel
BEHIND LOCKED DOORS .... Budd Boetticher
BEHIND THE GREAT WALL .... Carlo Lizzani
BEHIND THE MASK .... Phil Karlson
BEHIND THE RISING SUN .... Edward Dmytryk
BEHIND THE WALL .... Krzysztof Zanussi
BEHINDERTE ZUNKUFT .... Werner Herzog
BEHOLD A PALE HORSE .... Fred Zinnemann
BEING THERE .... Hal Ashby
BEING TWO ISN'T EASY .... Kon Ichikawa
BELIEVE IN ME .... Stuart Hagmann
BELINDA .... Richard Franklin
BELL, BOOK AND CANDLE .... Richard Quine
BELL JAR, THE .... Larry Peerce
BELLBOY, THE .... Jerry Lewis
BELLE MA POVERE .... Dino Risi
BELLE SOMMARS .... Elliot Silverstein
BELLE STARR (TF) .... John A. Alonzo
BELLS ARE RINGING .... Vincente Minnelli
BELLS HAVE GONE TO ROME, THE .... Miklos Jancso
BELLS OF SAN ANGELO .... William Witney
BELOW THE BELT .... Robert Fowler
BELSTONE FOX, THE .... James Hill
BEN .... Phil Karlson
BENEATH THE PLANET OF THE APES .... Ted Post

BENEATH THE VALLEY OF THE ULTRAVIXENS
....Russ Meyer
BENGAL BRIGADE ....Laslo Benedek
BENJI ....Joe Camp
BENNY & BARNEY: LAS VEGAS UNDERCOVER
(TF)...Ron Satlof
BENNY'S PLACE (TF) ....Michael Schultz
BEQUEST TO THE NATIONA ....James Cellan-
jones
BERLIN AFFAIR (TF)............David Lowell Rich
BERLIN TUNNEL 21 (TF) ....Richard Michaels
BERMUDA DEPTHS (TF), THE ....Tom Kotani
BERMUDA TRIANGLE, THE .... Dick Friedenberg
BERSAGLIO MOBILE.................Sergio Corbucci
BERSERKI ....James O'connolly
BERTOLDO BERTOLDINO E ... CACASENO.......
Mario Monicelli
BEST BOY (FD) ....Ira Wohl
BEST DEFENSE ....Willard Huyck
BEST FRIENDS.......................Noel Nosseck
BEST LITTLE GIRL IN THE WORLD (TF), THE....
Sam O'steen
BEST LITTLE WHOREHOUSE IN TEXAS, THE....
Colin Higgins
BEST MAN, THE ....Franklin J. Schaffner
BEST MAN WINS ....John Sturges
BEST OF ENEMIES, THE ....Guy Hamilton
BEST OF EVERYTHING, THE.....Jean Negulesco
BEST PLACE TO BE (TF), THE .... David Miller
BEST REVENGE........................John Trent
BETRAYAL ....David Jones
BETRAYAL (TF) ....Gordon Hessler
BETSY, THE ....Daniel Petrie
BETTA BETTA ....William Byron Hillman
BETTER LATE THAN NEVER ....Bryan Forbes
BETTER LATE THAN NEVER (TF)....................
Richard Crenna
BETTY CO-ED ....Arthur Dreifuss
BETWEEN FRIENDS.................Donald Shebib
BETWEEN FRIENDS (CTF).............. Lou Antonio
BETWEEN HEAVEN AND HELL ....
Richard Fleischer
BETWEEN MIDNIGHT AND DAWN ....
Gordon Douglas
BETWEEN THE LINES ....Joan Micklin Silver
BETWEEN TIME & TIMBUKTU (TF)................
Fred Barzyk
BETWEEN TWO BROTHERS (TF) ....
Robert M. Lewis
BETWEEN US GIRLS ....Henry Koster
BETWEEN WIFE AND LADY .... Kon Ichikawa
BEULAH LAND (MS) ....Virgil W. Vogel
BEWARE OF CHILDREN ....Gerald Thomas
BEWAREI THE BLOB ....Larry Hagman
BEWITCHED ....Arch Oboler
BEYOND AND BACK ....James L. Conway
BEYOND ATLANTIS ....Eddie Romero
BEYOND DEATH'S DOOR ....Henning Schellerup
BEYOND EVIL ....Herb Freed
BEYOND REASON ....Telly Savalas
BEYOND THE BERMUDA TRIANGLE (TF)..........
William A. Graham
BEYOND THE DOOR.................Liliana Cavani
BEYOND THE FOG ....James O'connolly
BEYOND THE LAW...............Norman Mailer
BEYOND THE LIMIT..............John Mackenzie
BEYOND THE POSEIDON ADVENTURE ....
Irwin Allen
BEYOND·THE REEF ....Frank C. Clark
BEYOND THE VALLEY OF THE DOLLS ....
Russ Meyer
BEYOND THIS PLACE ....Jack Cardiff
BIANCO, ROSSO E ....Alberto Lattuada
BIBLE ... IN THE BEGINNING, THE ....
John Huston
BIG BAD MAMA ....Steve Carver
BIG BIRD CAGE, THE ....Jack Hill
BIG BLACK PILL (TF), THE .... Reza Badiyi
BIG BLONDE (TF) ....Kirk Browning
BIG BOB JOHNSON AND HIS FANTASTIC
SPEED CIRCUS (TF)..................Jack Starrett
BIG BOODLE, THE ....Richard Wilson
BIG BOUNCE, THE ....Alex March
BIG BRAWL, THE ....Robert Clouse
BIG BREAK, THE ....Joseph Strick
BIG BUS, THE ....James Frawley
BIG CARNIVAL, THE ....Billy Wilder
BIG CAT, THE ....Phil Karlson
BIG CHIEF, THE ....Henri Verneuil
BIG CHILL, THE ....Lawrence Kasdan
BIG CITY BLUES ....Mervyn Leroy
BIG DEAL ON MADONNA STREET ....
Mario Monicelli
BIG DIG, THE ....Ephraim Kishon

BIG DOLL HOUSE, THE ....Jack Hill
BIG FIX, THE ....Jeremy Paul Kagan
BIG GAMBLE, THE ....Richard Fleischer
BIG HAND FOR THE LITTLE LADY, A ....
Fielder Cook
BIG HOUSE, U.S.A. .,.........Howard W. Koch
BIG JAKE ....George Sherman
BIG JOB, THE ....Gerald Thomas
BIG KNIFE, THE ....Robert Aldrich
BIG KNIGHT, THE.....................Joseph Losey
BIG LAND, THE.................Gordon Douglas
BIG LEAGUER, THE ....Robert Aldrich
BIG MO ....Daniel Mann
BIG MOUTH, THE ....Jerry Lewis
BIG RED ONE, THE ..../......Samuel Fuller
BIG RIP-OFF (TF), THE ....Dean Hargrove
BIG RISK, THE ....Claude Sautet
BIG ROSE (TF) ....Paul Krasny
BIG SCORE, THE ....Fred Williamson
BIG SHOW, THE ....James B. Clark
BIG SLEEP, THE ....Michael Winner
BIG STEAL, THE ....Don Siegel
BIG T.N.T. SHOW (FD), THE ....Larry Peerce
BIG TRUCK AND POOR CLARE.....................
Robert Ellis Miller
BIG WEDNESDAY ....John Milius
BIGAMIST, THE ....Ida Lupino
BIGGER SPLASH, A ....Jack Hazan
BIGGEST BUNDLE OF THEM ALL, THE ....
Ken Annakin
BIKE BOY ....Andy Warhol
BIKINI BEACH ....William Asher
BILITIS ....David Hamilton
BILL COSBY, HIMSELF .... William H. Cosby, Jr.
BILL: ON HIS OWN (TF)............Anthony Page
BILL (TF) ....Anthony Page
BILLIE ....Don Weis
BILLION DOLLAR BRAIN ....Ken Russell
BILLIONAIRE, A ....Kon Ichikawa
BILLY BUDD ....Peter Ustinov
BILLY IN THE LOWLANDS ....Jan Egleson
BILLY JACK ....Tom Laughlin
BILLY JACK GOES TO WASHINGTON ....
Tom Laughlin
BILLY LIAR ....John Schlesinger
BILLY: PORTRAIT OF A STREET KID (TF)..........
Steven Gethers
BILLY THE KID ....David Miller
BILLY TWO HATS ....Ted Kotcheff
BIM ....Hugh A. Robertson
BINGO LONG TRAVELING ALL STARS AND
MOTOR KINGS, THE ....John Badham
BIRCH INTERVAL ....Delbert Mann
BIRCH-WOOD, THE ....Andrzej Wajda
BIRD ON A WIRE (FD) ....Tony Palmer
BIRD WITH THE CRYSTAL PLUMAGE, THE.......
Dario Argento
BIRDMAN OF ALCATRAZ ...John Frankenheimer
BIRDMEN (TF), THE ....Philip Leacock
BIRDS DO IT ....Andrew Marton
BIRDS OF PREY (TF) ....William A. Graham
BIRTH ....Robert Kramer
BIRTH OF THE BEATLES (TF)......................
Richard Marquand
BIRTHDAY PARTY, THE...........William Friedkin
BIS ZUR BITTEREN NEIGE...........Gerd Oswald
BISCUIT EATER, THE .... Vincent Mceveety
BISHOP'S WIFE*, THE ....Henry Koster
BITCH ....Andy Warhol
BITCH, THE ....Gerry O'hara
BITE THE BULLET ....Richard Brooks
BITTER HARVEST (TF) ☆ ....Roger Young
BITTER TEA OF GENERAL YEN, THE ....
Frank Capra
BITTERSWEET LOVE ....David Miller
BJ & THE BEAR (TF) ....Bruce Bilson
BLACK 13 ....Kenneth "Ken" Hughes
BLACK ALLEYCATS (TF) ....Henning Schellerup
BLACK AND WHITE IN COLOR ....Jean-
jacques Annaud
BLACK AND WHITE LIKE DAY AND NIGHT ......
Wolfgang Petersen
BLACK ARROW, THE ....Gordon Douglas
BLACK BART ....George Sherman
BLACK BEAUTY ....James Hill
BLACK BEAUTY (MS) ....Daniel Haller
BLACK BELT JONES.................Robert Clouse
BLACK BIRD, THE ....David Giler
BLACK BUNCH, THE...........Henning Schellerup
BLACK CAESAR ....Larry Cohen
BLACK CASTLE, THE ....Nathan Juran
BLACK CAULDRON (AF), THE ....Art Stevens
BLACK CHRISTMAS ....Bob Clark
BLACK EYE ....Jack Arnold

BLACK FANTASY (FD)...............Lionel Rogosin
BLACK FIST ....Timothy Galfas
BLACK GIRL ....Ossie Davis
BLACK GOLD ....Leslie H. Martinson
BLACK HEAT ....Al Adamson
BLACK HOLE, THE .... Gary Nelson
BLACK JACK ....Kenneth Loach
BLACK JOY ....Anthony Simmons
BLACK MAMA, WHITE MAMA.....Eddie Romero
BLACK MARBLE, THE ....Harold Becker
BLACK MARKET BABY (TF) ....Robert Day
BLACK MIDNIGHT ....Budd Boetticher
BLACK MOON ....Louis Malle
BLACK NARCISSUS ....Michael Powell
BLACK NOON (TF)............Bernard L. Kowalski
BLACK ORCHID, THE ....Martin Ritt
BLACK PEARL, THE ....Saul Swimmer
BLACK PETER .... Milos Forman
BLACK RIVER ....Masaki Kobayashi
BLACK RODEO (FD) .... Jeff Kanew
BLACK ROOTS (FD) ....Lionel Rogosin
BLACK ROSE, THE ....Henry Hathaway
BLACK SAMSON.....................Chuck Bail
BLACK SAMURAI .... Al Adamson
BLACK SHAMPOO ....Greydon Clark
BLACK SIX, THE ....Matt Cimber
BLACK STALLION RETURNS, THE.................
Robert Dalva
BLACK STALLION, THE.............Carroll Ballard
BLACK STREETFIGHTER, THE .... Timothy Galfas
BLACK SUNDAY ....John Frankenheimer
BLACK TIGHTS ....Terence Young
BLACK WATER GOLD (TF) .... Alan Landsburg
BLACK WHIP, THE .....Charles Marquis Warren
BLACK WINDMILL, THE ....Don Siegel
BLACKBEARD'S GHOST .... Robert Stevenson
BLACKBOARD JUNGLE, THE .... Richard Brooks
BLACKENSTEIN ....William A. Levey
BLACKJACK KETCHUM, DESPERADO ....
Earl Bellamy
BLACKOUT ....Michael Powell
BLACKSNAKE .... Russ Meyer
BLACULA ....William Crain
BLADE RUNNER ....Ridley Scott
BLAME IT ON RIO ....Stanley Donen
BLANK GENERATION ....Ulli Lommel
BLAST OFF/JULES VERNE'S ROCKET TO THE
MOON .... Don Sharp
BLAZING SADDLES .... Mel Brooks
BLAZING STEWARDESSES .... Al Adamson
BLESS THE BEASTS & CHILDREN ....
Stanley Kramer
BLESS THIS HOUSE.................Gerald Thomas
BLIND ALLEY............................ Larry Cohen
BLIND AMBITION (TF)............George Schaefer
BLIND DATE ....Joseph Losey
BLINDED BY THE LIGHT (TF).....John A. Alonzo
BLINDMAN ....Ferdinando Baldi
BLISS OF MRS. BLOSSOM, THE......................
Joseph Mcgrath
BLITHE SPIRIT ....David Lean
BLODWEN HOME FROM RACHEL'S MARRIAGE
(TF) .... Alan Cooke
BLONDE FROM SINGAPORE, THE ....
Edward Dmytryk
BLONDE SINNER ....J. Lee Thompson
BLOOD AND GUTS ....Paul Lynch
BLOOD AND HONOR: YOUTH UNDER HITLER
(MS) ....Bernd Fischerauer
BLOOD AND ROSES ....Roger Vadim
BLOOD AND SAND ....Rouben Mamoulian
BLOOD ARROW ....Charles Marquis Warren
BLOOD BATH .... Jack Hill
BLOOD BEACH ....Jeffrey Bloom
BLOOD FEUD ....Lina Wertmuller
BLOOD FEUD (TF) ....Mike Newell
BLOOD FOR DRACULA ....Paul Morrissey
BLOOD OF DRACULA'S CASTLE.... Al Adamson
BLOOD OF GHASTLY HORROR...... Al Adamson
BLOOD OF OTHERS (CMS), THE ....
Claude Chabrol
BLOOD ON SATAN'S CLAW, THE...............
Piers Haggard
BLOOD ON THE MOON ....Robert Wise
BLOOD SPORT (TF) ....Jerrold Freedman
BLOODBROTHERS ....Robert Mulligan
BLOODY MAMA.....................Roger Corman
BLOOMFIELD ....Richard Harris
BLOSSOMS IN THE DUST ....Mervyn Leroy
BLOW JOB.......................Andy Warhol
BLOW OUT ....Brian De palma
BLOW-UP ★................Michelangelo Antonioni
BLUE ....Silvio Narizzano

335

BULLY ... Peter H. Hunt
BUNKER (TF), THE ... George Schaefer
BUNNY LAKE IS MISSING ... Otto Preminger
BUNNY O'HARE ... Gerd Oswald
BUONA SERA, MRS. CAMPBELL ... Melvin Frank
BURDEN OF DREAMS (FD) ... Les Blank
BURGLAR, THE ... Paul Wendkos
BURGLARS, THE ... Henri Verneuil
BURMA VICTORY (FD) ... Roy Boulting
BURMESE HARP, THE ... Kon Ichikawa
BURNI ... Gillo Pontecorvo
BURN, WITCH, BURN ... Sidney Hayers
BURNING, THE ... Tony Maylam
BURNT OFFERINGS ... Dan Curtis
BURY ME AN ANGEL ... Barbara Peeters
BUS II (FD) ... Haskell Wexler
BUS RILEY'S BACK IN TOWN ... Harvey Hart
BUS STOP ... Joshua Logan
BUSH CHRISTMAS ... Henri Safran
BUSHBABY, THE ... John Trent
BUSHIDO BLADE, THE ... Tom Kotani
BUSHWHACKERS, THE ... Rod Amateau
BUSTER AND BILLIE ... Daniel Petrie
BUSTER KEATON STORY, THE ... Sidney Sheldon
BUSTIN' LOOSE ... Oz Scott
BUSTING ... Peter Hyams
BUT I DON'T WANT TO GET MARRIEDI (TF) ... Jerry Paris
BUTCH AND SUNDANCE: THE EARLY DAYS ... Richard Lester
BUTCH CASSIDY AND THE SUNDANCE KID ★ ... George Roy Hill
BUTCH MINDS THE BABY ... Peter Webb
BUTCHER, BAKER, NIGHTMARE MAKER ... William Asher
BUTLEY ... Harold Pinter
BUTTERCUP CHAIN, THE ... Robert Ellis Miller
BUTTERFIELD 8 ... Daniel Mann
BUTTERFLIES ARE FREE ... Milton Katselas
BUTTERFLY ... Matt Cimber
BUZZARD, THE ... Chris Cain
BWANA DEVIL ... Arch Oboler
BY DESIGN ... Claude Jutra
BY LOVE POSSESSED ... John Sturges
BYE BYE BIRDIE ... George Sidney
BYE BYE BRAVERMAN ... Sidney Lumet
BYE BYE MONKEY ... Marco Ferreri

C

C.C. AND COMPANY ... Seymour Robbie
C'ERA UNA VOLTA ... Francesco Rosi
C'EST ARRIVE A PARIS ... John Berry
C.H.O.M.P.S. ... Don Chaffey
C.O.D. ... Michael Powell
CA VA BARDER ... John Berry
CABARET★★ ... Bob Fosse
CABIN IN THE SKY ... Vincente Minnelli
CABLE CAR MURDER (TF), THE ... Jerry Thorpe
CABOBLANCO ... J. Lee Thompson
CABRIOLA ... Mel Ferrer
CACTUS FLOWER ... Gene Saks
CADDIE ... Donald Crombie
CADDYSHACK ... Harold Ramis
CAESAR AND CLEOPATRA (TF) ... James Cellan-jones
CAFE EXPRESS ... Nanni Loy
CAGE WITHOUT A KEY (TF) ... Buzz Kulik
CAGED HEAT ... Jonathan Demme
CAGNEY & LACEY (TF) ... Ted Post
CAHILL, U.S. MARSHAL ... Andrew V. Mclaglen
CAINE MUTINY, THE ... Edward Dmytryk
CALAMITY JANE AND SAM BASS ... George Sherman
CALAMITY JANE (TF) ... James Goldstone
CALCUTTA (FD) ... Louis Malle
CALIFORNIA DREAMING ... John Hancock
CALIFORNIA GOLD RUSH (TF) ... Jack B. Hively
CALIFORNIA KID (TF), THE ... Richard T. Heffron
CALIFORNIA SPLIT ... Robert Altman
CALIFORNIA SUITE ... Herbert Ross
CALL HER MOM (TF) ... Jerry Paris
CALL HIM MR. SHATTER ... Michael Carreras
CALL ME BWANA ... Gordon Douglas
CALL ME GENIUS ... Robert Day
CALL NORTHSIDE 777 ... Henry Hathaway
CALL OF THE WILD ... Ken Annakin
CALL OF THE WILD (TF), THE ... Jerry Jameson
CALLAN ... Don Sharp
CALLAWAY WENT THATAWAY ... Melvin Frank
CALLIE & SON (TF) ... Waris Hussein
CALLIOPE ... Matt Cimber
CAMELOT ... Joshua Logan
CAMILLE 2000 ... Radley Metzger
CAMMINACAMMINA ... Ermanno Olmi
CAMOUFLAGE ... Krzysztof Zanussi
CAMP ... Andy Warhol
CAMP-FIRE GIRLS ... Henning Schellerup
CAMP ON BLOOD ISLAND, THE ... Val Guest
CAMPBELL'S KINGDOM ... Ralph Thomas
CAMPUS CALL ... William Byron Hillman
CAMPUS RHYTHM ... Arthur Dreifuss
CAN ELLEN BE SAVED? (TF) ... Harvey Hart
CAN HIERONYMOUS MERKIN EVER FORGET MERCY HUMPPE AND FIND TRUE HAPPINESS? ... Anthony Newley
CAN I SAVE MY CHILDREN? (TF) ☆ ... Walter C. Miller
CAN SHE BAKE A CHERRY PIE? ... Henry Jaglom
CAN'T STOP THE MUSIC ... Nancy Walker
CANADIANS, THE ... Burt Kennedy
CANAL ZONE (FD) ... Frederick Wiseman
CANCEL MY RESERVATION ... Paul Bogart
CANDIDATE, THE ... Michael Ritchie
CANDY TANGERINE MAN, THE ... Matt Cimber
CANNERY ROW ... David S. Ward
CANNIBAL GIRLS ... Ivan Reitman
CANNON FOR CORDOBA ... Paul Wendkos
CANNON (TF) ... George Mccowan
CANNONBALL ... Paul Bartel
CANNONBALL II ... Hal Needham
CANNONBALL RUN, THE ... Hal Needham
CANTATA ... Miklos Jancso
CANTERBURY TALE, A ... Michael Powell
CANTERVILLE GHOST, THE ... Jules Dassin
CAPE FEAR ... J. Lee Thompson
CAPER OF THE GOLDEN BULLS, THE ... Russell Rouse
CAPONE ... Steve Carver
CAPRICCIO ALL'ITALIANA ... Mario Monicelli
CAPRICORN ONE ... Peter Hyams
CAPTAIN AMERICA (TF) ... Rod Holcomb
CAPTAIN APACHE ... Alexander Singer
CAPTAIN NEMO AND THE UNDERWATER CITY ... James Hill
CAPTAIN NEWMAN, M.D. ... David Miller
CAPTAINS AND THE KINGS (MS) ... Allen Reisner
CAPTAINS COURAGEOUS (TF) ... Harvey Hart
CAPTIVE CITY, THE ... Robert Wise
CAPTIVE WILD WOMAN ... Edward Dmytryk
CAPTURE OF GRIZZLY ADAMS (TF), THE ... Don Keeslar
CAPTURE, THE ... John Sturges
CAR, THE ... Elliot Silverstein
CAR WASH ... Michael Schultz
CARAVAN TO VACCARES ... Geoffrey Reeve
CARAVANS ... James Fargo
CARBON COPY ... Michael Schultz
CARD, THE ... Ronald Neame
CARDINAL ★, THE ... Otto Preminger
CAREER ... Joseph Anthony
CARELESS YEARS, THE ... Arthur Hiller
CARETAKER, THE ... Clive Donner
CARETAKERS, THE ... Hall Bartlett
CAREY TREATMENT, THE ... Blake Edwards
CARLTON-BROWNE OF THE F.O. .. Roy Boulting
CARMEN ... Carlos Saura
CARMEN, BABY ... Radley Metzger
CARMEN JONES ... Otto Preminger
CARNABY, M.D. ... Ralph Thomas
CARNAL KNOWLEDGE ... Mike Nichols
CARNAVAL ... Henri Verneuil
CARNIVAL MAGIC ... Al Adamson
CARNIVAL ROCK ... Roger Corman
CARNY ... Robert Kaylor
CARO MICHELE ... Mario Monicelli
CARO PAPA' ... Dino Risi
CARPETBAGGERS, THE ... Edward Dmytryk
CARPOOL (TF) ... E.W. Swackhamer
CARRIE ... Brian De palma
CARRY ON ABROAD ... Gerald Thomas
CARRY ON ADMIRAL ... Val Guest
CARRY ON AGAIN, DOCTOR ... Gerald Thomas
CARRY ON AT YOUR CONVENIENCE ... Gerald Thomas
CARRY ON BEHIND ... Gerald Thomas
CARRY ON CABBY ... Gerald Thomas
CARRY ON CAMPING ... Gerald Thomas
CARRY ON CLEO ... Gerald Thomas
CARRY ON CONSTABLE ... Gerald Thomas
CARRY ON COWBOY ... Gerald Thomas
CARRY ON CRUISING ... Gerald Thomas
CARRY ON DOCTOR ... Gerald Thomas
CARRY ON EMMANUELLE ... Gerald Thomas
CARRY ON ENGLAND ... Gerald Thomas
CARRY ON HENRY ... Gerald Thomas
CARRY ON JACK ... Gerald Thomas
CARRY ON LOVING ... Gerald Thomas
CARRY ON MATRON ... Gerald Thomas
CARRY ON NURSE ... Gerald Thomas
CARRY ON REGARDLESS ... Gerald Thomas
CARRY ON SCREAMING ... Gerald Thomas
CARRY ON SERGEANT ... Gerald Thomas
CARRY ON SPYING ... Gerald Thomas
CARRY ON UP THE JUNGLE ... Gerald Thomas
CARRY ON ... UP THE KHYBER ... Gerald Thomas
CARS THAT ATE PARIS, THE ... Peter Weir
CARS THAT EAT PEOPLE, THE ... Peter Weir
CARSON CITY ... Andre De toth
CARTER'S ARMY (TF) ... George Mccowan
CARTOUCHE ... Philippe De broca
CARVE HER NAME WITH PRIDE ... Lewis Gilbert
CASA DEL TAPPETO GIALLO ... Carlo Lizzani
CASANOVA ... Federico Fellini
CASANOVA '70 ... Mario Monicelli
CASBAH ... John Berry
CASE AGAINST BROOKLYN, THE ... Paul Wendkos
CASE OF THE MISSING SCENE, THE ... Don Chaffey
CASE OF THE RED MONKEY, THE ... Kenneth "Ken" Hughes
CASE OF THE SMILING STIFFS, THE ... Sean S. Cunningham
CASEY'S SHADOW ... Martin Ritt
CASH AND COMPANY (MS) ... George Miller
CASH MCCALL ... Joseph Pevney
CASINO ROYALE ... John Huston
CASINO (TF) ... Don Chaffey
CASS TIMBERLANE ... George Sidney
CASSANDRA CROSSING, THE ... George Pan Cosmatos
CAST A DARK SHADOW ... Lewis Gilbert
CAST A GIANT SHADOW ... Melville Shavelson
CASTAWAY COWBOY, THE .. Vincent Mceveety
CASTAWAYS OF GILLIGAN'S ISLAND (TF), THE ... Earl Bellamy
CASTLE KEEP ... Sydney Pollack
CASTLE OF THE SPIDER'S WEB, THE ... Akira Kurosawa
CAT AND MOUSE ... Claude Lelouch
CAT AND THE CANARY, THE ... Radley Metzger
CAT BALLOU ... Elliot Silverstein
CAT CREATURE (TF), THE ... Curtis Harrington
CAT O'NINE TAILS ... Dario Argento
CAT ON A HOT TIN ROOF ★ ... Richard Brooks
CAT PEOPLE ... Paul Schrader
CATACOMBS ... Gordon Hessler
CATAMOUNT KILLING, THE ... Krzysztof Zanussi
CATCH-22 ... Mike Nichols
CATCH A PEBBLE ... James F. Collier
CATCH ME A SPY ... Dick Clement
CATCH MY SOUL ... Patrick Mcgoohan
CATCH, THE ... Nagisa Oshima
CATCH US IF YOU CAN ... John Boorman
CATERED AFFAIR, THE ... Richard Brooks
CATHOLICS (TF) ... Jack Gold
CATHY'S CHILD ... Donald Crombie
CATLOW ... Sam Wanamaker
CATTLE ANNIE AND LITTLE BRITCHES ... Lamont Johnson
CATTLE EMPIRE ... Charles Marquis Warren
CAUGHT ON A TRAIN (TF) ... Peter John Duffell
CAUSE TOUJOURS ... TU M'INTERESSE ... Edouard Molinaro
CAVALLO DELLA TIGRE, A ... Luigi Comencini
CAVE-IN I (TF) ... Georg J. Fenady
CAVEMAN ... Carl Gottlieb
CEDDO ... Ousmene Sembene
CELEBRITY (MS) ... Paul Wendkos
CEMENTHEAD (TF) ... Ralph L. Thomas
CENTENNIAL (MS) ... Bernard Mceveety
CENTENNIAL SUMMER ... Otto Preminger
CENTER FOLD GIRLS ... John Peyser
CEREMONY, THE ... Nagisa Oshima
CERTAIN SMILE, A ... Jean Negulesco
CERVANTES ... Vincent Sherman
CESAR AND ROSALIE ... Claude Sautet
CHADWICK FAMILY (TF), THE ... David Lowell Rich
CHAFED ELBOWS ... Robert Downey
CHAIN OF EVENTS ... Gerald Thomas
CHAINED HEAT ... Paul Nicolas
CHAIRMAN, THE ... J. Lee Thompson
CHALK GARDEN, THE ... Ronald Neame

CHALLENGE, THE..............John Frankenheimer
CHALLENGERS (TF), THE.....Leslie H. Martinson
CHAMBER OF HORRORS..............Hy Averback
CHAMP, THE..........................Franco Zeffirelli
CHAMPAGNE MURDERS, THE...Claude Chabrol
CHAMPIONS . . . A LOVE STORY (TF)..............
John A. Alonzo
CHAMPIONS, THE..........................John Irvin
CHAN IS MISSING.....................Wayne Wang
CHANCE MEETING....................Joseph Losey
CHANDLERTOWN.......................Bryan Forbes
CHANEL SOLITAIRE.............George Kaczender
CHANGE OF HABIT.............William A. Graham
CHANGE OF SEASONS, A...........Richard Lang
CHANGELING, THE......................Peter Medak
CHANGES.....................................Hall Bartlett
CHANT OF JIMMIE BLACKSMITH, THE............
Fred Schepisi
CHAPLINESQUE, MY LIFE AND HARD TIMES....
Harry Hurwitz
CHAPPAQUA............................Conrad Rooks
CHAPTER TWO..........................Robert Moore
CHARADE...............................Stanley Donen
CHARGE AT FEATHER CREEK, THE.................
Gordon Douglas
CHARGE OF THE LIGHT BRIGADE, THE...........
Tony Richardson
CHARIOTS OF FIRE ★................Hugh Hudson
CHARLES, DEAD OR ALIVE..........Alain Tanner
CHARLES & DIANA: A ROYAL LOVE STORY
(TF)..............................James Goldstone
CHARLES ET LUCIE......................Nelly Kaplan
CHARLESTON (TF)......................Karen Arthur
CHARLEY AND THE ANGEL... Vincent Mceveety
CHARLEY MOON........................Guy Hamilton
CHARLEY-ONE-EYE........................Don Chaffey
CHARLEY VARRICK........................Don Siegel
CHARLIE AND A HALF..............Boaz Davidson
CHARLIE AND THE GREAT BALLOON CHASE
(TF).....................................Larry Elikann
CHARLIE BUBBLES......................Albert Finney
CHARLIE CHAN THE CURSE OF THE DRAGON
QUEEN....................................Clive Donner
CHARLIE COBB: NICE NIGHT FOR HANGING
(TF)..................................Richard Michaels
CHARLIE MUFFIN............................Jack Gold
CHARLIE'S ANGELS (TF)...............................
John Llewellyn Moxey
CHARLIE SMITH AND THE FRITTER TREE (TF)...
David R. Loxton
CHARLOTTE...............................Roger Vadim
CHARLY....................................Ralph Nelson
CHARRO!....................Charles Marquis Warren
CHARULATA..............................Satyajit Ray
CHASE A CROOKED SHADOW.......................
Michael Anderson
CHASE, THE.................................Arthur Penn
CHATEAU EN SUEDE...................Roger Vadim
CHATO'S LAND......................Michael Winner
CHATTANOOGA CHOO CHOO.......Bruce Bilson
CHATTERBOX.........................Tom Desimone
CHE!..................................Richard Fleischer
CHE C'ENTRIAMO NOI CON LA RIVOLUZIONE?
....Sergio Corbucci
CHE SI DICE A ROMA..................Ettore Scola
CHEAP DETECTIVE, THE............Robert Moore
CHEAPER TO KEEP HER..............Ken Annakin
CHEAT, THE...........................George Abbott
CHECK IS IN THE MAIL, THE.........Joan Darling
CHECKERED FLAG OR CRASH.......Alan Gibson
CHECKPOINT..........................Ralph Thomas
CHEECH & CHONG AS THE CORSICAN
BROTHERS..........................Thomas Chong
CHEECH & CHONG'S NICE DREAMS...............
Thomas Chong
CHEECH & CHONG: STILL SMOKIN................
Thomas Chong
CHEERLEADERS' WILD WEEKEND.. Jeff Werner
CHELSEA GIRLS, THE..................Andy Warhol
CHERE LOUISE.................Philippe De broca
CHEROKEE TRAIL (TF), THE..........Kieth Merrill
CHERRY, HARRY AND RAQUEL......Russ Meyer
CHESS PLAYERS, THE..................Satyajit Ray
CHEYENNE SOCIAL CLUB, THE.......Gene Kelly
CHICAGO STORY (TF), THE..........Jerry London
CHICKEN CHRONICLES, THE......Francis Simon
CHIDIAKHANA..............................Satyajit Ray
CHIEDO ASILO.........................Marco Ferreri
CHIEF CRAZY HORSE............George Sherman
CHIEFS (MS)............................Jerry London
CHILD BRIDE OF SHORT CREEK (TF)..............
Robert M. Lewis
CHILD IN THE HOUSE........................Cy Endfield
CHILD IS WAITING, A...........John Cassavetes
CHILD OF DIVORCE..............Richard Fleischer
CHILD'S PLAY............................Sidney Lumet
CHILD STEALER (TF), THE.........Melvin Damski
CHILD UNDER A LEAF.........George Bloomfield
CHILDISH THINGS.........................John Derek
CHILDREN NOBODY WANTED (TF), THE..........
Richard Michaels
CHILDREN OF AN LAC (TF), THE.....................
John Llewellyn Moxey
CHILDREN OF DIVORCE (TF)...........Joanna Lee
CHILDREN OF RAGE..... Arthur Allan Seidelman
CHILDREN OF SANCHEZ, THE........Hall Bartlett
CHILDREN OF THEATRE STREET (FD), THE.......
Robert Dornhelm
CHILDREN'S WAR, THE.............Moshe Mizrahi
CHILDREN SHOULDN'T PLAY WITH DEAD
THINGS...Bob Clark
CHIMES AT MIDNIGHT...............Orson Welles
CHINA 9 LIBERTY 37..............Monte Hellman
CHINA GATE..........................Samuel Fuller
CHINA GIRL........................Henry Hathaway
CHINA IS NEAR.....................Marco Bellocchio
CHINA ROSE (TF)..........................Robert Day
CHINA SYNDROME, THE...........James Bridges
CHINA VENTURE..........................Don Siegel
CHINATOWN ★.......................Roman Polanski
CHINO.....................................John Sturges
CHISHOLMS (MS), THE...................Mel Stuart
CHISUM...........................Andrew V. Mclaglen
CHITTY CHITTY BANG BANG..........................
Kenneth "Ken" Hughes
CHLOE IN THE AFTERNOON..........Eric Rohmer
CHOICE OF WEAPONSA............Kevin Connor
CHOICE (TF), THE.....................David Greene
CHOICES.............................Silvio Narizzano
CHOICES OF THE HEART (TF)... Joseph Sargent
CHOIRBOYS, THE.....................Robert Aldrich
CHOOSE ME..........................Alan Rudolph
CHOSEN SURVIVORS.................Sutton Roley
CHOSEN, THE...................Jeremy Paul Kagan
CHRIST STOPPED AT EBOLI.....Francesco Rosi
CHRISTA.................................Jack O'connell
CHRISTIAN LICORICE STORE, THE..................
James Frawley
CHRISTIAN THE LION.....................James Hill
CHRISTINA................................Paul Krasny
CHRISTINE JORGENSEN STORY, THE.............
Irving Rapper
CHRISTMAS LILIES OF THE FIELD (TF)............
Ralph Nelson
CHRISTMAS MIRACLE IN CAUFIELD, U.S.A.
(TF)..Jud Taylor
CHRISTMAS STORY, A.....................Bob Clark
CHRISTMAS TO REMEMBER (TF), A.................
George Englund
CHRISTMAS TREE, THE...........Terence Young
CHRISTMAS WITHOUT SNOW (TF), A.............
John Korty
CHRISTO'S VALLEY CURTAIN (FD).................
Albert Maysles
CHRISTOPHER COLUMBUS (MS)....................
Alberto Lattuada
CHU CHU AND THE PHILLY FLASH................
David Lowell Rich
CHUKA................................Gordon Douglas
CHULAS FRONTERAS (FD)................Les Blank
CHUNG KUO (FD).........Michelangelo Antonioni
CIMARRON KID, THE...............Budd Boetticher
CINCINNATI KID, THE............Norman Jewison
CINDERELLA 2000........................Al Adamson
CINDERELLA LIBERTY....................Mark Rydell
CINDY (TF)......................William A. Graham
CINEMA-CINEMA (FD).................Krishna Shah
CIRCLE OF CHILDREN (TF), A..........Don Taylor
CIRCLE OF DECEIT.............Volker Schlondorff
CIRCLE OF IRON.....................Richard Moore
CIRCLE OF LOVE.........................Roger Vadim
CIRCLE OF POWER.......................Bobby Roth
CIRCLE OF TWO...........................Jules Dassin
CIRCLE, THE..........................Gerald Thomas
CIRCUS FRIENDS.....................Gerald Thomas
CIRCUS OF FEAR..........John Llewellyn Moxey
CIRCUS OF HORRORS..............Sidney Hayers
CIRCUS WORLD.....................Henry Hathaway
CISCO PIKE.............................B.W.L. Norton
CITADEL OF CRIME...............George Sherman
CITIZEN KANE..........................Orson Welles
CITIZENS BAND....................Jonathan Demme
CITY BENEATH THE SEA.........Budd Boetticher
CITY BENEATH THE SEA (TF)..........Irwin Allen
CITY GIRL, THE.....................Martha Coolidge
CITY IN FEAR (TF)..........................Jud Taylor
CITY IS DARK, THE....................Andre De toth
CITY NEWS..........................David Fishelson
CITY OF SHADOWS.................William Witney
CITY OF THE DEAD........John Llewellyn Moxey
CITY OF WOMEN.....................Federico Fellini
CITY ON FIRE!.............................Alvin Rakoff
CITY STREETS..................Rouben Mamoulian
CITY (TF), THE.............................Daniel Petrie
CLAIR DE FEMME.......................Costa Gavras
CLAIRE'S KNEE.............................Eric Rohmer
CLAMBAKE................................Arthur H. Nadel
CLARENCE, THE CROSS-EYED LION................
Andrew Marton
CLASH OF THE TITANS..........Desmond Davis
CLASS...............................Lewis John Carlino
CLASS OF '44...............................Paul Bogart
CLASS OF '63 (TF).........................John Korty
CLASS OF '74...............................Arthur Marks
CLASS OF 1984..........................Mark L. Lester
CLASS OF MISS MACMICHAEL, THE..............
Silvio Narizzano
CLAUDELLE INGLISH..............Gordon Douglas
CLAUDINE......................................John Berry
CLAY PIGEON...................................Lane Slate
CLAY PIGEON, THE..............Richard Fleischer
CLEAR AND PRESENT DANGER (TF) ☆, A........
James Goldstone
CLEO FROM 5 TO 7....................Agnes Varda
CLEOPATRA..................Joseph L. Mankiewicz
CLEOPATRA JONES......................Jack Starrett
CLEOPATRA JONES AND THE CASINO OF
GOLD...Chuck Bail
CLERAMBARD..............................Yves Robert
CLIMB UP THE WALL............Michael Winner
CLINIC, THE..............................David Stevens
CLINIC XCLUSIVE.........................Don Chaffey
CLOAK AND DAGGER.............Richard Franklin
CLOCK, THE........................Vincente Minnelli
CLOCKMAKER OF ST. PAUL, THE...................
Bertrand Tavernier
CLOCKWORK ORANGE ★, A..... Stanley Kubrick
CLONE MASTER (TF), THE...........Don Medford
CLOSE ENCOUNTERS OF THE THIRD KIND ★...
Steven Spielberg
CLOSE-UP..................................Jack Donohue
CLOSED CIRCUIT................Giuliano Montaldo
CLOSET, THE................................Andy Warhol
CLOUD DANCER..........................Barry Brown
CLOUDED YELLOW, THE...........Ralph Thomas
CLOWN MURDERS, THE............Martyn Burke
CLOWNS, THE........................Federico Fellini
CLUB, THE.............................Bruce Beresford
CLUE OF THE MISSING APE, THE....James Hill
COACH...................................Bud Townsend
COACH OF THE YEAR (TF)...........Don Medford
COAL MINER'S DAUGHTER........Michael Apted
COAST TO COAST.................Joseph Sargent
COBWEB, THE......................Vincente Minnelli
COCAINE AND BLUE EYES (TF)....................
E.W. Swackhamer
COCAINE COWBOYS.....................Ulli Lommel
COCAINE: ONE MAN'S SEDUCTION (TF)...........
Paul Wendkos
COCKFIGHTER.........................Monte Hellman
COCKLESHELL HEROES, THE.........Jose Ferrer
COCKTAIL MOLOTOV....................Diane Kurys
COCKTAILS IN THE KITCHEN.........................
J. Lee Thompson
CODE NAME: DIAMOND HEAD (TF)..................
Jeannot Szwarc
CODE NAME: HERACLITUS (TF)......................
James Goldstone
CODE NAME: TRIXIE...........George A. Romero
CODE RED (TF)....................J. Lee Thompson
COFFEE, TEA OR ME? (TF)......Norman Panama
COFFY..Jack Hill
COLD CUTS...............................Bertrand Blier
COLD FEET...........................Bruce Van Dusen
COLD NIGHT'S DEATH (TF), A.........................
Jerrold Freedman
COLD ROOM (CTF), THE..........James Dearden
COLD SWEAT......................Terence Young
COLD TURKEY..........................Norman Lear
COLD WIND IN AUGUST, A...Alexander Singer
COLDITZ STORY, THE................Guy Hamilton
COLLEGE CONFIDENTIAL.........Albert Zugsmith
COLONEL BLIMP.....................Michael Powell
COLONEL MARCH INVESTIGATES... Cy Endfield
COLORADO SUNSET.............George Sherman
COLOSSUS OF RHODES, THE......Sergio Leone
COLOSSUS: THE FORBIN PROJECT.................
Joseph Sargent
COLPO DI STATO......................Luciano Salce
COMA.................................Michael Crichton
COMANCHE.........................George Sherman
COMANCHE STATION.............Budd Boetticher

338

CRY FROM THE STREETS, A........Lewis Gilbert
CRY IN THE WILDERNESS (TF), A..................
    Gordon Hessler
CRY OF THE BANSHEE............Gordon Hessler
CRY OF THE INNOCENT (TF)..Michael O'herlihy
CRY PANIC (TF) ....James Goldstone
CRY RAPE I (TF) ....Corey Allen
CRY TERROR I ....Andrew L. Stone
CRY TOUGH ....Paul Stanley
CRY UNCLE I ....John G. Avildsen
CRYPT OF THE LIVING DEAD........Ray Danton
CUBA ....Richard Lester
CUENCA ....Carlos Saura
CUJO ....Lewis Teague
CUL-DE-SAC ....Roman Polanski
CULLODEN (TF)..................Peter Watkins
CULPEPPER CATTLE CO., THE ......Dick Richards
CUORE DI CANE ....Alberto Lattuada
CUORE (MS)..................Luigi Comencini
CURSE OF KING TUT'S TOMB (TF), THE ....
    Philip Leacock
CURSE OF THE BLACK WIDOW (TF)............
    Dan Curtis
CURSE OF THE CAT PEOPLE, THE..................
    Robert Wise
CURSE OF THE FLY ....Don Sharp
CURSE OF THE MUMMY'S TOMB, THE............
    Michael Carreras
CURSE OF THE PINK PANTHER ....
    Blake Edwards
CURTAINS ....Richard Ciupka
CUTTER AND BONE ....Ivan Passer
CUTTER'S TRAIL (TF)............ Vincent Mceveety
CUTTER'S WAY ....Ivan Passer
CUTTER (TF)....................Richard Irving
CAN YOU HEAR THE LAUGHTER? THE STORY
 OF FREDDIE PRINZE (TF)..Burt Brinckerhoff
CYCLONE KID, THE ....George Sherman
CYCLOPS ....Bert I. Gordon
CYRANO DE BERGERAC ....Michael Gordon

D

D.A.: CONSPIRACY TO KILL (TF), THE ....
    Paul Krasny
D.C. CAB ....Joel Schumacher
D-DAY, THE SIXTH OF JUNE........Henry Koster
DADDY, I DON'T LIKE IT LIKE THIS (TF)..........
    Adell Aldrich
DADDY LONG LEGS ....Jean Negulesco
DAGUERREOTYPES (FD) ....Agnes Varda
DAIN CURSE (MS) ☆, THE.....E.W. Swackhamer
DAISY KENYON ....Otto Preminger
DAISY MILLER ....Peter Bogdanovich
DALEKS - INVASION EARTH 2150 A.D. ....
    Gordon Flemyng
DALLAS COWBOYS CHEERLEADERS II (TF) ....
    Michael O'herlihy
DALLAS COWBOYS CHEERLEADERS (TF) ......
    Bruce Bilson
DAM BUSTERS, THE ....Michael Anderson
DAMIEN - OMEN II ....Don Taylor
DAMIEN ... THE LEPER PRIEST ....
    Steven Gethers
DAMN THE DEFIANT I—H.M.S. DEFIANT ....
    Lewis Gilbert
DAMN YANKEES ....George Abbott
DAMNATION ALLEY ....Jack Smight
DAMNED DON'T CRY, THE.....Vincent Sherman
DAMNED, THE ....Joseph Losey
DANCE HALL ....Charles Crichton
DANCE IN THE SUN ....Shirley Clarke
DANCE LITTLE LADY ....Val Guest
DANCE MOVIE ....Andy Warhol
DANCE OF THE DWARFS ....Gus Trikonis
DANCE OF THE SEVEN VEILS (TF), THE ....
    Ken Russell
DANCE OF THE VAMPIRES ...... Roman Polanski
DANDY, THE ALL-AMERICAN GIRL ....
    Jerry Schatzberg
DANGER IN PARADISE (TF) ....
    Marvin J. Chomsky
DANGER - LOVE AT WORK.......Otto Preminger
DANGER WITHIN ....Don Chaffey
DANGEROUS AGE, A................Sidney J. Furie
DANGEROUS COMPANY (TF)...Lamont Johnson
DANGEROUS DAVIES - THE LAST DETECTIVE
    Val Guest
DANGEROUS DAYS OF KIOWA JONES (TF),
 THE ....Alex March
DANGEROUS SUMMER, A ......Quentin Masters

DANIEL ....Sidney Lumet
DANTE'S INFERNO (TF) ....Ken Russell
DANTON ....Andrzej Wajda
DARBY O'GILL AND THE LITTLE PEOPLE..........
    Robert Stevenson
DARING DOBERMANS, THE......Byron Chudnow
DARING GAME ....Laslo Benedek
DARK ALIBI ....Phil Karlson
DARK AT THE TOP OF THE STAIRS, THE........
    Delbert Mann
DARK CORNER, THE ...... Henry Hathaway
DARK CRYSTAL, THE ....Frank Oz
DARK DID NOT CONQUER (TF), THE ....
    Paul Almond
DARK END OF THE STREET, THE .. Jan Egleson
DARK INTRUDER ....Harvey Hart
DARK NIGHT OF THE SCARECROW (TF)..........
    Frank De felitta
DARK ODYSSEY ....Radley Metzger
DARK OF THE SUN ...... Jack Cardiff
DARK PLACES ....Don Sharp
DARK SECRET OF HARVEST HOME (TF), THE ...
    Leo Penn
DARK SIDE OF INNOCENCE (TF), THE ....
    Jerry Thorpe
DARK SIDE OF TOMORROW, THE ....
    Barbara Peeters
DARK STAR........................John Carpenter
DARK SUNDAY ....Jimmy Huston
DARK, THE ....John "Bud" Cardos
DARK VICTORY (TF) ....Robert Butler
DARK WATERS ...... Andre De toth
DARKER SIDE OF TERROR (TF), THE ....
    Gus Trikonis
DARKER THAN AMBER ....Robert Clouse
DARKTOWN STRUTTERS ....William Witney
DARLING LILI ....Blake Edwards
DARLING ★ ....John Schlesinger
DARWIN ADVENTURE, THE .... Jack Couffer
DAS ABENTEUER DER THEA ROLAND............
    Henry Koster
DAS BOOT (THE BOAT) ★....Wolfgang Petersen
DAS FALSCHE GEWICHT ....Bernhard Wicki
DAS HASSLICHE MADCHEN ....Henry Koster
DAS TAGEBUCH DER GELIEBTEN ....
    Henry Koster
DAS WUNDER DES MALACHIAS ....
    Bernhard Wicki
DATELINE DIAMONDS ....Jeremy Summers
DAUGHTER OF THE MIND (TF) ....
    Walter Grauman
DAUGHTERSI DAUGHTERSI ....Moshe Mizrahi
DAUGHTERS OF JOSHUA CABE RETURN (TF),
 THE ....David Lowell Rich
DAUGHTERS OF JOSHUA CABE (TF), THE ......
    Philip Leacock
DAVID ....Peter Lilienthal
DAVID AND GOLIATH............Ferdinando Baldi
DAVID AND LISA ★ ....Frank Perry
DAVID COPPERFIELD (TF)..........Delbert Mann
DAVID HOLZMAN'S DIARY............Jim Mcbride
DAWN AT SOCORRO ....George Sherman
DAWN OF THE DEAD ......George A. Romero
DAWN: PORTRAIT OF A TEENAGE RUNAWAY
 (TF) ....Randal Kleiser
DAY AFTER HALLOWEEN, THE .. Simon Wincer
DAY AFTER (TF), THE ....Nicholas Meyer
DAY AND THE HOUR, THE ....René Clement
DAY CHRIST DIED (TF), THE ......James Cellan-
    jones
DAY FOR NIGHT ....Francois Truffaut
DAY FOR THANKS ON WALTON'S MOUNTAIN
 (TF), A ....Harry Harris
DAY IN THE DEATH OF JOE EGG, A ....
    Peter Medak
DAY MARS INVADED EARTH, THE..................
    Maury Dexter
DAY OF THE DOLPHIN, THE ....Mike Nichols
DAY OF THE EVIL GUN ....Jerry Thorpe
DAY OF THE JACKAL, THE ......Fred Zinnemann
DAY OF THE LOCUST, THE....John Schlesinger
DAY OF THE OUTLAW ....Andre De toth
DAY OF THE TRUMPET, THE.......Eddie Romero
DAY THE BUBBLE BURST (TF), THE ....
    Joseph Hardy
DAY THE EARTH CAUGHT FIRE, THE ....
    Val Guest
DAY THE EARTH MOVED, THE (TF)..................
    Robert M. Lewis
DAY THE EARTH STOOD STILL, THE ....
    Robert Wise
DAY THE FISH CAME OUT, THE..................
    Michael Cacoyannis

DAY THE LORD GOT BUSTED, THE ....
    Burt Topper
DAY THE LOVING STOPPED (TF), THE..............
    Daniel Mann
DAY THE WOMEN GOT EVEN, THE ....
    Burt Brinckerhoff
DAY THE WORLD ENDED, THE ..Roger Corman
DAY THEY GAVE BABIES AWAY, THE ....
    Allen Reisner
DAY THEY ROBBED THE BANK OF ENGLAND,
 THE ....John Guillermin
DAY TIME ENDED, THE ......John "Bud" Cardos
DAY TO REMEMBER, A .... Ralph Thomas
DAYS AND NIGHTS IN THE FOREST ....
    Satyajit Ray
DAYS OF HEAVEN ....Terrance Malick
DAYS OF WINE AND ROSES .....Blake Edwards
DAYTON'S DEVILS ....Jack Shea
DE CHE SEGNO SEI? ....Sergio Corbucci
DE GREY - LE BANC DE DESOLATION (TF)......
    Claude Chabrol
DE LA PART DES COPAINS ......Terence Young
DE SADE ....Cy Endfield
DEAD AND BURIED ....Gary A. Sherman
DEAD CERT ....Tony Richardson
DEAD DON'T DIE (TF), THE .... Curtis Harrington
DEAD END STREET ....Yaky Yosha
DEAD HEAT ON A MERRY-GO-ROUND..............
    Bernard Girard
DEAD KIDS ....Michael Laughlin
DEAD MAN ON THE RUN (TF)......Bruce Bilson
DEAD MEN DON'T WEAR PLAID .....Carl Reiner
DEAD MEN TELL NO TALES (TF) ....
    Walter Grauman
DEAD OF NIGHT ....Charles Crichton
DEAD ON ARRIVAL ....Charles Martin
DEAD PIGEON ON BEETHOVEN STREET ....
    Samuel Fuller
DEAD RINGER ....Allan Nicholls
DEAD ZONE, THE..................David Cronenberg
DEADFALL ....Bryan Forbes
DEADHEAD MILES ....Vernon Zimmerman
DEADLIER THAN THE MALE....... Ralph Thomas
DEADLIEST SEASON (TF), THE ....
    Robert Markowitz
DEADLIEST SIN, THE.... Kenneth "Ken" Hughes
DEADLINE AUTO THEFT ........H.B. Halicki
DEADLINE - U.S.A. ....Richard Brooks
DEADLOCK (TF)........................Don Weis
DEADLY AFFAIR, THE ....Sidney Lumet
DEADLY BEES, THE ....Freddie Francis
DEADLY BLESSING ....Wes Craven
DEADLY COMPANIONS, THE .....Sam Peckinpah
DEADLY DREAM (TF), THE ....Alf Kjellin
DEADLY ENCOUNTER (TF)....William A. Graham
DEADLY FORCE ....Paul Aaron
DEADLY GAME (TF) ....Lane Slate
DEADLY HARVEST (TF) ....Michael O'herlihy
DEADLY HERO ....Ivan Nagy
DEADLY HONEYMOON ....Elliot Silverstein
DEADLY HUNT (TF), THE............John Newland
DEADLY LESSONS (TF) ....William Wiard
DEADLY MANTIS, THE ....Nathan Juran
DEADLY STRANGERS ....Sidney Hayers
DEADLY TOWER (TF), THE ....Jerry Jameson
DEADLY TRAP, THE..................René Clement
DEADLY TRIANGLE (TF), THE.. Charles S. Dubin
DEADMAN'S CURVE (TF)........Richard Compton
DEAL OF THE CENTURY......William Friedkin
DEALING: OR THE BERKELEY-TO-BOSTON
 FORTY-BRICK LOST-BAG BLUES ....
    Paul Williams
DEAR BRIGITTE........................Henry Koster
DEAR DETECTIVE ....Philippe De broca
DEAR DETECTIVE (TF)..............Dean Hargrove
DEAR HEART ....Delbert Mann
DEAR INSPECTOR ....Philippe De broca
DEAR MR. WONDERFUL ......Peter Lilienthal
DEATH AMONG FRIENDS (TF) .... Paul Wendkos
DEATH AT LOVE HOUSE (TF) ....
    E.W. Swackhamer
DEATH BE NOT PROUD (TF)........Donald Wrye
DEATH BY HANGING................Nagisa Oshima
DEATH CAR ON THE FREEWAY (TF) ....
    Hal Needham
DEATH CRUISE (TF)..................Ralph Senensky
DEATH DIMENSION ....Al Adamson
DEATH HUNT ....Peter Hunt
DEATH IN CANAAN (TF), A .....Tony Richardson
DEATH IS NOT THE END.......Richard Michaels
DEATH JOURNEY ....Fred Williamson
DEATH LINE ....Gary A. Sherman
DEATH MOON (TF) ....Bruce Kessler

343

FOREVER AND A DAY .... Robert Stevenson
FOREVER FEMALE .... Irving Rapper
FOREVER (TF) .... John Korty
FOREVER YOUNG .... David Drury
FOREVER YOUNG, FOREVER FREE .... Ashley Lazarus
FORGOTTEN MAN (TF), THE .... Walter Grauman
FORMULA, THE .... John G. Avildsen
FORT APACHE, THE BRONX .... Daniel Petrie
FORT BOWIE .... Howard W. Koch
FORT DOBBS .... Gordon Douglas
FORTUNA .... Menahem Golan
FORTUNE AND MEN'S EYES .... Harvey Hart
FORTUNE COOKIE, THE .... Billy Wilder
FORTUNE, THE .... Mike Nichols
FORTUNES OF CAPTAIN BLOOD .... Gordon Douglas
FORTY DAYS FOR DANNY (TF) .... Robert Greenwald
FORTY-DEUCE .... Paul Morrissey
FORTY GUNS .... Samuel Fuller
FORTY GUNS TO APACHE PASS .... William Witney
FORTY-NINTH PARALLEL, THE ... Michael Powell
FOSSILS .... Masaki Kobayashi
FOSTER AND LAURIE (TF) .... John Llewellyn Moxey
FOUL PLAY .... Colin Higgins
FOUNTAINHEAD, THE .... Masaki Kobayashi
FOUR DAYS .... John Guillermin
FOUR DAYS OF NAPLES, THE .... Nanni Loy
FOUR DEUCES, THE ..... William J. Bushnell, Jr.
FOUR DIMENSIONS OF GRETA, THE .... Peter Walker
FOUR FEATHERS (TF), THE .... Don Sharp
FOUR FLIES ON GREY VELVET .... Dario Argento
FOUR FRIENDS .... Arthur Penn
FOUR GIRLS IN TOWN .... Jack Sher
FOUR HORSEMEN OF THE APOCALYPSE, THE .... Vincente Minnelli
FOUR IN THE MORNING .... Anthony Simmons
FOUR MUSKETEERS, THE .... Richard Lester
FOUR NIGHTS OF A DREAMER .... Robert Bresson
FOUR SEASONS, THE .... Alan Alda
FOUR STARS .... Andy Warhol
FOURTEEN HOURS .... Henry Hathaway
FOURTH MAN, THE .... Paul Verhoeven
FOURTH WISH, THE .... Don Chaffey
FOX AND THE HOUND (AF), THE .... Art Stevens
FOX IN THE CHICKEN COOP .... Ephraim Kishon
FOX, THE .... Mark Rydell
FOXES .... Adrian Lyne
FOXFIRE .... Joseph Pevney
FOXHOLE IN CAIRO .... John Llewellyn Moxey
FOXY BROWN .... Jack Hill
FOXY LADY .... Ivan Reitman
FRAGMENT OF FEAR .... Richard C. Sarafian
FRAMED .... Phil Karlson
FRANCES .... Graeme Clifford
FRANCESCO D'ASSISI (TF) .... Liliana Cavani
FRANCIS GARY POWERS: THE TRUE STORY OF THE U-2 SPY INCIDENT (TF) .... Delbert Mann
FRANCOIS REICHENBACH'S JAPAN (FD) .... Francois Reichenbach
FRANKENSTEIN - 1970 .... Howard W. Koch
FRANKENSTEIN (TF) .... Glenn Jordan
FRANKENSTEIN: THE TRUE STORY (TF) .... Jack Smight
FRANTIC .... Louis Malle
FRAULEIN .... Henry Koster
FRAULEIN DOKTOR .... Alberto Lattuada
FREAKY FRIDAY .... Gary Nelson
FRECKLES .... Andrew V. Mclaglen
FREDDIE STEPS OUT .... Arthur Dreifuss
FREE AND EASY .... George Sidney
FREE SPIRIT .... James Hill
FREE, WHITE AND 21 .... Larry Buchanan
FREE WOMAN, A .... Volker Schlondorff
FREEBIE AND THE BEAN .... Richard Rush
FREEDOM (TF) .... Joseph Sargent
FREEZE BOMB .... Al Adamson
FRENCH ATLANTIC AFFAIR (TF), THE .... Douglas Heyes
FRENCH CONNECTION II ... John Frankenheimer
FRENCH CONNECTION ★★, THE .... William Friedkin
FRENCH DRESSING .... Ken Russell
FRENCH LIEUTENANT'S WOMAN, THE .... Karel Reisz
FRENCH MISTRESS, A .... Roy Boulting
FRENCH POSTCARDS .... Willard Huyck
FRENCH WOMAN, THE .... Just Jaeckin
FRESCOS ON THE WHITE .... Emil Loteanu
FREUD .... John Huston
FRIDAY FOSTER .... Arthur Marks
FRIDAY THE 13TH .... Sean S. Cunningham
FRIDAY THE 13TH PART 2 .... Steve Miner
FRIDAY THE 13TH PART 3 .... Steve Miner
FRIEND IS A TREASURE, A .... Sergio Corbucci
FRIEND, THE .... Yilmaz Guney
FRIENDLY FIRE (TF) ☆☆ .... David Greene
FRIENDLY PERSUASION (TF) .... Joseph Sargent
FRIENDS .... Lewis Gilbert
FRIENDS OF EDDIE COYLE, THE ..... Peter Yates
FRIENDSHIP, SECRETS AND LIES .... Marlena Laird
FRIENDSHIPS, SECRETS AND LIES (TF) .... Ann Zane Shanks
FRIGHTENED BRIDE, THE .... Terence Young
FRIGHTMARE .... Peter Walker
FRISCO KID, THE .... Robert Aldrich
FRISKY .... Luigi Comencini
FRITZ THE CAT (AF) .... Ralph Bakshi
FROGS .... George Mccowan
FROM A FAR COUNTRY (POPE JOHN PAUL II) (TF) .... Krzysztof Zanussi
FROM BEYOND THE GRAVE .... Kevin Connor
FROM HELL TO TEXAS .... Henry Hathaway
FROM HERE TO ETERNITY (MS) .... Buzz Kulik
FROM HERE TO ETERNITY ★★ .... Fred Zinnemann
FROM NOON TILL THREE .... Frank D. Gilroy
FROM RUSSIA WITH LOVE .... Terence Young
FROM THE LIFE OF THE MARIONETTES .... Ingmar Bergman
FROM THE MIXED-UP FILES OF MRS. BASIL E. FRANKWEILER .... Fielder Cook
FROM THIS DAY FORWARD .... John Berry
FRONT PAGE, THE .... Billy Wilder
FRONT, THE .... Martin Ritt
FRONTIER FREMONT .... Dick Friedenberg
FRONTIER VENGEANCE .... George Sherman
FUCK .... Andy Warhol
FUGITIVE FAMILY (TF) .... Paul Krasny
FUGITIVE KIND, THE .... Sidney Lumet
FUGITIVES, THE .... Yilmaz Guney
FULL CIRCLE .... Richard Loncraine
FULL MOON HIGH .... Larry Cohen
FULL OF LIFE .... Richard Quine
FULL TREATMENT, THE .... Val Guest
FUN AND GAMES .... Ray Austin
FUN ON A WEEKEND .... Andrew L. Stone
FUN WITH DICK & JANE .... Ted Kotcheff
FUNERAL HOME .... William Fruet
FUNERAL IN BERLIN .... Guy Hamilton
FUNHOUSE, THE .... Tobe Hooper
FUNNY FACE .... Stanley Donen
FUNNY FARM, THE .... Ron Clark
FUNNY LADY .... Herbert Ross
FUNNY THING HAPPENED ON THE WAY TO THE FORUM, A .... Richard Lester
FUNNYMAN .... John Korty
FURTHER UP THE CREEK .... Val Guest
FURY AT SHOWDOWN .... Gerd Oswald
FURY, THE .... Brian De palma
FUTURE COP (TF) .... Jud Taylor
FUTUREWORLD .... Richard T. Heffron
FUTZ .... Tom O'horgan
FUZZ .... Richard A. Colla

G

G.I. HONEYMOON .... Phil Karlson
G'OLE! (FD) .... Tom Clegg
GABLE AND LOMBARD .... Sidney J. Furie
GABRIELA .... Bruno Barreto
GABRIELLA .... Mack Bing
GAILY, GAILY .... Norman Jewison
GAL YOUNG UN .... Victor Nuñez
GALAXINA .... William Sachs
GALAXY OF TERROR .... Bruce Clark
GALILEO .... Joseph Losey
GALLIPOLI .... Peter Weir
GAMBIT .... Ronald Neame
GAMBLER, THE .... Karel Reisz
GAME FOR THREE LOSERS, A .... Gerry O'hara
GAME FOR VULTURES .... James Fargo
GAME IS OVER, THE .... Roger Vadim
GAME OF DEATH .... Robert Clouse
GAME OF DEATH, A .... Robert Wise
GAMEKEEPER, THE .... Kenneth Loach
GAMES .... Curtis Harrington
GAMES GIRLS PLAY, THE .... Jack Arnold
GAMES MOTHER NEVER TAUGHT YOU (TF) .... Lee Philips
GAMES, THE .... Michael Winner
GANDHI ★★ .... Richard Attenborough
GANGSTER CHRONICLES (TF), THE .... Richard C. Sarafian
GANGSTER STORY .... Walter Matthau
GANITO KAMI NOON, PAANO KAYO NGAYON? .... Eddie Romero
GANJA & HESS .... Bill Gunn
GARAGE, THE .... Vilgot Sjoman
GARCON .... Claude Sautet
GARDEN OF DELIGHTS, THE .... Carlos Saura
GARDEN OF EVIL .... Henry Hathaway
GARDENER'S SON (TF), THE ...... Richard Pearce
GARGOYLES (TF) .... B.W.L. Norton
GARMENT JUNGLE, THE .... Vincent Sherman
GAS .... Les Rose
GAS-S-S-SI . . .OR IT BECAME NECESSARY TO DESTROY THE WORLD IN ORDER TO SAVE IT! .... Roger Corman
GATES TO PARADISE .... Andrzej Wajda
GATHERING OF EAGLES, A .... Delbert Mann
GATHERING, PART II (TF), THE .... Charles S. Dubin
GATHERING STORM (TF), THE ...... Herbert Wise
GATHERING (TF) ☆, THE .... Randal Kleiser
GATOR .... Burt Reynolds
GAUGUIN THE SAVAGE (TF) .... Fielder Cook
GAUNTLET, THE .... Clint Eastwood
GAWAIN AND THE GREEN KNIGHT .... Stephen Weeks
GAY DECEIVERS, THE .... Bruce Kessler
GAY DESPERADO, THE .... Rouben Mamoulian
GAY RANCHERO, THE .... William Witney
GAY SENORITA, THE .... Arthur Dreifuss
GAY SISTERS, THE .... Irving Rapper
GEMINI AFFAIR .... Matt Cimber
GEMINI MAN (TF) .... Alan J. Levi
GENE KRUPA STORY, THE .... Don Weis
GENERAL IDI AMIN DADA (FD) .... Barbet Schroeder
GENERAL SPANKY .... Gordon Douglas
GENERATION .... George Schaefer
GENERATION, A .... Andrzej Wajda
GENESIS II (TF) .... John Llewellyn Moxey
GENOCIDE (FD) .... Arnold Schwartzman
GENTLEMAN BANDIT (TF), THE .... Jonathan Kaplan
GENTLEMAN JOE PALOOKA .... Cy Endfield
GENTLEMAN MISBEHAVES, THE .... George Sherman
GENTLEMAN'S AGREEMENT ★★ .... Elia Kazan
GENTLEMAN'S FATE .... Mervyn Leroy
GEORGE WASHINGTON (MS) .... Buzz Kulik
GEORGIA PEACHES (TF) .... Daniel Haller
GEORGINAS GRUNDE (TF) .... Volker Schlondorff
GEORGY GIRL .... Silvio Narizzano
GERONIMO .... Arnold Laven
GERVAISE .... René Clement
GET CARTER .... Mike Hodges
GET CHARLIE TULLY .... Cliff Owen
GET CHRISTIE LOVE! (TF) .... William A. Graham
GET CRAZY .... Allan Arkush
GET DOWN AND BOOGIE .... William Witney
GET MEAN .... Ferdinando Baldi
GET OUT YOUR HANDKERCHIEFS .... Bertrand Blier
GET TO KNOW YOUR RABBIT .... Brian De palma
GETAWAY, THE .... Sam Peckinpah
GETTING AWAY FROM IT ALL (TF) .... Lee Philips
GETTING EVEN .... Harvey Hart
GETTING MARRIED (TF) .... Steven H. Stern
GETTING OF WISDOM, THE ..... Bruce Beresford
GETTING STRAIGHT .... Richard Rush
GHOST AND MR. CHICKEN, THE .... Alan Rafkin
GHOST AND MRS. MUIR, THE .... Joseph L. Mankiewicz
GHOST DANGING (TF) .... David Greene
GHOST IN THE INVISIBLE BIKINI, THE .... Don Weis
GHOST IN THE NOONDAY SUN .... Peter Medak
GHOST OF FLIGHT 401 (TF), THE .... Steven H. Stern
GHOST OF LOVE .... Dino Risi
GHOST STORY .... John Irvin
GHOST STORY OF YOUTH .... Kon Ichikawa
GHOST VALLEY RAIDERS .... George Sherman
GHOSTS OF BUXLEY HALL (TF), THE .... Bruce Bilson
GHOUL, THE .... Freddie Francis
GIACOMO L'IDEALISTA .... Alberto Lattuada

GIALLO NAPOLETANO ....Sergio Corbucci
GIANT LEECHES, THE........Bernard L. Kowalski
GIDEON'S TRUMPET (TF) ....Robert Collins
GIDGET..............................Paul Wendkos
GIDGET GETS MARRIED (TF) .... E.W. Swackhamer
GIDGET GOES HAWAIIAN..........Paul Wendkos
GIDGET GOES TO ROME ....Paul Wendkos
GIDGET GROWS UP (TF) ....James Sheldon
GIFT OF LIFE (TF), THE ....Jerry London
GIFT OF LOVE (TF), THE ....Don Chaffey
GIFT OF LOVE, THE ....Jean Negulesco
GIFT (TF), THE ....Don Taylor
GIGI ★ ....Vincente Minnelli
GIGOT ....Gene Kelly
GILDA LIVE (FD)............................Mike Nichols
GILDERSLEEVE ON BROADWAY .... Gordon Douglas
GILDERSLEEVE'S BAD DAY......Gordon Douglas
GILDERSLEEVE'S GHOST ....Gordon Douglas
GIMME SHELTER (FD)................Albert Maysles
GINGER...Don Schain
GINGER IN THE MORNING..........Gordon Wiles
GINZA VETERAN, A....................Kon Ichikawa
GIRL CALLED HATTER FOX (TF), THE............ George Schaefer
GIRL FROM LORRAINE, THE...... Claude Goretta
GIRL FROM PETROVKA, THE.................. Robert Ellis Miller
GIRL FROM THE DEAD SEA, THE .... Menahem Golan
GIRL GETTERS, THE ....Michael Winner
GIRL IN BLACK, A........ Michael Cacoyannis
GIRL IN BLACK STOCKINGS, THE .... Howard W. Koch
GIRL IN BLUE, THE ....George Kaczender
GIRL IN THE CROWD, THE ....Michael Powell
GIRL IN THE EMPTY GRAVE (TF), THE .... Lou Antonio
GIRL IN THE PICTURE, THE...........Don Chaffey
GIRL IN THE RAIN ....Alf Kjellin
GIRL IN THE RED VELVET SWING, THE .... Richard Fleischer
GIRL IN WHITE, THE ....John Sturges
GIRL MOST LIKELY TO ... (TF), THE............... Lee Philips
GIRL NAMED SOONER (TF), A ..... Delbert Mann
GIRL NAMED TAMIKO, A ....John Sturges
GIRL OF THE LIMBERLOST, THE.......Mel Ferrer
GIRL OF THE NIGHT.................. Joseph Cates
GIRL ON A MOTORCYCLE, THE.......Jack Cardiff
GIRL ON THE LATE, LATE SHOW (TF), THE...... Gary Nelson
GIRL ON THE RUN....................Richard L. Bare
GIRL RUSH........................Gordon Douglas
GIRL SAID NO, THE .... Andrew L. Stone
GIRL, THE GOLD WATCH AND DYNAMITE (TF), THE ....Hy Averback
GIRL, THE GOLD WATCH AND EVERYTHING (TF), THE .... William Wiard
GIRL WHO CAME GIFT-WRAPPED (TF), THE...... Bruce Bilson
GIRL WHO COULDN'T LOSE (TF)☆☆, THE.......... Mort Lachman
GIRL WITH GREEN EYES, THE.. Desmond Davis
GIRL WITH RED BOOTS ....Juan Buñuel
GIRLFRIENDS...............................Claudia Weill
GIRLS ....Just Jaeckin
GIRLS ARE FOR LOVING................Don Schain
GIRLS FOR RENT .... Al Adamson
GIRLS FROM WILKO, THE..........Andrzej Wajda
GIRLS IN THE NIGHT ....Jack Arnold
GIRLS IN THE OFFICE (TF), THE..........Ted Post
GIRLS OF HUNTINGTON HOUSE (TF), THE .... Alf Kjellin
GIRLS ON THE BEACH, THE......William Witney
GIRLS, THE ....Mai Zetterling
GIRLY ....Freddie Francis
GIRO CITY.......................................Karl Francis
GIROLIMONI - IL MOSTRO DI ROMA .... Damiano Damiani
GIVE A GIRL A BREAK ....Stanley Donen
GIVE HER THE MOON ....Philippe De broca
GIVE MY REGARDS TO BROAD STREET.......... Peter Webb
GIVE US THE MOON..........................Val Guest
GIVE US THIS DAY................Edward Dmytryk
GIZMO! (FD)...............................Howard Smith
GLADIATORS ....Peter Watkins
GLAMOUR GIRL.......................Arthur Dreifuss
GLASS HOUSES ....Alexander Singer
GLASS MENAGERIE (TF), THE... Anthony Harvey
GLASS MENAGERIE, THE............ Irving Rapper
GLASS WEB, THE .... Jack Arnold
GLEN AND RANDA.......................Jim Mcbride
GLI INTOCCABILI ....Giuliano Montaldo
GLI SPECIALISTI ....Sergio Corbucci
GLISSMENTS PROGRESSIFS DU PLAISIR .... Alain Robbe-Grillet
GLITTER DOME (TF), THE......... Stuart Margolin
GLOBAL AFFAIR, A .... Jack Arnold
GLORIA ....John Cassavetes
GLORY BOY ....Edwin Sherin
GLORY GUYS, THE ....Arnold Laven
GLOWING AUTUMN ....Masaki Kobayashi
GNOME-MOBILE, THE .... Robert Stevenson
GO ASK ALICE (TF) ....John Korty
GO-BETWEEN, THE ....Joseph Losey
GO TELL IT ON THE MOUNTAIN (TF).............. Stan Lathan
GO TELL THE SPARTANS ....Ted Post
GO WEST, YOUNG GIRL (TF) ....Alan J. Levi
GO WEST, YOUNG MAN .... Henry Hathaway
GOALIE'S ANXIETY AT THE PENALTY KICK, THE ....Wim Wenders
GOD IS MY PARTNER .... William F. Claxton
GOD'S ANGRY MAN (TD)..........Werner Herzog
GOD TOLD ME TO ....Larry Cohen
GODCHILD (TF), THE ....John Badham
GODFATHER, PART II★★, THE .... Francis Ford Coppola
GODFATHER★, THE ....Francis Ford Coppola
GODS MUST BE CRAZY, THE ....Jamie Uys
GODSEND, THE ....Gabrielle Beaumont
GODSPELL .... David Greene
GOIN' ALL THE WAY .... Robert Freedman
GOIN' COCONUTS ....Howard Morris
GOIN' DOWN THE ROAD ....Donald Shebib
GOIN' SOUTH ....Jack Nicholson
GOING APE! .... Jeremy Joe Kronsberg
GOING BERSERK.........................David Steinberg
GOING HOME .... Herbert B. Leonard
GOING IN STYLE ....Martin Brest
GOING PLACES ....Bertrand Blier
GOING STEADY (LEMON POPSICLE II) .... Boaz Davidson
GOLD .... Peter Hunt
GOLD DIGGERS OF 1933 .... Mervyn Leroy
GOLD FOR THE CAESARS ...... Andre De toth
GOLD OF THE AMAZON WOMEN (TF)............ Mark L. Lester
GOLD OF THE SEVEN SAINTS .... Gordon Douglas
GOLDEN AIRLINER, THE.................. Don Sharp
GOLDEN BLADE, THE .... Nathan Juran
GOLDEN BOY .... Rouben Mamoulian
GOLDEN DISC, THE............................ Don Sharp
GOLDEN GATE MURDERS (TF), THE............. Walter Grauman
GOLDEN GATE (TF) ....Paul Wendkos
GOLDEN GLOVES .... Edward Dmytryk
GOLDEN HONEYMOON (TF), THE..... Noel Black
GOLDEN HORDE, THE............George Sherman
GOLDEN MOMENT: AN OLYMPIC LOVE STORY (TF), THE ....Richard C. Sarafian
GOLDEN NEEDLES ....Robert Clouse
GOLDEN RENDEZVOUS............. Ashley Lazarus
GOLDEN SALAMANDER, THE .....Ronald Neame
GOLDEN SEAL, THE ....Frank Zuniga
GOLDEN VOYAGE OF SINBAD, THE................ Gordon Hessler
GOLDENGIRL ....Joseph Sargent
GOLDENROD (TF) ....Harvey Hart
GOLDFINGER .... Guy Hamilton
GOLDIE AND THE BOXER GO TO HOLLYWOOD (TF) .... David Miller
GOLDIE AND THE BOXER (TF)........ David Miller
GOLDSTEIN .... Philip Kaufman
GOLIATH AND THE VAMPIRES .... Sergio Corbucci
GOLIATH AWAITS (TF) .... Kevin Connor
GONE ARE THE DAYS!..........Nicholas Webster
GONE IN 60 SECONDS .... H.B. Halicki
GONE TO EARTH ....Michael Powell
GONE WITH THE WEST ....Bernard Girard
GONG SHOW MOVIE, THE........... Chuck Barris
GOOD AGAINST EVIL (TF).......... Paul Wendkos
GOOD AND BAD AT GAMES (TF) ..... Jack Gold
GOOD AND THE BAD, THE ....Claude Lelouch
GOOD-BYE, CRUEL WORLD........... David Irving
GOOD COMPANIONS, THE.....J. Lee Thompson
GOOD DAY FOR A HANGING...... Nathan Juran
GOOD DIE YOUNG, THE ....Lewis Gilbert
GOOD GUYS AND THE BAD GUYS, THE.......... Burt Kennedy
GOOD GUYS WEAR BLACK ....Ted Post
GOOD LUCK, MISS WYCKOFF .... Marvin J. Chomsky
GOOD MORNING ... AND GOODBYE .... Russ Meyer
GOOD MORNING, MISS DOVE ..... Henry Koster
GOOD NEIGHBOR SAM ....David Swift
GOOD SOLDIER (TF), THE .... Kevin Billington
GOOD SOLDIER, THE ....Franco Brusati
GOOD, THE BAD AND THE UGLY, THE............ Sergio Leone
GOOD TIMES.........................William Friedkin
GOOD TIMES, WONDERFUL TIMES (FD).............. Lionel Rogosin
GOODBYE AND AMEN...........Damiano Damiani
GOODBYE, CHARLIE ....Vincente Minnelli
GOODBYE, COLUMBUS ....Larry Peerce
GOODBYE GEMINI.........................Alan Gibson
GOODBYE GIRL, THE........................ Herbert Ross
GOODBYE - GOOD DAY.............. Kon Ichikawa
GOODBYE, MR. CHIPS ....Herbert Ross
GOODBYE, MY FANCY ....Vincent Sherman
GOODBYE, NORMA JEAN .... Larry Buchanan
GOODBYE PEOPLE, THE .... Herb Gardner
GOODBYE PORK PIE ....Geoff Murphy
GOODBYE, RAGGEDY ANN (TF) .....Fielder Cook
GOODNIGHT MY LOVE (TF)...........Peter Hyams
GOOPY GYNE BAGHA BYNE ....Satyajit Ray
GORDON PINSENT AND THE LIFE AND TIMES OF EDWIN ALONZO BOYD (TF) ....Les Rose
GORDON'S WAR ....Ossie Davis
GORKY PARK ....Michael Apted
GORP....................................... Joseph Ruben
GOSPEL (FD)..................................David Leivick
GOSPEL ROAD, THE.....................Robert Elfstrom
GOSSIP COLUMNIST (TF), THE.......................... James Sheldon
GRACE KELLY (TF) ....Anthony Page
GRADUATE ★★, THE.......................Mike Nichols
GRADUATION DAY.........................Herb Freed
GRAMBLING'S WHITE TIGER (TF)..................... Georg Stanford Brown
GRAND CANYON MASSACRE.........Albert Band
GRAND JURY ....Chris Cain
GRAND PRIX ....John Frankenheimer
GRAND SLAM ....Giuliano Montaldo
GRAND THEFT AUTO ....Ron Howard
GRANDVIEW, U.S.A. .... Randal Kleiser
GRASS IS ALWAYS GREENER OVER THE SEPTIC TANK (TF), THE ....Robert Day
GRASS IS GREENER, THE ....Stanley Donen
GRASSHOPPER, THE .... Jerry Paris
GRAVY TRAIN ....Jack Starrett
GRAY LADY DOWN....................David Greene
GREASE .... Randal Kleiser
GREASE 2 ....Patricia Birch
GREASED LIGHTNING.............. Michael Schultz
GREASER'S PALACE ....Robert Downey
GREAT AMERICAN BEAUTY CONTEST (TF), THE ....Robert Day
GREAT AMERICAN COWBOY (FD), THE .... Kieth Merrill
GREAT AMERICAN TRAFFIC JAM (TF), THE....... James Frawley
GREAT AMERICAN TRAGEDY (TF), A .... J. Lee Thompson
GREAT BANK HOAX, THE .... Joseph Jacoby
GREAT BANK ROBBERY, THE ....Hy Averback
GREAT BIG THING, A ....Eric Till
GREAT BRAIN, THE .... Sidney Levin
GREAT CASH GIVEAWAY GETAWAY (TF), THE ....Michael O'herlihy
GREAT CATHERINE.................Gordon Flemyng
GREAT CHESS MOVIE (FD), THE..... Gilles Carle
GREAT ESCAPE, THE ....John Sturges
GREAT EXPECTATIONS (TF) ....Joseph Hardy
GREAT EXPECTATIONS★.................David Lean
GREAT GATSBY, THE ....Jack Clayton
GREAT GILDERSLEEVE, THE .....Gordon Douglas
GREAT HOUDINIS (TF), THE .... Melville Shavelson
GREAT ICE RIP-OFF (TF), THE ....Dan Curtis
GREAT IMPOSTER, THE .... Robert Mulligan
GREAT MAN'S WHISKERS (TF), THE .... Philip Leacock
GREAT MAN, THE .... Jose Ferrer
GREAT MAN VOTES, THE............ Garson Kanin
GREAT MCGONAGALL, THE .....Joseph Mcgrath
GREAT MISSOURI RAID, THE ...Gordon Douglas
GREAT MUPPET CAPER, THE ....Jim Henson
GREAT NIAGARA (TF), THE............................ William "Billy" Hale
GREAT NORTHFIELD, MINNESOTA RAID, THE... Philip Kaufman
GREAT RACE, THE ....Blake Edwards
GREAT ROCK 'N' ROLL SWINDLE, THE .... Julien Temple

GREAT SANTINI, THE .... Lewis John Carlino
GREAT SCOUT AND CATHOUSE THURSDAY,
THE ....Don Taylor
GREAT SKYCOPTER RESCUE, THE ....
Lawrence D. Foldes
GREAT SMOKEY ROADBLOCK, THE ....
John Leone
GREAT TELEPHONE ROBBERY, THE ....
Menahem Golan
GREAT TEXAS DYNAMITE CHASE, THE ....
Michael Pressman
GREAT TRAIN ROBBERY, THE ....
Michael Crichton
GREAT VICTOR HERBERT, THE ....
Andrew L. Stone
GREAT WALDO PEPPER, THE ...George Roy Hill
GREAT WALLENDAS (TF), THE ..... Larry Elikann
GREAT WALTZ, THE .... Andrew L. Stone
GREAT WAR, THE ....Mario Monicelli
GREAT WHITE HOPE, THE ....Martin Ritt
GREATEST AMERICAN HERO (TF), THE ....
Rod Holcomb
GREATEST HEROES OF THE BIBLE (MS)..........
James L. Conway
GREATEST MAN IN THE WORLD (TF), THE ......
Ralph Rosenblum
GREATEST THING THAT ALMOST HAPPENED
(TF), THE ....Gilbert Moses
GREED IN THE SUN .... Henri Verneuil
GREEK TYCOON, THE ....J. Lee Thompson
GREEN BIRD, THE .... Istvan Szabo
GREEN-EYED BLONDE, THE ....Bernard Girard
GREEN EYES (TF) .... John Erman
GREEN FIRE .... Andrew Marton
GREEN ICE .... Ernest Day
GREEN MAN, THE .... Robert Day
GREEN MANSIONS .... Mel Ferrer
GREEN ROOM, THE ....Francois Truffaut
GREENGAGE SUMMER, THE ....Lewis Gilbert
GREENWICH VILLAGE STORY ....Jack O'connell
GREETINGS .... Brian De palma
GREGORY'S GIRL .... Bill Forsyth
GREMLINS .... Joe Dante
GRENOBLE (FD)...................Claude Lelouch
GREY FOX, THE .... Phillip Borsos
GREY GARDENS (FD)..............Albert Maysles
GREYEAGLE .... Charles B. Pierce
GREYFRIARS BOBBY .... Don Chaffey
GREYSTOKE: THE LEGEND OF TARZAN, LORD
OF THE APES .... Hugh Hudson
GRIFFIN AND PHOENIX (TF) .... Daryl Duke
GRIP OF THE STRANGLER ....Robert Day
GRISSOM GANG, THE .... Robert Aldrich
GROOVE TUBE .... Ken Shapiro
GROUNDSTAR CONSPIRACY, THE ....
Lamont Johnson
GROUP MARRIAGE...............Stephanie Rothman
GROUP, THE.......................... Sidney Lumet
GUARDIE E LADRI.................Mario Monicelli
GUENDALINA .... Alberto Lattuada
GUERRE SECRETE ....Carlo Lizzani
GUESS WHAT WE LEARNED IN SCHOOL
TODAY? ....John G. Avildsen
GUESS WHO'S COMING TO DINNER ★ ....
Stanley Kramer
GUESS WHO'S SLEEPING IN MY BED? (TF).....
Theodore J. Flicker
GUEST, THE .... Clive Donner
GUIDE FOR THE MARRIED MAN, A ....
Gene Kelly
GUIDE FOR THE MARRIED WOMAN (TF), A .....
Hy Averback
GUILTY OR INNOCENT: THE SAM SHEPPARD
MURDER CASE (TF) .... Robert M. Lewis
GUINEA PIG, THE........................ Roy Boulting
GULLIVER'S TRAVELS.................. Peter Hunt
GUMBALL RALLY .... Chuck Bail
GUN AND THE PULPIT (TF), THE .. Daniel Petrie
GUN IN THE HOUSE (TF), A .... Ivan Nagy
GUN RIDERS .... Al Adamson
GUN RUNNERS, THE .... Don Siegel
GUN (TF), THE .... John Badham
GUN THE MAN DOWN ......Andrew V. Mclaglen
GUNFIGHT, A .... Lamont Johnson
GUNFIGHT AT THE O.K. CORRAL ....
John Sturges
GUNFIGHT IN ABILENE...... William "Billy" Hale
GUNMAN'S WALK .... Phil Karlson
GUNN .... Blake Edwards
GUNPOINT .... Earl Bellamy
GUNS AT BATASI .... John Guillermin
GUNS FOR SAN SEBASTIAN ..... Henri Verneuil
GUNS OF NAVARONE ★, THE ....
J. Lee Thompson

GUNS OF THE MAGNIFICENT SEVEN..............
Paul Wendkos
GUNSLINGER, THE .... Roger Corman
GUNSMOKE................................Nathan Juran
GURU, THE .... James Ivory
GUS .... Vincent Mceveety
GUSTAVE MOREAU (FD) ....Nelly Kaplan
GUY, A GAL AND A PAL, A.....Budd Boetticher
GUYANA TRAGEDY: THE STORY OF JIM
JONES (TF) ☆.................William A. Graham
GUYS AND DOLLS......... Joseph L. Mankiewicz
GWENDOLINE .... Just Jaeckin
GYPSY .... Mervyn Leroy
GYPSY AND THE GENTLEMAN, THE ....
Joseph Losey
GYPSY COLT......................... Andrew Marton
GYPSY MOTHS, THE ....John Frankenheimer

H

H.O.G. ....Donald Wrye
H.O.T.S.............Gerald Seth Sindell
HADLEY'S REBELLION .... Fred Walton
HAIL, HERO! .... David Miller
HAIR .... Milos Forman
HAIRCUT .... Andy Warhol
HALAHAKA .... Avi Nesher
HALF A HERO ....Don Weis
HALF A SIXPENCE .... George Sidney
HALF PAST MIDNIGHT .... William F. Claxton
HALF-WAY TO HEAVEN ....George Abbott
HALLELUJAH TRAIL, THE ....John Sturges
HALLOWEEN ....John Carpenter
HALLOWEEN II ....Rick Rosenthal
HALLOWEEN III: SEASON OF THE WITCH ....
Tommy Lee Wallace
HALLS OF ANGER ....Paul Bogart
HAMBONE AND HILLIE ....Roy Watts
HAMLET .... Tony Richardson
HAMLET ★ ....Laurence Olivier
HAMMER .... Bruce Clark
HAMMERHEAD .... David Miller
HAMMERSMITH IS OUT ....Peter Ustinov
HAMMETT .... Wim Wenders
HAMSIN .... Daniel Wachsmann
HAND IN HAND ....Philip Leacock
HAND ME DOWN KID (TF), THE ....
Robert Mandel
HAND OF DEATH .... Gene Nelson
HAND, THE .... Oliver Stone
HANDFUL OF LOVE, A.............. Vilgot Sjoman
HANDGUN......................Tony Garnett
HANDLE WITH CARE.........Jonathan Demme
HANDS OF CORMAC JOYCE (TF), THE ....
Fielder Cook
HANDS OF THE RIPPER................Peter Sasdy
HANDS UP!.................. Jerzy Skolimowski
HANG 'EM HIGH ....Ted Post
HANGAR 18 .... James L. Conway
HANGED MAN (TF), THE .... Don Siegel
HANGMAN'S KNOT ....Roy Huggins
HANGUP .... Henry Hathaway
HANKY PANKY .... Sidney Poitier
HANNA K. .... Costa Gavras
HANNIBAL BROOKS .... Michael Winner
HANNIE CAULDER .... Burt Kennedy
HANOVER STREET ....Peter Hyams
HANS BRINKER (TF) .... Robert Scheerer
HAPPENING OF THE VAMPIRE, THE ....
Freddie Francis
HAPPENING, THE .... Elliot Silverstein
HAPPILY EVER AFTER.......... Robert Stevenson
HAPPILY EVER AFTER (TF) ...... Robert Scheerer
HAPPINESS AHEAD .... Mervyn Leroy
HAPPINESS CAGE, THE ....Bernard Girard
HAPPINESS IS A WARM CLUE (TF) ....
Daryl Duke
HAPPY ANNIVERSARY .... David Miller
HAPPY BIRTHDAY GEMINI ....Richard Benner
HAPPY BIRTHDAY TO ME......J. Lee Thompson
HAPPY ENDING, THE .... Richard Brooks
HAPPY ENDINGS (TF) .... Noel Black
HAPPY HOOKER GOES HOLLYWOOD, THE ....
Alan Roberts
HAPPY HOOKER GOES TO WASHINGTON, THE
.......................William A. Levey
HAPPY HOOKER, THE .... Nicholas Sgarro
HAPPY IS THE BRIDE .... Roy Boulting
HAPPY MOTHER'S DAY - LOVE, GEORGE ......
Darren Mcgavin
HAPPY NEW YEAR ....Claude Lelouch

HAPPY ROAD, THE .... Gene Kelly
HAPPY (TF) .... Lee Philips
HAPPY TIME, THE .... Richard Fleischer
HARAKIRI .... Masaki Kobayashi
HARBOR LIGHTS .... Maury Dexter
HARD CONTRACT .... S. Lee Pogostin
HARD COUNTRY .... David Greene
HARD DAY FOR ARCHIE, A..........Jim Mcbride
HARD DAY'S NIGHT, A............. Richard Lester
HARD, FAST AND BEAUTIFUL .... Ida Lupino
HARD FEELINGS .... Daryl Duke
HARD MAN, THE ....George Sherman
HARD PART BEGINS, THE.............. Paul Lynch
HARD RIDE, THE .... Burt Topper
HARD TIMES .... Walter Hill
HARD TO HANDLE .... Mervyn Leroy
HARD TO HOLD .... Larry Peerce
HARD WAY, THE .... Vincent Sherman
HARDCASE (TF)..........John Llewellyn Moxey
HARDCASTLE AND MCCORMICK (TF).............
Roger Young
HARDCORE......................Paul Schrader
HARDHAT AND LEGS (TF)...............Lee Philips
HARDLY WORKING .... Jerry Lewis
HARLAN COUNTY, U.S.A. (FD) ...Barbara Kopple
HARLEM GLOBETROTTERS ON GILLIGAN'S
ISLAND (TF), THE .... Peter Baldwin
HARLEQUIN........................... Simon Wincer
HARLOT .... Andy Warhol
HARLOW...................... Gordon Douglas
HARNESS FEVER .... Don Chaffey
HAROLD AND MAUDE .... Hal Ashby
HAROLD ROBBINS' 79 PARK AVENUE (MS) .....
Paul Wendkos
HAROLD ROBBINS' THE PIRATE (TF).............
Ken Annakin
HAROLD TEEN .... Mervyn Leroy
HARPER ....Jack Smight
HARPER VALLEY PTA ....Richard C. Bennett
HARPY (TF) ....Gerald Seth Sindell
HARRAD EXPERIMENT, THE .... Ted Post
HARRAD SUMMER, THE ....Steven H. Stern
HARRIET CRAIG .... Vincent Sherman
HARRY AND SON .... Paul Newman
HARRY AND TONTO................ Paul Mazursky
HARRY AND WALTER GO TO NEW YORK ....
Mark Rydell
HARRY'S WAR .... Kieth Merrill
HARRY TRACY ....William A. Graham
HART TO HART (TF) .... Tom Mankiewicz
HARUM SCARUM .... Gene Nelson
HARVEY .... Henry Koster
HARVEY GIRLS, THE .... George Sidney
HARVEY MIDDLEMAN, FIREMAN .. Ernest Pintoff
HASTY HEART, THE .... Vincent Sherman
HAT HET BOLDOGSAG .... Andre De toth
HATFIELDS AND THE MCCOYS (TF), THE ....
Clyde Ware
HATFUL OF RAIN, A................Fred Zinnemann
HAUNTED PALACE, THE .... Roger Corman
HAUNTED STRANGLER, THE ....Robert Day
HAUNTING OF JULIA, THE....Richard Loncraine
HAUNTING PASSION (TF), THE........John Korty
HAUNTING, THE........................Robert Wise
HAUNTS ....Herb Freed
HAUNTS OF THE VERY RICH (TF) ....
Paul Wendkos
HAVE ROCKET, WILL TRAVEL ....
David Lowell Rich
HAVING A WILD WEEKEND....John Boorman
HAVING BABIES II (TF) .... Richard Michaels
HAVING BABIES III (TF) .... Jackie Cooper
HAVING BABIES (TF) ....Robert Day
HAVING IT ALL (TF) ....Edward Zwick
HAWAII .... George Roy Hill
HAWAII FIVE-O (TF) .... Paul Wendkos
HAWK, THE .... Edward Dmytryk
HAWK THE SLAYER .... Terry Marcel
HAWKINS ON MURDER (TF)............ Jud Taylor
HAWMPS .... Joe Camp
HAYWIRE (TF) .... Michael Tuchner
HE IS MY BROTHER.............. Edward Dmytryk
HE KNOWS YOUR'RE ALONE ....
Armand Mastroianni
HE LAUGHED LAST ....Blake Edwards
HE RAN ALL THE WAY ....John Berry
HE WHO RIDES A TIGER .... Charles Crichton
HEAD....................... Bob Rafelson
HEAD OVER HEELS .... Joan Micklin Silver
HEADIN' FOR BROADWAY ....Joseph Brooks
HEADLINE HUNTERS ....William Witney
HEADS OR TAILS .... Robert Enrico
HEALTH .... Robert Altman
HEAR NO EVIL (TF) .... Harry Falk

HEARSE, THE ....George Bowers
HEART BEAT ....John Byrum
HEART IN HIDING (TF) ....Peter Levin
HEART IS A LONELY HUNTER, THE .....
............................Robert Ellis Miller
HEART LIKE A WHEEL............Jonathan Kaplan
HEART OF A CHILD ....Clive Donner
HEART OF A TYRANT...............Miklos Jancso
HEART OF GLASS ....Werner Herzog
HEART, THE ....Kon Ichikawa
HEARTACHES....................Donald Shebib
HEARTBEEPS ....Allan Arkush
HEARTBREAK KID, THE ....Elaine May
HEARTBREAKER ....Frank Zuniga
HEARTLAND ....Richard Pearce
HEARTS AND MINDS (FD) ....Peter Davis
HEARTS OF THE WEST ....Howard Zieff
HEAT ....Paul Morrissey
HEAT AND DUST ....James Ivory
HEAT LIGHTING ....Mervyn Leroy
HEAT OF ANGER (TF) ....Don Taylor
HEAT WAVE ....Kenneth "Ken" Hughes
HEATWAVE ....Phillip Noyce
HEATWAVE I (TF) ....Jerry Jameson
HEAVEN CAN WAIT ★ ....Buck Henry
HEAVEN KNOWS, MR. ALLISON....John Huston
HEAVEN'S ABOVE I................John Boulting
HEAVEN'S GATE ....Michael Cimino
HEAVEN WITH A GUN ....Lee H. Katzin
HEAVENLY BODIES ....Russ Meyer
HEAVY METAL (AF) ....Gerald Potterton
HEAVY TRAFFIC (AF) ....Ralph Bakshi
HEC RAMSEY (TF) ....Daniel Petrie
HEDDA ....Trevor Nunn
HEDY ....Andy Warhol
HEDY THE SHOPLIFTER ....Andy Warhol
HEIDI ....Luigi Comencini
HEIDI'S SONG (AF) ....Robert Taylor
HEIDI (TF) ....Delbert Mann
HEIST (TF), THE ....Don Mcdougall
HELEN AND TEACHER (TF) ....Alan Gibson
HELEN OF TROY ....Robert Wise
HELEN - QUEEN OF THE NAUTCH GIRLS (FD)...
............................James Ivory
HELL AND HIGH WATER ....Samuel Fuller
HELL BENT FOR LEATHER ......George Sherman
HELL DRIVERS ....Cy Endfield
HELL IN THE PACIFIC ....John Boorman
HELL IS A CITY ....Val Guest
HELL IS FOR HEROES ....Don Siegel
HELL IS SOLD OUT ....Michael Anderson
HELL NIGHT ....Tom Desimone
HELL'S ANGELS ON WHEELS ......Richard Rush
HELL'S BELLES ....Maury Dexter
HELL'S BLOODY DEVILS ....Al Adamson
HELL'S HEADQUARTERS ......Andrew L. Stone
HELL'S ISLAND ....Phil Karlson
HELL SQUAD ....Burt Topper
HELL TO ETERNITY ....Phil Karlson
HELL UP IN HARLEM ....Larry Cohen
HELL WITH HEROES, THE ......Joseph Sargent
HELLBENDERS, THE ....Sergio Corbucci
HELLCATS OF THE NAVY ....Nathan Juran
HELLDORADO ....William Witney
HELLE ....Roger Vadim
HELLFIGHTERS............Andrew V. Mclaglen
HELLGATE ....Charles Marquis Warren
HELLINGER'S LAW (TF) ....Leo Penn
HELLIONS, THE ....Ken Annakin
HELLO, DOLLY I ....Gene Kelly
HELLO DOWN THERE ....Jack Arnold
HELLO - GOODBYE ....Jean Negulesco
HELLSTROM CHRONICLE (FD), THE .....
............................Walon Green
HELP I ....Richard Lester
HELP WANTED: MALE (TF) ....William Wiard
HELTER SKELTER ....Ralph Thomas
HEMINGWAY'S ADVENTURES OF A YOUNG
MAN ....Martin Ritt
HENDERSON MONSTER (TF), THE .....
............................Waris Hussein
HENNESSY......................Don Sharp
HENRY GELDZAHLER ....Andy Warhol
HENRY IV ....Marco Bellocchio
HENRY V......................Laurence Olivier
HENRY VIII AND HIS SIX WIVES.....
............................Waris Hussein
HER BROTHER ....Kon Ichikawa
HER FIRST ROMANCE ....Edward Dmytryk
HER LAST AFFAIRE ....Michael Powell
HERBIE GOES BANANAS ....Vincent Mceveety
HERBIE GOES TO MONTE CARLO.....
............................Vincent Mceveety
HERBIE RIDES AGAIN ....Robert Stevenson

HERCULES ....Lewis Coates
HERE ARE LADIES..................John Quested
HERE COME THE HUGGETTS ....Ken Annakin
HERE COME THE TIGERS .....
............................Sean S. Cunningham
HERE COMES THE GROOM ....Frank Capra
HERE'S YOUR LIFE ....Jan Troell
HERE WE GO ROUND THE MULBERRY BUSH...
............................Clive Donner
HERETIC: EXORCIST II, THE ....John Boorman
HERITAGE OF THE DESERT .....Henry Hathaway
HERO AIN'T NOTHIN' BUT A SANDWICH, A.....
............................Ralph Nelson
HERO AT LARGE ....Martin Davidson
HERO'S ISLAND ....Leslie Stevens
HERO, THE ....Richard Harris
HEROES ....Jeremy Paul Kagan
HEROES OF ROCK AND ROLL (TD) .....
............................Andrew Solt
HEROES OF THE SADDLE ....William Witney
HESTER STREET ....Joan Micklin Silver
HEY BOYI HEY GIRLI......David Lowell Rich
HEY GOOD•LOOKIN' (AF) ....Ralph Bakshi
HEY, I'M ALIVE I (TF) ....Lawrence J. Schiller
HI DIDDLE DIDDLE ....Andrew L. Stone
HI-JACKERS, THE ....James O'connolly
HI-JINX ....James Komack
HI, MOM I ....Brian De palma
HI, NELLIE I ....Mervyn Leroy
HI-RIDERS ....Greydon Clark
HI-YO SILVER ....William Witney
HIBERNATUS ....Edouard Molinaro
HICKEY AND BOGGS ....Robert Culp
HIDDEN FEAR ....Andre De toth
HIDDEN FORTRESS, THE .....Akira Kurosawa
HIDDEN ROOM, THE.............Edward Dmytryk
HIDE AND SEEK ....Cy Endfield
HIDE IN PLAIN SIGHT ....James Caan
HIDEAWAYS, THE ....Fielder Cook
HIDING PLACE, THE ....James F. Collier
HIGH AND DRY ....Alexander Mackendrick
HIGH AND LOW ....Akira Kurosawa
HIGH ANXIETY ....Mel Brooks
HIGH BRIGHT SUN, THE ....Ralph Thomas
HIGH COMMISSIONER, THE ....Ralph Thomas
HIGH COST OF LOVING, THE........Jose Ferrer
HIGH COUNTRY, THE ....Harvey Hart
HIGH HEELS ....Claude Chabrol
HIGH ICE ....Eugene S. Jones
HIGH INFIDELITY ....Luciano Salce
HIGH MIDNIGHT (TF) ....Daniel Haller
HIGH NOON - PART II: THE RETURN OF WILL
KANE (TF)..................Jerry Jameson
HIGH NOON ★ ....Fred Zinnemann
HIGH PLAINS DRIFTER ....Clint Eastwood
HIGH POWERED RIFLE, THE .....Maury Dexter
HIGH PRESSURE ....Mervyn Leroy
HIGH RISK ....Stewart Raffill
HIGH RISK (TF) ....Sam O'steen
HIGH ROAD TO CHINA ....Brian G. Hutton
HIGH ROLLING ....Igor Auzins
HIGH SCHOOL (FD) ....Frederick Wiseman
HIGH SCHOOL HERO ....Arthur Dreifuss
HIGH SCHOOL U.S.A. (TF).........Rod Amateau
HIGH TIDE AT NOON ....Philip Leacock
HIGH TIME ....Blake Edwards
HIGH TREASON ....Roy Boulting
HIGH, WIDE, AND HANDSOME.....
............................Rouben Mamoulian
HIGH WIND IN JAMAICA, A.....
............................Alexander Mackendrick
HIGHLY DANGEROUS ....Roy Ward Baker
HIGHWAY 301 ....Andrew L. Stone
HIGHWAY DRAGNET ....Nathan Juran
HILL, THE ....Sidney Lumet
HILLS HAVE EYES, THE ....Wes Craven
HILLS RUN RED, THE ....Carlo Lizzani
HINDENBURG, THE ....Robert Wise
HINOTORI ....Kon Ichikawa
HIRED HAND, THE ....Peter Fonda
HIRELING, THE ....Alan Bridges
HIROSHIMA, MON AMOUR ....Alain Resnais
HIS LAND ....James F. Collier
HIS LORDSHIP ....Michael Powell
HISTOIRES EXTRAORDINAIRES .....
............................Federico Fellini
HISTORY OF POST-WAR JAPAN AS TOLD BY
A BAR HOSTESS (FD) .....Shohei Imamura
HISTORY OF THE WORLD, PART I... Mel Brooks
HIT I ....Sidney J. Furie
HIT AND RUN ....Charles Braverman
HIT LADY (TF) ....Tracy Keenan Wynn
HIT MAN ....George Armitage
HITCH-HIKER, THE ....Ida Lupino

HITCHHIKE I (TF).................Gordon Hessler
HITLER: A FILM FROM GERMANY ....Hans-
jurgen Syberberg
HITLER CONNAIS PAS..............Bertrand Blier
HITLER'S CHILDREN ....Edward Dmytryk
HITLER'S SON ....Rod Amateau
HOI ....Robert Enrico
HOA-BINH ....Raoul Coutard
HOBBIT (ATF), THE ....Arthur Rankin, Jr.
HOBSON'S CHOICE ....David Lean
HOFFMAN ....Alvin Rakoff
HOG WILD ....Les Rose
HOLE IN THE HEAD, A ....Frank Capra
HOLE, THE ....Kon Ichikawa
HOLIDAY CAMP ....Ken Annakin
HOLIDAY IN MEXICO ....George Sidney
HOLIDAY IN SPAIN ....Jack Cardiff
HOLLOW IMAGE (TF)......... Marvin J. Chomsky
HOLLOW, THE.........George T. Nierenberg
HOLLYWOOD BOULEVARD ....Allan Arkush
HOLLYWOOD KNIGHTS, THE ....Floyd Mutrux
HOLLYWOOD ON TRIAL (FD).....
............................David Helpern, Jr.
HOLOCAUST (MS)☆☆ .... Marvin J. Chomsky
HOLY MOUNTAIN, THE.. Alexandro Jodorowsky
HOMBRE ....Martin Ritt
HOME BEFORE DARK ....Mervyn Leroy
HOME BEFORE MIDNIGHT ....Peter Walker
HOME FOR THE HOLIDAYS (TF).....
............................John Llewellyn Moxey
HOME FROM THE HILL..........Vincente Minnelli
HOME IN INDIANA ....Henry Hathaway
HOME IS THE HERO.............Fielder Cook
HOME MOVIES ....Brian De palma
HOME OF OUR OWN (TF), A..........Robert Day
HOME TO STAY (TF) ....Delbert Mann
HOMEBODIES ....Larry Yust
HOMECOMING ....Mervyn Leroy
HOMECOMING (TF)☆, THE ....Fielder Cook
HOMECOMING, THE ....Peter Hall
HOMER ....John Trent
HOMETOWN, U.S.A. .... Max Baer, Jr.
HOMEWORK ....James Beshears
HONDO AND THE APACHES ....Lee H. Katzin
HONEY POT, THE..........Joseph L. Mankiewicz
HONEYBABY, HONEYBABY.......Michael Schultz
HONEYBOY (TF) ....John Berry
HONEYCOMB ....Carlos Saura
HONEYMOON ....Michael Powell
HONEYMOON WITH A STRANGER (TF).....
............................John Peyser
HONEYSUCKLE ROSE............Jerry Schatzberg
HONKY.................William A. Graham
HONKY TONK FREEWAY........John Schlesinger
HONKY TONK (TF)...............Don Taylor
HONKYTONK MAN ....Clint Eastwood
HONOR GUARD, THE ....Burt Kennedy
HONOR THY FATHER (TF) ....Paul Wendkos
HOODLUM PRIEST, THE ....Irvin Kershner
HOODWINK ....Claude Whatham
HOOPER ....Hal Needham
HOOTENANNY HOOT .... Gene Nelson
HOPE ....Yilmaz Guney
HOPELESS ONES, THE ....Yilmaz Guney
HOPSCOTCH ....Ronald Neame
HORIZONS WEST...........Budd Boetticher
HORNETS' NEST ....Phil Karlson
HORROR AT 37,000 FEET (TF), THE .....
............................David Lowell Rich
HORROR HOTEL.........John Llewellyn Moxey
HORROR OF FRANKENSTEIN, THE .....
............................Jimmy Sangster
HORROR OF THE BLOOD MONSTERS .....
............................Al Adamson
HORROR ON SNAPE ISLAND .....
............................James O'connolly
HORSE'S MOUTH, THE ....Ronald Neame
HORSE WITHOUT A HEAD, THE ....Don Chaffey
HORSEMEN, THE..............John Frankenheimer
HOSPITAL (FD)................Frederick Wiseman
HOSPITAL, THE................Arthur Hiller
HOSTAGE HEART (TF), THE ...Bernard Mceveety
HOSTAGE TOWER (TF), THE ...Claudio Guzman
HOT BUBBLEGUM (LEMON POPSICLE III) .....
............................Boaz Davidson
HOT CAR GIRL ....Bernard L. Kowalski
HOT DOG ... THE MOVIE...........Peter Markle
HOT ENOUGH FOR JUNE ....Ralph Thomas
HOT LEAD AND COLD FEET ....Robert Butler
HOT MARSHLAND, THE .... Kon Ichikawa
HOT MILLIONS ....Eric Till
HOT POTATO ....Oscar Williams
HOT ROCK, THE ....Peter Yates
HOT ROD GIRL ....Leslie H. Martinson

I

348

LA LOI ... Jules Dassin
LA LUPA ... Alberto Lattuada
LA MACCHINA CINEMA ... Marco Bellocchio
LA MADRIGUERA ... Carlos Saura
LA MAIN A COUPER ... Etienne Perrier
LA MAIN CHAUDE ... Gerard Oury
LA MAISON SOUS LES ARBRES ... René Clement
LA MAITRE D'ECOLE ... Claude Berri
LA MANDARINE ... Edouard Molinaro
LA MANDRAGOLA ... Alberto Lattuada
LA MARCIA SU ROMA ... Dino Risi
LA MAZZETTA ... Sergio Corbucci
LA MIA SIGNORINA ... Luigi Comencini
LA MOGLIE PIU BELLA ... Damiano Damiani
LA MORT D'UN BUCHERON ... Gilles Carle
LA MORT DE BELLE ... Edouard Molinaro
LA MURAGLIA CINESE (FD) ... Carlo Lizzani
LA NONNA SABELLA ... Dino Risi
LA NOSTRA GUERRA ... Alberto Lattuada
LA NOTTE ... Michelangelo Antonioni
LA NOTTE DI SAN LORENZO ... Paolo Taviani
LA NUIT AMERICAINE ★ ... Francois Truffaut
LA NUIT DE VARENNES ... Ettore Scola
LA PACIFISTA ... Miklos Jancso
LA PECCATRICE DELL'ISOLA ... Sergio Corbucci
LA PECORA NERA ... Luciano Salce
LA PELLE ... Liliana Cavani
LA PETITE FILLE EN VELOURS BLEU ... Alan Bridges
LA PILLOLE DE ERCOLE ... Luciano Salce
LA PIOVRA ... Damiano Damiani
LA PITIE DANGEREUSE (TF) .. Edouard Molinaro
LA PIU BELLA SERATA DELLA MIA VITA ... Ettore Scola
LA POINTE COURTE ... Agnes Varda
LA PORTIERA NUDA ... Lewis Coates
LA PRESIDENTESSA ... Luciano Salce
LA PROVINCIALE ... Claude Goretta
LA RAGAZZA DEL VAGONE LETTO ... Ferdinando Baldi
LA RAISON DU PLUS FOU (FD) ... Francois Reichenbach
LA RETOUR D'AFRIQUE ... Alain Tanner
LA RIMPATRIATA ... Damiano Damiani
LA RONDE ... Roger Vadim
LA ROUTE AU SOLEIL ... Philippe De broca
LA ROUTE DE CORINTHE ... Claude Chabrol
LA ROUTE DE ST. TROPEZ ... Michael Sarne
LA RUPTURE ... Claude Chabrol
LA SALAMANDRE ... Alain Tanner
LA SELVAGGIA (GEOMETRA PRINETTI SEL VAGGIAMENTEOSVALDO) ... Ferdinando Baldi
LA SFIDA ... Francesco Rosi
LA SIGNORA SENZA CAMELIE ... Michelangelo Antonioni
LA SPIAGGIA ... Alberto Lattuada
LA STANZA DEL VESCOVO ... Dino Risi
LA STEPPA ... Alberto Lattuada
LA STRADA ... Federico Fellini
LA STREGA IN AMORE ... Damiano Damiani
LA TÊTE DE NORMANDE ST. ... Gilles Carle
LA TABLE AUX CREVES ... Henri Verneuil
LA TECNICA E IL RITO ... Miklos Jancso
LA TERRAZZA ... Ettore Scola
LA TRATTA DELLA BIANCHE ... Luigi Comencini
LA TRAVIATA ... Franco Zeffirelli
LA VACHE ET LE PRISONNIER ... Henri Verneuil
LA VALIGIA DEI SOGNI ... Luigi Comencini
LA VICTOIRE EN CHANTANT ... Jean-jacques Annaud
LA VIE CONTINUE ... Moshe Mizrahi
LA VIE DEVANT SOI ... Moshe Mizrahi
LA VIE EST UN ROMAN ... Alain Resnais
LA VIE HEUREUSE DE LÉOPOLD Z ... Gilles Carle
LA VITA AGRA ... Carlo Lizzani
LA VITA CONTINUA (MS) ... Dino Risi
LA VOGLIA MATTA ... Luciano Salce
LACEMAKER, THE ... Claude Goretta
LACOMBE LUCIEN ... Louis Malle
LACY AND THE MISSISSIPPI QUEEN (TF) ... Robert Butler
LAD: A DOG ... Aram Avakian
LADIES AND GENTLEMEN ... THE FABULOUS STAINS ... Lou Adler
LADIES' MAN, THE ... Jerry Lewis
LADIES OF LEISURE ... Frank Capra
LADIES OF THE CHORUS, THE ... Phil Karlson
LADIES OF THE PARK, THE ... Robert Bresson
LADY AND THE MONSTER, THE ... George Sherman
LADY CAROLINE LAMB ... Robert Bolt
LADY CHATTERLEY'S LOVER ... Just Jaeckin
LADY COCOA ... Matt Cimber
LADY FOR A DAY★ ... Frank Capra
LADY FROM SHANGHAI, THE ... Orson Welles
LADY FROM TEXAS, THE ... Joseph Pevney
LADY GAMBLES, THE ... Michael Gordon
LADY IN A CAGE ... Walter Grauman
LADY IN CEMENT ... Gordon Douglas
LADY IN RED, THE ... Lewis Teague
LADY L ... Peter Ustinov
LADY LIBERTY ... Mario Monicelli
LADY OF THE HOUSE (TF) ... Ralph Nelson
LADY OSCAR ... Jacques Demy
LADY SINGS THE BLUES ... Sidney J. Furie
LADY TAKES A FLYER, THE ... Jack Arnold
LADY VANISHES, THE ... Anthony Page
LADYBUG, LADYBUG ... Frank Perry
LADYHAWKE ... Richard Donner
LADYKILLERS, THE ... Alexander Mackendrick
LANA TURNER ... Andy Warhol
LANCELOT AND GUINEVERE ... Cornel Wilde
LANCELOT OF THE LAKE ... Robert Bresson
LAND OF DESIRE, THE ... Ingmar Bergman
LAND OF FURY ... Ken Annakin
LAND OF SILENCE AND DARKNESS ... Werner Herzog
LAND RAIDERS ... Nathan Juran
LAND THAT TIME FORGOT, THE ... Kevin Connor
LAND UNKNOWN, THE ... Virgil W. Vogel
LANDFALL ... Ken Annakin
LANDLORD, THE ... Hal Ashby
LANDRU ... Claude Chabrol
LANDSCAPE AFTER BATTLE ... Andrzej Wajda
LANIGAN'S RABBI (TF) ... Lou Antonio
LARCENY ... George Sherman
LARRY (TF) ... William A. Graham
LAS VEGAS LADY ... Noel Nosseck
LAS VEGAS STORY, THE ... Robert Stevenson
LASERBLAST ... Michael Rae
LASSITER ... Roger Young
LAST ADVENTURE, THE ... Robert Enrico
LAST AMERICAN HERO, THE ... Lamont Johnson
LAST AMERICAN VIRGIN, THE ... Boaz Davidson
LAST ANGRY MAN (TF), THE ... Jerrold Freedman
LAST ANGRY MAN, THE ... Daniel Mann
LAST BLITZKRIEG, THE ... Arthur Dreifuss
LAST BRIDE OF SALEM (TF), THE ... Tom Donovan
LAST CHASE, THE ... Martyn Burke
LAST CHILD (TF), THE ... John Llewellyn Moxey
LAST CONVERTIBLE (MS), THE ... Gus Trikonis
LAST CRY FOR HELP (TF), A ... Hal Sitowitz
LAST DAY (TF), THE ... Vincent Mceveety
LAST DAYS OF MAN ON EARTH, THE ... Robert Fuest
LAST DAYS OF POMPEII (MS), THE ... Peter Hunt
LAST DETAIL, THE ... Hal Ashby
LAST DINOSAUR (TF), THE ... Alex Grasshoff
LAST EMBRACE ... Jonathan Demme
LAST ESCAPE, THE ... Walter Grauman
LAST FIGHT, THE ... Fred Williamson
LAST FLIGHT OF NOAH'S ARK, THE ... Charles Jarrott
LAST FOUR DAYS, THE ... Carlo Lizzani
LAST GIRAFFE (TF), THE ... Jack Couffer
LAST GRENADE, THE ... Gordon Flemyng
LAST HARD MEN, THE ... Andrew V. Mclaglen
LAST HOURS BEFORE MORNING (TF) ... Joseph Hardy
LAST HOUSE ON THE LEFT ... Wes Craven
LAST HUNT, THE ... Richard Brooks
LAST HURRAH (TF), THE ... Vincent Sherman
LAST MARRIED COUPLE IN AMERICA, THE ... Gilbert Cates
LAST METRO, THE ... Francois Truffaut
LAST MILE, THE ... Howard W. Koch
LAST MOVIE, THE ... Dennis Hopper
LAST MUSKETEER, THE ... William Witney
LAST NINJA (TF), THE ... William A. Graham
LAST OF SHEILA, THE ... Herbert Ross
LAST OF THE COMANCHEROS ... Al Adamson
LAST OF THE COMANCHES ... Andre De toth
LAST OF THE COWBOYS, THE ... John Leone
LAST OF THE FAST GUNS, THE ... George Sherman
LAST OF THE GOOD GUYS (TF) ... Theodore J. Flicker
LAST OF THE MOBILE HOT-SHOTS ... Sidney Lumet
LAST OF THE MOHICANS (TF), THE ... James L. Conway
LAST OF THE RED HOT LOVERS ... Gene Saks
LAST OF THE REDMEN ... George Sherman
LAST OUTLAW (MS), THE ... George Miller
LAST PICTURE SHOW ★, THE ... Peter Bogdanovich
LAST PLANE OUT ... David Nelson
LAST RIDE OF THE DALTON GANG (TF), THE ... Dan Curtis
LAST ROMANTIC LOVER, THE ... Just Jaeckin
LAST ROUND-UP, THE ... Henry Hathaway
LAST RUN, THE ... Richard Fleischer
LAST SAFARI, THE ... Henry Hathaway
LAST SHOT YOU HEAR, THE ... Gordon Hessler
LAST SONG (TF), THE ... Alan J. Levi
LAST STARFIGHTER, THE ... Nick Castle, Jr.
LAST SUMMER ... Frank Perry
LAST SUNSET, THE ... Robert Aldrich
LAST SURVIVORS (TF), THE ... Lee H. Katzin
LAST TANGO IN PARIS ★ .. Bernardo Bertolucci
LAST TENANT (TF), THE ... Jud Taylor
LAST TIME I SAW PARIS, THE ... Richard Brooks
LAST TRAIN FROM GUN HILL ... John Sturges
LAST TYCOON, THE ... Elia Kazan
LAST UNICORN (AF), THE ... Arthur Rankin, Jr.
LAST VALLEY, THE ... James Clavell
LAST VOYAGE, THE ... Andrew L. Stone
LAST WALTZ, THE ... Martin Scorsese
LAST WAVE, THE ... Peter Weir
LAST WINTER, THE ... Riki Shelach
LAST WOMAN ON EARTH, THE ... Roger Corman
LAST WOMAN, THE ... Marco Ferreri
LAST WORD, THE ... Roy Boulting
LAST YEAR AT MARIENBAD ... Alain Resnais
LATE GEORGE APLEY, THE ... Joseph L. Mankiewicz
LATE SHOW, THE ... Robert Benton
LATHE OF HEAVEN (TF), THE ... David R. Loxton
LATIN LOVERS ... Mervyn Leroy
LAUGHING POLICEMAN, THE ... Stuart Rosenberg
LAUGHTER IN THE DARK ... Tony Richardson
LAURA ... David Hamilton
LAURA ★ ... Otto Preminger
LAUTARY ... Emil Loteanu
LAVENDER HILL MOB, THE ... Charles Crichton
LAW AND DISORDER ... Charles Crichton
LAW AND JAKE WADE, THE ... John Sturges
LAW AND ORDER ... Nathan Juran
LAW AND ORDER (FD) ... Frederick Wiseman
LAW AND ORDER (TF) ... Marvin J. Chomsky
LAW OF THE LAND (TF) ... Virgil W. Vogel
LAW OF THE LAWLESS ... William F. Claxton
LAW (TF), THE ... John Badham
LAWLESS, THE ... Joseph Losey
LAWMAN ... Michael Winner
LAWRENCE OF ARABIA★★ ... David Lean
LAWYER, THE ... Sidney J. Furie
LAZARUS SYNDROME (TF), THE ... Jerry Thorpe
LAZYBONES ... Michael Powell
LE AMICHE ... Michelangelo Antonioni
LE BAISERS ... Claude Berri
LE BAL ... Ettore Scola
LE BEAU MARIAGE ... Eric Rohmer
LE BEAU SERGE ... Claude Chabrol
LE BONHEUR ... Agnes Varda
LE BOUCHER ... Claude Chabrol
LE BOULANGER DE VALORGUE ... Henri Verneuil
LE CAVALEUR ... Philippe De broca
LE CHÂTEAU DE VERRE ... René Clement
LE CHANCE ET L'AMOUR ... Claude Berri
LE CHEVAL D'ORGEUIL ... Claude Chabrol
LE CINEMA DU PAPA ... Claude Berri
LE CINQUE GIORNATE ... Dario Argento
LE COMPAGNON INDESIRABLE ... Robert Enrico
LE COPPIE ... Mario Monicelli
LE CORPS DE MON ENNEMI ... Henri Verneuil
LE COUP DU PARAPLUIE ... Gerard Oury
LE COUPLE TEMOIN ... William Klein
LE DEPART ... Jerzy Skolimowski
LE FARO DA PADRE ... Alberto Lattuada
LE FATE ... Luciano Salce
LE FIANCEE DU PIRATE ... Nelly Kaplan
LE FOU ... Claude Goretta
LE GAI SAVOIR ... Jean-Luc Godard
LE GANG ... Jacques Deray
LE GANG DES OTAGES ... Edouard Molinaro
LE GIGOLO ... Jacques Deray
LE GUERRIERE DEL SNO NUDA ... Terence Young
LE INFIDELI ... Mario Monicelli
LE ITALIANE E L'AMORE ... Marco Ferreri
LE JEU AVEC LE FEU ... Alain Robbe-Grillet

LITTLE SHEPHERD OF KINGDOM COME, THE ... Andrew V. Mclaglen
LITTLE SHOP OF HORRORS, THE ... Roger Corman
LITTLE SISTER (TF) ... Jan Egleson
LITTLE WOMEN ... Mervyn Leroy
LITTLE WOMEN (TF) ... David Lowell Rich
LITTLEST HORSE THIEVES, THE ... Charles Jarrott
LIVE A LITTLE, STEAL A LOT ... Marvin J. Chomsky
LIVE AGAIN, DIE AGAIN (TF) ... Richard A. Colla
LIVE AND LET DIE ... Guy Hamilton
LIVE FOR LIFE ... Claude Lelouch
LIVE WIRES ... Phil Karlson
LIVELY SET, THE ... Jack Arnold
LIVES OF A BENGAL LANCER★, THE ... Henry Hathaway
LIVES OF JENNY DOLAN (TF), THE ... Jerry Jameson
LIVING FREE ... Jack Couffer
LIVING PROOF: THE HANK WILLIAMS, JR. STORY (TF) ... Dick Lowry
LIZA ... Marco Ferreri
LLANTO POR UN BANDITO ... Carlos Saura
LO SCOPONE SCIENTIFICO ... Luigi Comencini
LO SVITATO ... Carlo Lizzani
LOCAL BOY MAKES GOOD ... Mervyn Leroy
LOCAL HERO ... Bill Forsyth
LOCH NESS HORROR, THE ... Larry Buchanan
LOCK, STOCK AND BARREL (TF) .. Jerry Thorpe
LOCK UP YOUR DAUGHTERS ... Peter Coe
LOCUSTS (TF) ... Richard T. Heffron
LOG OF THE BLACK PEARL (TF), THE ... Andrew V. Mclaglen
LOGAN'S RUN ... Michael Anderson
LOIS GIBBS AND THE LOVE CANAL (TF) ... Glenn Jordan
LOLA ... Jacques Demy
LOLITA ... Stanley Kubrick
LOLLIPOP COVER, THE ... Everett Chambers
LOLLY-MADONNA XXX ... Richard C. Sarafian
LONDON BLACKOUT MURDERS ... George Sherman
LONDON ROCK & ROLL SHOW (FD), THE ... Peter Clifton
LONE HAND, THE ... George Sherman
LONE STAR ... Vincent Sherman
LONE STAR RAIDERS ... George Sherman
LONE WOLF MCQUADE ... Steve Carver
LONELIEST RUNNER (TF), THE ... Michael Landon
LONELINESS OF THE LONG DISTANCE RUNNER, THE ... Tony Richardson
LONELY ARE THE BRAVE ... David Miller
LONELY GUY, THE ... Arthur Hiller
LONELY HEARTS ... Paul Cox
LONELY LADY, THE ... Peter Sasdy
LONELY PROFESSION (TF), THE ... Douglas Heyes
LONELY WIFE, THE ... Satyajit Ray
LONERS, THE ... Sutton Roley
LONESOME COWBOYS ... Andy Warhol
LONG AGO TOMORROW ... Bryan Forbes
LONG DAY'S JOURNEY INTO NIGHT ... Sidney Lumet
LONG DAYS OF SUMMER (TF), THE ... Dan Curtis
LONG DUEL, THE ... Ken Annakin
LONG GOOD FRIDAY, THE ... John Mackenzie
LONG GOODBYE, THE ... Robert Altman
LONG HAUL, THE ... Kenneth "Ken" Hughes
LONG HOT SUMMER, THE ... Martin Ritt
LONG JOURNEY BACK (TF) ... Melvin Damski
LONG, LONG TRAILER, THE ... Vincente Minnelli
LONG PANTS ... Frank Capra
LONG RIDERS, THE ... Walter Hill
LONG ROPE, THE ... William Witney
LONG SHIPS, THE ... Jack Cardiff
LONG SUMMER OF GEORGE ADAMS (TF), THE ... Stuart Margolin
LONG WAY HOME (TF), A ... Robert Markowitz
LONGEST 100 MILES (TF), THE ... Don Weis
LONGEST DAY, THE ... Andrew Marton
LONGEST NIGHT (TF), THE ... Jack Smight
LONGEST YARD, THE ... Robert Aldrich
LONGSHOT ... E.W. Swackhamer
LONGSTREET (TF) ... Joseph Sargent
LOOK BACK IN ANGER ... Tony Richardson
LOOK DOWN AND DIE ... Steve Carver
LOOK WHAT'S HAPPENED TO ROSEMARY'S BABY (TF) ... Sam O'steen
LOOKER ... Michael Crichton
LOOKIN' TO GET OUT ... Hal Ashby
LOOKING FOR JESUS ... Luigi Comencini
LOOKING FOR LOVE ... Don Weis
LOOKING FOR MR. GOODBAR ... Richard Brooks
LOOKING GLASS WAR, THE ... Frank Pierson
LOOKING UP ... Linda Yellen
LOOKS AND SMILES ... Kenneth Loach
LOOPHOLE ... John Quested
LOOPS ... Shirley Clarke
LOOSE CONNECTIONS ... Richard Eyre
LOOT ... Silvio Narizzano
LORD JIM ... Richard Brooks
LORD LOVE A DUCK ... George Axelrod
LORD OF THE FLIES ... Peter Brook
LORD OF THE RINGS (AF), THE ... Ralph Bakshi
LORDS OF DISCIPLINE, THE ... Franc Roddam
LORDS OF FLATBUSH, THE ... Martin Davidson
LORNA ... Russ Meyer
LORNA DOONE ... Phil Karlson
LOS CHICOS ... Marco Ferreri
LOS GOLFOS ... Carlos Saura
LOSER TAKES ALL ... Ken Annakin
LOSERS, THE ... Jack Starrett
LOSIN' IT ... Curtis Hanson
LOSS OF INNOCENCE ... Lewis Gilbert
LOST ... Guy Green
LOST AND FOUND ... Melvin Frank
LOST CONTINENT, THE ... Michael Carreras
LOST EMPIRE, THE ... Jim Wynorski
LOST HONOR OF KATHARINA BLUM, THE ... Volker Schlondorff
LOST HONOR OF KATHRYN BECK (TF), THE ... Simon Langton
LOST HORIZON ... Charles Jarrott
LOST IN THE DESERT ... Jamie Uys
LOST IN THE STARS ... Daniel Mann
LOST WEEKEND ★★, THE ... Billy Wilder
LOST WORLD, THE ... Irwin Allen
LOTNA ... Andrzej Wajda
LOTTE IN ITALIA (FD) ... Jean-Luc Godard
LOTTERY! (TF) ... Lee Philips
LOUIS ARMSTRONG - CHICAGO STYLE (TF) ... Lee Philips
LOUISIANA ... Phil Karlson
LOUISIANA (CMS) ... Philippe De broca
LOVE ... Annette Cohen
LOVE 65 ... Bo Widerberg
LOVE AFFAIR; OR THE CASE OF THE MISSING SWITCHBOARD OPERATOR ... Dusan Makavejev
LOVE AFFAIR: THE ELEANOR AND LOU GEHRIG STORY (TF), A ... Fielder Cook
LOVE AND ANARCHY ... Lina Wertmuller
LOVE AND BULLETS ... Stuart Rosenberg
LOVE AND DEATH ... Woody Allen
LOVE AND LARCENY ... Dino Risi
LOVE AND MONEY ... James Toback
LOVE AND PAIN AND THE WHOLE DAMNED THING ... Alan J. Pakula
LOVE AT FIRST BITE ... Stan Dragoti
LOVE AT FIRST SIGHT ... Rex Bromfield
LOVE AT TWENTY ... Andrzej Wajda
LOVE BAN, THE ... Ralph Thomas
LOVE BOAT II (TF), THE ... Hy Averback
LOVE BOAT (TF), THE ... Alan Myerson
LOVE BUG, THE ... Robert Stevenson
LOVE CHILD ... Larry Peerce
LOVE, DEATH ... Theodore Gershuny
LOVE FILM ... Istvan Szabo
LOVE FOR RENT (TF) ... David Miller
LOVE HAPPY ... David Miller
LOVE HAS MANY FACES ... Alexander Singer
LOVE, HATE, LOVE (TF) ... George Mccowan
LOVE IN A GOLDFISH BOWL ... Jack Sher
LOVE IN THE AFTERNOON ... Billy Wilder
LOVE IN THE CITY ... Alberto Lattuada
LOVE-INS, THE ... Arthur Dreifuss
LOVE IS A BALL ... David Swift
LOVE IS A FUNNY THING ... Claude Lelouch
LOVE IS A SPLENDID ILLUSION ... Tom Clegg
LOVE IS BETTER THAN NONE ... Stanley Donen
LOVE IS FOREVER (TF) ... Hall Bartlett
LOVE IS NOT ENOUGH (TF) ... Ivan Dixon
LOVE LETTERS ... Amy Jones
LOVE MACHINE, THE ... Jack Haley, Jr.
LOVE ME TONIGHT ... Rouben Mamoulian
LOVE ON A PILLOW ... Roger Vadim
LOVE ON THE RUN ... Francois Truffaut
LOVE'S DARK RIDE (TF) ... Delbert Mann
LOVE'S SAVAGE FURY (TF) ... Joseph Hardy
LOVE STORY (MS) ... Henri Safran
LOVE STORY ★ ... Arthur Hiller
LOVE STREAMS ... John Cassavetes
LOVE TAPES (TF), THE ... Allen Reisner
LOVE TEST, THE ... Michael Powell
LOVE WAR (TF), THE ... George Mccowan
LOVE WITH THE PROPER STRANGER ... Robert Mulligan
LOVED ONE, THE ... Tony Richardson
LOVELAND ... Richard Franklin
LOVELY TO LOOK AT ... Mervyn Leroy
LOVELY WAY TO DIE, A ... David Lowell Rich
LOVER, COME BACK ... Delbert Mann
LOVER LOTTERY, THE ... Charles Crichton
LOVER'S ROMANCE, A ... Andrei Konchalovsky
LOVER, THE ... Kon Ichikawa
LOVERS AND LIARS ... Mario Monicelli
LOVERS AND OTHER STRANGERS .. Cy Howard
LOVERS, HAPPY LOVERS! ... René Clement
LOVERS!, THE ... Herbert Wise
LOVES OF A BLONDE ... Milos Forman
LOVES OF ISADORA, THE ... Karel Reisz
LOVES OF ONDINE, THE ... Andy Warhol
LOVESCENE ... Bud Townsend
LOVESICK ... Marshall Brickman
LOVEY: A CIRCLE OF CHILDREN, PART II (TF) ... Jud Taylor
LOVIN' MOLLY ... Sidney Lumet
LOVING ... Irvin Kershner
LOVING COUPLES ... Jack Smight
LOVING YOU ... Hal Kanter
LOWER DEPTHS, THE ... Akira Kurosawa
LUCAN (TF) ... David Greene
LUCAS TANNER (TF) ... Richard Donner
LUCI DEL PO ... Alberto Lattuada
LUCK OF GINGER COFFEY, THE ... Irvin Kershner
LUCK OF THE IRISH, THE ... Henry Koster
LUCKY JIM ... John Boulting
LUCKY LADY ... Stanley Donen
LUCKY LUCIANO ... Francesco Rosi
LUCKY ME ... Jack Donohue
LUCKY STAR, THE ... Max Fischer
LUCY GALLANT ... Robert Parrish
LUDWIG: REQUIEM FOR A VIRGIN KING ... Hans-Jurgen Syberberg
LUI, LEI, MASCHIO E FEMMINA ... Sergio Corbucci
LUMIERE ... Jeanne Moreau
LUNA ... Bernardo Bertolucci
LUNA DE MIEL ... Michael Powell
LUNCH HOUR ... James Hill
LUNCH WAGON ... Ernest Pintoff
LUNCH WAGON GIRLS ... Ernest Pintoff
LUPE ... Andy Warhol
LUPO! ... Menahem Golan
LUPO GOES TO NEW YORK ... Boaz Davidson
LURE OF THE SWAMP ... Hubert Cornfield
LURE OF THE WILDERNESS ... Jean Negulesco
LUST FOR A VAMPIRE ... Jimmy Sangster
LUST FOR LIFE ... Vincente Minnelli
LUTHER ... Guy Green
LUV ... Clive Donner
LYDIA BAILEY ... Jean Negulesco
LYONS IN PARIS, THE ... Val Guest

M

M ... Joseph Losey
M.A.D.D.: MOTHERS AGAINST DRUNK DRIVERS (TF) ... William A. Graham
M*A*S*H ★ ... Robert Altman
M STATION: HAWAII (TF) ... Jack Lord
MACAHANS (TF), THE ... Bernard Mceveety
MACARTHUR ... Joseph Sargent
MACBETH ... George Schaefer
MACHINE GUN KELLY ... Roger Corman
MACHINE GUN MCCAIN ... Giuliano Montaldo
MACHO CALLAHAN ... Bernard L. Kowalski
MACISTE CONTRO IL VAMPIRO ... Sergio Corbucci
MACK, THE ... Michael Campus
MACKENNA'S GOLD ... J. Lee Thompson
MACKENZIE BREAK, THE ... Lamont Johnson
MACKINTOSH AND T.J. ... Marvin J. Chomsky
MACKINTOSH MAN, THE ... John Huston
MACON COUNTY LINE ... Richard Compton
MAD ABOUT MEN ... Ralph Thomas
MAD ADVENTURES OF 'RABBI' JACOB, THE ... Gerard Oury
MAD BOMBER, THE ... Bert I. Gordon
MAD BULL ... Walter Doniger
MAD DOG ... Philippe Mora
MAD DOG MORGAN ... Philippe Mora
MAD MAGAZINE PRESENTS UP THE ACADEMY ... Robert Downey

MAD MAX ..... George Miller
MAD MAX II ..... George Miller
MAD MONSTER PARTY (AF) ..... Jules Bass
MAD ROOM ..... Bernard Girard
MADAME BOVARY ..... Vincente Minnelli
MADAME CLAUDE ..... Just Jaeckin
MADAME CURIE ..... Mervyn Leroy
MADAME ROSA ..... Moshe Mizrahi
MADAME SIN (TF) ..... David Greene
MADAME WANG'S ..... Paul Morrissey
MADAME X ..... David Lowell Rich
MADAME X (TF) ..... Robert Ellis Miller
MADE ..... John Mackenzie
MADE FOR EACH OTHER ..... Robert B. Bean
MADE IN ITALY ..... Nanni Loy
MADE IN U.S.A. ..... Jean-Luc Godard
MADELEINE ..... David Lean
MADEMOISELLE ..... Tony Richardson
MADEMOISELLE FIFI ..... Robert Wise
MADIGAN ..... Don Siegel
MADMAN ..... Joe Giannone
MADO ..... Claude Sautet
MADRON ..... Jerry Hopper
MADWOMAN OF CHAILLOT, THE ..... Bryan Forbes
MAE WEST (TF) ☆ ..... Lee Philips
MAFIA ..... Damiano Damiani
MAFIOSO ..... Alberto Lattuada
MAFU CAGE, THE ..... Karen Arthur
MAGGIE, THE ..... Alexander Mackendrick
MAGIC ..... Richard Attenborough
MAGIC BOX, THE ..... John Boulting
MAGIC CARPET (TF) ..... William A. Graham
MAGIC CHRISTIAN, THE ..... Joseph Mcgrath
MAGIC FLUTE, THE ..... Ingmar Bergman
MAGIC OF LASSIE, THE ..... Don Chaffey
MAGIC SHOW, THE ..... Norman Campbell
MAGIC SWORD, THE ..... Bert I. Gordon
MAGICIAN OF LUBLIN, THE ..... Menahem Golan
MAGICIAN (TF), THE ..... Marvin J. Chomsky
MAGICIAN, THE ..... Ingmar Bergman
MAGNIFICENT AMBERSONS, THE ..... Orson Welles
MAGNIFICENT MAGNET OF SANTA MESA (TF) ..... Hy Averback
MAGNIFICENT MATADOR, THE ..... Budd Boetticher
MAGNIFICENT SEVEN RIDE!, THE ..... George Mccowan
MAGNIFICENT SEVEN, THE ..... John Sturges
MAGNIFICENT TWO, THE ..... Cliff Owen
MAGNIFICENT YANKEE, THE ..... John Sturges
MAGNUM FORCE ..... Ted Post
MAGNUM THRUST ..... Earl Bellamy
MAGUS, THE ..... Guy Green
MAHANAGAR ..... Satyajit Ray
MAHATMA AND THE MAD BOY ..... James Ivory
MAHLER ..... Ken Russell
MAHOGANY ..... Berry Gordy
MAHONEY'S ESTATE (TF) ..... Harvey Hart
MAID IN AMERICA (TF) ..... Paul Aaron
MAIDS, THE ..... Christopher Miles
MAIDSTONE ..... Norman Mailer
MAIL-ORDER BRIDE ..... Burt Kennedy
MAIN ATTRACTION, THE ..... Daniel Petrie
MAIN EVENT, THE ..... Howard Zieff
MAITRESSE ..... Barbet Schroeder
MAJOR AND THE MINOR, THE ..... Billy Wilder
MAJOR DUNDEE ..... Sam Peckinpah
MAJORITY OF ONE, A ..... Mervyn Leroy
MAKE ME AN OFFER (TF) ..... Jerry Paris
MAKE MINE LAUGHS ..... Richard Fleischer
MAKING IT ..... John Erman
MAKING LOVE ..... Arthur Hiller
MAKIOKA SISTERS, THE ..... Kon Ichikawa
MALAGA ..... Laslo Benedek
MALE COMPANION ..... Philippe De broca
MALE HUNT ..... Edouard Molinaro
MALE OF THE CENTURY ..... Claude Berri
MALIBU BEACH ..... Robert J. Rosenthal
MALIBU HIGH ..... Lawrence D. Foldes
MALIBU (TF) ..... E.W. Swackhamer
MALPAS MYSTERY, THE ..... Sidney Hayers
MALTESE BIPPY, THE ..... Norman Panama
MALTESE FALCON, THE ..... John Huston
MAME ..... Gene Saks
MAN, A WOMAN AND A BANK, A ..... Noel Black
MAN, A WOMAN, AND A KILLER, A ..... Wayne Wang
MAN AND A WOMAN ★, A ..... Claude Lelouch
MAN AND BOY ..... E.W. Swackhamer
MAN BEHIND THE MASK, THE ..... Michael Powell
MAN CALLED DAGGER, A ..... Richard Rush
MAN CALLED GANNON, A ..... James Goldstone
MAN CALLED HORSE, A ..... Elliot Silverstein
MAN CALLED PETER, A ..... Henry Koster
MAN COULD GET KILLED, A ..... Cliff Owen
MAN ESCAPED, A ..... Robert Bresson
MAN FOR ALL SEASONS ★★, A ..... Fred Zinnemann
MAN FRIDAY ..... Jack Gold
MAN FROM ATLANTIS (TF), THE ..... Lee H. Katzin
MAN FROM BITTER RIDGE, THE ..... Jack Arnold
MAN FROM CLOVER GROVE, THE ..... William Byron Hillman
MAN FROM GALVESTON, THE ..... William Conrad
MAN FROM SNOWY RIVER, THE ..... George Miller
MAN FROM THE ALAMO, THE ..... Budd Boetticher
MAN-HUNTER (TF), THE ..... Don Taylor
MAN IN 5A, THE ..... Max Fischer
MAN IN A COCKED HAT ..... Roy Boulting
MAN IN THE GLASS BOOTH, THE ..... Arthur Hiller
MAN IN THE IRON MASK (TF), THE ..... Mike Newell
MAN IN THE MIDDLE ..... Guy Hamilton
MAN IN THE SADDLE ..... Andre De toth
MAN IN THE SANTA CLAUS SUIT (TF), THE ..... Corey Allen
MAN IN THE SHADOW ..... Jack Arnold
MAN IN THE SKY, THE ..... Charles Crichton
MAN IN THE VAULT ..... Andrew V. Mclaglen
MAN IN THE WHITE SUIT, THE ..... Alexander Mackendrick
MAN IN THE WILDERNESS ..... Richard C. Sarafian
MAN IS NOT A BIRD ..... Dusan Makavejev
MAN OF A THOUSAND FACES ..... Joseph Pevney
MAN OF FLOWERS ..... Paul Cox
MAN OF IRON ..... Andrzej Wajda
MAN OF LA MANCHA ..... Arthur Hiller
MAN OF MARBLE ..... Andrzej Wajda
MAN OF THE FOREST ..... Henry Hathaway
MAN OF VIOLENCE ..... Peter Walker
MAN ON A STRING ..... Andre De toth
MAN ON A STRING (TF) ..... Joseph Sargent
MAN ON A SWING ..... Frank Perry
MAN ON A TIGHTROPE ..... Elia Kazan
MAN ON THE ROOF ..... Bo Widerberg
MAN ON THE RUN ..... Eddie Romero
MAN, THE ..... Joseph Sargent
MAN TO REMEMBER, A ..... Garson Kanin
MAN UPSTAIRS, THE ..... Don Chaffey
MAN VANISHES, A ..... Shohei Imamura
MAN WHO CHANGED HIS MIND, THE ..... Robert Stevenson
MAN WHO COULD TALK TO KIDS (TF), THE ..... Donald Wrye
MAN WHO DARED, THE ..... John Sturges
MAN WHO DIED TWICE (TF), THE ..... Joseph Sargent
MAN WHO FELL TO EARTH, THE ..... Nicolas Roeg
MAN WHO HAD POWER OVER WOMEN, THE ..... John Krish
MAN WHO LIES, THE ..... Alain Robbe-Grillet
MAN WHO LIVED AGAIN, THE ..... Robert Stevenson
MAN WHO LOVED CAT DANCING, THE ..... Richard C. Sarafian
MAN WHO LOVED WOMEN, THE ..... Blake Edwards
MAN WHO NEVER WAS, THE ..... Ronald Neame
MAN WHO SAW TOMORROW, THE ..... Robert Guenette
MAN WHO TALKED TOO MUCH, THE ..... Vincent Sherman
MAN WHO WANTED TO LIVE FOREVER (TF), THE ..... John Trent
MAN WHO WASN'T THERE, THE ..... Bruce Malmuth
MAN WHO WOULD BE KING, THE ..... John Huston
MAN WITH A MILLION ..... Ronald Neame
MAN WITH BOGART'S FACE, THE ..... Robert Day
MAN WITH CONNECTIONS, THE ..... Claude Berri
MAN WITH THE BALLOONS, THE ..... Marco Ferreri
MAN WITH THE GOLDEN ARM, THE ..... Otto Preminger
MAN WITH THE GOLDEN GUN, THE ..... Guy Hamilton
MAN WITH THE GUN ..... Richard Wilson
MAN WITH THE POWER (TF), THE ..... Nicholas Sgarro
MAN WITH TWO BRAINS, THE ..... Carl Reiner
MAN WITHOUT A COUNTRY (TF), THE ..... Delbert Mann
MAN WITHOUT NATIONALITY, THE ..... Kon Ichikawa
MAN, WOMEN AND CHILD ..... Dick Richards
MANCHU EAGLE CAPER MYSTERY, THE ..... Dean Hargrove
MANCHURIAN CANDIDATE, THE ..... John Frankenheimer
MANDABI ..... Ousmene Sembene
MANDINGO ..... Richard Fleischer
MANDRAKE (TF) ..... Harry Falk
MANDY ..... Alexander Mackendrick
MANEATER ..... Vincent Edwards
MANEATERS ARE LOOSE! (TF) ..... Timothy Galfas
MANGO TREE, THE ..... Michael Pate
MANHATTAN ..... Woody Allen
MANHATTAN ANGEL ..... Arthur Dreifuss
MANHUNTER (TF) ..... Walter Grauman
MANIAC ..... Michael Carreras
MANIMAL (TF) ..... Russ Mayberry
MANIONS OF AMERICA (MS), THE ..... Charles S. Dubin
MANOEUVRE (FD) ..... Frederick Wiseman
MANSLAUGHTER ..... George Abbott
MANTRAP, THE ..... George Sherman
MANUELA ..... Guy Hamilton
MARACAIBO ..... Cornel Wilde
MARAT/SADE ..... Peter Brook
MARATHON MAN ..... John Schlesinger
MARATHON (TF) ..... Jackie Cooper
MARCH OR DIE ..... Dick Richards
MARCIA NUNZIALE ..... Marco Ferreri
MARCIANO (TF) ..... Bernard L. Kowalski
MARCO ..... Seymour Robbie
MARCO POLO (MS) ..... Giuliano Montaldo
MARCUS-NELSON MURDERS (TF) ☆☆, THE ..... Joseph Sargent
MARCUS WELBY, M.D. (TF) ..... David Lowell Rich
MARGIN FOR ERROR ..... Otto Preminger
MARGO ..... Menahem Golan
MARIA CHAPDELAINE ..... Gilles Carle
MARIA'S LOVERS ..... Andrei Konchalovsky
MARIAGE ..... Claude Lelouch
MARIAN ROSE WHITE (TF) ..... Robert Day
MARIE-CHANTAL CONTRE LE DOCTEUR KHA ..... Claude Chabrol
MARILYN: THE UNTOLD STORY (TF) ..... Jack Arnold
MARITI IN CITTA ..... Luigi Comencini
MARJOE (FD) ..... Howard Smith
MARJORIE MORNINGSTAR ..... Irving Rapper
MARK, I LOVE YOU (TF) ..... Gunnar Hellstrom
MARK OF ZORRO (TF), THE ..... Don Mcdougall
MARK OF ZORRO, THE ..... Rouben Mamoulian
MARK, THE ..... Guy Green
MARLEY (FD) ..... Gary Weis
MARLOWE ..... Paul Bogart
MAROC 7 ..... Gerry O'hara
MAROONED ..... John Sturges
MARQUIS OF GRILLO, THE ..... Mario Monicelli
MARQUISE OF O . . . , THE ..... Eric Rohmer
MARRIAGE, A ..... Sandy Tung
MARRIAGE IS ALIVE AND WELL (TF) ..... Russ Mayberry
MARRIAGE OF A YOUNG STOCKBROKER ..... Lawrence Turman
MARRIAGE OF CONVENIENCE ..... Clive Donner
MARRIAGE ON THE ROCKS ..... Jack Donohue
MARRIAGE: YEAR ONE (TF) ..... William A. Graham
MARRIED COUPLE (FD), A ..... Allan King
MARRIED WOMAN, THE ..... Jean-Luc Godard
MARRY ME! MARRY ME! ..... Claude Berri
MARSEILLES CONTRACT, THE ..... Robert Parrish
MARTIAN CHRONICLES (TF), THE ..... Michael Anderson
MARTIN ..... George A. Romero
MARTIN'S DAY ..... Alan Gibson
MARTY ★★ ..... Delbert Mann
MARU MARU ..... Gordon Douglas
MARVA COLLINS STORY (TF), THE ..... Peter Levin
MARVIN AND TIGE ..... Eric Weston
MARY AND JOSEPH: A STORY OF FAITH (TF) ..... Eric Till
MARY JANE HARPER CRIED LAST NIGHT (TF) ..... Allen Reisner
MARY LOU ..... Arthur Dreifuss
MARY, MARY ..... Mervyn Leroy

MARY POPPINS ★ .... Robert Stevenson
MARY, QUEEN OF SCOTS .... Charles Jarrott
MARY WHITE (TF) .... Jud Taylor
MARYJANE .... Maury Dexter
MASCULINE FEMININE .... Jean-Luc Godard
MASK OF DIMITRIOS, THE .... Jean Negulesco
MASK OF SHEBA (TF), THE ... David Lowell Rich
MASK OF THE AVENGER .... Phil Karlson
MASQUE OF THE RED DEATH, THE .... Roger Corman
MASS APPEAL .... Glenn Jordan
MASSACRE HARBOR .... John Peyser
MASSACRE IN ROME .... George Pan Cosmatos
MASSARATI AND THE BRAIN (TF) .... Harvey Hart
MASTER GUNFIGHTER, THE .... Frank Laughlin
MASTER OF BALLANTRAE (TF), THE .... Douglas Hickox
MASTER OF THE WORLD .... William Witney
MASTER PLAN, THE .... Cy Endfield
MASTERMIND .... Alex March
MASTERWORK .... Miklos Jancso
MATATABI .... Kon Ichikawa
MATCHLESS .... Alberto Lattuada
MATCHMAKER, THE .... Joseph Anthony
MATILDA .... Daniel Mann
MATINEE IDOL, THE .... Frank Capra
MATING SEASON (TF), THE .... John Llewellyn Moxey
MATT HELM (TF) .... Buzz Kulik
MATT HOUSTON (TF) .... Richard Lang
MATTA DA SLEGARE .... Marco Bellocchio
MATTEI AFFAIR, THE .... Francesco Rosi
MATTER OF INNOCENCE, A .... Guy Green
MATTER OF LIFE AND DEATH (TF), A .... Russ Mayberry
MATTER OF LIFE AND DEATHA .... Michael Powell
MATTER OF PRIDE (FD), A .... Allan King
MATTER OF TIME, A .... Vincente Minnelli
MATTER OF WHO, A .... Don Chaffey
MATTER OF WIFE ... AND DEATH (TF), A .... Marvin J. Chomsky
MAURIE .... Daniel Mann
MAUSOLEUM .... Michael Dugan
MAUVAISE GRAINE .... Billy Wilder
MAX DUGAN RETURNS .... Herbert Ross
MAX ET LES FERRAILLEURS .... Claude Sautet
MAXIME .... Henri Verneuil
MAYA .... John Berry
MAYBE I'LL COME HOME IN THE SPRING (TF) .... Joseph Sargent
MAYDAY AT 40,000 FEET (TF) .... Robert Butler
MAYERLING .... Terence Young
MAYFLOWER: THE PILGRIMS' ADVENTURE (TF) .... George Schaefer
MAZEL TOV OU LE MARIAGE .... Claude Berri
MCCABE & MRS. MILLER .... Robert Altman
MCCLAIN'S LAW (TF) .... Vincent Mceveety
MCCLOUD: WHO KILLED MISS U.S.A.? (TF) .... Richard A. Colla
MCCONNELL STORY, THE .... Gordon Douglas
MCGUIRE, GO HOME! .... Ralph Thomas
MCLINTOCK! .... Andrew V. Mclaglen
MCMASTERS, THE .... Alf Kjellin
MCNAUGHTON'S DAUGHTER (TF) .... Jerry London
MCQ .... John Sturges
MCVICAR .... Tom Clegg
ME AND THE COLONEL .... Peter Glenville
MEADOW, THE .... Paolo Taviani
MEAN DOG BLUES .... Mel Stuart
MEAN JOHNNY BARROWS .... Fred Williamson
MEAN STREETS .... Martin Scorsese
MEAT (FD) .... Frederick Wiseman
MEATBALLS .... Ivan Reitman
MECHANIC, THE .... Michael Winner
MEDICAL STORY (TF) .... Gary Nelson
MEDICINE BALL CARAVAN (FD) .... Francois Reichenbach
MEDIUM COOL .... Haskell Wexler
MEDUSA TOUCH, THE .... Jack Gold
MEET DANNY WILSON .... Joseph Pevney
MEET JOHN DOE .... Frank Capra
MEET MARLON BRANDO (FD) .... Albert Maysles
MEET ME IN ST. LOUIS .... Vincente Minnelli
MEETINGS WITH REMARKABLE MEN .... Peter Brook
MEGAFORCE .... Hal Needham
MELANIE .... Rex Bromfield
MELINDA .... Hugh A. Robertson
MELODIE EN SOUS-SOL .... Henri Verneuil
MELODY .... Waris Hussein
MELODY PARADE .... Arthur Dreifuss
MELVIN AND HOWARD .... Jonathan Demme
MELVIN PURVIS: G-MAN (TF) .... Dan Curtis
MEMBER OF THE WEDDING, THE .... Fred Zinnemann
MEMED .... Peter Ustinov
MEMOIRS OF A SURVIVOR .... David Gladwell
MEMORIAL DAY (TF) .... Joseph Sargent
MEMORIES NEVER DIE (TF) .... Sandor Stern
MEMORY OF EVA RYKER (TF), THE .... Walter Grauman
MEMORY OF JUSTICE (FD), THE .... Marcel Ophuls
MEN OF ARNHEM (FD) .... Terence Young
MEN OF SHERWOOD FOREST .... Val Guest
MEN OF THE DRAGON (TF) .... Harry Falk
MEN OF THE FIGHTING LADY .. Andrew Marton
MEN OF TOHOKU, THE .... Kon Ichikawa
MEN, THE .... Fred Zinnemann
MEN WITHOUT WOMEN (FD) ... Derek Burbidge
MENACE, THE .... Gerard Oury
MEPHISTO .... Istvan Szabo
MEPHISTO WALTZ, THE .... Paul Wendkos
MERCENARIES, THE .... Jack Cardiff
MERCENARY, THE .... Sergio Corbucci
MERRILL'S MARAUDERS .... Samuel Fuller
MERRY ANDREW .... Michael Kidd
MERRY CHRISTMAS, MR. LAWRENCE .... Nagisa Oshima
MESSAGE, THE .... Moustapha Akkad
MESSAGE TO MY DAUGHTER (TF) .... Robert M. Lewis
MESSIAH OF EVIL .... Willard Huyck
MESSIDOR .... Alain Tanner
METALSTORM: THE DESTRUCTION OF JARED-SYN .... Charles Band
METEOR .... Ronald Neame
MEURTRE EN 45 TOURS .... Etienne Perrier
MEXICALI ROSE .... George Sherman
MEXICO MEXICO (FD) .... Francois Reichenbach
MI MANDA PICONE .... Nanni Loy
MICHAEL KOHLHAAS .... Volker Schlondorff
MICKEY ONE .... Arthur Penn
MICKEY SPILLANE'S MARGIN FOR MURDER (TF) .... Daniel Haller
MICKEY SPILLANE'S 'MURDER ME, MURDER YOU' (TF) .... Gary Nelson
MIDAS RUN .... Alf Kjellin
MIDDLE AGE CRAZY .... John Trent
MIDDLE OF THE NIGHT .... Delbert Mann
MIDDLE OF THE WORLD, THE .... Alain Tanner
MIDDLEMAN, THE .... Satyajit Ray
MIDDLETOWN (TD) .... Peter Davis
MIDNIGHT COWBOY ★★ .... John Schlesinger
MIDNIGHT EXPRESS ★ .... Alan Parker
MIDNIGHT LACE .... David Miller
MIDNIGHT LACE (TF) .... Ivan Nagy
MIDNIGHT MADNESS .... David Wechter
MIDNIGHT MAN, THE .... Burt Lancaster
MIDNIGHT OFFERINGS (TF) .... Rod Holcomb
MIDNIGHT STORY, THE .... Joseph Pevney
MIDNITE SPARES .... Quentin Masters
MIDSUMMER NIGHT'S DREAM, A .... Peter Hall
MIDSUMMER NIGHT'S SEX COMEDY, A .... Woody Allen
MIDWAY .... Jack Smight
MIKADO, THE .... Stuart Burge
MIKE'S MURDER .... James Bridges
MIKEY AND NICKY .... Elaine May
MILADY'S REVENGE .... Richard Lester
MILANO '83 (FD) .... Ermanno Olmi
MILAREPA .... Liliana Cavani
MILES TO GO BEFORE I SLEEP (TF) .... Fielder Cook
MILESTONES .... Robert Kramer
MILLE MILLIARDS DE DOLLARS .... Henri Verneuil
MILLHOUSE: A WHITE COMEDY .... Emile Deantonio
MILLION DOLLAR DIXIE DELIVERY (TF), THE .... Russ Mayberry
MILLION DOLLAR DUCK, THE .... Vincent Mceveety
MILLION DOLLAR FACE (TF), THE .... Michael O'herlihy
MILLION DOLLAR INFIELD (TF) .... Hal Cooper
MILLION DOLLAR MERMAID .... Mervyn Leroy
MILLION DOLLAR RIP-OFF (TF), THE .... Alexander Singer
MILLION POUND NOTE, THE .... Ronald Neame
MILLIONAIRE (TF), THE .... Don Weis
MIMI METALLURGICO FERITO NELL'ONORE .... Lina Wertmuller
MIND OF MR. SOAMES, THE .... Alan Cooke
MIND OVER MURDER (TF) .... Ivan Nagy
MIND SNATCHERS, THE .... Bernard Girard
MINI-SKIRT MOB, THE .... Maury Dexter
MINNESOTA CLAY .... Sergio Corbucci
MINNIE AND MOSKOWITZ .... John Cassavetes
MINSTREL MAN (TF) .... William A. Graham
MIO DIO COME SONO CADUTA IN BASSO .... Luigi Comencini
MIRACLE OF KATHY MILLER (TF), THE .... Robert M. Lewis
MIRACLE OF THE WHITE STALLIONS, THE .... Arthur Hiller
MIRACLE ON 34TH STREET (TF) .... Fielder Cook
MIRACLE ON ICE (TF) .... Steven H. Stern
MIRACLE, THE .... Irving Rapper
MIRACLE WOMAN, THE .... Frank Capra
MIRACLE WORKER ★, THE .... Arthur Penn
MIRACLE WORKER (TF), THE .... Paul Aaron
MIRAGE .... Edward Dmytryk
MIRAGE (TF) .... Gordon Flemyng
MIRANDA .... Ken Annakin
MIRROR CRACK'D, THE .... Guy Hamilton
MIRROR, MIRROR (TF) .... Joanna Lee
MIRROR, THE .... Andrei Tarkovsky
MIRRORS .... Noel Black
MISADVENTURES OF MERLIN JONES, THE .... Robert Stevenson
MISFITS, THE .... John Huston
MISS ALL-AMERICAN BEAUTY (TF) .... Gus Trikonis
MISS LONDON LTD. .... Val Guest
MISS LONELYHEARTS .... Michael Dinner
MISS PILGRIM'S PROGRESS .... Val Guest
MISS RIGHT .... Paul Williams
MISS ROBIN HOOD .... John Guillermin
MISS SUSIE SLAGLE'S .... John Berry
MISSING .... Costa Gavras
MISSING ARE DEADLY (TF), THE .... Don Mcdougall
MISSING CHILDREN: A MOTHER'S STORY (TF) .... Dick Lowry
MISSING IN ACTION .... Ted Kotcheff
MISSING JUROR, THE .... Budd Boetticher
MISSING LADY, THE .... Phil Karlson
MISSING PIECES (TF) .... Mike Hodges
MISSION MARS .... Nicholas Webster
MISSIONARY, THE .... Richard Loncraine
MISSISSIPPI '82 .... Bertrand Tavernier
MISSISSIPPI MERMAID .... Francois Truffaut
MISSOURI BREAKS, THE .... Arthur Penn
MISSOURI OUTLAW, A .... George Sherman
MISSOURI TRAVELER, THE .... Jerry Hopper
MISTER BUDDWING .... Delbert Mann
MISTER CORY .... Blake Edwards
MISTER DRAKE'S DUCK .... Val Guest
MISTER FREEDOM .... William Klein
MISTER JERICO (TF) .... Sidney Hayers
MISTER MOSES .... Ronald Neame
MISTER ROBERTS .... Mervyn Leroy
MISTER ROCK & ROLL .... Charles S. Dubin
MISTRESS OF PARADISE (TF) .... Peter Medak
MISTRESS PAMELA .... James O'connolly
MISTY .... James B. Clark
MISUNDERSTOOD .... Jerry Schatzberg
MITCHELL .... Andrew V. Mclaglen
MIXED COMPANY .... Melville Shavelson
MOB, THE .... Robert Parrish
MOBILE TWO (TF) .... David Moessinger
MOBY DICK .... John Huston
MODEL (FD) .... Frederick Wiseman
MODEL SHOP .... Jacques Demy
MODELS, INC. .... Gerry O'hara
MODERATOR CANTABILE .... Peter Brook
MODERN PROBLEMS .... Ken Shapiro
MODERN ROMANCE .... Albert Brooks
MODESTY BLAISE .... Joseph Losey
MOGLI PERICOLOSE .... Luigi Comencini
MOHAMMAD, MESSENGER OF GOD .... Moustapha Akkad
MOI JE .... Jean-Luc Godard
MOLE PEOPLE, THE .... Virgil W. Vogel
MOLLY AND LAWLESS JOHN .... Gary Nelson
MOLLY MAGUIRES, THE .... Martin Ritt
:MOM, THE WOLFMAN AND ME (TF) .... Edmond Levy
MOMENT BY MOMENT .... Jane Wagner
MOMENT OF LOVE, A .... Shirley Clarke
MOMENT OF TRUTH, THE .... Francesco Rosi
MOMENT TO MOMENT .... Mervyn Leroy
MOMENTS .... Michal Bat-Adam
MOMMIE DEAREST .... Frank Perry
MON ONCLE ANTOINE .... Claude Jutra
MON ONCLE BENJAMIN .... Edouard Molinaro
MON ONCLE D' AMERIQUE .... Alain Resnais
MONDO TEENO .... Richard Lester

MYSTERY BROADCAST .... George Sherman
MYSTERY IN MEXICO .... Robert Wise
MYSTERY IN SWING .... Arthur Dreifuss
MYSTERY IN THE MINE .... James Hill
MYSTERY OF KASPAR HAUSER, THE .... Werner Herzog
MYSTERY OF OBERWALD, THE .... Michelangelo Antonioni
MYSTERY SEA RAIDERS .... Edward Dmytryk
MYSTERY STREET .... John Sturges
MYSTIC WARRIOR (MS), THE .... Richard T. Heffron
MYSTIQUE/BRAINWASH/THE NAKED WEEKEND .... Bobby Roth

N

NADA .... Claude Chabrol
NADA GANG, THE .... Claude Chabrol
NAKED ALIBI .... Jerry Hopper
NAKED ANGELS .... Bruce Clark
NAKED BRIGADE, THE .... Maury Dexter
NAKED CAME THE STRANGER .... Radley Metzger
NAKED CITY, THE .... Jules Dassin
NAKED CIVIL SERVANT (TF), THE .... Jack Gold
NAKED EARTH, THE .... Vincent Sherman
NAKED EDGE, THE .... Michael Anderson
NAKED FACE, THE .... Bryan Forbes
NAKED KISS, THE .... Samuel Fuller
NAKED MAJA, THE .... Henry Koster
NAKED NIGHT, THE .... Ingmar Bergman
NAKED PARADISE .... Roger Corman
NAKED PREY, THE .... Cornel Wilde
NAKED RUNNER, THE .... Sidney J. Furie
NAKED UNDER LEATHER .... Jack Cardiff
NAME OF THE GAME IS KILL (TF), THE .... Gunnar Hellstrom
NAMU, THE KILLER WHALE .... Laslo Benedek
NANA .... Dan Wolman
NAPOLEON AND SAMANTHA .... Bernard Mceveety
NARROW MARGIN, THE .... Richard Fleischer
NASHVILLE GIRL .... Gus Trikonis
NASHVILLE GRAB (TF) .... James L. Conway
NASHVILLE ★ .... Robert Altman
NASHVILLE SOUND (FD), THE ... Robert Elfstrom
NASTY HABITS .... Michael Lindsay-Hogg
NATE AND HAYES .... Ferdinand Fairfax
NATIONAL LAMPOON'S ANIMAL HOUSE .... John Landis
NATIONAL LAMPOON'S CLASS REUNION .... Michael Miller
NATIONAL LAMPOON'S JOY OF SEX .... Martha Coolidge
NATIONAL LAMPOON'S MOVIE MADNESS .... Bob Giraldi
NATIONAL LAMPOON'S VACATION .... Harold Ramis
NATIVITY (TF), THE .... Bernard L. Kowalski
NATURAL ENEMIES .... Jeff Kanew
NATURAL, THE .... Barry Levinson
NAUGHTY BABY .... Mervyn Leroy
NAUGHTY STEWARDESSES, THE .. Al Adamson
NAUSICAA (TF) .... Agnes Varda
NAVAJO JOE .... Sergio Corbucci
NAYAK .... Satyajit Ray
NAZI AGENT .... Jules Dassin
NAZIS STRIKE (FD), THE .... Frank Capra
NEA .... Nelly Kaplan
NEA - A YOUNG EMMANUELLE .... Nelly Kaplan
NEARLY A NASTY ACCIDENT .... Don Chaffey
NEARLY EIGHTEEN .... Arthur Dreifuss
NECROMANCY .... Bert I. Gordon
NED KELLY .... Tony Richardson
NEGATIVES .... Peter Medak
NEGRO SOLDIER (FD), THE .... Frank Capra
NEIGHBORHOOD (TF), THE .... Lee H. Katzin
NEIGHBORS .... John G. Avildsen
NEIL SIMON'S ONLY WHEN I LAUGH .... Glenn Jordan
NEIL SIMON'S SEEMS LIKE OLD TIMES .... Jay Sandrich
NEITHER BY DAY NOR BY NIGHT .... Steven H. Stern
NEL NOME DEL PADRE .... Marco Bellocchio
NELSON AFFAIR, THE .... James Cellan-Jones
NEON CEILING (TF), THE .... Frank Pierson
NEPTUNE FACTOR, THE .... Daniel Petrie
NEST OF GENTRY, A .... Andrei Konchalovsky
NETWORK ★ .... Sidney Lumet
NEVADA SMITH .... Henry Hathaway
NEVADA SMITH (TF) .... Gordon Douglas
NEVADAN, THE .... Gordon Douglas
NEVER A DULL MOMENT .... Jerry Paris
NEVER CRY WOLF .... Carroll Ballard
NEVER-ENDING STORY, THE .... Wolfgang Petersen
NEVER GIVE AN INCH .... Paul Newman
NEVER LET GO .... John Guillermin
NEVER ON SUNDAY★ .... Jules Dassin
NEVER PUT IT IN WRITING .... Andrew L. Stone
NEVER SAY GOODBYE .... Jerry Hopper
NEVER SAY NEVER AGAIN .... Irvin Kershner
NEVER SO FEW .... John Sturges
NEVER TOO LATE .... Bud Yorkin
NEW ADVENTURES OF HEIDI (TF), THE .... Ralph Senensky
NEW CENTURIONS, THE .... Richard Fleischer
NEW DAUGHTERS OF JOSHUA CABE (TF), THE .... Bruce Bilson
NEW FRONTIER .... George Sherman
NEW GIRL IN TOWN .... Gus Trikonis
NEW INTERNS, THE .... John Rich
NEW KIND OF LOVE, A .... Melville Shavelson
NEW LAND, THE .... Jan Troell
NEW LEAF, A .... Elaine May
NEW LOVE BOAT (TF), THE .... Richard Kinon
NEW MAVERICK (TF), THE .... Hy Averback
NEW YEAR'S EVIL .... Emmett Alston
NEW YORK CONFIDENTIAL .... Russell Rouse
NEW YORK, NEW YORK .... Martin Scorsese
NEWMAN'S LAW .... Richard T. Heffron
NEWSFRONT .... Phillip Noyce
NEXT CHEECH & CHONG MOVIE, THE .... Thomas Chong
NEXT MAN, THE .... Richard C. Sarafian
NEXT ONE, THE .... Nico Mastorakis
NEXT STOP, GREENWICH VILLAGE .... Paul Mazursky
NEXT TIME I MARRY .... Garson Kanin
NIAGARA .... Henry Hathaway
NIAGARA FALLS .... Gordon Douglas
NICE GIRL LIKE ME, A .... Desmond Davis
NICHOLAS AND ALEXANDRA .... Franklin J. Schaffner
NICKEL RIDE, THE .... Robert Mulligan
NICKELODEON .... Peter Bogdanovich
NICKY'S WORLD (TF) .... Paul Stanley
NIGHT AMBUSH .... Michael Powell
NIGHT AND FOG IN JAPAN .... Nagisa Oshima
NIGHT AND THE CITY .... Jules Dassin
NIGHT CALL NURSES .... Jonathan Kaplan
NIGHT CALLER, THE .... Henri Verneuil
NIGHT CHASE (TF) .... Jack Starrett
NIGHT CRIES (TF) .... Richard Lang
NIGHT CROSSING .... Delbert Mann
NIGHT DIGGER, THE .... Alastair Reid
NIGHT EYES .... Robert Clouse
NIGHT FLIGHT TO MOSCOW .... Henri Verneuil
NIGHT GALLERY (TF) .... Steven Spielberg
NIGHT GAMES .... Mai Zetterling
NIGHT GAMES (TF) .... Don Taylor
NIGHT HEAVEN FELL, THE .... Roger Vadim
NIGHT HOLDS TERROR, THE .. Andrew L. Stone
NIGHT IN HEAVEN, A .... John G. Avildsen
NIGHT IS MY FUTURE .... Ingmar Bergman
NIGHT MOVES .... Arthur Penn
NIGHT MUST FALL .... Karel Reisz
NIGHT NURSE, THE .... Igor Auzins
NIGHT OF ADVENTURE, A .... Gordon Douglas
NIGHT OF DARK SHADOWS .... Dan Curtis
NIGHT OF PASSION .... Sidney J. Furie
NIGHT OF TERROR (TF) .... Jeannot Szwarc
NIGHT OF THE BLOOD BEAST .... Bernard L. Kowalski
NIGHT OF THE EAGLE .... Sidney Hayers
NIGHT OF THE FOLLOWING DAY, THE .... Hubert Cornfield
NIGHT OF THE GRIZZLY, THE ... Joseph Pevney
NIGHT OF THE IGUANA .... John Huston
NIGHT OF THE JUGGLER .... Robert Butler
NIGHT OF THE LEPUS .... William F. Claxton
NIGHT OF THE LIVING DEAD .... George A. Romero
NIGHT OF THE PARTY, THE .... Michael Powell
NIGHT OF THE SHOOTING STARS, THE .... Paolo Taviani
NIGHT PARTNERS (TF) .... Noel Nosseck
NIGHT PORTER, THE .... Liliana Cavani
NIGHT RIDER (TF), THE .... Hy Averback
NIGHT RIDERS, THE .... George Sherman
NIGHT SCHOOL .... Kenneth "Ken" Hughes
NIGHT SHADOWS .... John "Bud" Cardos
NIGHT SHIFT .... Ron Howard
NIGHT SLAVES (TF) .... Ted Post
NIGHT STALKER (TF), THE .... John Llewellyn Moxey
NIGHT STRANGLER (TF), THE .... Dan Curtis
NIGHT TERROR (TF) .... E.W. Swackhamer
NIGHT THAT PANICKED AMERICA (TF), THE .... Joseph Sargent
NIGHT THE BRIDGE FELL DOWN (TF), THE .... Georg J. Fenady
NIGHT THE CITY SCREAMED (TF), THE .... Harry Falk
NIGHT THE LIGHTS WENT OUT IN GEORGIA, THE .... Ronald F. Maxwell
NIGHT THE PROWLER, THE .... Jim Sharman
NIGHT THEY RAIDED MINSKY'S, THE .... William Friedkin
NIGHT THEY TOOK MISS BEAUTIFUL (TF), THE .... Robert M. Lewis
NIGHT TIDE .... Curtis Harrington
NIGHT TO REMEMBER, A .... Roy Ward Baker
NIGHT UNTO NIGHT .... Don Siegel
NIGHT VISITOR, THE .... Laslo Benedek
NIGHT WARNING/MOMMA'S BOY .... William Asher
NIGHT WAS OUR FRIEND .... Michael Anderson
NIGHT WATCH .... Brian G. Hutton
NIGHT WITHOUT SLEEP .... Roy Ward Baker
NIGHTCOMERS, THE .... Michael Winner
NIGHTHAWKS .... Bruce Malmuth
NIGHTINGALE SANG IN BERKELEY SQUARE, A .... Ralph Thomas
NIGHTKILL (TF) .... Ted Post
NIGHTMARE .... Freddie Francis
NIGHTMARE HONEYMOON .... Elliot Silverstein
NIGHTMARE IN BADHAM COUNTY (TF) .... John Llewellyn Moxey
NIGHTMARE IN CHICAGO (TF) .... Robert Altman
NIGHTMARE IN WAX .... Bud Townsend
NIGHTMARE (TF) .... William "Billy" Hale
NIGHTMARES .... Joseph Sargent
NIGHTS OF CABIRIA .... Federico Fellini
NIGHTSHADE FLOWER .... Kon Ichikawa
NIGHTSIDE (TF) .... Bernard L. Kowalski
NIGHTWING .... Arthur Hiller
NIJINSKY .... Herbert Ross
NIKKI, WILD DOG OF THE NORTH .... Jack Couffer
NINE DAYS A QUEEN .... Robert Stevenson
NINE LIVES OF FRITZ THE CAT (AF), THE .... Robert Taylor
NINE TO FIVE .... Colin Higgins
NINJA III: THE DOMINATION ... Sam Firstenberg
NINTH CONFIGURATION, THE .... William Peter Blatty
NO BLADE OF GRASS .... Cornel Wilde
NO CHILD'S LAND .... Marco Ferreri
NO DOWN PAYMENT .... Martin Ritt
NO DRUMS, NO BUGLES .... Clyde Ware
NO HIGHWAY .... Henry Koster
NO HIGHWAY IN THE SKY .... Henry Koster
NO KIDDING .... Gerald Thomas
NO LEAVE TO LOVE .... Charles Martin
NO LONGER ALONE .... Nicholas Webster
NO LOVE FOR JOHNNIE .... Ralph Thomas
NO, MAMA, NO (TF) .... Roland Joffe
NO MAPS ON MY TAPS (FD) .... George T. Nierenberg
NO MORE EXCUSES .... Robert Downey
NO, MY DARLING DAUGHTER .... Ralph Thomas
NO NAME ON THE BULLET .... Jack Arnold
NO OTHER LOVE (TF) .... Richard Pearce
NO PLACE TO GO .... Mervyn Leroy
NO PLACE TO HIDE .... Robert A. Schnitzer
NO PLACE TO HIDE (TF) .... John Llewellyn Moxey
NO PLACE TO RUN (TF) .... Delbert Mann
NO REGRETS FOR OUR YOUTH .... Akira Kurosawa
NO SEX PLEASE - WE'RE BRITISH ... Cliff Owen
NO SUN IN VENICE .... Roger Vadim
NO TIME FOR FLOWERS .... Don Siegel
NO TIME FOR SERGEANTS .... Mervyn Leroy
NO TIME TO BE YOUNG .... David Lowell Rich
NO TIME TO DIE .... Terence Young
NO TREES IN THE STREET .... J. Lee Thompson
NO WAY BACK .... Fred Williamson
NO WAY OUT .... Joseph L. Mankiewicz
NO WAY TO TREAT A LADY .... Jack Smight
NOB HILL .... Henry Hathaway
NOBODY LIVES FOREVER .... Jean Negulesco
NOBODY RUNS FOREVER .... Ralph Thomas
NOBODY'S PERFECT .... Alan Rafkin
NOBODY'S PERFEKT .... Peter Bonerz
NOI DONNE SIAMO FATTE COSI .... Dino Risi

OT ORA 40 1939, HUNGARIAN .... Andre De toth
OTHELLO .... Orson Welles
OTHER HALF OF THE SKY: A CHINA MEMOIR (FD), THE ....Claudia Weill
OTHER LOVER, THE............... Andre De toth
OTHER MAN (TF), THE............ Richard A. Colla
OTHER SIDE OF MIDNIGHT, THE .... Charles Jarrott
OTHER SIDE OF THE MOUNTAIN - PART 2, THE ....Larry Peerce
OTHER SIDE OF THE MOUNTAIN, THE............ Larry Peerce
OTHER SIDE OF THE WIND, THE.................... Orson Welles
OTHER, THE .... Robert Mulligan
OTHER VICTIM (TF), THE................ Noel Black
OTHER WOMAN (TF), THE.... Melville Shavelson
OTLEY ....Dick Clement
OTRO IL BENE E IL MALE ....Liliana Cavani
OUR FAMILY BUSINESS (TF).......Robert Collins
OUR LAST SPRING .... Michael Cacoyannis
OUR MAN FLINT..........................Daniel Mann
OUR MAN IN MARRAKESH .... Don Sharp
OUR MOTHER'S HOUSE .... Jack Clayton
OUR TIME ....Peter Hyams
OUR VERY OWN............................ David Miller
OUR WINNING SEASON .... Joseph Ruben
OUT OF IT .... Paul Williams
OUT OF SEASON........................ Alan Bridges
OUT OF THE BLUE .... Dennis Hopper
OUT OF THE SHADOW .... Michael Winner
OUT-OF-TOWNERS, THE............... Arthur Hiller
OUTBACK .... Ted Kotcheff
OUTCAST, THE........................William Witney
OUTER AND INNER SPACE .... Andy Warhol
OUTFIT, THE.................................John Flynn
OUTLAND...................................Peter Hyams
OUTLANDERS, THE ....Richard L. Bare
OUTLAW BLUES .... Richard T. Heffron
OUTLAW JOSEY WALES, THE .. Clint Eastwood
OUTLAWS OF PINE RIDGE........William Witney
OUTLAWS OF SONORA..........George Sherman
OUTPOST IN MALAYA................ Ken Annakin
OUTRAGE.. Ida Lupino
OUTRAGE ! (TF) .... Richard T. Heffron
OUTRAGE, THE ....Martin Ritt
OUTRAGEOUS ! ....Richard Benner
OUTSIDE CHANCE (TF) .... Michael Miller
OUTSIDE MAN, THE..................Jacques Deray
OUTSIDE THE LAW .... Jack Arnold
OUTSIDER (TF), THE ....Michael Ritchie
OUTSIDER, THE .... Delbert Mann
OUTSIDERS, THE .... Francis Ford Coppola
OUTTAKES ....Jack M. Sell
OVER THE BROOKLYN BRIDGE...................... Menahem Golan
OVER THE EDGE ....Jonathan Kaplan
OVER-THE-HILL GANG RIDES AGAIN (TF), THE ....George Mccowan
OVERBOARD (TF) .... John Newland
OVERLAND STAGE RAIDERS ...George Sherman
OVERLORD ....Stuart Cooper
OWAIN GLYNDWR - PRINCE OF WALES (TF).... James Hill
OWD BOB .... Robert Stevenson
OWEN MARSHALL, COUNSELOR AT LAW (TF) .... Buzz Kulik
OWL AND THE PUSSYCAT, THE .. Herbert Ross

P

P.J. ....John Guillermin
P'TANG, YANG, KIPPERBANG ..... Michael Apted
PACIFIC RENDEZVOUS .... George Sidney
PACK, THE ....Robert Clouse
PACKIN' IT IN (TF) .... Jud Taylor
PAD (... AND HOW TO USE IT), THE............ Brian G. Hutton
PADDY .... Daniel Haller
PADRE PADRONE.......................Paolo Taviani
PADRI E FIGLI ....Mario Monicelli
PAGE MISS GLORY .... Mervyn Leroy
PAID VACATION (TF), A ....Ralph L. Thomas
PAIN.. Yilmaz Guney
PAIN IN THE A–, A .... Edouard Molinaro
PAINT YOUR WAGON ....Joshua Logan
PAINTED BOATS..................... Charles Crichton
PAINTERS PAINTING (FD)........ Emile Deantonio
PAIR OF BRIEFS, A .... Ralph Thomas
PAJAMA GAME, THE.................George Abbott
PAJAMA PARTY ....Don Weis
PAL JOEY .... George Sidney
PALMERSTOWN, U.S.A. (TF) ....Peter Levin
PALS OF THE SADDLE ....George Sherman
PANACHE (TF)............................ Gary Nelson
PANAMA SAL.........................William Witney
PANDEMONIUM ....Alfred Sole
PANE, AMORE E ... .Dino Risi
PANE, AMORE E GELOSIA ....Luigi Comencini
PANIC BUTTON ....George Sherman
PANIC IN ECHO PARK (TF)............ John Llewellyn Moxey
PANIC IN NEEDLE PARK ....Jerry Schatzberg
PANIC IN THE STREETS .... Elia Kazan
PANIC ON THE 5:22 (TF) ....Harvey Hart
PANORAMA BLUE .... Alan Roberts
PANTALOONS ....John Berry
PAPA LES PETITS BATEAUX ....Nelly Kaplan
PAPER CHASE, THE..................James Bridges
PAPER DOLLS (TF) ....Edward Zwick
PAPER LION .... Alex March
PAPER MAN (TF) .... Walter Grauman
PAPER MOON .... Peter Bogdanovich
PAPER ORCHID .... Roy Ward Baker
PAPER TIGER .... Ken Annakin
PAPILLON........................ Franklin J. Schaffner
PAR UN BEAU MATIN D'ETE......Jacques Deray
PARADES ....Robert J. Siegel
PARADISE ....Stuart Gillard
PARADISE ALLEY .... Sylvester Stallone
PARADISE CONNECTION (TF) ....Michael Preece
PARADISE LAGOON ....Lewis Gilbert
PARALLAX VIEW, THE ....Alan J. Pakula
PARANOIAC............................Freddie Francis
PARAS PATHAR ....Satyajit Ray
PARASITE.................................Charles Band
PARATROOP COMMAND...........William Witney
PARATROOPER .... Terence Young
PARDON MON AFFAIRE .... Yves Robert
PARDON MON AFFAIRE, TOO! .... Yves Robert
PARENT TRAP, THE........................ David Swift
PARI E DISPARI ....Sergio Corbucci
PARIS BLUES ....Martin Ritt
PARIS HOLIDAY............................ Gerd Oswald
PARIS-PALACE-HOTEL .... Henri Verneuil
PARIS, TEXAS .... Wim Wenders
PARIS VU PAR ... .Claude Chabrol
PARIS WHEN IT SIZZLES........... Richard Quine
PARK ROW .... Samuel Fuller
PAROLA DI LADRO .... Nanni Loy
PAROLE (TF) ....Michael Tuchner
PARSIFAL................... Hans-Jurgen Syberberg
PART 2 SOUNDER ....William A. Graham
PART 2 WALKING TALL .... Earl Bellamy
PARTNER .... Bernardo Bertolucci
PARTNERS ....Andre Guttfreund
PARTNERS IN CRIME............Peter John Duffell
PARTNERS IN CRIME (TF) ....Jack Smight
PARTY CRASHERS, THE............Bernard Girard
PARTY'S OVER, THE................... Guy Hamilton
PARTY, THE.............................Blake Edwards
PASQUALINO SETTEBELLEZZE ★ .... Lina Wertmuller
PASSAGE HOME.................... Roy Ward Baker
PASSAGE, THE .... J. Lee Thompson
PASSAGE TO INDIA, A ....David Lean
PASSENGER, THE......... Michelangelo Antonioni
PASSION.................................Jean-Luc Godard
PASSION OF ANNA, THE........Ingmar Bergman
PASSION OF SLOW FIRE, THE .... Edouard Molinaro
PASSIONATE FRIENDS, THE...........David Lean
PASSIONATE THIEF, THE ....Mario Monicelli
PASSIONE D'AMORE .... Ettore Scola
PASSOVER PLOT, THE........... Michael Campus
PASSPORT TO CHINA ....Michael Carreras
PASSPORT TO SHAME .... Alvin Rakoff
PASSPORT TO SUEZ............. Andre De toth
PASSWORD IS COURAGE, THE............... Andrew L. Stone
PASTOR HALL .... Roy Boulting
PAT GARRETT & BILLY THE KID .... Sam Peckinpah
PATCH OF BLUE, A.......................... Guy Green
PATERNITY.............................David Steinberg
PATHER PANCHALI ....Satyajit Ray
PATHS OF GLORY .... Stanley Kubrick
PATRICIA NEAL STORY (TF), THE .... Anthony Harvey
PATRICK ....Richard Franklin
PATSY, THE .... Jerry Lewis
PATTERNS.....................................Fielder Cook
PATTON ★★.......................Franklin J. Schaffner
PAUL AND MICHELLE.................Lewis Gilbert
PAUL'S CASE (TF).................. Lamont Johnson
PAUL SWAN ....Andy Warhol
PAULINE AT THE BEACH .... Eric Rohmer
PAVLOVA .... Emil Loteanu
PAWNBROKER, THE .... Sidney Lumet
PAY-OFF, THE ....Arthur Dreifuss
PAY OR DIE ....Richard Wilson
PAYDAY...Daryl Duke
PEACEMAKER, THE...........................Ted Post
PEARL (TF) ....Hy Averback
PEAU D'ESPION .... Edouard Molinaro
PEDESTRIAN, THE ....Maximilian Schell
PEEPER ....Peter Hyams
PEEPING TOM .... Michael Powell
PEKING MEDALLION, THE ....James Hill
PELE (FD) ....Francois Reichenbach
PEMBERTON VALLEY (FD) ....Allan King
PENDULUM ....George Schaefer
PENELOPE .... Arthur Hiller
PENITENTIARY .... Jamaa Fanaka
PENITENTIARY II .... Jamaa Fanaka
PENNIES FROM HEAVEN............. Herbert Ross
PENNY GOLD .... Jack Cardiff
PENNY PRINCESS ....Val Guest
PEOPLE AGAINST O'HARA, THE ...John Sturges
PEOPLE NEXT DOOR, THE .... David Greene
PEOPLE (TF), THE ....John Korty
PEOPLE THAT TIME FORGOT, THE.................. Kevin Connor
PEOPLE WILL TALK........ Joseph L. Mankiewicz
PEPE.. George Sidney
PEPPERMINT FRAPPE .... Carlos Saura
PEPPERMINT SODA..................... Diane Kurys
PERCEVAL .... Eric Rohmer
PERCY .... Ralph Thomas
PERCY'S PROGRESS................. Ralph Thomas
PERFECT COUPLE, A .... Robert Altman
PERFECT FRIDAY ....Peter Hall
PERFECT FURLOUGH, THE ....Blake Edwards
PERFECT GENTLEMEN (TF) .... Jackie Cooper
PERFECT MATCH (TF), A ....Melvin Damski
PERFORMANCE .... Donald Cammell
PERIL FOR THE GUY .... James Hill
PERILOUS VOYAGE (TF).......William A. Graham
PERILS OF PAULINE, THE ... Herbert B. Leonard
PERIOD OF ADJUSTMENT ....George Roy Hill
PERSECUTION .... Don Chaffey
PERSECUTION AND ASSASSINATION OF JEAN-PAUL MARAT AS PERFORMED BY THE INMATES OF THE ASYLUM OF CHARENTON UNDER THE DIRECTION OF, THE............................. Peter Brook
PERSIANE CHIUSE ....Luigi Comencini
PERSONA.................................Ingmar Bergman
PERSONAL BEST ....Robert Towne
PERSONALITY KID ....George Sherman
PERSONALS, THE........................ Peter Markle
PERSUADERS, THE...............................Val Guest
PETE N' TILLIE...................................Martin Ritt
PETE'S DRAGON ....Don Chaffey
PETE SEEGER ... A SONG AND A STONE (FD) ....Robert Elfstrom
PETER .... Henry Koster
PETER AND PAUL (TF) ....Robert Day
PETER IBBETSON................... Henry Hathaway
PETER LUNDY AND THE MEDICINE HAT STALLION (TF) ED FRIENDLY .... Michael O'herlihy
PETER RABBIT & TALES OF BEATRIX POTTER ....Reginald Mills
PETULIA...................................... Richard Lester
PEUR SUR LA VILLE .... Henri Verneuil
PHAEDRA ....Jules Dassin
PHANTASM ....Don Coscarelli
PHANTOM COWBOY, THE ......George Sherman
PHANTOM INDIA (TD).......................... Louis Malle
PHANTOM LIGHT, THE .... Michael Powell
PHANTOM OF HOLLYWOOD, THE... Gene Levitt
PHANTOM OF THE OPEN HEARTH (TF), THE..... David R. Loxton
PHANTOM OF THE OPERA (TF)........................ Robert Markowitz
PHANTOM OF THE PARADISE.................... Brian De palma
PHAR LAP .... Simon Wincer
PHASE IV ....Saul Bass
PHENIX CITY STORY, THE ....Phil Karlson
PHILADELPHIA, HERE I COME .....John Quested
PHILIP MARLOWE - PRIVATE EYE .... David Wickes
PHILIP MARLOWE - PRIVATE EYE (CMS) .... Bryan Forbes
PHOBIA.. John Huston
PHOENIX (TF), THE ....Douglas Hickox

ROSSETTI AND RYAN: MEN WHO LOVE WOMEN (TF) .... John Astin
ROTHKO CONSPIRACY (TF), THE ... Paul Watson
ROTTEN TO THE CORE .... John Boulting
ROUGH CUT .... Don Siegel
ROUGH NIGHT IN JERICHO .... Arnold Laven
ROUGH SHOOT .... Robert Parrish
ROUGH TREATMENT .... Andrzej Wajda
ROUGHNECKS (TF) .... Bernard Mceveety
ROUND-UP, THE .... Miklos Jancso
ROUNDERS, THE .... Burt Kennedy
ROUSTABOUT .... John Rich
ROUSTERS (TF), THE .... E.W. Swackhamer
ROVIN' TUMBLEWEEDS .... George Sherman
ROYAL FLASH .... Richard Lester
ROYAL ROMANCE OF CHARLES AND DIANA (TF), THE .... Peter Levin
ROYAL SCANDAL, A .... Otto Preminger
ROYAL WEDDING .... Stanley Donen
RUBBER GUN, THE .... Allan Moyle
RUBLO DE LOS CARAS .... Etienne Perrier
RUBY .... Curtis Harrington
RUBY AND OSWALD (TF) .... Mel Stuart
RUDE BOY .... David Mingay
RUDOLPH AND FROSTY (ATF) .... Jules Bass
RULES OF MARRIAGE (TF), THE .... Milton Katselas
RULING CLASS, THE .... Peter Medak
RUMBLE FISH .... Francis Ford Coppola
RUMOR OF WAR (TF), A ...... Richard T. Heffron
RUN A CROOKED MILE (TF) .... Gene Levitt
RUN ACROSS THE RIVER ...... Everett Chambers
RUN, ANGEL, RUN! .... Jack Starrett
RUN, COUGAR, RUN .... Jerome Courtland
RUN FOR THE SUN .... Roy Boulting
RUN OF THE ARROW .... Samuel Fuller
RUN SILENT, RUN DEEP .... Robert Wise
RUN, SIMON, RUN (TF) .... George Mccowan
RUN WILD, RUN FREE .... Richard C. Sarafian
RUNAWAY BUS, THE .... Val Guest
RUNAWAY! (TF) .... David Lowell Rich
RUNAWAYS (TF), THE .... Harry Harris
RUNNER STUMBLES, THE .... Stanley Kramer
RUNNERS .... Charles Sturridge
RUNNING .... Steven H. Stern
RUNNING AWAY BACKWARDS (FD) .... Allan King
RUNNING BRAVE .... Donald Shebib
RUNNING FENCE (FD) .... Albert Maysles
RUNNING OUT (TF) .... Robert Day
RUNNING SCARED .... David Hemmings
RUSH TO JUDGMENT (FD) ...... Emile Deantonio
RUSS MEYER'S UP! .... Russ Meyer
RUSS MEYER'S VIXEN .... Russ Meyer
RUSSIAN ROULETTE .... Louis Lombardo
RUSSIANS ARE COMING THE RUSSIANS ARE COMING, THE .... Norman Jewison
RYAN'S DAUGHTER .... David Lean
RYAN'S FOUR (TF) .... Jeff Bleckner
RYNOX .... Michael Powell

S

S.A.S. MALKO "TERMINATE WITH EXTREME PREJUDICE" .... Raoul Coutard
S*H*E* (TF) .... Robert M. Lewis
S.O.B. .... Blake Edwards
S.O.S. PACIFIC .... Guy Green
S.O.S. TITANIC (TF) .... William "Billy" Hale
S*P*Y*S .... Irvin Kershner
S.W.A.L.K. .... Waris Hussein
SABOTEUR, CODE NAME "MORITURI", THE .... Bernhard Wicki
SABRINA ★ .... Billy Wilder
SACCO AND VANZETTI .... Giuliano Montaldo
SACKETTS (TF), THE .... Robert Totten
SACRED GROUND .... Charles B. Pierce
SAD HORSE, THE .... James B. Clark
SADAT (TF) .... Richard Michaels
SADDLE THE WIND .... Robert Parrish
SADGATI .... Satyajit Ray
SAFARI .... Terence Young
SAFARI 3000 .... Harry Hurwitz
SAFE AT HOME! .... Walter Doniger
SAFE PLACE, A .... Henry Jaglom
SAHARA .... Andrew V. Mclaglen
SAILOR FROM GIBRALTER, THE .... Tony Richardson
SAILOR OF THE KING .... Roy Boulting
SAILOR'S RETURN, THE .... Jack Gold
SAILOR WHO FELL FROM GRACE WITH THE SEA, THE .... Lewis John Carlino
SAINT JACK .... Peter Bogdanovich
SAINT JOAN .... Otto Preminger
SAIT-ON JAMAIS? .... Roger Vadim
SALAMANDER, THE .... Peter Zinner
SALEM'S LOT (TF) .... Tobe Hooper
SALESMAN (FD) .... Albert Maysles
SALLAH .... Ephraim Kishon
SALOME AND DELILAH .... Andy Warhol
SALT AND PEPPER .... Richard Donner
SALT TO THE DEVIL .... Edward Dmytryk
SALUT L'ARTISTE .... Yves Robert
SALVAGE GANG, THE .... John Krish
SALVAGE (TF) .... Lee Philips
SALVATE MIA FIGLIA .... Sergio Corbucci
SALVATORE GIULIANO .... Francesco Rosi
SALZBURG CONNECTION, THE ..... Lee H. Katzin
SAM HILL: WHO KILLED THE MYSTERIOUS MR. FOSTER? (TF) .... Fielder Cook
SAM MARLOW, PRIVATE EYE .... Robert Day
SAM'S SON .... Michael Landon
SAM WHISKEY .... Arnold Laven
SAME TIME, NEXT YEAR .... Robert Mulligan
SAMMY GOING SOUTH .... Alexander Mackendrick
SAMMY STOPS THE WORLD (FD) .... Melvin Shapiro
SAMSON .... Andrzej Wajda
SAMURAI REBELLION .... Masaki Kobayashi
SAMURAI (TF) .... Lee H. Katzin
SAN BABILA ORE 20: UN DELITTO INUTILE ..... Carlo Lizzani
SAN FERRY ANN .... Jeremy Summers
SAN FRANCISCO INTERNATIONAL AIRPORT (TF) .... John Llewellyn Moxey
SAN FRANCISCO STORY, THE ... Robert Parrish
SAN MICHELE AVEVA UN GALLO (TF) .... Paolo Taviani
SAN QUENTIN .... Gordon Douglas
SANCTUARY .... Tony Richardson
SANCTUARY OF FEAR (TF) .... John Llewellyn Moxey
SAND PEBBLES, THE .... Robert Wise
SANDCASTLES (TF) .... Ted Post
SANDPIPER, THE .... Vincente Minnelli
SANDPIT GENERALS, THE .... Hall Bartlett
SANDS OF THE KALAHARI .... Cy Endfield
SANJURO .... Akira Kurosawa
SANSHIRO AT GINZA .... Kon Ichikawa
SANSHIRO SUGATA .... Akira Kurosawa
SANSHIRO SUGATA - PART TWO .... Akira Kurosawa
SANTA CLAUS CONQUERS THE MARTIANS ..... Nicholas Webster
SANTA FE STAMPEDE .... George Sherman
SANTEE .... Gary Nelson
SANTIAGO .... Gordon Douglas
SAPS AT SEA .... Gordon Douglas
SARAH T. - PORTRAIT OF A TEENAGE ALCOHOLIC (TF) .... Richard Donner
SARGE: THE BADGE OR THE CROSS (TF) .... Richard A. Colla
SARONG GIRL .... Arthur Dreifuss
SASAMEYKI .... Kon Ichikawa
SASKATCHEWAN (TF), THE .... Daryl Duke
SATAN BUG, THE .... John Sturges
SATAN'S CHEERLEADERS .... Greydon Clark
SATAN'S SADISTS .... Al Adamson
SATAN'S SCHOOL FOR GIRLS (TF) .... David Lowell Rich
SATAN'S SKIN .... Piers Haggard
SATAN'S TRIANGLE (TF) .... Sutton Roley
SATANIC RITES OF DRACULA .... Alan Gibson
SATURDAY NIGHT AND SUNDAY MORNING .... Karel Reisz
SATURDAY NIGHT FEVER .... John Badham
SATURDAY'S CHILDREN .... Vincent Sherman
SATURDAY'S HERO .... David Miller
SATURDAY THE 14TH .... Howard R. Cohen
SATURN 3 .... Stanley Donen
SAUVE QUI PEUT LA VIE .... Jean-Luc Godard
SAVAGE EYE, THE .... Joseph Strick
SAVAGE GUNS, THE .... Michael Carreras
SAVAGE HARVEST .... Robert Collins
SAVAGE IS LOOSE, THE .... George C. Scott
SAVAGE MESSIAH .... Ken Russell
SAVAGE SEVEN, THE .... Richard Rush
SAVAGE SISTERS .... Eddie Romero
SAVAGE STREETS .... Daniel Steinmann
SAVAGE (TF) .... Steven Spielberg
SAVAGE WEEKEND .... David Paulsen
SAVAGES .... James Ivory
SAVAGES (TF) .... Lee H. Katzin
SAVANNAH SMILES .... Pierre Demoro
SAVE THE CHILDREN (FD) .... Stan Lathan
SAVE THE TIGER .... John G. Avildsen
SAWDUST AND TINSEL .... Ingmar Bergman
SAY AMEN, SOMEBODY (FD) .... George T. Nierenberg
SAY GOODBYE, MAGGIE COLE (TF) .... Jud Taylor
SAY HELLO TO YESTERDAY .... Alvin Rakoff
SAY IT IN FRENCH .... Andrew L. Stone
SAY IT WITH SABLES .... Frank Capra
SAYONARA ★ .... Joshua Logan
SBATTI IL MONSTRO IN PRIMA PAGINA .... Marco Bellocchio
SCALAWAG .... Kirk Douglas
SCALPHUNTERS, THE .... Sydney Pollack
SCALPLOCK (TF) .... James Goldstone
SCANDAL .... Akira Kurosawa
SCANDAL AT SCOURIE .... Jean Negulesco
SCANDAL IN SORRENTO .... Dino Risi
SCANDAL SHEET .... Phil Karlson
SCANDALE .... George Mihalka
SCANDALOUS .... Rob Cohen
SCANDALOUS JOHN .... Robert Butler
SCANNERS .... David Cronenberg
SCARAMOUCHE .... George Sidney
SCARECROW .... Jerry Schatzberg
SCARED STRAIGHT! ANOTHER STORY (TF) .... Richard Michaels
SCARFACE .... Brian De palma
SCARFACE MOB, THE .... Phil Karlson
SCARLET AND THE BLACK (TF), THE .... Jerry London
SCARLET COAT, THE .... John Sturges
SCARLET LETTER, THE .... Wim Wenders
SCARLET PIMPERNEL (TF), THE .... Clive Donner
SCARLET THREAD, THE .... Lewis Gilbert
SCARS OF DRACULA, THE ..... Roy Ward Baker
SCARY TIME, A .... Shirley Clarke
SCAVENGER HUNT .... Michael Schultz
SCENES FROM A MARRIAGE .. Ingmar Bergman
SCENT OF A WOMAN .... Dino Risi
SCENT OF MYSTERY .... Jack Cardiff
SCHERZO DEL DESTINO IN AGGUATO DIETRO L'ANGOLO COME UN BRIGANTE DI STRADA .... Lina Wertmuller
SCHIZOID .... David Paulsen
SCHLOCK .... John Landis
SCHOOL FOR SECRETS .... Peter Ustinov
SCORCHY .... Howard (Hikmet) Avedis
SCORE .... Radley Metzger
SCORPIO .... Michael Winner
SCOTT FREE (TF) .... William Wiard
SCOTT JOPLIN .... Jeremy Paul Kagan
SCREAM AND SCREAM AGAIN .... Gordon Hessler
SCREAM FOR HELP .... Michael Winner
SCREAM OF THE WOLF (TF) .... Dan Curtis
SCREAM, PRETTY PEGGY (TF) ... Gordon Hessler
SCREAMING MIMI .... Gerd Oswald
SCREAMING WOMAN (TF), THE ..... Jack Smight
SCREEN TEST .... Andy Warhol
SCREWBALLS .... Rafal Zielinski
SCROOGE .... Ronald Neame
SCRUBBERS .... Mai Zetterling
SCRUPLES (TF) .... Alan J. Levi
SCUOLA ELEMENTARE .... Alberto Lattuada
SE PERMETTE, PARLIAMO DI DONNE .... Ettore Scola
SEA AROUND US (FD), THE .... Irwin Allen
SEA FURY .... Cy Endfield
SEA GOD, THE .... George Abbott
SEA GULL, THE .... Sidney Lumet
SEA GYPSIES, THE .... Stewart Raffill
SEA OF GRASS .... Elia Kazan
SEA OF SAND .... Guy Green
SEA SHALL NOT HAVE THEM, THE .... Lewis Gilbert
SEA WOLVES, THE .... Andrew V. Mclaglen
SEABO .... Jimmy Huston
SEAGULLS OVER SORRENTO ...... John Boulting
SEANCE ON A WET AFTERNOON .... Bryan Forbes
SEARCH AND DESTROY .... William Fruet
SEARCH FOR ALEXANDER THE GREAT (MS), THE .... Peter Sykes
SEARCH FOR THE GODS (TF) .... Jud Taylor
SEARCH FOR THE NILE (MS), THE .... Richard Marquand
SEARCH ★, THE .... Fred Zinnemann
SEASIDE SWINGERS .... James Hill
SEBASTIAN .... David Greene
SEBASTIANE .... Derek Jarman
SECOND CHANCE .... Claude Lelouch

SECOND CHANCE (TF) ... Peter Tewksbury
SECOND HAND HEARTS ... Hal Ashby
SECOND THOUGHTS ... Lawrence Turman
SECOND TIME AROUND, THE ... Vincent Sherman
SECOND WIND ... Donald Shebib
SECONDS ... John Frankenheimer
SECRET CEREMONY ... Joseph Losey
SECRET DIARY OF SIGMUND FREUD, THE ... Danford B. Greene
SECRET FILE ... Arthur Dreifuss
SECRET FURY, THE ... Mel Ferrer
SECRET INVASION, THE ... Roger Corman
SECRET LIFE OF AN AMERICAN WIFE, THE ... George Axelrod
SECRET LIFE OF JOHN CHAPMAN (TF), THE ... David Lowell Rich
SECRET LIFE OF PLANTS (FD), THE ... Walon Green
SECRET NIGHT CALLER (TF), THE ... Jerry Jameson
SECRET OF CONVICT LAKE, THE ... Michael Gordon
SECRET OF MY SUCCESS, THE ... Andrew L. Stone
SECRET OF NIMH (AF), THE ... Don Bluth
SECRET OF SANTA VITTORIA, THE ... Stanley Kramer
SECRET OF THE INCAS ... Jerry Hopper
SECRET OF THE PURPLE REEF ... William Witney
SECRET PLACE, THE ... Clive Donner
SECRET POLICEMAN'S OTHER BALL (FD), THE ... Julien Temple
SECRET TENT, THE ... Don Chaffey
SECRET, THE ... Ann Hui
SECRET WAR OF HARRY FRIGG, THE ... Jack Smight
SECRET WAR OF JACKIE'S GIRLS (TF), THE ... Gordon Hessler
SECRET WAYS, THE ... Phil Karlson
SECRETS ... Gavin Millar
SECRETS OF A MOTHER AND DAUGHTER (TF) ... Gabrielle Beaumont
SECRETS OF A SECRETARY ... George Abbott
SECRETS OF THE GODS ... William Sachs
SECRETS OF THE LONE WOLF ... Edward Dmytryk
SECRETS OF THE PHANTOM CAVERNS ... Don Sharp
SECRETS OF THE WHISTLER ... George Sherman
SECRETS OF THREE HUNGRY WIVES (TF) ... Gordon Hessler
SECRETS OF WOMEN ... Ingmar Bergman
SECRETS (TF) ... Paul Wendkos
SEDUCTION OF JOE TYNAN, THE ... Jerry Schatzberg
SEDUCTION OF MIMI, THE ... Lina Wertmuller
SEDUCTION OF MISS LEONA (TF), THE ... Joseph Hardy
SEDUCTION, THE ... David Schmoeller
SEE HOW SHE RUNS (TF) ... Richard T. Heffron
SEE HOW THEY RUN (TF) ... David Lowell Rich
SEE NO EVIL ... Richard Fleischer
SEE THE MAN RUN (TF) ... Corey Allen
SEED OF INNOCENCE ... Boaz Davidson
SEED OF MAN, THE ... Marco Ferreri
SEEDING OF SARAH BURNS (TF), THE ... Sandor Stern
SEEKERS (TF), THE ... Sidney Hayers
SEEKERS, THE ... Ken Annakin
SEGUIN (TF) ... Jesus Salvador Trevino
SEIZURE ... Oliver Stone
SEIZURE: THE STORY OF KATHY MORRIS (TF) ... Gerald I. Isenberg
SEMI-TOUGH ... Michael Ritchie
SEMINOLE ... Budd Boetticher
SEMINOLE UPRISING ... Earl Bellamy
SEMMELWEIS ... Andre De toth
SEND ME NO FLOWERS ... Norman Jewison
SENDER, THE ... Roger Christian
SENIOR PROM ... David Lowell Rich
SENIOR TRIP (TF) ... Kenneth Johnson
SENIOR YEAR (TF) ... Richard Donner
SENIORS, THE ... Rod Amateau
SENSATIONS OF 1945 ... Andrew L. Stone
SENSE OF FREEDOM (TF), A ... John Mackenzie
SENSE OF LOSS (FD), A ... Marcel Ophuls
SENSITIVE, PASSIONATE MAN (TF), A ... John Newland
SENTINEL, THE ... Michael Winner
SENZA PIETA ... Alberto Lattuada
SENZA SAPERE NULLA DI LEI ... Luigi Comencini
SEPARATE PEACE, A ... Larry Peerce
SEPARATE TABLES ... Delbert Mann
SEPARATE WAYS ... Howard (Hikmet) Avedis
SEPPUKU ... Masaki Kobayashi
SEPTEMBER 30, 1955 ... James Bridges
SEPTEMBER GUN (TF) ... Don Taylor
SERAPHITA'S DIARY ... Frederick Wiseman
SERGEANT MATLOVICH VS. THE U.S. AIR FORCE (TF) ... Paul Leaf
SERGEANT RYKER ... Buzz Kulik
SERGEANT STEINER ... Andrew V. Mclaglen
SERGEANT, THE ... John Flynn
SERGEANTS 3 ... John Sturges
SERIAL ... Bill Persky
SERIOUS CHARGE ... Terence Young
SERPENT'S EGG, THE ... Ingmar Bergman
SERPENT, THE ... Henri Verneuil
SERPICO ... Sidney Lumet
SERPICO: THE DEADLY GAME (TF) ... Robert Collins
SERVANT, THE ... Joseph Losey
SESSIONS (TF) ... Richard Pearce
SESSO E VOLENTIERI ... Dino Risi
SESSOMATTO ... Dino Risi
SET THIS TOWN ON FIRE (TF) ... David Lowell Rich
SET-UP, THE ... Robert Wise
SEVEN ... Andy Sidaris
SEVEN ALONE ... Earl Bellamy
SEVEN ANGRY MEN ... Charles Marquis Warren
SEVEN BEAUTIES ... Lina Wertmuller
SEVEN BRIDES FOR SEVEN BROTHERS ... Stanley Donen
SEVEN BRIDES FOR SEVEN BROTHERS (TF) ... Gary Nelson
SEVEN CAPITAL SINS ... Claude Chabrol
SEVEN DAYS IN MAY ... John Frankenheimer
SEVEN DAYS TO NOON ... John Boulting
SEVEN IN DARKNESS (TF) ... Michael Caffey
SEVEN LITTLE FOYS, THE ... Melville Shavelson
SEVEN MEN FROM NOW ... Budd Boetticher
SEVEN MILES FROM ALCATRAZ ... Edward Dmytryk
SEVEN MINUTES, THE ... Russ Meyer
SEVEN NIGHTS IN JAPAN ... Lewis Gilbert
SEVEN-PER-CENT SOLUTION, THE ... Herbert Ross
SEVEN SAMURAI ... Akira Kurosawa
SEVEN THIEVES ... Henry Hathaway
SEVEN UPS, THE ... Philip D'antoni
SEVEN WONDERS OF THE WORLD ... Andrew Marton
SEVEN YEAR ITCH, THE ... Billy Wilder
SEVENTEEN YEARS OLD ... Alf Kjellin
SEVENTH AVENUE (MS) ... Richard Irving
SEVENTH CROSS, THE ... Fred Zinnemann
SEVENTH DAWN, THE ... Lewis Gilbert
SEVENTH SEAL, THE ... Ingmar Bergman
SEVENTH SIN, THE ... Ronald Neame
SEVERED HEAD, A ... Dick Clement
SEX AND THE MARRIED WOMAN (TF) ... Jack Arnold
SEX AND THE SINGLE GIRL ... Richard Quine
SEX AND THE SINGLE PARENT (TF) ... Jackie Cooper
SEX KITTENS GO TO COLLEGE ... Albert Zugsmith
SEX O'CLOCK USA (FD) ... Francois Reichenbach
SEX ON THE GROOVE TUBE ... Sean S. Cunningham
SEX SYMBOL (TF), THE ... David Lowell Rich
SEXTETTE ... Kenneth "Ken" Hughes
SGT. PEPPER'S LONELY HEARTS CLUB BAND ... Michael Schultz
SHADOW BOX (TF)☆, THE ... Paul Newman
SHADOW IN THE STREETS (TF), A ... Richard Donner
SHADOW LINE ... Andrzej Wajda
SHADOW OF THE HAWK ... George Mccowan
SHADOW ON THE LAND (TF) ... Richard C. Sarafian
SHADOW ON THE WINDOW, THE ... William Asher
SHADOW OVER ELVERON (TF) ... James Goldstone
SHADOW RIDERS (TF), THE ... Andrew V. Mclaglen
SHADOWED ... John Sturges
SHADOWS ... John Cassavetes
SHAFT ... Gordon Parks
SHAFT IN AFRICA ... John Guillermin
SHAFT'S BIG SCORE! ... Gordon Parks
SHAGGY D.A., THE ... Robert Stevenson
SHAKE HANDS WITH THE DEVIL ... Michael Anderson
SHAKEDOWN ... Joseph Pevney
SHAKESPEARE WALLAH ... James Ivory
SHAKIEST GUN IN THE WEST, THE ... Alan Rafkin
SHALAKO! ... Edward Dmytryk
SHALIMAR ... Krishna Shah
SHALOM ... Yaky Yosha
SHAME ... Ingmar Bergman
SHAME, SHAME, EVERBODY KNOWS HER NAME ... Joseph Jacoby
SHAMPOO ... Hal Ashby
SHAMROCK HILL ... Arthur Dreifuss
SHAMUS ... Buzz Kulik
SHANGHAI COBRA, THE ... Phil Karlson
SHAPE OF THINGS TO COME, THE ... George Mccowan
SHARK! ... Samuel Fuller
SHARK KILL (TF) ... William A. Graham
SHARK'S TREASURE ... Cornel Wilde
SHARKY'S MACHINE ... Burt Reynolds
SHARON: PORTRAIT OF A MISTRESS (TF) ... Robert Greenwald
SHE ... Avi Nesher
SHE CAME TO THE VALLEY ... Albert Band
SHE CRIED MURDER (TF) ... Bernard L. Kowalski
SHE DANCES ALONE ... Robert Dornhelm
SHE GODS OF SHARK REEF, THE ... Roger Corman
SHE LIVES (TF) ... Stuart Hagmann
SHE'S BACK ON BROADWAY ... Gordon Douglas
SHE'S DRESSED TO KILL (TF) ... Gus Trikonis
SHE'S IN THE ARMY NOW (TF) ... Hy Averback
SHE WAITS (TF) ... Delbert Mann
SHEEP HAS FIVE LEGS, THE ... Henri Verneuil
SHEILA LEVINE IS DEAD AND LIVING IN NEW YORK ... Sidney J. Furie
SHELL GAME (TF) ... Glenn Jordan
SHENANDOAH ... Andrew V. Mclaglen
SHEPHERD OF THE HILLS, THE ... Henry Hathaway
SHERIFF (TF), THE ... David Lowell Rich
SHIELD FOR MURDER ... Howard W. Koch
SHILLINGBURY BLOWERS, THE ... Val Guest
SHINING SEASON (TF), A ... Stuart Margolin
SHINING STAR ... Sig Shore
SHINING, THE ... Stanley Kubrick
SHINING VICTORY ... Irving Rapper
SHIP OF FOOLS ... Stanley Kramer
SHIRLEY THOMPSON VERSUS THE ALIENS ... Jim Sharman
SHIRTS/SKINS (TF) ... William A. Graham
SHIVERS ... David Cronenberg
SHOCK CORRIDOR ... Samuel Fuller
SHOCK TREATMENT ... Denis Sanders
SHOCK TROOPS ... Costa Gavras
SHOCK WAVES ... Ken Wiederhorn
SHOES OF THE FISHERMAN, THE ... Michael Anderson
SHOGUN (MS) ★ ... Jerry London
SHOOT ... Harvey Hart
SHOOT FIRST ... Robert Parrish
SHOOT-OUT ... Henry Hathaway
SHOOT-OUT AT MEDICINE BEND ... Richard L. Bare
SHOOT THE MOON ... Alan Parker
SHOOT THE PIANO PLAYER ... Francois Truffaut
SHOOT TO KILL ... Michael Winner
SHOOTING PARTY, THE ... Alan Bridges
SHOOTING STARS (TF) ... Richard Lang
SHOOTING, THE ... Monte Hellman
SHOOTIST, THE ... Don Siegel
SHOOTOUT IN A ONE-DOG TOWN (TF) ... Burt Kennedy
SHORT EYES ... Robert M. Young
SHOT IN THE DARK, A ... Blake Edwards
SHOUT AT THE DEVIL ... Peter Hunt
SHOUT, THE ... Jerzy Skolimowski
SHOW BOAT ... George Sidney
SHOWGIRL IN HOLLYWOOD ... Mervyn Leroy
SHOWMAN (FD) ... Albert Maysles
SHRIKE, THE ... Jose Ferrer
SHUTTERED ROOM, THE ... David Greene
SI C'ETAIT A REFAIRE ... Claude Lelouch
SI J'ETAIS UN ESPION ... Bertrand Blier
SIBERIADE ... Andrei Konchalovsky
SIBERIAN LADY MACBETH ... Andrzej Wajda
SICILIAN CLAN, THE ... Henri Verneuil
SICILIAN CONNECTION, THE ... Ferdinando Baldi
SIDDHARTHA ... Conrad Rooks
SIDE BY SIDE ... Bruce Beresford

STRANGE VENGEANCE OF ROSALIE, THE ....
                              Jack Starrett
STRANGER AT JEFFERSON HIGH (TF), THE......
                             Lyman Dayton
STRANGER IN BETWEEN, THE....................
                       Charles Crichton
STRANGER IN OUR HOUSE (TF) .... Wes Craven
STRANGER IS WATCHING, A ....
                    Sean S. Cunningham
STRANGER ON THE PROWL .... Joseph Losey
STRANGER ON THE RUN (TF)........Don Siegel
STRANGER'S KISS ....Matthew Chapman
STRANGER (TF), THE ....Lee H. Katzin
STRANGER, THE .... Orson Welles
STRANGER WHO LOOKS LIKE ME (TF), THE.....
                             Larry Peerce
STRANGER WITHIN (TF), THE ....Lee Philips
STRANGER WORE A GUN, THE ....
                          Andre De toth
STRANGERS IN 7A (TF), THE ..... Paul Wendkos
STRANGERS IN PARADISE............Ulli Lommel
STRANGERS' MEETING..............Robert Day
STRANGERS: THE STORY OF A MOTHER AND
  A DAUGHTER (TF)..........Milton Katselas
STRANGERS WHEN WE MEET ... Richard Quine
STRANGLER'S WEB........John Llewellyn Moxey
STRANGLER, THE........Burt Topper
STRATEGY OF TERROR..............Jack Smight
STRAW DOGS ....Sam Peckinpah
STRAWBERRY STATEMENT, THE ....
                         Stuart Hagmann
STRAY DOG ....Akira Kurosawa
STRAZIAMI DA MI BACI SAZIAMI ......Dino Risi
STREAMERS .... Robert Altman
STREET GIRLS .... Michael Miller
STREET KILLING (TF)...............Harvey Hart
STREET MUSIC .... Jenny Bowen
STREETCAR NAMED DESIRE ★, A.....Elia Kazan
STREETCAR NAMED DESIRE (TF), A ....
                           John Erman
STREETS OF FIRE .... Walter Hill
STREETS OF L.A. (TF), THE ...Jerrold Freedman
STREETS OF SAN FRANCISCO (TF), THE ....
                        Walter Grauman
STRESS EN TRES TRES.............. Carlos Saura
STRICTLY DISHONORABLE........... Melvin Frank
STRIKING BACK......................William Fruet
STRIP POKER ....Peter Walker
STRIPES ....Ivan Reitman
STRIPPER, THE ....Franklin J. Schaffner
STROHFEUER .... Volker Schlondorff
STROKER ACE .... Hal Needham
STRONG MAN, THE .... Frank Capra
STRONGER THAN THE SUN (TF) ....
                        Michael Apted
STRONGEST MAN IN THE WORLD, THE ....
                      Vincent Mceveety
STROSZEK ....Werner Herzog
STRUCTURE OF CRYSTALS, THE....................
                      Krzysztof Zanussi
STUBBY ....Bo Widerberg
STUCK ON YOU!....................Michael Herz
STUD BROWN .... Al Adamson
STUD, THE .... Quentin Masters
STUDENT BODIES.................Mickey Rose
STUDENT NURSES, THE.....Stephanie Rothman
STUDENT TEACHERS, THE.....Jonathan Kaplan
STUDS LONIGAN (MS) ....James Goldstone
STUDY IN TERROR, A ....James Hill
STUNT MAN ★, THE...........Richard Rush
STUNT SEVEN (TF)...............John Peyser
STUNTS .... Mark L. Lester
STUNTS UNLIMITED (TF) .... Hal Needham
SUBJECT WAS ROSES, THE ....Ulu Grosbard
SUBMARINE ....Frank Capra
SUBMARINE X-1 ....William A. Graham
SUBURBIA ....Penelope Spheeris
SUCCESS ....William Richert
SUCH A GORGEOUS KID LIKE ME ....
                      Francois Truffaut
SUCH GOOD FRIENDS ....Otto Preminger
SUCKER, THE .... Gerard Oury
SUDDEN DANGER .... Hubert Cornfield
SUDDEN DEATH ....Eddie Romero
SUDDEN FEAR .... David Miller
SUDDEN IMPACT..............Clint Eastwood
SUDDEN TERROR................John Hough
SUDDEN WEALTH OF THE POOR PEOPLE OF
  KOMBACH, THE ....Volker Schlondorff
SUDDENLY LAST SUMMER ....
                    Joseph L. Mankiewicz
SUDDENLY, LOVE (TF)............Stuart Margolin
SUDDENLY SINGLE (TF).................Jud Taylor
SUGAR COOKIES ....Theodore Gershuny

SUGAR HILL..................Paul Maslansky
SUGARLAND EXPRESS, THE ..Steven Spielberg
SUICIDE .... Andy Warhol
SUICIDE'S WIFE (TF), THE..........John Newland
SULLIVAN'S EMPIRE................Harvey Hart
SULLIVANS (MS), THE ...... David Stevens
SULTAN'S DAUGHTER, THE ...... Arthur Dreifuss
SUMMER AND SMOKE.............Peter Glenville
SUMMER GIRL (TF) ....Robert M. Lewis
SUMMER HOLIDAY .... Peter Yates
SUMMER IN THE CITY ....Wim Wenders
SUMMER LOVERS .... Randal Kleiser
SUMMER MADNESS★...................David Lean
SUMMER OF '42 ....Robert Mulligan
SUMMER OF MY GERMAN SOLDIER (TF) ....
                      Michael Tuchner
SUMMER OF SECRETS ....Jim Sharman
SUMMER SCHOOL TEACHERS ....
                      Barbara Peeters
SUMMER (TF)...............Dezso Magyar
SUMMER WISHES, WINTER DREAMS ....
                      Gilbert Cates
SUMMER WITHOUT BOYS (TF), A ....
                      Jeannot Szwarc
SUMMERSPELL..................Lina Shanklin
SUMMERTIME...................David Lean
SUMMERTREE ....Anthony Newley
SUN'S BURIAL, THE .... Nagisa Oshima
SUNBURN ....Richard C. Sarafian
SUNDAY BLOODY SUNDAY ★........................
                      John Schlesinger
SUNDAY IN NEW YORK ....Peter Tewksbury
SUNDAY IN THE COUNTRY ....John Trent
SUNDAY LOVERS .... Bryan Forbes
SUNDAY PUNCH..................... David Miller
SUNDAY WOMAN ....Luigi Comencini
SUNDOWN .... Henry Hathaway
SUNDOWNERS ★, THE ....Fred Zinnemann
SUNNY SIDE OF THE STREET .... Richard Quine
SUNNYSIDE .... Timothy Galfas
SUNSET BOULEVARD ★★..............Billy Wilder
SUNSET COVE .... Al Adamson
SUNSET LIMOUSINE (TF)............Terry Hughes
SUNSET PASS .... Henry Hathaway
SUNSHINE BOYS, THE .... Herbert Ross
SUNSHINE CHRISTMAS (TF)........ Glenn Jordan
SUNSHINE PATRIOT (TF), THE .. Joseph Sargent
SUNSHINE (TF) .... Joseph Sargent
SUNSTROKE .... Yaky Yosha
SUPER COPS (TF) .... Gordon Parks
SUPER COPS, THE .... Gordon Parks
SUPER DUDE .... Henry Hathaway
SUPER FUZZ ....Sergio Corbucci
SUPERCOCK .... Gus Trikonis
SUPERDAD .... Vincent Mceveety
SUPERDOME (TF) ....Jerry Jameson
SUPERFLY T.N.T. .... Ron O'neal
SUPERGIRL ....Jeannot Szwarc
SUPERMAN .... Richard Donner
SUPERMAN II .... Richard Lester
SUPERSTARS IN FILM CONCERT (FD) ....
                      Peter Clifton
SUPERVIXENS ....Russ Meyer
SUPPERMAN III ....Richard Lester
SUPPORT YOUR LOCAL GUNFIGHTER............
                      Burt Kennedy
SUPPORT YOUR LOCAL SHERIFF.................
                      Burt Kennedy
SUPPOSE THEY GAVE A WAR AND NOBODY
  CAME? ....Hy Averback
SURF ....Don Chaffey
SURF II ....Randall Badat
SURF PARTY .... Maury Dexter
SURFACING .... Claude Jutra
SURPRISE PACKAGE ....Stanley Donen
SURPRISE PARTY ....Roger Vadim
SURVIVAL '67 ....Jules Dassin
SURVIVAL OF DANA (TF)...........Jack Starrett
SURVIVOR, THE...........David Hemmings
SURVIVORS, THE ....Michael Ritchie
SUSPECT ....John Boulting
SUSPIRIA ....Dario Argento
SUZANNE ....Robin Spry
SVEGLIATI E UCCIDI ....Carlo Lizzani
SVENGALI (TF) ....Anthony Harvey
SWALLOWS AND AMAZONS ....
                      Claude Whatham
SWAMP THING........................ Wes Craven
SWAMP WOMAN ....Roger Corman
SWAN SONG (TF) ....Jerry London
SWARM, THE .... Irwin Allen
SWASHBUCKLER ....James Goldstone
SWASTIKA (FD) ....Philippe Mora
SWEDISH FLY GIRLS ....Jack O'connell

SWEDISH MISTRESS, THE.........Vilgot Sjoman
SWEENEY .... David Wickes
SWEENEY 2 ....Tom Clegg
SWEET ADELINE ....Mervyn Leroy
SWEET AND THE BITTER, THE....James Clavell
SWEET BIRD OF YOUTH ....Richard Brooks
SWEET CHARITY ....Bob Fosse
SWEET GENEVIEVE ....Arthur Dreifuss
SWEET GINGER BROWN ....Garry Marshall
SWEET HOSTAGE (TF)...................Lee Philips
SWEET HOURS ....Carlos Saura
SWEET JESUS, PREACHER MAN ....
                      Henning Schellerup
SWEET LOVE, BITTER.............Herbert Danska
SWEET MOVIE................Dusan Makavejev
SWEET NOVEMBER............Robert Ellis Miller
SWEET REVENGE ....Jerry Schatzberg
SWEET RIDE, THE ....Harvey Hart
SWEET SMELL OF SUCCESS ....
                    Alexander Mackendrick
SWEET SOUNDS .... James Ivory
SWEET SUZYI ....Russ Meyer
SWEET, SWEET RACHEL (TF) .... Sutton Roley
SWEET SWEETBACK'S BAADASSSSSS SONG
                    Melvin Van Peebles
SWEET TORONTO ................D.A. Pennebaker
SWEET WILLIAM ....Claude Whatham
SWEETHEART OF THE CAMPUS ....
                    Edward Dmytryk
SWEPT AWAY BY AN UNUSUAL DESTINY IN
  THE BLUE SEA OF AUGUST ....
                    Lina Wertmuller
SWIMMER, THE .... Frank Perry
SWIMMING POOL, THE ....Jacques Deray
SWING PARADE OF 1946 ....Phil Karlson
SWING SHIFT...............Jonathan Demme
SWINGER, THE .... George Sidney
SWINGERS' PARADISE .... Sidney J. Furie
SWINGIN' MAIDEN, THE .... Gerald Thomas
SWINGING AT THE CASTLE ....Alf Kjellin
SWINGING BARMAIDS, THE..........Gus Trikonis
SWINGING CHEERLEADERS, THE....... Jack Hill
SWISS CONSPIRACY, THE .... Jack Arnold
SWISS FAMILY ROBINSON.......... Ken Annakin
SWISS FAMILY ROBINSON (TF), THE ....
                    Harry Harris
SWITCH (TF).....................Robert Day
SWITCHBLADE SISTERS .... Jack Hill
SWORD AND THE ROSE, THE ...... Ken Annakin
SWORD AND THE SORCERER, THE ....
                    Albert Pyun
SWORD IN THE DESERT ....George Sherman
SWORD IN THE STONE (AF), THE ....
                    Wolfgang Reitherman
SWORD OF ALI BABA, THE ......Virgil W. Vogel
SWORD OF D'ARTAGNAN, THE ....
                    Budd Boetticher
SWORD OF LANCELOT, THE ....Cornel Wilde
SWORD OF THE VALIANT ....Stephen Weeks
SWORDSMAN OF SIENA ....Etienne Perrier
SYBIL (TF) .... Daniel Petrie
SYLVIA ....Gordon Douglas
SYMPATHY FOR THE DEVIL...Jean-Luc Godard
SYMPHONY FOR A MASSACRE ....
                    Jacques Deray
SYNANON .... Richard Quine
SYSKONBADD 1782 .... Vilgot Sjoman
SYSTEM, THE .... Michael Winner
SZERELEM, ELEKTRA .... Miklos Jancso

T

T.J. HOOKER (TF) ....Clifford Bole
T.R. BASKIN .... Herbert Ross
TABLE FOR FIVE .... Robert Lieberman
TABOO .... Vilgot Sjoman
TAG ....Nick Castle, Jr.
TAIL GUNNER JOE (TF) ☆ .... Jud Taylor
TAILOR'S MAID, THE.................Mario Monicelli
TAKE A GIANT STEP .... Philip Leacock
TAKE A GIRL LIKE YOU ... Jonathan Miller
TAKE CARE OF MY LITTLE GIRL ....
                    Jean Negulesco
TAKE DOWN .... Kieth Merrill
TAKE HER, SHE'S MINE.............. Henry Koster
TAKE MY LIFE ....Ronald Neame
TAKE THE HIGH GROUND ....Richard Brooks
TAKE THE MONEY AND RUN ....Woody Allen
TAKE THIS JOB AND SHOVE IT....Gus Trikonis
TAKE YOUR BEST SHOT (TF) ...... David Greene

THIS INSTANT ... Emil Loteanu
THIS IS A HIJACK ... Barry Pollack
THIS IS ELVIS (FD) ... Andrew Solt
THIS IS MY STREET ... Sidney Hayers
THIS MAN MUST DIE ... Claude Chabrol
THIS MAN STANDS ALONE (TF) ... Jerrold Freedman
THIS PROPERTY IS CONDEMNED ... Sydney Pollack
THIS REBEL BREED ... Richard L. Bare
THIS SAVAGE LAND (TF) ... Vincent Mceveety
THIS SIDE OF THE LAW ... Richard L. Bare
THIS SPORTING LIFE ... Lindsay Anderson
THIS WAY - THAT WAY ... Kon Ichikawa
THOMAS CROWN AFFAIR, THE ... Norman Jewison
THORN BIRDS (MS)☆, THE ... Daryl Duke
THORN IN THE HEART ... Alberto Lattuada
THORNWELL (TF) ... Harry Moses
THOROUGHLY MODERN MILLIE ... George Roy Hill
THOSE DARING YOUNG MEN IN THEIR JAUNTY JALOPIES ... Ken Annakin
THOSE FANTASTIC FLYING FOOLS ... Don Sharp
THOSE LIPS, THOSE EYES ... Michael Pressman
THOSE MAGNIFICENT MEN IN THEIR FLYING MACHINES ... Ken Annakin
THOSE WERE THE HAPPY TIMES ... Robert Wise
THOSE WHO MAKE TOMORROW ... Akira Kurosawa
THOSE WHO TREAD ON THE TIGER'S TAIL ... Akira Kurosawa
THOU SHALT NOT COMMIT ADULTERY (TF) ... Delbert Mann
THOU SHALT NOT KILL (TF) ... I.C. Rapoport
THOUSANDS CHEER ... George Sidney
THREE ... James Salter
THREE BAD MEN IN A HIDDEN FORTRESS ... Akira Kurosawa
THREE BROTHERS ... Francesco Rosi
THREE CAME HOME ... Jean Negulesco
THREE CARD MONTE ... Les Rose
THREE COINS IN THE FOUNTAIN ... Jean Negulesco
THREE GUNS FOR TEXAS ... David Lowell Rich
THREE HATS FOR LISA ... Sidney Hayers
THREE HUNDRED MILES FOR STEPHANIE (TF) ... Clyde Ware
THREE IN THE ATTIC ... Richard Wilson
THREE LIVES OF THOMASINA, THE ... Don Chaffey
THREE LOVES ... Masaki Kobayashi
THREE MEN IN A BOAT ... Ken Annakin
THREE MEN ON A HORSE ... Mervyn Leroy
THREE MUSKETEERS, THE ... George Sidney
THREE ON A COUCH ... Jerry Lewis
THREE ON A DATE (TF) ... Bill Bixby
THREE ON A MATCH ... Mervyn Leroy
THREE ON A SPREE ... Sidney J. Furie
THREE RESURRECTED DRUNKARDS ... Nagisa Oshima
THREE RING CIRCUS ... Joseph Pevney
THREE'S A CROWD (TF) ... Harry Falk
THREE SECRETS ... Robert Wise
THREE SISTERS ... Laurence Olivier
THREE SISTERS, THE ... Paul Bogart
THREE SMART GIRLS ... Henry Koster
THREE SMART GIRLS GROW UP ... Henry Koster
THREE STARS ... Miklos Jancso
THREE STRANGE LOVES ... Ingmar Bergman
THREE STRANGERS ... Jean Negulesco
THREE TEXAS STEERS ... George Sherman
THREE TO GO ... Peter Weir
THREE WARRIORS ... Kieth Merrill
THREE WISE KINGS ... Sergio Corbucci
THREE WORLDS OF GULLIVER, THE ... Jack Sher
THRESHOLD ... Richard Pearce
THRILL OF IT ALL, THE ... Norman Jewison
THRILLING ... Carlo Lizzani
THRONE OF BLOOD ... Akira Kurosawa
THROUGH A GLASS DARKLY ... Ingmar Bergman
THROUGH NAKED EYES (TF) ... John Llewellyn Moxey
THROUGH THE MAGIC PYRAMID (TF) ... Ron Howard
THUMB TRIPPING ... Quentin Masters
THUNDER ALLEY ... Richard Rush
THUNDER AND LIGHTNING ... Corey Allen
THUNDER IN THE SUN ... Russell Rouse
THUNDER OVER THE PLAINS ... Andre De toth
THUNDER ROCK ... Roy Boulting
THUNDERBALL ... Terence Young
THUNDERBOLT ... John Sturges
THUNDERBOLT AND LIGHTFOOT ... Michael Cimino
THUNDERHOOF ... Phil Karlson
THUNDERING HERD, THE ... Henry Hathaway
THUNDERSTORM ... John Guillermin
THURSDAY'S CHILD (TF) ... David Lowell Rich
THURSDAY'S GAME (TF) ... Robert Moore
THX 1138 ... George Lucas
TI HO SPOSATO PER ALLEGRIA ... Luciano Salce
TIARA TAHITI ... Ted Kotcheff
... TICK ... TICK ... TICK ... Ralph Nelson
TICKET TO HEAVEN ... Ralph L. Thomas
TICKLISH AFFAIR, A ... George Sidney
TIFFANY JONES ... Peter Walker
TIGER AND THE PUSSYCAT, THE ... Dino Risi
TIGER BAY ... J. Lee Thompson
TIGER IN SMOKE ... Roy Ward Baker
TIGER MAKES OUT, THE ... Arthur Hiller
TIGHT LITTLE ISLAND ... Alexander Mackendrick
TIGHT SPOT ... Phil Karlson
TILL MARRIAGE US DO PART ... Luigi Comencini
TILL SEX DO US PART ... Vilgot Sjoman
TILL THE CLOUDS ROLL BY ... Vincente Minnelli
TILL THE END OF TIME ... Edward Dmytryk
TILT ... Rudy Durand
TIM ... Michael Pate
TIME AFTER TIME ... Nicholas Meyer
TIME BANDITS ... Terry Gilliam
TIME FOR DYING, A ... Budd Boetticher
TIME FOR KILLING, A ... Phil Karlson
TIME FOR LOVING ... Christopher Miles
TIME FOR MIRACLES (TF), A ... Michael O'herlihy
TIME GENTLEMEN PLEASE! ... Lewis Gilbert
TIME IS MY ENEMY ... Don Chaffey
TIME LIMIT/SPEED LIMIT 65 ... Yaphet Kotto
TIME LOST AND TIME REMEMBERED ... Desmond Davis
TIME MACHINE (TF), THE ... Henning Schellerup
TIME OF THE JACKALS ... Damiano Damiani
TIME TO DIE, A ... Matt Cimber
TIME TO RUN ... James F. Collier
TIME TO SING, A ... Arthur Dreifuss
TIME TRAVELERS (TF) ... Alexander Singer
TIME WALKER ... Tom Kennedy
TIME WITHOUT PITY ... Joseph Losey
TIMELOCK ... Gerald Thomas
TIMERIDER ... William Dear
TIMES SQUARE ... Allan Moyle
TIMESLIP ... Kenneth "Ken" Hughes
TIN DRUM, THE ... Volker Schlondorff
TINKER, TAILOR, SOLDIER, SPY (TF) ... John Irvin
TITANIC ... Jean Negulesco
TITFIELD THUNDERBOLT, THE ... Charles Crichton
TITICUT FOLLIES (FD) ... Frederick Wiseman
TITLE SHOT ... Les Rose
TO ALL MY FRIENDS ON SHORE (TF) ... Gilbert Cates
TO BE A CROOK ... Claude Lelouch
TO BE OR NOT TO BE ... Alan Johnson
TO CATCH A KING (CTF) ... Clive Donner
TO COMMIT A MURDER ... Edouard Molinaro
TO DIE IN PARIS (TF) ... Allen Reisner
TO'E MORTA LA NONNA ... Mario Monicelli
TO FIND A MAN ... Buzz Kulik
TO FIND MY SON (TF) ... Delbert Mann
TO FORGET VENICE ... Franco Brusati
TO HAVE AND TO HOLD ... Herbert Wise
TO JOY ... Ingmar Bergman
TO KILL A CLOWN ... George Bloomfield
TO KILL A COP (TF) ... Gary Nelson
TO KILL A MOCKINGBIRD ★ ... Robert Mulligan
TO LOVE AGAIN ... Kon Ichikawa
TO RACE THE WIND (TF) ... Walter Grauman
TO SIR, WITH LOVE ... James Clavell
TO THE DEVIL A DAUGHTER ... Peter Sykes
TO THE ENDS OF THE EARTH ... Robert Stevenson
TO THE ENDS OF THE EARTH (FD) ... William Kronick
TO THE LAST MAN ... Henry Hathaway
TO THE VICTOR ... Robert Stevenson
TO TRAP A SPY ... Don Medford
TOBRUK ... Arthur Hiller
TODAY'S FBI (TF) ... Virgil W. Vogel
TOGETHER ... Sean S. Cunningham
TOGETHER BROTHERS ... William A. Graham
TOGETHER FOR DAYS ... Michael Schultz
TOKYO OLYMPIAD (FD) ... Kon Ichikawa
TOKYO SAIBAN (FD) ... Masaki Kobayashi
TOM ... Greydon Clark
TOM BROWN'S SCHOOLDAYS ... Robert Stevenson
TOM, DICK AND HARRY ... Garson Kanin
TOM HORN ... William Wiard
TOM JONES ★★ ... Tony Richardson
TOM SAWYER ... Don Taylor
TOMA (TF) ... Richard T. Heffron
TOMAHAWK ... George Sherman
TOMB OF LIGEIA, THE ... Roger Corman
TOMMY ... Ken Russell
TOMORROW ... Joseph Anthony
TOMORROW IS THE FINAL DAY ... Yilmaz Guney
TOMORROW'S CHILD (TF) ... Joseph Sargent
TONIGHT FOR SURE ... Francis Ford Coppola
TONIGHT OR NEVER ... Mervyn Leroy
TONINO NERA ... Carlo Lizzani
TONY ROME ... Gordon Douglas
TOO FAR TO GO (TF) ... Fielder Cook
TOO HOT TO HANDLE ... Don Schain
TOO LATE BLUES ... John Cassavetes
TOO LATE THE HERO ... Robert Aldrich
TOO MANY GIRLS ... George Abbott
TOO SOON TO LOVE ... Richard Rush
TOO YOUNG TO MARRY ... Mervyn Leroy
TOOMORROW ... Val Guest
TOOTSIE ★ ... Sydney Pollack
TOP O' THE MORNING ... David Miller
TOP OF THE HEAP ... Christopher St. John
TOP OF THE HILL (TF), THE ... Walter Grauman
TOP SECRET! ... David Zucker
TOP SECRET (TF) ... Paul Leaf
TOP SPEED ... Mervyn Leroy
TOPKAPI ... Jules Dassin
TOPO GIGIO E SEI LADRI ... Kon Ichikawa
TOPPER (TF) ... Charles S. Dubin
TOPRINI NASZ ... Andre De toth
TORA! TORA! TORA! ... Richard Fleischer
TORCH SONG ... Tom Wright
TORMENT ... John Guillermin
TORMENTED ... Bert I. Gordon
TORMENTOR, THE ... John Llewellyn Moxey
TORN BETWEEN TWO LOVERS (TF) ... Delbert Mann
TORPEDO RUN ... Joseph Pevney
TORTURE GARDEN ... Freddie Francis
TOTO CERCA CASA ... Mario Monicelli
TOTO E CAROLINA ... Mario Monicelli
TOTO E I RE DI ROMA ... Mario Monicelli
TOUCH AND GO ... Philippe De broca
TOUCH OF CLASS, A ... Melvin Frank
TOUCH OF EVIL ... Orson Welles
TOUCH OF LARCENY, A ... Guy Hamilton
TOUCH OF LOVEA ... Waris Hussein
TOUCH OF THE TIMES, A ... Michael Roemer
TOUCH OF ZEN, A ... King Hu
TOUCH, THE ... Ingmar Bergman
TOUCHED ... John Flynn
TOUCHED BY LOVE ... Gus Trikonis
TOUCHEZ PAS LA FEMME BLANCHE ... Marco Ferreri
TOUGH ENOUGH ... Richard Fleischer
TOUGHEST GUN IN TOMBSTONE ... Earl Bellamy
TOURIST (TF) ... Jeremy Summers
TOURIST TRAP ... David Schmoeller
TOUT ALLURE, A ... Robert Kramer
TOUT CASSER, A ... John Berry
TOUT PRENDE, A ... Claude Jutra
TOUT VA BIEN ... Jean-Luc Godard
TOUTE UNE VIE ... Claude Lelouch
TOWARD THE UNKNOWN ... Mervyn Leroy
TOWER OF LONDON ... Roger Corman
TOWERING INFERNO, THE ... Irwin Allen
TOWN CALLED BASTARD, A ... Robert Parrish
TOWN CALLED HELLA ... Robert Parrish
TOWN LIKE ALICE (MS), A ... David Stevens
TOWN OF LOVE AND HOPE, A ... Nagisa Oshima
TOWN ON TRIAL ... John Guillermin
TOWN THAT DREADED SUNDOWN, THE ... Charles B. Pierce
TOY, THE ... Richard Donner
TOY TIGER ... Jerry Hopper
TOYS IN THE ATTIC ... George Roy Hill
TRA MOGLIE E MARITO ... Luigi Comencini
TRACCO DI VELENO IN UNA COPPA DI CHAMPAGNE ... Gordon Hessler
TRACKDOWN ... Richard T. Heffron

TRACKDOWN: FINDING THE GOODBAR KILLER (TF) ....Bill Persky
TRACKERS (TF), THE..................Earl Bellamy
TRACKS ....Henry Jaglom
TRADER HORN......................Reza Badiyi
TRADING PLACES ....John Landis
TRAGEDY OF A RIDICULOUS MAN ....
　　　　　　　　　　Bernardo Bertolucci
TRAGICO FANTOZZI ....Luciano Salce
TRAIL BLAZERS, THE ....George Sherman
TRAIL OF THE LONESOME PINE, THE ....
　　　　　　　　　　　Henry Hathaway
TRAIL OF THE PINK PANTHER ...Blake Edwards
TRAIL RIDE, THE ....William Byron Hillman
TRAIN OF EVENTS ....Charles Crichton
TRAIN ROBBERS, THE ....Burt Kennedy
TRAIN, THE ....John Frankenheimer
TRAITOR'S GATE ....Freddie Francis
TRAMPLERS, THE ....Albert Band
TRANS-EUROP-EXPRESS ......Alain Robbe-Grillet
TRANSIT ....Daniel Wachsmann
TRANSPLANT (TF) ....William A. Graham
TRAP, THE ....Norman Panama
TRAPPED ....Richard Fleischer
TRAPPED BENEATH THE SEA (TF) ....
　　　　　　　　　　　William A. Graham
TRAPPED (TF) ....Frank De felitta
TRASH ....Paul Morrissey
TRAUMA CENTER (TF) ....Thomas Carter
TRAVELING EXECUTIONER, THE ....Jack Smight
TRAVELLER'S JOY ....Ralph Thomas
TRAVELLERS, THE ....Richard L. Bare
TRAVELS WITH ANITA ....Mario Monicelli
TRAVIS LOGAN, D.A. (TF) ....Paul Wendkos
TRAVIS MCGEE (TF) ....Andrew V. Mclaglen
TRE NOTTE D'AMORE......Luigi Comencini
TRE TIGRI CONTRA TRE TIGRI ....
　　　　　　　　　　　Sergio Corbucci
TREASURE ISLAND ....John Hough
TREASURE OF MATECUMBE, THE...............
　　　　　　　　　　　Vincent Mceveety
TREASURE OF PANCHO VILLA, THE ....
　　　　　　　　　　　George Sherman
TREASURE OF SAN GENNARO ....Dino Risi
TREASURE OF THE FOUR CROWNS ....
　　　　　　　　　　　Ferdinando Baldi
TREASURE OF THE SIERRA MADRE ★★, THE ....
　　　　　　　　　　　John Huston
TREATISE IN JAPANESE BAWDY SONGS, A ....
　　　　　　　　　　　Nagisa Oshima
TREE GROWS IN BROOKLYN, A ....Elia Kazan
TREE GROWS IN BROOKLYN (TF), A...............
　　　　　　　　　　　Joseph Hardy
TREE OF WOODEN CLOGS, THE ....
　　　　　　　　　　　Ermanno Olmi
TREE, THE ....Robert Guenette
TRENCHCOAT ....Michael Tuchner
TRESPASSERS, THE ....John Duigan
TRIAL OF BILLY JACK, THE ....Frank Laughlin
TRIAL OF CHAPLAIN JENSEN (TF), THE ....
　　　　　　　　　　　Robert Day
TRIAL OF JOAN OF ARC, THE...Robert Bresson
TRIAL OF LEE HARVEY OSWALD (TF), THE...............
　　　　　　　　　　　David Greene
TRIAL OF THE CATONSVILLE NINE, THE ....
　　　　　　　　　　　Gordon Davidson
TRIAL RUN (TF) ....William A. Graham
TRIAL, THE ....Orson Welles
TRIALS OF OSCAR WILDE, THE ....
　　　　　　　　　　Kenneth "Ken" Hughes
TRIANGLE FACTORY FIRE SCANDAL (TF), THE ....
　　　　　　　　　　　Mel Stuart
TRIBE (TF), THE ....Richard A. Colla
TRIBES (TF) ☆ ....Joseph Sargent
TRIBUTE.............................Bob Clark
TRIBUTE TO A BAD MAN ....Robert Wise
TRICK BABY ....Larry Yust
TRIGGER TRIO, THE ....William Witney
TRILOGY ....Frank Perry
TRILOGY OF TERROR (TF) ....Dan Curtis
TRILOGY: THE AMERICAN BOY (TF) ....
　　　　　　　　　　　Noel Black
TRIO ....Ken Annakin
TRIP, THE ....Roger Corman
TRIPLE CROSS ....Terence Young
TRIPLE DECEPTION ....Guy Green
TRIPLE ECHO, THE ....Michael Apted
TRISTAN AND ISOLT ....Tom Donovan
TRIUMPHS OF A MAN CALLED HORSE...............
　　　　　　　　　　　John Hough
TROG................................Freddie Francis
TROIS HOMMES A ABBATRE .....Jacques Deray
TROJAN WOMEN, THE .... Michael Cacoyannis
TRON...........................Steven Lisberger

TROOPER HOOK ....Charles Marquis Warren
TROPIC OF CANCER..................Joseph Strick
TROUBLE COMES TO TOWN (TF)...............
　　　　　　　　　　　Daniel Petrie
TROUBLE IN HIGH TIMBER COUNTRY (TF) ....
　　　　　　　　　　　Vincent Sherman
TROUBLE IN MOLOPOLIS ....Philippe Mora
TROUBLE MAN ....Ivan Dixon
TROUBLE SHOOTER (MS)............Henri Safran
TROUBLE WITH ANGELS, THE .... Ida Lupino
TROUBLE WITH GIRLS, THE....Peter Tewksbury
TROUBLEMAKER, THE ....Theodore J. Flicker
TROUPE, THE .... Avi Nesher
TROUT (LA TRUITE), THE ....Joseph Losey
TRUCK STOP WOMEN ....Mark L. Lester
TRUCK TURNER..............Jonathan Kaplan
TRUE CONFESSIONS ....Ulu Grosbard
TRUE GLORY, THE ....Garson Kanin
TRUE GRIT ....Henry Hathaway
TRUE GRIT: A FURTHER ADVENTURE (TF) ....
　　　　　　　　　　　Richard T. Heffron
TRUE STORY OF ESKIMO NELL, THE ....
　　　　　　　　　　　Richard Franklin
TRUNK CRIME ....Roy Boulting
TRUNK TO CAIRO ....Menahem Golan
TUCSON ....William F. Claxton
TUDOR ROSE ....Robert Stevenson
TUGBOAT ANNIE ....Mervyn Leroy
TULIPS ....Mark Warren
TULSA KID, THE ....George Sherman
TUMBLEWEED ....Nathan Juran
TUNES OF GLORY ....Ronald Neame
TUNISIAN VICTORY (FD) ....Frank Capra
TUNNEL OF LOVE, THE ....Gene Kelly
TUNNELVISION ....Brad Swirnoff
TURKISH DELIGHT ....Paul Verhoeven
TURN ON TO LOVE ....John G. Avildsen
TURNING POINT OF JIM MALLOY (TF), THE .....
　　　　　　　　　　　Frank D. Gilroy
TURNING POINT ★, THE ....Herbert Ross
TURNOVER SMITH (TF)......Bernard L. Kowalski
TUSK ....Alexandro Jodorowsky
TUTTO A POSTE E NIENTE IN ORDINE ....
　　　　　　　　　　　Lina Wertmuller
TWELVE ANGRY MEN ★ ....Sidney Lumet
TWELVE CHAIRS, THE ....Mel Brooks
TWELVE CHAPTERS ABOUT WOMEN ....
　　　　　　　　　　　Kon Ichikawa
TWENTY MILLION MILES TO EARTH ....
　　　　　　　　　　　Nathan Juran
TWICE IN A LIFETIME (TF) ....
　　　　　　　　　　　Herschel Daugherty
TWICE ROUND THE DAFFODILS ....
　　　　　　　　　　　Gerald Thomas
TWICE UPON A TIME (AF) .....Charles Swenson
TWILIGHT FOR THE GODS ....Joseph Pevney
TWILIGHT'S LAST GLEAMING ....Robert Aldrich
TWILIGHT TIME ....Goran Paskaljevic
TWILIGHT ZONE - THE MOVIE .... George Miller
TWIN DETECTIVES (TF)................Robert Day
TWINKY ....Richard Donner
TWINS OF EVIL ....John Hough
TWIRL (TF) ....Gus Trikonis
TWIST OF FATE...................David Miller
TWIST OF SAND, A ....Don Chaffey
TWISTED NERVE ....Roy Boulting
TWO A PENNY ....James F. Collier
TWO AND TWO MAKE SIX ......Freddie Francis
TWO BLONDES AND A REDHEAD ....
　　　　　　　　　　　Arthur Dreifuss
TWO BROTHERS (TF) ....Burt Brinckerhoff
TWO COLONELS ....Sergio Corbucci
TWO CROWDED HOURS ....Michael Powell
TWO DAUGHTERS ....Satyajit Ray
TWO DOWN AND ONE TO GO (FD) ....
　　　　　　　　　　　Frank Capra
TWO ENGLISH GIRLS.........Francois Truffaut
TWO-FIVE (TF), THE ....Bruce Kessler
TWO FLAGS WEST ....Robert Wise
TWO FOR THE MONEY (TF) ....
　　　　　　　　　　　Bernard L. Kowalski
TWO FOR THE ROAD ....Stanley Donen
TWO FOR THE SEESAW ....Robert Wise
TWO GENTLEMENT SHARING ......Ted Kotcheff
TWO GUN SHERIFF................George Sherman
TWO-HEADED SPY, THE ....Andre De toth
TWO KINDS OF LOVE (TF)............Jack Bender
TWO-LANE BLACKTOP.............Monte Hellman
TWO LEFT FEET ....Roy Ward Baker
TWO LIVES OF CAROL LETNER (TF), THE ....
　　　　　　　　　　　Philip Leacock
TWO MARRIAGES (TF)............Joseph Hardy
TWO MEN OF KARAMOJA.......Eugene S. Jones
TWO-MINUTE WARNING ....Larry Peerce

TWO MULES FOR SISTER SARA .....Don Siegel
TWO OF A KIND ....John Herzfeld
TWO OF A KIND (TF) ....Roger Young
TWO OF US, THE ....Claude Berri
TWO ON A BENCH (TF)................ Jerry Paris
TWO ON A GUILLOTINE ....William Conrad
TWO ON THE TILES...............John Guillermin
TWO OR THREE THINGS I KNOW ABOUT HER ....
　　　　　　　　　　　Jean-Luc Godard
TWO PEOPLE ....Robert Wise
TWO ROSES AND A GOLDEN ROD ....
　　　　　　　　　　　Albert Zugsmith
TWO SECONDS ....Mervyn Leroy
TWO SISTERS FROM BOSTON.....Henry Koster
TWO SMART PEOPLE ....Jules Dassin
TWO TICKETS TO TERROR ....Al Adamson
TWO-WAY STRETCH ....Robert Day
TWO WEEKS IN ANOTHER TOWN...............
　　　　　　　　　　　Vincente Minnelli
TWO WORLDS OF JENNY LOGAN (TF), THE.....
　　　　　　　　　　　Frank De felitta
TWONKY, THE ....Arch Oboler
TYLER (TF)....................Ralph L. Thomas
TZANANI FAMILY, THE ....Boaz Davidson

U

U-BOAT 29 ....Michael Powell
U-TURN ....George Kaczender
UBERNACHTUNG IN TIROL (TF)...............
　　　　　　　　　　　Volker Schlondorff
UFO INCIDENT (TF), THE.........Richard A. Colla
UFORIA ....John Binder
UGLY AMERICAN, THE ....George Englund
ULTIMATE IMPOSTER (TF), THE .....Paul Stanley
ULTIMATE SOLUTION OF GRACE QUIGLEY, THE ....Anthony Harvey
ULTIMATE THRILL, THE ....Robert Butler
ULTIMATE WARRIOR, THE ....Robert Clouse
ULYSSES ....Joseph Strick
ULZANA'S RAID ....Robert Aldrich
UMBRELLAS OF CHERBOURG, THE ....
　　　　　　　　　　　Jacques Demy
UN AMORE A ROMA ....Dino Risi
UN AMOUR DE SWANN......Volker Schlondorff
UN BORGHESE PICCOLO PICCOLI ....
　　　　　　　　　　　Mario Monicelli
UN CERTO GIORNO ....Ermanno Olmi
UN CHAMBRE EN VILLE ....Jacques Demy
UN COEUR GROS COMME CA (FD)...............
　　　　　　　　　　　Francois Reichenbach
UN DOLLARO A TESTA ....Sergio Corbucci
UN EROE DEI NOSTRI TEMPI ....Mario Monicelli
UN ETE A SAINT TROPEZ (FD) ....
　　　　　　　　　　　David Hamilton
UN FILM COMME LES AUTRES ....Jean-luc Godard
UN FIUME DI DOLLARI.................Carlo Lizzani
UN GENIO, DUE COMPARI, UN POLLO ....
　　　　　　　　　　　Sergio Corbucci
UN GIORNO DA LEONI ....Nanni Loy
UN HOMME DE TROP ....Costa Gavras
UN HOMME QUI ME PLAIT.......Claude Lelouch
UN NEVEU SILENCIEUX...........Robert Enrico
UN PAPILLON SUR L'EPAULE ....Jacques Deray
UN PEU ... BEAUCOUP ... PASSIONEMENT ....
　　　　　　　　　　　Robert Enrico
UN UOMO DA BRUCIARE........Paolo Taviani
UN UOMO IN GINOCCHIO .....Damiano Damiani
UNA RAGAZZA PIUTTOSTO COMPLICATA...............
　　　　　　　　　　　Damiano Damiani
UNA STORIA MODERNA: L'APE REGINA...........
　　　　　　　　　　　Marco Ferreri
UNA VITA DIFFICILE.........................Dino Risi
UNCHAINED.......................Hall Bartlett
UNCLE JOE SHANNON.....Joseph C. Hanwright
UNCLE, THE ....Desmond Davis
UNCLE VANYA ....Andrei Konchalovsky
UNCOMMON VALOR (TF) .... Rod Amateau
UND DAS AM MONTAGMORGEN ....
　　　　　　　　　　　Luigi Comencini
UNDEAD, THE ....Roger Corman
UNDEFEATED, THE ....Andrew V. Mclaglen
UNDER AGE ....Edward Dmytryk
UNDER CALIFORNIA SKIES ....William Witney
UNDER FIRE ....James B. Clark
UNDER MILK WOOD ....Andrew Sinclair
UNDER MY SKIN ....Jean Negulesco
UNDER TEXAS SKIES...........George Sherman
UNDER THE RAINBOW ....Steve Rash
UNDER THE TONTO RIM .... Henry Hathaway

UNDER THE VOLCANO .... John Huston
UNDER THE YUM YUM TREE .... David Swift
UNDER YOUR SPELL .... Otto Preminger
UNDERCOVER .... David Stevens
UNDERCOVER GIRL .... Joseph Pevney
UNDERCOVERS HERO .... Roy Boulting
UNDERCURRENT .... Vincente Minnelli
UNDERGROUND .... Arthur H. Nadel
UNDERGROUND ACES .... Robert Butler
UNDERGROUND AGENT .... Michael Gordon
UNDERGROUND (FD) .... Emile Deantonio
UNDERGROUND MAN (TF), THE .... Paul Wendkos
UNDERSEA GIRL .... John Peyser
UNDERWATER! .... John Sturges
UNDERWATER WARRIOR .... Andrew Marton
UNDERWORLD INFORMERS .... Ken Annakin
UNDERWORLD STORY, THE .... Cy Endfield
UNDERWORLD U.S.A. .... Samuel Fuller
UNE FEMME DOUCE .... Robert Bresson
UNE FEMME FIDELE .... Roger Vadim
UNE FILLE ET DES FUSILS .... Claude Lelouch
UNE FILLE POUR L'ETE .... Edouard Molinaro
UNE MANCHE ET LA BELLE .... Henri Verneuil
UNE PARTIE DE PLAISIR .... Claude Chabrol
UNE RAVISSANTE IDIOTE .... Edouard Molinaro
UNE SEMAINE DE VACANCES .... Bertrand Tavernier
UNEARTHLY STRANGER, THE .... John Krish
UNFAITHFUL, THE .... Vincent Sherman
UNFAITHFULLY YOURS .... Howard Zieff
UNFINISHED DANCE, THE .... Henry Koster
UNFORGIVEN, THE .... John Huston
UNHOLY DESIRE .... Shohei Imamura
UNHOLY PARTNERS .... Mervyn Leroy
UNHOLY ROLLERS .... Vernon Zimmerman
UNIDENTITIED FLYING ODDBALL .... Russ Mayberry
UNION CITY .... Mark Reichert
UNITED KINGDOM (TF) .... Roland Joffe
UNIVERSAL SOLDIER .... Cy Endfield
UNKNOWN TERROR, THE .... Charles Marquis Warren
UNMAN, WITTERING & ZIGO .... John Mackenzie
UNTAMED YOUTH .... Howard W. Koch
UNTIL SEPTEMBER .... Richard Marquand
UNTIL SHE TALKS (TF) .... Mary Lampson
UNTIL THEY SAIL .... Robert Wise
UNWED FATHER (TF) .... Jeremy Paul Kagan
UNWED MOTHER .... Walter Doniger
UOMINI CONTRO .... Francesco Rosi
UOMINI MERCE .... Carlo Lizzani
UP FROM THE BEACH .... Robert Parrish
UP FROM THE DEPTHS .... Charles B. Griffith
UP IN SMOKE .... Lou Adler
UP IN THE CELLAR .... Theodore J. Flicker
UP JUMPED A SWAGMAN .... Christopher Miles
UP PERISCOPE .... Gordon Douglas
UP THE CREEK .... Robert Butler
UP THE DOWN STAIRCASE .... Robert Mulligan
UP THE SANDBOX .... Irvin Kershner
UP TIGHT .... Jules Dassin
UP TO HIS EARS .... Philippe De broca
UPRISING, THE .... Peter Lilienthal
UPS AND DOWNS .... Paul Almond
UPSTAIRS AND DOWNSTAIRS .... Ralph Thomas
UPSTATE MURDERS, THE .... David Paulsen
UPTOWN SATURDAY NIGHT .... Sidney Poitier
URANIUM CONSPIRACY, THE .. Menahem Golan
URBAN COWBOY .... James Bridges
URGH! A MUSIC WAR (FD) .... Derek Burbidge
USED CARS .... Robert Zemeckis
USERS (TF), THE .... Joseph Hardy
UTTERLY MONSTROUS MIND-ROASTING SUMMER OF O.C. AND STIGGS, THE .... Robert Altman
UTU .... Geoff Murphy
UTVANDRARNA ★ .... Jan Troell

V

V (TF) .... Kenneth Johnson
VACANZE COL GANGSTER .... Dino Risi
VACATION DAYS .... Arthur Dreifuss
VACATION IN HELL (TF), A .... David Greene
VALACHI PAPERS, THE .... Terence Young
VALDEZ HORSES, THE .... John Sturges
VALDEZ IS COMING .... Edwin Sherin
VALENTINE MAGIC ON LOVE ISLAND (TF) .... Earl Bellamy
VALENTINE (TF) .... Lee Philips
VALENTINO .... Ken Russell
VALERIE .... Gerd Oswald
VALIANT ONES, THE .... King Hu
VALIANT, THE .... Roy Ward Baker
VALLEY FORGE (TF) .... Fielder Cook
VALLEY GIRL .... Martha Coolidge
VALLEY (OBSCURED BY CLOUDS), THE .... Barbet Schroeder
VALLEY OF GWANGI, THE .... James O'connolly
VALLEY OF THE EAGLES .... Terence Young
VALUE FOR MONEY .... Ken Annakin
VAMOS A MATAR COMPAÑEROS .... Sergio Corbucci
VAMPIRA .... Clive Donner
VAMPIRE LOVERS, THE .... Roy Ward Baker
VAMPIRE (TF) .... E.W. Swackhamer
VAN MORRISON IN IRELAND (FD) .... Michael Radford
VAN NUYS BLVD. .... William Sachs
VANISHED (TF) .... Buzz Kulik
VANISHING POINT .... Richard C. Sarafian
VARIETY LIGHTS .... Alberto Lattuada
VAULT OF HORROR, THE .... Roy Ward Baker
VEDO NUDO .... Dino Risi
VEGA$ (TF) .... Richard Lang
VEILS OF BAGDAD .... George Sherman
VELVET UNDERGROUND AND NICO, THE .... Andy Warhol
VELVET VAMPIRE, THE .... Stephanie Rothman
VENDETTA .... Mel Ferrer
VENETIAN AFFAIR, THE .... Jerry Thorpe
VENETIAN BIRD, THE .... Ralph Thomas
VENEZIA, LA LUNA E TU .... Dino Risi
VENGA A PRENDERE IL CAFFE DA NOI .... Alberto Lattuada
VENGEANCE .... Freddie Francis
VENGEANCE IS MINE .... Shohei Imamura
VENGEANCE OF FU MANCHU, THE .... Jeremy Summers
VENGEANCE OF SHE, THE .... Cliff Owen
VENOM .... Peter Sykes
VERA CRUZ .... Robert Aldrich
VERA VERAO .... Michael Sarne
VERBOTEN! .... Samuel Fuller
VERDICT ★, THE .... Sidney Lumet
VERDICT, THE .... Don Siegel
VERNO: USO GIRL (TF) ☆ .... Ronald F. Maxwell
VERY CURIOUS GIRL, A .... Nelly Kaplan
VERY FRIENDLY NEIGHBORS, THE .... Albert Zugsmith
VERY HAPPY ALEXANDER .... Yves Robert
VERY IMPORTANT PERSON .... Ken Annakin
VERY LIKE A WHALE .... Alan Bridges
VERY MISSING PERSON (TF), A .... Russ Mayberry
VERY PRIVATE AFFAIR, A .... Louis Malle
VERY SPECIAL FAVOR, A .... Michael Gordon
VIALE DELLA SPERANZA .... Dino Risi
VICE AND VIRTUE .... Roger Vadim
VICE SQUAD .... Gary A. Sherman
VICE SQUARD .... Arnold Laven
VICE VERSA .... Peter Ustinov
VICIOUS CIRCLE, THE .... Gerald Thomas
VICTIM (TF), THE .... Herschel Daugherty
VICTIMS (TF), THE .... Jerrold Freedman
VICTOR/VICTORIA .... Blake Edwards
VICTORIA .... Bo Widerberg
VICTORS, THE .... Carl Foreman
VICTORY .... John Huston
VICTORY MARCH .... Marco Bellocchio
VIDEODROME .... David Cronenberg
VIEW FROM THE BRIDGE, A .... Sidney Lumet
VIGILANTE .... William Lustig
VIGILANTE FORCE .... George Armitage
VIKING QUEEN, THE .... Don Chaffey
VIKING WOMEN AND THE SEA SERPENT, THE .... Roger Corman
VIKINGS, THE .... Richard Fleischer
VILLA! .... James B. Clark
VILLA RIDES! .... Buzz Kulik
VILLAGE OF THE GIANTS .... Bert I. Gordon
VILLAIN .... Michael Tuchner
VILLAIN, THE .... Hal Needham
VINCENT, FRANCOIS, PAUL AND THE OTHERS .... Claude Sautet
VINCENT THE DUTCHMAN .... Mai Zetterling
VINYL .... Andy Warhol
VIOLATION OF SARAH MCDAVID (TF), THE .... John Llewellyn Moxey
VIOLATORS, THE .... John Newland
VIOLENCE AT NOON .... Nagisa Oshima
VIOLENT ENEMY, THE .... Don Sharp
VIOLENT FOUR, THE .... Carlo Lizzani
VIOLENT MOMENT .... Sidney Hayers
VIOLENT ROAD .... Howard W. Koch
VIOLENT SATURDAY .... Richard Fleischer
VIOLETTE .... Claude Chabrol
VIOLETTE NOZIERE .... Claude Chabrol
VIRGIN AND THE GYPSY, THE .... Christopher Miles
VIRGIN QUEEN, THE .... Henry Koster
VIRGIN SOLDIERS, THE .... John Dexter
VIRGIN SPRING, THE .... Ingmar Bergman
VIRGIN WITCHES .... Ray Austin
VIRGINIA HILL STORY (TF), THE .... Joel Schumacher
VISA TO CANTON .... Michael Carreras
VISIONQUEST .... Harold Becker
VISIONS OF EIGHT (FD) .... Claude Lelouch
VISIONS ... (TF) .... Lee H. Katzin
VISIT, THE .... Bernhard Wicki
VISIT TO A CHIEF'S SON .... Lamont Johnson
VISITORS, THE .... Elia Kazan
VITA DA CANI .... Mario Monicelli
VIVA ITALIA! .... Dino Risi
VIVA KNIEVEL! .... Gordon Douglas
VIVA LA MUERTE ... TUA! .... Sergio Corbucci
VIVA LA VIE .... Claude Lelouch
VIVA LAS VEGAS .... George Sidney
VIVA MARIA! .... Louis Malle
VIVA MAX! .... Jerry Paris
VIVA ZAPATA! .... Elia Kazan
VIVEMENT DIMANCHE .... Francois Truffaut
VLADIMIR ET ROSA .... Jean-Luc Godard
VOGLIAMO I COLONNELLI .... Mario Monicelli
VOICE OF THE TURTLE, THE .... Irving Rapper
VOICES .... Kevin Billington
VOLTATI EUGENIO .... Luigi Comencini
VOLUNTEER, THE .... Michael Powell
VON RICHTOFEN AND BROWN .. Roger Corman
VOTE FOR HUGGETT .... Ken Annakin
VOYAGE OF THE DAMNED .... Stuart Rosenberg
VOYAGE OF THE YES (TF), THE .... Lee H. Katzin
VOYAGE ROUND BY FATHER (TF), A .... Alvin Rakoff
VOYAGE TO GRAND TARTARIE .... Jean-CHARLES TACCHELLA
VOYAGE TO THE BOTTOM OF THE SEA .... Irwin Allen
VULTURE, THE .... Yaky Yosha
"W" .... Richard Quine

W

W.C. FIELDS AND ME .... Arthur Hiller
W.E.B. (TF) .... Harvey Hart
W.W. AND THE DIXIE DANCEKINGS .... John G. Avildsen
WABASH AVENUE .... Henry Koster
WACKO .... Greydon Clark
WACKY WORLD OF MOTHER GOOSE (AF), THE .... Jules Bass
WAGNER (MS) .... Tony Palmer
WAIKIKI (TF) .... Ron Satlof
WAIT FOR US AT DAWN .... Emil Loteanu
WAIT TILL YOUR MOTHER GETS HOME (TF) .... Bill Persky
WAIT UNTIL DARK .... Terence Young
WAITRESS! .... Michael Herz
WAKE IN FRIGHT .... Ted Kotcheff
WAKE ME WHEN IT'S OVER .... Mervyn Leroy
WAKE ME WHEN THE WAR IS OVER (TF) .... Gene Nelson
WALK A CROOKED MILE .... Gordon Douglas
WALK IN THE SPRING RAIN, A .... Guy Green
WALK LIKE A DRAGON .... James Clavell
WALK ON THE WILD SIDE .... Edward Dmytryk
WALK PROUD .... Robert Collins
WALK SOFTLY, STRANGER .... Robert Stevenson
WALK TALL .... Maury Dexter
WALK WITH LOVE AND DEATH, A .... John Huston
WALKABOUT .... Nicolas Roeg
WALKING HILLS, THE .... John Sturges
WALKING STICK, THE .... Eric Till
WALKING TALL .... Phil Karlson
WALKING THROUGH THE FIRE (TF) .... Robert Day
WALKOVER .... Jerzy Skolimowski
WALL OF DEATH .... Lewis Gilbert
WALL OF NOISE .... Richard Wilson
WALL (TF), THE .... Robert Markowitz
WALL, THE .... Yilmaz Guney
WALLS OF HELL, THE .... Eddie Romero
WALLS OF MALAPAGA, THE .... René Clement

WALTZ ACROSS TEXAS .... Ernest Day
WALTZ OF THE TOREADORS ... John Guillermin
WANDA NEVADA .... Peter Fonda
WANDERERS, THE .... Philip Kaufman
WANTED: THE SUNDANCE WOMAN (TF)..........
　　　　　　　　　　　　　　　　 Lee Philips
WAR AND PEACE .... Sergei Bondarchuk
WAR ARROW ....George Sherman
WAR BETWEEN MEN AND WOMEN, THE ....
　　　　　　　　　　　　 Melville Shavelson
WAR BETWEEN THE TATES (TF), THE ....
　　　　　　　　　　　　　　　　 Lee Philips
WAR GAME, THE ....Peter Watkins
WAR GODDESS ....Terence Young
WAR HUNT ....Denis Sanders
WAR IS HELL ....Burt Topper
WAR LORD, THE ....Franklin J. Schaffner
WAR LOVER, THE ....Philip Leacock
WAR OF CHILDREN (TF) ☆, A ....
　　　　　　　　　　　　　　 George Schaefer
WAR OF THE COLOSSAL BEAST ....
　　　　　　　　　　　　　　　　 Bert I. Gordon
WAR OF THE SATELLITES .... Roger Corman
WAR WAGON, THE .... Burt Kennedy
WARE CASE, THE .... Robert Stevenson
WARGAMES .... John Badham
WARLOCK .... Edward Dmytryk
WARLORDS OF ATLANTIS .... Kevin Connor
WARM DECEMBER, A .... Sidney Poitier
WARNING SHOT .... Buzz Kulik
WARRENDALE (FD) .... Allan King
WARRIORS, THE .... Walter Hill
WARUM SIND SIE GEGEN UNS? ....
　　　　　　　　　　　　　　 Bernhard Wicki
WASHINGTON: BEHIND CLOSED DOORS (MS)
☆ .... Gary Nelson
WASHINGTON MISTRESS (TF)......Peter Levin
WASN'T THAT A TIME! (FD) .... Jim Brown
WASP WOMAN, THE .... Roger Corman
WASTREL, THE .... Michael Cacoyannis
WAT ZIEN IK .... Paul Verhoeven
WATCH THE BIRDIE .... Jack Donohue
WATCH YOUR STERN .... Gerald Thomas
WATCHER IN THE WOODS, THE ... John Hough
WATER BABIES, THE .... Lionel Jeffries
WATER UNDER THE BRIDGE (MS) ...Igor Auzins
WATERFRONT.....................Michael Anderson
WATERFRONT WOMEN .... Michael Anderson
WATERHOLE #3 .... William A. Graham
WATERLOO ....Sergei Bondarchuk
WATERLOO BRIDGE .... Mervyn Leroy
WATERMELON MAN ...... Melvin Van Peebles
WATERSHIP DOWN (AF)............Martin Rosen
WATTS MONSTER, THE .... William Crain
WATTSTAX (FD).......................Mel Stuart
WAVE, A WAC AND A MARINE, A ....
　　　　　　　　　　　　　　　　 Phil Karlson
WAVE (FD), THE ....Fred Zinnemann
WAVELENGTH .... Mike Gray
WAY HE WAS, THE .... Mark L. Lester
WAY OF THE STRONG, THE .... Frank Capra
WAY ... WAY OUT! ....Gordon Douglas
WAY WE LIVE NOW, THE ....Barry Brown
WAY WE WERE, THE .... Sydney Pollack
WAY WEST, THE ....Andrew V. Mclaglen
WAYS IN THE NIGHT ..... Krzysztof Zanussi
WE ALL LOVED EACH OTHER SO MUCH ....
　　　　　　　　　　　　　　　　 Ettore Scola
WE ARE THE LAMBETH BOYS .... Karel Reisz
WE LIVE AGAIN .... Rouben Mamoulian
WE OF THE NEVER NEVER ....Igor Auzins
WE'RE FIGHTING BACK (TF) ..... Lou Antonio
WE'RE NOT THE JET SET (FD) .... Robert Duvall
WE WERE STRANGERS ....John Huston
WE WILL ROCK YOU (FD).........Saul Swimmer
WEAK AND THE WICKED, THE ....
　　　　　　　　　　　　　 J. Lee Thompson
WEAKER SEX, THE................Roy Ward Baker
WEAPON, THE ....Val Guest
WEB OF EVIDENCE .... Jack Cardiff
WEB OF PASSION/A DOUBLE TOUR ....
　　　　　　　　　　　　　　 Claude Chabrol
WEB, THE .... Michael Gordon
WEBSTER BOY, THE .... Don Chaffey
WEDDING, A .... Robert Altman
WEDDING IN BLOOD ....Claude Chabrol
WEDDING IN WHITE ....William Fruet
WEDDING MARCH .... Kon Ichikawa
WEDDING NIGHT ....Piers Haggard
WEDDING ON WALTON'S MOUNTAIN (TF), A ...
　　　　　　　　　　　　　　　　 Lee Philips
WEDDING PARTY, THE .... Brian De　palma
WEDDING, THE ....Andrzej Wajda
WEDNESDAY'S CHILD .... Kenneth Loach

WEEK'S VACATION, A .... Bertrand Tavernier
WEEKEND ....Jean-Luc Godard
WEEKEND A ZUYDCOOTE.......... Henri Verneuil
WEEKEND AT DUNKIRK .... Henri Verneuil
WEEKEND, ITALIAN STYLE ....Dino Risi
WEEKEND OF TERROR (TF) .... Jud Taylor
WEEKEND SUN (TF), THE........Jeannot Szwarc
WELCOME HOME, BROTHER CHARLES ....
　　　　　　　　　　　　　　 Jamaa Fanaka
WELCOME HOME, JOHNNY BRISTOL (TF) ......
　　　　　　　　　　　　　 George Mccowan
WELCOME HOME, SOLDIER BOYS ....
　　　　　　　　　　　　　 Richard Compton
WELCOME TO BLOOD CITY...........Peter Sasdy
WELCOME TO HARD TIMES ...... Burt Kennedy
WELCOME TO L.A. .... Alan Rudolph
WELFARE (FD) .... Frederick Wiseman
WELL, THE .... Russell Rouse
WEREWOLF OF WASHINGTON, THE ....
　　　　　　　　　　 Milton Moses Ginsberg
WEST 11 .... Michael Winner
WEST SIDE KID, THE ....George Sherman
WEST SIDE STORY ★★.........Jerome Robbins
WEST TEXAS .... Alan Gadney
WESTBOUND .... Budd Boetticher
WESTWORLD ....Michael Crichton
WHALE FOR THE KILLING (TF), A ....
　　　　　　　　　　　　 Richard T. Heffron
WHAT? ....Roman Polanski
WHAT A CRAZY WORLD.......Michael Carreras
WHAT A WAY TO GO! .... J. Lee Thompson
WHAT ARE BEST FRIENDS FOR? (TF).........
　　　　　　　　　　　　　　 Jay Sandrich
WHAT CHANGED CHARLEY FARTHING? ....
　　　　　　　　　　　　　　 Sidney Hayers
WHAT COLOR IS THE WIND........Frank Zuniga
WHAT DID YOU DO IN THE WAR, DADDY? .....
　　　　　　　　　　　　　　 Blake Edwards
WHAT DO YOU SAY TO A NAKED WOMAN?...
　　　　　　　　　　　　　　　　 Allen Funt
WHAT EVER HAPPENED TO AUNT ALICE? ....
　　　　　　　　　　　　　　 Lee H. Katzin
WHAT EVER HAPPENED TO BABY JANE? ....
　　　　　　　　　　　　　　 Robert Aldrich
WHAT HAPPENED AT CAMPO GRANDE?..........
　　　　　　　　　　　　　　　　 Cliff Owen
WHAT PRICE MURDER .... Henri Verneuil
WHAT'S A NICE GIRL LIKE YOU ... ? ....
　　　　　　　　　　　　　　　　 Jerry Paris
WHAT'S GOOD FOR THE GOOSE ....
　　　　　　　　　　　　　　 Menahem Golan
WHAT'S HAPPENING: THE BEATLES IN THE
USA (FD)....................Albert Maysles
WHAT'S NEW PUSSYCAT? .... Clive Donner
WHAT'S THE MATTER WITH HELEN? ....
　　　　　　　　　　　　　 Curtis Harrington
WHAT'S UP, DOC?......Peter Bogdanovich
WHAT'S UP, TIGER LILY?....... Woody Allen
WHEELER DEALERS, THE .... Arthur Hiller
WHEN A STRANGER CALLS .... Fred Walton
WHEN DINOSAURS RULED THE EARTH ....
　　　　　　　　　　　　　　　　 Val Guest
WHEN EIGHT BELLS TOLL........ Etienne Perrier
WHEN EVERY DAY WAS THE FOURTH OF
JULY (TF)....................Dan Curtis
WHEN HELL WAS IN SESSION (TF)...........
　　　　　　　　　　　　　　 Paul Krasny
WHEN MICHAEL CALLS (TF) .... Philip Leacock
WHEN SHE WAS BAD ... (TF) ....Peter H. Hunt
WHEN THE LEGENDS DIE..............Stuart Millar
WHEN TIME RAN OUT .... James Goldstone
WHEN WOMEN KILL (CTD) ....Lee Grant
WHEN YOU COMIN' BACK, RED RYDER? ....
　　　　　　　　　　　　　　 Milton Katselas
WHEN YOUR LOVER LEAVES (TF)...........
　　　　　　　　　　　　　　 Jeff Bleckner
WHERE DOES IT HURT? .... Rod Amateau
WHERE EAGLES DARE .... Brian G. Hutton
WHERE HAVE ALL THE PEOPLE GONE? (TF)...
　　　　　　　　　　　　 John Llewellyn Moxey
WHERE IT'S AT .... Garson Kanin
WHERE LOVE HAS GONE .... Edward Dmytryk
WHERE'S JACK? .... James Clavell
WHERE'S POPPA? .... Carl Reiner
WHERE THE BOYS ARE .... Hy Averback
WHERE THE BUFFALO ROAM........... Art Linson
WHERE THE GREEN ANTS DREAM ....
　　　　　　　　　　　　　　 Werner Herzog
WHERE THE HOT WIND BLOWS ...Jules Dassin
WHERE THE LADIES GO (TF)..........
　　　　　　　　　　　　　 Theodore J. Flicker
WHERE THE LILIES BLOOM ....
　　　　　　　　　　　　　 William A. Graham
WHERE THE SIDEWALK ENDS ..Otto Preminger

WHERE THE SPIES ARE..................Val Guest
WHERE WERE YOU WHEN THE LIGHTS WENT
OUT? ....Hy Averback
WHEREVER SHE GOES .... Michael Gordon
WHICH WAY IS UP? .... Michael Schultz
WHICH WAY TO THE FRONT? ...... Jerry Lewis
WHIFFS ....Ted Post
WHIRLPOOL ....Otto Preminger
WHISKEY GALORE! ...... Alexander Mackendrick
WHISPERERS, THE .... Bryan Forbes
WHISTLE DOWN THE WIND ....Bryan Forbes
WHITE BUFFALO, THE ....J. Lee Thompson
WHITE DAWN, THE .... Philip Kaufman
WHITE DOG .... Samuel Fuller
WHITE GAME, THE ....Bo Widerberg
WHITE LIGHTNING .... Joseph Sargent
WHITE LINE FEVER .... Jonathan Kaplan
WHITE LIONS, THE ....Mel Stuart
WHITE MAMA (TF) .... Jackie Cooper
WHITE ROCK (FD) .... Tony Maylam
WHITE SHEIK, THE .... Federico Fellini
WHITE SISTER .... Alberto Lattuada
WHITE TRAP, THE .... Sidney Hayers
WHITE WATER REBELS (TF)...........Reza Badiyi
WHITE WITCH DOCTOR .... Henry Hathaway
WHO? ....Jack Gold
WHO AM I THIS TIME? (TF)...Jonathan Demme
WHO ARE THE DE BOLTS? .... AND HOW
DID THEY GET 19 KIDS? (FD) ......John Korty
WHO DARES WINS ....Ian Sharp
WHO FEARS THE DEVIL .... John Newland
WHO HAS SEEN THE WIND ....Allan King
WHO IS HARRY KELLERMAN AND WHY IS HE
SAYING THOSE TERRIBLE THINGS ABOUT
ME? ....Ulu Grosbard
WHO IS KILLING THE GREAT CHEFS OF
EUROPE? .... Ted Kotcheff
WHO IS THE BLACK DAHLIA? (TF) ....
　　　　　　　　　　　　　 Joseph Pevney
WHO KILLED JENNY LANGBY? (TF)..........
　　　　　　　　　　　　　 Donald Crombie
WHO KILLED MARY WHAT'S'ERNAME ....
　　　　　　　　　　　　　　 Ernest Pintoff
WHO KILLED TEDDY BEAR?........ Joseph Cates
WHO'LL SAVE OUR CHILDREN? (TF)...........
　　　　　　　　　　　　　 George Schaefer
WHO'LL STOP THE RAIN .... Karel Reisz
WHO'S AFRAID OF VIRGINIA WOOLF? ★ ....
　　　　　　　　　　　　　　 Mike Nichols
WHO'S BEEN SLEEPING IN MY BED? ....
　　　　　　　　　　　　　　 Daniel Mann
WHO'S GOT THE ACTION? ....Daniel Mann
WHO'S MINDING THE MINT? .... Howard Morris
WHO'S THAT KNOCKING AT MY DOOR? ....
　　　　　　　　　　　　　 Martin Scorsese
WHO SAW HIM DIE? .... Jan Troell
WHO SLEW AUNTIE ROO? .... Curtis Harrington
WHO WAS THAT LADY? .... George Sidney
WHO WILL LOVE MY CHILDREN? (TF) ☆☆ ....
　　　　　　　　　　　　　　 John Erman
WHOLE TRUTH, THE ....John Guillermin
WHOLE WORLD IS WATCHING (TF), THE ....
　　　　　　　　　　　　　 Richard A. Colla
WHOLLY MOSES ....Gary Weis
WHOSE LIFE IS IT ANYWAY? .....John Badham
WHY....................................Nanni Loy
WHY BRING THAT UP? ....George Abbott
WHY ME? (TF) ....Fielder Cook
WHY SHOOT THE TEACHER ... Silvio Narizzano
WHY WOULD I LIE? ....Larry Peerce
WICKED AS THEY COME ....
　　　　　　　　　　　　 Kenneth "Ken" Hughes
WICKED LADY, THE .... Michael Winner
WICKED, WICKED ....Richard L. Bare
WICKED WOMAN .... Russell Rouse
WICKER MAN, THE .... Robin Hardy
WIDE BOY .... Kenneth "Ken" Hughes
WIDOW (TF).........................J. Lee Thompson
WIFE WANTED.................................Phil Karlson
WILBY CONSPIRACY, THE ....Ralph Nelson
WILD 90.......................... Norman Mailer
WILD AFFAIR, THE .... John Krish
WILD AND THE BRAVE (FD), THE ....
　　　　　　　　　　　　　 Eugene S. Jones
WILD AND THE FREE (TF), THE......James Hill
WILD AND THE INNOCENT, THE ...... Jack Sher
WILD AND THE WILLING, THE ... Ralph Thomas
WILD AND WONDERFUL ......Michael Anderson
WILD AND WOOLY (TF)............Philip Leacock
WILD ANGELS, THE .... Roger Corman
WILD BUNCH, THE .... Sam Peckinpah
WILD CHILD, THE ....Francois Truffaut
WILD COUNTRY, THE.................Robert Totten
WILD DUCK, THE..........................Henri Safran

373

WILD GEESE, THE............Andrew V. Mclaglen
WILD HEART, THE ....Michael Powell
WILD HORSE HANK ....Eric Till
WILD HORSE MESA ....Henry Hathaway
WILD HORSE RODEO ....George Sherman
WILD MCCULLOCHS, THE ....Max Baer, Jr.
WILD ON THE BEACH ....Maury Dexter
WILD ONE, THE ....Laslo Benedek
WILD PACK, THE ....Hall Bartlett
WILD PARTY, THE ....James Ivory
WILD RACERS, THE ....Daniel Haller
WILD RIVER ....Elia Kazan
WILD ROVERS ....Blake Edwards
WILD SEED ....Brian G. Hutton
WILD SIDE, THE ....Penelope Spheeris
WILD STRAWBERRIES ....Ingmar Bergman
WILD STYLE ....Charlie Ahearn
WILD TIMES (TF) ....Richard Compton
WILD WILD WEST REVISITED (TF), THE .....
..........................Burt Kennedy
WILD WOMEN OF CHASTITY GULCH (TF), THE
.....................................Philip Leacock
WILD WOMEN (TF)..................Don Mcdougall
WILDERNESS FAMILY PART II, THE.............
....Frank Zuniga
WILDMAN ....Geoff Murphy
WILL ANY GENTLEMAN? ......Michael Anderson
WILL: G. GORDON LIDDY (TF) ....
...........................Robert Lieberman
WILL THERE REALLY BE A MORNING? (TF) .....
...........................Fielder Cook
WILLA (TF) ....Claudio Guzman
WILLARD ....Daniel Mann
WILLIAM COME TO TOWN ....Val Guest
WILLIE AND PHIL ....Paul Mazursky
WILLIE DYNAMITE ....Gilbert Moses
WILLMAR 8 (FD), THE ....Lee Grant
WILLY MCBEAN AND HIS MAGIC MACHINE
(AF) ....Arthur Rankin, Jr.
WILLY WONKA AND THE CHOCOLATE
FACTORY ....Mel Stuart
WILMA (TF) ....Bud Greenspan
WINCHESTER '73 (TF) ......Herschel Daugherty
WIND AND THE LION, THE ......John Milius
WIND CANNOT READ, THE........ Ralph Thomas
WIND FROM THE EAST.........Jean-Luc Godard
WIND IN THE WILLOWS (ATF), THE ....
..........................Arthur Rankin, Jr.
WINDFALL IN ATHENS ......Michael Cacoyannis
WINDOM'S WAY ....Ronald Neame
WINDOWS ....Gordon Willis
WINDS OF AUTUMN, THE .....Charles B. Pierce
WINDS OF KITTY HAWK (TF), THE ....
..........................E.W. Swackhamer
WINDS OF WAR (MS)☆, THE............Dan Curtis
WINDWALKER ....Kieth Merrill
WINDY CITY ....Armyan Bernstein
WING AND A PRAYER...........Henry Hathaway
WINGS OF FIRE (TF)............David Lowell Rich
WINGS OF THE HAWK ....Budd Boetticher
WINIFRED WAGNER (FD) ....Hans-
JURGEN SYBERBERG
WINNER TAKE ALL (TF) ....Paul Bogart
WINNING ....James Goldstone
WINSTON CHURCHILL - THE WILDERNESS
YEARS (MS)...................Ferdinand Fairfax
WINTER A GO-GO ....Richard Benedict
WINTER KILL (TF) ....Jud Taylor
WINTER KILLS ....William Richert
WINTER LIGHT ....Ingmar Bergman
WINTER OF OUR DISCONTENT (TF), THE ......
...........................Waris Hussein
WINTER OF OUR DREAMS.........John Duigan
WINTER WIND....................Miklos Jancso
WINTERHAWK ....Charles B. Pierce
WISE BLOOD ....John Huston
WISE GUYS, THE...................Robert Enrico
WITCH WHO CAME FROM THE SEA, THE.......
..........................Matt Cimber
WITCHCRAFT.........................Don Sharp
WITCHING HOUR, THE ....Henry Hathaway
WITH LOVE FROM TRUMAN (FD) ....
............................Albert Maysles
WITH SIX YOU GET EGGROLL .. Howard Morris
WITH THIS RING (TF) ....James Sheldon
WITHOUT A TRACE ....Stanley Jaffe
WITHOUT ANESTHETIC ....Andrzej Wajda
WITHOUT RESERVATIONS ....Mervyn Leroy
WITHOUT WARNING ....Arnold Laven
WITNESS FOR THE PROSECUTION ★............
..........................Billy Wilder
WITNESS FOR THE PROSECUTION (TF)...........
............................Alan Gibson
WIVES AND LOVERS......................John Rich

WIZ, THE ....Sidney Lumet
WIZARD OF BAGHDAD, THE ...George Sherman
WIZARDS (AF) ....Ralph Bakshi
WOLF HUNTERS, THE ....Budd Boetticher
WOLF LAKE ....Burt Kennedy
WOLFEN ....Michael Wadleigh
WOLFHEAD ....John Hough
WOMAN CALLED GOLDA (TF), A.. Alan Gibson
WOMAN CALLED MOSES (TF), A ....
.........................Paul Wendkos
WOMAN FOR ALL MEN, A...........Arthur Marks
WOMAN HATER......................Terence Young
WOMAN HUNT ....Maury Dexter
WOMAN HUNT, THE ....Eddie Romero
WOMAN HUNTER (TF), THE ....
.........................Bernard L. Kowalski
WOMAN IN A DRESSING GOWN ....
.........................J. Lee Thompson
WOMAN IN HIDING ....Michael Gordon
WOMAN IN RED ....Gene Wilder
WOMAN IS A WOMAN, A ......Jean-Luc Godard
WOMAN NEXT DOOR, THE ...Francois Truffaut
WOMAN OBSESSED ....Henry Hathaway
WOMAN OF THE YEAR (TF) ....Jud Taylor
WOMAN ON PIER 13, THE ... Robert Stevenson
WOMAN'S DECISION, A ....Krzysztof Zanussi
WOMAN'S TESTAMENT, A...........Kon Ichikawa
WOMAN'S WORLD, A ....Jean Negulesco
WOMAN UNDER THE INFLUENCE★, A.............
.........................John Cassavetes
WOMAN WHO TOUCHED THE LEGS, THE.......
.........................Kon Ichikawa
WOMAN WHO WOULDN'T DIE, THE ....
.........................Gordon Hessler
WOMBLING FREE....................Lionel Jeffries
WOMEN AT WEST POINT (TF) ....
.........................Vincent Sherman
WOMEN IN CHAINS (TF)....Bernard L. Kowalski
WOMEN IN LOVE ★ ....Ken Russell
WOMEN IN REVOLT ....Andy Warhol
WOMEN IN WHITE (MS) ....Jerry London
WOMEN OF SAN QUENTIN (TF) ....
.........................William A. Graham
WOMEN'S ROOM (TF), THE ... Glenn Jordan
WON TON TON, THE DOG WHO SAVED
HOLLYWOOD......................Michael Winner
WONDER WOMAN (TF)........ Vincent Mceveety
WONDERFUL COUNTRY, THE ..... Robert Parrish
WONDERFUL CROOK, THE ... Claude Goretta
WONDERFUL TO BE YOUNG!...Sidney J. Furie
WOODCUTTERS OF THE DEEP SOUTH (FD)......
.........................Lionel Rogosin
WOODSTOCK (FD) ....Michael Wadleigh
WORD (MS), THE ....Richard Lang
WORD OF HONOR (TF).........Melvin Damski
WORK IS A FOUR LETTER WORD .....Peter Hall
WORKING GIRLS, THE ....Stephanie Rothman
WORLD ACCORDING TO GARP, THE.............
.........................George Roy Hill
WORLD CHANGES, THE ....Mervyn Leroy
WORLD FOR RANSOM ....Robert Aldrich
WORLD IN MY POCKET...............Alvin Rakoff
WORLD OF APU, THE ....Satyajit Ray
WORLD OF HENRY ORIENT, THE ....
.........................George Roy Hill
WORLD OF SUZIE WONG, THE .. Richard Quine
WORLD'S GREATEST ATHLETE, THE ....
.........................Robert Scheerer
WORLD'S GREATEST LOVER, THE ....
.........................Gene Wilder
WORLD WAR III (TF) ....David Greene
WOW! ....Claude Jutra
WOYZECK ....Werner Herzog
WR - MYSTERIES OF THE ORGANISM ....
.........................Dusan Makavejev
WRATH OF GOD, THE ....Ralph Nelson
WRECK OF THE MARY DEARE, THE............
.........................Michael Anderson
WRECKING CREW, THE ....Phil Karlson
WRIGHT BROTHERS (TF), THE ..... Arthur Barron
WRONG ARM OF THE LAW, THE ... Cliff Owen
WRONG BOX, THE...................Bryan Forbes
WRONG IS RIGHT..................Richard Brooks
WRONG MOVE, THE.................Wim Wenders
WRONGDOERS, THE ....Yilmaz Guney
WUSA ....Stuart Rosenberg
WUTHERING HEIGHTS................Robert Fuest
WYOMING OUTLAW ....George Sherman
WYOMING WILDCAT.............George Sherman

X

X-15 ....Richard Donner
X MARKS THE SPOT ....George Sherman
X-RAY ....Boaz Davidson
"X" - THE MAN WITH THE X-RAY EYES ....
.........................Roger Corman
X Y & ZEE ....Brian G. Hutton
XALA ....Ousmene Sembene
XANADU ....Robert Greenwald
XAOS ....Paolo Taviani

Y

YAKUZA, THE ....Sydney Pollack
YANGTSE INCIDENT ....Michael Anderson
YANKEE PASHA...................Joseph Pevney
YANKS ....John Schlesinger
YEAR OF LIVING DANGEROUSLY, THE.............
.........................Peter Weir
YEHUDI MENUHIN - ROAD OF LIGHT (FD) ....
.........................Francois Reichenbach
YELLOW BALLOON, THE...J. Lee Thompson
YELLOW CAB MAN, THE ....Jack Donohue
YELLOW CANARY, THE ....Buzz Kulik
YELLOW HAIR AND THE PECOS KID ....
.........................Matt Cimber
YELLOWBEARD ....Melvin Damski
YELLOWSTONE KELLY ....Gordon Douglas
YENTL ....Barbra Streisand
YES, GIORGIO ....Franklin J. Schaffner
YES SIR, THAT'S MY BABY ....George Sherman
YESTERDAY'S CHILD (TF)..............Corey Allen
YESTERDAY'S ENEMY ....Val Guest
YIELD TO THE NIGHT...........J. Lee Thompson
YOJIMBO ....Akira Kurosawa
YOL ....Yilmaz Guney
YOLANDA AND THE THIEF ....Vincente Minnelli
YOU AND ME........................David Carradine
YOU BETTER WATCH OUT ....Lewis Jackson
YOU CAN'T GO HOME AGAIN (TF) ....
.........................Ralph Nelson
YOU CAN'T TAKE IT WITH YOU★★ ....
.........................Frank Capra
YOU FOR ME ....Don Weis
YOU KNOW WHAT SAILORS ARE ....
.........................Ken Annakin
YOU LIE SO DEEP, MY LOVE (TF)...............
.........................David Lowell Rich
YOU LIGHT UP MY LIFE.........Joseph Brooks
YOU'LL LIKE MY MOTHER ......Lamont Johnson
YOU'LL NEVER SEE ME AGAIN (TF) ....
.........................Jeannot Szwarc
YOU MUST BE JOKING!..........Michael Winner
YOU ONLY LIVE TWICE ....Lewis Gilbert
YOU'RE A BIG BOY NOW ....
.........................Francis Ford Coppola
YOU'RE IN THE NAVY NOW ... Henry Hathaway
YOU'RE LYING ....Vilgot Sjoman
YOUND ADVENTURERS, THE...David Hemmings
YOUNG AMERICANS (FD) ..... Alex Grasshoff
YOUNG AND DANGEROUS .. William F. Claxton
YOUNG AND WILD ....William Witney
YOUNG AND WILLING ....Ralph Thomas
YOUNG AT HEART.................Gordon Douglas
YOUNG BESS ....George Sidney
YOUNG BILLY YOUNG ....Burt Kennedy
YOUNG CAPTIVES, THE..............Irvin Kershner
YOUNG CASSIDY ....Jack Cardiff
YOUNG COUNTRY (TF), THE.......Roy Huggins
YOUNG DOCTORS IN LOVE ....Garry Marshall
YOUNG DOCTORS, THE...........Phil Karlson
YOUNG FRANKENSTEIN ....Mel Brooks
YOUNG GENERATION, THE .... Kon Ichikawa
YOUNG GIRLS OF ROCHEFORT, THE ....
.........................Jacques Demy
YOUNG GUNS OF TEXAS ....Maury Dexter
YOUNG GUNS, THE ....Albert Band
YOUNG IDEAS ....Jules Dassin
YOUNG JESSE JAMES .... William F. Claxton
YOUNG JOE, THE FORGOTTEN KENNEDY (TF)
.........................Richard T. Heffron
YOUNG LADY CHATTERLEY ...... Alan Roberts
YOUNG LAWYERS (TF), THE ....Harvey Hart
YOUNG LIONS, THE ....Edward Dmytryk
YOUNG LOVE.................Michal Bat-Adam
YOUNG LOVE, FIRST LOVE (TF)...............
.........................Steven H. Stern
YOUNG LUST ....Gary Weis

374

A

ABRAMS RUBALOFF & ASSOCIATES
8075 W. Third Street, Suite 303
Los Angeles, CA 90048
213/935-1700

ADAMS, RAY & ROSENBERG
9200 Sunset Blvd—PH 25
Los Angeles, CA 90069
213/278-3000

AGENCY FOR THE PERFORMING ARTS, INC., (APA)
9000 Sunset Blvd., 12th Floor
Los Angeles, CA 90069
213/273-0744

203 N. Wabash Avenue
Chicago, IL 60601
312/664-7703

7630 Biscayne Blvd.
Miami, FL 33188
305/758-8731

120 West 57th Street
New York, NY 10019
212/582-1500

BUDDY ALTONI TALENT AGENCY
3901 MacArthur Blvd., Suite 115-D
Newport Beach, CA 92660
714/851-1711
Mr. Buddy Altoni

CARLOS ALVARADO AGENCY
8820 Sunset Blvd., Suites A & B
Los Angeles, CA 90028
213/652-0272
Carlos Alvarado, Monalee Schilling

FRED AMSEL & ASSOCIATES, INC.
291 S. La Cienega Blvd., Suite 3
Beverly Hills, CA 90211
213/855-1200
Mr. Fred Amsel

THE ARTISTS AGENCY
10000 Santa Monica Blvd.
Los Angeles, CA 90067
213/277-7779
Mr. Mickey Frieberg

ARTISTS CAREER MANAGEMENT
9157 Sunset Blvd., Suite 206
Los Angeles, CA 90069
213/278-9157
Mr. Edgar Small

ARTISTS GROUP, LTD.
10100 Santa Monica Blvd., Suite 310
Los Angeles, CA 90067
213/552-1100
Mr. Arnold Soloway

B

BARSKIN AGENCY
11240 Magnolia Blvd., Suite 202
No. Hollywood, CA 91601
213/985-2992
Mr. Doovid Barskin

BAUMAN & HILLER
9220 Sunset Blvd., Suite 202
Los Angeles, CA 90069
213/271-5601

250 W. 57th Street, Suite 803
New York, NY 10019
212/757-0098

BEAKEL & JENNINGS AGENCY
427 N. Canon Drive, Suite 205
Beverly Hills, CA 90210
213/274-5418
Mr. Walter Beakel, Mr. Tom Jennings

GEORGE BEAUME
3 Quai Maiaquais
Paris 75006, France
325-2759
Mr. George Beaume

BERKUS, COSAY, HANDLEY & STEIN
(See LEADING ARTISTS, INC.)

BLAKE-GLENN AGENCY
409 N. Camden Drive
Beverly Hills, CA 90210
213/278-6885

BLOOM, LEVY & SHORR ASSOCIATES
800 S. Robertson Blvd., Suite 9
Los Angeles, CA 90035
213/659-6160

HARRY BLOOM AGENCY
8833 Sunset Blvd., Suite 202
Los Angeles, CA 90069
213/659-5985

J. MICHAEL BLOOM LTD.
9200 Sunset Blvd., Suite 1210
Los Angeles, CA 90069
213/275-6800

400 Madison Avenue, 20th Floor
New York, NY 10017
212/932-6900

PAUL BRANDON & ASSOC.
9046 Sunset Blvd.
Los Angeles, CA 90069
213/273-6173

BERNIE BRILLSTEIN & CO.
9200 Sunset Blvd., Suite 428
Los Angeles, CA 90069
213/275-6135
Mr. Bernie Brillstein

BRODER/KURLAND AGENCY
9046 Sunset Blvd., Suite 202
Los Angeles, CA 90069
213/274-8291
Mr. Bob Broder

C

CAREY-PHELPS-COLVIN
1407 N. La Brea Avenue
Los Angeles, CA 90028
213/874-7780

CENTURY ARTISTS, LTD.
9744 Wilshire Blvd., Suite 206
Beverly Hills, CA 90212
213/273-4366
Mr. Louis Bershad

CHARTER MANAGEMENT
9000 Sunset Blvd., Suite 1112
Los Angeles, CA 90069
213/278-1690

CHASIN-PARK-CITRON
9255 Sunset Blvd., Suite 910
Los Angeles, CA 90069
213/273-7190
Mr. George Chasin, Mr. Tom Chasin

CHASMAN & STRICK ASSOCIATES
6725 Sunset Blvd., Suite 506
Los Angeles, CA 90028
213/463-1115
Ms. Tanya Chasman, Ms. Shirley Strick

COLEMAN-ROSENBERG
667 Madison Avenue
New York, NY 10021
212/838-0734

KINGSLEY COLTON & ASSOCIATES
321 S. Beverly Drive
Beverly Hills, CA 90212
213/277-5491

POLLY CONNELL & ASSOCIATES
4605 Lankershim Blvd., Suite 213
North Hollywood, CA 91602
213/985-6266
Ms. Polly Connell

CONTEMPORARY-KORMAN ARTISTS
132 Lasky Drive
Beverly Hills, CA 90212
213/278-8250
Mr. Ronald Lief

BEN CONWAY & ASSOCIATES, INC.
999 N. Doheny Drive, Suite 403
Los Angeles, CA 90069
213/271-8133
Mr. Ben Conway

THE COOPER AGENCY
1900 Avenue of the Stars, Suite 2535
Los Angeles, CA 90067
213/277-8422
Mr. Frank Cooper

CREATIVE ARTISTS AGENCY (CAA)
1888 Century Park East-14th Floor
Los Angeles, CA 90067
213/277-4545

LIL CUMBER ATTRACTIONS AGENCY
6515 Sunset Blvd., Suite 300A
Los Angeles, CA 90028
213/469-1919

CURTIS-BROWN, LTD.
575 Madison Avenue
New York, NY
212/755-4200

D

DADE/ROSEN ASSOCIATES
9172 Sunset Blvd., Suite 2
Los Angeles, CA 90069
213/278-7077
Mr. Mike Rosen

DALLAS INTERNATIONAL ARTISTS
8383 Stemmons Fwy - #148
Dallas, TX 75247
214/484-4800

DAVID, HUNTER, KIMBLE, PARSEGHIAN & RIFKIN
7319 Beverly Blvd., Suite 1
Los Angeles, CA 90036
213/857-1234
Mr. Arnold Rifkin, Mr. Stephen Destanady

165 W. 46th Street, Suite 710
New York, NY 10036
212/869-2880

DENNIS, KARG, DENNIS & CO.
470 S. San Vicente Blvd.
Los Angeles, CA 90048
213/651-1700

DIAMOND ARTISTS, LTD.
9200 Sunset Blvd., Suite 909
Los Angeles, CA 90069
213/278-8146
Mr. Abby Greshler

E

EISENBACH-GREENE, INC.
760 N. La Cienega Blvd.
Los Angeles, CA 90069
213/659-3420

F

JACK FIELDS & ASSOCIATES
9255 Sunset Blvd., Suite 1105
Los Angeles, CA 90069
213/278-1333

FILM ARTISTS ASSOCIATES
9200 Sunset Blvd., Suite 431
Los Angeles, CA 90069
213/275-6193

FILM ARTISTS MANAGEMENT ENTERPRISES (F.A.M.E.)
1800 Avenue of the Stars
Los Angeles, CA 90067
213/556-8071

THE SY FISCHER COMPANY
10960 Wilshire Blvd., 10th Floor
Los Angeles, CA 90024
213/557-0388
Mr. Sy Fischer, Ms. Diane Cairns

KURT FRINGS AGENCY, INC.
415 N. Crescent Drive
Beverly Hills, CA 90210
213/274-8881
Mr. Kurt Frings

G

GAGE GROUP
9229 Sunset Blvd., Suite 306
Los Angeles, CA 90069
213/859-8777

1650 Broadway
New York, NY 10019
212/541-5250

DALE GARRICK INTERNATIONAL AGENCY
8831 Sunset Blvd., Suite 402
Los Angeles, CA 90069
213/657-2661
Mr. Dale Garrick

GELFAND, RENNERT & FELDMAN
1880 Century Park East, Suite 900
Los Angeles, CA 90067
213/553-1707

GENERAL MANAGEMENT CORP.
9000 Sunset Blvd., Suite 400
Los Angeles, CA 90069
213/274-8805
Ms. Helen Kushnick

ROY GERBER & ASSOCIATES
9200 Sunset Blvd., Suite 620
Los Angeles, CA 90069
213/550-0100

THE GERSH AGENCY
222 N. Canon Drive, Suite 201
Beverly Hills, CA 90210
213/274-6611
Mr. Phil Gersh

J. CARTER GIBSON
9000 Sunset Blvd., Suite 811
Los Angeles, CA 90069
213/274-8813

GOLDFARB-LEWIS AGENCY
8733 Sunset Blvd., Suite 202
Los Angeles, CA 90069
213/659-5955

GOTLER AGENCY
9100 Sunset Blvd., Suite 360
Los Angeles, CA 90069
213/273-2811
Mr. Joel Gotler

IVAN GREEN AGENCY
1888 Century Park East, Suite 908
Los Angeles, CA 90067
213/277-1541
Mr. Ivan Green

LARRY GROSSMAN & ASSOCIATES
211 S. Beverly Drive, Suite 206
Beverly Hills, CA 90212
213/550-8127

GROSSMAN-STALMASTER
10100 Santa Monica Blvd., Suite 310
Los Angeles, CA 90067
213/552-0905
Mr. Hal Stalmaster

H

REECE HALSEY AGENCY
8733 Sunset Blvd., Suite 101
Los Angeles, CA 90069
213/652-2409
Ms. Dorris Halsey

JAMES HARPER
13063 Ventura Blvd.
Studio City, CA 91604
213/872-0944
Mr. James Harper

MARK HARRIS MANAGEMENT
10100 Santa Monica Blvd., Suite 310
Los Angeles, CA 90067
213/552-0658
Mr. Mark Harris

HENDERSON/HOGAN AGENCY, INC.
247 S. Beverly Drive, Suite 102
Beverly Hills, CA 90212
213/274-7815
Ms. Lynne Radmin

200 57th Street
New York, NY 10019
212/765-5190

HESSELTINE-BAKER ASSOCIATES
165 W. 46th St., Suite 409
New York, NY 10019
212/921-4460

ROBERT G. HUSSONG AGENCY
721 N. La Brea Ave., Suite 201
Los Angeles, CA 90038
213/655-2534

I

GEORGE INGERSOLL AGENCY
6513 Hollywood Blvd., Suite 217
Los Angeles, CA 90028
213/874-6434
Mr. George Ingersoll

INTERNATIONAL CREATIVE MANAGEMENT (ICM)
8899 Beverly Blvd.
Los Angeles, CA 90048
213/550-4000

111 North-West 183rd St.
Miami, FL 33169
305/550-4000

22 Champs-Elysee
Paris 75008, France
723-9066

40 West 57th St.
New York, NY 10019
212/556-5600

38 Via Siacci
Rome 75008, Italy
806-041

22 Grafton Street
London W1 England
01-629-8080

K

MERRILY KANE AGENCY
9171 Wilshire Blvd., Suite 310
Beverly Hills, CA 90210
213/550-8874

KAPLAN-STAHLER AGENCY
119 N. San Vicente Blvd.
Beverly Hills, CA 90211
213/653-4483

PARTRICIA KARLAN AGENCY
3815 W. Olive Ave., Suite 202
Burbank, CA 91505
213/954-8848

PAUL KOHNER, INC.
9169 Sunset Boulevard
Los Angeles, CA 90069
213/550-1060
Paul Kohner

L

THE CANDACE LAKE OFFICE
1103 Glendon Avenue
Los Angeles, CA 90024
213/824-9706

THE LANTZ OFFICE, INC.
9255 Sunset Blvd., Suite 505
Los Angeles, CA 90069
213/858-1144

888 Seventh Avenue
New York, NY 10106
212/586-0200
Mr. Robert Lantz

IRVING PAUL LAZAR AGENCY
211 S. Beverly Drive, Suite 110
Beverly Hills, CA 90212
213/275-6153
Mr. Irving Paul Lazar

One East 66th Street
New York, NY 10021
212/355-1177

LEADING ARTISTS, INC.
1900 Avenue of the Stars, Suite 1530
Los Angeles, CA 90067
213/277-9090

JACK LENNY & ASSOCIATES
9701 Wilshire Blvd., Suite 800
Beverly Hills, CA 90212
213/271-2174

140 W. 58th Street
New York, NY 10019
212/582-0270

LITKE/GROSSBART MANAGEMENT
8500 Wilshire Blvd., Suite 506
Beverly Hills, CA 90211
213/657-5562
Mr. Marty Litke, Mr. Jack Grossbart

ROBERT LITTMAN COMPANY, INC.
(See LEADING ARTISTS, INC)

STERLING LORD AGENCY
660 Madison Avenue
New York, NY 10021
212/751-2533

LUND AGENCY
6515 Sunset Blvd., Suite 204
Los Angeles, CA 90028
213/466-8280
Mr. Reginald Lund

GRACE LYONS AGENCY
204 S. Beverly Drive, Suite 102
Beverly Hills, CA 90212
213/652-5290

M

MAJOR TALENT AGENCY
11812 San Vicente Blvd., Suite 510
Los Angeles, CA 90049
213/820-5841

CHRISTOPHER MANN, LTD.
39 Davies Street
London, WI England
01/493-2810
Mr. Christopher Mann

MCCARTT, ORECK & BARRETT
9200 Sunset Blvd., Suite 1009
Los Angeles, CA 90069
213/278-6243

JAMES MCHUGH AGENCY
8150 Beverly Blvd., Suite 303
Los Angeles, CA 90048
213/651-2770

FRED MESSENGER AGENCY
8235 Santa Monica Blvd., Suite 315
Los Angeles, CA 90046
213/654-3800
Mr. Fred Messenger

GEORGE MICHAUD AGENCY
4950 Densmore Avenue, Suite 1
Encino, CA 91436
213/981-6680
Mr. Arthur Dreifuss

MILLER AGENCY
4425 Riverside Dr., Suite 200
Burbank, CA 91505
213/849-2363
Mr. Tommy Miller

WILLIAM MORRIS AGENCY
151 South El Camino Dr.
Beverly Hills, CA 90212
213/274-7451

1350 Avenue of the Americas
New York, NY 10019
212/586-5100

2325 Crestmoore Road
Nashville, TN 37215
615/385-0310

147-149 Wardour Street
London, WI England
01/734-9361

Lamonstrasse 9
Munich 27, Germany
47/608-1234

Via Nomentha 60
Rome, Italy
86-8551

MARVIN MOSS, INC.
9200 Sunset Blvd., Suite 601
Los Angeles, CA 90069
213/278-8483
Marvin Moss

N

SKIP NICHOLSON AGENCY, INC.
13701 Riverside Drive, Suite 314
Sherman Oaks, CA 91423
213/906-2700

NOVEMBER NINTH MANAGEMENT
9021 Melrose Ave., Suite 301
Los Angeles, CA 90069
213/652-9800

O

FIFI OSCARD AGENCY
19 West 44th Street
New York, NY 10036
212/764-1100
Ms. Fifi Oscard, Mr. Charles Hunt

P

ANTHONY JONES PETERS
London 01-839-2556
Mr. Anthony Jones Peters

PICKMAN COMPANY, INC.
9025 Wilshire Blvd., Suite 214
Beverly Hills, CA 90212
213/273-8273
Mr. Milton Pickman

PROGRESSIVE ARTISTS AGENCY
400 S. Beverly Drive
Beverly Hills, CA 90212
213/553-8561

R

RAPER ENTERPRISES
9441 Wilshire Blvd., Suite 620D
Beverly Hills, CA 90212
213/273-7704

RICHLAND AGENCY
1888 Avenue of the Stars - Suite
Los Angeles, CA 90067
213/553-1257
Mr. Dan Richland, Mr. Joe Richland

THE ROBERTS COMPANY
427 N. Canon Drive
Beverly Hills, CA 90210
213/275-9384

FLORA ROBERTS AGENCY
65 East 55th St.
New York, NY 10022
212/355-4165

ROBINSON-LUTTRELL ASSOCIATES
141 El Camino Drive
Beverly Hills, CA 90212
213/275-6114
Mr. Bill Robinson

ROBINSON-WEINTRAUB & ASSOCIATES
554 S. San Vicente Blvd., Suite 3
Los Angeles, CA 90048
213/652-5802

STEPHANIE ROGERS & ASSOCIATES
9100 Sunset Blvd., Suite 340
Los Angeles, CA 90069
213/278-2015
Ms. Stephanie Rogers

ROLLINS-JOFFE
Paramount Studios/5555 Melrose Avenue
Los Angeles, CA 90038
213/462-6677

130 W. 57th St.
New York, NY
212/582-1940
Mr. Jack Rollins, Mr. Charles Joffe

HAROLD ROSE ARTISTS, LTD.
190 N. Canon Drive, Suite 202
Beverly Hills, CA 90210
213/652-3961

JACK ROSE AGENCY
6430 Sunset Blvd., Suite 1203
Los Angeles, CA 90028
213/461-4911 or 213/463-7300
Mr. Jack Rose

HOWARD ROTHBERG
P.O. Box 10657
9701 Wilshire Blvd.
Beverly Hills, CA 90213
213/273-9100

S

SACKHEIM AGENCY
9301 Wilshire Blvd., Suite 606
Beverly Hills, CA 90210
213/858-0606

IRVING SALKOW AGENCY
9350 Wilshire Blvd., Suite 214
Beverly Hills, CA 90210
213/276-3141
Mr. Irving Salkow

SANFORD-BECKETT AGENCY
1015 Gayley Avenue - Suite 301
Los Angeles, CA 90024
213/208-2100
Mr. Geoffrey Beckett, Ms. Brenda
Beckett

IRV SCHECHTER & CO.
9300 Wilshire Blvd., Suite 410
Beverly Hills, CA 90212
213/278-8070
Mr. Irv Schechter

**DON SCHWARTZ &
ASSOCIATES**
8721 Sunset Blvd., Suite 200
Los Angeles, CA 90069
213/657-8910
Ms. Anita Haeggstrom

SELECTED ARTISTS AGENCY
12711 Ventura Blvd., Suite 460
Studio City, CA 91604
213/763-9731
Ms. Flo Joseph

**DAVID SHAPIRA &
ASSOCIATES, LTD.**
15301 Ventura Blvd., Suite 345
Sherman Oaks, CA 91403
213/906-0322
Mr. David Shapira

SHAPIRO-LICHTMAN AGENCY
2049 Century Park East, Suite
1320
Los Angeles, CA 90067
213/557-2244

SHAPIRO/WEST
141 El Camino Drive, Suite 295
Beverly Hills, CA 90212
213/278-8896
Mr. George Shapiro

LEW SHERRELL AGENCY, LTD.
7060 Hollywood Blvd., Suite 610
Los Angeles, CA 90028
213/461-9955

**SMITH-FRIEDMAN &
ASSOCIATES**
9869 Santa Monica Blvd., Suite
207
Beverly Hills, CA 90212
213/277-8464
Ms. Susan Smith

**CRAYTON SMITH-RAY
GOSNELL AGENCY**
20154 Pacific Coast Highway
Malibu, CA 90265
213/456-6641
Mr. Crayton Smith, Mr. Ray
Gosnell

STE REPRESENTATION, LTD.
211 S. Beverly Dr., Suite 201
Beverly Hills, CA 90212
213/550-3982
Mr. David Eidenherg

888 Seventh Avenue
New York, NY 10019
212/246-1030
Mr. Clifford Stevens

**CHARLES H. STERN AGENCY,
INC.**
9220 Sunset Blvd., Suite 218
Los Angeles, CA 90069
213/273-6890
Mr. Charles H. Stern

STONE-MASSER AGENCY
1052 Carol Drive
Los Angeles, CA 90069
213/275-9599

H. N. SWANSON, INC.
8523 Sunset Boulevard
Los Angeles, CA 90069
213/652-5385

T

**TALENT MANAGEMENT
INTERNATIONAL**
6380 Wilshire Blvd., Suite 910
Los Angeles, CA 90048
213/273-4000
Mr. Lawrence Becksey

HERB TOBIAS & ASSOCIATES
1901 Avenue of the Stars, Suite
840
Los Angeles, CA 90067
213/277-6211
Herb Tobias

**TWENTIETH CENTURY
ARTISTS**
13727 Ventura Blvd., Suite 211
Studio City, CA 91604
213/990-8580
Ms. Diane Davis

U

**THE HARRY J. UFLAND
AGENCY**
190 N. Canon Drive, Suite 202
Beverly Hills, CA 90210
213/273-9441
Mr. Harry Ufland

W

ELLIOT WAX & ASSOCIATES
9255 Sunset Blvd., Suite 612
Los Angeles, CA 90069
213/273-8217
Mr. Elliot Wax

**LEW WEITZMAN &
ASSOCIATES**
14144 Ventura Blvd., Suite 200
Sherman Oaks, CA 91423
213/995-4400

PHILIP WELTMAN
425 S. Beverly Drive
Beverly Hills, CA 90212
213/556-2081

SYLVIA WOSK AGENCY
439 S. La Cienega Blvd.
Los Angeles, CA 90048
213/274-8063

WRITERS & ARTISTS AGENCY
11726 San Vicente Blvd., Suite
300
Los Angeles, CA 90049
213/820-2240
Ms. Joan Scott

Z

ZIEGLER, DISKANT, INC.
9255 Sunset Blvd., Suite 1112
Los Angeles, CA 90069
213/278-0070
Mr. Martin Hurwitz

Index of Advertisers

A special thanks to the following advertisers whose support allowed us to bring you this expanded edition

RESERVE YOUR ADVERTISING SPACE NOW

in the 1985 edition of FILM DIRECTORS: A Complete Guide

382

FEELING LEFT OUT???

The 1985 Third International Edition of FILM DIRECTORS: A Complete Guide will be published in December 1984. We update our records continuously during the year. If you are a director and you qualify to be listed (please read the introduction for qualifications), then send us your information as soon as possible. Our editorial deadline is August 31, 1984. **PLEASE DO NOT WAIT UNTIL THEN.** Our computer **loves** getting up-dated information all year long.

Send all listing information to:

FILM DIRECTORS: A Complete Guide
Lone Eagle Publishing
9903 Santa Monica Blvd. - Suite 204
Beverly Hills, CA 90212
Phone: 213/274-4766 or 213/277-9616

Or, just fill out the post-paid tear-out card in the front of the book and drop in the mail. We'll send you the information form.

EDITOR/COMPILER

Michael Singer, 31, has worked in motion pictures for eleven years as a producer's assistant, writer, publicist, story analyst, researcher and journalist. A native of New York City, he now resides in Los Angeles.